Advanced Technologies for Microfinance:
Solutions and Challenges

Arvind Ashta
Groupe ESC Dijon Bourgogne, France

BUSINESS SCIENCE REFERENCE

Hershey · New York

Director of Editorial Content: Kristin Klinger
Director of Book Publications: Julia Mosemann
Acquisitions Editor: Lindsay Johnston
Development Editor: Christine Bufton
Publishing Assistant: Deanna Jo Zombro
Typesetter: Deanna Jo Zombro
Production Editor: Jamie Snavely
Cover Design: Lisa Tosheff

Published in the United States of America by
        Business Science Reference (an imprint of IGI Global)
        701 E. Chocolate Avenue
        Hershey PA 17033
        Tel: 717-533-8845
        Fax: 717-533-8661
        E-mail: cust@igi-global.com
        Web site: http://www.igi-global.com/reference

Library of Congress Cataloging-in-Publication Data

Advanced technologies for microfinance : solutions and challenges / Arvind Ashta, editor.   p. cm.
   Includes bibliographical references and index.   Summary: "This book offers research on the microfinance movement that is providing poor people around the world an opportunity to take responsibility for their lives by providing them complementary elements such as financial capital and guidance"--Provided by publisher.   ISBN 978-1-61520-993-4 -- ISBN 978-1-61520-994-1 (ebk.) 1. Microfinance. 2. Technological innovations. I. Ashta, Arvind. II. Title.

    HG178.3.A34 2011
    332--dc22
                                    2009052754

British Cataloguing in Publication Data
A Cataloguing in Publication record for this book is available from the British Library.

All work contributed to this book is new, previously-unpublished material. The views expressed in this book are those of the authors, but not necessarily of the publisher.

Table of Contents

Section 1
Information Technology for MFIs
Introduction by Raghavan Kunigahalli, Navy Federal Credit Union, USA

Section 2
Mobile Banking
Introduction by Kevin Day, Riskebiz Microfinance Solutions, Canada

Section 3
Online Financing for Microfinance

Introduction by Arvind Ashta, Burgundy School of Business (Groupe ESC Dijon-Bourgogne), France

Section 4
Technical, Regional and Sectoral Issues

Introduction by Glòria Estapé-Dubreuil, Universitat Autònoma de Barcelona, Spain

Detailed Table of Contents

Section 1
Information Technology for MFIs
Introduction by Raghavan Kunigahalli, Navy Federal Credit Union, USA

Chapter 1
Krishna Nyapati, Microsense Software, India

The chapter looks at the MFI context which is characterized by multiple stakeholders, with a variety of often divergent goals / requirements at a systems level. It examines the key stakeholders in the MFI context and their high level requirements. These requirements, which are typically complex and abstract, are then a into elementary attributes, which are amenable to quantification and measurement. While the discussion addresses multiple stakeholders, the detailed analysis is restricted to MFIs and their clients (borrowers of micro credit). The discussion also addresses a few promising technologies which have the potential of improving availability and accessibility of technological solutions in engaging MFI clients.

Chapter 2
Britta Augsburg, The Institute for Fiscal Studies (Centre for Evaluation of Development
    Policies), UK
Jan Philipp Schmidt, United Nations University MERIT, The Netherlands
Karuna Krishnaswamy, Independent Consultant, India

In this chapter the authors investigate the potential of open source software to increase the impact of microfinance (MF) especially for the very poor. They argue that small and medium organizations play a crucial role, because they are more flexible in operations and familiar with the local context. They consider how new information and communication technology (ICT) can increase outreach of MF to the very poor within a self-sustainable holistic approach. They consider the potential of free/open source software projects to address the computing needs of small and remote MFIs, and describe the reasons why no suitable solutions have emerged yet.

Chapter 3
S. Mohd. Najmullah Quadri, IT Professional, Singapore
Vikas Kumar Singh, IT Professional, Singapore
Kishen Parthasarathy Iyengar, University of Colorado at Boulder, USA

In order to increase the outreach of MFI, institution will have to go a step further and start their operation in the rural areas. Implementing sustainable IT infrastructure in such areas is a challenge with numerous obstacles. Further, employee training also poses challenges that are unique to the microfinance industry. In this chapter, the authors articulate some of the challenges faced by microfinance institutions and some potential solutions with the help of real world case studies. They also propose a framework, which will help microfinance institutions implement IT based management information systems effectively.

Chapter 4
Saleh Khan, ASA International, Nigeria

With increasing attention given to Microfinance Institutions (MFIs) by global thought leaders and policy makers alike, the entire sector stands under increasing scrutiny and demands for transparency. This increasing attention coupled with the intrinsic need for MFIs to be efficient in their operations, leads to more and more MFIs adopting Information Technology (IT) tools to automate and streamline their operations. Whilst automating their operations, MFIs need to be careful in keeping some of the basic tenets of sustainable microfinance operations intact – including human contact that is important in ensuring timely repayments. This chapter examines some basic business processes followed by MFIs in their lending operations and evaluates the possible impacts and implications of automating these processes and discusses the extent to which automation is feasible for a MFI and its implications on the sustainability of the organization.

Chapter 5
Puspadhar Das, Asomi, India

Mifos is an open source enterprise solution for microfinance. This chapter is a practitioner's point of view on implementation of Mifos in an organization, based on the author's experience in implementing Mifos at Asomi, a microfinance institution operating in the state of Assam, India. The factors to be considered in selection and implementation of Mifos are discussed. Various inputs, analyses and resources required for implementation are discussed. Any organization must have a concrete set of operational strategies that enables it to track its borrowers and loan portfolio effectively and on time in order to succeed.

Chapter 6

Abu Saleh Mohammad Musa, South Asian Microfinance Network (SAMN), Bangladesh
Mostafa Saidur Rahim Khan, Stamford University, Bangladesh

Adoption of Information Technology (IT) in Microfinance Institutes (MFIs) has become one of the key indicators to ensure good governance and transparency to the stakeholders. Though the cost of investment in IT is a matter of concern, it has manifold benefit ranging from productivity improvement to socio economic development of the target clients. This chapter focuses on the adoption of IT in MFIs and its possible benefits in operation, cost reduction and stakeholder relationship through an evaluation of a small-scale MFI, Come to Save (CTS), operating in Bangladesh. This chapter reinforces that timely implementation of IT reduces cost of operation, attains economies of scale and increases outreach through increased staff productivity.

Section 2
Mobile Banking
Introduction by Kevin Day, Riskebiz Microfinance Solutions, Canada

Chapter 7

Prateek Shrivastava, Monitise Group PLC, UK

Mobile banking is one of the newest approaches to the provision of financial services made possible by the widespread adoption of mobile phones in low income countries. However, reports show that potential users may not be using these systems despite already being available. This study extends the Luarn & Lin mobile banking adoption model by adding two additional constructs: "Enhancement of image" and the "enhancement of quality of life by having access to financial service" to test the attitude toward mobile banking. This study concludes that mobile banking can indeed be a channel to reach out to low income groups.

Chapter 8

Nandu Kulkarni, Independent Consultant, Banking Technology, India

The microfinance sector is seeing a rapid expansion in terms of geographical reach, and an explosive growth in terms of the number of service providers and customers. Given that Information Technology (IT) is a critical enabler for this growth, there is a large rush of IT providers eager to service this market, bringing in a) the risk that inappropriate or substandard IT solutions are implemented, resulting in wastage of resources, and b) the potential for misuse and fraud. This chapter makes a case for creating an IT requirements and governance framework at a policy level, in order to ensure that the needs of this market are properly serviced, and resources are optimally and efficiently deployed, so that the benefits of Information Technology flow through to the grassroots level.

This chapter explains how M-PESA, an application that was designed for money transfers, is being used for savings in Kenya. It uses data from a collection of financial diaries that captured the savings practices of fourteen M-PESA users for a period of one month. They were part of a fourteen month ethnographic study that examined the adoption, usage and impact of M-PESA in two locations: an urban slum and a rural village. The study reveals that informants held a portfolio of savings mechanisms. M-PESA was used in conjunction with the other mechanisms and held a vital place in the portfolio— somewhere between the bank and home bank. The chapter suggests how mobile money applications can be designed to better suit the unique savings needs of the resource poor.

Chapter 10

The purpose of this chapter is to analyse how ICT can influence MFI performance. In this regard, three aspects of MFI performance are studied: efficiency, risk management and customer relationship management. The results of the survey conducted with MFI professionals in developing and emerging countries show that the implementation of ICTs enables MFIs to significantly improve their microfinance services, while enhancing work efficiency and customer relationship management in the same way as in other branches of financial services in general. However, the results give no empirical support to the contribution of ICTs in risk management or risk reduction.

Section 3
Online financing for MFIs
Introduction by Arvind Ashta, Burgundy School of Business (Groupe ESC Dijon-Bourgogne), France

The marketing trends of the emerging sector of peer-to-peer microlending websites have been left largely unexplored during its rise to recognition. Based on a sample of nine popular social lending sites, this exploratory chapter uses observational research methods to analyze the uncontrollable and controllable marketing elements of online social lending websites in order to better understand its present and future tendencies. A more comprehensive understanding based on similarities and differences of the marketing movement within this industry will be a more reliable prediction of the future it holds.

Chapter 12

Arvind Ashta, Burgundy School of Business (Groupe ESC Dijon-Bourgogne), France
Djamchid Assadi, Burgundy School of Business (Groupe ESC Dijon-Bourgogne), France

The main objective of this chapter was to investigate whether peer to peer online lending transactions are integrated to support a higher level of social interactions and associations with a promise of reducing (transaction) costs through disintermediation and risk reduction. The authors find that "peer to peer" lending consists of diverse websites of microcredit (Kiva, Wokai, Babyloan), social investing (MicroPlace) as well as small loans at market rates (Prosper, Zopa, Lending Club), and even lending between friends and family members (Virgin Money). It finds that most of the so called "peer-to-peer" lenders are in fact intermediaries between the peers (lender and borrowers) and there is little direct contact between the peers. The impact on transaction costs should therefore be very little as there is neither disintermediation nor risk reduction.

Chapter 13

Daniel Brett, EDA CapitalConnect, USA
Nikias Stefanakis, EDA CapitalConnect, USA

EDA CapitalConnect (EDACC) has developed an online platform that allows social enterprises and institutional funders to communicate with one another, initiate financial transactions, and analyze market trends. The platform seeks to increase deal flow and transparency in the social enterprise space by facilitating information dissemination and the exchange of funding offers between capital providers and seekers of all sizes. As the platform develops, the challenges of achieving financial sustainability and scale will require EDACC to continue to fine-tune its services to meet the evolving needs of the social enterprise community. EDACC's experience in its nascence suggests that technology providers to microfinance institutions and social enterprises – particularly start up organizations – must pay close attention to the behavior of their target users, and modify their services based upon trends in usage and market perceptions.

This chapter presents credit scoring as a technology meant to improve micro lending significantly. Credit scoring can be efficient only in massive homogeneous markets such as those addressed by microfinance. On the other hand, quantitative measurements, required for statistical developments, suffer from the fact that micro-entrepreneurs operate mostly in the informal or semi-formal sectors. The authors describe in detail possible applications of credit scoring in micro lending. They explain themain technical aspects and point out expected benefits versus implementation and maintenance efforts.

This chapter presents an application of systemic-fuzzy models to evaluate the social impact of a microcredit program. The goal is to supply a complement to effectiveness indicators (traditionally based on profitability and portfolio quality) by measuring personal and family achievements, and through consideration of the economic consequences derived from microcredit. The method proposes a more complete and transparent image of the activity of such institutions.

Microfinance has demonstrated great success in poverty-relief in less-developed countries and is experiencing rapid growth and interest in developed countries. Descriptive analysis is used in this chapter to infer that microfinance must be redesigned to meet developed country socio-economic conditions, if it is to avoid a reputation of being too poorly focused, ineffective, and inefficient. This chapter reviews current-performance concerns of developed country microfinance, discusses how it can still effectively relieve poverty, examines how regulatory and other socio-economic factors affect micro-enterprise, and concludes that microfinance should be refocused before developed countries commit to further developing/adapting it.

This chapter analyzes the relationships between IT and microfinance, focusing on the microfinance sector in Spain. It shows that the microfinance sector's basic IT infrastructures are above the Spanish average. Two main uses of IT tools are revealed: (1) to provide information, both to prospective clients and to those sustaining microfinance, and (2) as a management and support tool, including on-line direct support to would-be entrepreneurs. Strategic use of IT is less widespread, related primarily to financial transparency issues, more clearly shown by MFIs linked to the social economy. Finally, depth of outreach related to the actual IT use in the sector is also discussed.

Chapter 18

2.5 billion people do not have access to a toilet; instead they have no choice but to practice open defecation, having a potentially detrimental effect on their health. The chapter asks whether microfinance and IT can play a role in tackling the problem. Drawing on the experience of Grameen Telephone it is argued that this is analogous with attempts to promote the purchase of toilets, in particular the technological leap where expensive infrastructure is bypassed. Drawing on three case studies we show that such a process is underway and while there are a limited number of microfinance providers engaged in this market it is insufficient to address the myriad of both organizational and cultural problems.

Foreword

In 1976, few would have guessed that Muhammad Yunus's small action research project would ultimately drive the global spread of microfinance and earn him a Nobel Prize. But today, the writing is on the wall.

M-PESA, Safaricom's pervasive mobile money service in Kenya, is the Grameen Bank of the next decade. It is proof that technology will take microfinance mainstream and it has accelerated a global movement to take advantage of technology's power.

Whereas Grameen Bank demonstrated that even very poor people are creditworthy (still a revolutionary idea among many bankers) M-PESA has demonstrated how to bring financial services profitably to nearly everyone. Cheaper to operate than bank branches and ATMs, and more accessible to the poor than the Internet, the M-PESA channel uses mobile phones and thousands of airtime resellers to let anyone conduct transactions electronically. Eventually, billions of people (yes, billions!) will use services like M-PESA to borrow and repay loans, and save for their future.

Like the Grameen Bank, M-PESA is an inspiration. The "imitators," banks and mobile operators in dozens of markets, seek to replicate its success by adapting the model for local markets. Examples include Orange and MTN across Africa, ANZ Royal in Cambodia's WING service, and others. The innovators are beginning to design and deliver services such as banking, health and trading differently – now that nearly half of all adults in Kenya can make small payments anytime, anywhere.

But mobile phone networks are not the only technology that will transform microfinance. Already, new ways of communicating information, analyzing data, and writing software are increasing the sophistication, scale and diversity of financial services for poor people. For example, several microfinance software providers including global leaders such as IBM are working to host their applications and store customer data "in the cloud." Online lending platforms such as Kiva and MyC4 have begun to consider mobile-based person-to-person lending models.

This book is the first to systematically address technology's impact on microfinance. Ably compiled and edited by Professor Arvind Ashta, it covers a range of technology applications that will define the "next generation" of the microfinance movement. Most importantly, it tackles "tough questions" around technology: what are the disadvantages of technology-enabled microfinance, and what will this mean for the inclusiveness and empowerment of the service, among others.

It may be years, even a decade before we really understand the power of technology and its limits. Indeed, many still grapple with the true impact that access to credit – Prof. Yunus's early insights – has for the poor. But as an early proponent of efforts to track, advance and pioneer technology for microfinance, I am rewarded by successes like M-PESA and the growing appetite to tackle these questions.

Whether you are an imitator or an innovator – both are needed – you will find this book useful. It is pioneering, like the Grameen Bank and M-PESA, and I hope it will also be inspiring.

Gautam Ivatury
Strategic Advisor, CGAP
Partner, Signal Point Partners
New York, USA

Gautam Ivatury *is a Strategic Advisor to CGAP, the global microfinance resource center housed at the World Bank, and the founder of Signal Point Partners, a global investment and advisory firm in the mobile services space. From 2003 through 2008, he led CGAP's work in microfinance and technology, including setting up and managing the $26 million CGAP Technology Program co-funded by the Bill and Melinda Gates Foundation. Gautam's team designed, funded, and researched experimental mobile-banking businesses with firms such as Globe Telecom (Philippines), Tameer Bank (Pakistan), Equity Bank (Kenya), WIZZIT (South Africa), and XacBank (Mongolia). As a member of CGAP's management team, Gautam helped shape the organization's strategic and operational decisions. Before joining CGAP, Mr. Ivatury helped manage SKS Microfinance, India's largest microfinance institution (now serving 5m+ households). He has also worked in investment and commercial banking at Donaldson Lufkin & Jenrette (now Credit Suisse) and the International Finance Corporation.*

Preface

This book is set in a background of efforts to create a decent global society providing all people a fair chance, and to remedy disparities of power and opportunity, through a democratic and market based process. The microfinance movement is about providing poor people, the world over, an opportunity to take responsibility for their lives by providing them complementary elements such as financial capital and guidance.

To help poor women across the world escape poverty through entrepreneurship, Microfinance Institutions started offering small loans since the early 1970s. These loans help finance working capital or small investments in a very tiny business. Innovative, group monitoring and peer group pressure based contracts, among others, increased the probability of success and ensured that loans were repaid. The high repayment rates of the poor borrowers approaching 98% in good times, has got financers as well as donors the world over to take notice of the Microfinance movement (Morduch, 1999). Armendariz & Morduch (2005) and Ashta (2009) explain why the MFIs succeeded where banks feared to tread.

Very briefly, the crux of this explanation (Ashta, 2009) indicates that banks were not able to lend to poor people owing to high transaction costs and high risk from information asymmetry. As a result, the Marginal Revenue curve of the poor was way below the Marginal cost curve of the banks (called the supply of credit curve) and the two did not meet, as shown in Figure 1. However, the marginal cost curve of money lenders was lower, and illustrated by the dashed line, partly because they were living in the same area and therefore had lower transaction costs and partly because their families knew the credit history of the borrowers and therefore there were lower asymmetric information costs. Therefore, the marginal cost curve intersected with the marginal revenue curve at D, but being a monopoly in each village, the money lender could charge high interest rates of R_{MLm}. The essential point is that if poor entrepreneurs take loans at such high interest rates, their businesses cannot survive.

The advent of microfinance essentially resulted in lower interest rates to a level where the poor could borrow and expect a small profit in their businesses, as illustrated in Figure 2 (Ashta, 2009). In this figure the original supply curve of the banks has been taken out, and the supply of credit curve is that of the moneylenders. The dashed portion of the curve shows that MFIs were able to reduce this supply cost further. They were able to do this by innovative group lending schemes, progressive lending and other incentives, all of which were aimed at reducing information asymmetry. Moreover, in addition to reducing risk, these MFIs got funds from donors and loans from commercial banks at rates lower than those available, if at all, to moneylenders. For both these reasons, the supply curve shifted down. At the same time, group lending may also have led to better business performance owing to Hawthorne effect (people are watching you, so you perform better) or owing to the fact that other group members had to monitor and advise to ensure the success of the borrowers. This may have shifted the marginal revenue curve of the poor entrepreneurs outwards to MR' in the figure. The final result is that if the MFI is in a

Figure 1. Why money lenders lend at high interest rates

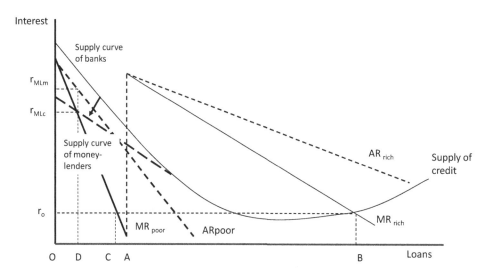

Moneylenders have lower transaction costs and lower information asymmetry. As a result, they push down the supply curve for poorer borrowers to the dashed line shown in the diagram. They charge high interest rates r_{ML}, much higher than the interest rates r_o charged by the competitive organized sector to the wealthier borrowers. (Source: Ashta, 2009)

monopoly position it can charge, r_{MFIm}, which is lower than the interest rates charged by money lenders. If the MFI is in competition, it may lower interest rates further to r_{MFIc}, as shown in Figure 2.

Therefore, donor capital, initially, and loans and private investments more recently, have pushed the number of microfinance borrowers to about 150 million, mostly women. With an average family size of five, it is estimated that about 750 million people are covered by microfinance. The success of the movement has brought fame and prestige, and a Nobel Peace prize was awarded to one of the pioneers of this movement, Prof. Muhammad Yunus, along with his microfinance institution, the Grameen Bank. Many institutions started as NGOs and have become for-profit financial institutions and some have converted themselves into banks to attract deposits. On the other hand, the success in outreach has also attracted banks to downscale to serve poorer borrowers.

This success and visibility have made people wonder whether the movement needs donor funds, social capital, socially responsible investment or, perhaps, even commercial investment. So far, barely 2% of the 10,000 estimated Microfinance Institutions (i.e., 200 MFIs) are profitable and financially sustainable. But among those which are, profits can be extremely high.

An Initial public offering by Compartamos in 2007 was a visible landmark. The share capital of Compartamos floated in 2000 was $ 6 million, its book value in 2006 was $126 million and the IPO valued the company at $1,500 million. The issue was over-subscribed thirteen times and two days later, market capitalization jumped to $ 2 billion.

This success made people wonder how Compartamos grew so fast. They noticed that the valuation was based on high expected growth rates, based on high past growth rates of about 50% per annum. These high growth rates were made possible by high retained earnings and a high return on equity. The high return on equity was based on high interest rates approaching 100% per annum with Value Added Tax. As was shown in Figure 2, monopoly interest rates can be charged even by MFIs, even if

Figure 2. Why MFIs are able to lower interest rates

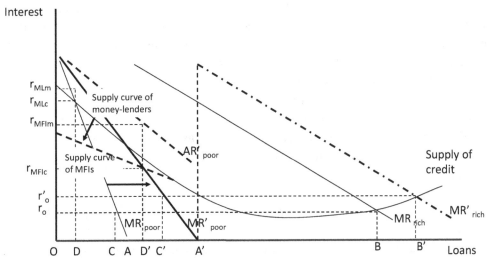

Microfinance institutions have lower cost of capital and they overcome information asymmetry. As a result, they push down the supply curve for poorer borrowers further to the dotted line shown in the diagram. At the same time, group monitoring and involvement may actually boost the performance on projects and push the MR curve of the poor to MR'. The MFIs charge interest rates r_{MFIc}, or r_{MFIm}, depending on whether there is competition or monopoly in the local market, in either case much higher than the interest rates r_o charged by the organized sector to the wealthier borrowers, but much lower than the interest rates r_{ML} charged by money-lender. (Source: Ashta, 2009)

these may be lower than rates charged by money lenders. The question which has been hotly debated in academic and practitioner circles is whether such high rates of 100% are ethical (Ashta & Bush, 2009; Ashta & Hudon, 2009; Granger, 2009; Lewis, 2008; Rhyne & Guimon, 2007; Rosenberg, 2007; Smith & Epstein, 2007). On the one hand, such lucrative profits would encourage commercial investments into Microfinance which should eventually bring down interest rates through competition. On the other hand, such high interest rates and the unethical perception may make donors, social investors and socially responsible investors look elsewhere. It may also bring governments to cap interest rates to what would be considered acceptable levels by the citizens. Such externally exposed caps, it is often argued, may create capital rationing and limit the microfinance movement (Helms & Reille, 2004; Honohan, 2004), but there is evidence also that lifting usury caps does not necessarily lead to spectacular growth of Microfinance (Ashta, Attuel-Mendes & Ditter, 2008).

A recent CGAP study (Rosenberg, Gonzalez & Narain, 2009) reported on interest rate levels in 2006. It found that in the three years (2003 to 2006) median interest rates have reduced from 36% per annum to 28% per annum, although the median varies from continent to continent and country to country. Although the CGAP study took pains to indicate that Compartamos was an outlier (less than 1% of MFIs charge such high interest rates), interest rates of 28% seem high, and would seem unethical to donors in developed countries who are witnessing near zero interest rates. The CGAP study details the median broad components of interest rates (28%) into financing costs (8%), operating costs (13%), loan loss provisions (2%) and profits (2% of assets, 13% of equity). (The totals do not necessarily add up since median figures are used, the denominator is not the same, and other methodological reasons). The crux of this CGAP finding is that for operating costs, about 13%, to reduce further, we need technology. Therefore, if MFIs are to remain sustainable, interest rates cannot go down much below 28% per annum without new technology.

This book is situated primarily in this perspective. What can technology do for microfinance and its mission to help poor people take responsibility for their lives? How can it bring down interest rates by reducing costs directly? More indirectly, can technology increase outreach and then bring economies of scale, which would also decrease costs? Or will technology lead to losses of revenues as microfinance becomes more impersonal and repayment rates fall. These different considerations are presented in Figure 3. As can be seen, the technology option increases the initial fixed costs. This could be the costs of purchasing the MIS, the costs of designing the online lending or mobile payment platform. Therefore the average fixed cost curve moves from AFC1 to AFC2.

At the same time, if the MFI is increasing these costs, it is because it is expecting transaction cost savings. For the moment, we have illustrated these as savings in variable costs. Thus, it would cost much less to process each loan application. Therefore, variable costs are shown as moving down from AVC1 to AVC2.

The final situation in costs depends on the tradeoffs between these two movements in the two cost curves. The final average total cost may be above or below the initial ATC1 curve. Thus, both ATC2 and ATC3 are possible.

Finally, it is possible that technology may lead to some loss in revenue owing to depersonalization. Loan repayments may be dependent on group lending incentives as well as personal relationships with the borrowers. If this is so, and if the technology option may push microfinance firms to increase the

Figure 3. Tradeoffs in using technology for Microfinance

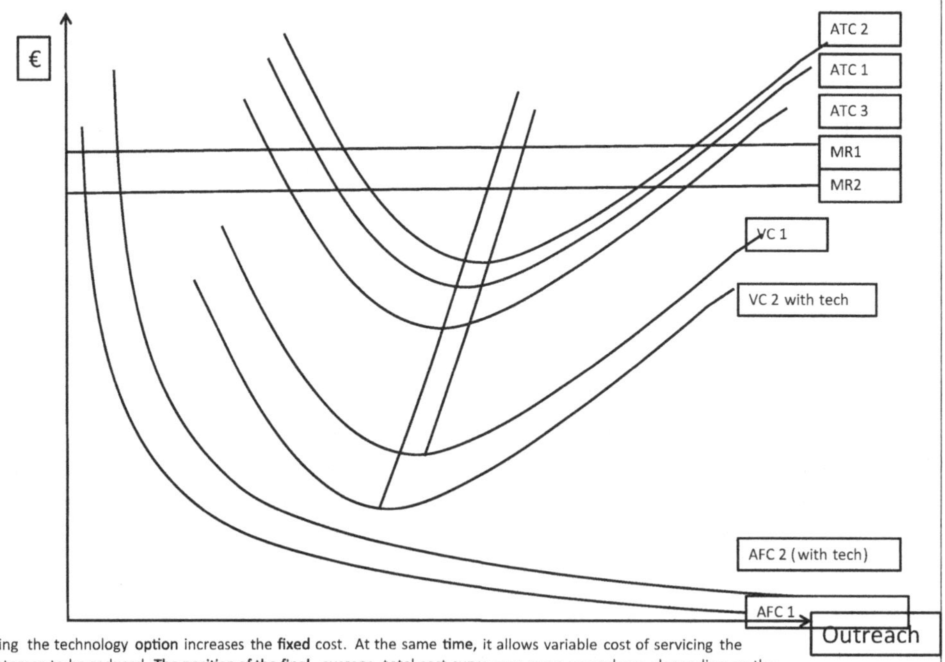

Using the technology option increases the fixed cost. At the same time, it allows variable cost of servicing the customer to be reduced. The position of the final average total cost curve may move up or down depending on the exact increases in costs. However, if the loss of personalisation may lead to lower repayment and this means the MR curve moves down (assumed as flat, but its more likely to be monopoly position and sloping downwards.)My thanks to Andrew Plantingas for discussion on this way of presenting the arguments.

number of clients served by each loan officer, the relationships may suffer and reimbursement rates would go down. This is illustrated in the figure by the MR curve moving down. From MR1 to MR2. These curves are indicated as flat for this illustration, but if the MFI is alone, as is often the case, the MR curve may be downward sloping and the effects could be even more complicated.

The exact impact of such technologies therefore depends on a myriad of factors and far more research is required on these questions than can be modeled by researchers external to an enterprise without exact information on costs.

Perhaps technology will lead to new forms of disruptive or radical innovation permitting peer to peer interaction, new ecosystems or platforms, new forms of crowdsourcing and recombinant innovations as businesses network and offer new kinds of business processes made possible by this new technology.

The first three sections of the book deal with chapters which would address these issues. Section 1, introduced by Raghavan Kunigahalli, contains six chapters by different authors, dealing with information technologies or management information systems and how they are contributing to microfinance. These technologies include improved MIS, more specific MIS adapted to microfinance, and sharing the MIS with other MFIs in the Software as a Service concept.

Section 2, introduced by Kevin Day, contains four chapters dealing with mobile phones and how they are contributing to increasing the outreach of microfinance. These chapters concern countries which have already implemented some form of mobile banking as well as countries where it is being tested and those which are thinking about it.

I myself introduce the three chapters in Section 3 dealing with online financing solutions and how they may permit microfinance to reach out to more investors and retail investors. A marketing analysis of the existing online microfinance players is followed by trying to understand if the web 2.0 tools do indeed lower costs. A case study of a more general website looks at how to bring institutional investors into contact with NGOs and for-profit entities with social objectives, including those in microfinance.

Gloria Estape-Dubreuil introduces the last five chapters constituting Section 4 and dealing with questions which do not fit into this perspective but are also related to technology and microfinance. Two of these papers are on techniques for risk management, two on adapting the microfinance perspective to developed countries, and the last paper is on using microfinance to finance appropriate technologies. It is important, at the end, to remember that we are all working to harness technology for a reason, and that is to improve the lives of the millions of poor people, whether they are in developed and poor countries.

The introductory notes to each of these parts will provide more details on the specific chapters included and the authors of each of these chapters.

The chapters bring out the fact that while the deployment of technology based solutions certainly offers cost reduction, it also offers better transparency, auditability, timeliness of data and enrichment of the engagement model with clients, all of which have the potential for long term impacts. On the one hand, all of these improve the image of the sector and reduce the ethical risks inherent in working with people from different cultures. On the other hand, they increase outreach not only to more poor borrowers, but outreach to the investors who are financing the microfinance sector, be they donors, lenders or investors.

All of these people, on the two ends of the microfinance supply chain as well as the stakeholders within the supply chain, in fact practically the whole world, is watching closely the deontology as well as the teleology of the microfinance movement. We are wondering whether the movement contributes to reducing poverty and whether it can do so through free, democratic, market-based solutions. This book is on how technology can add to both these solutions.

Arvind Ashta
Groupe ESC Dijon-Bourgogne, France

REFERENCES

Armendariz, B., & Morduch, J. (2005). *The Economics of Microfinance*. Cambridge, MA: MIT Press.

Ashta, A. (2009). Microcredit Capital Flows and Interest Rates: An Alternative Explanation. *Journal of Economic Issues (M.E. Sharpe Inc.), 43*(3), 661-683.

Ashta, A., Attuel-Mendes, L., & Ditter, J.-G. (2008). Another "French Paradox": Explaining Why Interest Rates To Microenterprises Did Not Increase With The Change In French Usury Legislation. *European Microfinance Week*. Luxemburg.

Ashta, A., & Bush, M. (2009, November). Ethical Issues of NGO Principals in Sustainability, Outreach and Impact of Microfinance: Lessons in Governance from the Banco Compartamos' I P O., *Management Online REview,* 1-18.

Ashta, A., & Hudon, M. (2009). To whom should we be fair? Ethical issues in Balancing Stakeholder Interests from Banco Compartamos Case Study. *CEB Working Paper*. Brussels: Centre Emile Bernheim, p. 34.

Granger, B. (2009). Évaluer la microfinance après le scandale Compartamos. *Rapport sur l'argent dans le Monde, Ed Association d'économie financière Juin 2009.*

Helms, B., & Reille, X. (2004). Interest Rates Ceilings and Microfinance: The Story So Far. Washington D.C.: CGAP/ The World Bank Group.

Honohan, P. (2004). Financial Sector Policy and the Poor: Selected Findings and Issues. World Bank

Lewis, J.C. (2008). Microloan Sharks. *Stanford Social Innovation Review,* 54-59.

Morduch, J. (1999). The Microfinance Promise. *Journal of Economic Literature, 37*(4), 1569-1614.

Rhyne, E., & Guimon, A. (2007). The Banco Compartamos Initial Public Offering. *Accion Insight* Accion.

Rosenberg, R. (2007). CGAP Reflections on the Compartamos Initial Public Offering: A Case Study on Microfinance Interest Rates and Profits. Washington D.C.

Rosenberg, R., Gonzalez, A., & Narain, S. (2009). The New Moneylenders: Are the Poor Being Exploited by High Microcredit Interest Rates? *Occasional Paper, vol. 15*. Washington, D.C.: CGAP.

Smith, G., & Epstein, K. (2007). The Ugly Side of Microlending. *Business Week*.

Acknowledgment

This book could not have been finished without the support of family, friends, colleagues, acquaintances and even people who I have never met except virtually. Some of them gave me time to finish this work while they took on added responsibilities. Others offered me their network to get in touch with authors and reviewers. Still others joined in for a while as authors or reviewers but finally the pressure of business did not allow them to stay in. They probably do not realize how much their presence, brief or long, with the project added to the overall enthusiasm.

Although I may have forgotten to add a dozen names, here are the ones who are still top of the mind.

Family: Emmanuelle, Amélie, Kavi, Amandine and Etienne (all Ashta).

Colleagues: First and foremost, Murielle Thibierge-Batude who joined in and looked at all the formatting of the papers. Laurence Attuel-Mendes, Stéphan Bourcieu, Isabelle Demay, Sophie Reboud, Christine Sinapi, Emmanuelle Zenou and Marie-Jo Albert-Batt and the international relations department.

School friends: Shrikant Krishan, Manna Mandana, and Mani P. Sam.

Microfinance experts: Scott Bales, Philippe Breul, Sankar Datta, Radhika Gajjala, Venkatramana Gajjala, Malika Hamadi, Gregory A. Kuhlemeyer, Robert Lensink, Deepak Luthra, Antoine Melo, Nikhil Mhapankar, Felix Ngoussou, Shweta Pandey, Ajay Kumar Pillai, Jim Rosenberg, Scott Sobel , Regi Varghese, Arnaud Ventura and Meenu Verma.

Information Technology expert: Peter C. Knight

Publisher: Special thanks to Christine Bufton for her reactivity and positive attitude.

Graphic Designer: Lisa Tosheff

Institutions: Banque Populaire de Bourgogne-Franche Comté, Burgundy School of Business, CERMI, CGAP, European Microfinance Network, European Microfinance Platform, Microfinance Focus, LinkedIn, PlaNet Finance.

Finally, I would like to thank the authors for writing and the editorial and technical advisory board members, who reviewed the papers, along with the authors and the editor. Some were strict, some were lenient, but after each paper had been reviewed by four people at least, all the authors had enough material to improve their chapter and this book is the final outcome of all these efforts.

Arvind Ashta
Editor

Section 1
Information Technology for MFIs

Introduction

Raghavan Kunigahalli
Navy Federal Credit Union, USA

Daily income of 80% of the world population is estimated to be less than $10.00[1]. Self employment encompasses more than half of the labor force in developing countries[2]. Even with more than 2 billion people still lacking access to formal financial services a lot of time and energy is being spent on just the right or wrong way to go about assisting poor with no access to formal financial services (Brix 2009). Traditional banking and financial service practices with brick-and-mortar branches are inherent with high operational expenses (Kunigahalli, 2008). Although the total revenue from servicing one hundred loans worth $100 does not differ greatly from the revenue that result from delivering one loan of $10,000 the fixed cost of processing a loan of any size is considerable. Regardless of the loan size banks and financial services organizations have to perform several activities related to assessment of potential borrowers, their repayment prospects, administration of outstanding loans and collection from delinquent borrowers. Therefore, traditional approaches to banking and financial services could lose money on *high-volume low-value* financial services thus severely restricting opportunities to offer Microfinance services to assist poor with no access to formal financial services. Due to limited options available, poor people in developing countries rely on relatives or a local money lender whose interest rates can be extremely high. A majority of Informal Money Lending rates in Asia, Latin America and Africa exceed 10% per month[3].

However, in light of the global financial crisis, even large banks and financial institutions world-wide are examining several opportunities for cutting the operational costs of brick-and-mortar branches and tapping new revenue opportunities from unbanked population (Kunigahalli 2009). Information Technology combined with innovative techniques in the area of Microfinance offer significant potential to drive profitable business with *high-volume low-value* banking and financial service offerings in developing countries. However, adoption of innovative techniques in Microfinance that utilize advances in Information Technology and Communications in developing countries requires careful analysis of several factors such as adequacy of technology and communications infrastructure, availability of computing devices and skill levels of consumers. A formal stakeholder analysis framework to identify the right solution, while taking into account aforementioned factors, can add significant value in promoting innovative techniques that adapt Information Technology to drive profitable business with *high-volume low-value* financial service offerings. A formal Microfinance stakeholder analysis framework facilitates Microfinance institutions to identify, prioritize and quantify the requirements of technology solutions to ensure that the business objectives are clearly met.

Total Cost of Ownership (TCO) of any Information Technology initiative to support or enable Microfinance activities must be extremely low to help lower the fixed cost of processing loans and maintaining accounts. Lowered TCO can be achieved by optimizing hardware, software licensing and support costs. Hardware cost optimization can be accomplished by adapting virtualization or utilizing shared on-demand hosting services whereas software cost is dependent on software products. Open Source software, on the other hand, can substantially reduce the software licensing cost to Microfinance institutions. However, organizations must understand the implications in terms of support and maintenance of Open Source solutions before embarking on full-fledged implementation. There are several Open Source solutions available at various different levels to address the needs of Web Servers, Application Servers and Database Servers. In addition to Open Source software available to develop Microfinance business applications, there are specialized Open Source Software solutions tailored to Microfinance business transactions. As an example, Mifo, an Open Source Microfinance Software solution has been implemented successfully in a Microfinance institution in Assam, India. It is extremely important for Microfinance institutions to review lessons-learned from such case studies and understand the analysis and resources required for deployment and operations of Open Source Software solutions like Mifos.

Even with promising growth and advances in Information Technology and Communications area, it is extremely important to realize that the Information Technology is just an enabler to improve the efficiency and lower the operational costs of banking and financial services. The process-oriented approach to examine the maturity of a Microfinance institution in terms of its preparedness to adapt Information Technology and automation without any major impact or interruptions to the existing business is crucial to the success of Information Technology and automation initiatives. It is extremely critical to demonstrate the Return on Investment (ROI) and ensure buy-in from the senior management and business stakeholders before embarking on a major Information Technology initiative. Adoption of Information Technology for microfinance services can help establish accountability and governance while ascertaining transparency to the stakeholders. Improvement in stakeholder relationship, operational cost reduction and socio economic benefits of target clients have been reported from early adapters of small scale MFIs in Asia.

Emerging Technology approaches such as on-demand services, cloud computing and Software as a Service (SaaS) can reduce time to market as Microfinance institutions do not have to set up and operate the Information Technology services essential for network, infrastructure and security stack. Agile development methodologies with iterative approaches can help organizations to evolve towards next-generation financial service offerings using innovative techniques that adapt advancement in Information Technology and Communications in developing countries.

In Chapter 1 titled *"Stakeholder Analysis of IT Applications for Microfinance"*, Krishna Nyapati presents stakeholders analysis from the context of Microfinance institutions. High-level requirements of Microfinance stakeholders are broken down into elementary attributes to facilitate quantification and measurement. Key IT system level requirements and their decomposition and representational aspects are clearly outlined to facilitate stakeholder analysis of Microfinance applications.

In Chapter 2 titled *"Free & Open Source Software for Microfinance: Increasing Efficiency and Extending Benefits to the Poor"*, Britta Augsburg, Jan Philipp Schmidt & Karuna Krishnaswamy examine the potential of Free Open Source Software (FOSS) to address the Information Technology application needs of small to medium sized Microfinance institutions. Key components of a FOSS ecosystem and challenges phased by Open Systems initiative from an esteemed Microfinance institution are highlighted. Contemporary opportunities such as Software as a Service (SaaS) to lower the capital and operational costs of MFIs are presented.

In Chapter 3 titled *"IT and MIS in Microfinance Institution: Effectiveness and Sustainability issues"*, S.Mohd. Najmullah Quadri, Vikas Kumar Singh & Kishen Parthasarathy Iyengar outline a Framework for appropriate governance of Information Technology initiatives of MFIs. Some of the current challenges associated with rural areas are elaborated using real-world case studies.

In Chapter 4 titled "*Automating MFIs: How far Should We Go?*" Saleh Khan scrutinizes basic business process of lending operations of MFIs and presents an impact analysis of automating MFI business processes. The chapter examines the landscape of MFI investors and examines the high borrowing costs of MFIs and the need for automation to do more with less capital while expanding the outreach. The chapter highlights the fact that one size does not fit all and outlines various levels of automation that MFIs can adapt to facilitate proper alignment with the business objectives while taking into account practical constraints.

In Chapter 5 titled "*A Case Study of Mifos Implementation at Asomi*", Puspadhar Das provides an overview of a specific implementation of open source IT application to improve the productivity of a renowned MFI in India. The chapter describes various layers of the MFI open source application and elaborates on the technology components at Web, Application and Data tiers using Model View Controller (MVC) paradigm.

In Chapter 6 titled "*Implementing Point of Sale Technology in Microfinance: An Evaluation of Come To Save (CTS) Cooperatives, Bangladesh*" Abu Saleh Mohammad Musa & Mostafa Saidur Rahim Khan outline operational cost savings realized by adaptation of Point of Sale (POS) devices used in Field Force operating in remote areas. The chapter analyzes effectiveness of POS in terms of staff productivity and efficiency gains, error reduction and lowered cost with high return on investment for POS devices.

REFERENCES

Brix, L. (2009, June). What is Microfinance. *CGAP Microfinance Blog*. Retrieved from at http://microfinance.cgap.org

Kunigahalli, R. (2008, November 18). Banks should address challenges with Creativity. *Kenya Times*.

Kunigahalli, R. (2009, February 3). Security Solutions for Mobile Banking Services. *Nairobi Standard – Financial Journal Section*.

ENDNOTES

[1]   The World Poverty Statistics, http://worldpovertystatistics.com
[2]   Discussion Topic on "Role of Microcredit and Microfinance in the Eradication of Poverty", UN General Assembly 2: Economic and Financial Forum
[3]   "Poverty" – Wikipedia at http://en.wikipedia.org/wiki/Poverty

Chapter 1
Stakeholder Analysis of IT Applications for Microfinance

Krishna Nyapati
Microsense Software, India

ABSTRACT

Microfinance Institutions (MFI) currently service over 130 million clients worldwide (World Bank, 2009), while potentially 3 billion people could benefit from the services offered by this sector. This huge base of clients, and the corresponding transactions which they generate, offer a significant potential for MFI operators to utilize Information Technology (IT) based applications in order to reduce costs and expand services. At the same time, a host of factors including inadequate infrastructure, such as the low penetration of computers and limited availability of data communication services in many geographies, and illiteracy and lack of skills, present significant challenges in being able to realize such potential. The present discussion uses a framework of stakeholder analysis, in order to identify specific problems and possible solutions impacting the future of IT applications in the MFI sector. Stakeholder analysis is a well known technique which is used to design and construct large and complex systems. The present discussion looks at the MFI context which is characterized by multiple stakeholders, with a variety of often divergent goals / requirements at a systems level. Such requirements need to be identified, prioritized and quantified, in order to ensure that they are effectively addressed in the several downstream phases, such as design, development, implementation and ongoing support. The present discussion examines the key stakeholders in the MFI context and their high level requirements. These requirements, which are typically complex and abstract, are then decomposed into elementary attributes, which are amenable to quantification and measurement. While the discussion addresses multiple stakeholders, the detailed analysis is restricted to MFIs and their clients (borrowers of micro credit). Clients are the most important category of stakeholders in any proposed system and the detailed discussion looks at some of the unique characteristics of this group, challenges they pose to designers of IT applications, and some possible ideas which have the potential to make significant impact in future systems. Specific attributes discussed include accessibility, availability and unique identity. The usage of computers and

DOI: 10.4018/978-1-61520-993-4.ch001

Management Information Systems (MIS) in the MFI sector has been growing rapidly, with an estimated 82% of all MFIs using some form of automation (CGAP, 2009 a) as per recent surveys. However, most of the currently deployed MIS solutions address back office functions and do not engage their clients directly or through intermediaries, using technology based solutions. The present discussion examines a few specific technologies and design ideas which have the potential to improve availability and accessibility of technology based solutions to the client base of MFIs, thereby enhancing the scope of automation in this sector.

INTRODUCTION

One of the major challenges facing the Microfinance sector is to engage its huge client base, now numbering over 130 million worldwide, effectively, using IT applications. Looking at the Indian context, with a user base exceeding 50 million, the challenge is to address the specific problems of poor, illiterate populations, dispersed across geographic areas with poor access to infrastructural services such as electricity, computing platforms and connectivity. Given that transactional frequencies are high, with daily collections in some cases, it is clear that automating certain identified aspects of the transaction processing system, using suitable IT based solutions could deliver significant benefits in terms of cost efficiencies, timeliness of data, and services to clients.

Recent statistics for 2007 (Srinivasan, 2008) indicate that Self Help Group (SHG) clients number around 40 million and MFI clients account for around 14 million in India. At a global level, the latest report of the Consultative Group to Assist the Poor (CGAP, 2009 b), provides estimates for 2004, 2005 and 2007, arrived at by different methods, with 133 million users for 2007. These estimates are not strictly comparable, due to differences in estimation methodology, as also differences in definition. However, it is sufficient for this discussion to note that the number of MFI users globally is already over one hundred million, and growing rapidly.

It has also been reported that as per recent surveys that only 13% of the population with annual income levels of Rs 50,000 or less (US $ 1,000) are availing credit facilities from banks, while 28.3% of this income segment have bank accounts. This leaves millions "unbanked and unaddressed" as mentioned by Dr Chkarabarty, deputy Governor of India's Reserve Bank, in a recent speech[1].

What kinds of benefits can technology be expected to deliver to MFI stakeholders, and what is the experience of MFIs in adopting technology?

As per a recent survey (May 2009) of 152 MFIs by CGAP (CGAP, 2009 a), an increasing number of MFIs are computerizing their operations, particularly for tracking transactions and loans. Currently, only 18% use manual systems, compared to 46% who were doing so as per an earlier survey in 2004 conducted by CGAP. The same survey also reports that currently 53% of respondents use customized software, while 29% use off the shelf commercial software packages. Thus, there is a clear indication that MFIs recognize the need for automation, and are rapidly moving in this direction. It has been reported (www.microfinancereport.com, 2009 a) that smart phones, biometrics and mobile phones are making MFIs more efficient and cost effective. Indeed, it is no exaggeration to say that some technologies like mobile banking have revolutionized the microfinance landscape, empowering hundreds of millions of poor clients with access to banking and financial services, which would have otherwise remained out of their reach (www.microfinancereport.com, 2009 b).

In the following discussion, our view of IT applications is based on the customer as a key stakeholder and user. It is recognized that IT applications currently used by MFIs primarily focus on data processing and back office applications, and do not address the client as a user. There are several good reasons for this state of affairs, some of which are discussed in detail in later sections. However, we believe that going forward, IT applications will have to address the client as user, sooner rather than later, and in the process, also solve a number of problems.

The discussion of requirements creates major challenges for systems designers, and we consider a few promising technologies, which have the potential of playing significant roles in meeting the requirements stakeholders in the MFI sector.

The following sections include a discussion of the background of stakeholder analysis and IT applications in MFIs followed by the main section which addresses some key, system level requirements, their decomposition and representational aspects.

BACKGROUND

Stakeholder Analysis

The term "stakeholder" has been widely used in management literature, and may be traced to Freeman's seminal book, "Strategic Management: A Stakeholder Approach" (1984).Freeman defined stakeholders as any identifiable group of individuals, who can affect the achievement of an organization's objectives, or be affected by the organization's objectives. Some of the key ideas in the stakeholder framework are that the management needs to specifically recognize and cater to the needs of all stakeholders, going beyond the traditional boundaries of investor, customer, vendor and employee. In many contexts, the term is also associated with corporate responsibility, since such a definition of stakeholders is inclusive of the public at large, civil society organizations and the Government.

Stakeholders include not only financial claimants, but also employees, customers, communities, governmental officials, ("and, under some interpretations, the environment, terrorists, blackmailers, and thieves.") (Jensen, 2000, p. 1)

Stakeholder Analysis has been used in a number of contexts, and has been found to be very useful where multiple stakeholders are involved. It has been argued (Jensen, 2000), that there is a need to maximize the overall *value* across multiple stakeholders. Indeed, Jensen, a professor at the Harvard Business School, raises fundamental questions regarding what one is trying to achieve, and how one can measure impact qualitatively and quantitatively. This highlights the centrality of defining goals, and the ability to measure actual achievement or performance against such goals.

In a paper on "Stakeholder Value Metrics" (Mize and Hallam, MIT), the authors stress the importance of explicitly recognizing stakeholders in a system, defining high level requirements (such as *Customer Satisfaction*), decomposing such complex requirements into lower level requirements (Product / Service Quality; Relationship with Corporation; Cost of ownership; cycle time), and specific metrics (acquisition cost, operating cost, maintenance cost, supply lead time, rejection rate), and finally mapping performance against importance levels, in order to derive overall values.

Another discussion on stakeholder analysis (Berry, Hungate and Temple, IBM, December 2003) looks at User Engineering and User Centered Design (UCD) as specific techniques used in IBM, for the same purpose. UCD, which is a cornerstone of User Engineering, positions user needs as the driving force behind all design activities, explicitly recognizes that setting business goals includes a determination of user needs, evaluates designs based on user feedback, and integrates user needs into overall product plans and product engineering.

The area of decomposition, quantification and representation of multiple stakeholder requirements has been treated in detail (Gilb, 2005) in his book "Competitive Engineering". Gilb has also proposed a structured representational language, called *Planguage*, developed specially for representing quantified requirements.

Thus we see that stakeholder analysis is a well known and well proven method, applicable to situations involving multiple stakeholders, values and metrics.

The purpose of stakeholder analysis, as applied to IT applications, is that such an analysis will explicitly identify all those who determine the success of such systems, and will also identify and analyze the specific requirements of each such group. Stakeholders' requirements serve as the goals of the system, and are critical in defining what the system must do in order to be considered successful.

Stakeholder analysis, the elicitation of requirements and their quantification are also critical in all the downstream processes involved in systems development, such as design, construction, testing / validation, implementation, operation and ongoing support and maintenance.

Stakeholder analysis will also facilitate the early identification of conflicting requirements. Such conflicts may arise within the requirement set specified by one class of stakeholder, or, more commonly, between requirements of different stakeholders. For example, there may often be a tradeoff between price and performance, and stakeholder analysis helps in early stage identification and resolution of such conflicts.

The overall perspective of this discussion is to use stakeholder analysis in order to discuss some of the main stakeholders and their key requirements. We then look at the problem of decomposing complex and abstract requirements of potential users, such as Accessibility, Affordability and Availability. The goal of such an exercise is to reduce complex requirements to elementary, quantifiable and measurable requirements which can be made operational. Once such goals have been identified, they need to be represented in a structured manner in order to facilitate the level of specification required by architects and designers of IT systems. This is the representational aspect of the problem, and this is also discussed with reference to a specific method called Planguage, which was developed by Tom Gilb.

The following sections will examine some of the key stakeholders in the MFI context, from the perspective of stakeholder analysis. Based on this analysis, we identify some critical problem areas and discuss a few promising technologies for the future, that have the potential to improve the effectiveness and efficiency of MFIs in the future. While the current discussion focuses on the requirements of customers / borrowers as a type of stakeholder, we note that a similar analysis in respect of other types of stakeholders and their requirements is a very useful exercise, in the context of design of IT applications.

Technology in the Microfinance Sector

The need for technology in the MFI sector has been well recognized, and studies also indicate the increasing rate of adoption of these technologies by MFIs.

Any discussion regarding technology and microfinance inevitably includes mobile phones and the variety of services being supported on them. The rapid growth of mobile phone users, coupled with technological advancements which support a growing number of services and solutions on this platform, has led to mobile phones becoming a de facto standard in terms of end user access in a few countries. Of particular importance is the ability to execute transactions on mobile phones, which has been successfully implemented in India and in Indonesia. It has also been reported that the deployment of technologies such as smart phones and biometrics is making MFIs more efficient and cost effective. Biometrics applies biological authentication systems, such as those based on fingerprints, in order to execute secure transactions. Smart cards contain real time financial data, enabling users to interact directly with biometric teller machines (BTMs) and ATMs. ICICI bank in India and Danamon in Indonesia have successfully deployed these technologies, and these initiatives are a clear indication that technology can be effectively used in reaching poor and underserved segments of the population.

However, as we discuss in the following sections, a number of other technologies, such as Interactive Voice Response systems (IVRS), support for Indian languages, text to speech technology (TTS) and WiMax, among others, offer great promise in terms of making IT applications accessible, available and affordable to the target user groups.

STAKEHOLDER ANALYSIS & QUANTIFICATION OF KEY REQUIREMENTS

In the following sections, we identify some of the major stakeholders, and some of their main requirements in the MFI context. The MFI System, as used here, includes all the major stakeholders including MFIs, their Agents, Clients, Investors, Regulators and Employees. As indicated in Figure 1, such stakeholders include current and potential borrowers, service providers, investors, agents, regulators and employees.

Now, let us consider two types of stakeholder for further analysis, and identify some of their high level requirements. We have considered two types of stakeholders, namely, clients and investors and some of the main requirements of each of these stakeholders are indicated below in Figure 2. These requirements are termed as high level requirements, identified at an abstract level. For example, it appears axiomatic that a given service must be affordable. It is not possible to measure affordability per se, but we may see that affordability is a function of the cost of the service and the income levels of the user group.

If the usage of technology based solutions were to be a chargeable service, then the criterion we would look for is *Affordability*. Here, one could go on to say that affordability could be defined and measured using some other, proxy, attributes, such as:

a. User fees as a % of the transaction value.
b. User fees as a % of the relationship value
c. User fees as a % of average monthly income of the target segment.

These proxy attributes are easy to define, quantify and measure, and hence may be used instead of the high level requirement, namely, affordability. In the process of deriving elementary attributes from affordability, we have also defined

Figure 1. Some Stakeholders in the MFI system

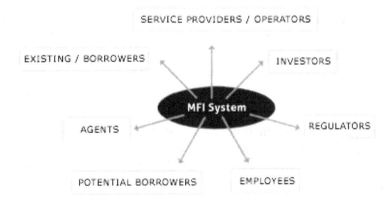

Figure 2. Need for user interfaces relevant to MFI customer

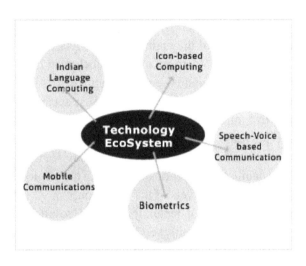

Table 1. Main requirements for two types of stakeholders

Clients / Borrowers: Main Requirements	Investors: Main Requirements
Availability	Availability
Affordability	Scalability
Accessibility	Security
Functionality	Integrity
Usability	Auditability
	Profitability

the requirement in precise, numerical terms, necessary for very many other related processes.

Scalability

As mentioned earlier, over 50 million households in India already benefit from microfinance. In the global context, it is estimated that over 130 million households are clients of the MFIs. These large numbers highlight the issues related to *Scalability* and *Performance*. Software system scalability is an important requirement in a context where the user base is large and growing rapidly. It is important that the system should have adequate capability to handle high traffic levels without adversely affecting the user experience. It may also be noted that this requirement is of critical importance to Service Providers, even though it is also of interest to investors and clients.

Availability

This is another key requirement from the user's perspective. It is evident that in order for a system to be effectively used, it must be available for the intended user. Thus, if one considers ATMs,

it is easy to see that only if they are *easily available*, that they are likely to be used. Let us now consider how we may quantify this requirement, and express it in clear, measurable terms. Here are a couple of possibilities:

Availability: A function of the distance the user needs to travel in order to access the service;
A function of the time taken (transport time + queuing time);
A function of the cost incurred.

If we apply these criteria, to, say, our ATM example, we can see that each of these three measures (time, cost, distance) are likely to have "ceilings", beyond which the user will not find it worthwhile to make use of the service. In similar fashion, we may postulate specific numbers for these *elementary attributes*, and specify that the system availability must be below specified ceiling values.

Next, if we consider the geographic spread of the target population, it turns out that important "catchment areas" lie in rural and semi urban areas. Referring once again to the Indian context, we note that the basic communication and power infrastructure, required for supporting computer based applications, is absent in large parts of the country, much of it in the catchment area for MFIs. Consider for example, that the Internet penetration rate for India as a whole is just 5.2%, and also the fact that a large proportion of this group comprises urban dwellers, not in the target population for MFIs. While the internet penetration rate varies across countries, the rates are just 5% for Africa and 17% for Asia, with the world averaging 23%. Since traditional online information systems require basic internet connectivity infrastructure, we may see that the *Availability* of the IT application, in target geographic areas, is another key requirement. Hence, we note that making IT systems available to the target segment poses immense challenges to systems designers and technologists, given the mismatch between what current technology ecosystems require and the ground reality.

Accessibility

Continuing our analogy of ATMs, given that the service is affordable and available, as defined in detail in earlier sections, there is one more important condition to be met, namely, the intended user should be able to interact with the ATM, and carry out a given set of actions, in order to meet the criterion of *Accessibility*. If we consider the example of visually handicapped persons, then films, for example, are not accessible to this group. Similarly, the set of services which MFIs intend to provide to their customers through technological interventions, must meet the criterion of *Accessibility*.

Let us consider now some relevant statistics from India. A large proportion of target customers lack English language skills, computer literacy and indeed, literacy of any kind. Looking at the indicators for India, of a total population of 1.147 billion, 61% (55% for women) are literate, 10% are English speaking and 6% are computer literate (http://www.nlm.nic.in/lsi.htm). Given that most current IT applications are based on an English language interface, it is clear that such an approach would exclude *90% of the target country's population*. Hence, we see that *Accessibility* is a key high level requirement, which needs to be addressed

in the design of information systems. While the proportion of literacy varies widely, ranging from 99.8% for Cuba (ranked No 1) to 25.7% in Chad (ranked 174), the need to provide access, is a key requirement worldwide. If one considers the female literacy rates and socioeconomic profiles of target users, it is obvious that the accessibility issue assumes even greater importance. Hence, the issue of making information systems accessible to target groups, who currently lack the skills which such systems demand, is another key challenge for systems design. Here again, we may use the approach of decomposing accessibility into some of its elementary attributes, which may be quantified. Thus, we may postulate that:

Accessibility: A function of % of target population, in the target geography, with the ability to perform a defined set of operations, with error rates less than defined rates.

While we shall discuss this particular aspect of quantification in a later section, it may be noted that this approach helps in specifying measurable outcomes, which are in turn derived from the higher level requirements.

In the following sections, we discuss some important requirements of other types of stakeholder, and one of the aspects to be noted that a specific requirement may be, and often is, relevant to multiple stakeholders.

Usability

This is an important attribute to be considered in any discussion regarding the usage of technology based solutions, and refers to *how well* a typical user is able to perform a defined set of functions. It is useful to consider learning and operation as two separate aspects of usability, and common metrics used in assessing usability include ease of learning, ease of use, and error rates. Ease of learning and ease of use, in turn, may be measured by the time taken to learn a defined set of functions and the time taken to perform a set of defined functions, while the measure of error rate is self explanatory. We may formulate requirements for usability as follows:

A function of the (% of target population which is able to learn a set of defined functions within a defined time period, % of the target population which is able to perform a defined set of functions within a specified period of time, % of target population which is able to perform a defined set of functions with error rates of less than 1%).

Functionality

This is another key requirement from the perspective of users, and refers to the set of tasks which may be performed by the user. For example, a user of an MFI may be permitted to obtain his account balance, payment history, make or receive payments, purchase insurance products, and these constitute the systems' functionality as seen by the user.

Unique Identity

One of the problems faced by clients, MFIs, regulators and investors is related to the fact that a large proportion of the target segment does not possess credible proof of identity. From the customer's perspective, this is a serious problem, since it restricts access to formal credit channels to begin with, even though she may otherwise be eligible for such credit facilities, and despite the fact that formal channels typically charge lower interest rates, often because of specific credit subsidies from the Government. Hence, from the customer's point of view, lack of identification may be seen as something which restricts entitlement. The gap between entitlement and provisioning is a serious problem affecting large segments of the population.

From the MFI operator's perspective, customers' lack of identification is an equally serious issue, since it brings in a risk factor related to the same customer availing multiple lines of credit, from different sources, without disclosing

her current debt status and repayment ability. In private conversations, executives from the MFI sector speak about the kite flying syndrome, which they use to describe the act of a borrower taking multiple loans, using one loan to repay another.

This is also a critical requirement for the Regulator a stakeholder in the context of monitoring the flow of funds with a view to controlling money laundering and terrorism related funding.

We see that the issue of unique identity is an important requirement for both the customer and the MFI. It may also be observed that in order to make such unique identities operational, it becomes necessary for all the MFIs in a given area to cooperate and share their databases, much in the way that credit rating agencies operate. Indeed, this is a very important requirement for the MFI system as a whole, when viewed from the perspective of technological interventi

Looking at the Indian context, it is reported that the number of Below Poverty Line (BPL) cards issued actually exceeds the total number of families in several states. Now, the BPL card is an important form of identification, which entitles the holder to a variety of benefits including subsidized food and fuel, and the entire system has been demonstrably compromised. The same holds with Permanent Account Number (PAN) cards issued by the Income Tax department, with millions of fake cards and numbers being unearthed by investigative agencies. It is important to understand the serious problem faced in ground level implementation by Governmental agencies which are charged with the responsibility of issuing such critical forms of identity proof. Recognizing the criticality of this problem, the Government of India has constituted an Authority to issue Unique Identities to all Indians, and has appointed Nandan Nilekani, one of the founders and former CEO of Infosys Technologies, as the Chairman of the Authority, with the rank of a Cabinet Minister, in order to lead a high priority national Unique Identification Authority.

Decomposition and Quantification

I often say that when you can measure what you are speaking about, and express it in numbers, you know something about it. (Lord Kelvin, Lecture to the Institution of Civil Engineers, May 1883)

In the foregoing sections, we have identified important stakeholders, and some of their main requirements, such as accessibility, availability and identity. These requirements, when applied to the microfinance context, generate major challenges for designers and operators of IT systems, which have also been discussed briefly. Our discussion also introduces ideas as to how these requirements can be identified and quantified, explaining the need for decomposing complex requirements (such as availability and accessibility) into elementary attributes of the system.

In this section, we discuss the operations of decomposition and quantification in greater depth, with particular reference to the attributes which have already been identified.

We illustrate the approach of decomposition and quantification by considering two very important client requirements, namely *availability* and *usability*, represented in Table 2.

The first process in decomposition is to recognize those elementary attributes which make sense, in serving as a proxy for the "original" attribute. It may also be noted that a given high level attribute (like availability) may be represented by a number of elementary attributes, as represented in Figure 3. Thus, we may consider local language support, and availability of infrastructure, as two proxy attributes for availability.

Having identified relevant proxy attributes, we then need to identify suitable scales of measure for each such attribute. For example, if we consider the availability of infrastructure, it is logical to look at the % of target population, which is able to access infrastructure, within 30 minutes, and (in the Indian context) within Indian Rs 10 of expenditure, and hence these become the scales of measure. Similarly, usability may be represented by the average time taken by the target group *to learn* a defined set of functions, the time taken to *perform* a defined set of functions, and the error rate. We also need to identify the meter (the instrument for measuring the identified attribute) and the method of recording the readings, but we do not intend discussing these any further, except to note that in choosing a suitable scale, one also needs to ensure that they are able to measure and record the identified usability metrics.

Let us consider the general case, with n stakeholders. Each stakeholder has a certain number of key requirements, represented as $R(i,j)$. This represents the requirement(i) belonging to stakeholder(j).

The approach of decomposing complex and abstract requirements may be represented as follows:

{Availability} = f {(travel time), (travel cost), (transaction cost), (others)}

Table 2. Elementary attributes for availability and usability

Elementary attributes for: Availability	Elementary attributes for: Usability
System availability in urban, semi-urban and rural areas	Time to learn [defined functions][defined skills]
Access to data communication infrastructure	Time to perform [defined functions][defined conditions]
Customers literate versus less-literate	Error rate
Language support: Local / regional	
Local assistance	

Or,

$R(i,j) = f\{r(i,j,1)..r(i,j,m)\}$ where the requirement $R(i,j)$ is decomposed into m elementary attributes represented as $r(i,j,x)$ where x varies from 1 to m.

It may be seen that the *elementary* attributes, such as travel time, or travel cost can be easily quantified and measured, and the overall idea is that *a set of identified elementary attributes serves as a proxy for the corresponding high level requirement.*

Once we define the elementary attributes which make up a given complex requirement, it becomes much easier to *specify* what we want. For example, we may specify that at least 90% of the target segment should be able to avail the IT application (or ATM in our other example) in less than 45 minutes of travel AND incurring less than $ 1 in cost. Given such a precise, quantified specification, it becomes possible to *test* whether a given system satisfies such a requirement. It also enables systems designers to use such a specification as an input in designing their solutions.

We have provided a summary of a few high level requirements related to users and investors in the following figure, which also indicate how elementary attributes are associated with and derived from the higher level requirements. For example, profitability, which is a requirement from the investor's perspective, may be specified in terms of Return on Investment (RoI), Internal Rate of Return (IRR), or Net Present Value (NPV). Similarly, Security, which is a requirement for investors as also clients, may be decomposed into compliance with specified security policies, and success rate in planned vulnerability assessments.

Structured Representation

Now that we have discussed the *process* of decomposition, we still need to be able to represent the requirement in a structured manner, using necessary qualifiers, entities and concepts.

Table 3. Associating investor requirements with quality attributes requirements

	Quality Measures
Integrity	% Discrepancy under defined conditions
Auditability	Availability of information / documentation under defined conditions
Profitability	ROI, IRR, NPV
Security	Compliance with defined policies
	% Success in breaching security under defined conditions

Given below is an illustration of representing the *Availability* attribute. The representation uses the *Planguage* constructs developed by *Tom Gilb.*

Representing the Availability Attribute

Our discussion regarding the Accessibility attribute may be represented using Planguage, developed by Tom Gilb, as illustrated in Table 4 for the Indian context. Planguage uses a well defined set of key words, such as Type, Scope, Ambition, and Scale, as also Goal, Past and Fail.

A summary of commonly used Planguage terms and symbols is provided below:

- GIST: A short, simple description of the concept contained in the Planguage statement
- SCALE: The scale of measure used to quantify the statement
- METER: The process or device used to establish location on a SCALE
- PLAN: The level at which good success can be claimed
- MUST: The minimum level required to avoid failure
- FAIL: Level below defined acceptance level.
- GOAL: Level of achievement which is targeted.
- PAST: An expression of previous results for comparison

Table 4. A Planguage illustration of the 'Availability' attribute

Type	Key system level requirement.
Scope	For information systems in the MFI domain.
Context	Many clients of MFIs are likely to reside in rural communities with limited infrastructure in terms of data connectivity and electricity. The challenge then is to identify technologies which are "available" to such a group
Ambition	Make MFI IT systems actually available in practice, to all potential 'clients'.
Scale	% probability that a defined [Customer type] with defined [Literacy] using defined [Agents] can get defined [Service levels] within a defined [Time: default 24 hours] using defined [Devices: default PC] within defined [Geography].
Past	[Customer = {Village, Woman, New Client}, Literacy = None, Agents = Village MF Agent, Service = All New, As Of = 2009] < 5%
Fail	[Customer = {Village, Woman, New Client}, Literacy = None, Agents = Village MFI Agent, Service = All New, As Of = 2011] < 50%,
Goal 1	[Customer = All, Literacy = {English, Written}, Agents = None, Service = All, Device = Smart phone, As Of = 2012] > 95%
Goal 2	[Customer = {Village, New Client}, Literacy = {Any Major Indian Language, Oral}, Agents = MF Agent, Service = {Application, Application Status}, As Of = 2013, Device = {Smartphone, PC, Office Visit}, As Of = 2012] > 99%

- TREND: An historical range or extrapolation of data
- RECORD: The best known achievement
- WISH: A desirable level of achievement that is not yet thought to be attainable through available means
- DEFINED: The official definition of a term
- Fuzzy concepts requiring more details: *<fuzzy concept>*
- Qualifiers (used to modify other keywords): [*when, which, ...*]
- A collection of objects: {*item1, item2, ...*}

The importance of this technique may be understood by looking at the definition of Scale.

Firstly, we note that in any decomposition exercise, as we identify elementary attributes, we also need to identify a suitable scale of measure. In this particular case, we suggest a scale which is the % of the target population able to access a particular service. Here, we also see the use of qualifiers, such as geography, time scale and services. The idea is to make the representation as precise as possible.

Some of the key words such as Goal, Past and Fail help to provide a context for the requirement, as also to provide criteria for testing whether the system is a success or a failure. Thus, in Table 4, if the target population able to access defined services is less than 50%, then it counts as a failure.

Design Ideas for Improved Availability and Accessibility

The foregoing discussion highlights certain very unique and challenging characteristics and system level requirements, which apply in the MFI sector.

Against this background, we discuss a few design ideas, which have the potential to deliver huge impacts in the MFI sector.

Voice Based Technologies

Voice based technologies have the potential of impacting accessibility in a significant manner, since they do not require literacy, English language skills and computer literacy as pre requisites to be met by potential users. It may also be noted that the specific technologies which are discussed here, have been well proven in other contexts, mitigating possible risk factors associated with new technologies. In other words, these technologies present proven applications, worthy of serious consideration by system designers, developers and operators.

The two specific technologies discussed here are *Interactive Voice Response Systems (IVR)* and *Text to Speech (TTS)*.

Interactive Voice Response IVR) Systems and Voice Portals

IVR solutions have been successfully deployed in various sectors such as banking, insurance, credit cards and other financial products, as also in several retail segments, by service providers, and utilities. It may be seen that these sectors represent a large number of retail users and a range of functions which are supported. The development of related technologies such as Voice XML has led to the next generation of Voice Portals, which enable richer functionality.

Another encouraging aspect of this technology is the support for Indian languages, which has already been implemented by several commercial organizations. For example, Telsima offers a range of products, including Telespeech, which supports 10 Indian languages, making these products accessible to almost 90% of the country's population (www.telsima.com). An Indian insurance Company, Max New York, recently launched IVR services in 10 Indian languages. Bhrigus Software Pvt Ltd, a Company based in Hyderabad, India, has announced a range of products and platforms to support Indian languages, including Text-to-speech (TTS) applications. HISAAB, an open source initiative for the development of Open Source software applications for Microfinance, has been experimenting with the design paradigm of numeric interfaces. These numeric interfaces only require the user to be familiar with numbers and not necessarily literate, in order to be able to use the solutions. It is possible to conceptualize an application which combines voice and numeric interfaces, in order to support a variety of functions, including queries, reports, requests and even other types of support.

The above cited developments represent a significant potential for the MFI sector, in terms of being able to reach out to its clients and potential clients, in delivering informational and transactional services, using voice and numeric interfaces.

Text to Speech (TTS) Solutions

The problem of converting text to speech has received considerable attention in recent years, and Acharya, an initiative of IIT Madras has made significant progress in this area (www.iitm.ac.in). The phonetic nature of Indian languages facilitates the generation of synthetic speech, which is easily comprehended. One of the drivers for these developments is to enable visually challenged people, but it is equally relevant in communicating with groups lacking in literacy. Bhrigus Software Pvt Ltd, a Company based in Hyderabad, India, has emphasized support Indian languages, including TTS applications.

Computing Platforms and Connectivity

Availability is the other major system attribute which we discussed earlier in the analysis of stakeholder requirements. The basic issue here is that the system needs to provide a good level of availability to users and potential users, which meet some defined criteria of time and cost to begin with. For example, one could postulate that a computing platform with suitable connectivity should be available to 80% of the target population in a defined geographic area, within 30 minutes of travel time and at a cost of Indian Rs 10 or less.

Advancements in mobile telephone technology have transformed the voice communication scenario in India, and in much of the world. Currently, the mobile user segment in India numbers over 400 million, with monthly additions in the range of 15 million (http://www.zdnetasia.com/insight/specialreports/india/.) Given this background, one needs to consider whether this technology offers options for data connectivity, as required for access to IT applications.

Wireless broadband (WBA) represents another connectivity option, particularly well suited for data connectivity. The technologies to consider in this category include Wireless Fidelity (WiFi), Worldwide Interoperability Microwave Access (WiMax) and 3G services.

The following sections discuss the status of these technologies and their suitability in addressing the needs of the Microfinance customer community.

Cellular / Mobile Phones

The key advantages of this technology include high penetration rates and acceptance levels in the target population, service availability which is practically ubiquitous, low entry and operating costs and support for data services.

However, there are some key negative factors which need to be considered as well. The first problem we face is that the two major technologies,

GSM (Global System for Mobile communications) and CDMA *(Code-Division Multiple Access)*, currently offer low data rates, in comparison with broadband alternatives, such as DSL and WBA, which are far better suited for high speed data connectivity. Thus any solution which is built on these technologies will need to contend with data speeds of around 230 kbps, which is indeed a low threshold, and corresponds to the first generation of wireless data networking, referred to as 1X. Current technologies, which are at 3X offer much higher connect speeds, with CDMA 2000 3 X offering downlinks up to 3.1 Mbits per second and uplink speeds of up to 1.8 Mbits per second. Similarly, GSM with Evolved Edge supports peak data rates of 1Mbit per second and typical rates of 400 kbits per second. It is expected that mobile phone networks will upgrade data services to 3X levels in the near future, thereby improving connectivity to a significant extent.

It has also been the experience of many countries and service providers that the revenues from data services account for less than 5% of their total revenues, while consuming a disproportionate amount of bandwidth, which constitutes a major part of the service provider's costs. This combination of high prices and low bandwidth is certainly a constraint in the usage of data services by the MFIs' target population.

Another possible negative factor arises from the relatively high prices of phones with data connectivity and computing environment support, commonly referred to as Smart phones. Currently, most such models cost US $ 250 or more in India, compared to entry level phones, which cost around $ 20. This represents a huge gap, and the high prices of smart phones constitute an entry barrier, which needs to be addressed.

WiMax and Wireless Broadband

This group of technologies holds great promise in terms of enabling high speed and reliable data connectivity to underserved geographies and the corresponding potential users. Currently, WiFi (Wireless Fidelity) technology has gained popularity and has penetrated consumer devices such as laptops and smart phones, to a significant level. The service availability is also good, and all these factors have certainly helped in making WiFi a mainstream networking technology.

A major drawback of WiFi is its range, which is limited to a few hundred meters (typically 300 to 500 meters), and hence the service is typically available in pockets or zones, such as airports, hotels, offices and homes. This is the problem which is well addressed by WiMax (Worldwide Interoperability for Microwave Access), which has a range of a few kms (typically 5 to 8 kms) for each tower, thereby making it possible to provide ubiquitous coverage over large areas. Mobile WiMax is already available in various forms, and holds the promise of delivering wireless broadband services, much in the same way that mobile voice services are currently delivered.

The potential significance of WiMax is that it is capable of providing broadband internet access to remote areas, and rural settlements, which are otherwise outside the coverage of wire line technologies, such as Digital Subscriber Line (DSL) and E1 links. The importance of broadband connectivity is that it is capable of supporting a variety of services, such as data, voice and video, thus empowering rural populations.

Wi Max has already been deployed by over one hundred operators and is available in 50 countries. The deployment of this technology in India has been significantly delayed due to issues in spectrum allocation, and even as of October 2009, such deployment appears to be at least 12 to 18 months away.

Kiosks / Shared Infrastructure Solutions / Common Service Centres

Kiosks are composite computing facilities, comprising hardware, software and data connectivity, which are being deployed in small towns and villages in India, as part of private and publicly funded initiatives. Such kiosks are meant to offer a number of citizen services, including, for example, land records and identity cards in Karnatka state. These kiosks address a number of high level requirements of their clients including affordability, availability and accessibility from the user's perspective. One interesting initiative from Drishtee has combined the kiosk model with entrepreneurship development and has promoted 1700 entrepreneurs in 10 Indian states, as per a World Bank report. Comat, another organization active in e-governance, has set up over 2,000 kiosks in Karnataka state alone. E-Governance refers to initiatives by government organizations and private operators to deliver a variety of citizen services, using the Internet, and shared computing infrastructure. By some estimates, there are as many as 150 rural PC-kiosk projects across India, some of which already have, or are planning, thousands of installations. (Toyama et al., 2004). Most of these projects were started within the last five years, riding on India's booming IT industry. Reflecting the nation's diversity, these initiatives differ in goals, models, operating paradigms, and geographic distribution. Every sector is involved – large enterprise, entrepreneurs, universities, government, and NGOs – with motives ranging from turning a commercial profit, to driving socio-economic growth, to streamlining government bureaucracy.

In a recent interview with Business Line, India's Minister for IT, Sachin Pilot, mentioned that there were already 40,000 kiosks in operation and that the Government plans to install another 100,000 kiosks rapidly. He also said that the low internet penetration in India would not be an obstacle for users, since such shared infrastructure would become available across the country.

From the perspective of MFIs, kiosks present an immediate possibility, for connecting with dispersed populations of clients and potential clients.

Envisioning the Technology Ecosystem

We summarize some of the concepts which have been discussed in the foregoing sections, and attempt to synthesize them into our prediction of how the MFI sector technology ecosystem will evolve, given its unique requirements.

These predictions arise from the perspective that IT based solutions in the future will leverage available technologies in order to improve the attributes of Availability, Affordability and Accessibility, as discussed in the foregoing sections.

First, we expect that current and traditional methods of computing, with English language interfaces and a requirement of basic computer literacy, will not have much relevance to users of MFIs. There is a need for providing *voice based communication,* in the *local language,* to support a set of defined interactions. There is also scope for deploying *numeric interfaces* which are language independent, and which will also support a defined set of functions. Thus, we are likely to see radically different user interfaces, and perhaps even the base products are likely to change substantially.

Next, we see that *mobile phones* and *kiosks* are likely to be the access devices of choice, representing a level of convergence between computing and communication. We also expect that high speed, ubiquitous, wireless communication infrastructure, based on *3G and WiMax*, to become available in the near future. Even today, we have satisfactory levels of security implemented in mobile payment systems, and hence this is not expected to pose any significant difficulty. Kiosks are also expected to play a major role in making services available in remote and rural areas.

We expect that biometrics will play a key role, in establishing identity and uniqueness. One can think of a solution in which each user of the MFI service, is provided with a smartcard, which also contains his fingerprint, and details of his accounts.

Such a system will permit the use of shared devices, and even community devices, and kiosks with multiple user access, which is the expected mode of functioning.

FUTURE RESEARCH DIRECTIONS

Non-English Language Computing

This is a major requirement, to make the IT systems accessible to a very large segment of the target market for MFIs. In India (and in other regions of the world as well) the many languages and scripts with which MFIs target users to communicate pose significant challenges to designing user interfaces which are easily accessible to these target users. However, developing user interfaces in languages comprehended by MFI clients and target clients is not the only challenge facing designers of IT systems; such solutions also need the ability to search, sort, compute, report and print in many non-English languages. There are several approaches available at present and there is a need to evaluate current technologies and products, in order to define further work which is needed.

Voice Based Communication

We have discussed the key role which voice based communication can play, again in the province of accessibility. There is tremendous scope for interactive voice based communications in foreign languages, which can solve the problems of lack of English skills and lack of computer literacy. It is indeed encouraging to note that Interactive Voice Response solutions in Indian languages are already available from several commercial solution vendors, and they have also been deployed in pockets. The challenge is to develop more functionality and capability by deploying Voice and related services supporting multiple Indian languages.

Access Products

Given the scale of operations in the MFI sector, we believe there is a good potential for design, development and deployment of purpose specific computing devices, targeting users in this sector. Such devices need to incorporate the required data communication functions, voice and icon based interfaces, as also biometrics, and multi user scenarios. There are many examples of kiosks which have been designed specifically to provide services in remote areas, which are indicative of this particular line of development.

CONCLUSION

Technology based solutions have the potential of improving service levels and operational efficiencies in the MFI sector, by making such solutions more accessible and easily available to their clients. Designers and operators of such technology based solutions will need to address specific and significant challenges arising from characteristics of the target users, as also from limitations in terms of certain elements of infrastructure.

The present discussion uses stakeholder analysis to examine certain key requirements from the clients' perspective, namely availability and accessibility. These requirements will need to be satisfied by any IT based solution in order to effectively engage their clients. Stakeholder analysis, combined with techniques of decomposition and quantification, as used in the present discussion, facilitates the specification of such high level requirements at an operational level. The challenge to designers and operators of IT based solutions is to design and build innovative solutions, using appropriate technology components, in order to improve availability and accessibility to their clients, leading to improved efficiencies and enhances services.

REFERENCES

Berry, D., Hungate, C., & Temple, T. (2003). *Delivering Expected Value to Users and Stakeholders with User Engineering*. IBM Systems Journal.

Gilb, T. (2005). *Competitive Engineering*. Oxford, MA: Butterworth Heinemann.

Jensen, M. C. (2000). *Value Maximization and Stakeholder Theory* (Working Paper-HBS Working Knowledge). Cambridge, MA: Harvard Business School.

Mize, J., & Hallam, C. (2002). *Stakeholder Value Metrics (Module to support Team Assignment in Course 16.852J/ESD.61.J-Fall 2002 "Integrating the Lean Enterprise")*. Cambridge, MA: Massachusetts Institute of Technology.

Srinivasan, N. (2008). *Microfinance India: State of the Sector Report 2008*. New Delhi, India: Sage Publications.

ADDITIONAL READING

Freeman, R. E. (1984). *Strategic Management: A Stakeholder Approach*. London: Pitman Publishing.

Robinson, M. S. (2001). *The Microfinance Revolution: Sustainable Finance for the Poor*. Washington, DC: International Bank for Reconstruction and Development.

Start, D., & Hovland, I. (2004). *Tools for Policy Impact: A Handbook for Researchers*. London: Overseas Development Institute.

WEBSITES

http://www.cgap.org/p/site/c/template.rc/1.11.1792/

http://www.cgap.org/p/site/c/template.rc/1.26.10622/

http://www.microfinancereport.com/2008/01/biometrics-and.html

http://www.microfinancereport.com/2008/01/the-rise-of-mob.html

www.drishtee.com

www.indiamicrofinance.com

www.microfinance.in

www.microfinancefocus.com

www.microfinancegateway.org

www.microfinanceindia.org

www.telsima.com

www.worldbank.org

ENDNOTE

[1]   Available at http://www.microfinancefocus.com/news/2009/08/16 last accessed on 14 Oct, 2009.

Chapter 2

Free & Open Source Software for Microfinance:
Increasing Efficiency and Extending Benefits to the Poor

Britta Augsburg
The Institute for Fiscal Studies (Centre for Evaluation of Development Policies), UK

Jan Philipp Schmidt
United Nations University MERIT, The Netherlands

Karuna Krishnaswamy
Independent Consultant, India

ABSTRACT

In this chapter we investigate the potential of open source software to increase the impact of microfinance (MF) especially for the very poor. We argue that especially small and medium organizations play a crucial role, because they are more flexible in operations and familiar with the local context. We consider how new information and communication technology (ICT) can increase outreach of MF to the very poor within a self-sustainable holistic approach. We consider the potential of free/open source software projects to address the computing needs of small and remote MFIs, and we describe the reasons why no suitable solutions have emerged yet. While the use of FOSS and ICTs in general can help increase outreach, we feel the need to draw attention to the challenges that come with it; one should not forget that access to basic financial services is not all that is needed by the very poor.

[...] our agenda [The Millennium Development Goals] is still achievable globally and in most or even all countries — but only if we break with business as usual and dramatically accelerate and scale up action until 2015 [...]

UN Secretary General Kofi Annan; Annan (2005, p. 11)

INTRODUCTION: DIFFICULTIES OF PROVIDING FINANCIAL SERVICES TO THE POOR

In this chapter we consider two important issues, which are widely discussed in the literature on microfinance, in the context of information and communications technology (ICT). The first issue

DOI: 10.4018/978-1-61520-993-4.ch002

concerns the outreach of institutions, mainly the outreach to the rural poor, including the ultra poor who are usually left out and do not profit from the microfinance industry. The second issue concerns the delivering institutions and their financial self-sustainability. Usually, increasing outreach and becoming financial self-sustainable is seen as a trade-off. Targeting the very poor comes at high costs, so that institutions that aim for the former usually depend on donor funds and subsidies. Morduch (2000) refers to this debate as the "microfinance schism", which centers on whether in order to achieve self-sufficiency, microfinance institutions (MFIs) must target marginally-poor or non-poor clientele so as to capture economies of scale and cover costs.

Most of the very poor live in rural areas with poorly developed infrastructure. It can take a full day to reach the closest bank and the opportunity costs by and large outweigh the benefit of such a lost day. Furthermore, many institutions have come to realize that their poor clients, just like anyone else, are in need of more than purely credit. A diverse range of financial instruments is needed to build assets, stabilize consumption and protect against risks. Microcredit developed into microfinance, including not only credit but also other financial services such as savings and insurance and one observes a further broadening of the concept to include services such as training, food programs, etc. Credit delivery in combination with such other services is often referred to as an integrated or holistic approach and has become increasingly popular over the last years. One of the main contributors to this development is Vijay Mahajan, Chairman of BASIX India, based in Hyderabad, who fostered, together with Tomas Dichter, the idea of livelihood promotion. The success of this integrated model has spurred similar projects in other countries such as Kenya and Papua New Guinea.

In the next background section, we argue that especially small organizations play a crucial role within the holistic approach. We describe the ICT

needs and challenges of microfinance institutions, and consider the case of BASIX India, before focusing on the special technology needs of the important small institutions. We then turn to the main section where we introduce free/open source software as a solution to provide a common technology platform to increase efficiency of smaller MFIs. The final section presents future research directions and conclusions.

BACKGROUND: WHY SMALL MICROFINANCE ORGANIZATIONS ARE NEEDED

While we are safe to say that microfinance is a successful and important tool in alleviating poverty, it is difficult, if not impossible, to track how many institutions are involved. The issue starts by defining what a "microfinance institution" actually refers to. The term is mostly used for all types of formal and semi-formal institutions that offer microfinance services but does not specify how many of their operations should be devoted to microfinance services and how their client profile should look like. This leaves a wide range of institutions including, but not limiting to, banks1, regulated MFIs2, (micro) credit companies3, credit (and savings) cooperatives and credit unions4 and Development NGOs and other non-profit microfinance intermediary facilitators.

The formal sector in India includes apex institutions such as the National Bank for Agriculture and Rural Development (NABARD), Small Industries Development Bank of India (SIDBI), and Rashtriya Mahila Kosh (RMK). At the retail level, Commercial Banks, Regional Rural Banks, and, Cooperative banks provide micro finance services. In 2004, the estimated number of such retail credit outlets of the formal banking sector comprised 60,000 in the rural areas. Of these 60,000 about 12,000 were branches of district level cooperative banks, over 14,000 were branches of the Regional Rural Banks (RRBs) and over 30,000 were rural and semi-urban branches of commercial banks. In addition almost 90,000 cooperatives credit societies at the village level were in operation. These numbers imply that on an average, there is at least one retail credit outlet for about 5,000 rural people. (Rao, 2004)

For the informal sector on the other hand it is much more difficult to get a hold of accurate numbers since there is no published data on private MFIs operating in the country. Rao (2004) reports that the estimate for these is about 800, split up in legal forms as displayed in Figure 1.

Of these 700 to 800 MFIs, only ten institutions (between one and two percent) report to have an outreach of 100,000 microfinance clients.

This distribution is reflected all over the world. A campaign launched by the Microcredit Summit in 1997 undertakes every year a survey of microfinance institutions and find that in 2005 about 73% of surveyed institutions serve fewer than 2,500 clients, as displayed in Figure 2.[5]

Despite their relatively low number of poorest clients (see Figures 1 and 2) there are a number of reasons why we consider the small institutions as especially crucial for alleviation of poverty. First, "small institutions appear more likely to enter the microfinance market" (ADB, 2000). Considering that 90 percent of the poor in the world is estimated to have no access to credit yet, the need for more microfinance institutions in the market becomes obvious and if small organiza-

Figure 1. Legal form of private MFIs in India (Source: Adapted from Rao (2004))

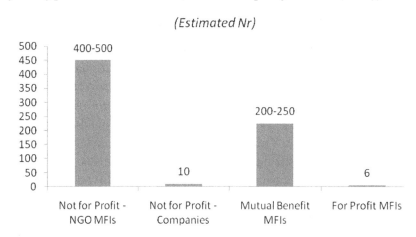

Figure 2. Nr of institutions by their size (Source: Bases on Microcredit Summit Campaign Report 2005, pg. 25, Table 3)

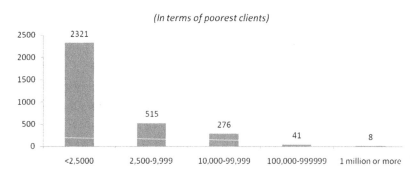

tions show more entrepreneurship then we must ask how they can be supported. In addition, it is the small and local organizations that have the potential of servicing those clients that are often left out by microfinance - the ultra poor. Institutions too often either do not prioritize or do not successfully reach this group. Reasons include the high costs of servicing the poorest (since the very poor are not the most attractive clients for standard financial services), which clashes with the increasing pressure of becoming financially self-sustainable. The ultra poor struggle with the most basic problems of food security and health and their primary concern is survival. It is not obvious how providing simple loans to this group can end the circle of poverty they are trapped in. A much more integrated approach, one that has the overall goal of establishing a regular source of income is needed; this can include financial services but more often starts with much more resource intensive activities, such as training and food assistance. In order to address the variety of needs many microfinance institutions have started to diversify their portfolio of products and services. Since studies (see for example Morduch, 1998) show that the ultra-poor are still left out, the question arises whether institutions operating on a large scale are flexible enough to give the very poor the specialized attention they need, since this does not only demand time but also precise knowledge of the environment - something which small and localized institutions can offer.

In developing countries like India - mainstream approaches and institutions fail to reach the poorest, especially in remote and less developed regions like northeastern and eastern India. Many voluntary non government organizations (NGOs) play a significant role in fostering meaningful opportunities for the poor, particularly in innovating ways for them to work together towards self reliance and to deal effectively usually with the mainstream. NGOs depend heavily on foreign funds in the absence of indigenous sources of

non government funding and highly bureaucratic and schematized nature of government funding. Consequently, smaller NGOs often closest to poor people, cannot raise funds as they lack access to international donors. Much potential for outreach and innovation thus remains unharnessed.

From the purpose of the MFI called Rashtriya Gramin Vikas Nidhi (RGVN)6

Information and Communication Technology and Microfinance

It is estimated that about 400-500 million poor people have demand for microfinance services (Global Envision, 2006). While this is a considerable number, it is only 16% of those that could benefit - only one sixth of the three billion poor people of working age have access to formal financial services.7 These numbers naturally imply the need to reach further and deeper and the need for a whole range of institutions that focus on very poor people and innovate to reach more of them in sustainable ways.

With current grant-based practices, nonstandard data and the lack of infrastructure, microfinance institutions seeking growth will have difficulty even doubling their operations. New business practices and innovative solutions that do not require constant infusions of donor funds need to be applied if the industry is to achieve a breakthrough in scale, (Sanchez, 2003)

The use of new information and communication technology (ICT) offers opportunities to lower the cost of financial services provision. We go a step further and argue that it is especially beneficial in increasing the outreach of (holistic) microfinance interventions to the very poor. The ICT needs of microfinance institutions mainly focus on three objectives: (1) exchanging information with remote clients, (2) processing and managing data at the institutional level, both at central offices and in remote locations, and (3) reducing the potential for loss during monetary transactions (collection/delivery) in remote areas. A Management Information System (MIS) that addresses the needs of MFIs consists of different components, including hardware components (desktop and server computers, hand-held devices, mobile phones, etc.), network components and protocols (GSM or other mobile cellular networks, Internet, local area networks, etc.) and software components (user interfaces, databases, etc.). The particular business needs of an MFI define what is the most appropriate solution at all three layers. However, the particular focus of this chapter is the software layer, which most directly represents the codified business processes of an institution.

The previous analysis of types and numbers of microfinance institutions provides a taste of the complexity that comes with the topic. This complexity is further enriched through the wide range of services offered by the institutions. Looking at financial services alone, there are different lending methodologies within microfinance, including for example village banking, solidarity groups and individual lending. Also, the methods for interest and payment calculations vary from one institutional model to the next and so do the number of loan products offered. At the front-office level, organizations that work with local agents in rural areas need to take into account their literacy levels and consider the use of indigenous languages. At the back-office level, where transactions are processed and assets tracked, an MIS needs to allow integration with different processing protocols that are in use by national banks and provide interfaces to upstream financial service providers. This complexity is exacerbated given that many of these variations occur inside the same institution. Furthermore social, political, economic, regulatory, legal, and cultural aspects shape the environments that organizations operate in, and differ substantially between states, countries, and regions. All these issues are of relevance when talking about the

right type of software for an institution. Moreover, MFIs are spread all over the world so that different currencies, languages, and reporting requirements come into play (Mainhart, 1999).

Technology needs differ between organizations of different size, and at different stages of their development. Waterfield & Ramsing (1998) suggest considering different software needs in the following three categories: (1) small-scale efforts with less than 2,000 clients, (2) institutions undergoing transition into large-scale institutions, serving between 2,000 and 10,000 clients, and (3) large-scale microfinance institutions, with more than 10,000 clients. Small MFIs, those that fall within the first category, may manage their operations with manual ledgers or spreadsheets and often do so since they simply do not have the institutional capacity - either in terms of computer sophistication, staff skills, or budget in order to install and maintain a full-featured software package. Not least because manual data input is time consuming and error-prone, most MFIs eventually need custom-built or commercially-available MIS software to track financial transactions and create reports for management, donors, and regulators (CGAP Donor Brief No. 23, 2005). Expanding institutions go through "growing pains: The need to deal with substantial increase in activity and resources, as well as the need to become more systematic in their operating procedures in order to handle a much larger volume of information. Their technology requirements now include security provisions, the recording and reporting of auditing information, and ability to reliably handle much larger volumes of transactions. At the same time, these organizations often lack the managerial and technical skills to implement and use such sophisticated systems" (Waterfield & Ramsing, 1998).

Not only the diverse needs of today's societies, but also a fast changing environment and pressure to innovate present challenges for software solutions and require the possibility for new features to be bolted on. New technologies that may make a dramatic difference to how microfinance institutions deliver services to their clients emerge rapidly. Latest developments include the adoption of handheld devices, the increasing diffusion of automatic teller machines (ATMs) and mobile banking - the use of mobile phones to execute transactions. In Africa, the major cell-phone carriers are starting to offer banking services to their customers, some of which are currently unbanked. For example, in March 2009 MTN announced the roll-out of its MobileMoney service to 80 million subscribers in 21 African countries, some of which are currently unbanked.8 Ketley & Duminy (2003, p.2) go as far as stating that "... the message is clear technology is changing the entire banking landscape. The poor are more and more becoming a viable target market for conventional banks. MFIs need to understand this challenge or risk becoming irrelevant."

Hence, in order for a software solution, to be appropriate to the needs of diverse organisations and settings, and to ensure its adequacy in the future, must be customizable. Only then will software be able to adapt to new institutional structures, higher volumes of activity, new pricing methods, new reporting standards, or any other relevant changes (Waterfield & Ramsing, 1998).

The Case of BASIX

One example that provides an illustration of some of the issues just described is the experiences of BASIX India9. BASIX India is an institution established in 1996, promoting the generation of livelihoods, working with almost 200,000 poor households in 44 districts and eight states across India and can hence clearly be classified in the third "software-need" category, having even had a system developed from scratch. Based on the particular needs of BASIX, FAMIS (Financial Accounting and Management Information System) was developed in 199510. During the following eight years that their operations ran on this software, several alterations had to be made

in order to increase functionality and robustness. Besides being adapted for their own use, BASIX supplied their software to several external MFIs, which in each case required tailoring to issues such as different lending technologies and interest calculation methods. One of these external users is for example Rashtriya Gramin Vikas Nidhi (RGVN) an institution that is lending to groups of individuals serving about 32,000 active borrowers11 as well as to small NGOs. Business analysts spent a lot of time with the organization and its staff in order to understand processes crucial for the adaptation of the software and translate them into software functionality. This was the case for every organization they worked with, increasing the number of different versions and hence the complexity greatly. To deal with this problem, FAMIS PLUS, a unified version was developed that supports credit, savings and insurance. FAMIS was well suited for the needs of a small MFI, but did not scale well to accommodate the significant growth BASIX experienced. To take account of future scalability, a new solution named Delphix was developed. After almost five years of running pilots, fixing problems that occurred when migrating data and further adapting the software, BASIX completed migration to Delphix in 2005. Advantages of this system include extremely rich reporting features, and its flexibility regarding terminology, interest calculation method and lending/saving methodology. This set of more powerful features has led to the software being used by more than 50 organizations today. The case of BASIX illustrates that software can be developed, which meets the demand of different microfinance institutions. It also shows though that even with custom-made software, continuous adaptation is of great importance - be it for different approaches taken, to include or change to new technologies or simply to handle growth of the organization. This obviously weighs heavily on an institutions budget. But not only costs form an obstacle. Drawing again on the experience of BASIX, other challenges, such as time-constraints are exemplified and determine what technology choices exist. For example, in 2005, BASIX launched urban operations in Hyderabad which called for the handling of new functionalities. Instead of going through the process of implementing modifications in Delphix, they chose to implement an existing (but separate) solution. Another example is IDIAS, which stands for Insurance Distribution and Administration System. This software was entirely developed in-house and BASIX is only working today on implementing these features into Delphix, although the software is already used for almost four years. The urge to offer the health, rainfall and livestock insurance that the software handles, outweighed the advantages of delaying its implementation. In several other cases, BASIX was dictated by expediency in their decision to opt for banking software called BankSoft even though that made substantial customization efforts necessary.

The ICT Needs of Small MFIs

Most existing software for MFIs is developed by and for large organizations, often with significant financial support from donors, and not with the needs of smaller rural organizations in mind. In addition, these solutions are typically proprietary (or built on top of proprietary technology), which means their owners charge licensing fees for use of the software and control who can make changes to it. This is particularly unfortunate since even in cases where the owners do not charge for use of the software (Regy & Mahajan, 2006) the costs for training and customization can be significant. This prevents access to the technology especially for smaller and remote organizations that cannot afford the required capital investment and are unable to modify existing packages to suit their needs. We see the case of BASIX as a good example of challenges and of how some of them can be tackled. Nevertheless, BASIX was in a unique position to respond to these challenges, since significant budget and expertise were available.

In sum, mature software packages and ICT solutions for MFIs already exist, but they are usually not suitable or affordable for the small institutions we are focusing on. There are several obstacles specific to these small organizations. Firstly, small institutions often lack technology leadership in-house to make correct strategic decisions as well as the staff skilled to support the MIS and vendors supplying solutions at an affordable price. A second obstacle is the paucity of funds to procure and update/upgrade technology. Furthermore, poor IT decisions may lead to "patchwork software" – software with several parts, not well integrated to each other. -, This leads easily to delays, technical defects, lack of automated data flows from the branches; and such patched software is usually not scalable to handle growth of the institution. Finally, institutions lack of basic infrastructure such as power and internet pose another obstacle.

According to the 2008 Technology Survey by CGAP12 40% of the MFIs reported that their MIS was preventing them from reaching their operating goals and 56% did not make the needed software investments due to lack of funding.

In the next section, we will elaborate how Free and Open Source Software could become a solution that has the potential of tackling the problems and challenges just illustrated.

MAIN TOPIC: FREE AND OPEN SOURCE SOFTWARE

During the past decade a new model for development of software has emerged and holds promise for the computing needs of small and remote MFIs. Free/Open Source Software (FOSS), is "software which is liberally licensed to grant the right of users to study, change, and improve its design through the availability of its source code" (Wikipedia, 2006). More specifically FOSS is developed by an international community of volunteer contributors, in a commons-based peer production model (Benkler, 2002) and makes explicit the rights that are otherwise typically reserved by copyright. These include (1) the right to modify the software; (2) to use the software with almost no restrictions; (3) to freely share the software with others; and, in order to enable modifications, (4) the right to inspect the source code. FOSS alternatives for many of the popular proprietary software products exist, and are used by private and public sector organizations in developing and developed countries. In some areas, such as web server software, FOSS applications are market leaders.

A FOSS Ecosystem

Successful FOSS projects are community efforts. They are supported by users and developers. Users report problems and bugs that they experience, request new features, and support each other in the use of the software. Developers (this category is usually broken down into further hierarchical levels) fix the reported bugs, discuss how to best improve the software, and develop new features. FOSS projects often bring together the private and public sectors, academia, and non-profit organizations. These actors participate for difference reasons, they respond to different incentives, and they expect different outcomes. From the above discussion it becomes clear that a comprehensive

approach is required to develop and support a core FOSS solution for MFIs and enable customization and deployment into a wide range of use-cases. In what follows we give a rough sketch of the key components of a FOSS ecosystem and depict this system adapted to the microfinance context in Figure 3. The exact interaction between different agents and the appropriate intervention by policy-makers strongly depends on the local context.

For one, there are the developers. Both, hired/paid and volunteer developers are needed to design and write the software code for the application. The developer community may be spread out geographically and diverse. Hired programmers may be needed for building the initial version of the core system, as well as for deployment at an MFI.

The MFIs themselves are the users. A set of early adopters to give feedback on the software for improvements and next a critical mass of users to keep the momentum of enhancements and bug fixes going. We argue that in the microfinance context, it is the small, local institutions that can keep this momentum going, while it is rather the large MFIs that need to give their support in the design stages.

Also the service providers are divided according to the size of the institution as depicted in Figure 3. Training, customization, technical support and

Figure 3. A FOSS ecosystem

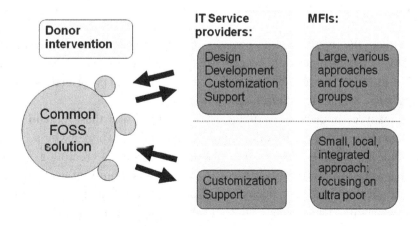

change management services are crucial factors that determine the success of technology, not only in the MF sector. Service providers need to be present in remote locations where MFIs operate. A centralized champion team to maintain the repository, deliver releases, coordinate version changes will be needed.

And then there are communities: in successful FOSS projects, the above actors form part of a larger community. Creating such a community intentionally requires careful attention to the needs and motivations of individual actors and finding the right balance between providing support and structure and letting the community find its own structures.

Based on the experience of free/open source software projects in other areas we can identify a few advantages that the FOSS model holds in the microfinance context.13FOSS saves profit mark-ups. Most small MFIs lack the financial means to purchase proprietary software licenses and donors might be reluctant to purchase software licenses for each MFI that they work with. If a network, instead, provides the seed investment and promotes a FOSS software, the profit mark-up that a traditional vendor might impose is saved.

FOSS enables the pooling of resources - networks of users contribute their expertise to design the system, and share the cost of development and maintenance and bringing more skills to the table. Some literature suggests that larger numbers of users also lead to better detection and fixing of bugs and errors, however conclusive evidence is missing.14

FOSS comes without the requirement to pay a license fee.15 This is the case not only when the software is first installed, but also considering any future upgrades. In addition, FOSS can be installed on as many computers as desired, enabling an organization to share it with others, or a donor to distribute it to all of its partners. It is important to note that while FOSS is free of charge since it removes application software licenses from total cost of ownership, deployment of the

FOSS software is not free of cost, since deployment requires hardware, supporting software and migration and deployment costs. Ghosh (2003) notes that application software license costs do matter when adjusted to the local earning potential.

The combination of no license costs with the ability to share and distribute creates an interesting mechanism for donor intervention and funding. The potential multiplier effect of paying for software development once, and then sharing it with all of one's partner organizations is attractive to donors, who are reluctant to pay software license costs in each of the projects they support. While resource pooling enables the creation of a common basic core solution, the cornerstone of FOSS remains the ability to inspect and change the source code. Every user remains free to make changes, develop extensions or custom modules for her specific needs (or hire someone to do it). This enables the development of customized solutions, and is cost-effective since a common basic starting point exists and can be used free of charge. Ideally these contributions are then shared back with the community, increasing the value of the software to all participants.

Availability of a FOSS solution can stimulate development of a local support and service sector. Rural MFIs will require training, technical support and adaptation of the software. Small local entrepreneurs and companies (who, in the FOSS model, are granted full access to the source code) can best address these needs, because they understand the local context. These local entrepreneurs can benefit from the free transfer of knowledge that is embedded in a software application and capture a much larger share of the value-added than resellers of proprietary software can (Ghosh, 2005).

Considering these potential advantages one cannot fail to wonder why a FOSS solution has not succeeded in creating a full-fledged MIS or build a community of users and developers that could support the effort in sustainable fashion. We must ask what the reasons are that hold back development efforts of a FOSS solution, and how they could be overcome. Some of the most important factors, especially in the context of MF, are mentioned below.

For one, the FOSS community is not users of the system – FOSS works best if the programmers developing the product also use it or have domain knowledge, permitting them to think of enhancements and incentivize them to make the product better. These factors are reduced in the case of programmers developing an MFI portfolio management software. Further the team would not have the domain knowledge and would rely on another source to come up with the functional specifications, which is not easy to come up with at a global level.

A second reason that holds back the development of a FOSS solution is that sometimes an early version of an application is not mature – The first versions of the product can be immature and is often believed not to be handled as professionally as by a private firm. If true, this translates into the early adopting MFIs having to endure the teething problems which keep them from adopting and delay further feedback from users for improving the software. Nevertheless, this holds true for all software – if the application is poorly written and not ready yet, the users will have problems.

Third, there is a lack of awareness - Despite its success in many areas of computing perception of FOSS is still clouded by misconceptions. Especially outside of technical circles, it is not often considered a credible alternative for proprietary software that can enable sustainable local software ecosystems.

FOSS applications are continuously improved and new versions tend to be released more frequently than for proprietary software – One of the key areas for improvement in the past few years has been the development of package managers, which greatly simplify the installation and update of software applications. However, especially for less widely used applications, the ongoing development of the software by a community of volunteers has both benefits (improvements are quickly passed on to users) and brings challenges (the effort required to maintain an up-to-date system might go beyond the capacity of a small MFI)

There is also lack of donor support for software development activities – Many donors fund capacity development, or infrastructure projects, but rarely the salaries of software engineers who develop FOSS.

A third lack relates to computer engineering skills in many developing countries – While India boasts a thriving IT sector that is exporting services and products, most other developing countries are struggling to find the skilled labor needed to support their economies internal needs. It is difficult for MFIs to attract and retain the talent needed to modify and maintain advanced software products if used in the software. Further technical leadership needs to be present at the MFI to undertake the project, which is always in short supply in most MFISs. Finally, in a complex project, software deployment and post deployment administration can be quite complex, costly and requires skills not easily found.

Moreover, difficulties to adapt management strategies hamper the development of a FOSS solution - FOSS projects require very different approaches to management, structure and hierarchy than closed source software development, where paid programmers develop applications that are designed by their managers. FOSS development processes are community-based, with clear hierarchies, and sets of roles (Lee & Cole 2003, Raymond, 2000), but it is not well understood how individuals take on certain roles. It is not an easy task to create a vibrant FOSS community and there are numerous examples of failed projects on the sourceforge.org website, which offers free hosting of FOSS development projects.

And a final obstacle is the reluctance to commit initial investment - While FOSS projects are community-based, they are usually started and managed, by a small group of individuals or organisations, who invest resources in developing a first version of the software. As Eric Raymond explains in his seminal piece (2000) on FOSS development in the real world of software solutions for MFIs, a basic prototype must be developed in a small group as a starting point for community involvement. According to Raymond it is sufficient if the software will "(a) run, and (b) convince potential co-developers that it can be evolved into something really neat in the foreseeable future (Raymond, 2000, p. 10). In the MFI context a higher level of usability might be required to convince potential partners of the value of joining the effort.

The Case of Grameen Foundation Technology Center

The Grameen Foundation has been one of the most active supporters of a FOSS micro-finance application. In their first attempt, the Microfinance Open Architecture Project (MOAP) was started with a strong community approach and invited active participation in design and development. However, the project highlighted the difficulties of steering a software development project that aims to integrate a community of self-motivated (and self-selected) software developers. At one point the lead developer left the project and publicly announced his dissatisfaction with the direction the project was taking. Clearly a discouraging moment for an organization that is investing resources into the development of a community good. Grameen took the opportunity to learn from the experience and decided to close the development process in order to revisit its original strategy. They subsequently engaged Aditi, an Indian software development firm, to build the first release of the MIFOS portfolio management software. Once the product has reached satisfactory levels of functionality and stability it will be released into the community under an open source license. Grameen aims to complement the technology platform, with efforts to build a community of MFIs that will use the software and support each other, and a network of volunteer programmers,

who contribute development time to the project.16 However at the moment, despite product maturity, adoption by MFIs has been slow and building a network of volunteers remains a challenge. MIFOS is an example of private/open community partnership. Private firms were engaged for the technical work to deploy MIFOS at an MFI and support it post-deployment.

Software as a Service

The microfinance sector is leaning towards centralized server architecture for their portfolio management needs. This is an order of magnitude more complicated to deploy and maintain than simpler desktop applications often currently used. The costs of renting a data center and purchasing servers are significant and administering it needs advanced skills that an MFI might not be able to attract. This points to the potential for building FOSS applications on a multi-tenant model. In this model, the software is designed and deployed at a data center in such a way that multiple MFIs can simultaneously and securely use the software residing on the same server. This may be compared to many email users being able to create gmail accounts on the same gmail server. While the software may be developed by the FOSS community, its deployment and customer support needs to be done by a dedicated third party such as an MF network or association. The MFIs pay on a pay-as-you-go model, based on a per transaction fee or per customer fee. This avoids the larger upfront investment and team hiring needs on the MFI. The PinoyMe Foundation has recently launched MIFOS on such a "software as a service" model called MiFITS for MFIs in the Philippines.

FURTHER RESEARCH DIRECTIONS

In this study we look at how new ICT, namely free/open source software, can increase outreach of microfinance – through small and large MFIs – within a self-sustainable approach

It is clear that many challenges have to be tackled to succeed in the match of this technology and the microfinance movement. There is little empirical research that unravels these challenges as well as the prospects inherent in the fusion of ICT and the complex context of microfinance, where human practices and social relations play a major role. More research is needed to get behind these relationships to understand how the proposed amalgamation can be successfully put in action.

CONCLUSION

While technology remains a challenge for MFIs by and large, it has the potential to increase outreach to more customers and reduce operating costs. While this goal is of interest to many developing countries, transition countries are in promising positions. Brazil or India have great experience with successful microfinance projects, but are under pressure to extend the benefits and improve living conditions of their many rural poor. In addition these countries have relatively well-developed ICT sectors and software development capacity, and this local availability of skills presents an opportunity to create the affordable and adaptable software solution that is needed by the small rural MFIs in developing countries. The public sector can play a crucial role in supporting the diffusion of MF services to the poor, by supporting/ funding collaborative software development for MFIs, facilitating knowledge networks between MFIs, raising awareness of the advantages of a collaborative approach that is built on FOSS. At the same time, this is a time of opportunity for the private sector, both large MFIs as well as small local organizations and service providers who could support and maintain the IT infrastructure of small remote organizations. We have stressed the importance of providing affordable and appropriate technology to increase outreach of holistic MF services to the very poor. At the same time we are cautious as to the measurable impact of such intervention. It remains a crucial research need to find out more about the individuals that are being reached and the impact on their living conditions, to avoid equating simple increase in numbers of clients with real impact on livelihood. This can only be achieved through carefully designed monitoring and ongoing evaluation efforts. First, it is important to know 'who' is being reached and consider the trade-off between increasing outreach and reaching the very poor. We argue that this trade-off is important and that it is the reason why a diverse set of institutions is needed: large institutions that can serve the poor and not-so pure on a large scale and small and local institutions that concentrate on the ultra poor. Policy-makers need to consider the special support that these smaller institutions might need since their operations are struggling to become self-sustainable. In order to increase the number of such small organizations, governments should lower barriers of entry in this market specifically. This can be done through adjusting the regulatory framework or providing support and services. We argue that the development of a FOSS MIS for these smaller organizations would facilitate their scaling up, and allow them to implement stricter evaluation and reporting standards, which in turn would enable access to donor funding. In addition, government should encourage the collaboration between MFIs of different sizes and at different stages of development. Providing a common technology platform and standards for exchange of data would greatly facilitate this process.

REFERENCES

Annan, K. (2005). *In larger freedom: towards development, security and human rights for all. Report of the Secretary-General, 21 March 2005.* United Nations.

Benkler, Y. (2002). Coase's Penguin, or, Linux and The Nature of the Firm. *The Yale Law, 112.*

Ghosh, R. A. (2005). *Free/Libre/Open Source Software for developing countries: skills, employment and costs.* Paper presented at International Conference on Open Source ICOS 2005, Taipei. November 10, 2005. Retrieved October 20, 2009 from http://www.infonomics.nl/FLOSS/papers/20051110/rishabGHOSH-icos05.pdf

Global Envision. (2006). The Basics on microfinance. Retrieved October 20, 2009 from http://www.mcenterprises.org/userimages/file/basics_on_microfinance_global_envision_2006.pdf

Haaland, R. (2003). Licence fees and GDP per capita: the case for open source in developing countries. *First Monday, 8*(12). Retrieved October 20, 2009 from http://firstmonday.org/htbin/cgiwrap/bin/ojs/index.php/fm/issue/view/165

Ketley, R., & Duminy, B. (2003). Meeting the Challenge the Impact of Changing Technology on MicroFinance Institutions (MFIs). *MicroSave Briefing.* Retrieved October 10, 2009 from http://www.microsave.org/

Lee, G. K., & Cole, R. E. (2003). From a firm-based to a communitybased model of knowledge creation: The case of the Linux kernel development. *Organization Science, 14*, 633–649. doi:10.1287/orsc.14.6.633.24866

Mainhart, A. (1999). *Management Information System for Microfinance: An Evaluation Framework.* A work supported by the U.S. Agency for International Development, Bureau for Global Programs, Center for Economic Growth and Agricultural Development, Office of Microenterprise Development, through funding to the Microenterprise Best Practices (MBP) Project, contract number PCE-C-00-96-90004-00. Retrieved August 6, 2006 from http://www.cgap.org

Morduch, J. (1998). *Does Microfinance Really Help the Poor? New Evidence on Flagship Programs in Bangladesh.* MacArthur Foundation project on inequality working paper, Princeton University, draft. Retrieved April 17, 2006 from http://www.nyu.edu/projects/morduch/documents/microfinance/Does_Microfinance_Really_Help.pdf

Morduch, J. (2000). The Microfinance Schism. *World Development, 28*(4), 617–629. doi:10.1016/S0305-750X(99)00151-5

Rao, K. M. (2004). *Microfinance Institutions in India.* An article presented at the APRACA Seminar on Regulation of MFIs, Manila, Philippines.

Regy, P.V. & Mahajan, V. (2006). IT at BASIX: Successes and Failures, a Retrospective, *Information for Development, 4*(5).

Sanchez, E. C. (2003). Microfinance and technology: The way to greater financial access Retrieved August 1, 2006 from http://www.itmatters.com.ph/features.php?id=091503

Waterfield, C. & Ramsing, N. (1998). *Handbook for Management Information Systems for Microfinance Institutions.*, CGAP Technical Tool Series No. 1, February 1998.

ADDITIONAL READING

Arsenault, N. (2003). *Answering the Top 5 Myths about Selecting Software for Microfinance Institutions,* [White Paper] Retrieved on August 6, 2006 from http://www.microfinancegateway.org/gm/document-1.9.25595/3812_arsenault.pdf

Asian Development Bank. (2000). *The Role of central Banks in Microfinance in Asia and the Pacific.* Asian Development Bank.

Cascio, J. (2006, February 10). *Open Source Microcredit, Revisited*. The Tech Bloom Collaborative and Emergent Technologies. Retrieved August 8, 2006 from http://www.worldchanging.com/archives/004095.html

CGAP (April 2005). *Funding Microfinance Technology*. CGAP Donor Brief No. 23. Washington, D.C: CGAP.

Coleman, B. E. (2002). *Microfinance in Northeast Thailand: Who benefits and how much?* Economics and Research Department, Asian Development Bank. Working Paper Series No.9.

Dailey-Harris, J. (2005). *State of the microcredit Summit Campaign Report 2005*. Washington, DC, USA: The Microcredit Summit Campaign.

Foster, D. (2005). What C.E.O.s Need to Know About Software Selection. *MicroSave Briefing* Note # 43. Retrieved October 20, 2009 from http://www.microsave.org/briefing_notes/briefing-note-43-what-ceos-need-to-know-about-software-selection

Heckman, J. J., & LaLonde, R. J. (1999). The Economics and Econometrics of Active Labor Market Programs. In Ashenfelter, O., & Card, D. (Eds.), *Handbook of Labor Economics* (*Vol. 3*).

Lee, M.-J. (2005). *Micro-Econometrics for Policy, Program and Treatment Effects*. New York: Oxford University Press Inc. doi:10.1093/0199267693.001.0001

Parikh, T. (2005). *Rural Microfinance Service Delivery: Gaps, Inefficiencies and Emerging Solutions*. University of Washington. Retrieved August 6, 2006 from http://www.fdc.org.au/Electronic%20Banking%20with%20the%20Poor/3%20Parikh.pdf

Pitt, M., & Khandker, S. (1998). The Impact of Group-Based Credit Programs on Poor Households in Bangladesh: Does the Gender of Participants Matter? *The Journal of Political Economy*, *106*(5), 958–996. doi:10.1086/250037

Prasad, G. (2001, July 26). *Yes, you can do Business with Open Source*. FreeOS.com. Retrieved August 9, 2006 from http://www.zdnetindia.com/techzone/linuxcentre/stories/32999.html

Raymond, E. S. (2000). The Cathedral and the Bazaar. Retrieved October 10, 2009 from http://catb.org/~esr/writings/homesteading/cathedral-bazaar/

Steve, L. (2005, July 3). Model Credit Bureau. *Open Source Solution Being tested in Morocco*. Retrieved August 8, 2006 from http://www.nextbillion.net/newsroom/2005/07/03/model-creditbureau-open-source-solution-being-tested-in-morocco

ENDNOTES

[1]　companies that fall under national banking laws with considerable microfinance activities (Banco del Desarrollo in Chile, Banco Solidario in Ecuador, but also the rural banks - BPRs - in Indonesia)

[2]　financial intermediaries that are subject to government or Central Bank rules and regulations but are not banks (EDPYMEs in Peru, Fondos Financieros Privados in Bolivia).

[3]　non-regulated companies involved in microfinance (Share Microfin Ltd. in India, Cambodian Entrepreneur Building Ltd.).

[4]　formally registered cooperatives and unions that provide microfinance services to their members (SACCOs in Kenya, MACAPFs in Bulgaria).

[5]　Network numbers given in the table "include data from three large networks: the National Bank for Agriculture and Rural Development (NABARD), see footnote 14, in India; the Association of Asian Confederation of Credit Unions (ACCU), which has 3,137,398 total and poorest clients, and the Bangladesh Rural Development Board

(BRDB) which has 3,713,728 total clients and 3,528,041 poorest. These entities are not individual microfinance institutions, but they report the aggregate number of clients served to the Microcredit Summit and are included accordingly in our report, after we have eliminated any double counting." (Microcredit Summit Campaign Report, 2005, p.25)

[6] http:// www.rgvnindia.org/genesis.htm. RGVN was founded as an autonomous, non profit organization in April, 1990 and is today working in 14 states of India, providing support and capacity building to Indian NGOs as well as credit and saving facilities directly to the people.

[7] The estimate of how many poor people are not being reached differ by sources and country considered. Muhammed Yunus states at the International Seminar on Attacking Poverty with Microcredit in Dhaka, Bangladesh, January, 2003, that "In most countries it [microfinance] has not even reached 10% of the poor families within that country."

[8] http:// africa.tmcnet.com / news / 2009 / 03/ 16/4059454.htm

[9] This case study draws heavily on Regy & Mahajan (2006).

[10] The development partner for the software is the company Sadguru Management Consultants, who have subsequently been involved with other BASIX software development projects.

[11] http:// www.mixmarket.org

[12] www.cgap.org, accessed June 2009.

[13] Some good starting points are the community access project in the Extremadura region of Spain, or the development of the Open Office suite of applications.

[14] The positive influence of having more people inspect the source code is typically referred to as "Linus Law", http://en.wikipedia.org/wiki/Linus's law, last accessed August 2006.

[15] While FOSS licenses do not prevent sales of the software, most licenses mandate the availability of source code and the right to redistribute, which reduces the potential market to one customer.

[16] http:// www.gfusa.org/ technology center/ MIFOS/ beta release/

Chapter 3
IT and MIS in Microfinance Institution:
Effectiveness and Sustainability Issues

S. Mohd. Najmullah Quadri
IT Professional, Singapore

Vikas Kumar Singh
IT Professional, Singapore

Kishen Parthasarathy Iyengar
University of Colorado at Boulder, USA

ABSTRACT

According to a recognized survey, only 11% of the world's 240 million poorest families are currently served by Microfinance Institution (Daley-Harris, 2002). In order to increase the outreach of MFI, institution will have to go a step further and start their operation in the rural areas. Implementing sustainable IT infrastructure in such areas is a challenge with numerous obstacles. Further, employee training also poses challenges that are unique to the microfinance industry. In this chapter, we articulate some of the challenges faced by microfinance institutions and some potential solutions with the help of real world case studies. We also propose a framework, which will help microfinance institutions implement IT based management information systems effectively.

INTRODUCTION

"The Millennium Development Goals can be met by 2015 but only if all involved break with business as usual and dramatically accelerate and scale up action now." These words of erstwhile UN Secretary General Kofi Annan suggest that there is a need for every industry, including mi-

DOI: 10.4018/978-1-61520-993-4.ch003

crofinance institutions (MFIs) to go a step further to increase its outreach.

With current practices, nonstandard data and the lack of infrastructure, microfinance institutions seeking growth will have difficulty in even doubling their operations which is imperative to widen their scope. As a result, new business practices and innovative solutions by harnessing the benefits of technology are preeminent to achieve the breakthrough in the scale. The solution to this is integrating MFI with a management information system (MIS) but, there are many challenges and sustenance issues to be dealt with. Further, judicious use of MIS can be a boon for any MFI whereas, if not used wisely the same MIS can be encumbrances for the MFI.

In this chapter we intend to consider three very important points which are widely discussed among the fraternity of microfinance, in the context of management information system (MIS). The first point concerns the basic challenges any MFI has to face in integrating management information system. By definition, most of the poor live in rural areas with poorly developed infrastructure. Hence, it becomes imperative to find out different ways to mitigate the impediments coming in the way of any MFI in establishing MIS in the absence of basic infrastructure. The second point concerns the factors that can be included in order to have a sustainable MIS for any MFI. Once the challenges are met in establishing MIS within an MFI, the institution has to confront the sustainability issues from maintaining financial viability to maintenance of infrastructure. We try to discuss diverse range of ways and measures that can be adopted to help MFI sustain its MIS. The third issue concerns the methodologies that can be incorporated for having an effective MIS in MFI. Every MFI seeks some objectives from MIS. Only an effective MIS will be able to promise the following points like fast exchange of information with remote clients, processing and managing of data at the institutional level, both at central offices and in remote clients, reduction in the potential for loss during financial transactions, be it collection or delivery in the remote areas and finally, effective reporting. All these fulfilments will help the MFI to reach further and deeper and help in serving the needy in a much more focused way. We bring forth some of the points including the discussion of a framework which will help in the set-up of an effective MIS. (Augsburg & Schmidt, 2006)

BACKGROUND: CHALLENGES IN SUSTAINING MIS IN MFIS

The last decade has been marked by the increasing influence of Information Technology and Communications in all walks of life. The Microfinance Industry is no exception, but inculcating MIS in MFIs is not an easy task at hand due to various factors that will be discussed in this section.

MFIs usually operate in remote and rural areas and therefore, employees are predominantly not well educated. Further, MFIs have low budgets, making it difficult to build and operate MIS that can have a positive impact. The major challenges such firms face are that MFIs are significantly different from commercial banks, existence of infrastructure issues in implementing MIS in MFIs, lack of IT support in MIS in MFIs, lack of organized training in IT for the MFI employees and lack of standardization in procedures in the MIS. Each of these challenges is described below. (Ahmad, The First MicrofinanceBank Ltd., 2008) (Murthy and Bagchi – Java Softech Private Ltd, http://www.microfinancegateway.org/gm/document-1.9.26112/38547_file_38.ppt)

Challenge I: MFIS are Different from Commercial Banks

Microfinance is significantly different from Commercial and Retail banking in its approach and operational structure. Since Microfinance is a relatively new concept, as compared to commercial financing, very little attention has been given to its organization and structure. Furthermore, account officers working in MFIs are not that well trained in their realm, as compared to their counterparts in the banking sector.

The kind of information that MIS need to capture is another factor that makes Microfinance different from regular banking. In regular banking, banks obtain proof of the client's identity and certain relevant information like KYC (Know Your Client) before doing any financial business with the client. Also, in regular banking there is a concept of keeping financial history for the clients. On other hand, microfinance client information is much more detailed and it includes information about the socio-economic status, household member details and background checks. Thus, implementing an MIS in such institutions, where requirements are not fixed, is a challenge. (Charitonenko and Campion (all Chemonics), http://www.basis. wisc.edu/rfc/documents/Summary%20and%20 Notes%20-%20session%205.pdf).

One of the reasons for the less organized nature of MFIs is that the industry is still in its inception phase. Further, up until now, MFIs have eluded the attention of commercial bankers, who may be more capable to improve on the structure and processes of MFIs. This may be attributed to the fact that not much money flows in for a MFI in the initial stages of institution set up, when it is trying to sustain itself.

In a number of countries, commercial banks have been compelled by their governments to provide financial services, especially credit, to sectors such as small or agricultural enterprises that are considered social priorities. However, the use of moral or legal compulsion in general, has not led to sustainable models. Sustainable models for the Microfinance sector may only come about when commercial banks find microfinance to be an imperative investment.

The entry of commercial banks into MFIs is already underway with some banks entering the microfinance market because they see sustainable profit and growth opportunities. Furthermore, commercial banks are facing increasing competition in their markets, leading to shrinking margins. This pressure is leading forward-thinking banks to explore new potential markets. To many commercial banks, microfinance is a potential market with the capacity to generate growth in clients at acceptable profit margins.

The entry of big banks into microfinance may help increase the financial status and legitimacy of the sector. Further, the IT experience and financial

acumen of such large banks will help in designing and implementing systems within MFIs that are sustainable.

We describe a case study below, which elucidates how the entry of big commercial banks can help microfinance institutions build MIS.

How IBM – FINO Helped MFIs in India?

FINO (Financial Information Network and Operation Ltd.), promoted by ICICI Bank, is a technology solutions company that is among the first to provide a solution to reach millions of underserved people through MFIs.

FINO was founded on July 13th 2006, with the objective of building technologies that enable financial institutions to serve the under-served unbanked rural sector. Since its inception, the firm has been on a rapid growth journey. IBM has partnered with FINO to deploy a low cost core banking and end-to-end smart card solution for MFIs based in India.

The technology facilitates online and offline transactions at an affordable cost so that it can be used in rural areas where the infrastructure is inadequate. The customers access the system using a biometric-enabled multi-functional personalized card, which also serves as the proof of identity and as an electronic passbook for them.

FINO, which was established by 17 bankers from ICICI bank, has now come up with many specialized products, one of which is the FINO– MITRA. FINO – MITRA is a comprehensive package of mobile-enabled banking solutions enables the enrollment as well as banking transactions through the use of mobile technology thereby increasing capability at reduced costs. With the initial thrust and support, FINO has also managed to offer products like Tijori (a biometric smart card based no frills saving account product designed), Saral (a loan management system) and Sayana Ravi (a credit scoring solution for banks). (http:// www.indiamicrofinance.com/ - FINO Launches MITRA page)

With initiatives such as this, big commercial banks can open up new strategic areas of investment, while serving the under-served. *Source: EFY News, March 2007*

Challenge II: Infrastructure Issues in Implementing MIS, in MFIS

It is an unavoidable fact that MFIs will face infrastructure issues. How big the infrastructure issue is, solely depends on how big the institution itself is.

In the words of Mohammed Yunus, the founder of Grameen Bank, "People should not come to the bank; the bank should go to the people". So to serve better, a Microfinance institution has to be in rural areas where access to basic infrastructure is limited in terms of power, internet access and phone lines. IT based information system would require such an infrastructure to be in place. Therefore, MFIs face a challenge in implementing systems where the infrastructure is lacking.

When faced with problems, one of the best strategies is to learn from other firms. Microfinance institutions should look to how other similar organizations overcome such infrastructure constraints.

One simple strategy to handle the infrastructure issues is to plan appropriately. For example, some MFIs tackle the lack of power by clustering 20-30 branches into one regional center, which serves as a data entry point. The field staff submits a weekly collection sheet to the cluster center, where data entry operators enter all information about loans and collections for the week. This process circumvents the need to establish and maintain IT systems in all branches. Similar workarounds may be possible for other infrastructure issues.

Another methodology developed is the Branch Office Franchise Model. In this approach, the MFI links to the third-party merchants in the remote areas. These third –party franchisees manage transactions on the behalf of the bank, they then receive an agreed payment for service on a per-transaction basis. The key advantages of having franchisees are that they are long-term businesses, respected and trusted in their communities thereby helping MFI to convince the local people. A recent player in the Branch Office Franchise, notably in India, is the rural telecentre networks that are particularly suited to serving as retail outlets for a distributed microfinance network.

Challenge III: Lack of IT Support in MFIS

It is often said that a majority of the costs are accrued in the maintenance of the system, rather than building or implementing it. Two major issues in the maintenance phase, described below, have the potential to increase costs for the organization. First there are hardware/software issues in which IT based systems may face fatal errors and fail due to hardware or software crashes or malfunctions. Secondly there can be changes in the requirement of the organization during the implementation or post-implementation of the MIS. These changes basically arise because of the change in the process model, growth of the organization or change in the strategic focus.

As mentioned previously, the post-implementation maintenance and support activities are a potential drain on the resources of the organization. The extent of costs for such activities depends on the issues faced. In general, early detection of problems alleviates the costs. Thus, organizations that plan support protocols, for various problem scenarios, have the best chance at reducing costs.

In the following sections, we outline some scenarios that an organization could face, and measures that the organization could incorporate in order to reduce costs. We will illustrate this using various case studies. While it is virtually impossible to plan for all eventualities, we will discuss some of the most common ones below. Awareness of these common issues will help in developing responses aimed at resolving the issues quickly and lower cost.

Database Crash

The term, database, refers to the repository of data in the organization. Unlike manual spreadsheets which have only a two-dimensional structure to store the data, a database can store data on three or more dimensions. If an institution is growing larger, then a computerized database is vastly preferable.

As an organization grows, the amount of data to be stored also increases. The exponential growth in data poses the challenge of storage and protection from accidental deletions and disasters, as well as complying with regulatory requirements. These challenges are usually handled in one of the two different ways. The first method is called as 'backup'. Backup technologies have long provided effective recovery options for systems subject to data loss from human error, hardware failure or major natural disasters. They are ideally suited for quick restoration of large amounts of lost information and can return complete systems to full operational capacity in a short period of time. Any organization, however small, can make backup copies of its database. If there are chances of a power failure breakdown during the backup process itself, then there should be a provision of small battery back-up in the form of UPS (Uninterruptible Power Supply). The UPS will enable the user to at least control the backup process which can be continued once power restoration happens. The copies of the data can then be stored at an offsite location. Thus, in case there is a loss of the database due to any reason, the organization can rely on the copy stored elsewhere. Another method uses 'archiving'. Archiving is very similar to backup, except that archives are implemented with long-term access and retrieval in mind.

A Microfinance Institution can plan on implementing either of the two methodologies, based on its requirements. Bigger organizations can incorporate both together to minimize costs. (Smeaton,http://www.augsd.org/sampleapps/ Splitting%20a%20Database.ppt)

Hardware or Software Crash

Typically, at the time of their establishment, microfinance institutions do not have clear plans for growth or the extent of their expansion. They also lack any kind of planning for the procurement of hardware and software. The ad-hoc procurement of hardware and software leads to higher costs and inefficiencies. Moreover, because procurement procedures are not in place, firms end up with low quality hardware and software. Such poor quality IT infrastructure often leads to systems that are prone to breakdowns. Furthermore, these organizations lack personnel with adequate IT knowledge to solve such issues.

A simple solution to prevent frequent hardware and software failures is to plan for the implementation of IT based systems well in advance, cognizant of the growth potential of the organization. Such plans need to be backed up by adequate budget allocation. This will help in laying the IT foundations that satisfy not only current requirements, but also fulfill future needs. Obviously, small MFIs will not be privileged enough to earmark budget because of restricted financial resources. For such cases, small MFIs should take advantage of the initiatives taken by big banks to promote microfinance. In India, private Institutions like ICICI banks, HDFC banks and many more have helped smaller MFIs to plan their future growth.

Another prevention method could be to bundle the software with suitable, no frills, low-cost hardware, especially for the institutions with multiple branches. This would involve the concept software bundling, wherein, the organization rolls out boxes with original software loaded for deployment.

Another step that MFIs should take is to ensure the quality of the hardware and software in its implementation. Licensed and authentic hardware and software sold by reputable vendors are typically accompanied by warranties. Such warranties ensure immediate resolution to hardware and software failures. Furthermore, counterfeit hardware and software are heavily prone to failures, and lack any warranties. Thus, firms should purchase only licensed authentic IT hardware and software to minimize the occurrence of failures. Another important advantage of purchasing licensed software and hardware is to get installation support from the vendor.

Further, there are some vendors who provide customizable software. One of the examples is the 'Exceptional Assistant' software from Common-Goals Software. There are other instances when software was customized owing to the needs of various MFIs. (http://www.commongoals.com/ - Exceptional Assistant FAQ page)

Evolution of Delphix as a Full-Fledged MIS Solution from BASIX

BASIX India is an institution established in 1996, promoting the generation of livelihoods, working with almost 200,000 poor households in 44 districts and eight states across India. Based on the particular needs of BASIX, FAMIS (Financial Accounting and Management Information System), a MIS supporting solution was developed in 1995. The following eight years BASIX's operations ran on FAMIS and several alterations had to be made in order to increase functionality and robustness. Besides being adapted for their own use, BASIX supplied their software to several external MFIs, which in each case required customizing to issues such as different lending technologies and interest calculation methods. One of these external users was Rashtriya Gramin Vikas Nidhi (RGVN), lending to groups as well as to small NGOs, and serving about 32,000 active borrowers.

Business analysts spent a lot of time with the organization and its staff in order to understand processes crucial for the adaptation of the software and translate them into software functionality. This was the case for every organization they worked with, increasing the number of different versions and hence the complexity greatly. To deal with this problem another version of FAMIS was developed known as FAMIS PLUS. This version

was an upgraded version which supported credit, savings and insurance together.

FAMIS PLUS suited to the needs of BASIX for some time but with the growing needs and with the widening of the scopes, and in response to the widening needs a new solution named Delphix was developed. After almost five years of running pilots, fixing problems that occurred when migrating data and further adapting the software, BASIX completed migration to Delphix in 2005. Advantages of this system include extremely rich reporting features, and its flexibility regarding terminology, interest calculation method and lending/saving methodology. This set of more powerful features has led to the software being used by more than 50 organizations today.

The case of BASIX illustrates that software can be developed, which meets the demand of different microfinance institutions. This also shows that software can evolve through customizations and tailoring in different forms to support wide range of needs for different MFIs. However, it also shows that even with custom-made software, continuous adaptation is of great importance - be it for different approaches taken, to include or change to new technologies or simply to handle growth of the organization. (Augsburg & J. Schmidt, September 2006)

Complex Functionality of the Application

Since MFIs are located in predominantly remote rural areas, users of technology in such organizations lack both IT and financial skills. Therefore, it becomes imperative to design a system that is simple to understand by such users. Figure 1 is a snapshot of an application that illustrates such a simple design adapted from one of the MFI.

System Slowdown

There can be many reasons for the slowdown of a system. While it is virtually impossible to list all possible reasons, one of the most common reasons is slow disk speed. Sometimes system slowdown happens when the disk arrays aren't able to handle Input/output requests quickly enough. Some other reasons can be like the System is starved for memory, so that applications are forced to swap to disk which can slow down the response or the System is out of processor power. At other times even the network interface is also overloaded. Sometimes the software itself is so complex that the processing of the input to generate the output complicates and hence slows down the system. Another, very threatening cause can be viruses.

A system slowdown can often be prevented. One effective way is to plan for future expansion of the institution by mapping resource requirements, thereby building efficient and sustainable systems. Such planning is possible by looking at the trends of resource consumption in past data. Further, the organization should ensure communication between its functional area and technology area. Such communication goes a long way in helping IT plan for future expansion of business operations.

Challenge IV: Lack of Organized Training in IT for the MFI Employees

Microfinance is an emerging industry. Due to its nature, it faces some unique human resource prob-

lems. Information system employees require expertise in both, technical and functional aspects of the business. Since MFI's operate in remote areas, it does not attract highly qualified professionals. Such organizations end up relying on personnel who are not well trained. Training procedures, even if they exist, are only ad-hoc. One potential solution to this problem is to have a simplified MIS that is easily understandable by the field staff. Preferably, the application and support could be in the local language. Another tactic could be to set up a communication protocol/procedure for the field staff to interact with the technical help. This is particularly helpful in cases when the local branches do not have an expert technical resource who can manage the MIS, on site. Staff, even if not trained in technology, can then coordinate to the MIS expert in the nearest branch.

Owing to the unique challenges faced, microfinance organizations need to think beyond traditional approaches for training employees. To encourage the employees to learn the basics of the business logic and computer skills, an organization should provide incentives to encourage employee learning. These skills should also be criteria for the promotion in the organization. Such an atmosphere

Figure 1. Snapshot of a system in an MFI

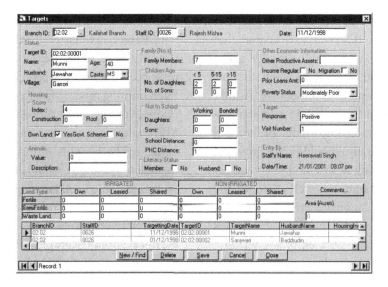

will create a sense of competition which can help to get the best out of the employees.

Apart from the above, the organization can take other steps to ensure streamlining of its training procedures. In order to do so, it needs to define different employee roles, and decide on the skills set that each category should be trained in. Two roles are particularly necessary in most scenarios. The *field staff* has the responsibility to interact with the MFI clients and get the loan proposals for the client. Furthermore, the staff disburses the loans and also collects the loan repayments. Sometimes, the field staff also owns the responsibility of entering the data into the system. The *branch manager* is an employee who supervises the field staff, and manages all the administrative and operational activities of the branch. S/he also approves the loan proposals and also coordinates with the head office to distribute funds. The training for each of the two roles could be divided into courses. There can be courses according to the institutions basic structure and architecture. For a generic view, following can be the structure of the course packages. The branch manager should be trained in all the three packages described below. The field staff should be trained in packages I and II.

Package I: Basic Computer Training

Computer Basic training should cover the following lessons. First, starting and switching Off of system: mostly the field staffs are laymen that supposedly do not have much knowledge about the computer system. Educating them to start and shut down a computer is imperative. A little carelessness can lead to the data loss or application crash. Moreover, the knowledge of the UPS (Unlimited Power Supply) should also be provided to them. Second, using mouse and keyboard: at times, the field staffs are not well aware of the letters of the English language. Hence, educating them to how to use keyboard and mouse becomes important. Third, basic data entry knowledge: The field staff should have the knowledge of the

application and should be able to enter the data. Fourth, internet connection: some of the MFIs have internet access which helps them to get connected to the other branches and garner data. The field staff should know how to do this. Fifth, maintenance of system: knowledge of MIS will help the field staff to perform the maintenance of the system. Maintenance of the system includes learning to support both Hardware and Software of the MIS. Maintenance of keyboard, mouse, UPS (Uninterrupted Power Supply), network cables is considered as Hardware support. Learning to take regular backups and frequent archival of the organization's data comes under the software support. Sixth, MS Office: applications like MS Excel and MS Word are sometimes helpful.

It would particularly useful if the training kit is available in local regional languages and more helpful if the trainer can converse in the local language. Below is a case study where-in training was given to the MFI employees, in the local language.

PlaNet Finance University for Microfinance Training

PlaNet University has established a full range of training courses in Microfinance. The course contents of this training catalogue are created to serve diversified range of people. Training activities are conjointly planned and implemented with Paris headquarter, local operational offices (Brazil, China, India, Mexico, Benin, Senegal) and resources and training centers (Morocco, Togo). Each training module is adjusted by local experts in order to best meet the specific needs of local MFIs and to respond to the particular country context. The benefits of this module design are that each training session is localized into easily understandable local language and responds well to geographical, cultural and social particularities of different countries.

In one of the examples, PlaNet Finance, with the support of Citi Foundation has built a thorough

Arabic Curriculum consisting of 50 modules aimed at the top and middle managers of MFIs that are active in Arab Region.

Another achievement from PlaNet Finance is the development of software named MicroFit has been sold since 2000 and is currently implemented in 12 MFIs. MicroFit is ranked 3rd in the world ranking of the CGAP software reviews.

One of the greatest advantages of MicroFit is that it is designed using the industry standard tools and is multi-currency, multi-branch and is fully integrated. This enables the MFIs to readily use the software at any part of world. Further, MicroFit has a translation module which allows translating the software into any language. This is a big leap towards the dissemination of the MIS, as with such software in place will make introduction and usage of MIS more acceptable. *Source: PlaNet Finance,* http://www.planetfinancegroup.org

Package II: Portfolio Software Training

The prerequisite of this training is knowledge about microfinance business and basic knowledge of computer operation. It will cover these topics. First, entry of target client information: field staff collects the targeted client information manually in form and they have to do data entry of all client related information in Portfolio system. An example to this is keying-in of the Client Identification Code in the field 'Client ID'. Second, formation of groups: microfinance sometimes uses the concept of Self Help Group (SHG). SHG is nothing but a village based financial intermediary usually composed between 5 to 10 members. Third, entry of loan application- field staff enters the loan details into the loan application. Fourth, daily collection sheet and disbursement sheet: every morning, the field staff officer goes to the clients' location to collect the repayments. To get the details about the daily collection, the field staff usually takes a printout of the Daily Collection Sheet which is a report giving details about the

clients and the repayment to be garnered on behalf of the loan against their names.

Package III: Account Software Training

The prerequisite of this training is knowledge of basic accounting. It will cover below topics. First, daily voucher entry: branch manager has the responsibility for Voucher Entry in the Accounts. One such task is 'daily expenditures' entry. Second, chart of accounts and basic ledger- in the account model, chart of accounts contains all the account codes related to voucher and ledger entry. Third, fund accounting: fund accounting tracks the sources of fund provided by bankers and investors to the MFIs. An example is each fund source having fund source code in application. Fourth, financial statements: branch manager monitors the financial statement of the branch. Ex: - balance sheet, ledger details et al. Fifth, tally between Portfolio System and Accounts System: branch manager tallies the disbursed loan amount and repayment of all the funds, on daily basis.

Challenge V: Lack of Standardization of Processes and Procedures

The microfinance industry does not have a long history of implementing technology. Therefore, there are not many standardized processes or rules in place. There have been some initiatives that have been taken to address the challenge of lack of standardization and regulation. Some of the initiatives are mentioned here. First, Conferences held on the standardization of Microfinance industry across the globe. There have been many developments on this front. One of them is the regional Consultation held in Cebu City on 8th May 2008. Around 32 organizations participated in the conference discussing the agenda 'to provide the overview of MIS, its benefits and the institutionalization'. MFIs from all parts of world participated in the conference and articulated their organizations' experiences with MIS.

Second, providing rating for the microfinance institution. Institutions like M-CRIL (Micro – Credit Ratings International Limited) regularly undertake long-term (3-7 years) and short-term (1-2 years) performance monitoring of MFIs across countries on behalf of multi-lateral and bilateral developments organizations, donor organizations and financial institutions. M-CRIL sets performance targets for an MFI, monitors the performance and makes recommendations to address areas of weakness. Longer term monitoring and hand holding enables an MFI build sustainable microfinance operations.

Third is the setting up of discussion boards. One such initiative is Solutions Exchange Community, which has a discussion board. Another successful initiative on this front is an organization named SeaMo. The main idea of this organization is to display in its application all the events (with regards to Microfinance) taking place across the globe. A major portion of the application is about the developments and issues in the MIS for MFIs. What makes this site very effective is that it easily brings Microfinance experts on the same page and enables them to discuss and suggest solutions on various issues.

Fourth are initiatives taken by country government to establish a regulatory authority. For example, a Microfinance bill has been presented in Parliament of India to help National Bank for Rural and Agricultural Development (NABARD) to regulate the microfinance sector in India. Finally, the microbanking standard project collects financial data and tracks performance of more than 150 MFIs around the world to create standards of performance. It also supports the local networks in developing the national level benchmarks and also provides bi-annually results in MicroBanking Bulletin (MBB). Microfinance Information Exchange (MIX) publishes this bulletin. (Microfinance Information eXchange, http://www.themix.org/)

A SUSTAINABLE MIS FOR MICROFINANCE

Up until now, we have discussed various challenges which MFIs face in implementing MIS. Still, some MFIs are successfully running MIS. A rigorous study of their experiences helps us to understand how small MFIs can also be self-reliant in implementing MIS and what steps are needed to make it sustainable.

In-House Development of MIS Application

Some MFIs prefer to develop MIS software, in-house. Developing in-house applications may provide the following advantages. First, In-house development affords quick and seamless interaction between the software development team and the stake-holders. This will alleviate any confusion in requirements development and expected service standards. Hence, better understanding of products and application. Second, In-house software development teams have comprehensive knowledge of the application. This will translate into lower time and resource consumption for support activities. Furthermore, in-house teams are more able to modify, or enhance, the software, if the business model changes. Hence, this causes easy maintenance and support. Third, initial costs to set up a software development team in-house may be expensive. However, an in-house product has the potential of breaking even, over time, thereby making it cost-effective. Fourth, software developed in-house can be implemented in multiple branches, without any licensing issues. This is especially advantageous for MFI's which experience high growth rates.

On more practical lines, it is generally observed that in the case of in-house development, there are chances of requirements going wrong. One strong reason for this is, on one hand, the internal IT staff (to implement MIS) is not well trained in the concepts of Microfinance and on the other hand, the experts of Microfinance are generally not much interested in learning new technologies. Hence, only after careful scrutiny and through proper considerations, the decisions to go for in-house development should be taken.

Another important factor (as discussed above) is the cost. Both small and big MFIs have their own reasons for counting on in-house development methodology, especially, in the initial phases of their MIS implementation. Small MFIs obviously have fewer budgets and less exposure towards MIS, hence they hire a resource who understands the requirements, and starts implementing the basic necessities, like storing and maintaining the important records. As the organization grows, it is in a position to decide whether to resort to outsourcing methodology or continue with in-house technique. This has been followed in many MFIs, including SKS Microfinance.

The reasons for a big MFI to count on in-house methodology are the impact on infrastructure and data security issues. With outsourcing, there will be more network traffic between the MFI and the outsourced service provider than there would be with an in-house system, so careful planning of the available infrastructure should be done. Data security is another major concern to the MFI and hence, in the earlier stages, the MFI tends to keep the MIS installation with itself. Still, there is no fixed rule for that and it depends on the management to decide which methodology suits the organization better.

Outsourcing the MIS Application, or Purchasing Off-the-Shelf Software

The organization can outsource the development of the MIS, or consider purchasing off-the-shelf applications. A number of factors need to be considered by MFIs in selecting software. Some of such factors are, firstly, matching of the business needs. It is imperative that the software meets business requirements. It is likely that the organizations may have to consider customization of the software. The extent of customization may impact resource consumption. Further, business requirements themselves may change. Therefore, the organization needs to clearly understand its current and future business requirements. Second, selecting from different software. Currently MFIs need three kinds of software in order to operate effectively. Often, these applications need to be compatible with each other, and work together in a seamless fashion. Portfolio Tracking Application: An application which can track all the client details, product details, daily transaction, branch Information etc. Accounting Module: An application which can manage MFIs day to day account processes. Ex: - Lenders money, Daily expenditure etc. Performance/Reporting Application: An application which can consolidate all the data from different branches and is able to generate various kind of operational and portfolio report required for the management. Third, costs are a major consideration in all software purchases. Purchases typically end up requiring compromises on cost or quality. Maximizing the utility of the purchase is possible if the organization adopts due diligence in its purchasing procedures. Furthermore, service level agreements (SLAs) may help in ensuring quality from vendors. Finally, maintenance and support costs must be factored in to any decision. (Mathison, The Foundation for Development Cooperation (FDC), 2009)

The following four points should be considered before going for Outsourcing of MIS implementation. First, if an MFI plans to grow or plans to offer a more complex suite of services, then outsourcing should be considered. Secondly, with outsourcing, an MFI may still need to scale-up its Internet services as there will be increase in the traffic over internet connection. Thirdly, the IT staff should be an integral part of the evaluation and selection process for the outsourcing provider, and fourth, one should always select a system with a history of positive customer references. New products should be usually avoided unless the vendor promises a long warranty support for the software installation.

Open Source Software for Microfinance

During the past decade, a new model for development of the software has become popular which holds considerable promise for the computing needs for the MIS. Free and Open Source Software (FOSS) is software that gives complete authority and unrestricted permission to the users to customize the software. The FOSS provides the following four rights to the user, to have the right to modify the software, to use the software with almost no restrictions, to freely share the customized software, and to inspect the source code of the software.

Most MFIs lack the basic financial means to purchase proprietary (licensed) software. FOSS projects, based on networks of users across the globe sharing their expertise, have the potential to reduce costs dramatically by spreading it across many users. Furthermore, every individual MFI will have the freedom to customize such software to fit its own unique needs, thereby circumventing the need for licensing. Implementing such open-source based solutions may also be cheaper. It may be argued that MFIs may give up the potential for strategic advantage against competitors by sharing software. However, MFIs are not primarily concerned with profit motive, and therefore, such a collaborative effort may be advantageous.

As one of the initiatives for the FOSS, Grameen Foundation's Technology Center built an Open Source Technology Platform for the microfinance industry. Mifos is a freely available product, which is a world class MIS that provides the core functionality required by the MFIs. The product is flexible and scalable enabling it to simultaneously standardize common processes, accommodate regional variations and scale for new innovation in future.

Based on the current records, more than a dozen MFIs are working on Mifos. There is also a plan to develop Mifos Community Edition. Grameen's Foundation Technology Center also looks forward to establishing a local office for support in Philippines. (MicroFinance Open Source, http://www.mifos.org/about)

This way, many new initiatives can be taken to understand the problems faced by many small and big MFIs in implementing MIS and ultimately help them to extend their reach to serve the poor.

Hardware for Sustaining MIS

Most MFIs lack the financial clout to support the infrastructure required for sustaining MIS. One such infrastructure component is hardware. One effective option for procuring cheap hardware for MFIs is to purchase used systems that are in good condition. There are some not-for-profit organizations, like Second byte, that aim to assist non-governmental organizations (NGOs) and MFIs in accessing second hand computers and hardware peripherals. Second byte assists in the procurement, refurbishing, and enhancement of hardware from IT companies and international donors. Many large for-profit firms have a surplus of used hardware. These companies are not aware of the needs of potential beneficiaries. Therefore, such used hardware is typically auctioned to dealers for a very low price. Such dealers refurbish the hardware and resell it for a profit. The only other choice that large companies have is the indiscriminate disposal of their used hardware to not-for-profit organizations.

The procurement of used hardware can be done in two ways. First, organizations such as Second byte can create a network of corporate companies who would be partners in donating second hand computers to the development sector. Second byte I.T Ltd is a non-profit social enterprise based in Scunthorpe that specializes in the collection of redundant I.T and electrical waste throughout the North of England and Midlands. The company was established in 2003, and now the company's clients include many big NGOs, MFIs, colleges, universities and multinationals. Second byte I.T is committed to the provision of a range of systems, support and technical information for social enterprises, charities and communication groups. Second, further, such entities/communities can also serve as a middle-man, certifying donated computers as being usable like SecondByte does.

Maintenance

The work involved in MFI branches is very information intensive. Such information, be it loan applications or client payments, needs to be input into the MIS. In such a scenario, staff may encounter issues that require support and maintenance.

Software Maintenance

Software maintenance is required in many situations, including regular troubleshooting and in scenarios where the business model undergoes change. For MFIs, endogenous growth may necessitate changes in existing software systems. Such changes need to be tested thoroughly, before they are implemented throughout the organization. For MFIs, implementing such changes may involve the software development team traveling to each branch. Below, we discuss a case study involving such a scenario in a MFI organization.

How the MIS Team of SKS Microfinance Managed MIS

Until September 2005, SKS microfinance was a non-governmental organization (NGO) which served the savings and loan markets. It was converted into a non-banking financial corporation (NBFC) in September 2005. As per Indian law, an NBFC can have loan services in its portfolio, but cannot serve the savings market. Thus, SKS microfinance faced a change in their business model.

In order to meet the new challenge, the IT team gathered requirements from the operations team and modified the existing system to reflect the organizations current needs. The newer version of the software system was tested thoroughly and was installed in all branches successfully. The MIS team at SKS was also successful in developing a software utility.

Branch splitting tool: - As the number of client grows, it becomes very difficult to manage the operations within one branch. In such a scenario, the functional team requests IT to split the branch into two separate units. In order to handle such requests, the MIS team in SKS developed a branch splitting tool, which splits the database of one branch in two. One of the imperative checks in the branch splitting for the operations team is to verify the operational and financial statements for the branch before splitting and the statements after splitting. There should not be any discrepancy in the two statements.

Hardware Maintenance

Hardware typically lasts for a specific period before which systems will need to be replaced. Moreover, processing capacity increases exponentially, making it imperative to replace hardware, thus improving efficiency. Hardware changes may also be driven by software upgrades, which require more processing power. Establishing LANs and other networks may require other hardware such as routers, modems etc. Finally, printers are extremely resource intensive, and require high maintenance. Some MFIs are located in tropical countries, and operate in non air-conditioned atmosphere. Thus, many a hardware failure is a direct result of overheating.

EFFECTIVE MIS

While we have elaborated on some of the challenges faced by MFIs in implementing MIS, we discuss other aspects which will lead to effective systems within the organization. An MIS may be considered to be effective if it improves productivity and efficiency, among other aspects, of the organization. The following criteria should be considered in evaluating the effectiveness of an MIS. First is increased information accuracy. The system should be able to avoid data inconsistencies. The application should ensure that modifying records follow the right procedures. Second is increased processing speed. MIS should expedite the processing speed of important tasks like the data entry, updates, calculations, sorting and reporting. Third is increased productivity. Productivity is simply the ratio of inputs and outputs. Thus, there is an increase in productivity if there is an increase in output for the same amount of input. Information systems are particularly effective in increasing labor productivity. This is achieved by automating many human resource intensive activities such as ledger maintenance and audit.

Increased Productivity with Effective MIS

Information systems have the potential to help MFIs become efficient and effective. A case in point is First Microfinance Bank Ltd (FMFB). FMFB was formed as the first regulated private-sector MFI in Pakistan. FMFB came about as a growing transformation of a development program undertaken over the last twenty years in the remote and rural northern areas, by the Aga Khan Rural Support Program (AKRSP). The growth of FMFB from a NGO to a microfinance bank posed challenges on the technology front that were addressed effectively, making it one of the most advanced within its peer group. The challenges that arose from transforming manual operations to an automated, technology based MIS were addressed are establishment of a strong IT department, short-term solution that involved integration of an off-the-shelf application with its existing portfolio management system, and long-term plan

to build an enterprise MIS with the functionality to deliver all banking and microfinance services, and flexible enough to meet the current and future technology requirements of the bank. (Ahmad, The First MicrofinanceBank Ltd., 2008)

In addressing these challenges, the FMFB management demonstrated their understanding and commitment in making IT its strategic imperative. This in turn, made for a positive impact on its business model and led to its growth.

Below, we elaborate on three other aspects that will help in building and operating effective MIS within microfinance institutions.

Effective MIS with Operation in the Local Languages

Financial institution managers and information systems staff generally don't speak the same language. Compounding this communication problem are heavy staff workloads and a tendency to compartmentalize operations. The result, despite the best of intentions, is often a misinterpretation of management requests and a system that does not meet its users' needs.

Further, the use of application can become easier and hence more effective if the application has the description written in the local language along with English. There are some of the software development organizations who are working to provide the Operating System also in the regional languages. This will prove to be helpful for the MFIs.

One of the initiatives known as Mahakalasm is a project which takes on the responsibility of assembling an open-source, easy to use MIS for the MFIs. One of the parts of this project is the documentation of the procedures in the form of manuals. The Manual introduces the role of MIS in managing group finances and operations, provides step-to-step instructions for collecting data in order to generate the reports. This manual is currently available in local languages like Hindi and Tamil. (Parikh, Department of Computer Science, University of Washington)

Effective MIS: Adhering to Processes for Efficient MIS Performance

For MIS to perform smoothly, it is imperative that processes and procedures are followed. While processes are not hard and fast rules, they usually encapsulate best practices that are learnt by the organization over time. Below, we discuss some processes that may increase the effectiveness of the MIS within the organization. The first one is the 'Day Starting Process'. The Financial and banking applications have initialization processes, which enable users to start the application for a particular day. MFI applications should also follow a day starting process, thereby enabling tracking of day-to-day transactions. Further, the applications should have the flexibility to backdate entries, in cases where field staff is not available on a given day. Branch managers need to start the day initialization processes for the account and portfolio applications. The second process is 'Day Closing Process'. Similar to the day starting process, the day closing process of all applications will ensure streamlined processes. Branch managers or cashiers could be in charge of the closing process. The third process is 'Tally Process'. Portfolio application tracks the client and loan details and the accounting application tracks fund details for loans, daily expenditure for the branch etc. Generally portfolio application sends a daily automated voucher for disbursed loan and repayments. It is the duty of Branch Manager/Cashier to tally the total disbursed loan and repayments in both applications. The fourth process is 'Backup Policy'. The IT department relies on backups to generate operational and financial statements to be issued by senior management. Each day, the bank manager or the cashier should make a backup of database of Portfolio and Account Application. The IT department should provide instructions on the backup process to the bank managers and cashiers, and these backups should be sent to the head office on the last working day of the month.

To explain the above mentioned practices, we include a case study that will explain how IT Team of SKS Microfinance set up a standard process to set up and run a branch in an effective manner.

Case Study for the Standard Set Up of MIS in a Branch

SKS Microfinance is a well known Indian Microfinance Institution with around 1300 branches across India. Like most growing firms, SKS had to expand, opening branches in remote locations. At such times, the organization made use of the standard processes by which it ensured authentic and robust installation of hardware and software in the branch. Below is a glimpse of the process that was usually followed in SKS Microfinance.

Before starting a new branch, SKS addresses many aspects including hardware and software issues. It has to take care of several factors such as authenticity of the software and hardware, procurement of hardware and software, budget allocation, hardware and software testing, etc

When a new branch is to be opened within the organization, the IT team gets the information from the operations team. The operations team will also provide the target date by which the MIS should be installed in the branch. The IT team will then get details about the new branch including its location, number of employees, hardware and software requirements as well as fund allocations.

Based on the final requirement analysis performed, the IT team approaches the vendor and puts out a request for quotation. Reasonable and the best option are selected for the purchase, after ensuring that the purchase delivery will be timely. On finalization of the quotation and accounting department approval, the vendor delivers the machines and system to the IT Team.

Once the purchases are delivered, the hardware is tested. Each individual hardware component, such as printers, UPS etc., are tested separately first, and then tested in conjunction with each other. This ensures that there are no compatibility issues. In case there are problems, the vendor is notified and a timely replacement is ensured.

The IT team installs the software next. First, a licensed operating system (Windows XP) is installed, followed by applications including portfolio tracker, account application, etc. Finally, the database is created for the branch. This process includes creating branch ID, as well as the input of branch employee credentials and information. This forms the basis for user access rights and passwords that are set up within the system.

Once all the testing activity is completed, the system is dismantled again and sent to the new branch. One of the members of the IT team accompanies the system to help to install the system in the branch. After installation, the branch manager and staff are provided their respective passwords. If required, the IT team member stays in the new branch for some time, ensuring that the MIS works without any hitches.

Finally, a handbook of IT policies to be adhered to (including information on day starting and ending processes, backup policy, tallying process, etc) is provided to the manager. (Swayam Krushi Sangam, http://sksindia.com)

Effective Reporting

Apart from the above, an important aspect of MIS is to produce useful and effective reports. MIS is supposed to provide the information in a form which is easily understandable, which is represented in a standard format. This representation of information in standard format is called a report. Reports are extremely important for the MFI as they enable the institution to run the operation effectively by helping the users to make the appropriate decisions. Moreover, reports can also help manage risks, forecast market trends, and help forecast any changes in business plans. In today's competitive MFI market, an institution

needs to get timely and accurate reports in order to be effective.

There are many different types of users of an information system within an MFI. Such users include field staff, cashiers, branch managers, area managers, investors, and executives. Each user type may require different types of reports to be generated. The unique requirements of each user must be considered, such that the reports generated satisfy information requirements. Further, given that the MFI industry is growing at a rapid pace, reporting requirements are likely to change. Information system reports are likely to provide information that may reflect market trends.

While an MIS could track data and transactions efficiently, its true utility is achieved when information is conveyed to the staff in the form of useful reports. The information that these reports hold need to be understood by the users. Therefore, effective reports and user training become prerequisites for an effective MIS within any organization.

In organizations of substantial size, the same information might have to be presented at different levels of aggregation. For example, portfolio quality might be reported for each loan officer in a branch office report, for each branch office in a regional office report, and for each region in a report to the board. Since, designing a sophisticated report can be time-consuming and information can be presented and analyzed in unlimited ways, a microfinance institution must decide which approaches to organizing information it will use regularly—for example, by officer or branch office—and invest in automating these reports.

It is likely that the same information can be used in different format for different set of users. It may be helpful to characterize information based on the purpose of its use. Although the characterization of the information will mostly depend on the organization, one basic characterization is to distribute information at four levels, namely, strategic, management, operational and external.

Strategic information is predictive. It is oriented toward the long term. Strategic information is used primarily by the institution's board and senior management. Information such as, the national distribution of micro-entrepreneurs, trends in the informal economy, and the institution's coverage, helps decision-makers determine whether the institution is meeting its ultimate objectives. It also supports decision-making on the acquisition and allocation of resources, such as planning and budgeting for growth, opening and closing branch offices, and developing new financial products.

Management information is used primarily by the executive director, chief financial officer, and senior department heads. These managers need information on the use of resources and whether or not resources are being used as planned. Financial reports and activity reports that compare actual performance with budgets and annual objectives help fulfill this need. Decision makers need management information to maintain control of the institution's activities and performance.

Operational information is different from strategic information as it focuses on the short term. Staff, responsible for day-to-day activities needs operational information that enables them to accomplish their tasks. Examples of such activities include disbursing loans, collecting payments, carrying out training programs and paying bills. Operational information enables the user to take action. For example, a delinquent client report identifies which clients a loan officer needs to visit. Similarly, a delinquent loan follow-up report will enable a supervisor to ensure the corrective action to be undertaken.

An example of a report is shown below. The report is a daily collection sheet which tabulates loan and client details at one center. Such a report will be effective in conveying relevant information to staff, and thus, will help them execute their activities efficiently.

External parties may include entities such as investors, bankers, clients, regulators or even other MFIs. A report intended for an external party, such as a donor, may contain information such as the local inflation rate, cost recovery, or even human interest stories about how MFI's have an impact.

However, an important point to be noted here is that the detailed reporting standard mentioned above is merely a standard and not a rigid reporting benchmark. The MFI itself should decide which reports to generate and store in its database. A small scale MFI may aim to store simply the basic clients' details rather than his/her financial status. Similarly, a bigger MFI may even choose to store more information than has been mentioned here.

Framework for Effective MIS

Developing a MIS is a complex task for an MFI. Development of MIS involves many assessment questions like, what does the MFI want to accomplish? How does it go about its task? How is success determined? Creating a successful MIS tailored to the needs of the institution thus requires an integrated, forward-looking approach.

A framework helps the organization to understand what it needs and also helps in documenting the entire structure and architecture of the institution. The benefits of having a MIS framework are as follows first, providing a blueprint/layout to the MFI, second, separating different sets of modules, thereby, making the structure simpler, third, giving the initial idea of the flow of information across the MFI, fourth, making maintenance easier thereby reduces the cost of maintenance, fifth, helping to reduce the dependency on the external parties thereby reducing cost, and sixth, providing a vision for the MFI. (Charles Waterfield and Nick Ramsing, 1998)

The framework mentioned in Figure 3 closely followed the handbook developed by Consultative Group to Assist the Poor (CGAP) titled 'Management Information Systems for Micro Finance Institutions'. Particular care was taken toward applying a systematic approach in light of

Figure 2. Daily collection sheet report

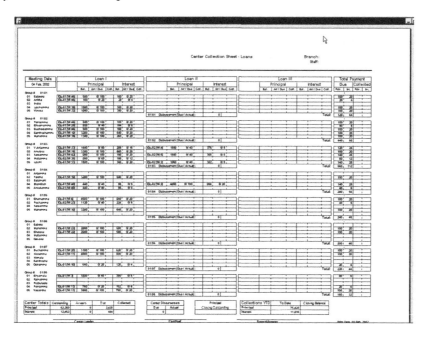

various prior unsuccessful efforts at developing and implementing effective and cost-effective computerization solutions across the global micro finance sector.

In Figure 3, there are six major entities. Details are provided below:

First, *Portfolio Tracker System*- A portfolio tracker is an application that keeps all the client details, MFI product information, loan and payment details. It should have all policy and procedures which need to run the operation in MFI. The portfolio tracker is integrated with Account system and HR and payroll system. The portfolio tracker daily sends a consolidated voucher of loan and repayments into the account module. Second, *Accounts System*- Accounts system keeps fund details, voucher and ledger entry for all the expenses of branches. This application should meet the requirements of international accounting standards. Third, *Performance Monitor*- This application is used to consolidate all the branch data and provide a performance report at the

organization level. This application gets the data from Central Data Server. Fourth, *HR and Payroll System*- This application keeps the details of all employee of MFI. It is also used to generate the payroll of all employees. This application is also integrated with Portfolio Tracker which provides all staff details in the portfolio tracker application. Fifth, *Central Data Server*- Central Data server is a data server in Head office which keeps all the branch data at one place. This data is used in performance monitoring to generate various kinds of reports at organization level. Sixth, *Handheld Device Data capture*- This application is used for handheld device. An example of this is the PDA or mobile phones. Some MFIs use handheld devices instead of daily collection sheet. They download the client repayment details from Portfolio Tracker and visit the villages to collect the loans. Field staffs do the loan collection entry in handheld devices. After coming to branch, they upload the same data in Portfolio Tracker application.

Figure 3. MIS framework for microfinance institutions

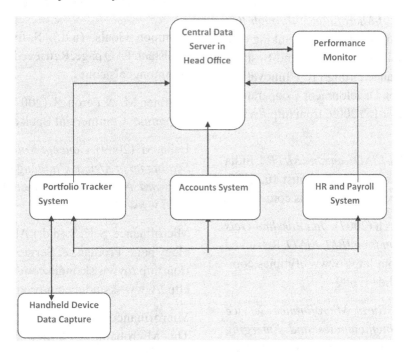

CONCLUSION

It is well understood that implementing MIS can play an imperative role for the MFIs. But the benefits of technology in the form of MIS are still under-realized. There are some challenges that need to be dealt with a focus to help the entire microfinance community. These challenges can be addressed by innovations in methodologies and processes that address the unique nature of microfinance. Such innovations have the potential to help even small microfinance institutions in their mission to help serve the poor.

REFERENCES

Ali, A. (2008). *Managed Information System (MIS) for Microfinance.* The First Microfinance-Bank Ltd. BWTP Network. Retrieved December 25, 2008 from http://www.bwtp.org/pdfs/arcm/5Ahmad.pdf

Augsburg, B., & Schmidt, J. P. (2006). *Free & Open Source Software for Microfinance: Increasing Efficiency and Extending Benefits to the Poor.* Policy Innovations Retrieved September 15, 2008, from http://www.policyinnovations.org

Charitonenko, S. & Campion (2003). *Expanding Commercial Microfinance in Rural Areas: Constraints and Opportunities. A. Rural Finance Expansion: Experience in Commercialization.* Chemonics Int. Retrieved September 25, 2009, from http://dec.usaid.gov

Daley-Harris, S. (2002). State of the Microcredit Summit Campaign Report 2002. Retrieved October 5, 2009, from http://www.microcreditsummit.org

Fleisig, H. W., & de la Peña, N. (2003). *Legal and Regulatory Requirements for Effective Rural Financial Markets.* Paper presented at the USAID/WOCCU International Conference on Best Practices: Paving the Way Forward in Rural Finance, Washington, D.C. Retrieved October 10, 2009, from www.fao.org

Mathison, S. (2007). *Increasing the Outreach and Sustainability of Microfinance through ICT Innovation*. Papers from Electronic Banking with the Poor: Increasing the Outreach and Sustainability of microfinance through ICT Innovation, The Foundation for Development Cooperation. Retrieved on August 15th 2009, from http://www.fdc.org.au/

Naagesh, N. (2009). *FINO launches MITRA*. India Microfinance News Retrieved August 10, 2009, from http://www.microfinancefocus.com

News, E. F. Y. March (2007). *Janalakshmi Gets Smart Card Solution from IBM, FINO*. Retrieved March 7, 2007, from http://www.efytimes.com/e1/fullnews.asp?edid=17699

Parikh, T. (2005). *Rural Microfinance Service Delivery: Gaps, Inefficiencies and Emerging Solutions*, University of Washington. Retrieved October 5, 2009, from http://www.fdc.org.au

Ramana-Murthy, G. V., & Bagchi, S. (2005). *Delimiting Microfinance through Effective MIS*. Paper presented at ICT for Communities: Learning Workshop Series - I, 2005 MIS for Community Based Financial Institutions - Innovations & Experiences. Retrieved April 25, 2009, from www.microfinancegateway.org

Smeaton, R. (2003). *Splitting of database: How and why*. The Access User Group of San Diego (AUGSD). Retrieved August 15, 2008, from http://www.augsd.org/sampleapps/Splitting%20a%20Database.ppt

Waterfield, C., & Ramsing, N. (1998). Handbook for Management Information Systems for Microfinance Institutions, CGAP Technical Tool Series No. 1, February 1998 Retrieved August 19, 2009, from www.microfinancegateway.org

ADDITIONAL READING

Common Goals. (n.d.). Software Exceptional Assistant. FAQ page. Retrieved from http://www.commongoals.com

Delfiner, M., & Peron, S. (2007). *Central Bank of Argentina*. Commercial Bank and Microfinance.

Leila, M. (2009). *Concept Note on Microfinance Scaling up in Africa: Challenges Ahead and Way Forward*. African Development Bank. Retrieved from www.afdb.org

Microfinance, S. K. S. (n.d.). About SKS Methodology page, Products & Services page. Retrieved from http://www.sksindia.com/methodology.htm, http://www.sksindia.com/products.htm

Microfinance Information eXchange. (n.d.). The Microbanking Bulletin. Retrieved from http://www.themix.org/microbanking-bulletin/microbanking-bulletin.

MicroFinance Open Source (Mifos). (n.d.). About Mifos, Need for Mifos, Why Open Source. Retrieved from http://www.mifos.org/about/need-for-mifos, http://www.mifos.org/about/open-source-technology

Nazirwan, M. (2003). *The Way Forward: Future Direction and Strategies for Building a Sustainable Microfinance*. Retrieved from http://adsindonesia.or.id

PlaNet Finance. CFM (n.d.). Retrieved from http://www.planetfinancegroup.org/EN/activites.php.

Putzeys, R. (2002). *Micro Finance in Vietnam*. Belgian Technical Cooperation. BTCCTB Belgian Development Cooperation Agency. Retrieved from http://www2.btcctb.org/vietnam/docs/microfinance.pdf

Second Byte 2ndByte Organisation Mission & Vision (n.d.). Retrieved from http://orgs.tigweb.org/22

Sumeeta, B., & Anjum, K. (2007). Poverty. Microfinance Resource, Microfinance Community, UN Solution Exchange, India. Retrieved from www.solutionexchange-un.net.in

Chapter 4

Automating MFIs:
How Far Should We Go?

Saleh Khan
ASA International, Nigeria

ABSTRACT

Over the last few decades Microfinance has emerged from being an experiment in poverty reduction to a proven mechanism for providing access to sustainable financing to those who have none. With increasing attention given to Microfinance Institutions (MFIs) by global thought leaders and policy makers alike, the entire sector stands under increasing scrutiny and demands for transparency. This increasing attention coupled with the intrinsic need for MFIs to be efficient in their operations, leads to more and more MFIs adopting Information Technology (IT) tools to automate and streamline their operations. Whilst automating their operations, MFIs need to be careful in keeping some of the basic tenets of sustainable microfinance operations intact – including human contact that is important in ensuring timely repayments. This chapter examines some basic business processes followed by MFIs in their lending operations and evaluates the possible impacts and implications of automating these processes. The chapter also discusses the extent to which automation is feasible for a MFI and its implications on the sustainability of the organization.

INTRODUCTION

Over the last few decades, Microfinance has emerged from being an experiment in poverty reduction to a proven mechanism for providing access to sustainable financing to those who have none. In the context of national development,

there is rarely a gathering of professionals where the concepts and ideas of microfinance are not discussed and debated.

There are those who believe that microfinance should be cornerstone for a poverty reduction strategy in any corner of the world and then there are those who think it is a mechanism for exploiting the poor. Whatever personal convictions may be the global proliferation of MFIs stand as testament

DOI: 10.4018/978-1-61520-993-4.ch004

to the robustness of its basic concept and its ability to address the needs of the poor.

While the basic tenet of microfinance remains the same, service delivery mechanisms, lending methodologies and products offered vary widely between Microfinance Institutions (MFIs). These changes are made to differentiate themselves from the competition and serve their client's needs better.

Increasingly, MFIs find that they have the potential to reach more clients than they have the capacity to lend to – mostly due to a shortage of capital required to reach these people. Government funds and donor funds do not have the volumes required by these MFIs and therefore the private sector has stepped in to provide them with access to capital markets and the funding they require. Accessing funding from these formal financial institutions, however, comes with multiple pre-conditions – one of which is the need for information transparency.

A project proposal by the Asian Development Bank (ADB, 2007) which aims at providing financing to MFIs and small business banks states that although small business banks are frequently more transparent from the standpoint of operations and transparency than MFIs, they are often equipped with substandard information technology and management information systems, which have difficulty producing the sophistication of reporting on issues like portfolio-at-risk and liquidity management, which would give confidence to foreign investors.

This aptly summarizes the position of investors to the microfinance sector as a whole where the lack of information transparency, especially in small and medium MFIs, can be deal breakers. One of the most efficient ways of having any level of information transparency is through the use of robust Information Technology (IT) systems.

MFIs are therefore encouraged to adapt Information Technology (IT) tools for the purpose of enhancing transparency, streamlining recordkeeping, ensuring financial compliance, improving lending efficiencies and improve managerial planning, among others. It is at this juncture that MFIs are faced with the need for changing their traditional manual process to IT based systems. Adopting these IT tools often calls for changes in their business processes which inevitably lead to these MFIs grappling with technical and change management challenges that they are neither prepared for nor equipped to take on.

This chapter explores the emerging trends in automating MFIs, including m-Banking, and matches it against the core lending principles followed by Bangladeshi MFIs. The chapter also examines benefits that MFIs can gain from automating and the extent to which automation could be viable. Finally it provides some key recommendations on the extent to which MFIs should be automated and some basic steps that need to be followed to ensure that automation is successful.

BACKGROUND

Commercialization of Microfinance

In 2008, World Bank recalibrated the poverty line and defined extreme poverty to be at incomes less than USD 1.25 a day; revised from the previous USD 1 a day. This revision has changed the global poverty map and according to the new measures there are 1.4 billion people living in extreme poverty around the world – more than a quarter of the developing country's population (World Bank 2008). People living on less than USD 2 a day is nearly half of the population of these developing countries at 2.5 billion people. Over the last two decades, the percentage of population living in extreme poverty has decreased globally – the greatest decline of which has been in Asia and the Pacific.

In spite of successes, reaching such a large number of people living in poverty is a challenge that governments and international development institutions face alike. To improve the quality of lives of the poor, Non-government Organizations (NGOs) and Civil Society Organizations (CSOs) are doing their part with the help of governments and development partners. It is under their aegis that Microfinance Institutions (MFIs) are fostered as a vehicle to provide seed capital for the poor to engage in income generating activities (IGAs). These MFIs mostly start up with grant funding from donors or development finance institutions, while some are started with special funding provided by governments and some are established with private funds.

Accessing government funding to start up MFIs remains a challenge in most developing countries. In these countries, the governments are faced with multi-faceted development challenges and are often found balancing priorities between education, health, sanitation, infrastructure and reducing income poverty. Large chunks of their development budgets are therefore not directed towards microfinance simply because visible results and successes often outweigh the intangible results provided by microfinance – it is easier to quantify the number of schools built and students enrolled or the decrease in child mortality rates than the impact a USD 100 loan has on a poor family.

MFIs are therefore often not prioritized for access to national development resources and have to resort to either donor resources or commercial sources of funds. Most MFIs are able to borrow from commercial sources, such as banks and development financial institutions, and the general trend of commercially investing in MFIs through funds or intermediaries is increasing. CGAP in a Press Release (CGAP, 2008) states that, "Investments (in MFIs) have more than doubled since last year. If the growth rate continues through 2009, we would expect asset under management of microfinance investment vehicles (MIVs) to reach almost $20 billion by that time."

Dieckmann (2007), based on information disclosed by MFIs, estimates that the current volume of loans provided by MFIs globally is around USD 25 billion. Taking global poverty estimates into account, a total of USD 275 billion is required to meet the needs of the microfinance market in the forms of debt, equity, deposits and guarantees. From this, we can estimate that there is a current funding gap / demand of USD 250 billion.

While aggregating this amount of money is not entirely impossible, it would be difficult for development institutions and development finance institutions to allocate this volume of funds while ignoring priorities such as health, education and combating disease.

With such a large funding gap, it is of no surprise that more and more investors are entering the field of funding microfinance initiative around the world. Reille & Forster (2008) segmented investors into three broad categories:

- **Public investors:** traditional bilateral donors such as USAID (United States) or CIDA (Canada) or KfW (Germany), but also other investors include Development Finance Institutions (DFIs) comprising of multilateral organizations such as the World Bank and IFC as well as organizations such as OPIC (United States);
- **Individual investors:** those who invest either through Web 2.0 initiatives, such as Kiva.org, or subscribe to mutual fund offers, such as those offered by responsAbility. High net-worth individuals invest in MFIs through foundations such as the Bill and Melinda Gates Foundation or the Omidyar-Tufts Microfinance Fund; and
- **Institutional investors:** comprising of international banks, pension funds, and insurance companies have begun investing in the microfinance sector.

A finding by CGAP (2008) suggests that a total of USD 11.6 billion has been committed by a mix of donors, Development Finance Institutions (DFIs), institutional investors and individual investors.

For MFIs to grow and reach the target clients, they need access to capital in volumes bigger than what is available through traditional funding sources – donors, government funds, special poverty reduction or microfinance funds, etc. This is where the formal financial sector comes in. By proving that they are an asset class worthy of investment, MFIs can tap into a potentially unlimited amount of funds from capital market institutions.

Reille & Forster (2008) further goes on to state that funding so far has taken forms that are familiar in capital markets such as - Initial Public Offerings (IPO), bond issue, Collateralized Debt Obligations (CDO) and securitizations. Private sector debt and equity microfinance funds have also started up, both managed and un-managed. These offer the investors a level of comfort though investment instruments and mechanisms that they are familiar with. This familiarity coupled with a favorable risk to return ratio, backed by low default rates in the microfinance industry, has encouraged a lot of investors to step forward in to this 'new' investment opportunity.

This linkage between the formal financial sector (the 'banking' sector) and the more informal microfinance sector leads to the oft quoted 'commercialization of microfinance.' Christen & Drake (2002) explains commercialization in microfinance as "the movement of microfinance out of the heavily donor-dependent arena of subsidized operations into one in which microfinance institutions "manage on a business basis" as part of the regulated financial system."

This 'commercialization of microfinance' movement is gathering steam as MFIs around the world acquire capital funds from commercial sources rather than from funds subsidized by DFIs or host governments.

Use of Information Technology in MFIs

Microfinance Institutions (MFIs) have to pay higher costs when seeking funds from commercial sources since commercial entities expect market (or near market) returns on their investments. This increase in operating cost puts pressure on the MFIs to maintain their margins and internal rates of return. As a result, most MFI pass on this additional cost to borrowers by increasing their lending rates or charging extra fees.

Passing on this cost to borrowers has raised a spirited debate centered on whether MFIs are becoming overtly commercial, exploitative, and charging higher rates than they need to. MFIs usually address these concerns by streamlining their operations and cutting down on operating cost, so that they can reduce (or at least keep at the same level) lending rates charged to borrowers whilst remain financially viable.

It is often at this juncture, driven by a need to cut costs, that Information Technology (IT) tools come into play for a MFI. They also look towards IT for a number of other equally compelling reasons.

Lending relationships between formal financial sector entities and MFIs is almost always based on tried and tested rules of the formal financial system. Banks and commercial funding institutions have, over the years, developed industry wide systems for risk assessment and management – most of which rely on IT tools since these are generally considered to be less error prone than manual systems. It is therefore not surprising that, for a lot of these financial transactions, having an IT system in place is a pre-requisite.

Banks and other financial institutions are also heavily dependent on their IT system for operating and reporting, often as part of regulatory requirement. Their interaction with capital markets is based on the information generated by the interconnectivity, transparency and auditing ability provided by a seamless IT system. When these financial institutions go on to fund MFIs, they expect much of the same system to be in place as part of their comfort in lending.

As an example, in a landmark deal where Citi Bank NA securitized a portion of BRAC Bangladesh's microfinance portfolio, the entire eligible loan identification and portfolio monitoring system was structured around data extracted from BRAC's Microfinance Management Information System (MF MIS). Ongoing portfolio performance monitoring was also done through this system.

One of the major reasons why securitization of microfinance portfolios, especially in a mature market such as Bangladesh, has not been as widespread as expected because of the lack of mature MF MIS in Bangladeshi MFIs.

Beyond this partnership, calls for transparency and accountability also make a MFI turn to IT solutions. Government regulators are interested in timely reports from MFIs that are accurate and audited – both of which can be achieved better though a MF MIS system rather than a paper based system. Development partners and donors, who provide grants to MFIs, sometimes also require IT systems to be in place as it promotes better quality reporting and strengthens the institutional capacity of the MFI.

Some development partners encourage the use of IT by MFIs as a mechanism for developing the private sector. One of ADB's projects (ADB, 2007) that aim at providing funding for MFIs and small business banks clearly states that these entities should "ideally have investors or creditors that include international finance institutions (IFIs) that demand certain levels of transparency and information disclosure." ADB states in its development outcomes that these requirements are beneficial for the sector since it will lead to private sector development, especially in "encouraging such mechanisms as enhanced disclosure and accounting standards at MFIs."

The Consultative Group to Assist the Poorest (CGAP), a consortium of public and private development agencies hosted by the World Bank, has issued a set of disclosure guidelines on MFI financial reporting requirements (Rosenberg, Mwangi, Christen, & Nasr, 2003). However, these guidelines are not accounting policies and do not command any particular format for financial reporting. Instead, they simply indicate the minimum information that should be included in MFI financial reports.

Additionally, for a MFI to maximize its potential and expand – to include more clients or branch out geographically – it needs access to timely and accurate information. An effective MIS is crucial for managers during this expansion stage as it assists in better fund management and in diagnosing problems.

Levels of Automation in MFIs

At present, most Microfinance Institutions (MFIs) around the world (and certainly in Bangladesh) follow the traditional model of operations with limited use of technology. MFIs maintain their operational information on paper forms with either no or minimal Management Information Systems (MIS) use; or on a hybrid system where paper based records are entered into a spreadsheet application (typically MS Excel) and then exchanged via e-mail.

In a typical non-automated Bangladeshi MFI, Loan Officers collect transaction information from clients, mostly on paper forms, and submit a daily transaction report to the Branch Offices. Branch Managers then summarize the information collected from all Loan Officers and send it either directly to the Head Office or via a Regional Office. The information flow from the Branch Office to the Head Office is done manually or partially electronically on a weekly or monthly basis. The Head Office accumulates all information from all Branch Offices and stores it in a large spreadsheet or a paper register – or both. The Head Office manages its entire operations structure based on this information exchange and faces operational challenges when it does not have up-to-date information.

As shown in Figure 1, automation in MFIs can be classified in five broad categories. The MFI's typically start their operations with little or no Automation where it runs purely on paper based system for both internal record keeping and for external reporting. This is the de-facto status of most small MFIs in Bangladesh.

The first level of automation usually takes place at the Head Office level where non-networked computer stations are available. Reports from the field and regions are compiled manually from paper based records and passed on to the Head Office where the manual records are entered into pre-configured spreadsheets for reporting purposes. Most medium to large MFIs in Bangladesh are in this stage.

Maturing MFIs then embark on automating their 'First Tier' or regional offices where they compile paper based records and send them electronically, either via e-mail or through physical media, to the Head Office where the information is compiled for reporting. Data compilation at the Head Office can be though a customized database application or using an extensive spreadsheet and intensive staff effort. The Head Office might be networked and connected to the Internet, which makes sector reporting easier. Some of the large and giant MFIs in Bangladesh have been able to reach this stage.

Some mature MFI's are 'Fully Automated' and computerization is present throughout the organization, from the Head Office to the Branch level. Branches are automated to handle daily collection entry and other 'back office' functions such as accounting and personnel. Data reporting is done either directly to the Head Office or through regional offices and is usually over the Internet. The Head Office itself is networked and connected to the Internet that allows staff to share data, both internally and with external stakeholders, with ease. At this level, the MFI usually has a customized software platform which could either be developed in-house or be purchased off-the-shelf and then customized. The giant MFIs in Bangladesh (ASA, BRAC, and Grameen) are yet to reach this stage to exploit the full potential of IT tools, although some have partially achieved this stage.

The pinnacle of automation for a MFI is when it can conduct e-transactions. Data is captured directly from the client and uploaded automatically to the Head Office to generate performance reports– often in real-time. This process could be achieved through a Centralized MIS Platform, a networked server running at the Head Office or through mobile banking (m-Banking) mechanisms. This process could be automated to the point where clients can make loan re-payments though mobile phones and collect their loans through Automated Teller Machine (ATM) networks or

Figure 1. Levels of automation in microfinance institutions

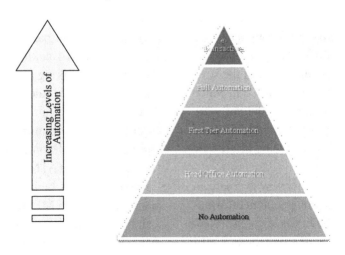

intermediary banking agents. For various reasons, most MFIs are yet to reach this stage.

At the sector level in Bangladesh, information relating to performance is fragmented, based on information provided by MFIs without any verification, and dissemination is infrequent. The limited use of technology stops potential benefits for the overall industry. Each MFI reports a summarized form of client and portfolio information on a voluntary basis in response to paper surveys sent out by the microfinance network. Information is collected and summarized from paper surveys and is disseminated in paper form for review by the Government and other industry stakeholders.

Emerging Trends in Microfinance MIS

The use of technology tools by MFIs is steadily increasing due to decreasing costs of computers equipment and connectivity. An entire industry is growing up around the Information Technology (IT) needs of the MFIs by developing appropriate software applications and custom hardware solutions. Some of the emerging trends in this sector include MFIs adopting free and open source software (FOSS), using 'on-demand' software services, and creating centralized MIS platforms.

Free and Open Source Software (FOSS) is modeled on the community contribution model. These software applications are usually created by a group of dedicated, and mainly, volunteers who provide the software free of cost for anyone to use or improve. A community of skilled programmers contributes towards the development of the software and continually works to improve it. Since the contributors are all voluntary, the software itself is free but customizing it or training staff on how to use it effectively might be offered by companies for a fee.

At least two efforts are under way to create an open source Microfinance Management Information System (MF MIS). The first is Mifos, a project of Grameen Foundation, aimed at creating a MFI

MIS that supports the Grameen methodology of operations and is being currently implemented in India and Kenya. The Second is Octopus Micro-Finance Solution (OMFS), which is being implemented in a number of Central Asian countries.

With the improvement in tele-connectivity and tele-reach in most developing countries, "on-demand" software applications, that follow a 'Software as a Service' (SaaS) model, is gaining popularity. This is a hosted solution where a company creates common software platform and offers it for use by multiple users or companies. Salesforce.com, which has been recognized for essentially creating this model, has launched a Microfinance Edition as a shared platform and has demonstrated the power of this platform though pilot projects.

Another form that SaaS applications could take is as a centralized MIS platform, which combine a mix of software applications with an online (or 'over the wire') service delivery system. This allows the MFI to 'subscribe' to a platform and the software application is customized to meet the needs of the MFI. This makes automation less hardware and application development. The focus for a central technology platform is to provide an easy-to-use solution that is capable of serving the entire microfinance industry, at an affordable price, though easy-to-access channels such as mobile phones.

An example of a centralized platform that is being talked about in the banking industry is m-Banking, or mobile banking. Tiwari & Buse (2007, p. 73) define m-Banking as "the provision and availment of banking and financial services with the help of mobile telecommunication devices." Individual clients can therefore transact directly with their banks though mobile phones without the need for traditional branches or Automatic Teller Machines (ATMs).

m-Banking is being extended to the micro-banking aspect of MFI operations, where clients can have financial transactions directly with the MFI via mobile phones without having to deal with loan officers or MFI staff. m-Banking also opens up the opportunity of 'branchless banking' – where distribution channel are setup (via mobile phones) to deliver financial services without having to rely on bank branches. Branchless banking offers an opportunity to dramatically slash transactions costs and expand geographic coverage of formal financial services.

HOW FAR SHOULD WE AUTOMATE MFIS?

This section reviews the use of IT in microfinance institutions (MFIs) and the challenges faced by them. It further reviews lending methodologies and whether IT tools can have a detrimental influence on them.

IT tools, or technology as a whole, is often viewed as panacea for all the problems that besiege a Microfinance Institution (MFI) – especially those relating to efficiency, internal control, transparency and accountability.

That being said, technology tools can never solve the problems of an inefficient or poorly managed institution.

Automating an inefficient process does not, by itself, make the process efficient or add value to the institution – it merely speeds up an inefficient process. The main challenge lies in having efficient core business processes that adds value to the overall institutional goal at every step and that are not there because 'that is how things have always been done.'

Challenges Faced by MFIs in Adopting IT Tools

In the 2008 Microfinance "Banana Skins" (CSFI, 2008) microfinance practitioners from all over the world cited cost as a major barrier to getting the most benefit out of technology which was followed by the shortage of the right skills needed to adopt technology within a MFI. Practitioners

from Asia cited management of technology as the highest anticipated risk in the years to come whilst management and staff quality also featured in the top 5 concerns in the sector.

These findings will come as no surprise to microfinance practitioners and researchers. These issues have long been recognized as major challenges to implementing an automation project within a MFI. Based on research and anecdotal evidence, I believe that the three main challenges that MFIs face in adopting IT tools.

The first challenge usual arises from the lack of explicit support for, or understanding of the benefits of, automation by senior managers. This can be future compounded by perceived high cost of automation projects and lack of skilled manpower within the MFI to drive the automation project forward. While these might seem easily remedied issues, things are rarely straightforward in practice. A closer examination should provide better insight for non-practitioners.

One of the findings of CSFI (2008) is that "… MFIs tend to be dominated by 'visionaries' who are strong on charisma but less so on management skills and strategic flexibility." This aptly summarizes the situation within most MFIs around the world, and certainly for most Bangladeshi MFIs, which tend to be centered on a single individual – the promoter or the chief executive. This charismatic individual usually creates the MFI from scratch and effortlessly toils over the years to bring it to a stage where it can sustain and grow. He or she, therefore, instills their own views and beliefs within the organization and defines the organizational culture and attitude towards technology.

If the Chief Executive is either skeptical about adopting technology or feels that it is being imposed upon the MFI by an external factor (perhaps as pre-requisite for a loan), then the implementation process becomes complex, tedious and often headed for failure. First line managers too have to be fully committed towards adopting technology and be willing to 'see the process through,' i.e. carry the process forward even in the face of complexities and challenges that might often seem to slow the implementation process down.

Another recurring issue cited by MFIs is the high cost of acquiring and implementing technology tools. While is it true that 'exotic' solutions – such as acquiring a Core Banking Software (CBS) and giving Personal Digital Assistants (PDAs) to credit officers – will be unreasonably expensive for a small or medium MFI; cost effective and appropriate solutions are now available that can be adopted. The issue that then remains is the awareness that automation brings long term tangible and intangible benefits for the MFI and is well worth the money being spent.

In the interest of cost minimization and having a lean operation, most MFIs would happily do away with IT tools that are often seen as non-productive and hugely expensive. In most cases, even if a MFI can afford the cost of automation, they think of it as an unnecessary expenditure and thus look towards external assistance, such as donor funding or grants, to meet this expense. It is this dependence on external funding sources that has long run implications on the sustainability of the organization.

While donor funding can meet the 'one-time acquisition cost' for a technology platform, it is the recurring cost of maintaining hardware, paying for personnel and software licenses / upgrades / customization that most MFIs fail to factor into their operating cost estimates. In the end, it is this recurring cost that hurts the cash flow (and thus the profitability / sustainability) of the MFI.

MFIs should, therefore, pay for the technology platform partially (with a subsidy from a donor) or completely to factor in the expenses such a system entails in their operations. The MFI needs to be aware of the cost for both one-time acquisition and running costs. The ability of a MFI to successfully absorb the cost of automation into the regular operational expenditure and still remain sustainable is a critical challenge.

The third major challenge MFIs face is the lack of skilled manpower to drive the automation process. Skilled manpower is not restricted to having technical staff within the MFI; it extends to include people within the MFI who are 'tech-savvy', know project management and can deal with business process reengineering or change management. Even the best IT Manager cannot carry a process very far within an organization that is naturally resistive to change and lacks a buy in to technology.

Beyond the technical aspect of the project, microfinance operations managers within the MFI also need to know how to assist in implementing a technology project and have the mindset to tackle challenges that will inevitably come up. Change managers need to actively work in making the staff aware of the progress and ensure their 'buy-in' into the system. An effective IT system can only function and sustain within a MFI if staff at all level accepts it and realizes its potential.

Beyond the institutional factors, the very nature of microfinance operations might pose a problem towards adopting IT Tools. In partnerships between formal financial institutions and MFIs, IT Tools are often required to be in place (for example, in the case of securitizing microfinance portfolio). There is the potential for a clash of methodologies between the formal financial sector, which has evolved over the years into structured institutions with rigid rules and requirements, and MFIs who tend to grow organically. In most cases this disagreement centers on recordkeeping and financial discipline, which are standardized in formal financial institutions and monitored transparently through the use of IT tools.

Can Lending Methodologies Limit Automation?

Certain aspects of the methodology used in microfinance lending could also, possibly, limit the extent to which technology can be used by a MFI.

Microfinance operation is dependent entirely on human relationships – more specifically the entire process of lending and recovery is dependent on the relationship between the Loan Officer and the client. This relationship is made even more important by the fact that, by its very nature, almost all microfinance lending is free of financial collateral. While there are exceptions to this, most MFIs around the world rely on 'social collateral' to safeguard their loans.

In the traditional 'group lending' or 'individual lending' approach, Loan Officers are exclusively relied upon to carry out a number of critical tasks. They start with a preliminary assessment of the area within which the branch is located and identify potential clients; then they move on to contact clients, market products and services of the MFI, and motivate member to join. Once the client has agreed to join the MFI, the Loan Officer assesses the income capacity of a client and recommends the amount of loan a client is eligible for and advises them on how best to utilize the loan and how to protect themselves from economic shocks.

After the loan has been disbursed, s/he then motivates clients in making timely repayments and contributes towards voluntary savings schemes. In case of non-payment, they motivate clients into regularizing repayments and in case of outright default, assess the economic condition and earning potential of a client and recommend to the branch manager whether the loan can be partially recovered (in which case a new repayment schedule is set up) or be completely written off.

While this is not an exhaustive list of tasks carried out by a Loan Officer, these are some that illustrates the 'human' relationship aspects to microfinance operations. These tasks require a Loan Officer to meet with clients, often on a one on one basis, and explain to them the situation and propose solutions. This approach of being a 'bank with a human face' is probably what has contributed the most towards the successes of microfinance and is certainly a key element to the phenomenal recovery rates seen in MFIs.

Replacing this human interaction between Loan Officers and clients with technology, either partially or completely, could pose its own set of challenges for a MFI.

Microfinance and m-Banking

Ivatury & Mas (2008) provide some interesting insight into the experience of branchless banking, both m-banking as well as other channels, which have been tried so far. They observe that while branchless banking can substantially reduce transaction costs, as compared to traditional banking, it is being used mainly for making payments and not for savings or credit purposes. They also state that few unbanked people (less than 10 percent of branchless banking customers are poor) use the branchless banking to access financial services.

Ivatury & Mas also state that, in their findings, m-Banking initiatives are being led by mobile phone operators and that Microfinance Institutions (MFIs) are being left out of this process. Reasons behind this include the lack of specialized human capacity within a MFI to implement such a process and the lack of specialized core banking applications.

A CGAP survey conducted in South Africa found that roughly half said they preferred to deal face-to-face with a person for their banking transactions rather than with an electronic device, even if the device is quicker. Interestingly, the responses were similar between m-Banking customers and people who have a mobile phone but do not use it to conduct transactions (Ivatury & Mas, 2008).

While m-Banking can offer the comfort and ease of making financial transactions from anywhere, the informal financial service providers that poor people use, such as MFIs, depend heavily on human interaction and personal or community relationships. This personal touch and relationship is expected by the clients as seen from the results of this survey.

The basic tenet of Grameen Bank's model (and of most group lending models) is to focus heavily on the Client-Loan Officer relationship – starting right from loan application evaluation to recovery of bad debt.

It is therefore of no surprise that Reille in a conference paper (SANABEL, 2008) states that, based on findings from m-Pesa in Kenya (a popular m-Banking model), joint liability of microborrowers were degraded when using m-Banking solutions. He goes on to say that uptake of m-Banking in MFIs has been low because the MFIs do not know how to match technology with group lending methodology.

Lending Methodologies

Most people recognize Grameen Bank in Bangladesh as the institutions that pioneered microfinance lending methodology centered on group liability. The "Grameen Bank Model" has since been adopted by numerous MFIs around the world. The strength of this model is said to lie in its successful use of social collateral to not only ensure timely repayments, but also in improving the client selection and loan monitoring ability of a MFI.

The mechanisms of using group liability in microfinance lending has been credited with improving repayment rates and lowering transaction costs by providing incentives for peers to screen, monitor and enforce timely repayments for each other's loans. Because clients will potentially be held financially liable for his/her group members' loan defaults, they have incentives to screen their peers so that only trustworthy individuals are allowed into the group. Timely repayments are also enforced through clients as individual defaulters face peer pressure to repay their loans.

The newer "Grameen II" Model, however, abandons this Group guaranteed lending methodology. Under this new model, the group is no longer financially liable for individual loans and group members no longer have to provide a 'financial guarantee' for the loan taken by its other members. Instead, Grameen Bank loans are now provided to individual clients against a 'flexible loan contract.'

Under this new methodology, each borrower must still belong to a group but the group is not required to give any guarantee (legal or financial) for a loan to its member i.e. group members are not responsible for paying on behalf of a defaulting member. The onus of repaying the loan is on an individual borrower. The group acts in enforcing social control, overseeing that everyone maintains group discipline and no one gets into repayment problem.

ASA Bangladesh has long been using an individual lending model that focused on 'social collateral,' reinforced by group structures, rather than financial collateral. In the current ASA model, Loan Officers are required to induct new members into an existing group or start up a new group if sufficient new members are found; this allows a new member to be verified by the 'social screening' mechanisms intrinsic to the group lending methodology. Lending is done against individual contracts where group members are not required to provide any financial pledge to protect against loan default by the new members. The members are, however, 'morally responsible' for ensuring that the newly inducted member pays off her loan.

Causes of Default

Even with protections and guarantees and all the social screening, defaults in loan repayment are an operational challenge faced by Microfinance Institutions (MFIs) all over the world. MFIs are well aware of the impact defaults have on cash flow and accept this phenomenon as an operational challenge that will have to meet.

The causes of loan repayment defaults in microfinance are numerous and can range from true income poverty to outright fraud caused by collusion between a Loan Officer and a client. Based on anecdotal evidence, defaults also traditionally increase in mature markets where 'overlapping' – a single client borrowing from alternative credit sources, mostly from multiple MFIs – becomes an issue.

Armendariz & Morduch (2005) report anecdotal evidence from Bangladeshi microfinance providers suggesting that microfinance contracts with less frequent repayment saw higher client default; i.e. the longer the loan repayment cycle the higher the risk of default. This is corroborated by anecdotal evidence from microfinance practitioners who prefer to design microcredit products with weekly repayment installments rather than monthly repayments. Their logic being that the increased contact between Loan Officers and clients discourages clients from defaulting on payments.

Davies & Roy (2008) state in a presentation, based on their research, there is no significant increase in defaults by clients making weekly repayments versus clients on monthly repayment schedules. However, those who paid monthly installments still attended weekly meetings (pp. 5), indicating that the frequent meetings might still be a factor that affects the little variation in default rates.

A study carried out by ASA Bangladesh (1997) attempted to identify some of the core reasons for defaults; the respondents were ASA's clients who were asked to rank what they perceived to be causes for defaults. Responses indicate that defaults occur due to various reasons, including irregular attendance of group members to group meetings, lack of mutual relationships between group members, lack of adherence to group rules, and repayment through others. Operating policies such as inadequate time allocated to form groups which leads to weak group cohesion, and frequent MFI staff transfer erodes group cohesion and motivation also plays a role in this regard as does limited staff skills which leads to wrong selection of group members, improper formation of groups, and limited ability of the Loan Officer in motivating the group.

Addressing Default

Whatever the cause of default may be, the overriding priority for any MFI is to recover the outstanding loan – either partially or completely. The onus for this process of recovery is almost always on the Loan Officer since s/he was the one initially responsible for assessing the client's financial worth and recommending the loan. In addition, the Loan Officer is in the best position to access the client and evaluate the cause for default.

Based on literature review cited above and anecdotal evidence from the field, one can identify 'decrease in contact frequency between clients and Loan Officers' as one of the leading cause for loan defaults. While this is certainly not THE major cause for default, one can hypothesize that this is one of the major conditions that can lead a client to default on her / his loan.

In the case of a client defaulting on her / his loan, the action recommended by ASA's operations manual is clear and unequivocal – maintain communication / contact with the client above all else. Loan Officers are further instructed to motivate the client to regularly attend group meetings even if s/he is unable to pay. Beyond this, Loan Officers are supposed to visit the client's house on a regular basis to try and motivate them into repaying the loan. This is to be bolstered by providing institutional notices and visits by senior officers if necessary.

This strategy is followed by most, if not all, MFIs as the basic mechanisms for dealing with cases of default. Legal enforcement (either a visit by policemen or taking the client to court) is usually avoided since this builds a 'bad brand image' whilst strong arm tactics to recover the loans is unpleasant and is something everyone wants to avoid.

Other Challenges of Using IT Tools

While increasing Client to Loan Officer contact is the logical thing to do in order to avoid the risk of defaults, certain technological advancement seems to aim at decreasing this. IT tools that extends beyond back office automation to improve transaction efficiency, seeks to decrease the Client to Loan Officer interaction times, perhaps even remove it altogether.

However, as we have noted, within the group lending methodology, Loan Officers travel to a center meeting where all the clients arrive to make their repayments. This is the spot where Client – Loan Officer interactions take place and is the primary mechanism for enforcing group discipline, including motivating defaulters to pay.

Perhaps the greatest risk from IT tools, therefore, comes from the *possibility* that in their zeal to streamline operational processes, MFI (or its Loan Officers) may sacrifice Client to Loan Officer contact in favor of faster transaction times – which will allow a Loan Officer to cater to more clients.

Assessing the risk of existing and upcoming technologies, we can see that while using PDA or other digital devices to speed up the financial transaction process, will certainly improve operational efficiency, the Loan Officers might be tempted to reduce time spend interacting with clients during center meetings driven by their need to cover more clients in a day.

In using an online platform such as m-Banking, clients might prefer human-to-human interactions instead of transacting through mobile phones and it certainly puts at risk the human face of microfinance. Clients might also need advice, or want to reschedule a payment, or pay partially (all of which are acceptable in a group meeting where it can be negotiated with a Loan Officer) – the chances for which might not be available to them in a m-Banking solution.

For true branchless banking, which represents the pinnacle of m-banking where clients receive payments through ATM network and repay through mobile phones, the clients are at risk of being completely alienated from the MFI and its Loan Officers. This is almost certain to increase defaults and impact loan recovery.

While all of these risks can easily be mitigated they pose a challenge which, if not addressed properly, might negatively impact operations.

Solutions and Recommendations

After evaluating the information presented thus far, the questions that remain are: Should MFIs automate? How do they go about it? And how much of their processes should they automate?

Should MFIs Automate?

Yes, MFIs should automate – there is no escaping it as the global microfinance sector comes to age and forges partnerships with the formal financial sector.

There might be difference causes for automation – internal need to streamline or cut costs, or external requirement by a funding institution – but MFIs should all look towards eventually automating their operations.

MFIs will, however, benefit immensely from mastering their operations relying on manual systems before automating. This process of working with manual systems can ensure that a core group of staff learn the nitty-gritty details of business processes before automation takes over and simplifies procedures. This will also allow these individuals to design processes which will be unique to the MFI and innovate rather than align themselves with prescribed operations in an IT platform.

MFIs are also better off being automated since this will enable them to tap into funding from formal financial institutions right off the start rather than signing up for the funding first and then embarking on automation (as is the case with most MFIs now). An automation project is inherently complex and tedious – the implementation process itself can often be long dawn out and has the potential to disillusion funding entities, who are not used to the challenges of automating a MFI.

How Should MFIs Approach Automation?

The Consultative Group to Assist the Poorest (CGAP) website has a sub-section dedicated to technology that provides information on various Management Information System (MIS) tools and houses valuable resources on how a MFI should implement a MIS solution. Some of these resources, like the Information Systems: Implementation Guidelines (CGAP, undated), outline step by step the tasks that need to be completed and persons who should be responsible for each step. The discussion here is not exhaustive and does not cover all the steps critical to a systems design / implementation process – it merely highlights what should be some of the more important steps in this entire process.

That being said, a critical step in the entire process is probably the need to instill within the staff of *all level* an awareness of the added advantage IT tools can bring to their work. Most automation project will fail if this change management process – which is far more important than most people realize – is not properly addressed.

A Cost Benefit Analysis must be carried out to demonstrate the long term financial impact of adopting an IT system, any cost savings it can bring and whether the MFI can sustain itself when paying for the system. The issue of sustainability is critical here since a MFI must find the correct juncture within its financial evolution timeline to automate – the question should never be automate or sustain.

Once the decision to automate is taken, the remaining challenge is to either acquire the human capacity required or train existing staff to see this process through. MFIs often assume that hiring a single Systems Engineer or a Software Developer or a System Administrator will solve all the requirements of the automation project. The actual requirement for such an automation process is usually far more multi-disciplinary and multi-skills intensive than appreciated.

The skills required are not limited to only technical realms such as systems architecture or network design or software development but more basic skills such as project management. MFIs traditionally lack project management, change management and the 'soft skills' required to make any systems implementation project a success. Designing the technical architecture is usually the simplest step in this process – the more challenging and complex tasks is to identify and translate business processes that needs to be automated, identifying and streamlining business rules, and equipping the staff within the MFI to handle this change.

Figure 2 provides a graphical representation of the elements that an automation project should incorporate into the implementation process.

These steps are essentially linear, as management acceptance and buy-in is a pre-requisite to the change management process. Similarly, change management exercise should be carried out well before the systems analysis, development and implementation process begins.

How Far Should MFIs Automate?

By saying 'how far' we essentially mean how prevalent or pervasive technology is expected to be entrenched in a MFI.

Figure 2. Steps that should be included in the IT implementation process

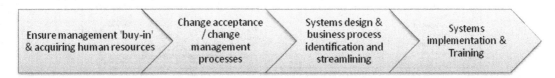

MFIs have a multitude of options on how far to automate that has been outlined in Figure 1. Hybrid systems, which fall in between these tiers, are also common in MFIs that are in the process of being automated.

Based on personal experience and anecdotal evidence from the field, the most effective way for a MFI to automate should be down to the Loan Officer level – i.e. the internal / back office processes are automated, even to the level of a Loan Officer carrying a hand-held device to the collection centers, but client to institution interactions remain face-to-face/non-automated.

The reason behind this is the demonstrated need to nurture human relationships between a MFI and its clients. In addition, this is also to ensure that in the process of being efficient MFIs do not lose their 'human face' – a characteristic that makes them different from formal financial institutions.

To address these operational issues, the status of MFI's operations should be as shown in Figure 3.

FUTURE RESEARCH DIRECTIONS

Over the last few years, a large amount of hype has been built up surrounding the automation of Microfinance Institutions (MFIs). For an emerging field in technology that is keeping pace with microfinance's increasing popularity, this is an understandable phenomenon.

While technology companies around the world are scrambling to mould existing technology to fill the needs of MFIs, the institutions themselves are reviewing lessons learned and evaluating successes and failures. At this juncture more research is needed to evaluate how technology can impact the core business processes of MFIs – not just in efficiency and cost or time savings but also in other areas such as client satisfaction, development impact, and need based product development.

Some possible areas of future research could be on the impact of automating client-MFI interactions on client satisfaction; whether decrease in contact time between Loan Officers and clients actually increase defaults; whether decreased in client-Loan Officer contact time, or frequency, increase defaults and whether technology get abandoned or does the way in which MFIs conduct their business get reengineered?

While conducting research on these topics, researchers must keep in mind that first time borrowers will exhibit different characteristic from second or third time (mature) borrowers. There will also be variations in urban and rural places which will determine frequency of meetings and how comfortable with technology the clients will be.

As has been pointed out, MFIs, like many start ups, need to scale up in order to sustain. This scaling up requires large investment in working capital and at the same time make rather large investments in information systems. Further areas of research could be to find decision criteria on prioritizing

Figure 3. Automated interactions by MFIs

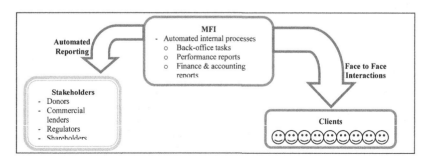

these needs to guide MFIs, cost benefit analysis for small or mid-sized MFIs and the impact (both tangible and intangible) that automation can have on a MFI.

CONCLUSION

With the inevitable need to automate, Microfinance Institutions (MFIs) must pay attention to ensure that they get the most value out of technology tools. They must learn to appreciate the advantage IT tools can bring into an institution and how to streamline business processes using these tools.

In undertaking this process, MFIs must be careful in ensuring that the right people are involved, the proper process is followed and expectations are clearly managed. And they must keep in mind that the overarching objective of a MFI is to serve its clients whist achieving institutional sustainability – tools that could, potentially, distance them from clients should be avoided.

The focus, therefore, should be on automating the internal business processes and ensures that operational efficiency is improved and staff are able to better manage their times in productive tasks rather than clerical tasks. Back-office automation, that has little or no impact on the Client-Loan Officer relationship, can improve operational efficiency whilst outright replacing human contact can prove detrimental for a MFI in the long run.

REFERENCES

Armendariz, B., & Morduch, J. (2005). *The Economics of Microfinance*. Cambridge, MA: MIT Press.

ASA. (1997). *Causes of Default in Microcredit*. Dhaka, Bangladesh: ASA.

Asian Development Bank. (2007). *Proposed Loans and Guarantees REG: Micro- and Small Enterprise Financing Facility: Report and Recommendation of the President to the Board of Directors*. Asian Development Bank.

Centre for the Study of Financial Innovation (CSFI). (2008). *Microfinance Banana Skins 2008*. UK: CSFI.

CGAP. (2008). *Press Release: Study on Evolving Opportunities for Microfinance Investment Funds*. Retrieved September 6, 2009 from http://www.cgap.org/p/site/c/template.rc/1.26.3406/. Washington, D.C.: CGAP.

CGAP. (2008). *2008 Microfinance Funders Survey, Global Results*. Washington, D.C.: CGAP.

Christen, R. P., & Drake, D. (2002). Commercialization: The New Reality of Microfinance? In Drake, D., & Rhyne, E. (Eds.), *The Commercialization of Microfinance: Balancing Business and Development*. ACCION International.

Davies, E., & Roy, A. (2008). *Does Meeting Repay? Early Repayment and Default in Microfinance: Evidence from India*. Presentation made by the Institute for Financial Management and Research (IFMR), India.

Dieckmann, R. (2007). *Microfinance: An emerging investment opportunity*. Frankfurt, Germany: Deutsche Bank Research.

Ivatury, G., & Mas, I. (2008). *The Early Experience with Branchless Banking*. Washington, D.C.: CGAP.

Reille, X. (2008). *Technology Revolutionizing the Industry*. Presentation made at SANABEL 5th Annual Conference; "State of the Industry and Presentation of the Conference Themes." Tunis, Tunisia.

Reille, X., & Forster, S. (2008). *Foreign Capital Investment in Microfinance: Balancing Social and Financial Returns. Focus Note 44*. Washington, D.C.: CGAP.

Rosenberg, R., Mwangi, P., Christen, R. P. & Nasr, M. (July 2003). *Disclosure Guidelines for Financial Reporting by Microfinance Institutions.* Washington D.C.: CGAP.

The World Bank. (2008). *World Development Indicators 2008: Poverty Data, A supplement to World Development Indicators 2008.* Washington, D.C.: Development Data Group, The World Bank.

Tiwari, R., & Buse, S. (2007). *The Mobile Commerce Prospects: A Strategic Analysis of Opportunities in the Banking Sector.* Hamburg, Germany: Hamburg University Press.

Pellegrina, D. Lucia (2007). *Microfinance and Investment: a Comparison with Bank and Informal Lending.* Working Papers 20070401, Università degli Studi di Milano-Bicocca, Dipartimento di Statistica.

Rahman, R., & Mohammed, S. S. (2007). *BRAC Micro Credit Securitization Series I: Lessons from the World's First Micro-Credit Backed Security.* Boston, USA: MF Analytics Ltd.

Rutherford, S. (2000). *The Poor and Their Money.* New Delhi, India: Oxford University Press.

Zaman, S. & Kairy, S. N. (2007). Building Domestic Capital Markets: BRAC's AAA Securitization. *MicroBanking Bulletin*, 14.

ADDITIONAL READING

Campion, A., & Halpern, S. S. (2001). *Automating Microfinance: Experience in Latin America, Asia and Africa.* The Microfinance Network, Occasional Paper No. 5.

Coppoolse, M. (2007). *Microfinance: An Emerging Asset Class for Equity and Debt Investors.* Article in Microcapital.org.

Dowla, A., & Barua, D. (2006). *The Poor Always Pay Back.* Connecticut, USA: Kumarian Press, Inc.

Field, E., & Pande, R. (2007). Repayment Frequency and Default in Micro-finance: Evidence from India. *Journal of the European Economic Association, 2-3*(4-5), 501–509.

Ghatak, M. (1999). Group lending, local information and peer selection. *Journal of Development Economics, 60*(1), 27–50. doi:10.1016/S0304-3878(99)00035-8

ENDNOTES

[1]   CGAP (Undated) *Information Systems: Implementation Guidelines - A practical guide to the development life cycle of microfinance information systems.* Accessed from "http:// www.cgap.org/ gm/document1.9.5064/ IS_Implementation_Guidelines%5B1%5D. pdf" on 24 October 2009. Washington, D.C.: CGAP.

[2]   This chapter represents the views of the author alone and does not necessarily reflect the opinions or positions of either ASA International or any other organization he may be associated with. The author can be reached at saleh.khan@gmail.com.

APPENDIX

Glossary of Abbreviations

ICT	Information and Communication Technology
IT	Information Technology
m-Banking	Mobile Banking
MFI	Microfinance Institution
MIS	Management Information System

Chapter 5
A Case Study of Mifos Implementation at Asomi

Puspadhar Das
Asomi, India

ABSTRACT

Mifos is an open source enterprise solution for microfinance. This chapter is a practitioner's point of view on implementation of Mifos in an organization, based on the author's experience in implementing Mifos at Asomi, a microfinance institution operating in the state of Assam, India. The factors to be considered in selection and implementation of Mifos are discussed. Various inputs, analyses and resources required for implementation are discussed. Any organization must have a concrete set of operational strategies that enables it to track its borrowers and loan portfolio effectively and on time in order to succeed. Wrong assumptions and choice of wrong technology may only aggravate MIS implementation. Development of technology has removed all the barriers to technologies and has enabled organizations to develop computerised systems streamlined to their operational needs and not the other way round. It is attempted to justify this by using the case of Mifos.

INTRODUCTION

Microfinance has become a dominant force in the field of financial services targeted to the poor who do not have access to formal credit. Access to basic financial services (such as credit, savings, and insurance) is most likely to develop the entrepreneurial skills and opportunities among those poor who are currently outside the perimeter of such financial markets and services (Sundaresan, 2008).

There are certain developments in the microfinance industry that necessitate the implementation of computerised management information system (MIS). Foremost is the increasing level of competition. The last few decades have witnessed a tremendous growth in the number of such service providers. At the same time, there has also been an increase in the reach of the older service providers. This increased competition leads to a number of

DOI: 10.4018/978-1-61520-993-4.ch005

difficulties like increasing non-performing assets and phantom loans which are the results of reduced loan repayments. Information asymmetry may lead to adverse selection which will ultimately affect the viability of the business. In such a scenario, borrowers' information and tracking of accounts in a timely manner becomes very critical to the success of a microfinance institution (MFI).

"Methodological issues, staff development, and even financing are frequently not proving to be the critical constraints to growth. Rather, an institution's ability to track the status of its portfolio in a timely and accurate manner is often the most pressing need." (Waterfield & Ramsing, 1998, p.2).

The ability to track portfolio, in turn, depends upon several factors including operational strategy and information storage and retrieval system. An MFI's portfolio is characterized by a large number of loans with small amount.

The sector is also undergoing profound structural changes. Convergence is occurring between microfinance and mainstream banking as MFIs grow in size and sophistication and commercial banks enter the market (Microfinance Banana Skins 2009).

Asomi, an MFI working in Assam, India, is a growing MFI. Prior to implementing Mifos, the organization used spreadsheets and a software package developed in-house in order to manage its data. As the client base increased and the types of services offered to its clientele increased, it was felt that a more robust information management system was the need of the hour. Out of the several options available, Mifos was chosen for implementation for loan portfolio management.

Although Mifos needs improvement in several aspects, it incorporates the whole concept of SHG movement and microfinance. So many things that are required to be done in the process of development or implementation of an MIS, including system analysis and design, can be omitted in this discussion and one can start with customization of the Mifos system for specific requirements of the organization as outlined in the operational manual of the organization.

This chapter outlines the various factors considered in the process of selection of an MIS, the process of Mifos implementation, and also the key learnings from the implementation process. This chapter should provide basic guidelines to a person overseeing the implementation of Mifos in an organization.

BACKGROUND

An information system is the set of people, procedures, and resources that collects, transforms, and disseminates information in an organization (O'Brien, 1996). Management information system is the series of processes and actions involved in capturing raw data, processing the data into usable information, and disseminating the information to users in the form needed. (Waterfield & Ramsing, 1998, p.3). It may either be manual, computerised or a combination of both.

One of the major benefits of a good MIS is the improvement of operational efficiency, which gets reflected in a multiplicity of factors like human resource productivity and better loan repayment tracking. This is possible by reducing the number of manual entries to be made, and by minimizing the possibility of human errors.

MFIs serve a market that is spread sparsely and loan amounts are small. This gives rise to increased transaction cost which leads to a relatively higher interest rate charged by the MFIs. Thus another imperative of using an MIS is to reduce costs.

Computerised MIS in any organization has three types, categorized based upon the level of computerization. The first type is the use of computer for normal calculations and data compilation. Here, spreadsheet and word processor based systems are used where data are stored manually and final reports are prepared by entering and compiling data in software packages like

Microsoft Office. It may still be called a manual system because the spreadsheets are mainly used for compilation, are inefficient and labour intensive. (Waterfield & Ramsing, 1998, p11).

The second type is the use of off-the-shelf software packages developed for standardized processes of MFIs. There are standard software packages for various functions like book keeping, accounting, payroll, loan portfolio tracking etc. Many MFIs follow standard procedures and use off-the-shelf packages for specific purposes.

There are a host of software solutions to cater to the diverse needs of organizations. *IS Fund* lists more than 60 such solutions serving different regions of the world. (CGAP, 2009). These are mostly packages implementing standardized processes.

The third type is the development and use of customizable software packages. The need of such a software package emerges when the requirements of the organization are mostly non-standard and when the organization is growing. This is more true of MFIs as microfinance is a comparatively new phenomenon and the MFI organization develops its system and style of work in conformity with the working style of the founders of the organization.

These three types may co-exist as organizations develop and move completely to type three.

When an organization decides to be in type three, the other existing systems should also be maintained for a certain period of time till the customized software becomes more mature and stable. This also helps to test the newly developed system. When software packages are tested during development, they are tested for correctness of the programme codes only and not from the factual point of view of organizational requirements. When both manual and computerized systems are run parallelly, factual correctness of the stored data gets tested and the manual system works as a backup in case something goes wrong with the new system.

Historically, it was argued that implementation of an MIS goes beyond software and entails willingness to evaluate and change the way the institution works. However Langer (Langer, 2008) argues that the only successful approach to analysis is to accept what exists in the user's environment, however far from ideal those conditions may be, and work within those limitations. Once it is known that the organization has a concrete operational manual and that has been followed and taught to the field staff, it will be difficult to change the way things are done. This is a great challenge and one of the main reasons behind failure of MIS in organizations. So, in order to make MIS initiative successful, one must have an MIS strategy that fits the reality of the environment rather than force the environment to change.

This is also reflected by the statement that MFIs will need to ensure that their systems and use of IT are closely aligned with their business strategies, both in the short and longer term (Ledgerwood & White, 2006). Although this was said in the context of an MFI in the process of transformation, this is valid even otherwise.

An important decision to make at this stage is which activities and operations to computerize and in what way. A typical MFI would have groups and individual borrowers as clientele, a field force to manage the client accounts, a management team to oversee operations, strategies, finances, and human resources. The major activities that require computerization are portfolio tracking system and accounting system (Waterfield & Ramsing, 1998, p.4).

Mainhart (1999) provides another framework for evaluating MIS where a hierarchical list of categories is used. The major categories are functionality and expandability, usability, reporting, standards and compliance, administration and support, technical specification and correctness and cost.

A study conducted by Adamson and Shine (2003) revealed that in a mandatory environment the perceived ease of use was a marginally stronger influencer than the usefulness of the system. This implies that the ease of use of a system is a very important criterion in selection of an MIS.

Table 1 outlines the criteria for evaluating an MIS (Waterfield & Sheldon, 1997). These were originally developed for loan tracking software evaluation which however can be used for evaluating an MIS system in general. Since the information technology scenario has considerably changed since 1997, some of the evaluation criteria will require recasting.

This chapter attempts to argue that Mifos is a system that does not require restructuring the organizational processes, products and scopes. It has sufficient built-in flexibility and scalability to manage almost any kind of loan portfolio that an MFI seeks to venture into. It also discusses how the evaluation criteria outlined in Table 1 are met by Mifos.

A difference analysis, and not a gap analysis, is required in order to successfully implement Mifos in an organization that has a proper operational strategy in place.

Table 1. Criteria for evaluating an MIS

Ease of use	Features
Documentation Tutorials Error handling Help screens Interface	Language Setup options Methodology issues Loan product definitions Branch management and consolidation Linkage between accounting and portfolio
Software and hardware issues	**Security**
Programming language Data storage format Network support Operating system Access speed	Password and levels of authorization Data modification Backup procedure Audit trails
Reports	**Technical support**
Existing reports New reports Print preview Printers supported Width of reports	Customization available Training Cost issues

Source: Waterfield & Sheldon, 1997

About Mifos

Mifos is a management information system developed to meet the requirements of the microfinance industry. Its architecture is based on Software as a Service (SaaS) framework and delivered through the Internet. The Mifos Initiative was launched in 2006 by the Grameen Foundation's Grameen Technology Center under the leadership of Mr. George Conard. The flexibility and scalability of the product means that one will be able to simultaneously standardize common processes, accommodate regional variations, and scale for new innovations in the future.

From operational point of view, Mifos is a portfolio tracking and reporting system. Although, other organizational activities, like finance and human resources, are being integrated, Mifos still has a long way to go to become an enterprise level software. Mifos being a community effort, new features are being added every day and many developers from different parts of the world are contributing their efforts to add new features.

It uses open source technology and is released under Apache 2.0 license. As of version 1.1, Mifos consists of open source technologies outlined in Table 2. Mifos is deployed as a SaaS software serving various offices through network.

Table 2. Technologies used in Mifos

Technology	Purpose
Java	Programming platform
MySQL	Relational Database management system (RDBMS)
Hibernate	Object Relational Mapping (ORM)
Struts	Model-View-Controller (MVC) framework
Java Server Pages (JSP)	Views
Apache Tomcat	Web application container
Subversion	For version control of codebase
Ant	Build tool

Mifos is a web application built around the concept of Model-View-Controller (MVC) framework. MVC is the concept introduced by Smalltalk's inventors (Trygve Reenskaug and others) of encapsulating some data together with its processing (the model) and isolate it from the manipulation (the controller) and presentation (the view) part that has to be done on a user interface. According to Reenskaug (Reenskaug, 1979), models represent knowledge. In MFI perspective, all entities like clients, groups and loan products and they way they behave will be put under the model. For example, the loan products of Asomi will have properties like interest rate and loan amounts and methods for calculation of interest rate, generation of repayment schedule. All these are done in the Model component.

A view is a visual representation of its model. Through the view various entities will be displayed to the user.

A controller is the link between a user and the system. It provides the user with input by arranging for relevant views to present themselves in appropriate places on the screen. It provides means for user output by presenting the user with menus or other means of giving commands and data.

Mifos uses Java, an object-oriented programming language for its model component. The work on the model part of the framework in Mifos is quite extensive. All the entities are encapsulated in the form of Javabeans and these are reusable. Each entity like clients, groups and loan accounts would be encapsulated into a Javabean and they possess various properties and methods as dictated by the requirements of an MFI or as it is observed in the real world.

For storage of data, MySQL, an open source database, is used in Mifos. The main application interacts with the database using another piece of component that maps the properties of the Java objects with the relation (tables) in the database through an object relational mapper called Hibernate. Hibernate also provides transaction

management and works perfectly with object oriented paradigm of Java.

Struts is the framework that implements the MVC design pattern. Struts helps in building web applications that uses the MVC framework.

Starting from version 1.3 of Mifos, the MVC framework has been moved to Spring framework which is an alternative to Struts. However the underlying business model in Java, that encapsulates the entities, remains the same.

Mifos uses Java Server Pages (JSP) for the view component. JSP provides ways to create dynamic web pages leveraging on the existing business system. A JSP page can contain both HTML tags and scripts to call methods and properties of Java objects. When a JSP page is accessed, it will contain all the information in simple HTML tags.

Mifos uses Ant as the build tool. It uses configuration files which are XML-based (eXtended Markup Language) where tasks to be performed are defined. This tool can be used for a wide range of routine functions like compiling, creating web application, deploying to server and even managing various maintenance activities. Starting from version 1.3, it has moved to Maven, which is a project management and comprehension tool.

The compiled codes and views are deployed in a servlet container. The most widely used application container is Apache Tomcat. Tomcat implements the Java servlet and JSP specifications from Sun Microsystems and provides an environment for Java codes to run.

Figure 1 depicts a simplified version of frameworks used in Mifos.

Background on Asomi

Asomi is a MFI operating in the state of Assam, India. With its administrative office located at Guwahati, it manages close to 200 loan officers through a network of 50 branches spread over the state of Assam.

It has been using computers since it started its operation in 2001, albeit in a very small way

Figure 1. Mifos framework

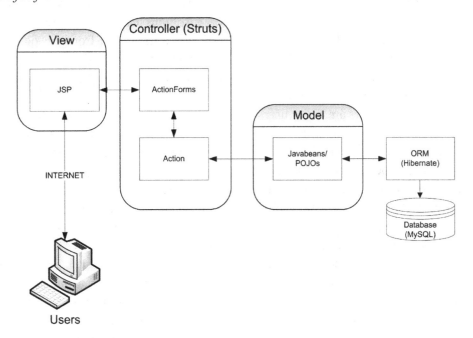

at the beginning. Earlier, spreadsheets were used to store and compile data on clients and loan accounts. After some years of operation, a standalone software package was built in-house for management of data. As operations of the organization and size of the data to be managed grew, it became unwieldy. Also, since it was installed in every PC in the branches, maintenance and upgradation of the package became more difficult as the number of branches grew. Parallelly, the manual system of data storage was also continued.

The organization hierarchy is depicted in Figure 2.

The organization's coverage is geographically divided into areas and areas are subdivided into branches. An area is supervised by a Business Development Manager (BDM) and a BDM oversees 5 to 10 branches. The branches are the main activity centers, manned by the field staff and dealing directly with the groups and clients. Groups are formed by ten or more individuals. There may also be individuals (clients) without any group association. The groups and clients

outside groups are attached to routes (similar to centers in microfinance parlance).

Figure 2. Organizational hierarchy of Asomi

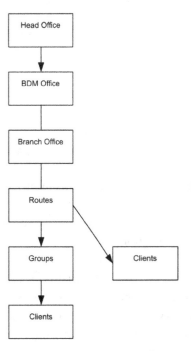

EVALUATING MIFOS

Based on the criteria outlined in Table 1, Mifos was evaluated. The following paragraphs briefly describe the criteria and how they are met in Mifos.

Ease of use is one very important criterion. Loan officers and credit officers are major users of Mifos and given the level of computer literacy of the loan officers and credit officers, the system should be easy to use. Processes should be well documented. Errors and exceptions should be handled properly, displaying the right error message through proper validation. Mifos runs in web browsers like Internet Explorer and Firefox. People are very familiar with these and the form elements of these browsers. The underlying technology (Struts) manages the flow of processes from one step to the other. Mifos can also display configurable error messages that convey the reason behind any unsuccessful operation. Mifos also shows a preview of data entered before committing any data to the database. These features make Mifos very user-friendly.

Features in Mifos are exhaustive and in line with the operational procedures of the organization. It supports creation of new products, groups, offices, and other entities. Custom properties for each of them can be defined.

The languages are configurable and terminologies used can be customized at the functional level.

Reports are an integral part of any system. Reporting system should be customizable and should allow the implementing organization to add new reports as and when required. Application and database being de-linked in any enterprise application, reporting system development is not a problem as database structure would be known to the organization.

Hardware and software issues are getting diluted. With the rise in popularity of open source technologies, the choice of software technology to be used has widened. As open source concept gains momentum, software support from companies is no longer a major issue. Also, with the decreas-

ing cost of hardware and networking equipment, organizations can go for internetworking and collect real-time data from the field. Now, it is only a matter of selecting the best technologies and hardware and using them most efficiently and effectively.

The software base required for Mifos is open source and works perfectly in most versions of Linux and Windows, the most popular operating systems. Being Java-based, it requires a Java virtual machine for running the application, an application container like Apache Tomcat, an RDBMS like MySQL and a web browser. These are all open source packages and are freely downloadable from the Internet. These products are easy to install and operate and a lot of resources are available in the Internet.

From the operational point of view, the major constraint is the connectivity. The limit is posed by the development of Internet infrastructure in a region. Mifos is not a data-intensive software, it is a process-intensive software and all processing takes place in the server, with inputs supplied by the client side users. As a result, the volume of data transfer is comparatively lower (approximately 100 kilobytes per page).

Session management is another crucial aspect of Mifos. Mifos uses Hyper Text Transfer Protocol (HTTP) which is stateless, and so the information between two page requests is not maintained in HTTP. By using session management in Java, the period for which a user is logged on is maintained allowing authorized users to work smoothly. The duration of an idle session is configurable and depending upon requirements, it can be set to any limit. So, even if the Internet connectivity is erratic, session attributes are maintained and a system user can seamlessly work in a flow.

Mifos is platform independent. As long as the server platform supports Java, and other components of the Mifos technology pack (e.g., MySQL), Mifos will work. On the client side too, one needs to access the application using a web browser and all pages are HTML compliant.

So, almost all the major browsers can be used to access the application. There may, however, be a compatibility issue related to Javascript. But this is a minor problem and whatever Javascript has been used is quite standard and supported by almost all the major browsers.

Information Security is a major concern. Being a SaaS application, Mifos is exposed to both internal and external security issues. Biskup (2009, pp. 17) defines a computing system to be secure if and only if it satisfies the intended purpose without violating relevant informational or other rights. In the following paragraphs, an attempt has been made to examine whether Mifos is secure from the point of view of the five generally accepted security goals: availability, confidentiality, integrity, authenticity and non-repudiation.

Availability of data and activities to be performed by Mifos is guaranteed by the hardware and server environment in place. The selection of a software environment like Java and MySQL also ensures that the system runs uninterrupted. The only scheduled non-availability Mifos is only when the batch jobs run. This is generally scheduled to occur when no user is using the system (typically at midnight in working environments).

Information classified on a wide range of variables like date, personnel and office can be derived from the database, thus adding to availability of data.

Confidentiality of information is managed by credential-based access control. Access control is implemented at database level, program access level, and data access level. At the database level, the security is managed by the underlying database system, MySQL in this case. Also, since the database is accessed locally by Mifos and this connection is hidden for an outside user, this does not pose a serious security threat as access to MySQL. Access to the database can be controlled by security features available in the operating system and also the in-built MySQL security features. At the program and data access

level, Mifos uses credential-based access control to give various levels of access to the system.

Permission to perform various activities in Mifos is controlled through its system of roles and privileges. One can define various roles like loan officers, credit officers, branch managers etc each with their respective roles and responsibilities as defined in the operational manual. For example, a data entry personnel will have the responsibility of creating accounts and a higher official like business development manager will have the responsibility of approving it.

The data in the database must represent correct content to the point of data entry. This kind of integrity is important as correct content should be maintained under all update operations and, accordingly, also messages containing query answers should enjoy this kind of integrity with regard to content (ibid, pp. 41). Mifos has several mechanisms to maintain data integrity. The first is the referential integrity constraints in the database. Various relations in the database maintain certain referential integrity that enables the system to maintain data in correct state. For example, the accounts of a group cannot be deleted unless the members listed under it are either removed or transferred to other groups.

Concurrent access to the same data may lead to two or more parties updating it and thus leading to a wrong data entry. This is prevented by checking version mismatch and then allowing or disallowing the data update accordingly.

The business logic component of Mifos controls various states of the customers (centers, groups and clients) and various accounts and operations can be performed only according to the current state of the entity. For example, the system does not allow creation loan account for a group if it is not in the approved state.

The access control system in Mifos helps to establish authenticity of data. Every data entered into Mifos is checked against the sender's credentials and accordingly the update is performed or aborted depending upon the access level.

Mifos maintains a log of all additions and updates. This forces the user not to repudiate in case a dispute happens. This also helps in increasing traceability of particular changes, which is an essential criterion of ISO quality standards.

Cost is one major consideration for the implementing company. The three major cost components are software customization, hardware and maintenance. Being open source, there is no initial license fee or royalty fee. However, during the initial days of implementation, a software developer having good domain knowledge, both in microfinance and in the software technologies used in Mifos, may be required. The development cost can be greatly reduced as Mifos is a community effort and a lot of developers are available for specific queries related to the codes of Mifos. Developers from Grameen Technology Center and other organizations implementing Mifos are also easily accessible for help.

An organization implementing Mifos will require investment in hardware in the form of servers, computers and network connectivity. The system including the application and database reside on a server which is accessed by users through the Internet using desktop computers as terminals. The server is generally connected to the Internet through a static IP address. Table 3 outlines typical hardware requirement and their typical costs

The majority of the maintenance cost is the cost of Internet connectivity. A high speed connection with a static IP address will cost somewhere around Rs. 10,000 per month. This will be

Table 3. Typical hardware costs

Particulars	Approximate cost
Server	Rs. 250,000
Internet connection	Rs. 50,000
Server environment including climate controlled room and rack	Rs. 300,000
Uninterrupted power supply	Rs. 120,000
Desktop computer	Rs. 35,000

required for the server. The branches will require normal Internet connection. With Internet connectivity tending to be very erratic, two connections from two different service providers should ideally be provided. For each branch, the total connectivity cost is in the range of Rs. 2,000 per month. The other recurring costs are costs of electricity and hardware maintenance cost.

From the human resources front, the organization needs to engage personnel f or reconciling data, and coordinating with branch offices in order to rectify and update any errors found.

The initial steps for the development of an MIS have already been done in Mifos. An analysis is required to find out the differences between the way operations were handled by Mifos and the way operations were done in the organization. Mifos does not force an institution to reassess and rearticulate issues that reach to its core. The basic philosophy of microfinance is ingrained in it. The organization just needs to harness the enabling power of Mifos in order to manage various processes.

Mifos Implementation

Starting with the operations manual, Asomi has been customizing Mifos in order to meet its requirements. Mifos was finally deployed in February 2009, interconnecting 10 BDM offices which serve the respective branches under them.

Figure 3 shows the activities performed in the implementation of Mifos at Asomi.

The process of Mifos implementation starts with the operations manual. Developers need not necessarily be made a part of the operational manual preparation process. Once the operations manual is ready, a difference analysis and subsequently Mifos customization and implementation work can be initiated. Other steps in the process can overlap each other. For example, feature requests keep coming even after deployment and an analysis is needed vis-à-vis existing features of Mifos.

Figure 3. Mifos implementation process at Asomi

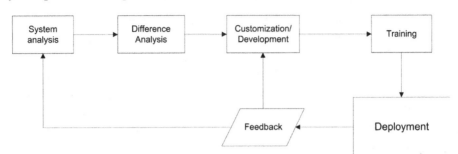

Before the implementation, the selection of developers is the most important task. Success of any software implementation depends upon the specialist team of developers that is selected for the job. The role of the developer(s) is important as the developer(s) need(s) to play multiple roles. The first and foremost role is to understand the requirements of the organization and translate it to the language of software. The second is communicating any requirements that may arise to the larger community of developers. Since Mifos is a community effort, and a lot of people are constantly working to improve it, any organization implementing Mifos can take assistance from the community developers if the organization is not able to find or employ a dedicated team of developers.

The third role is implementing any changes done at the community level. Mifos keeps evolving. Any organization implementing Mifos needs to start from a particular version of the code base of Mifos, after which both developments may go in different directions. So, from time to time, the developers may need to incorporate the changes made by the original Mifos developers into the Mifos system as being developed by the organization. With proper authorization, some feature may also be contributed back to the community Mifos so that other MFIs will be able to use.

An operational manual is a prerequisite for implementing Mifos. This is because Mifos customization and configuration should be done in accordance with the guidelines provided in the operational manual. The operational manual outlines the various processes related to employees, clients, products, etc. It is also a reflection of the overall content and quality of the vision, mission and objective of the organization. Processes and products are defined according to the strategies of the organization. What the organization strives to achieve and what Mifos does should be in alignment.

The manual is the reference point for all the staff members in the field for carrying out their day-to-day responsibilities. Hence the way Mifos will behave will strictly be dictated by the operational manual. If there is incongruity between what happens in the field and what is done in the system, then the perceived usefulness of the software will be eroded and there may be resistance from the field force to use it.

If the organization does not have an operational manual, a manual must be prepared and approved by the management outlining the key activities and products/ services of the organization.

Difference Analysis

The Mifos website suggests that implementations should start with a gap analysis. However Mifos has reached quite a mature state and there is not much of a gap between what is there in Mifos and what an organization would require. The issue is how it is done in Mifos. So, instead of calling it gap analysis, a more appropriate term would be difference analysis. The primary objective of this analysis is to differentiate the way operations are perceived by Mifos developers and the way it actually happens in the implementing organization.

The most important document required for doing the difference analysis is the Operations Manual of the organization. It determines the organization's control structure, flow of information, roles and responsibilities of various personnel, office structure and various other operational aspects of the organization. Drawing cues from it, the difference analysis can be performed. The first step is to design the process map as per the manual. By using a systems approach to problem solving (O'Brien, Indian Reprint 1996, p. 64), one can then determine how to do it in Mifos.

As an example, let us take the system of group loan approval. A portion of the process is depicted in Figure 4. The group applies for loan and the Loan Officer (LO) or the Credit Officer (CO) recommends. The Branch Manager (BM) verifies the details (step 1). These activities take place at the branch office (unit office) level (step 2). Once the Business Development Manager (BDM) at the area office level receives the application, reviews the loan application and if all the criteria are met, sanctions the loan amount (step 3).

In Mifos, the loan application process is merely a data entry process. There are other features in it that makes it a great piece of work.

The first is the set of statuses that a loan accounts would pass through. Any account may be in one of the several statuses depicted in Figure 5. When a loan application is entered for the first time, the application can be stored in the partial application state (more data need to be collected) or pending approval state requiring approval of personnel having approval privilege. From partial or pending approval state, an application can be cancelled. From the pending approval state, the state can be changed to approved or active state. For a loan account, the active state means that loan has been disbursed and normal activities like installment collection can be done. Under some circumstances, account may also be put on hold state, in which case, the normal activities like loan payment entries cannot be performed. The account can be closed if obligations are met or the loan is categorised as non-performaning.

A closer look the two figures above (Figure 4 and Figure 5), shows striking similarity between the states through which the loan application goes through and the various states of a loan account. The difference is in the use of terminologies. At

Figure 4. Portion of the loan application process

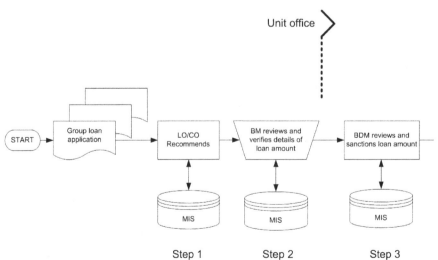

Figure 5. Account statuses in Mifos

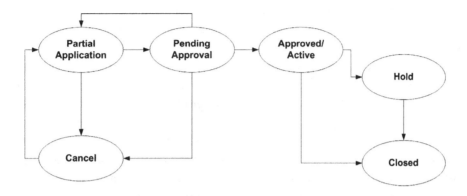

Asomi, the various states described in Figure 5 are rechristened to represent the way they are described in the operational manual.

The second is the privileges of various levels of persons. Roles like Loan Officers and Branch Managers corresponding to each level of officers in the organization can be defined and varying roles and responsibilities assigned as outlined in the operational manual. Now, combining these two, one gets what is expected from the MIS: Loan accounts changing states and being done by authorized personnel.

Thus, the issue is not whether the feature is there or not, the issue is how it is done in Mifos and how one need to modify it for the organization's requirements. A gap analysis will enable us to find what is there and what is required, whereas a difference analysis will enable us how to streamline the process in the MIS and the way the process happens in practice.

A tentative format for doing difference analysis has been provided in Table 4. The table has the following columns: Process, elements, how it is done in the organization, how it is done in Mifos and what is the level of customization required.

The process column outlines the name of the process. In column 2, the major elements in the process are outlined. The following are some representative elements for the loan approval process:

- **Personnel:** These are the personnel involved in the process. For a loan approval process, the persons responsible for the range of activities from loan creation to loan disbursal are listed.
- **Operational:** The various organizational constraints to be met. An example is whether the loan can be disbursed on a non-meeting date.

Table 4. Format for difference analysis

Process	Elements	How it is done in the organization	How it is done in Mifos	Level of customization required
1	2	3	4	5
Name of the process	Personnel/ Organizational inputs	Organizational processes	Mifos functionalities	Possible options are: 1. Code level 2. Configuration level 3. Functional level

• **Product related:** The various product features as designed by the MFI to suit the needs of the target customer. Product definition features in Mifos are quite extensive and a variety of products for groups and individual clients can be designed.

In Table 5, the difference analysis loan application process is illustrated.

Column 3 and 4 are self explanatory. How it is handled in the organization is described in short statements in column 3. In column 4, the process as done in Mifos is described. These two will enable to determine the level of customization required.

Customization

There are three levels of customization: configuration level, code level and functional. Code level customization means changes in the source codes. It may also mean change in database structure. Only a few things require code level customization.

The way earlier processes were run in the organization is very important. Major changes may not be acceptable as people are generally more adapt to doing things in the conventional ways. For example, in the previous system at Asomi, the Loan Officer used to give codes to groups serially. The group codes will be in numerical order: 1, 2, 3 and so on. But once Mifos was implemented, the group coding scheme was universalized and all the groups received system-generated codes and the groups under the same loan officer would not have their group codes in order, making it more difficult to memorize the group codes. Now, one does not have to remember the codes as details of any group and client can be viewed by searching with the name of the entity.

Configuration Customization

There are three groups of settings which require configuration. The first before Mifos is run, the second before the users start using the system and the third, on an ongoing basis and whenever some configuration level customization are required. The mutability of the settings in the first two groups is said to be trapdoor as it cannot changed to any arbitrary value. Many of the settings are mutable at any point in time and are of the third group. Due to evolving needs of an organization,

Table 5. Difference analysis for loan application

Process	Elements	How it is done in the organization	How it is done in Mifos	Level of customization required
Loan approval process	Personnel	Loan created by: Loan recommended by: Loan approved by: Loan disbursed by:	Flexible Define roles Define privileges for different roles Create users with different roles Create loans and change status according to defined roles	Configuration level
Loan approval process	Product related	Loan amounts Interest Repayment	Flexible Need to define products	Configuration level
Loan approval process	Operational	Any organizational constraints	Various constraints and validations are in-built	Configuration level For extra constraints, code level customization will be required.

sometimes Mifos may require reconfiguration, which falls under the third group of configuration level customization.

Most important in the first group is the Chart of Accounts. This must be done before Mifos is deployed and cannot be done after it is live. When Mifos runs for the first time, it writes some configuration values to the database. Some of these values can be changed later and some cannot. Specifically, the values from the Chart of Accounts can only be written to the database once. So, while preparing the chart of accounts, accounting policy of the organization should be considered. The General Ledger codes for each type of financial transactions must be outlined in the chart.

Similarly, trapdoor properties in the application configuration file can only be assigned non-default values once, before Mifos is run for the first time. After that point, a trapdoor property value can only be changed to its default setting.

For the first two types of configuration, the Mifos website can be consulted. The link is http://www.mifos.org/developers/wiki/ConfiguringMifos.

Functional Customization

Functional customizations are related to product definitions, report formats, etc. These are more of a strategic nature and should be done in consultation with the operational manual and generally the developers will have minimal role to play. Functional customization is done for entities, processes, messages and reports.

The entities in Mifos are loan products, savings products, centers, groups, clients, personnel and offices. All these products can be customized by the organization.

Various types of products can be defined in Mifos. All relevant product parameters can be defined, including interest rate, interest calculation method, grace period, fees, processing fees, etc.

For each of these entities, there is a standard set of properties. For example, a client will have a name, date of birth, father's name, address, etc. In addition to these, one can also define additional properties. If one wishes to collect information on the amount of land holding for each client, an additional field can be defined for the client and may make it mandatory in which case the informa-

Table 6. Some configuration parameters in Mifos

Property name	Mutability	Options	Default
Localization			
Language Code	Always	EN, ES, FR, and so on	EN
Accounting Rules			
Currency Code	Trapdoor	EUR, GBP, INR, etc	
Number of Interest Days	Always	360 or 365	365
Fiscal Calendar Rules			
Working Days		All days of week	Except Sunday
Client Rules			
Client can Exist outside Group	Trapdoor	Yes/ No	Yes
Process Flow			
Group Pending Approval State Enabled	Trapdoor	Yes/ No	Yes
Reporting			
Back Dated Transactions Allowed	Always	Yes/ No	Yes

tion must be collected before client information can be saved to the database.

Most of the processes are standardized. The way groups are formed, meetings are organized, loans are created and approved, repayments are collected are all standardized. One only needs to configure certain aspects of the processes in the configuration. Once these values are configured, processes will be dictated by those values. For example, if Mifos is configured to allow the possibility of loan repayments on a non-meeting day, one will have to input the meeting days separately for the repayment schedule and the system will calculate the schedule automatically.

There is another set of options which is defined at the functional level, once Mifos is up and running. These may either be labels or look-up options.

Mifos allows one to configure the labels attached to various entities. For example, at Asomi, the concept of center is not followed, instead a modified form of center called the route is followed. Operationally they are the same things with minor difference and do not require any code level customization. So, with this feature of defining labels, the label center is displayed as route. Another example is that the area level office has been renamed as BDM office and that label is displayed everywhere in place of Area Office.

Look-up options are various options which are configurable at functional level. For example, the list of possible occupations can be entered into the system using the Define Look-op options feature. There are around 11 such parameters which can be enriched depending upon the environmental consideration of the organization.

Code Level Customization

Apart from the customization that is possible through Mifos Admin interface and configuration values, some programming level customizations are also required in order to meet specific organizational requirements. The developer can play a major role in understanding the programming

requirement and then implementing it or asking for assistance from the community.

A lot of work is required to be done on reporting as reporting framework varies widely across organization.

For successfully completing customization, the developer has to have a good understanding of the various business processes of the organization and also a good understanding of the structure of Mifos. The developers should also have strong technical knowledge, especially, on the frameworks listed in Table 2.

A dedicated developer is required as new feature requests keep coming and only after deployment many more new requirements are discovered. The developer need to respond to these feature requests as fast as possible as any delay will have cascading effect and errors will multiply, which, as time passes, may become unmanageable.

There will be interaction with other departments like operations and finance, however, those interactions will only be exchange of information and validation of processes that has been analysed and undertaken for implementation.

Training

Mifos is a philosophy, metaphorically. The whole system is built around the concept of microfinance, where there will be groups with members attached to a center under a loan officer. Any literate person, well-conversant with Internet browsing and having some knowledge of the way the SHG model works, will be able to work with Mifos with little training. For a normal user, the core processes are creation and management of group/ client accounts, loan/ savings accounts and report preparation. These are done in Mifos using standard web interfaces which are easy to understand, are consistent and follow a seamless flow.

However training may be necessary if the users are not computer literate. In such a scenario, the focus of the training would be on the use of computer and not Mifos. This will also entail a shift in the way the target audience perceives computers.

Training is also required to read the information from the database. Whatever is generated and displayed or reported by Mifos are mere data unless the field staff knows how to use it. This type of training is more related to overall development of the personnel than a Mifos-related issue.

Deployment

Deployment is the process of actually making the system available to the users. Before actual deployment, all the configurations should be completed. Server(s) to run the web application and the database server and necessary server infrastructure to locate the server(s) and to make the server accessible in the Internet must be installed at a central location. Java Runtime Environment, MySQL server, Apache Tomcat application container and the Mifos web application should be installed. For details, the Mifos website may be consulted.

At the branches, Mifos can be accessed remotely through Internet.

It is advisable to test deploy Mifos before going for full scale organization-wide deployment. For this purpose, a branch may be selected and all the activities, like loan account creation, approval, loan tracking may be done through Mifos. This will help in further fine-tuning and streamlining Mifos with the operational procedures of the company.

Maintenance

System maintenance is a regular activity. Some maintenance jobs in Mifos happen automatically. For example, if a holiday is declared, the repayment schedules and meeting schedules of the groups and clients are rescheduled during the batch job run based on the declared holiday. By default, the batch job is run at midnight every day.

As a precautionary measure, data should be backed up on a regular basis and archived, so that in the event of data loss, due to hard disk crash or other system problem, data loss is minimal.

The frameworks used in Mifos are quite robust and do not allow incomplete transactions. So, data integrity is never lost. It may so happen that a transaction in the database was wrongly entered. Though this is rare, if it happens, it may affect the quality of data in the database. As part of maintenance, periodic checks of the data must be conducted and the outcomes compared with other available sources of data. The other sources of data may include the cashbook that is maintained at the branch.

Finally, in order to accommodate inherent and periodic changes in the organization, some personnel doing system administration functionality may be required. For example, if a loan officer gets transferred to another branch, his or her existing loan accounts should be assigned to other loan officers. On request from the branch office, the system administrator should perform the transfer action in the system by transferring the client and other related accounts to other loan officers, closing the routes under the loan officer and then transferring loan officer to another branch.

Change in the system may also be requested in case of programming bugs, or if some flaws were noticed in the way the programmers perceived a certain issue. These circumstances require immediate attention, as continuance of such occurrences will have a cascading effect on the errors and may violate integrity of the database that gets created. As this increases, time and energy required to rollback such errors may increase.

Development and incorporation of features and functionalities to Mifos is very important as it eases the tasks of the users and increases productivity and adoption. Changes in the operational manual is a strategic and less frequently occurring event. New products may be introduced. However it is unlikely that the product parameters will ever be outside of the features built in Mifos. For example, it is unlikely that a product will be developed for members of a group which will have a frequency of meeting different from their group meetings. If that happens, from an operations perspective, this will mean that for the same person, one will have to meet twice with the same person: once for collecting installment for the group loan and another time for collecting installment for the individual loan. However, if there is only one meeting scheduled for the same client, the operations cost will greatly reduce.

Major Challenges in Implementation

Mifos implementation is not without impediments. In the following few paragraphs, an attempt has been made to describe the major challenges faced and how Asomi has overcome them.

Connectivity and power supply are the most burning issues in the context of Asomi. Per se, Mifos has centralized application and database management system. An organization having branches throughout a region will have to use the same server in order to completely utilize the power of Mifos. However, all the branches do not have connectivity and the quality of both the Internet and power supply is erratic and irregular.

Asomi has opted to interconnect until the BDM office level is in the first phase. Branches will submit all records and information at the BDM office, where a data entry operator will key in the information into the system.

Even though Mifos is easy to use, getting the Loan Officers accustomed to the system, more specifically, to computers, does take some time. Since both the existing system and the new system run concurrently, time also becomes a major constraint.

Since Asomi is uploading information from the area office level, it does not have to appoint a data entry operator in each branch. There will be one data entry operator at the area office for all the branches under the area office. As the number of clients and products grow, the organization will have to provide connectivity to the branch level. In order to achieve this, training should also be

provided to the loan officers, thus reducing the burden on the data entry operators at the area office level.

FUTURE RESEARCH AND DEVELOPMENT

Mifos is basically a portfolio tracking software and work on incorporating accounting and financial system is not yet complete. Many organizations use a different package for accounting and financial management. Work is going on in the Mifos community as well for implementation of accounting package. As of 2009, basic features like chart of accounts and general ledger (GL) codes are already implemented. During transactions related to loan portfolio and savings portfolios, the financial and accounting related tables are also updated. Additionally, interface for entering office and other expenses, purchases, payments, bank accountrelated information would greatly help in automating branch report preparation. Reports in various financial and accounting formats, like balance sheets, profit and loss accounts, bank reconciliation statements, cash flows and fund flows would then be generated automatically.

If human resource management can be incorporated into Mifos, a lot of processes get automated. For example, production of paychecks will automatically update the relevant accounts and generate payroll reports. Another important aspect, viz., performance appraisal can also be made a part of the system. In Mifos, already performance-related information are stored in the database and by extracting these information, they can be input to the incentive management system.

Another good feature would be a messaging system. From time to time, the users may be required to provide feedback to personnel in the MIS department and vice versa. If a messaging system is implemented, this will greatly reduce the time and cost of interaction between users and administrators.

Planning is very important for any organization. As an anonymous quote says, if you do not know where you are going, you are never going to reach there. So, the people in the field should have an idea as to what are the villages that they are going to cover in the upcoming year, or even better, in the next two years. In order to enable this, a village database can be incorporated and assigned to the branches. The assigned branch, on the other hand, can assign those villages to loan officers in an efficient way so that those villages can be well covered.. This input can also be used for an estimation of the manpower requirement.

Integration of new technologies, like handheld devices, biometric solutions and mobile technologies can greatly improve operational efficiency and control. Since Mifos is quite extensible, these features can be added easily. As a first step, simple mobile technologies using GPRS connectivity can be implemented, enabling loan officers to feed repayment data straight from the field. Gradually, other more secure transaction cost reducing technologies can also be integrated to Mifos.

CONCLUSION

In this chapter, an attempt has been made to outline the experience of Asomi in the process of the customization and implementation of Mifos in the organization. The Asomi case history example shows that Mifos enables an organization to install a system streamlined to the operational procedures of the organization. The flexibility and scalability of Mifos enables an organization to adopt operational strategies as demanded by the market environment. Starting with the operational manual, Asomi has been able to customize Mifos without having to change its operations manual. This also helps in reducing the change management process that is generally seen when implementing a new system.

Mifos incorporates the concept of microfinance in toto and enables an organization to implement

it with customization mostly at configuration and functional level. Mifos, being an open source initiative, means less investment in software development. So, if any code level customization is required, the community developers can be requested to make necessary customization.

REFERENCES

Adamson, I., & Shine, J. (2003). *Extending the New Technology Acceptance Model to measure the End User Information Systems Satisfaction in a Mandatory Environment: A Bank's Treasury*. Taylor & Francis Ltd.

Biskup, J. (2009). *Security in Computer Systems: Challenges, Approaches and Solutions*. Berlin, Heidelberg: Springer-Verlag.

Center for the Study of Financial Innovations. (2009). *Microfinance Banana Skins 2009: Confronting Crisis and Change*. New York: Center for the Study of Financial Innovations.

CGAP. (2009). *Software Product Dashboard*. Retrieved from CGAP: http://collab2.cgap.org/gm/ISFund_Software_Product_Dashboard

Langer, A. M. (2008). *Analysis and Design of Information Systems*. London: Springer-Verlag.

Ledgerwood, J. (1998). *Microfinance Handbook*. Washington, DC: The World Bank. doi:10.1596/978-0-8213-4306-7

Ledgerwood, J., & White, V. (2006). *Transforming Microfinance Institutions*. IBRD/ World Bank.

Mainhart, A. (1999). *Management Information Systems for Microfinance*. Development Alternatives, Inc.

O'Brien, J. (Indian Reprint 1996). *Management Information Systems*. New Delhi: Galgotia Publications.

Reenskaug, T. (1979). MODELS - VIEWS - CONTROLLERS. http://folk.uio.no/trygver/1979/mvc-2/1979-12-MVC.pdf

Sundaresan, S. (Ed.). (2008). *Microfinance: Emerging Trends and Challenges* (1st ed.). Cheltenham, UK: Edward Elgar Publishing Limited.

Waterfield, C., & Ramsing, N. (1998). *Management Information Systems for Microfinance Institutes: A Handbook*. CGAP.

Waterfield, C., & Sheldon, T. (1997). *Assessing and Selecting Loan Tracking Software Systems*. New York: Women's World Banking.

ADDITIONAL READING

Bergsten, H. (2002). *JavaServer Pages*. O'Reilly.

Brooks, D. R. (2007). *An Introduction to HTML and Javascript*. London: Springer.

Dai, N., Mandel, L. & Ryman, Arthur (2007): *Eclipse Web Tools Platform: Developing Java Applications*. Upper Saddle River, NJ: Addison-Wesley.

Heffelfinger, D. R. (2006). *JasperReports for Java Developers*. Birmingham: Packt Publishing.

Holmes, J. (2004). *Struts: The Complete Reference*. McGraw-Hill/Osborne.

Iverson, W. (2004). *Hibernate: A J2EE™ Developer's Guide*. Upper Saddle River, NJ: Addison-Wesley.

Minoli, D. (2008). *Enterprise Architecture A to Z*. Boca Raton: CRC Press. doi:10.1201/9781420013702

Peh, D., Hannemann, A., & Hague, N. (2006). *BIRT- A Field Guide to Reporting*. Upper Saddle River, NJ: Addison-Wesley.

Schekkerman, J. (2004). *How to survive in the jungle of Enterprise Architecture Framework*. Canada: Trafford.

Schildt, H. (2002). *Java ™ 2: The Complete Reference*. McGraw-Hill/ Osborne.

Weathersby, J., French, D., Bondur, T., Tatchell, J., & Chatalbasheva, I. (2006). *Integrating and Extending BIRT*. Upper Saddle River, NJ: Addison-Wesley.

APPENDIX

Abbreviations

BDM	Business Development Manager
CGAP	Consultative Group to Assist the Poor
JSP	Java Server Pages
MFI	Microfinance Institutes
MIS	Management Information System
MVC	Model-View-Controller
NGO	Non-governmental organizations
ORM	Object Relational Mapping
SHG	Self Help Groups

Chapter 6

Implementing Point of Sale Technology in Microfinance:
An Evaluation of Come to Save (CTS) Cooperatives, Bangladesh

Abu Saleh Mohammad Musa
South Asian Microfinance Network (SAMN), Bangladesh

Mostafa Saidur Rahim Khan
Stamford University, Bangladesh

ABSTRACT

Adoption of Information Technology (IT) in Microfinance Institutes (MFIs) has become one of the key indicators to ensure good governance and transparency to the stakeholders. Though the cost of investment in IT is a matter of concern, it has manifold benefit ranging from productivity improvement to socio economic development of the target clients. This chapter focuses on the adoption of IT in MFIs and its possible benefits in operation, cost reduction and stakeholder relationship through an evaluation of a small-scale MFI, Come to Save (CTS), operating in Bangladesh. This chapter reinforces that timely implementation of IT reduces cost of operation, attains economies of scale and increases outreach through increased staff productivity.

INTRODUCTION

Microfinance Institutions (MFIs) are facing increasing pressure to reduce cost to become self dependent on the eve of reduction of donor funding and long term subsidized funding. MFIs are in need of increasing productivity and efficiency in their operation to attain sustainability also. Adoption of Information Technology (IT) in the production process is deemed to have a positive effect on efficiency. Use of IT has been successful to enhance productivity in the formal banking sector. A wide range of use of IT in MFIs is believed to improve efficiency, track operations more accurately, increase transparency and reach new customers. IT can be useful to track financial transactions and create reports for the management, donors and other stakeholders. IT is also helpful to keep client records, analyze data to predict client behavior and transmit data among staff and branches. Large MFIs can use delivery

DOI: 10.4018/978-1-61520-993-4.ch006

technologies like Automated Teller Machine (ATM), Point of Sale (POS) networks and mobile phone banking.

Family Economic Security (FES) Program, a program domain of Plan Bangladesh has been promoting flexible microfinance programs to provide financial support to the poor and extreme poor in a sustainable manner. Come to Save (CTS), an MFI, is implementing this program as a partner organization of Plan Bangladesh with extensive technical and financial support from Plan. CTS had been partnering with Plan since 1998 and offering a demand driven, savings led, flexible microfinance program targeting the poorest of the poor.

To reach the extremely poor as a financially sustainable MFI, CTS is striving to develop a group of professionals at senior management and front line operation positions, giving emphasis on developing human resources, strengthening infrastructural facilities, and introducing modern technology. In view of this, Plan in consultation with CTS management agreed to introduce handheld Point of Sale (POS) as part of technology innovation to reduce human error and to increase staff productivity at the operational level.

The chapter essentially focuses on the following key objectives by presenting a case study. Firstly, it identifies the cost effectiveness of the handheld POS in terms of staff productivity; secondly, it reviews the performance of the handheld POS in the areas of reducing human error and increasing client satisfaction at field level; and thirdly, it analyzes critically the strengths, weaknesses, opportunities and threats in relation to operational and technical viability of the microfinance program implemented by CTS. The background section provides details of microfinance, technology and the key organizations involved. The main topic section looks at the pilot implementation of POS by CTS and the learning from it. Finally, we concluded with the future research directions, suggested for further strengthening of POS implementation in CTS.

BACKGROUND

Microfinance is considered as one of the development interventions, which have been recognized as powerful instrument for poverty reduction of the low income households. Microfinance has enabled the poor to build assets, increase income, and reduce their vulnerability. There are still relatively few financially sustainable MFIs with significant breadth and depth in outreach in Asia including Bangladesh. It has been widely recognized that the main constraint for the sector is not the lack of funds but the lack of capacity in operating sustainable institutions (Setboonsarng & Zhang, 2006). As a means, information and communication technologies (ICT) have emerged as a powerful tool to reduce operating costs, making it viable for financial institutions to expand into rural and low-income areas. ICT innovations such as a personal computer connected to the internet, a mobile phone, ATM or POS device located at a retail, may be less expensive to establish than branches located in rural areas and more convenient for customers (Ivatury, 2005). Unlike pure cash based transactions, ICT-based transactions can take place with less time or with no time required from a teller. Rather than hand over cash to a teller when making a deposit or loan repayment, a customer can give cash to a store clerk, swipe a debit card through a POS card reader, and input an identification number to authorize the transaction. The store's account at the financial institution would be debited by an amount equivalent to the cash deposit, and the customer's would be credited. Since the transaction is electronic, from the institution's perspective, it is less costly to process.

Arrival of the Personal Digital Assistant (PDA) unlocked the potential to use ICT in MFIs. With the help of these pocket computers, loan officers and collectors can fill out forms containing customer information and can provide an initial indication of whether loan would be approved, thereby automating the information gathering process (Silva, 2002). An article by Steve Whelan, for The

Consultative Group to Assist the Poorest (CGAP), talks of the various technological devices that are currently being used around the world (Whelan, 2003). These articles highlight devices such as ATMs, interactive voice response technology (IVRs), smart cards and PDAs.

Information technology can be useful to MFIs through a number of channels, all of which lead to increased efficiency and /or cost reduction. By processing large amounts of data timely and accurately, IT enables managers to take better decisions. IT also helps to improve predictability by analyzing data. Trough data transmission technologies, data can be made available among the branches and key decision makers instantaneously, which is faster and cheaper than physical data transfer. Microfinance initiatives involve more people, customers as well as operating staff than traditional banking system. As a result, MFIs are required to keep records of a wide range of data that further requires analysis to serve the stakeholders (Majewsky & Usoro, 2006). Providing financial services under conditions, where more people are involved with small sum of money is often costly to the MFIs (Ivatury, 2006). Because of these issues, implementation of technology in MFIs was a pressing demand. However, implementation of technology at this level requires investment, which might seem to be costly. An analysis, however, revealed that successful implementation of IT improves customer convenience, lower processing cost, reaches areas with no branch, generates more revenues and collects more savings (Majewsky & Usoro, 2008).

Technology can be used at three levels in microfinance: institutional level, client interface level and sectoral level. Proper synchronization of IT use at these levels will generate maximum benefit. While the importance and utility of the technology can be underscored, one needs to ask the question as to why the use of technology has not percolated significantly within some MFIs (Arunachalam, 2007). At the client interface level, IT can benefit MFIs through appraising borrowers' credit worthiness effectively, which will lead to reduce loan default, contributing to reduce operational costs. Prediction of payment behavior of the borrower can also be analyzed and supported by information technology. Mithas, Krishnan and Fornell (2005) investigated the impact of IT on customer satisfaction. They also attempted to see whether customer satisfaction that comes out of IT investment differs industry wise. Based on the analysis of longitudinal data on 50 firms, they found positive association between IT investment and customer satisfaction. They also reported that the impact can be differential for the service sector.

At the institutional level, implementation of IT usually requires fundamental changes in the MFIs' business and significant planning. Before implementing IT, the organization must be clear about vision, mission, goals and operational procedures. The critical phases an MFI shall carefully pass through to introduce and implement IT are project preparation, need analysis, design, selection, implementation and management. The amount invested to introduce and implement IT should be evaluated as other usual areas of investment. There should be logical expectation of positive return from the implementation of IT. Kaufman and Kriebel (1988) attempted to establish linkage between information technology and business value. They found investment in IT creates the desired higher order economic impact. It was revealed that use of ATM by the commercial banks substantially increase the deposits made by customers in their current deposit accounts.

Mithas, Ramasubbu & Sambamurthy (2008) developed a model to find the linkage between information management capability with three important organizational capabilities (customer management capability, process management capability, and performance management capability) that mediate the links between informantion management capability and several measures of firm performance. They found that information management capability has significant influence on customer management capability, process management capability, and firm management capability. In turn, these capabilities affect customer, financial, human resources, and organizational effectiveness-related measures of firm performance.

It has been revealed by research that implementation of IT increases outreach and improves sustainability. Application of ICT in the back office in the form of MIS is helpful to monitor the quality, efficiency of the loan portfolio, development impact, manage general administrative task, etc. (Mathison, 2005).

Use of ICT to ensure proper governance of institutions has become a common phenomenon in corporate and formal banking sector. Throughout the globe, the sweep of information and communication technology offers unprecedented opportunities for the advancement of the governance and the firm. However, information and communication technology alone are inadequate to foster such benefits (Fountain, 2003). For getting maximum benefit from ICT, the support of core business systems is also required (Matthews, 2007).

Parent Organization: Plan Bangladesh and Microfinance

Plan Bangladesh implements microfinance programs through its partners under Family Economic Security (FES) Program in line with Plan's core approach called Child Centered Community Development (CCCD) Approach. Plan is working on the strategies to give its community development approach a livelihood framework to ensure the sustainability of the CCCD effort. Research has been taken as the core strategy of this program and the development of all components under this program are developed through research participated by the community, Plan and partners directly. The systematic action research is in place to monitor the program and also to improve the quality of the program continuously. Plan provides financial and technical supports to partner MFIs to work

with the extreme poor through financial innovation in a sustainable manner. Plan has identified *Safe*Save approach as a core model for partners to adopt in the rural area of Northern Bangladesh through an intensive and well designed action research framework.

The implementation strategy of Plan's microfinance programs[1] is working through local partner organizations backed by a systematic action research and technical support protocol. The overall microfinance strategy is geared towards ensuring flexible and demand driven financial services to reach the poor and the extreme poor. The balance between institutional sustainability and client impact has been maintained to make the program unique and exemplary.

The key implementation strategies are to experiment innovative financial products and approaches that support organizational growth with sustainability in order to reach the poor and extreme poor with positive impact through in-depth action research and learning. Along with this, to enhance social, technical and managerial competence of partner MFIs committed to reaching the poorest and incorporating microfinance innovations, a set of high quality training, technical tools and intense technical support is provided to facilitate lateral learning and transfer of skills. For the purpose of dissemination of the experiences and to facilitate cross-fertilization of ideas in the area of innovation and reaching the poorest, regular workshops/seminars, research and experimentation is done in collaboration with other key players in Bangladesh.

Come to Save (CTS) Cooperatives: An Innovative MFI

Come to Save (CTS) is a pro-poor institution, registered as a cooperative that works in Dinajpur district in the Northern part of Bangladesh. CTS offers financial services to poor men, women and children, especially the extreme poor. CTS is implementing a microfinance program as a partner organization of Plan Bangladesh with extensive technical and financial support from Plan. CTS had been partnering with Plan since 1998 and offering a demand driven, savings led, flexible microfinance program targeting the poorest of the poor. CTS is registered as an independent cooperative operating since 1998 and aims to provide flexible financial services to the community with a special focus to reach the poorest. The institution is both funded and conceptualized by Plan and now has become a full-fledged independent institution providing demand driven microfinance to the extreme poor on a sustainable basis.

CTS products and mechanisms were designed to provide flexible and convenient financial services, while helping the clients to maximize their savings capacity. CTS now has 8 branches in two upzillas (sub-district) of Dinajpur District. In each CTS branch there is one Branch Manager, one Data Entry Operator, one Field Organizer and 12 to 16 Collectors (frontline staff) based on the numbers of villages covered by each branch. One Area Manager is responsible to look after 4 branches and the Director of CTS is in charge of performing the supervisory role to all staff and CTS's field operations. The whole organization is led by the Director with management support

from an Executive Board consisting of 11 Board Members. The organization chart is depicted in Figure 1 (Hasan, Nuremowla and Musa, 2004).

CTS provides its clients' with a different mix of flexible financial services by creating the option to save or by giving out loans. The decision of either saving or taking loan is totally dependant on individual's planning, willingness and ability to forecast the future events. CTS's loan terms and rules are flexible, while the service charge for accessing the loan covers the cost of providing savings service and profit (interest) on that savings.

CTS frontline staff visits the clients everyday at their door-steps and collects the savings, loan repayment and loan fees, which the clients keep aside after meeting the daily expenses. These amounts can be any amount, including zero, and can vary based on the clients' income on that particular day. The clients are allowed to withdraw any amount, immediately, without any significant restriction, when required.

CTS also give out loans to the clients when demanded, if all rules and conditions for taking a loan are satisfied. All loan rules and conditions are provided to the clients in writing when they are recruited. Clients rely on CTS that they will

Figure 1. Organization chart of CTS

receive such service as CTS promised. Loan repayment terms and methods are very flexible and friendly, trying to respond to the clients' needs; with a maximum loan term of one year. However, the clients must exercise the financial discipline to repay regularly and within the loan term. The interest on the loan is due each month, and clients should pay that amount to CTS in full and can repay the principal amount simultaneously.

CTS's mission statement is to "increase income and create savings habit among the targeted population, especially the extreme poor", while the long term objective of CTS is to provide demand driven financial services through a sustainable financial institution to the people by expanding the working area according to the need of the community.

History of the Organization

CTS – a local cooperative – has started its operation in Dublia village of Goaldihi Union of Khansama Upuzilla in Dinajpur in 1998 as a joint pilot project of Plan, an international humanitarian organization and Come to Work, a local NGO operating in Dinajpur area. CTS is registered as an independent cooperative and aims to provide flexible financial services to the community with a special focus to reach the extreme poor. This project was both funded and conceptualized by Plan Bangladesh and was basically implemented to experiment with rural adaptation of *Safe*Save. However, it was registered as an independent co-operative, rather than continuing as a confused institution jointly managed by CTW and Plan Bangladesh. CTS is now a full-fledged independent institution providing demand driven microfinance to the extreme poor on sustainable basis. CTS products and mechanisms were designed by modifying *Safe*Save products to provide flexible and convenient services, while helping them to maximize their savings capacity.

When CTS was going through some operational difficulties, Plan appointed a technical advisor to recuperate the institution from its problems. After lots of technical inputs and hands-on technical support to CTS in the area of microfinance and organization development, CTS has become one of the most innovative local MFIs in Bangladesh. With the leadership of the technical advisor, the FES technical team of Plan Bangladesh has been providing continuous technical support to develop CTS as an institution. This technical support includes providing training for staff and clients' capacity building, designing and developing demand-driven flexible financial services, effectively implementing program, analyzing financial statements, regular monitoring of target versus achievement and developing guideline and framework for achieving long-term organizational goals.

Operating Framework

CTS works exclusively in low-income residential and market areas, and attracts the poor and very poor individuals in those areas by offering products that are designed and priced specifically for them. It is this participatory product design focus, which allows CTS to work with the poor and very poor. Any person living within the working area of a CTS branch may use CTS's services, although children under 15 may not borrow. Table 1 presents the basic features of the microfinance program of CTS (Hasan, Nuremowla and Musa, 2004).

CTS's experience shows that a daily opportunity to save at home or at work maximizes a poor person's ability to save and repay loans (Hasan, Nuremowla and Musa, 2004). If one allows savings amounts to vary each day (or be zero), it will not scare off the very poor, who make good clients and reliable borrowers. Working with individuals instead of groups allows each client to use services at their own pace, and according to their own particular needs. CTS also experienced that if realistic interest rates are set, supported by a low-cost working environment in a disciplined manner, it is possible to be commercially viable and serve poor clients (Hasan, Nuremowla and

Table 1. Basic features of the microfinance program of CTS

Features	CTS
Poverty Targeting	• CTS targets the extreme poor people by Participatory Wealth Ranking (PWR)[2] with assistance and consultation with other stakeholders • Special focus is given to reach the extreme poor at all staff and work levels of CTS, so that the poor people can enjoy different and diversified financial services to meet their different financial needs and to cope up with vulnerability.
Account Opening and Members	• Clients are recruited as individuals: there is no group formation and no cross guaranteeing of loans. There are therefore no meetings. • Clients may be men, women or children, though children may only borrow if they are at least 15 years of age • There can be more than one savings account per household.
Interface between CTS and its clients	• CTS's bank workers, known as Collectors, are responsible for visiting each of their clients once a day, six days a week. These collectors are hired from the community. • A Collector is encouraged to work with about 120-150 clients • All financial transactions between CTS and the client take place on the client's doorstep. Branch manager at branch level disburses loans. • CTS product rules specify the timing and value of withdrawals and loans and the charging or paying of interest. This means that employees have no discretion over whether a client may borrow or not and thus helps to prevent 'rent-seeking'[3] behavior by employees.
Savings	• There is a simple savings account in which clients may save as much as they like, when they like, at the daily visit. • There is a longer-term savings or bond account on which clients may earn interest.
Loans	• Clients may pay down loan principal in whatever value they wish during the daily visit. • Clients are obliged to pay loan interest on a monthly basis; this is the one transaction that they are required to make on a fixed timetable. • There will be one loan tied with the long-term savings and one loan will be free. However, loan size of later loans will definitely be less. • Clients have to return the whole principal within the loan period. Collectors usually remind and motivate the clients to pay back the loan principal • Loans are not renewable and zero-tolerance strategy applies for the loan term. • Not more than one general loan may be taken in any one calendar month. • Interest on loans is calculated on flat basis. • Loans are forgiven, net of savings, if the borrower dies.

Musa, 2004). CTS designs all its products through Participatory Product Development in cooperation between membership and senior staff, and implemented by the Director. When product rules are changed, all clients will be given at least one month written notice. Field operations staff may never modify product rules for any reason.

Legal Identity, Ownership and Governance

Come To Save (CTS) is a Cooperative Society, registered with the Cooperative Department of the Government of the Peoples Republic of Bangladesh, dated February 2001.

CTS is governed by a set of bylaws approved by the Registrar of Cooperatives. Presently the governing body of CTS has thirty-seven seats. To become a member of the governing body, a person needs to purchase shares of CTS with a nominal value of Taka 10 per share. However, no one can purchase more than 10% of CTS's 500,000 shares at any given time. Meetings of the general membership occur not less than one time per year. At other times, the Executive Committee can be called as needed. The General Secretary will call and minute all meetings of the governing body and executive committee.

Financial Management

CTS maintains all required primary accounting records, namely cash book and general ledger with supporting receipts and payment vouchers. Books are maintained on a daily basis. The primary responsibility of maintaining books lies with a Data Processing Officer who is assisted by Field Officers. A Branch Manager is responsible for ensuring that the books are updated timely.

Double entry book keeping is used for recording financial transactions. In addition to primary financial records mentioned above, several other subsidiary ledgers and supporting documents are maintained. These are individual loan ledger (collector wise), contract saving register (collector wise), vouchers, receipts, money receipt book and daily saving register (computer software under construction/testing).

The main record for daily savings is the collection sheet which doubles as the ledger. Same data is also collected through the POS and then entered into the MIS software CTS currently uses. The set of reports CTS regularly prepares are at a glance report (a portfolio report), statement of clients and savings (collector wise), statement of borrowers and loans (collector wise), statement of fees/interests (collector wise), receipts and payments statement, income statement, balance sheet, bank reconciliation statement and budget variance analysis.

Plan, being the single donor to CTS, introduced the reporting formats for CTS as part of its technical inputs. These cover all relevant aspects for an MFI except the trial balance. CTS also reinvests the surplus generated through its regular microfinance operations. Financial statements are prepared for all branches individually. However, CTS's practice is to prepare the income statements with accumulated figures for the period from its inception to date, which helps the users of the reports to understand the current performance as well as the cumulative profit/loss realized by CTS.

As part of being registered as a cooperative CTS is subject to external audit by the department of co-operative. Apart from that, CTS also employed an independent external auditor to conduct audits on an annual basis.

MAIN TOPIC: STUDY ON POS IMPLEMENTATION

Methodology

The study was conducted based on the secondary information made available by Plan Bangladesh and CTS. While conducting the study, primary data was also collected from the two geographic locations where the handheld POS is being piloted. Participatory tools and techniques were used to ensure substantial consultation with the stakeholders.

The study was conducted at two geographic locations, where two Program Units of Plan Bangladesh are providing support to CTS to pilot the handheld POS. These are Chirirbandar and Khanshama Units of Dinajpur district of Bangladesh. The key stakeholders consulted to collect primary data and to validate secondary data were Plan Bangladesh, CTS and microfinance clients served by CTS.

For the purpose of data collection, qualitative methods were mostly used. The key methods used to collect relevant data include key informant interview, Focus Group Discussion, process observation and review of documents.

The interviews of key informants were essentially informal, open-ended individual interviews with Plan management, who led the piloting phase. The Director, Area Managers, Branch Managers, Data Entry Operators and Field Officers of CTS were also interviewed. Focus Group Discussions were conducted with the frontline staff of CTS, who are the end-users of the handheld POS. Besides, the clients were divided into three different categories based on demographic classification for Focus Group Discussions. The group combination was for female, male and children to ensure symmetry of the data collected through the Focus Group Discussions. One plenary session was conducted at CTS Head Office in presence of multiple stakeholders like CTS and Plan management, local elites and representatives of other MFIs working in the same locality.

As part of the methodology to collect relevant data, the study team, in close attachment with the end-users and Data Entry Operators, observed the whole implementation process of the handheld POS from field to branch office level. The existing Management Information System (MIS) for data transfer from the POS, input by the Data Entry Operators and analysis for management use were also observed. While reviewing and observing the process, focus was given on time allocation for each unit of data transferred. Relevant documents like meeting minutes, periodic reports, manual documentation of transactions, collection sheets and internal monitoring checklist were also reviewed.

Current State of Technology use in Bangladesh

For last few years, MFIs are concentrating on the potential benefits of ICT to be derived. The focus on ICT has taken on even greater urgency as institutions are trying to serve clients efficiently, particularly in rural areas. In recent years, large amount of institutional capital and donor funds have been invested in MFIs to excel their operation. This section focuses on the current level of ICT usage by the MFIs in Bangladesh.

*Safe*Save is considered as the pioneer of implementing technology as a tool for increasing program efficiency. It is the first organization of its kind, who started implementation of Personal Digital Assistants (PDAs) back in 2003 at its Kurmitola branch office. The objective was to raise the efficiency of the loan officers, reduce the approval time and cost. *Safe*Save used PDAs for performing field level transactions. Though *Safe*Save has been successfully implementing PDAs in its branches, from a global perspective, it was reported that some of the users of PDAs have failed to realize expected benefit from PDAs, especially in improving revenues, product quality and information flow (Lui, et al, 2006).

Many MFIs in Bangladesh are currently using mobile phones as a means of improving communication between clients and offices located at different geographic locations. This has resulted in stronger facilitation of transactions, collection of overdue loans and stronger internal control. Globally, MFIs are using mobile phones for payment for goods and services, cash back, deposits, money transfer, checking account balances etc., while in Bangladesh the scope, so far, is limited to communication only. The benefits of mobile phones are widely available for large MFIs, while small MFIs working in the extremely rural areas are still to get the benefit from it.

In recent years, POS has emerged as advancement to ATM technology with a broader variety of transactions. The POS technology is mainly used for payment for goods and services, cash back, deposits, account transfer, balance enquiry, savings etc. One major advantage of POS over ATM is that POS is supported by on-site staff. As a result, clients feel more comfortable with POS as they can talk to the employee if any problem arises. Both the technologies issue receipts for transaction. However, presence of staff is a key element in establishing trust between clients and technology in case of deposits made by the clients. CTS is a bright and only example using this technology in Bangladesh since December 2007.

Though biometrics and voice recognition technology are being used in some MFIs, presence of these technologies are still not available for MFIs in Bangladesh. Apart from the cases of *Safe*Save and CTS mentioned above, there is no evidence and record of using technology widely by the MFIs in Bangladesh. However, many MFIs are using customized software and computerized record keeping system.

CTS and Technology Introduction

CTS serves its clients individually. The clients do not need to form any group for accessing the financial services offered by CTS. All transactions take place at the doorsteps of the clients during the daily visits by CTS frontline staff. The savings deposited and loans repaid by the clients are not in fixed installment amounts (please see Table 1 for details). The option of daily transaction resulted in larger numbers of transaction than that of traditional group based model, as the clients have the flexibility to deposit more money when available and even more than once a day, if felt necessary. It was realized by both CTS and Plan management that without having an automated MIS, handling of such large number of information and transaction may become difficult. The idea of automated MIS was supported by a set of management staff at Plan Country Office in Dhaka, who promoted technology for day-to-day functions of the office. Encouraged by the success of *Safe*Save, the core microfinance model Plan advocates for, in using PDAs for microfinance operation, Plan decided to implement similar technology innovation for its rural microfinance programs, through CTS.

With all these factors influencing the situation, Plan management assigned a team to develop customized microfinance software and started searching for a suitable device that will accelerate the field level transaction in combination with the software. Necessary programming required for synchronization of the software of the possible technology options were sorted out by the Information System and Technology team of

Plan. Meantime, another team was involved in identifying a low-cost, suitable technology to facilitate the field level transaction of CTS. Plan received a positive response from an Indian vendor, who had been delivering handheld POS to some MFIs in Mumbai and Pune, who seem to meet the requirement specified by the technical team.

Plan Bangladesh sent one of its staff to India to physically check the facilities offered by the vendor. Upon getting a positive feedback on the device, Plan decided to acquire the technology and brought CTS into the process. The technical team at Plan and the Indian vendor, over a period of six months, developed the technical design of the software and the POS. The POS devices were then imported under direct involvement of Plan and were handed over to CTS for piloting in two of its branch offices.

CGAP Suggested POS Model

CGAP Technology Center has identified three distinctive models of POS technology (Hishigsuren, 2006). The models are: (1) Customers use their debit or credit cards to make payments to vendors. The

POS device does not allow withdrawals or deposits. Customers must visit bank branches to apply for loans, deposit cash, or open a new ac-

Figure 2. Data flow of the handheld POS used by CTS

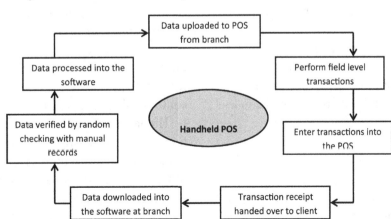

count. In this model, the POS technology requires no handling of cash by the customer or the retail outlet that has the POS device. (2) Customers can deposit and withdraw cash, and possibly transfer money to other account-holders. The POS device identifies and authenticates the client and authorizes the transaction, but the cash counting, handling and storage are the responsibility of the retailer's staff or a store employee dedicated for this purpose. Clients have less need to visit bank branches, and can transact at more convenient times and places. However, they must still visit branches to open accounts and handle more complicated transactions, such as applying for credit cards or term loans. The bank must ensure that the retailer is properly handling cash on its behalf. Five of the seven institutions that provided detailed information to CGAP on their POS devices reported using this model. (3) A full service channel provides the full range of banking services to retail or postal outlets that may be nearer to clients. Again, the POS handles the transaction processing and the human attendant performs basic cash handling and customer service functions. But in this case, customers are allowed to open new accounts and apply for loans. In some cases, an MFI or other third party may perform loan appraisal and follow up or monitoring functions.

The POS devices used by CTS largely resemble Model 2 of CGAP, as described above. However, during the pilot stage of the POS, CTS is only offering deposits, withdrawals and balance enquiry through the devices. It has a plan to extend the potential use of the devices, if improved technology is not found upon completion of the piloting. The possible extensions would enable the clients to transfer money from one account to another, pay for goods and services, as said by the management of CTS.

Analyses and Findings[4]

This part of the chapter focuses on the analyses and key findings on the pilot implementation of

handheld POS by CTS. As a summary of findings, it was observed that the manual workload of the staff at frontline level has reduced significantly. By effective synchronization of the POS data with the software, CTS is producing various reports i.e. client and collector wise information, for detail analysis of staff performance. A fully automated system, backed up by use of the POS and software, is enabling CTS to strengthen its existing internal control system through reduction of fraud and cases of manual data entry mistakes.

It was seen that the POS are quite user-friendly and the collectors can learn the operation of the POS very quickly. The operation of the devices resembles with the operation of calculators, which enables the relatively low qualified frontline staff to operate it smoothly. Collectors were also found saying that they feel comfortable and empowered using the devices in remote rural areas, where such technology are almost non-existent.

Effectiveness Analysis

While analyzing effectiveness of the handheld POS, the indicators taken into consideration were staff productivity, staff efficiency, human error, fraud, clients' satisfaction and MIS and FIS.

To assess productivity of staff, careful comparative analysis between piloting branches and non-piloting branches was done through discussion with CTS management and frontline staff and review of secondary documents. It was revealed that the POS is user-friendly, allowing the frontline staff to perform more transactions within their daily work time. At the same time, the level of inspiration towards work requiring less effort and pride to use advanced technology contributed towards increased staff efficiency.

Human errors in recording field level transactions have significantly reduced after introduction of the POS. The data transfer and client interface has become stronger than ever, as a 'three-step checking' takes place. The printed transaction receipt given to the clients confirms that transactions are rightly recorded at the first step, while at the second step the Data Entry Operators at the branch office checks all incoming data with the manual record. The final checking involves the branch managers, who pays daily visits and cross checks office record with the clients' record through random sampling. As part of CTS' existing program monitoring system combined with the use of technology, this three-step checking also has contributed towards reduction of rent-seeking behavior of the frontline staff and cases of fraud. CTS experienced improvement in client selection process, where nepotism by the frontline staff resulted in recruitment of clients with poor transaction profile and poor financial discipline. Before implementation of the POS, CTS occasionally experienced financial misappropriation by the frontline staff in case of depositing the daily collection at the branch office. For example, a Collector collected Tk 1,500 on any given day from the field, but deposited Tk. 1,200 at the branch office. This accounts for a misappropriation of Tk. 300 at the Collector level simply by not entering the collection of equivalent amount in the collection sheet. The only way to identify such cases by CTS management was to cross-check each client's passbook information with the collection sheet. This had been a very time consuming process, as well as expensive on the part of the organization. With the introduction of technology, CTS could reduce such cases by 100%, as the POS records all transaction and generates a daily collection report. A Collector now cannot tamper the records kept in the POS memory.

Interview with individual clients and discussion with group of clients, frontline and management staff of CTS revealed that satisfaction is high both at clients and organization levels. Clients expressed that they found instantaneous delivery of money receipt and balance update very useful. Clients also have expressed that introduction of the POS has significantly increased their trust towards CTS. They explained that an organization making such an investment is less likely to pull away from operation, which had been experienced by Bangladesh microfinance industry several times. The interface between CTS frontline staff and the clients was strengthened further through introduction of the handheld POS. One Collector at Tetulia Branch was found saying *"Our clients know that the handheld POS are Machines and to their understanding Machines can never make any mistakes in recording our financial transactions."*

Traditionally, MFI staff responsible for reporting spends much time consolidating and analyzing the information collected from field. The study team observed that to transfer data from POS to the customized MIS of CTS takes approximately three minutes on an average per device per day i.e. less than an hour to process all transactions of 12-15 collectors. The manual entry of a day's transaction would take about three to four hours per day. The 'three-step checking' ensures that the transferred data is accurately recorded and processed. By giving few simple commands using the software, CTS can produce all sorts of reports for internal and external use.

Cost Structure Analysis

The cost structure analysis put emphasize on cost effectiveness of the POS from the viewpoints of investment cost, operational cost, maintenance cost and capacity building cost.

Through document review, FGDs, interviews and comparative analysis of financial reports; the study team came to a conclusion that introduction of technology enabled CTS to reduce costs. While the initial investment to purchase one unit of POS is approximately USD 500, the operational and maintenance cost per unit were found to be significantly lower. Per month cost incurred by CTS for maintenance and usage of the POS stands at less than USD 10, which is less than manual record keeping (USD 19). This figure was drawn by an internal assessment team after analyzing relevant information from CTS' financial statements for a period of one year (January to December 2007).

The annual Return on Investment is, therefore, 21.6% *(9×12÷500)*.

Besides, the frontline staff was given on-job-training by Plan technical persons involved in the piloting process. The man hours consumed for developing frontline staffs' capacity did not incur additional costs, as the time of Plan technical persons is usually dedicated for supporting regular program implementation of CTS.

The comparative analysis of financial reports produced by CTS before and after piloting of POS revealed that operational costs were reduced by 13% in six months (from December 2007 to June 2008) after the piloting began. At the same time, it was reported by the frontline staff and the Data Entry Operators of CTS that per day transactions made by the clients of the pilot branches have increased by 7% during the reporting period (December 2007 to June 2008).

Limitations of the POS

Technology does not only contribute towards increased efficiency, but also comes with some limitations. The study team carefully focused on identifying the limitations of the piloting of handheld POS by CTS. Few of these limitations can be fixed by strengthening internal capacity of the organization, while the others need immediate attention before going into full fledged roll out of technology.

The net weight of the POS is 800 Grams. Though the POS comes with a carrying bag, the frontline staffs sometimes find it difficult to carry the device for the whole day and hold it when the transaction is being recorded. The small and monochrome display of the device also causes difficulty in viewing the records entered into the POS during dull weather and at places where less light is available. Protection from rain during rainy seasons is considered as another risky area by the users of the device, as the device is not water resistant.

CTS operates in remote rural areas of a northern district of Bangladesh, where the supply of regular accessories like ink, cartridge, ribbon, etc. needed for the POS is limited. When CTS would think of fully fledged implementation of the POS in all its branches, which is four times higher than that of current POS coverage, unavailability of regular accessories might result in optimum use of the POS. Both CTS and Plan has jointly arranged for a mechanism to ensure supply of the accessories from the capital city of Dhaka, which in the long-run does not support expansion of the POS implementation.

The POS records transactions and produces receipts in English. The clients, who are mostly village peasants, find it difficult to understand the language and need to take help from others to validate if their transactions were recorded properly. CTS may think of changing the language into Bengali with support from its funding organization and the POS vendor. The data transfer cable for the POS is COM/serial port. The newer computer hardware uses USB ports. This can pose difficulty in transferring data to and from the POS to computer if old hardware is replaced by CTS.

The current programming of the device supports recording of 5-digit transactions i.e. a maximum of Taka 99,999. Considering the current growth of the program, when the loan size of matured clients reaches Taka 100,000, the existing devices would soon become obsolete if digit limit is not increased. CTS currently is thinking of introducing microenterprise loans, where the average loan size will be approximately Taka 100,000 and CTS will be unable to use the existing technology support to record the transactions of the microenterprise loanees. The current programming allows CTS to record transactions on only 5 fields. CTS, being a progressive microfinance service provider, is planning to offer more financial services in the form of micro-insurance and micro-leasing. Currently there is no provision to include new fields of transaction.

CTS's flexible microfinance program philosophy allows clients to deposit, withdraw and repay more than once, if possible, in one day. The device does not support multiple transactions from one client within the same day.

FUTURE RESEARCH DIRECTIONS

The handled POS, which has completed one year piloting, has been proved to give desired level of outcome with few limitations in the piloting phase. However, it remains a major challenge for CTS to implement the technology in wider scale. This relates to the limitations of the existing technology as mentioned earlier. Successful implementation of technology depends largely on how suitably it has been planned for. If the planning is not flexible or depends on wrong assumptions, future implementation can face a lot of obstacles. CTS planned implementing handheld POS at a time when it has got momentum in loan disbursement and customer accumulation. In near future, when the loan size and number of clients are expecting to increase, the chances of using the current technology might not be suitable for CTS. If CTS still decides to continue using the POS for all branches, as planned, the potential cost of replacement in future seems very high. Implementation of the POS by CTS was facilitated by external donor funding, in absence of which it might become challenging for CTS to invest large sum of money from within the organization, given its current financial condition as a growing MFI.

CTS has still not decided about expanding the technology to other branch offices and would continue piloting with the existing branches for another year. Once the piloting is completed, more lessons based on more data would be generated. This chapter is part of the documentation process of the lessons learnt that has recently started and is expected to contribute towards giving CTS a more solid base to analyze the performance of the pilot phase.

CTS is considering vertical and horizontal expansion through its current 5-year business plan, which is up to the year 2012. It is another concern to link the investment in technology and expansion strategy. How far handheld POS can create value for the expanded CTS is another major question. CTS may think of moving from existing POS devices to a cheaper, easier and locally available technology that will contribute towards the expansion plan in a cost-effective way.

CONCLUSION

The piloting process of handheld POS did not leave room for CTS to stop manual record keeping. CTS management was conservative on this issue, as manual records could support/retrieve any data, shall the piloting face difficulty in adaptation. Keeping this in mind, the handheld POS could not generate promised level of performance. However, it is still evident from the analyses and findings that the POS could create certain level of impact on operational and financial aspect of CTS. At the same time, the piloting enabled CTS to suggest their customized requirements to the vendor, as well as Plan, for further improvement and increased utility of the POS. At the initial stage of pilot implementation of POS, sufficient effort to document the learning was absent, resulting in lack of information during evaluation of the piloting. Thus, many important issues and learning were forgotten. This chapter tries to fill in the gap of this documentation.

REFERENCES

Arunachalam, R. S. (2007). *Microfinance and Technology – Critical Issues, Lessons and Future Implications*. MCG Research Note Series in Low Income Financial Services, Research Note # 1. Tamil Nadu, India, Microfinance Consulting Group (MCG).

Fountain, J. E. (2003). *Information, Institutions and Governance: Advancing a Basic Social Science Research Program for Digital Government.* Working paper series No. RWP 03-004, John F. Kennedy School of Government, Cambridge, MA, USA.

Hasan, M. E., Nuremowla, S. A., & Musa, A. S. M. (2004). *Come To Save (CTS) Cooperatives Limited – A Vision: A Case Study on Poverty Focused Microfinance Program.* Dhaka: Plan Bangladesh.

Hishigsuren, G. (2006). *Information and Communication Technology and Microfinance: Options for Mongolia.* ADB Institute Discussion Paper No. 42. Tokyo, Japan, Asian Development Bank.

Islam, R., et al. (2008). *Internal Assessment of CTS: Microfinance Software and Handheld Device.* Unpublished, Plan Bangladesh and Come To Save (CTS) Cooperatives Limited, Bangladesh.

Ivatury, G. (2005). Using Electronic Payments to Build Inclusive Financial Systems. *CGAP Technology Center.* Retrieved March 17, 2009, from www.cgap.org/technology.html

Ivatury, G. (2006). Using Technology to Build Inclusive Financial Systems. *Microfinance Gateway Library.* Retrieved March 17, 2009, from http://www.microfinancegateway.org/p/site/m/library.html

Kaufman, R. J., & Kriebel, C. H. (1988). *Identifying Business Value Linkages for Information Technology: An Exploratory Application to Treasury Workstations.* Information Systems working paper series, NYU working paper no. IS-88-47. NY, USA.

Lui, A., Pertet, R., & White, V. (2006). *Technology for the Poor: Challenges and Benefits of PDAs, ATMs and More for Microfinance Institutes.* Paper presented at a USAID Learning Conference: Microenterprise Development in a Global World. USAID.

Majewsky, G., & Usoro, A. (2008). *Microfinance Monitoring, Reporting and Group Lending as Challenges for the Data Warehousing Technology.* Paper presented at eRA – 3 Proceedings: The Contribution of Information Technology to Science, Economy, Society & Education. T. E. I. of Piraeus, Spetses Island, Greece.

Mathison, S. (2005). *Increasing the Outreach and Sustainability of Microfinance through ICT Innovation.* Brisbane, Australia, Foundation for Development Cooperation (FDC).

Matthews, P. (2007). Platform for Improving Service Delivery or an Expensive Distraction. *Rural e-services.* Retrieved March 19, 2009, from http://linux.odi.org.uk/eservblog/?

Mithas, S., Krishnan, M. S., & Fornell, C. (2005). *Effect of Information Technology Investments on Customer Satisfaction: Theory and Evidence.* Stephen M. Ross School of Business working paper no. 971, University of Michigan, MI, USA.

Mithas, S., Ramasubbu, N., & Sambamurthy, V. (2008). *Information Management Capability and Firm Performance: An Empirical Analysis.* Robert H. Smith School of Business Research Paper No. RHS 06-071, University of Maryland, MD, USA.

Plan Bangladesh. (2007). *Annual Report 2007.* Dhaka: Plan Bangladesh.

Setboonsarng, S., & Zhang, J. (2006). *Using ICT in Capacity Building for Poverty Reduction in Asia: Lessons Learned from the Microfinance Training of Trainers Course.* ADB Institute Discussion Paper No. 50. Tokyo, Japan, Asian Development Bank.

Silva, S. (2002). *Quantum Leap: Microcredit Boosted by Technology.* Microenterprise Americas Magazine. Friday, May 27, 2005/Saturday, June 4, 2005.

Whelan, S. (2003). CGAP IT Innovation Series: Smart Cards. *CGAP Technology Center.* Retrieved March 15, 2009, from www.cgap.org/technology.html

ADDITIONAL READING

Arunachalam, R. S., Katticaren, K., Swarup, V., & Iyer, K. (2007). *Enhancing Financial Services Flow to Small Scale Marine Fisheries Sector*. A study for FAO/UNTRS. Chennai: United Nations Team for Tsunami Recovery Support, UN India.

Banker, R. D., & Kaufman, R. J. (1991). *Quantifying the Business Value of Information Technology: An Illustration of the 'Business Value Linkage' Framework*. NYU working paper No. IS-91-21, NY, USA.

Blancas, E. (1982). Let the People Identify the Poor. *Rural Reconstruction Review, 4*, 10–11.

Come to Save. (2004). *Operational Manual of Come To Save (CTS)*. Dinajpur, Bangladesh: Cooperatives Limited.

Hasan, M. E. (2003). Implication of Financial Innovation for the poorest of the Poor in the Rural area: Experience from Northern Bangladesh. *Journal of Microfinance, 5*(2). Humanities Publishers, UK.

Hasan, M. E., & Iglebaek, M. (2005). *Profitability and Poverty Alleviation Agenda for Microfinance Operators: Trade-off and Complementary Debate*. Dhaka: Plan Bangladesh.

Hulme, D., & Mosley, P. (1997). Finance for the poor or poorest? Financial Innovations, Poverty and Vulnerability in Wood, G. D./Sharif, I. (Ed.) *Who Needs Credit? Poverty and Finance in Bangladesh* (pp 96-129). University Press Limited, Dhaka and Zed Books, UK.

Kusakabe, M. (2005). *Developing ICT Strategy for Economic Growth*. Paper presented at the International Workshop on Workforce Development for Knowledge Economy, Seoul, Korea.

Kusakabe, M. (2005). *ICT and National Innovation System: Is ICT Engine of Growth?* Paper presented at the International Workshop on Workforce Development for Knowledge Economy, Seoul, Korea.

Lee, J. (2005). *Opening Remarks*. Delivered at the Conference on Community Information Services for the Poor, Colombo, Sri Lanka.

Meyer, R. L. (2002). *Track Record of Financial Institutions in Assisting the Poor in Asia*. ADB Institute Research Paper: 49. Tokyo, Japan, Asian Development Bank.

Musa, A. S. M. (2004). *Participatory Wealth Ranking (PWR): Identifying the Chronic and Extreme Poor to Improve Poverty Outreach. Plan Bangladesh Microfinance Technical Paper*. Dhaka: Plan Bangladesh.

Plan Bangladesh. (2002). *Plan Bangladesh's Approach for Child Centered Community Development (CCCD). CCCD Handbook* (p. 43). Dhaka: Plan Bangladesh.

Rutherford, S. (2000). *The Poor and Their Money*. Oxford Press.

Wijesiriwardana, I., & Musa, A. S. M. (2004). *Costing and Financial Management Review of Plan Microfinance Partners*. Dhaka: Plan Bangladesh.

ENDNOTES

[1] The implementation strategy of Plan's microfinance programs is working through local partner organizations backed by a systematic action research and technical support protocol. The overall microfinance strategy is geared towards ensuring flexible and demand driven financial services to reach poor and the extreme poor. The balance between institutional sustainability and client impact has been maintained to make the program unique and exemplary one. The key implementation strategies are – *Action Research & Innovation:* Experiment of innovative financial products and approaches that support organizational growth with sustainability in order to reach the poor and extreme poor

with positive impact through in-depth action research and learning. *Capacity Building:* Enhance social, technical and managerial competence of partner microfinance institutions committed in reaching the poorest and microfinance innovations, through a set of high quality training, developing technical tool series and technical support; and also facilitate lateral learning and transfer of skills through study tours and field exposure. *Dissemination, Capitalization and Adaptation of Learning:* Facilitate cross-fertilization of ideas and sharing of experiences in the area of innovation and reaching the poorest through regular workshops/seminars, research and experimentation in collaboration with other key players in Bangladesh (Hasan, Nuremowla and Musa, 2004).

[2] To conduct PWR, CTS, under direct guidance and support from Plan, follows the ABCD technique, which is an improvisation of ABC method of Rural Reconstruction Review (RRR) (Blancas, 1982). This process is carried out by the adolescents and also adults, which in many cases demonstrates the potential of children. Here, "A" stands for the better-off families in a community,

"B" stands for the middle-level families, and "C" stands for the poor, "D" and "E" stands for Extreme and chronically poor families, where "E" category households are landless and most vulnerable to shocks. The indicators and criteria for the ranking are decided by the community through participatory exercise (Musa, 2004).

[3] 'Rent-seeking' behavior refers to the frontline staff's intention to manipulate field level transactions, especially in approving or issuing loans. The collectors of CTS are hired to work in their own communities, so chances maybe there for such manipulation by loan syndication. CTS specifies the product rules in simple, easily understandable language and distributes those to all clients. This minimizes the potential cases of frauds and loan syndication that may arise otherwise.

[4] All information provided in this section of the chapter are collected from an internal evaluation of the pilot implementation of handheld POS, conducted by Plan and CTS in December 2008. The evaluation was done as the first step of documentation of the piloting and lessons learnt from it.

Section 2
Mobile Banking

Introduction

Kevin Day
Riskebiz Microfinance Solutions, Canada

Mobile banking has been seen as the potential panacea for delivering banking services to the 83% of the poor population which remains unbanked. However, despite the proven technical ability to provide banking services over mobile phones, many potential users are not using systems which are already available. In order to effectively utilize mobile banking solutions, it is critical to understand customers' reasons behind adopting the mobile banking services. In Chapter 7, Prateek Shrivastava attempts to understand the reasons behind the major perceived and real obstacles in the willingness of the consumer to embrace mobile banking. What is discovered is that often the reasons behind adoption are the opposite of what would have been expected.

One of the negative side effects of the enormous growth of information technology to support microfinance is the risk that many inappropriate solutions will be developed to meet the need at the expense of impeding the functioning and growth of the microfinance market. If technology solutions are implemented in a haphazard way, the chances of failure are high and the objectives of financial inclusion will not be met. Operational efficiency, the ability to scale and low cost units are some of the key characteristics of a successful microfinance technology. Even though the size of a typical microfinance transaction is very small and the customer is often an unsophisticated user, the requirements with respect to the technology and systems needed for supporting the microfinance market are complex. In Chapter 8, Nandu Kulkarni examines two case studies of technology implementation and analyzes the results to provide a better understanding of how both selecting the right solution can help an organization and a poor technology selection can hinder it. A third example looks at the shared services platform (SaaS) model as another option growing in both popularity and importance.

M-PESA is one of the most well known, and successful, mobile money transfer systems utilized in the microfinance market today. However, beyond simply moving money, M-PESA is increasingly being used as a sales mechanism by individuals in Kenya. How M-PESA is being used for savings varies depends on a variety of factors. In Chapter 9, Olga Morawczynski looks at the difference in M-PESA use for savings between an urban slum and a rural. Beyond the location difference, this chapter uses data from a collection of financial diaries to show not only how M-PESA is being used for savings, but how mobile money mechanisms can also act as a platform on which multiple savings mechanisms can and are being used.

In Chapter 10, Fred Jawadi, Nabila Jawadi & Ziane Ydriss address the question of whether communication technologies can improve the performance of microfinance programs by examining results from existing implementations. Although there is no shortage of research material on the use of ICT, few have been focused on the correlation between the use of technology and the enhancement of MFI performance. This chapter will show that ICT's are effective in enhancing work efficiency, improving risk management, developing customer relationship management and overall reducing transaction costs thus making MFIs better able to meet their objectives both financially and socially. However, challenges such as access to ICTs, cost, skills, etc. make it difficult for MFIs to effectively use technology. The results of a detailed survey regarding the implementation of ICTs has been analyzed in this chapter and provides evidence to support the conclusions regarding ICT effectiveness and challenges outlined above.

Chapter 7
Predicting the Attitude toward Mobile Financial Services in Developing Countries

Prateek Shrivastava
Monitise Group plc, UK

ABSTRACT

Globally, only about a sixth of the 3 billion poor people of working age currently have access to formal financial services. This translates to 17% coverage of the market, leaving 83% under-served or "unbanked". Addressing the needs of these people is the "self-sustaining approach" to microfinance. Mobile banking is one of the newest approaches to the provision of financial services made possible by the widespread adoption of mobile phones in low income countries. However, reports show that potential users may not be using these systems despite already being available. This study was conducted in 2008. It extends the Luarn & Lin mobile banking adoption model by adding two additional constructs: "Enhancement of image" and the "enhancement of quality of life by having access to financial service" to test the attitude toward mobile banking. In order to test these constructs, 11 hypotheses are proposed. The chapter successfully applies Luarn & Lin's model in a new geographic and economic context. Consistent with their study, perceived usefulness, perceived credibility, perceived ease of use and perceived self-efficacy were found to be significant antecedents. Perceived financial costs, however, was found to have a positive relationship with attitude. This finding is diametrically opposite to Luarn & Lin's study. Perceived enhancement to quality of life showed a strong relationship and Perceived enhanced image showed a weak relationship with the attitude toward mobile banking. The control group analysis showed the previously unbanked group (Mzansi) had the highest expectation of mobile banking and also found the idea most attractive. This study therefore concludes that mobile banking can indeed be a channel to reach out to low income groups.

DOI: 10.4018/978-1-61520-993-4.ch007

INTRODUCTION

Financial institutions help mobilise savings and provide payments services that facilitate the exchange of goods and services. Without inclusive financial systems, poor individuals and small enterprises need to rely on their personal wealth, internal resources or debilitating lines of credit to invest in their education, become entrepreneurs, or take advantage of promising growth opportunities. The bulk of the evidence, globally, suggests that improving access to finance is likely not only to accelerate economic growth, but also to reduce income inequality and poverty (Aghion et al, 2005).

According to research conducted in 2007 by Demirguc-Kunt, Beck, & Honohan of the World Bank, the majority of the population in the developing world does not have access to savings accounts, do not receive credit, and do not have any type of insurance and seldom make or receive payments through formal financial institutions. Globally, only about 25% of the world's population has an account with a financial institution.

Their research showed that China, India, Brazil and South Africa's population is less than 60% banked. Collectively, these four countries alone account for over 42% of the world's population. Across Sub-Saharan Africa, about 10% of the population has access to formal bank services. Another 15% have access to alternative financial services like microfinance. The remainder are "unbanked".

One of the approaches to providing financial products to the unbanked is financial institutions "down-scaling" their operations i.e. introducing new approaches to provide services to a poorer clientele. The business requirement for downscaling exists but the feasibility of doing so is suspect due to the large scale of human resource needed to support it (Ivatury & Pickens, 2006).

A possible solution is to use technology to reduce the cost per transaction of providing financial services. Possible technology solutions include ATMs, smart cards and mobile phone based banking (Whelan, 2003).

The growth of mobile telephony has been rapid, and has extended access well beyond already connected customers in developing countries (Gray, 2007). In 2006, the mobile phone became the first communications technology to have more users in developing countries than in developed ones. More than 800 million mobile phones were sold in developing countries between 2005 and 2008. In the last two quarters of 2008, India added an average of 9 million new users per month and China added an average of 8.5 million users per month.

This rapid growth of mobile phone users especially in developing countries offers a new low-cost alternative for firstly the financial institutions to still make a profit while dealing with small money transfers and payments (BAI, 2004; Booz Allen, 2003) and secondly consumers themselves to use since they no longer need to use scarce time and financial resources to travel to distant bank branches.

Many financial service providers in USA, UK, India and South Africa are successfully using mobile phones to inform customers about their balances, transaction histories, SMS based alerts when specific events occur (withdrawals, balance drops below a set threshold, etc.). In addition, in places such as East Africa and The Philippines, mobile phones have proven themselves as a great tool to transfer money remotely as either payments or remittances.

The development and successful deployment of financial services via mobile phones has shown willingness from financial service providers to develop and provide such products. However, there seems to be major perceived / real obstacles in the willingness of the consumer to adopt these products (Ivatury & Pickens, 2006). Therefore, the need to understand customer's reasons behind adopting these services becomes obvious.

The author will propose a model that provides a framework to empirically test the attitudes of customers (current and potential) towards mobile financial services. However, before that we provide a brief background on some basic concepts to situate the model.

BACKGROUND

This section offers a critical review of the current literature about the technologies currently used to reach out to the unbanked and the theories of technology adoption.

Reaching Out

Due to the relatively few banked customers in the emerging economies, it is imperative to provide a financial tool that is easy for people to obtain and operate.

Banks in many countries have created basic bank accounts with fewer Know Your Customer (KYC) requirements than a regular account. A few examples are the UK's "Basic Bank Account" and the "Universal Bank Account", India's "No-Frills Account" and South Africa's "Mzansi Account". These initiatives are the result of either having to comply with Central Bank regulations or overcome commercial pressures to increase customer numbers. For each of these accounts, each bank has to reach out to the prospective customer through mass-marketing followed by customer recruitment campaigns that could involve teams of people going from town to town signing people up whilst ensuring the strict KYC norms are met. Subsequently, each bank has to provide the means to operate the account – for example build a new branch with all its associated costs[1] or tie up with the post office network or provide mobile bank branches or use point-of-sale and other devices in retail outlets as "branchless banking" networks (a seminal example is Brazil's Banking Correspondent network).

Pre-paid or stored-value cards are widely seen as another vehicle to reach out to the unbanked. Some countries have pilots to deploy cheap ATMs (Gramateller INDI), other machines designed to dispense and load prepaid cards with basic facilities like tracking account balances. Some organisations are using point of sale terminals and associated smart cards to reach out to the unbanked (Zipp card, etc.). These are of incredible value and have had limited success since a card-based infrastructure (secure manufacturing and distribution and electricity at the point of service, etc.) is required in order to use these solutions.

An alternative is to use the mobile phone as the device to reach out to customers using a Mobile-Wallet ("m-wallet"). This has been done either by linking basic bank accounts to a mobile phone number (Wizzit, ABSA), linking a pre-paid card to a mobile phone number (SMART cash) or link a non-bank e-money[2] account to a mobile phone number (M-Pesa, Globe, MobiPawa, LUUP, etc.)

In its purest form, an m-wallet is essentially an aggregator of payment instruments on a mobile phone. It is a data repository that houses consumer data sufficient to facilitate a financial transaction from a mobile handset, and the applicable intelligence to translate an instruction from a consumer through a mobile handset/bearer/application into a message that a financial service provider can use to debit or credit bank accounts or other payment instruments. (see Figure 1)

Although the implementation of the e-money m-wallet varies from country-to-country, there usually are the following players in the supply chain: the customer, the bank, the m-wallet provider and a retail outlet to perform face-to-face transactions. Customers can open their accounts at a retail outlet. These accounts are stored and managed by the provider. The customer can deposit funds into and withdraw cash from their m-wallet at any authorised outlet. Commercial banks are often used to hold the real cash against the e-money issued by the m-wallet provider.

The majority of deployments of this solution have been mobile network operators ("MNO") rather than banks. This is unsurprising since MNOs with their large network of retail outlets

Figure 1. Typical m-wallet provider setup

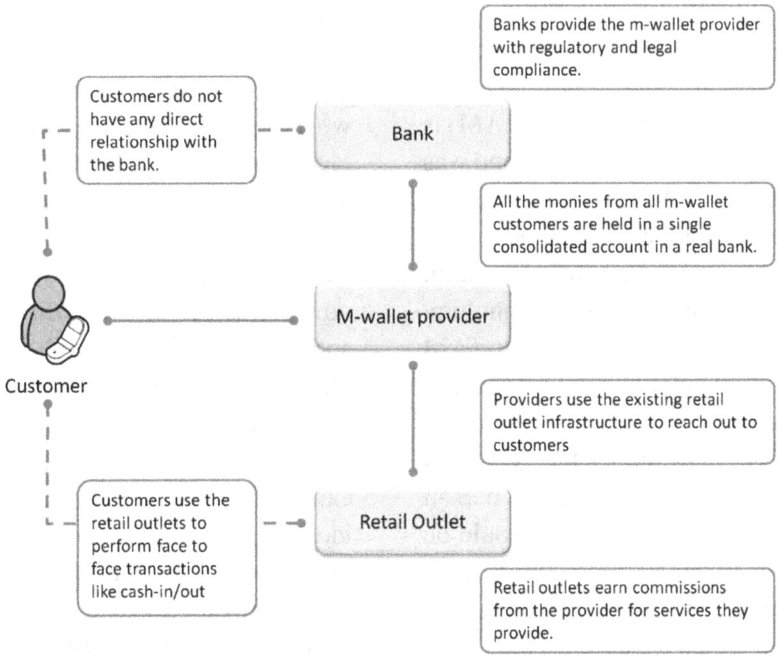

and existing customer base can easily offer m-wallet based e-money accounts as a value-added service to essentially decrease the rate of churn or attract new customers.

The success of MNO-led m-payment systems using different flavours of the above setup has been phenomenal. Globe Cash and SMART Money in the Philippines have over 3.5 million customers. M-Pesa has over 6.5 million registered users in Kenya alone. It has become a vital tool for many of the most vulnerable people in the economy. However, in most cases, these have become parallel financial systems that are not regulated by the relevant financial authorities. Due to this, central banks of many countries are beginning to regulate e-money to cover the receipt and transmittal of electronic cash on mobile phones to prevent fraud and money laundering.

As probably the current most famous example, there were circa 3 million bank accounts in Kenya as of January 2009. As of September 2009, there were circa 6.5 million registered M-Pesa customers that could operate their accounts at over 9,000

outlets (Camner & Sjoblom, 2009). To put this in perspective, banks in Kenya were first established in 1896 whereas M-Pesa was first established in January 2006. This example clearly shows the power of technology reaching out to the unbanked.

Theory of Adoption of Technology

The literature reviewed reveals that information technology adoption and acceptance theories can be applied to identify factors relevant to adoption of mobile financial services. This section summarises the four main theories of technology adoption: Theory of Reasoned Action, Technology Acceptance Model, Theory of Planned Behaviour and the Diffusion of Innovations.

The Theory of Reasoned Action is a widely studied model from social psychology, which is concerned with the determinants of consciously intended behaviours (Fishbein & Ajzen, 1975 and Ajzen & Fishbein, 1980). It states that the individual's Behavioural Intention to perform an action is jointly determined by the individual's

Attitude toward performing the Behaviour and Subjective Norm, which is the overall perception of what relevant others think the individual should or should not do.

The Technology Acceptance Model (TAM) is based on the Theory of Reasoned Action and was first proposed by Davis in 1989. TAM is one of the most applied models explaining technology adoption and use within information systems research. Developed to predict individual users' technology acceptance within an organizational context, TAM proposes that two particular beliefs: ease of use and usefulness determine the user acceptance of technology. Davis (1989) defines the perceived ease of use as "the degree to which a person believes that using a particular system would be free of effort" and the perceived usefulness as "the degree to which a person believes that using a particular system would enhance his or her job performance". These two beliefs form a person's attitude toward using the technology. TAM further posits that attitude and usefulness jointly determine the intention to use a technology and the intention then leads to actual system use. According to the TAM, system usage behaviour is determined by the intention to use a particular system, which in turn, is determined by the perceived usefulness and perceived ease of use of the system.

The Theory of Planned Behaviour (Ajzen, 1991) enhances the Theory of Reasoned Action with a third construct affecting behavioural intention and actual behaviour. The construct is perceived behavioural control, which includes an individual's perceptions on the presence or absence of requisite resources and opportunities to perform the behaviour.

Diffusion of innovations initially postulated by Rogers in 1962 is a multidisciplinary theory frequently applied in information systems acceptance research. Based on a synthesis of a considerable body of adoption research Rogers formulated the general theory to explain adoption of various types of innovations (Rogers, 1983, p. 215). Diffusion of innovations determines five innovation characteristics (Rogers, 1995, pp. 212-251) that affect the adoption: Relative Advantage, Complexity, Compatibility, Trialability and Observability. Relative advantage is the degree to which an innovation is perceived as better than the idea it supersedes. Relative advantage has been measured in terms of economic benefits, social prestige, status, convenience, and satisfaction. Complexity describes the degree to which an innovation is perceived as difficult to understand and use. Perceived complexity has a negative effect on the adoption. Compatibility denotes the degree to which an innovation is perceived as being consistent with the existing values, past experiences, and needs of potential adopters. An idea that is incompatible with the values and norms of a social system will not be adopted as rapidly as an innovation that is compatible. Trialability is the degree to which the innovation may be experimented with on a limited basis. A possibility to try an innovation before adoption will reduce the uncertainty and increase the likelihood of the adoption. Observability is the degree to which the results of an innovation are visible and communicable to others. The easier it is for individuals to see and discuss the results of an innovation, the more likely they are to adopt it.

Theories Applied to Mobile Financial Services

Brown (2003) hypothesised that mobile-banking is an extension of internet banking but with its own unique characteristics given that a cell phone is used rather than a web browser on a personal computer. In order to test their hypothesis, they extended the framework for the proposed by Tan and Teo (2000) to include Relative advantage, Compatibility, Complexity, Trialability, Banking needs, Risk, Self-efficacy, and Facilitating conditions. The study concluded that factors that would influence the initial adoption of cell phone banking include its perceived relative advantage, the ability to try and experiment with the innovation first (trialability), and the diversity of banking needs of a potential user. The perceived sense of risk was a major factor inhibiting adoption.

Among the different models that have been proposed, the TAM appears to be the most widely accepted among information systems researchers. The main reason for its popularity is perhaps its parsimony, as well as its wealth of recent empirical support (Agarwal & Prasad, 1999). Luarn and Lin (2005) extended the TAM to include one trust based construct "perceived credibility" and two resource based constructs – "perceived self-efficacy" (defined as the judgment of one's ability to use mobile financial services) and "perceived financial cost". In their study, they found perceived usefulness, ease of use, credibility, self-efficacy and financial resources to have positive influence on the behavioural intention (BI). Both perceived credibility and perceived financial resources were found to have a stronger effect on BI rather than the traditional TAM variable: ease of use.

PREDICTING THE ATTITUDE TOWARD MOBILE FINANCIAL SERVICES

The author will use the TAM as extended by Luarn and Lin (2005) to develop and test hypotheses to understand the antecedents that drive customer adoption of mobile financial services.

Research Model & Hypotheses

Perceived usefulness: The ultimate reason people would be interested in mobile financial services is that they find them useful (Luarn & Lin, 2005). There is also significant research in the IT community that shows the effect of perceived usefulness on usage intention. Therefore, the following hypotheses were tested:

H1. *Perceived usefulness will have a positive effect on attitude toward mobile financial services.*

Perceived ease of use: Venkatesh & Davis (1996) and Jackson, Chow, & Leitch (1997) researched the effect of perceived ease of use on usage intention within IT systems. Tan & Teo (2000) found this construct to be a significant antecedent to the perceived credibility of Internet banking. Luarn & Lin (2005) used this construct to test the behavioural intent to use mobile phone based banking in Taiwan. A greater perceived ease of use will lead to greater perceived usefulness, credibility and eventually the attitude to use mobile phone based banking. Thus, the following three hypotheses were tested:

H2. *Perceived ease of use will have a positive effect on the perceived usefulness of mobile financial services.*

H3. *Perceived ease of use will have a positive effect on the perceived credibility of mobile financial services.*

H4. *Perceived ease of use will have a positive effect on the attitude towards mobile financial services.*

Perceived credibility: Security and privacy would be paramount while designing and using new technologies for financial transactions (McKnight, Choudhury, & Kacmar, 2002). The need for security of personal details and financial information is therefore critical to the success of mobile phone banking. According to Wang et al. (2003), perceived credibility is defined as the extent to which a person believes that the use of mobile financial services will have no security or privacy threats. Luarn & Lin (2005) found that perceived credibility had a significant positive influence on the attitude toward mobile phone based banking. Thus, the following hypothesis was tested.

H5. *Perceived credibility will have a positive effect on the attitude towards mobile financial services.*

Perceived self-efficacy: This construct refers to the confidence an individual has in their ability to use a specific technology (Agarwal, Sambamurthy, & Stair, 2000). They further demonstrate the importance of self-efficacy in their study of user behaviour with information technology. In this context, perceived self-efficacy is defined as the judgment of one's ability to use mobile financial services. Luarn & Lin (2005) found that perceived self-efficacy had a significant positive influence on the attitude to use mobile phone based banking. Thus the following hypotheses were tested:

H6. *Perceived self-efficacy will have a positive effect on the perceived ease of use of mobile financial services.*

H7. *Perceived self-efficacy will have a positive effect on the attitude towards mobile financial services.*

Perceived financial cost is defined as the extent to which a person believes that using mobile financial services will cost money. Indeed, economic motivations and outcomes are most often the focus of IS acceptance studies. Perceived financial resources were also found to be a significant antecedent of the behavioural intention to use an information system (Mathieson, Peacock, & Chin, 2001). Therefore, the following hypothesis was tested:

H8. *Perceived financial cost will have a negative effect on the attitude towards mobile financial services.*

Perceived Enhanced Image: Moore and Benbasat (1991) define image as "the degree to which use of an innovation is perceived to enhance one's status in one's social system". It is the degree to which usage of mobile financial services is perceived to enhance one's image or status in one's social system. Therefore the following hypothesis was tested:

H9. *Expectation of enhanced image has a positive effect on attitude toward mobile financial services.*

Perceived improvement in quality of life: According to Prahalad (2004), access to a well-functioning financial system can economically and socially empower poor and low income people and micro and small enterprises and also actively contributes to their human and economic development. Thus, the following hypotheses were tested:

H10. *A perceived increase in quality of life will have a positive influence on perceived usefulness of mobile financial services.*

H11. *A perceived increase in quality of life will have a positive influence on the attitude towards mobile financial services.*

Figure 2 shows the resulting research model.

Research Methodology

The study was conducted in South Africa in 2008 for three reasons: firstly, South Africa has detailed demographic and financial data available through FinScope; secondly, with almost all banks and some third party providers in the country offering some form of mobile financial services, it is one of the most vibrant and competitive environments in the world; and thirdly, mainstream banks are interested in this technology as a new channel to reduce their cost while reaching out to the unbanked.

The potential customer base for mobile financial services in South Africa is a function of the unbanked population and the number of mobile phones. As of July 2008 the population of South Africa stood at 48.7 million of which 33 million were over 16 years of age (SSA, 2008). Of these, 12 million are unbanked (Finscope, 2008). 15.5% of the unbanked population also have a cell phone (Finscope, 2006). This gives us a potential market of at least 1.86 million currently unbanked con-

Figure 2. Research model

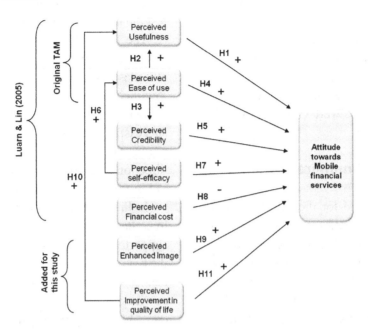

sumers that can be targeted with mobile financial services.

This study was sponsored by ABSA, South Africa's largest bank since they wanted to establish whether the mobile phone is a valid and sustainable channel when dealing with low income or previously unbanked customers. The respondents were unaware about whom the survey was being conducted for.

Universe and Sample Size

Due to time and resource constraints, the universe for sample selection was ABSA's current banking customers. The survey was designed to elicit responses from four different groups (see Table 1):

The control group consisted of customers who are current (active) mobile phone banking customers. This group gives us a statistically valid sample size to gain an impression of attitude toward mobile financial services. However, findings should not be considered true of all mobile financial services users. This is true since some of the poorest users may have been excluded since they

are more likely to live in areas with poor network coverage. They may also have been more likely to reject a call from an unknown phone number to avoid a charge, or may own a SIM card that they use in another person's mobile phone.

The three experimental groups consisted of a previously unbanked and the first two tiers of low income customers: *Mzansi* - a colloquial South African expression meaning "south" - is a basic, standardised, debit card-based transactional and savings account. It extends banking to low-income earners and those living beyond the reach of banking services by lowering the barriers to open an account. These accounts are open only

Table 1.

Group	Called (in this chapter)
Current mobile phone banking users	Control group
Mzansi account holders	Group A
Income <R2,500 per month	Group B
Income <R5,000 per month	Group C

to individuals who have previously never had a bank account.

The other two groups were chosen from the FinScope segmentation based on income levels.

As a pre-requisite, all respondents had to have access to a mobile phone. 100 completed responses of each type were expected to give a total of 400 responses.

Design of Questionnaire

The questions selected for the constructs were largely adapted from prior studies in order to ensure content validity. They were modified to make them relevant within the context of mobile financial services and produced in 5 languages – English, Afrikaans, Sesotho, Xhosa and Zulu. The questionnaire was pilot tested with 10 respondents representative of the sample groups. The test found that the applied Likert scale became "lost in translation" in the different languages and had to be simplified into 3 possible choices – "Yes", "No" and "Maybe". The reliability of the new scale was successfully proven after testing for the Cronbach's alpha on the responses to the pilot tests.

Data Capture

The purpose of this study was to obtain a wide respondent base to obtain a wide breadth of opinions. This needed a wide variety of people, from various locations and backgrounds. (see Table 2)

Situational intercepts were applied where necessary. Specifically, interviews on a one-on-one basis were conducted at the point of contact or point at which respondents moved around or interacted with one another for example: at taxi ranks, car washes, Shebeens (traditional bars and coffee shops) or in shopping malls.

Findings and Discussion

Due to the non-parametric scales used in the survey, the author was restricted to using Chi-square,

Kruskal-Wallis and Spearman's rho analyses to test the hypotheses proposed in this study.

The findings supported the appropriateness of using the proposed model to understand the attitudes of previously unbanked or people with low-income towards mobile financial services. It also proved the Luarn & Lin model can be successfully applied in very different parts of the world. The Chi-square values and strength and direction of the paths in the model are presented in Figure 3.

In line with Luarn and Lin (2005) findings, hypotheses H1, H2, H3, H4, H5, H6, and H7 were supported. Hypothesis H8 was also supported but the type of relationship between perceived financial cost and attitude toward mobile financial services changed from a negative one to a positive one. This is a key finding from this analysis. Both hypotheses H9 and H11 have a positive influence, albeit a weak one, on the Attitude toward mobile financial services. H10 has shown there is no link between the two constructs. Significant effects influencing the attitude from perceived usefulness, the ease of use, credibility, self-efficacy and financial costs were observed.

The Need to be Useful

The Perceived usefulness of mobile financial services service was defined as "convenient, cheap and offered the necessary banking transactions".

This perception of usefulness had the strongest influence on the attitude toward mobile financial services. The responses [$\rho = 0.429$, n=400, p < 0.0001] described a story of expectation that is being met: the Control Group agreed that mobile financial services gave them better control over their banking activities and was more convenient than going to a branch or ATM.

However they did not all agree about the range of services that should be available via a mobile phone: Group A was more optimistic than even the Control group regarding the types of transactions that could be conducted over the mobile.

Table 2. Key demographics within the sample set

Key demographics	Users	Non users	Group A	Group B	Group C
	n=100	n=300	n=100	n=100	n=100
Income < R2,500 per month	22.00%	54.50%	62.0%	100.0%	-
Income < R5,000 per month	72.00%	45.50%	32.0%	-	100.0%
Own a mobile phone	99.00%	96.00%	91.0%	97.0%	100.0%
Male	73.00%	62.30%	48.0%	67.0%	72.0%
Age groups:					
16-24	8.00%	13.00%	14.0%	15.0%	10.0%
25-34	51.00%	42.00%	43.0%	41.0%	42.0%
35-49	37.00%	32.00%	34.0%	31.0%	31.0%
50+	4.00%	13.00%	9.0%	13.0%	17.0%
Areas					
Gauteng	33.0%	37.7%	40.0%	38.0%	35.0%
Durban	10.0%	9.7%	14.0%	8.0%	7.0%
Cape Town	13.0%	11.7%	7.0%	17.0%	11.0%
Northern Cape	2.0%	0.7%	1.0%	1.0%	3.0%
Eastern Cape	2.0%	3.7%	3.0%	5.0%	9.0%
Limpopo	9.0%	9.0%	8.0%	10.0%	13.0%
North West	6.0%	8.7%	10.0%	3.0%	16.0%
Mpumalanga	21.0%	12.7%	12.0%	10.0%	5.0%
Free State	4.0%	6.0%	5.0%	8.0%	1.0%

Figure 4 shows many of the tasks performed by the non-user groups are similar to the types of transactions used by the current users[3].

Credibility

Perceived credibility – the safety of money and personal information – had the next strongest influence [$\rho = 0.349$, n=400, p < 0.0001] on attitude of all groups toward mobile financial services. 76% of users agreed with the credibility of the current mobile financial services service offered by ABSA. 78% of the same users felt more comfortable if a mobile financial services solution was backed by a bank. A majority (circa. 61%) were either against or unsure about cell-phone companies backing the mobile financial services offering. This could be influenced by the fact that the only companies allowed to offer mobile financial services in South Africa are banks or other regulated financial institutions as opposed to other parts of Africa where network operators can offer money transfer services to their customers.

The non users expected the service to be secure. Dissecting this further, at 65%, Mzansi account holders had the highest expectation followed by 52% of those with income less than R2,500. Only 43% of those with income between R2,500 and R5,000 thought the service would be secure.

Ensuring Ease of Use

South Africa is a multilingual environment with 8 different languages (Zulu, Xhosa, Afrikaans, Se-

Figure 3. Research model with results

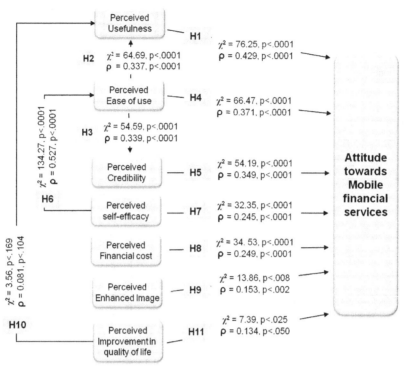

pedi, English, Setswana, Sesotho, and Xitsonga). The mobile financial services tool needs to be able to offer services in many different languages.

Literacy rates are at 86.4% (CIA, 2008) and this makes the task easier. The mobile financial services tool needs to be simple and straight forward

Figure 4. Comparison between transactions used by different groups

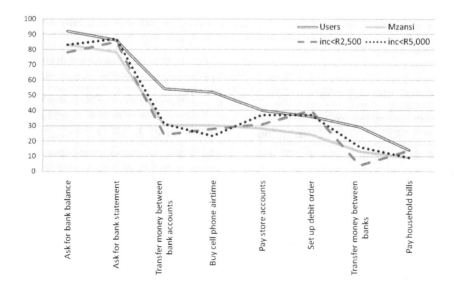

to use with as few keystrokes as possible. This is also linked to educating the customer.

The responses to the "Perceived ease of use" [$\rho = 0.371$, n=400, p < 0.0001] demonstrated the expectation that mobile financial services should be easy to use. The Control Group found that the system was easy to use already.

A Question of Money

The author expected a negative relationship between "Perceived financial cost" and the attitude toward mobile financial services – that is a perception of high cost would negatively influence the attitude toward such services. The survey showed this to be untrue. Responses from the Control Group showed costs like airtime definitely were a consideration due to their experience but the majority of respondents tended to agree that, all things considered, it was cheaper than having to go to the bank.

Responses [$\rho = 0.249$, n=400, p < 0.0001] demonstrated that they were willing to use mobile financial services due to the perception that such services would be cheaper than what they currently used (ATMs, branches, telephone banking, etc.). It could be inferred that the expected convenience far outweighed the perceived cost. The study showed the expectation of relatively lower cost was driving the positive attitude toward mobile financial services.

Boosting Customer Confidence

"Perceived self-efficacy" was found to have a significant effect on perceived ease of use, which in turn had positive influences on perceived usefulness, perceived credibility and attitude. These findings support prior research, which found that computer self-efficacy influenced perceived ease of use

(Agarwal, Sambamurthy, & Stair, 2000; Hong, Thong, Wong, & Tam, 2001; Venkatesh

& Morris, 2000) and that perceived ease of use influenced both perceived usefulness (Davis, 1989) and perceived credibility (Wang, Wang, Lin, & Tang, 2003).

Specifically, Mzansi account holders felt almost the same as the current users about feeling more comfortable with mobile financial services if they understood the technology better through tools like on-board "help" systems and even someone showing them how to use the services. The other experimental groups agreed with this as well. The opportunity to the business is to ensure people are educated about the possibilities of mobile financial services. As suggested by Luarn & Lin, management attention should be focused on the "development" of perceived self-efficacy by, for instance, organising short introductory courses when a customer takes out a new contract. These courses can still help customers develop positive usefulness; ease of use and credibility beliefs in the system, which in turn can influence attitude to use the services.

A Better Quality of Life

The study found between 94.16% and 98.44% of the population[4] will positively link bank accounts to an enhanced quality of life. This was judged by asking respondents whether having a bank account made them feel secure about the future by keeping their money safe and whether it helped them save money for their families. An average of 95% of respondents agreed about having a bank account gave them a feeling of security with regard to the future. The same percentage agreed that having a bank account would help keep their money safe. 96.75% believe that having a bank account helps them save money for their families. 89.50% say that having a bank account helps them transfer funds safely and cheaply. However, it also needs to be noted that the sample was taken from ABSA's customer database. They would be more likely to agree with bank accounts being a factor in their quality of life. Therefore, a very strong link between the perceived enhancement of quality of life and having access to financial services was found. This reinforces the need for financial services to be scaled "down" to this level of the economy thus validating Prahalad (2004) in a South African context.

A Question of Image

The cultural construct of mobile financial services as an enhancer of the image of the customer was not proven by this study. This agreed with Moore and Benbasat's (1991) finding that image was a weak predictor of adoption. However, both Groups A and B felt positively about mobile financial services being an image enhancer. The Control Group and Group C seemed to be unsure about it how much value would mobile financial services add to their social image.

Increasing Awareness

Awareness of mobile financial services is a critical question. Over 66% of non-users polled said they had heard about mobile financial services. When asked what did cell phone banking (mobile financial services) mean to the respondent, the answers varied from: "Mobile phone banking is dialling a number to your bank and asking them to transfer money to another person's account using your mobile phone" to "It's a way to connect with the bank to put money from one bank to another and they also notify you by SMS if there is any activity in your account". A majority of responses expect mobile financial services to be an information based service – "To check balance on the phone" or "When the bank sends you SMS about account". This shows a lack of consistency or understanding about what mobile financial services is about.

Figure 5 is a breakdown of how those polled had heard of mobile financial services. About 36% had found out about it a bank and about 25%

from friends and family. Over 15% had heard of it through television. It is a good indicator of how to market the product. The main difficulty would be to ensure the message is consistent across different groups and "educate the masses".

Expectation Management

The model has shown the strongest causal links are perceived usefulness, perceived ease of use and perceived credibility. Thus, these areas should be the focus to promote the use of mobile financial services. These are influenced by perceived self-efficacy of the consumers. In the case of Mzansi account holders and people with a monthly income <R2,500, the overall expectation may be too high.

In summary, if expectations are managed through education of the potential customer using different marketing channels, a greater number of prospects will become customers. However, if mobile financial services need to be moved from an "information-only" tool to a "transaction" one, greater education (to increase self-efficacy) along with increased flexibility (to increase usefulness) is needed. This has to be managed effectively to avoid customer disappointment. The study also shows the product has to be marketed differently to each of the different groups surveyed here.

Will They Use It?

The aim of this study was to test the attitude toward mobile financial services. For non-users, this was measured by the question "Are you interested in cell phone banking based on what you have heard". The response was one of three – yes (positive), no (negative) or maybe (neutral). For users, however, attitude was deemed to be a function of usage level and number of transactions conducted over the mobile financial services channel. For example, the 3 activities of checking balances (92% of the population), viewing statements (86% of the population) and a basic transaction like buying airtime for the phone (52% of the population)

Figure 5. Where have people heard of mobile financial services

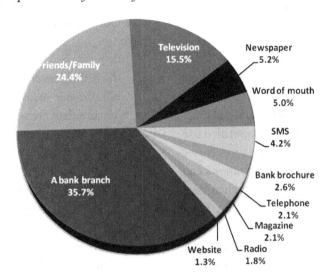

were in the majority of responses. Three transactions were considered as the baseline level of usage. If any user regularly (at least once a month) performed more than 3 types of transactions on the phone, he was deemed to have a Positive attitude towards the additional features of mobile financial services. If he performed only 3 types of transactions, he was deemed to be Neutral towards mobile financial services otherwise he was Negative towards mobile financial services. Both Goups A (Mzansi account holders) and B (those earning less than R2500 p.m.) showed a positive attitude toward mobile financial services. Group C (those earning less than R5000 p.m.) demonstrated a positive, albeit weaker, attitude toward using mobile financial services. However, this tool may not be for all. As can be seen in Table 3, as the income level increased, the attitude

toward mobile financial services tended to the negative. Further investigation revealed this was due to the perception that the bank will provide personalised services to more affluent people and that self-service tools such as mobile banking is meant only for those customers which the bank deems unprofitable or even unimportant.

Age based demographic analysis showed those aged between 25 and 34 had a positive attitude across all groups in the study. Age was not a distinguishing feature in Group A where a majority of respondents are positive about mobile financial services. However, it is interesting to note that 16-24 year olds were overwhelmingly positive about mobile financial services in Groups A and B as well as the Control group.

Table 3. Attitude toward mobile financial services across groups

			Group			
		Mznsi	Inc<R2500	Inc<R5000	User	Average
Attitude toward m-banking	Positive	67%	56%	39%	58%	55%
	Neutral	16%	19%	15%	17%	17%
	Negative	17%	25%	46%	25%	28%

Applying these Findings to the Microfinance Arena

Consumers' attitude toward using mobile financial services has been clearly demonstrated by this study. Microfinance institutions (MFIs) are limited by resources to reach out to their clients. Like formal banks, these institutions can also use the mobile phone to bring financial services closer to their clients. For example, the institutions can create an m-wallet account per client when they approve the loan or open a savings account. They can recruit local retail outlets as agents. Clients can then use these outlets to withdraw cash and make remote loan repayments or deposits into their accounts. Clients will be able to use the m-wallet to check their balances or get SMS reminders when their loan repayment is due. This application brings cost savings to the microfinance institution by reducing the need to send out their officers to the communities for the task of collecting repayments. The retail outlet benefits from commissions paid for services rendered as well as an increased footfall in their store.

The key to reaching out to low income clients is to find innovations that reduce the cost of supply so that revenue from clients can cover costs in the long term. New technologies can yield efficiency improvements due to streamlined systems and reduced labour costs. And, due to their almost ubiquitous nature, mobile phones are the most logical choice for mobile financial services. For the consumer, it is an everyday device that affords them convenience.

However, it was difficult to find full-scale organisation-wide mobile financial services deployed by MFIs. There are several well known pilots notably SKS in India, Equity and Faulu in Kenya to name a few. In early 2009, there have been a few MFIs successfully deploying their services through Globe and Smart networks in the Philippines. It is worth considering some of the risks associated with the use of such technology by MFIs:

If the MFI were to purchase technology from a vendor and manage the solution itself, it would have to:

- host the servers in a data centre and have all disaster recovery in place,
- ensure data connections to the network operators and banks are failsafe and robust,
- link the system to their internal core banking system or other solution,
- test the application works on at least 80% of the most popular mobile handsets in the country,
- keep abreast of the myriad new devices that are regularly released and continually update the service to match,
- work with the network operator to ensure data/SMS costs are lower or even zero-rated to allow their clients to use the solution for free,
- ensure regulatory compliance regarding know-your-customer and anti-money-laundering,
- ensure security of the service from risks such as man-in-the middle, phishing attacks, etc.,
- ensure the clients and agents are trained to use the solution,
- run a call centre in case of problems that clients or agents face (resetting lost passwords for example),
- fraud management systems,
- develop compelling new products that attract clients to use the service,
- etc.

Many of these can be outsourced or contracted out to reliable third parties. However, it is important to state here that such technical capabilities would be within the reach of only a handful of large MFIs. Thus the total cost of ownership of a system that is fully hosted, run and managed by the MFI itself could prove very expensive with a very long payback.

Another approach would be for an MFI to use an already-deployed mobile financial service. It is a well known fact that M-Pesa was initially created with delivering MFI services for Faulu in Kenya. In a very short while, Faulu discovered the cost of using M-Pesa's money transfer and cash-out service was too high compared to its existing process. The result was Faulu and M-Pesa moved apart and the M-Pesa we know today was born. This is a very good example of where an MFI finds it prohibitively expensive to use an existing service. However, it is important to note that there are success stories such as SMART Money in the Philippines which has begun to offer services to a large number of MFIs spread across the archipelago along with Microventures Inc. through their HAPINOY program. These MFIs have considerably lowered costs. A full report can be found on the CGAP blog (http://technology.cgap.org/2009/05/07/microfinance-mobile-banking-and-barangays).

Probably the most prudent approach for smaller and medium sized MFIs would be to use a managed service offered by "ecosystem" providers like Monitise or Moneybox (Sybase 365). Such organisations fully host the solution and develop products for a number of parties thereby harnessing economies of scale. This approach allows MFIs to offer mobile financial services using their own brand, choose (and help develop) products they want, use the hub's a shared agent network, shared call centre, shared security systems and infrastructure. This approach truly outsources the entire enterprise on a pay-as-you-go model allowing the MFI to build propositions for its clients rather than morphing into a mobile services company. Unfortunately, there are very few such hubs deployed around the world as of 2009. There are such hubs in UK and USA already and these organisations have announced plans to start services in India, Africa, Asia and South America.

FUTURE RESEARCH DIRECTIONS

This chapter has highlighted the opportunities of brining mobile financial services to the unbanked and low-income groups in South Africa. The following aspects require further investigation:

1. This study was not exhaustive from a global perspective. The cultural and regulatory differences in different countries within Africa, let alone globally, are vast. The infrastructure for mobile financial services is in many countries but the antecedents to adoption of the service are going to be influenced by cultural dimensions. A study that uses a similar model in Brazil, India and other parts of Africa would add further to the knowledge to the field.

2. A study exploring the perception of mobile financial services vs. traditional bank accounts would also help to understand how to better package the mobile financial services offering.

3. The model is cross-sectional; that is, it measures perceptions and intentions at a single point in time. However, perceptions change over time as individuals gain experience (Mathieson et al., 2001; Venkatesh & Davis, 1996). This change has implications for researchers and practitioners interested in understanding the antecedents to a positive attitude toward mobile financial services.

4. A longitudinal study would prove extremely useful to the field of mobile financial services.

5. An analysis of perceived security risks and the perception of fraud will allow providers to better inform customers and create more compelling propositions.

6. Using this model to perform a critical review of existing mobile payment services.

Figure 6. Comparison between Mzansi and current users

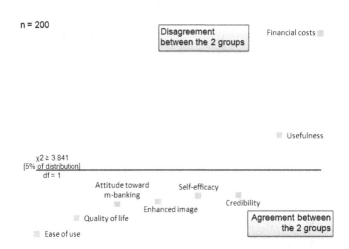

CONCLUSION

Will Mobile Phones Help Reach Out to Low Income Clients?

Mzansi account holders were specifically chosen in this study to understand their perception toward mobile financial services and extrapolate these findings to the broader unbanked population. Figure 6 is the result of the Kruskal-Wallis test to demonstrate the differences in perception between the Mzansi account holders and the current users.

As can be seen, the two groups are in agreement when it comes to a majority of the constructs and crucially the attitude toward mobile financial services itself.

The two constructs where they differ significantly are the perceived usefulness and the perceived financial costs. This is due to the fact that the Mzansi account holders have an expectation that mobile financial services will lower their overall financial costs. They also have an expectation that mobile financial services will be a very useful tool. These two expectations will have a positive effect on the potential customer to sign up for mobile financial services.

It seems that both these expectations are higher to the experience of users. Some differences are highlighted below:

- 76% of Mzansi account holders are willing to start mobile financial services even if there are costs, like airtime, involved. 59% of current users agreed with this statement.
- 86% of Mzansi account holders expect that mobile financial services are cheaper than other forms of banking whereas 82% of current users agreed with this statement.
- 76% of Mzansi account holders expect mobile financial services to be more convenient than going to a branch or ATM. 88% of current users agreed with this statement.
- 64% of Mzansi account holders expect mobile financial services to give them more control over their banking activities. 81% of current users agreed with this.

Figure 7 shows the overall perceptions, split by group, of each construct in the model. As can be seen, the Mzansi account holders lead the nonuser groups on every construct.

In summary, this study shows the Mzansi account holders have a great expectation of mobile financial services and some of these expectations are indeed being met by the offering (as reported by the current users). If these expectations are managed well and the recommended actions to help increase their self-efficacy of using the tool are implemented, more unbanked people can be

Figure 7. Comparison of perceptions across groups

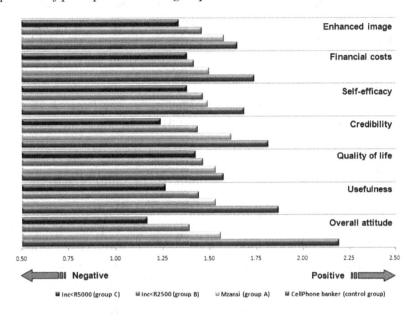

brought on board as Mzansi account holders and mobile financial services can indeed be a valid channel.

REFERENCES

Agarwal, R., & Prasad, J. (1999). Are individual differences germane to the acceptance of new information technologies? *Decision Sciences*, *30*(2), 361–391. doi:10.1111/j.1540-5915.1999. tb01614.x

Agarwal, R., Sambamurthy, V., & Stair, R. M. (2000). Research report: The evolving relationship between general and specific computer self-efficacy – An empirical assessment. *Information Systems Research*, *11*(4), 418–430. doi:10.1287/ isre.11.4.418.11876

Aghion, P., Howitt, P., & Mayer-Foulkes, D. (2005). The Effect of Financial Development on Convergence: Theory and Evidence. *The Quarterly Journal of Economics*, *120*, 173–222.

Ajzen, I. (1991). The theory of planned behavior. *Organizational Behavior and Human Decision Processes*, *50*, 179–211. doi:10.1016/0749-5978(91)90020-T

Ajzen, I., & Fishbein, M. (1980). *Understanding the attitudes and predicting social behaviour*. Englewood Cliffs, NJ: Prentice-Hall Inc.

BAI. (2004). *Transaction Cost per Distribution Channel*. Chigaco: BAI.

Booz Allen. (2003). *Processing Cost per Transaction*. New York: Booz Allen.

Brown, I., Cajee, Z., Davies, D., & Stroebel, S. (2003). Cell phone banking: predictors of adoption in South Africa-an exploratory study. *International Journal of Information Management*, *23*, 381–394. doi:10.1016/S0268-4012(03)00065-3

CIA. (2008). *South Africa*. Retrieved Nov 10, 2008, from CIA - World Fact Book: https://www. cia.gov/library/publications/the-world-factbook/ geos/sf.html

Davis, F. (1989). Perceived usefulness, perceived ease of use, and user acceptance of information technology. *Management Information Systems Quarterly, 13*, 318–339. doi:10.2307/249008

Demirguc-Kunt, A., Beck, T., & Honohan, P. (2007). *Policy research report on Access to Finance*. Washington, DC: World Bank.

Finscope. (2006). *FinScope SA 2005 Survey Findings Launch.* Johnnesburg: FinScope.

Finscope. (2008). *FinScope SA 2008 Survey Findings Launch.* Johannesburg: FinMark Trust.

Fishbein, M., & Ajzen, I. (1975). *Belief, attitude, intention and behavior: An introduction to theory and research.* Reading, MA: Addison-Wesley.

Gray, V. (2007). *Africa, ICT Indicators, 2007.* Retrieved on 1 November 2009 from http://www.itu.int/ITU- D/ict/statistics/at_glance/af_ictindicators_2007.html ITU

Hong, W., Thong, J. Y., Wong, W. M., & Tam, K. (2001). Determinants of user acceptance of digital libraries: An empirical examination of individual differences and system characteristics. *Journal of Management Information Systems, 18*(3), 97–124.

Ivatury, G., & Pickens, M. (2006). *Mobile Phone Banking and Low-Income Customers: Evidence from South Africa.* Washington, DC: CGAP.

Jackson, C. M., Chow, S., & Leitch, R. A. (1997). Toward an understanding of the behavioral intention to use an information system. *Decision Sciences, 28*(2), 357–389. doi:10.1111/j.1540-5915.1997.tb01315.x

Luarn, P., & Lin, H. (2005). Toward an understanding of the behavioural intention to use mobile banking. *Computers in Human Behavior, 21*, 873–891. doi:10.1016/j.chb.2004.03.003

Mathieson, K. (1991). Predicting user intentions: comparing the technology acceptance model with the theory of planned behaviour. *Information Systems Research, 2*, 173–191. doi:10.1287/isre.2.3.173

Mathieson, K., Peacock, E., & Chin, W. W. (2001). Extending the technology acceptance model: The influence of perceived user resources. *ACM SIGMIS Database, 32*(3), 86–112. doi:10.1145/506724.506730

McKnight, D., Choudhury, V., & Kacmar, C. (2002). Developing and validating trust measures for e- commerce: An integrative typology. *Information Systems Research, 13*(3), 334–359. doi:10.1287/isre.13.3.334.81

Moore, G. C., & Benbasat, I. (1991). Development of an Instrument to Measure the Perceptions of Adopting an Information Technology Innovation. *Information Systems Research, 2*(3), 192–222. doi:10.1287/isre.2.3.192

Prahalad, C. (2004). *The Fortune at the Bottom of the Pyramid: Eradicating Poverty Through Profits.* Wharton, USA: Wharton School Publishing.

Rogers, E. M. (1983). *Diffusion of Innovations* (3rd ed.). New York: The Free Press.

Rogers, E. M. (1995). *Diffusion of Innovations* (4th ed.). New York: The Free Press.

SSA. (2008). *Mid-year population estimates.* South Africa: Statistics South Africa.

Tan, M., & Teo, T. (2000). Factors influencing the adoption of Internet banking. *Journal of the Association for Information Systems, 1*(5), 1–42.

Venkatesh, V., & Davis, F. D. (1996). A model of the antecedents of perceived ease of use: Development and test. *Decision Sciences, 27*(3), 451–481. doi:10.1111/j.1540-5915.1996.tb01822.x

Venkatesh, V., & Morris, M. G. (2000). Why don't men ever stop to ask for directions? Gender, social influence, and their role in technology acceptance and usage behavior. *Management Information Systems Quarterly, 24*(1), 115–139. doi:10.2307/3250981

Wang, Y., Wang, Y.-M., Lin, H.-H., & Tang, T. I. (2003). Determinants of user acceptance of internet banking: An empirical study. *International Journal of Service Industry Management, 14*(5), 501–519. doi:10.1108/09564230310500192

Whelan, S. (2003). *Smart Cards*. Washington, DC: CGAP.

ADDITIONAL READING

Association, G. S. M. (2009, March 01). *South Africa - Coverage Map*. Retrieved April 5, 2009, from http://gsmworld.com/roaming/gsminfo/cou_za.shtml

Chau, P., & Hu, P. (2001). Information technology acceptance by individual professionals: a model comparison approach. *Decision Sciences, 32*(4), 699–719. doi:10.1111/j.1540-5915.2001.tb00978.x

Taylor, S., & Todd, P. (1995). Understanding information technology usage: a test of competing models. *Information Systems Research*, 144–176. doi:10.1287/isre.6.2.144

Teo, T., & Pok, S. (2003). Adoption of WAP-enabled Mobile Phones Among Internet Users. *Omega, 31*(6), 483–498. doi:10.1016/j.omega.2003.08.005

Tornatzky, L. G., & Klein, K. J. (1982). Innovation Characteristics and Innovation Adoption-Implementation: A Meta-Analysis of Findings. *IEEE Transactions on Engineering Management, 29*(1), 28–45.

ENDNOTES

[1] In Pakistan, for example, the average monthly running cost of a branch is US$28,000. In the Philippines, a typical transaction through a bank branch costs the bank US$2.50. Banco de Credito in Peru estimates that a cash transaction at a branch costs about US$0.85. (ref. "Early Experience with Branchless Banking", CGAP, April 2008)

[2] The European Union's Electronic Money Institutions Directive (2000) defines e-money as the "monetary value as represented by a claim on the issuer which is: (i) stored on an electronic device; (ii) issued on receipt of funds of an amount not less in value than the monetary value issued; (iii) accepted as a means of payment by undertakings other than the issuer". Most emerging markets require e-money to be held on a device in the customer's possession.

[3] The comparison is the number of responses from the current users of ABSA's mobile financial services and the number of transactions conducted by other groups using other banking methods (branch, ATM, phone banking, etc.)

[4] Over 94% (at ±2.14% margin of error at 95% confidence) of respondents linked access to financial services to "enhanced quality of life".

Chapter 8

A Technology Requirements and Governance Framework for Rural Microfinance:
An Indian Perspective

Nandu Kulkarni
Independent Consultant, Banking Technology, India

ABSTRACT

Governments and Financial Institutions in the emerging economies have recognized the enormous untapped potential of human capital at the "Bottom of the Pyramid," for fuelling the growth of the economy, and have identified easy access to capital as a key factor in realizing this potential. Many of the central banks and financial services trade associations are also in the process of creating a regulatory and governance framework that is conducive for financial services players to fulfil the need and the potential of this market, at the same time minimising the risks for all stakeholders. The Microfinance sector is thus seeing a rapid expansion in terms of geographical reach, and an explosive growth in terms of the number of service providers and customers. Given that Information Technology (IT) is a critical enabler for this growth, there is a large rush of IT providers eager to service this market. This brings with it (a) the risk that inappropriate or substandard IT solutions are implemented, resulting in wastage of resources, and (b) the potential for misuse and fraud. This chapter makes a case for creating an IT requirements and governance framework at a policy level, in order to ensure that the needs of this market are properly serviced, and resources are optimally and efficiently deployed, so that the benefits of Information Technology flow through to the grassroots level.

INTRODUCTION

It would be a truism to state that Information Technology is of crucial importance as an infrastructural component to support the smooth operation of the

DOI: 10.4018/978-1-61520-993-4.ch008

Microfinance market – both for the supply side and the demand side of the equation. As for the supply side (the financial institutions providing micro finance), it is critical for increasing the outreach, extending geographical jurisdiction, enhancing operational efficiency, optimising utilisation of internal resources (manpower, money and time), and providing accurate management information to the financial institution. On the demand side at the Bottom of the Pyramid, technology has the potential to mobilise savings and make capital more easily accessible by bringing financial products to the doorstep of the customer.

As a natural result of the enormous opportunity created by the Microfinance market for hardware and software solutions, there is the risk that a large number of players would enter the market, many of them trying to sell "half cooked" or inappropriate solutions in order to cash in on the opportunity. This could impede the functioning and growth of the market. This chapter outlines a framework for laying down and enforcing a set of functional and technology standards that Microfinance Institutions are required to follow, for procurement and implementation of technology solutions.

BACKGROUND

The microfinance sector has seen explosive growth in India in the last decade, and is poised for even more aggressive growth in the coming few years, due to various policy initiatives of the Ministry of Finance, the Reserve Bank of India and other government owned financial institutions. In India, microfinance is provided by a variety of entities, including banks (commercial banks, Regional Rural Banks, Co-operative Banks) and Microfinance Institutions (MFIs, that include Non Banking Finance Companies, Not for Profit companies, trusts and societies). The number of Self Help Groups (SHG) that got access to accounts in commercial banks is a telling indicator of this growth. The National Bank for Agricultural and Rural Development (NABARD) launched a Self Help Group – Bank Linkage Program (SBLP) in the early 1990's as an initiative to promote financial inclusion for the poor. Under this project, the total number of SHGs services by banks increased from 33,000 during 1992-99 to 264,000 in 2000-01 and 2,239,000 in 2005-06, and the cumulative

bank loans disbursed went up from Indian Rupees. 570 million (roughly US$ 10.4 million at today's exchange rate of Indian Rupees.50 to the US dollar) in 1992-99 to Indian Rupees. 4.81 billion (US$ 96.2 million) in 2000-01, and Indian Rupees. 113.98 billion (US$ 2.27 billion) (Reserve Bank of India Report, 2008, Chapter V.58). There is no definitive data on the number of MFIs operating in the country, but the Report of the Committee on Financial Inclusion (January, 2008, Para 105) set up by the RBI under the chairmanship of Dr. C. Rangarajan estimates that there are about 1,000 Non Government Organizations (NGO) operating as MFIs, and around 20 company MFIs. The company MFIs dominate the scene, with about 80% of the outstanding loans portfolio. Another estimate, as per the Bharat Micro Finance Report of Sa-Dhan, (March 2008), the 223 member MFIs of Sa-Dhan had an outreach of 14.1 million clients with an outstanding micro finance portfolio of Indian Rupees.59.54 billion (approximately US$ 1.2 billion).

These numbers seem miniscule in comparison to the overall loans portfolio of the banking sector in the country - the aggregate of Loans and Advances in the balance sheets of all Scheduled Commercial Banks (SCBs) in the country reads at Indian Rupees. 24.77 trillion, or US$ 495 billion as of March 2008, of which personal loans constituted Indian Rupees. 486 billion, or roughly US$ 9.72 billion. (Reserve Bank of India's Report on Trend and Progress of banking in India 2007-2008). However, the numbers must be seen in light of the fact that a large proportion of the population in India still remains outside the purview of the financial systems in the country, formal or informal. In other words, they do not have access to any sort of financial services in the form of credit, savings, insurance, payments, etc. Looking just at the population involved in the agricultural sector alone, "...45.9 million farmer households in the country (51.4%), out of a total of 89.3 million households do not access credit, either from institutional or non-institutional sources. Further, despite the vast network of bank branches, only 27% of total farm households are indebted to formal sources (of which one-third also borrow from informal sources)...." The Committee on Financial Inclusion has therefore recommended setting up of a National Rural Financial Inclusion Plan (NRFIP) with the explicit target of providing comprehensive access to financial services to at least 50% of the households that are currently financially excluded, and the remaining by 2015. (Committee on Financial Inclusion Report, January 2008)

The objective of quoting the above numbers is to illustrate the enormity of the problem of financial exclusion in India, which translates into a huge untapped "opportunity" for players in the Financial Services space, such as public and private sector banks as well as Microfinance Institutions. Recognising the crucial role of Information and Communications Technologies, the Committee on Financial Inclusion has set up, with a lot of foresight, a Financial Inclusion Technology Fund with an initial corpus of Indian Rupees. 5 billion (approximately US$ 100 million) in order to provide the support that is bound to be required to fund the promotional and developmental activities required to make the vision a reality.

THE CASE FOR A TECHNOLOGY REQUIREMENTS AND GOVERNANCE FRAMEWORK

From an Information Technology perspective, the hardware, networking and software solutions required for the operational and MIS needs of commercial banks have matured and stabilised over the last decade or so. In compliance with the directives of the RBI, all scheduled commercial banks (including all foreign banks, private banks and a majority of branches of public sector banks) have now implemented core banking applications. All commercial banks have now provided their customers access to their accounts through

Automated Teller Machines (either their own, or shared with other banks) and most have made internet, phone and mobile banking facilities available to customers for balance and transaction enquiries, funds transfers and bill payments. Many have implemented sophisticated Business Intelligence (BI) solutions to satisfy their MIS and regulatory needs, including Basel I and II reporting requirements.

Almost as a corollary, most core banking implementation projects have had their share of technology and implementation problems and consequent delays and project overruns. Although there have not been any published studies to prove it, anecdotal evidence suggests that many of the implementation problems and delays can be traced to the huge amount of customisation that solution vendors have had to do to their products. While some of the customisation was necessary to satisfy the requirements of Indian banking practises and regulations, a substantial portion has been forced upon the software product vendors by the insistence on the part of banks' operations staff and management to stick to existing practises and processes, rather than reengineering the processes. It is fair to say that bank managements as well as technology and solution vendors and consultants have learnt their lessons from these problems, and importantly, the software solutions have stabilised after having been customised to meet most of the Indian banking and regulatory requirements.

That, however, is not the case for the Microfinance market, which is comparatively much more fragmented, less developed, and where no standards exist for the technology platform, not even any de-facto standards. Many of the MFIs use home grown solutions developed by technology providers in the "unorganized" sector, where the most important criterion in the choice of technology provider may have been cost.

It would be pertinent at this stage, to look at some statistical data derived from extensive research into the success and failure track record of software implementation projects in general, as it could provide useful lessons for MFIs. The best known such data is from the Chaos Report, first published in 1995 by the Standish Group, based on extensive surveys of software implementation projects in small, medium and large companies. The report states that "..a staggering 31.1% of projects will be cancelled before they ever get completed. Further results indicate 52.7% of projects will cost over 189% of their original estimates..." The report further states, ".On the success side, the average is only 16.2% for software projects that are completed on-time and on-budget. In the larger companies, the news is even worse: only 9% of their projects come in on-time and on-budget. And, even when these projects are completed, many are no more than a mere shadow of their original specification requirements..." The respondents ranked "incomplete requirements" as the top reason why implementation projects are challenged and ultimately get cancelled. "Lack of planning", "lack of IT management" and "technology illiteracy" were the other causes of failure stated among the top ten.

Since that is not the subject of this chapter, we refer the reader to the large body of research contained in the references at the end of this chapter, on software project failure statistics and the reasons for project success and failure. It is our belief, however, that if technology solutions are implemented in the vast and fragmented Microfinance market in a haphazard way, the chances of project failure are very high, and the desired objectives of financial inclusion initiatives will not be met. It is important to recognise that solutions implemented for the commercial banking business will not fit the requirements of the Microfinance market exactly as they are. Hence the functional requirements of Microfinance from an operational and MIS perspective must be assessed and designed into the solution. In order to ensure uniformity, the process of evaluation and implementation of vendor solutions must be standardized with expert help, and implemented with proper checks and balances.

The rollout of the chosen solution offers an opportunity to standardise and streamline manual processes for field level as well as back-office operations, and this opportunity must be utilised, rather than allowing the software solution to be customised to suit existing manual processes, due to pressure from users. Lastly, robust project management processes must be instituted for the implementation of the technology solutions.

The Microfinance Market and Characteristics of Technology Solutions Required

The Bottom of the Pyramid or "BOP" segment of the economy represents a huge storehouse of entrepreneurial energy, and also throws up some major challenges for the players in this segment. This market comprises of a large population based largely in rural areas, but also in urban and semi-urban areas, often very poorly served by roads and rail, but fairly well served by cellular/mobile phones: hence the technology employed for offering the services must "bring the bank to the doorstep of the customer"

The report on Financial Inclusion cited above states that "...In countries with a large rural population like India, financial exclusion has a geographic dimension as well. Inaccessibility, distances and lack of proper infrastructure hinder financial inclusion. Vast majorities of population living in rural areas of the country have serious issues in accessing formal financial services..." In India, only about 18% of the villages had access to a bank branch within 2 km distance of the village, and about 23% of villages required their inhabitants to travel over 10 km to access banking facilities, as per data collected by the National Sample Survey Organisation of India (2002). Although the latest data is available only as of 2002, the situation is unlikely to have dramatically improved today.

On the other hand, the total number of mobile phone connections in India was around 277 million as of February 2009, and the rate of growth is a staggering 3.4% per month! There are several examples in India and around the world, of mobile phones being used as a channel for providing basic banking facilities to the unbanked. This explosive growth of mobile communications in India can be leveraged to dramatically increase the outreach of financial products, and "take the bank to the doorstep of the customer."

Since the target population has a low income and low literacy levels, the financial products offered must be low in complexity, and easy to understand. Operational ease is of utmost importance. The Committee on Financial Inclusion has very consciously made a very simple and modest definition of financial services facilities: "... it may include a basic no frills banking account for making and receiving payments, a savings product suited to the pattern of cash flows of a poor household, money transfer facilities, small loans and overdrafts for productive, personal and other purposes, etc." Some of the financial inclusion success stories in India, such as banks under the FINO shared platform umbrella, BASIX, SKS Microfinance, SEWA Bank, etc., reflect this philosophy of offering financial products that are simple, straightforward and easily appreciated by the target consumer of the products.

Since the market is characterised by extremely large volumes but low ticket sizes of transactions, operational efficiency, ability to scale, and low unit costs are necessary to make the services viable. Some of the statistical data presented in the Background section, relating to the potential size of the market if the targets set by the Committee on Financial Inclusion are met, should highlight the scale of the demands on the Information Technology infrastructure. It is evident from these numbers that at the back-end, robust systems are needed to accurately and efficiently process the huge number of financial transactions resulting from the low-value, high-volume transaction mix that characterises this market. The credit appraisal processes and systems must be able to assess the risk profiles of the customers, giving more weight

to the experience and judgement of the agents in the field. The Management Information Systems must be capable of handling the large volumes of raw data and distilling information, in order to highlight potential problem areas in terms of credit quality and fraud potential.

The typical Microfinance customer has different earning and spending patterns, as compared to the middle class segment of the market, which retail financial institutions are typically geared up to serve: hence the software and technology must be flexible enough to adapt to the borrowing and repayment needs of this market. The financial products, especially on the lending side, and the back-end processing systems must accommodate the functional requirements typical to the borrowing and repayment behaviour in this market- quite different from the typical home loan and vehicle loan type of loans. They must be able to accommodate the vegetable vendor who wants to use part of her daily sales to repay the loan taken, and the small time contractor, who may have a more predictable stream of income.

As a large majority of these customers are not reached by commercial banks, and often dependent on money-lenders, who use assets such as land, immovable and movable property as security: hence the financial products offered must be such that they liberate the population from the debt traps created by the money lenders. Although this is not a technology issue, the ability of the lender to offer loans at low interest rates is very much dependent on the cost of processing the loan, or keeping accounting records of the institution.

From a credit risk perspective, the social structures in the this segment of the population can be leveraged for offering new lending and credit models, such as group lending: hence the credit rating infrastructure has to be modified to take this factor into account. The borrowing, repayment and security practices associated with Self Help Groups and Joint Liability Groups, that are prevalent with Microfinance, are quite different from the age old commercial lending practices.

Hence the processing applications have to cater to these requirements, peculiar to Microfinance.

The Microfinance market entails a high risk of fraud and abuse, because of the huge volumes of customer transactions: hence the technology and processes used must provide robust protection from fraud. The absence of a National Identity card in India makes the KYC (Know Your Customer) processes more challenging. The Government of India has recently launched an initiative called Unique Identification Authority of India to issue Unique IDs to every citizen of the country. All other Identification numbers such as the Permanent Account Number issued by the Income Tax department, passport number, voters ID and ration card number will be linked to this UID. Although getting a UID will not be mandatory, all services such as bank accounts and loans, access to the Public Distribution System for food rations, etc. will be available only with a UID, making it mandatory in practise to get a UID. There have been initiatives by various governments in the past to issue some kind of national identity token, they have not been successful. Some of the emerging technologies like biometric authentication, as well as existing and well developed technologies like smart-cards/chip-cards can be employed to provide adequate protection from fraud. Interestingly, the ability of chip-cards to store large amounts of personal information can be leveraged for offering other allied services like insurance and health care.

Hence the requirements with respect to the technology and systems needed for supporting the Microfinance market are far from trivial, even though the ticket size of transactions is very small, and the end customer is often an unsophisticated user. Concomitant with this is the need to keep per unit transaction costs to the very minimum, and the initial investments in the technology at the lowest possible level, since the institutions involved in providing Microfinance are typically small players and NGOs. Although the managements of these institutions appreciate the need to have good processes and systems supported by modern technology, they do not necessarily have the technical expertise available at hand to choose the right solution, or the project management skills to implement the chosen solution. As a result, they have a strong inclination to pick the most readily available, and often the cheapest solution, or even worse, to build the solutions in house from scratch. Many institutions then end up implementing technology solutions after numerous problems and delays without getting the desired benefits, as the technology or the solution was inappropriate in the first place. Some end up abandoning the chosen solution after long delays and much frustration, and seem to be in a perpetual search for the "right" solution. Two of the case studies cited below illustrate this predicament that small institutions find themselves in. One of the case studies has a happy ending as they did finally implement a solution successfully that seems to serve their requirements.

The requirement to keep transaction costs low and the capital investment to the minimum, also suggests the need to create a shared technology services platform that can be a kind of a utility shared by multiple MFIs. This will also serve the twin objectives of preventing the proliferation of multiple solutions and standardisation of the technology and the software solution. The experience of the only initiative in India that we are aware of, for creating such a shared services platform for MFIs has been less than successful. The reasons for this need to be analysed, and the lessons learnt should be used for fine tuning the model. We have included this case study as well.

Case Studies

The first two case studies are intended to illustrate how the right (or wrong) choice of an enabling technology platform and implementation approach can aid (or hamper) the operations of the organisation. The third example is meant to provide food for thought for solution providers as well as policy planners, for research on the success factors for a shared services platform as a SAAS model.

Annapurna Parivar: India

Annapurna NBFC (Non-banking Finance Company) is an MFI focusing on micro-lending and deposit taking in three urban centers in Maharashtra state in India. It is part of a larger group of NGOs working with poor self-employed women and their families in large urban slums offering a comprehensive package of various services, designed to empower the beneficiaries. So far Annapurna has given micro loans ranging from Indian Rupees.3,000 to Indian Rupees.1,00,000 (roughly US$600 to US$2,000) to around 200,000 borrowers, a majority of whom are women. The loan portfolio is around Indian Rupees.40 Million (around US$800,000) Borrowers are organised as Joint Liability Groups consisting of 5 women or men. Borrowers are expected to keep a deposit amounting to 10% of the loan outstanding, on which Annapurna pays 6% interest currently. For deposits higher than the minimum required, customers get interest at 7%. The deposits serve as security, to be drawn upon in case of repayment default. For depositors, their savings with Annapurna are a source of comfort and give them a sense of achievement and self-worth. They therefore look for constant assurance that the money is in safe hands and is not being touched unless they default on repayment. Their trust in Annapurna is contingent upon this assurance.

Realising the need for computerisation to run its operations efficiently, Annapurna initially chose a DOS, Foxpro based solution, which was later ported to a Windows platform. The limitations of this solution soon became apparent and became an inhibiting factor for productivity, customer service and growth. The following sections list some of limitations.

Most importantly, the system did not have the concept of "Group" and Group Liability, a functional requirement fundamental to a Microfinance solution. The users implemented a "workaround" to this, namely, to prefix the Group Number to the borrower's name, so that the members of a group would be bunched together in the screens. However, this approach had some obvious, serious limitations that made some of the essential functions very cumbersome. For example, group liability analysis, to ensure that sufficient savings balance is maintained, was extremely difficult. Some of the basic operations fundamental to the working of the Microfinance market, like transferring funds from one member to some other member in a group to make up for loan default, group disbursement and collections, group recognition tests, and tracking of group attendance for mandatory meetings were very difficult, if not impossible.

The other serious limitation was that the system did not have a way to link savings accounts to loan accounts of borrowers. Hence, at the Head Office, two accounts were created for each person – loan and savings account. Data had to be entered separately in the two accounts increasing the work and the chances of errors. The monthly report available to the field staff could not give the savings balance of each member. This lack of "transparency" led to many arguments and accusations against the organization of stealing money from the members. In case of a default by a member, the funds had to be transferred from the savings account to the loan account. This had to be done in two steps – withdrawal from savings followed by a credit to the loan account. A clear case of duplication of work. Further, there was no way to ensure that the minimum balance required for the loan was maintained in the savings account – increasing the risk profile of the member. Such a member is at high risk of default. However, due to the limitations of the software such members could not be identified.

As the system did not have the proper names of the members (prefixed as they were with the group name) there were cases of fraud where members joined different groups to get multiple loans which then had to be written off. Due to the problem with names, the system could not maintain a complete history of the loans of a member (as she may have changed groups).

From an administrative perspective, there was major data editing involved if a field staff member left or the group was re-assigned to another field staff member. Each record had to be edited. Also, there was no integration with Payroll module. This meant that incentives for field staff had to be done by hand. Staff loans had to be created under a dummy branch/group.

Because of the limitations of the platform, the system would slow down when the data entry volumes peaked. In order to complete the work on time, the organisation would hire more data entry operators, slowing down the system even further.

After using the system for about five years, when the limitations of the system became debilitating for the organisation, the Annapurna management decided to look for alternative technology solutions. Fortunately they had good technical expert guidance available this time, helping them to evaluate and select the right technology partner. They went through an evaluation process to weigh alternatives, including product solutions, and partners for developing a custom built solution. Based on the evaluation, the contract was awarded to a local software vendor called Quantum Software Solutions with software product expertise, to develop a solution addressing the shortcomings of the existing solution, and taking into account future plans of the organisation. Annapurna's own technical advisory team was involved in the evaluation and implementation process, to validate and screen functional requirements before they found their way into the features being incorporated in the product. This helped maintain focus, and prevented the problem of scope creep, the cause of many software project failures. Quantum built the solution after a detailed understanding of Annapurna's requirements and current operational and MIS issues, but keeping in mind the objective of building a product solution that would serve the needs of other similar small and medium sized MFIs. They also took this opportunity to build other useful features to aid operation efficiency, such as a hierarchy of field staff with the ability to change the hierarchy as well as personnel involved, and a hierarchy of customers into a branch, center, group and individual structure, with a linkage to the field force hierarchy, with the ability to change it easily. An integrated loan/savings account for each member was incorporated, allowing for Compulsory Savings Deposit to be collected with monthly loan instalment, and with the facility of a single screen for all loan details with the facility to approve loans at a group level. A single receipt can be printed from the Head Office, listing the amount of money to be collected from the member each month, eliminating time-consuming manual receipt generation work of field-staff.

Annapurna has plans to launch a micro-insurance product, linked to Microfinance. Quantum has built an insurance module, integrated into the Microfinance solution.

Current Status

Annapurna went live with the new solution in June 2009, and has got back into a growth phase, now that system limitations are not an inhibiting factor. They now plan to build the micro loans portfolio to 25,000 ongoing borrowers, with a social security program to cover 100,000 people, and a Business Development and Job Placement service to help 5000 more young people with low skills. They are planning day care centres in Mumbai and Pune to take care of 1,000 children from slums and a sponsorship to be given to 500 more children of single mothers. All in all, Annapurna plan to reach out to 25% of the poorest families in designated areas in the region.

Annapurna, under the guidance of its technical advisory team, and with help from its technology partner, Quantum, is now in the process of looking at mobile based tools to further improve operational efficiency and customer service.

Lessons Learnt

The ICT journey travelled by Annapurna has some very important learning to offer. Firstly, computerisation and investment in technology by itself does not guarantee benefits, if the operational and business requirements are not adequately addressed by the solution. It becomes an inhibiting factor for growth. Secondly, Management, even with the best of intentions, requires guidance from experienced professionals with knowledge and understanding of system selection and implementation, in order to derive the potential benefits from ICT. Most importantly, one wrong choice of a technology solution need not be the end of the road. What is important is to learn from mistakes.

Development Initiative for Self Help and Awakening (DISHA): India

DISHA was launched around the year 2000 with funding support from Jankidevi Bajaj Gram Vikas Sanstha (JBGVS), part of a large and well known industrial house in India, with the objective of providing financial assistance to the economically disadvantaged sections of society in the rural areas. The focus would be mostly on women micro-entrepreneurs like vegetable vendors, shopkeepers, snack bar owners, etc., to help them use the funds provided as capital for income generating activities. The initiative was launched on the Grameen Bank Model, after some of the management and staff had undergone training in implementation and running of the model to, at the operations of Grameen Bank in Bangladesh. The initial funding from the donor organisation was around Indian Rupees.15 million (around US$300,000). There were 4 branch offices set up in and around Pune in Maharashtra state, and the lending portfolio was around Indian Rupees.10 million, among roughly 10,000 borrowers.

The management realised that in order to scale up, it was essential to computerise and automate some of the manual tasks, paperwork etc., and contracted the work to a small software development company after a brief, informal selection process around 2005. The contractor, who evidently did not have the requisite expertise in Microfinance requirements or formal software development processes, began software development from scratch, after discussions with the users to understand the requirements, and build the software based on the understanding, and deliver modules to the users. This turned out to be a difficult and tedious process for both sides, as the requirements were poorly understood, and the software delivered could not meet even some of the basic requirements of the user community, and was often ridden with bugs. After the project progressed in fits and starts for about three years, the DISHA management decided to abandon the project. Fortunately, the amount paid to the contractor for fees was a small portion of the total contracted amount, but three years had been lost. Without the support of an automated solution, managing the operations has proved more and more difficult, and the Disha management has decided to wind down the loan portfolio as existing loans get repaid, and has suspended fresh lending.

Current Status

The DISHA management, after considerable internal debate and discussion, has now decided to restructure operations and follow the Self Help Groups model instead of the Grameen Bank model. Issuing of fresh loans has been suspended, and after the existing loans on the books are repaid, DISHA will migrate to the SHG model, with a revitalised team. Importantly, the management has now decided to acquire and adopt the software solution developed by BASIX, one of the oldest and most successful organisations in the field, and arguably a role model for financial institutions engaged in Microfinance and financial inclusion related activities.

Lessons Learnt

DISHA can be considered to be a fairly typical example among the multitude of NGOs and small financial institutions operating in the country with the common goal of spreading financial inclusion in the country. While there may have been several reasons for the organisation not being able to realise the vision of its founders and senior management, it is evident that the lack of technology expertise led to the wrong choice of a solution vendor, and wastage of precious time and resources. With the right guidance, if DISHA had made the decision they made now, the growth and outreach would have been far more.

Financial Information Network and Operations (FINO): India

FINO (www.FINO.co.in) was launched in July 2006 to provide a technology platform for Microfinance Institutions, as a shared services platform running on the Application Service Provider (ASP) model that exploits economies of scale to drive down cost per transaction for its customers and partners, and allows financial institutions to launch and run operations without having to make the large initial investments in creating the technology infrastructure. It was incorporated as a limited company, under the leadership of ICICI Bank as the main promoter. It is now jointly owned by a set of international investors, and Indian public sector and private sector institutions (40%, 30% and 30% respectively.)

FINO has structured a set of financial products that its customers (the financial institutions using the FINO platform) can offer to their end customers. The products are simple to use and even have brand names like Tijori (a safe, or locker typically used by households in India to safely store cash, valuables, documents etc.) and Tatkal (prompt, or instant) that the end customers can quickly understand and relate to. The delivery channels allow user transaction to be completed online as well as offline, using a simple Point of Transaction (POT) device, and a smart card that every customer is issued. The smart cards are used for storing demographic and financial information

about the user, and also contain the user's fingerprint image which is used for authentication.

All the products use the same biometrically enabled smart card for storing information as well as for authenticating the end user and the Business Correspondent or Agent that provides the financial service at the doorstep of the end customer. Thus, the card becomes the focal instrument for performing any type of transaction, and is even positioned as a sort of an identity card (branded as FINO Parichay, or identity).

An essential component of the infrastructure underlying all the FINO services is a robust technology platform, that enables the Distribution system (the Smart Cards, the Point of Transaction devices and the communications network), the Core system (the back-end processing and record keeping engine) and the Information system (Management Information System and Credit Bureau). The biometrically enabled smart card reader terminals (POTs) and the smart cards issued to customers and to staff are key to the concept of "taking the bank to the customer" in a user friendly and yet secure way that customers can trust. The software that supports the financial products can be parameterized, allowing the individual Financial Institutions to fine tune the product to their own needs. The MIS allows participating institutions to get information needed for planning and managing day-to-day operations.

FINO went through an intensive and rigorous process of evaluation of the technology options available, before arriving at the choice of solution vendor for the smart card based front-end, the core processing engine and Management Information System, as also the hosting provider for owning, running and managing data centre operations. The target platform was designed taking into account the expected number of customers and transaction volumes over a five year planning horizon (projected at 600 million customers), and the hardware and processing capacity required to handle the scale of operation. The entire project was managed by a System Integrator responsible for overall management of the project, deliverables from the multiple vendors involved, and for integrating the different solutions from a functional and technical point of view, as well as for managing the "on boarding" process of new customers (financial institutions) as they were acquired.

As one would expect while undertaking a project of this scale, FINO faced several challenges in its journey towards realizing the vision of creating a robust and scalable platform, for enabling financial institutions to provide financial services to the enormous unbanked population of the country, at the lowest possible cost. FINO chose a core banking software product from a reputed banking product company with a large installed base internationally as well as in India. It was soon realised that the software would have to undergo a great deal of customisation to make it suitable to the needs of the Microfinance segment. The change management process of identifying the changes required, prioritising them, changing and testing the software was quite a major challenge. In its endeavour to provide multiple products and services to its customers, FINO has to continue investing in technology and applications. Being a pioneer in this field, FINO had to build a team that brought in knowledge and experiences from conventional banking to be applied to the micro-customer segment. This segment needs exactly the same quality as is available to conventional customers. The challenge here is to make the service offering sellable and scalable.

The initial vision of FINO was to create this platform specifically for Microfinance Institutions (MFIs), to enable them to leverage off the outsourced technology platform, without having to make the large investment in technology, and scale up on a "pay as you use" basis. The primary challenge was "selling" the concept to the 250-odd targeted Microfinance institutions, in spite of the fact that they would get a ready made platform at a very low cost per transaction cost, without the headache of having to manage the platform. Because of the slow uptake from MFIs, FINO then

had to scale back the target make a mid-course correction, and shift the strategy to offering Business Correspondent services to banks, insurance companies, and other financial institutions.

Current Status
The following list summarises the current reach of FINO.

- No. of Customers: 11 banks, 20 MFIs, 3 Insurance companies and 4 government entities
- No. of locations served: Over 1400 locations
- No. of FINO transaction points: over 4,000
- No. of states and districts in which FINO has presence: 16 states and 120 districts

Since its launch, the company has been continuously rolling out innovative solutions to leverage the power of the latest technology to take banking to the doorstep of the poor. The latest example is FINO's partnership with NCR Corporation, to install a smart card and biometric authentication based microdeposit solution, branded as EasyPoint 70 "Tijori" The plan is to roll out 30,000 such machines in the next five years.

Lessons Learnt
A shared services platform with a "pay as you use" model would appear to be the most obvious and intuitively logical solution for MFIs, for whom availability of a best of breed solution with practically no up-front investment, should have seemed like a boon. However, in spite of the commitment of resources and management support of a large organisation like ICICI Bank, and with no competition in that space, the reasons for the lack of expected response from MFIs for the shared services platform created by FINO should be a subject of analysis for academics and researchers.

The other document, "Management Information Systems for Microfinance Institutions, a Handbook" is a useful guide for the definition and creation of MIS reports for accounting and performance.

The CGAP website also contains a list of IT vendors for Microfinance, and reviews of their products, which should be an excellent starting point for an institution embarking on an IT program.

CGAP launched an IS Fund in 2004 for the purpose of supporting MFIs to hire independent consultants for activities such as creating a technology strategy, selecting and implementing a new software solution, and managing a new technology channel. The list of projects has a couple of Indian examples.

The next section wraps up the discussion with the salient solutions and recommendations.

Solutions and Recommendations

It should be evident from the discussions above that IT is going to be a crucial factor in the realisation of the vision for financial inclusion of India's population, the ambitious target for 2015, set by the government. Inadequate focus on the management of the IT planning and execution process can only result in a huge wastage of precious resources, and jeopardise the vision. This section outlines the salient features of a governance structure and mechanism for IT implementation among the financial institutions involved in Microfinance.

The recommendations address four aspects of the Technology Requirements and Governance framework. Firstly, an organisation mandated with the responsibility for creating and monitoring compliance to the technology standards should be set up. This organisation must first determine the areas that the standards cover, and define the technology standards. For MFIs to truly comply with the standards, an enabling ecosystem is needed, and lastly, enforcement and monitoring mechanisms for MFIs to comply with the standards must be set up.

Standards Organisation

The challenge here is to create an organisation that is not an overhead on the system and a bureaucratic hurdle that MFIs must cross, but an enabling organisation with the sole purpose of being a catalyst to realise the vision of Financial Inclusion. The organisation could be made up with participation from the principal stakeholders, such as the government and central bank, the institutions that will be the "agents" for Financial Inclusion, and representatives of the main beneficiaries. There are several existing organisations that could potentially play these roles: NABARD or SIDBI, (representing the government), a trade association such as Sa-Dhan (representing the MFIs), a reputed NGO that is working in the field (representing the beneficiaries) and experts in the field, such as academicians from National Institute of Bank Management (NIBM), India or an international organisation like CGAP

The legal and organisational structure of the organisation is not within the scope of this chapter, and is not being dealt with here.

Coverage of Standards

There has been some amount of effort focussed on creating standards for Information Technology selection and implementation, and we briefly cover two such initiatives. It must be said, though, that there is little evidence in literature of these standards having been institutionalised or adopted in practise.

Sa-Dhan Defined Standards

Sa-Dhan is an association of Microfinance stakeholders in India, formed in July 1999 with the objective of creating a platform to enable the participants to communicate and collaborate amongst themselves and with various government entities. The mandates of Sa-Dhan include, among other things, to provide research, consultancy and training, and define minimum standards relating to development and financial performance. Although the mandate does not explicitly talk about technology standards, there is a publication entitled "How to choose computerized Management Information Systems (MIS)-A Guide for MFI Managers" published in September 2008, and a set of standards and best practices available on Sa-Dhan's website for downloading.

However, many of the documents are a bit dated, and need review and updating to make them usable in practise. For example, the document entitled "Management Information Systems for Microfinance – An Evaluation Framework" is a study funded by USAID, and is dated November 1999. It covers quite comprehensively, a set of minimum functional and technical requirements that can be used to create a Request for Proposal (RFP) for vendor selection. Given that it is nearly ten years old, and the available technology options have grown exponentially in the intervening period, it needs updating through a fresh h study.

Consultative Group to Assist the Poor (CGAP) Defined Standards

CGAP is an independent policy and research centre supported by over 30 international developmental agencies, and is housed in the World Bank premises. CGAP clearly recognises the central role of innovation and technology in reaching the poor, and lays an overarching emphasis on technology encompassing distribution, back-end processing and MIS/analytics. Its website is replete with case studies, white papers, and research reports, and has a lively blog focused on the role of technology in Microfinance. CGAP actively partners with financial institutions, technology vendors and other stakeholders, as part of its Technology Program, funded by the Bill and Melinda Gates foundation. For example, it is supporting WIZZIT Bank mentioned above, in its initiative to deliver banking services to the poor in South Africa through the use of mobile technology.

CGAP's website has a set of standards documents created by professionals in the field and sponsored by CGAP. Among them, the implementation guidelines and MIS handbook are two documents that deserve a special mention. "Information Systems (IS) Implementation Guidelines" is a valuable resource for institutions planning to undertake a fresh implementation or upgrade of their technology infrastructure, as it contains a step-by-step description of the typical project life cycle.

Recommended Standards

In order for the standards to serve as a benchmark that proposed solutions and implementation plans can be evaluated against, they must address the following aspects of technology implementation at a minimum. They must lay down the basic common minimum requirements (functionality, operations, and MIS related) that must be addressed by all solutions. It would be of great value for MFIs looking to revamp their technology, to have a demonstrable Proof of Concept of the recommended technologies, implemented for a "Model MFI." The standards must also lay down an implementation methodology and processes with focus on best practices for requirements management, technology deployment, project budgeting and cost management, with case studies from successful implementation projects, and an IT and operations organisation structure for institutions with in house IT as well as those using shared IT services, during project implementation phase and in steady state maintenance and support mode. It would also help to provide guidelines and benchmarks for technology budgets for MFIs as a function of assets, account and transaction volumes. The standards could also list the vendors and software packages that are "certified" by the organisation to meet the above mentioned requirements for the Indian market.

Ecosystem Required

As part of its proposal to fund the SIDBI Foundation for Microcredit (SFMC), the International Fund for Agricultural Development (IFAD) commissioned BASIX' consulting wing to carry out a study of the parameters affecting the success (or otherwise) of ten MFIs around the country. Among other things, the report states: "...The case studies show that all MFIs require capacity building inputs, although the level varies across them. Hence careful assessment of each of them is called for..." It further states: "...all MFIs need technical assistance in the form of better computerised management information systems, particularly for tracking loan portfolios and delinquency management. They also need to upgrade their appraisal and fund management skills. The SFMC can play an important role in providing both of these types of capacity building inputs..."

The Information Technology fund of Indian Rupees. 5 billion (US $100 million) proposed by The Committee on Financial Inclusion is a step in the right direction, but the proper utilisation of these funds to effectively meet the objectives of the fund is critical, and should be planned and monitored with the same foresight that it was set up with. It is recommended here that the fund is allocated for the following purposes in a proportion that could be arrived at after analysis:

Firstly, a substantial portion of the fund should be used for setting up a shared technology services platform, or enhancing an existing platform like FINO mentioned above. The benefits of this would be evident from the case study covered above – standardisation of the technology as well as the methodology is implicitly enforced for the participants. The funds should be used for the initial investment, but the operation of the platform should be self-sustaining, as the provider would charge participants for the usage of the platform. Part of the fund should be set aside for funding MFIs that for some valid reason cannot use the shared services; to support them to set up or en-

hance their own technology platform. This could be done in the form of a low interest loan to the MFIs which they can repay as they start reaping the benefits, without straining their cash flows. MFIs availing of these funds would be required to satisfy criteria for operational and management best practices defined by this organisation, and would be open to monitoring and scrutiny. Given the criticality of good project management, part of the corpus should be used for supporting MFIs to access technology and project management services from reputed and accredited Indian and International consultants, on the lines of the IS fund set up CGAP, as mentioned above.

It is also recommended that the MFIs themselves be organised into "Self Help Groups" of 5-10, with one MFI among them that has successfully implemented technology and demonstrated its benefits, playing a lead role as a catalyst and facilitator for other MFIs to follow their lead. The groups should ideally consist of institutions operating in similar demographic regions, so that the success of one can be easily replicated across the group

Creating an ecosystem on these lines would create an enabling environment for successful implementation of Information Technology by MFIs.

Enforcement and Monitoring Mechanism

The most effective enforcement and monitoring mechanism would be a periodic reporting requirement from all MFIs, similar to what all commercial banks are subjected to. Stringent monitoring of financial and performance reports would ensure that all MFIs adopt technology for at least back office processing and MIS, if not for the front-end user facing functions.

Apart from the basic "regulatory" reports from Financial and operational performance parameters, an initiative must be undertaken to institutionalise the impact of MFIs on social and developmental indicators among the population served by the MFIs. The USAID report on impact MIS provides useful pointers for implementing this.

FUTURE RESEARCH DIRECTIONS

There are a few areas that emerge from the above study, as interesting areas for research:

Shared Services Platform: Critical Success Factors

It would be instructive and of great practical use to study the Critical Success Factors for a Shared Technology Services Platform based on a Software as a Service (SAAS) model. The FINO case study cited above illustrates that creating such a platform such as this, even with the operational, marketing and funding support of a large bank does not guarantee traction from the beneficiaries of the initiative, namely the MFIs.

Impact Analysis: Correlation of Microfinance Impact with Operational Practices

There are several parameters that govern the success of an MFI in financial performance terms as well as in terms of its outreach, and consequently the impact that it has on the population that it is meant to serve. The most important and obvious parameters include the integrity and quality of the promoters and the management, the professional practices they employ in the management of the enterprise, the efficacy of the model they adopt (SHG, JLG, Grameen Bank) for the socio-economic milieu they operate in, and the delivery channels they use to reach out to their clientele. While some of the parameters would be difficult to quantify and measure, the technology employed for the delivery channels could be measured more objectively. This has been done to some extent in

the USAID case studies mentioned earlier, and in various anecdotal forms on the CGAP blogs.

While impact measurement is of great interest to practitioners, and more importantly to donor organisations, we feel that an analysis of the correlation of the developmental indices measured, with the operational practices employed by the Microfinance Institutions would provide a powerful tool to standardise on the best practices that MFIs can be encouraged to adopt.

There has been a large amount of research on measurement of the impact of Microfinance on economic, social and other development indices, with respect to the methodologies and tools for measuring the impact, and on definition of developmental indices to measure the impact. We feel that a correlation between the parameters and their impact on the developmental indices is an interesting area for future research.

Self Help Groups of MFIs

One of the recommendations made above, is to organise MFIs themselves as SHGs to form synergistic relationships amongst themselves in order to learn from each others' successes and failures, especially where it comes to the adoption of technology. This is an interesting area of future research, to form such groups on an experimental basis, assess the results, and fine tune the model.

CONCLUSION

Given the criticality of technology in the success of India's vision of Financial Inclusion for its enormous population, this Chapter makes a case for putting in place a requirements and governance framework at a policy level, in order to ensure that the risk from inappropriate or incomplete technology solutions jeopardising the success of the Financial Inclusion program is minimised. The risk is illustrated through a set of real life examples of successful and unsuccessful implementation of technology from the Indian and International context. A set of recommendations based on four "pillars" for such a framework is proposed, namely, a standards organisation, the "body of knowledge" or the standards themselves, an enabling ecosystem, and the necessary enforcement and monitoring mechanisms.

Finally, three topics are suggested as areas of interest for future research. They are, analysis of the Critical Success Factors for a Shared Technology Services Platform for MFIs, Creation of a model for impact analysis of the operational practices adopted by MFIs, on the desired developmental indicators and finally, creating a formal "Self Help Group" structure of groups of MFIs that do not compete with each other, for adoption of best practices from each other's experience.

REFERENCES

Ministry of Statistics and Program Implementation. (2002). *Report on Village Facilities.* New Delhi, NCR: National Sample Survey Organisation of India

NABARD. (2008). *Report of the Committee on Financial Inclusion.* New Delhi, NCR: NABARD

(2008). *Rekha Misra Reserve Bank of India.* Mumbai, Maharashtra: Annual Report of the Reserve Bank of India.

Rekha Misra Sa-Dhan Association. (2008). *Bharat Micro Finance Report.* New Delhi, NCR: Sa-Dhan Microfinance Resource Centre

Reserve Bank of India (2007-2008). *Report on Trend and Progress of banking in India.* Mumbai, Maharashtra.

ADDITIONAL READING

Consultative Group to Assist the Poor (CGAP). (n.d.). Retrieved from www.cgap.org

Ivatury, G. (2006). *Using Technology to Build Inclusive Financial Systems.* CGAP.

Chapter 9
Saving through the Mobile:
A Study of M–PESA in Kenya

Olga Morawczynski
The University of Edinburgh, UK[1]

ABSTRACT

This chapter will explain how M-PESA, an application that was designed for money transfers, is being used for savings in Kenya. It uses data from a collection of financial diaries to make its arguments. These diaries captured the savings practices of fourteen M-PESA users for a period of one month. They were part of a fourteen month ethnographic study that examined the adoption, usage and impact of M-PESA in two locations: an urban slum and a rural village. The study reveals that informants held a portfolio of savings mechanisms. M-PESA was used in conjunction with the other mechanisms and held a vital place in the portfolio—somewhere between the bank and home bank. The chapter will also use the empirical findings to suggest how mobile money applications can be designed to better suit the unique savings needs of the resource poor. In particular, it will suggest that M-PESA can be much more than just a mechanism in the savings portfolio. Rather, it can act as the platform on which the entire portfolio resides.

INTRODUCTION

In the past five years, there have been two interesting shifts within the development finance community. The first is a focus on branchless banking models, which extend the reach of financial services to poor people who cannot be reached through traditional networks of bank branches (Lyman et al., 2006; Ivatury & Lyman, 2007; Ivatury & Mas, 2008). These models rely on third party outlets, such as retail shops or post offices, to act as agents and provide financial services beyond the physical bank branch. They also rely on technology infrastructure (POS, internet, mobile phones) to provide transactional security and to extend the reach of services. Secondly, there is recognition that credit may not be the appropriate tool for all households to manage their financial

DOI: 10.4018/978-1-61520-993-4.ch009

needs. Rather, appropriate savings mechanisms are also important to sustain and improve livelihoods.

These two trends are coming together. New strategies are being cultivated to mobilize savings via branchless banking models in general, and the mobile phone in particular. There is a recognition that savings, probably more than any other financial service, requires proximity and immediacy for the customer. Loans have built-in discipline mechanisms (regularity of payments, penalties in the event of non-payment), which make people willing to travel some distance or otherwise incur some personal cost to repay a loan that they had taken out in a time of need. But people may forgo the possibility of banking a portion of their cash receipts if doing so entails enough distance and inconvenience. If a formal savings vehicle is not available conveniently at or near the point where money is earned, it is likely that the money will either go into a range of competing uses or will remain stored informally. Therefore, there is increasing recognition that formal small-balance savings can only be mobilized effectively for the bulk of the population if branchless channels are leveraged.

Much of this recent interest towards savings via the mobile phone has been sparked by the stunning success of a Kenyan mobile money service called M-PESA. This service was introduced in March of 2007 by Safaricom, the country's largest mobile operator. It has since acquired over 7 million users and extended its agent base to over 10,000. Although M-PESA was designed as a money transfer service there is evidence that it is also being used for savings. For example, a study funded by FSD-Kenya of over 3000 households in Kenya revealed that the application was being used to store money (GSMA, 2009).

The portfolio of savings mechanisms is shown in Figure 1. The study further found that M-PESA was one of the most popular mechanisms for savings amongst the sample, even beating out the mattress for M-PESA users. These results raise some interesting questions. In particular, why did M-PESA beat out the mattress and other popular savings mechanisms? Is M-PESA becoming a substitute for these other mechanisms? How are the savings patterns of the poor changing as they begin to store money with M-PESA? This chapter will address these questions. The chapter will begin by reviewing the conceptual arguments around the relevance of savings and mobile money in poor peoples' daily lives. It will then examine the evidence from a collection of financial diaries, which captured the savings practices of 14 M-PESA users for a period of one month. These diaries were part of a fourteen month ethnographic study that examined the adoption, usage and impact of M-PESA in two locations: an urban slum and a rural village. Finally, the empirical findings will

Figure 1. Use of savings instruments in Kenya (Source: GSMA (2009), quoting study funded by FSD Kenya

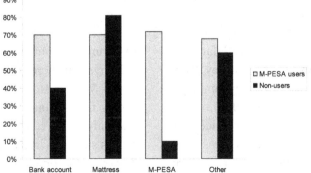

be used to suggest how mobile money applications can be designed to better suit the needs and interests of poor savers.

BACKGROUND

The Development of M-PESA

From its inception, the M-PESA application was designed to foster "sustainable development". It was intended to provide MFIs with an efficient mechanism for the collection of customer loans. Before the application was introduced, however, a pilot was run in conjunction with a local MFI called Faulu Kenya. During this pilot, customer needs and transaction patterns were assessed and an interesting discovery was made. People were sending mobile phone credit, which was purchased via M-PESA, to their relations upcountry. When this was investigated in more detail, the mobile service provider found that most Kenyans made similar transfers, not only with mobile phone credit, but also with cash.

Safaricom also noted a significant gap in the domestic remittance market. Most Kenyans used informal channels to transfer money. The most popular of these were family and friends, bus and matatu companies and the post office. However, there were complaints of these channels being both risky and costly. In a survey conducted shortly before the launch of M-PESA, over half the respondents said that they preferred to make the transfer themselves (FSD Kenya, 2007). Many complained that money and goods often failed to reach the final destination when they used the other channels. To address this gap, Safaricom identified the "send money home" as the key value proposition, and focused their marketing campaign in this direction (Hughes & Lonie, 2007).

As was mentioned above, the service has acquired over 7 million customers in less than three years. Such growth rates are even more impressive than those of the mobile phone. It took

Safaricom nearly 10 years to build a user base of 8 million. The competitive pricing structure noted here is one reason for such rapid growth. Several other factors should also be considered. Firstly, the service accelerates the speed at which money can be transferred. This is because money is being transferred in electronic rather than physical form. M-PESA works as follows. To transfer money individuals must register at one of the retail agent outlets, and deposit cash. This cash is thereafter reflected as e-money in a virtual account that is attached to the sender's SIM card. After a balance is established, e-money value can be transferred to the recipient's phone. The recipient thereafter visits an agent to convert the e-money balance back into cash. The actual transfer happens almost instantaneously.

The success of the application can also be attributed to the wide agent network. As mentioned in the introduction, there are over 10,000 of these agents in Kenya. These agents are located in small shops, petrol stations, banks and post offices. There is a high concentration in Nairobi and other urban centres. Many are also located in the villages. Safaricom estimates that almost half of their agents are located outside urban centres. There are some areas in Northern and Eastern Kenya where agents cannot offer the service because there is no network coverage. However, according to Safaricom this segment is small. 81 percent of the population receives network coverage, and can thus potentially access M-PESA services.

This wide agent network has provided M-PESA users with numerous points at which they can cash in and cash out. Many of these areas are unserved or underserved by financial institutions. There are, for example, about 11 times more M-PESA agents in Kenya than there are bank branches (Leishman, 2009). Many customers within these areas cannot access formal financial services. It is estimated that only 19 percent of the adult population can access such services through the banks. Another 8 percent are served by microfinance institutions (MFIs) and savings and credit cooperatives (SAC-

COs). This is low in comparison to mobile phone penetration. It is estimated that 55 percent of Kenyans own or have access to a mobile phone.

Conceptualizing the Role of Savings and Mobile Money in Poor People's Lives

A significant amount of empirical evidence suggests that resource-poor households usually save (Ashraf et al, 2008; Dupas & Robinson, 2009; Shipton, 1995; Rutherford, 1999; Collins et al., 2009). They do so by making small and irregular contributions into a variety of savings mechanisms. These accumulated amounts create new livelihood strategies; they are used to recover from shocks, smooth consumption and broaden investment opportunities. The evidence further notes that the poor are willing to pay a significant premium for savings. In some instances, they take out high interest loans to force themselves to accumulate cash (Dupas & Robinson, 2009; Collins et al, 2009). Many also receive negative interest for having others hold their money.

Why are millions of poor willing to pay these high costs to save? Research shows that there is a need to remove the cash from the household economy, where it is prone to the demands of spouses and other community members (Dupas & Robinson, 2009; Shipton, 2007). There is also a need to render savings illiquid for a particular period in time to avoid the risk of misuse (Shipton, 1989; 2007). Some are also willing to pay for mechanisms that instil discipline. This is why money collectors are popular in many developing countries. These collectors will make scheduled visits to the saver and collect a predetermined amount (Collins et al, 2007). The result is an accumulated amount at month-end. Regular contributions are also common in group savings schemes. These use peer pressure and trust built upon reciprocity between group members to encourage contributions (Ambec & Treich, 2007; Ashraf et al., 2003; Gugerty, 2007).

The research also highlights the various barriers to savings. The most frequently mentioned are the under-representation of financial services and the lack of appropriate savings mechanisms. Many of the formal service offerings demand minimum balances, and charge high monthly fees (Collins et al, 2009). This quickly wipes out any small savings. Socially imposed barriers have also been noted. The literature makes clear that savings is not just economic in nature. It is also submerged in social life (McNamara & Shipton, 1995; Collins et al., 2009). As a result, those storing cash have to find means of conserving their wealth without appearing selfish. This is why material forms of savings (from jewellery to cattle) that are indivisible and separated from such claims are popular (Shipton, 1989; 1995). These material forms have a significant advantage over other informal methods—they offer interest. For example, some prefer to convert their cash into livestock because the animals breed and can produce milk. The research also notes that these material forms have some serious drawbacks. They are less liquid and may generate less worth if sold in a hurry.

We can formalize the characteristics of various savings instruments with reference to two major attributes. The first is liquidity. Savings positions can be added to, or liquidated, easily. This is subject to any commitment features built into the product to drive savings discipline. The second is preservation of value. That is, whether the wealth held has a risk of erosion over time. Such value can be shaped by a number of different things. This includes: safety (low risk of theft, fraud or disappearance of funds), low entry and exit costs (total cost of depositing and withdrawing money), and net return on balances held (interest earned less inflation less administration fees).

Because each of the common savings mechanisms has its own unique set of advantages in terms of the above attributes, they are often used in conjunction. The research has also shown that the poor build up a reserve of financial instruments to manage their cash flows (Collins et al., 2009). For example, a saver with limited income may decide to keep some of their savings in a bank, some under the mattress, and purchase a goat with the rest of the cash. What has not been made clear within these studies is why particular mechanisms are integrated into the savings portfolio and just how they mutually reinforce each other. This will be discussed in the empirical findings. These findings will further make clear how a mobile money application can fit into this portfolio of financial mechanisms, and just what types of benefits it offers to poor savers. Such discoveries were made through the financial diaries, which are described below.

MAIN TOPIC: EVIDENCE FROM THE FINANCIAL DIARIES OF M-PESA USERS IN KENYA

Methodology

The financial diaries were a collection of notebooks that were handed out during the latter stage of a fourteen month ethnographic study. These diaries were meant to capture how M-PESA fit into, and altered, the financial habits of the users. Although twenty five of these diaries were handed out, only fourteen were used for the final analysis. The remaining eleven had incomplete entries, did not attend the weekly meetings or voluntarily decided to drop out of the project. Although the financial diaries sample size was small, the data provided in-depth information regarding the daily financial habits of the resource poor. Such data was important to substantiate some of the findings that emerged from the general ethnography. It must be noted that the sample size was significantly higher during the ethnography. Over 350 informants were interviewed and over 21 focus groups were organized. In some cases, these informants were interviewed more than once.

The majority of the participants were frequent users. These users made several transactions per week. Some even conducted transactions on a daily basis. The results presented here thus represent more intensive usage patterns than usual. Table 1 provides more information about the participants.

Eight of the participants came from Kibera, an informal settlement on the outskirts of Nairobi and six from villages in Western Kenya. Seven of the urban participants were male. Nearly all of the rural participants were female, and married to urban migrants in Kibera. This is with the exception of Joyce, the shop owner who stayed in Kibera with her husband. The majority of the urban participants were informally employed as tradesmen. Many operated small businesses within Kibera. Only two participants had found employment within the formal sector. Both worked as security guards. In the villages, most of participants sold goods from their farm to make extra money. Some sold these goods on the local market, whilst others sold to their neighbours and friends.

These participants were asked to make daily entries detailing their financial practices for the period of one month. These entries were made in two columns—money in and money out. They were also asked to maintain a balance in the two columns. This facilitated the analysis of not only expenditure but also savings patterns. Two in-depth interviews were conducted with the diary holders. The first interview was held before the diaries were handed out. During this interview participants were questioned about their employment activities, household structure, savings mechanisms, and money transfer channels. The participants were also interviewed after the diary was collected and analyzed. During this second interview all questions and concerns related to the diary were addressed. There was also a series of weekly meetings. These served two purposes. The first was to monitor the diaries and identify any missing or duplicate entries. The second was

Table 1. Financial diaries participants

Name	Location	Job	M-PESA User/Non user	Relation to Diary Participant
Wyclif	Urban- Kibera	Barber	Non User-sender	Married to Eunice
Eunice	Rural- Chamarmar	Farm work, fetch water	Non user	Married to Wyclif
Lawrence	Urban-Kibera	Painter	User-sender	
Brown	Urban-Kibera	Security guard	User-sender	Married to Betty
Betty	Rural-Bukura	Sold goods from farm	User-recipient	Married to Brown
Violet	Rural-Bukura	Not working	User-recipient	Betty's friend
Gaudezina	Rural-Shangalangwi (near Bukura)	Sold goods from farm	User-recipient	Betty's Mother
John	Urban-Kibera	Security guard and shop owner	User-sender	
Sylvesta	Urban-Kibera	Security guard and shop owner	User-sender	Married to Elizabeth
Elizabeth	Rural-Sikarira	Sold goods on market-table cloth etc.	User-recipient	Married to Sylvesta
Martin	Urban-Kibera	Shoe repair	User-sender	Married to Margaret
Margaret	Rural-Masiro	Sold goods from farm	User-recipient	Married to Martin
Joyce	Urban-Kibera	Shop owner	User-recipient	
Patrik	Urban-Kibera	Pastor	User-sender and recipient	

to keep the participants motivated to continue making daily entries.

The financial diaries methodology used here differs from that of Rutherford (2002), Ruthven (2002) and Collins (2005). These studies did not give the participants a diary in which they made entries. Instead the participants were interviewed, usually on a bi-weekly basis, for the period of one year. They were asked to describe their monetary inflows and outflows during these interviews. They did not keep a diary, as was done in this research. This method is best suited to the analysis of financial patterns over a longer period of time. It is less appropriate for capturing daily financial practices, which is the goal of this chapter. Furthermore, these studies focused on household rather than individual financial practices. Such an analysis would not be as appropriate in the Kenyan context because it is more difficult to define a household. Many are organized across space. There is evidence of strong ties between urban and rural based individuals, and a two-way flow of resources. The term "multi-spatial" household is often used in the literature to describe this type of arrangement (Owuor, 2005; 2006). To understand these multi-spatial ties and flows, urban migrants who sent money back home were given diaries. These migrants then encouraged the recipients in the rural areas, usually their wives, to also complete a diary.

THE FINDINGS

A Variety of Savings Mechanisms were Integrated into the Savings Portfolios of the Participants

The diaries confirmed that the poor use a combination of savings mechanisms to manage their limited income and to meet their unique savings needs. The average amount of savings mechanisms used by the participants for the storage of cash was just over two. The findings further illustrated that the poor were very strategic when cultivating their savings portfolios. The mechanisms included usually acted as complements to the others. As will be shown below, most of the participants who were banked continued to store money at home. These home savings were more accessible, and often used for daily consumption. The bank was appropriate for the accumulation of savings over time. This facilitated the purchase of future items, usually of greater value. It also provided the participants with an accumulated amount, which could be accessed during an emergency.

Many also appropriated these various mechanisms to keep track of their finances. For example, John used four mechanisms to store his cash. He explained that this made it easier for him to organize and "spread out" his savings:

"I have many accounts. I have the jamii bora (MFI). I deposit money there so that I can get a loan to boost my business. I have Equity [bank]. Salary for my askari [security guard] job comes through equity...Cash for big purchases also goes to Equity....M-PESA is for the business transactions, like buying goods. Home bank is for small cash. My wife can get money from there as well when she needs to buy chai [tea] and ugali [maize porridge]."

For John, each of these accounts served a different function and provided him with some type of benefit. For example, the home bank[2] allowed John to have immediate access to his cash. The bank gave him a place where he could save cash for larger purchases. M-PESA facilitated the separation of John's business and personal finances. He explained that this made it easier for him to organize and "keep track" of his finances.

Some of the informants also appropriated more than one mechanism to avoid the risk of money being lost. For example, Sylvesta kept money in both M-PESA and the bank. After he was paid his salary, he would withdraw a substantial amount from the bank and would deposit the money into his M-PESA account. Sylvesta explained that he did not fully trust the banks in Kenya with his money. He had heard "stories" that his savings would be lost if the bank crashed. He explained that such stories were especially prevalent during the post-election crises:

Sylvester: Guys were telling me to take my money out of Equity [name of his bank]. They were sure that it was going down...Many had already taken their money out because they were scared. They were keeping the cash at home. I was scared to keep any of the cash at home...They were fighting and looting all over...So I took my cash and put it in M-PESA.

Interviewer: You weren't afraid that your money would be lost when saved with M-PESA?

S: No, only the banks are greedy for money.

Sylvester was not alone in his distrust of banks. Many other informants confirmed this finding during the fieldwork. This distrust was especially common prior to the presidential elections of December 2007. This period was characterized by heightened tensions between ethnic communities within the informal settlement. There was a rumour circulating around Kibera that the head of Equity bank, who was Kikuyu like the President, was using the "common man's" money to fund the presidential campaign. Many were warned that Equity would soon crash. Informants took a variety of measures to protect their cash during the period. Some claimed that they took most, and sometimes all, of their savings from the banks and deposited the money into M-PESA and their home bank. They explained that they reduced the risk of money being lost by spreading out their savings.

Many also used M-PESA as a complement, or in some cases substitute, to home savings. As will be described below, many asserted that money saved in the home was at greater risk of being stolen. Some were also concerned that their home would burn down, and their money would be lost. They thus preferred to keep some money in savings outside of the home to reduce these risks. In-kind savings were also held. However, there were attempts to limit these savings to render wealth less visible. This would limit the requests for money that would be from friends and neighbours. This will also be described below.

Table 2 formalizes the advantages and disadvantages perceived by Kenyans on the main savings instruments that are available to them.

In Urban Areas, M-PESA and the Home Bank were the Most Popular Savings Mechanisms

There were some substantial differences between financial portfolios in urban centres and rural areas. In Kibera, the most widely used mechanism for savings was M-PESA as well as the home bank. Many of those informants who had steady flow of income also had an account with a formal bank or MFI. However, because there were no formal financial institutions within Kibera, the residents had to leave the informal settlement to transact. Many noted that this was a significant disadvantage of having such an account.

In regards to frequency of transactions, the home bank was the most popular. All of the urban participants kept some money in their home savings and many would make daily deposits and withdrawals. Most often, the money was used to purchase items for household consumption around Kibera. Lawrence kept nearly half of his income at home because it was easily accessible. He did not need to leave Kibera to transact. When asked whether he was afraid of losing money stored in the home, he said no. He explained that he had "hidden the money well" and did not "fear" theft by intruders. (see Figure 2)

Although the number of transactions was higher for the home bank, the value stored was lower than M-PESA. The diaries revealed that an average of 4 percent of total income was deposited into home savings. This compares to nearly 18 percent that was put into M-PESA. Two of the

Table 2. The savings portfolio of low-income Kenyans

Savings mechanism	Advantages	Disadvantages
Home bank	- Free to transact and highly accessible	- Risky-money stored in the home can be stolen by household members or outsiders -Puts the family at risk from home invasion - No interest is gained on the money stored at home
ROSCA	-Allows for the rapid accumulation of funds - Support to save is provided from other community members	- Risky-money can be lost if group dissolves - Time consuming-regular meetings are often required by group members
Bank	- Secure method of savings - Interest provided on savings - Potential for credit	- High transaction and maintenance fees - Difficult to access, especially in rural areas
M-PESA	- Free to deposit and store money - Highly accessible - Secure-customer ID and PIN is needed to access money	- No interest on money stored - Cash shortages in rural areas can sometimes make it difficult to withdraw money - Not regulated as a savings mechanism, thus funds of customer are not protected - Money virtual rather than physical and therefore subject to be erased or otherwise tampered with if security is not strong.
In-kind	- Material interest gained on some forms of material savings (i.e. Egg, milk)	- Maintenance fees sometimes required (i.e. animal feed) - Low liquidity on some material savings - Potential loss of value over time

Figure 2. Savings portfolio of urban diarists

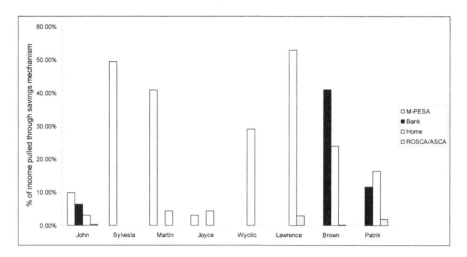

financial diaries participants, Martin and Sylvesta, stored nearly half of their income inflows with M-PESA. Both men asserted that they preferred this method because it was "safer" than the other savings mechanisms. Martin explained:

"I used to store all the cash at home, but that was no good. Thieves could come in the night to steal the money...Your cash could also be wiped in fire. I store with M-PESA because it is safe... Guys can't get at my cash unless they know my PIN. Even when my phone is stolen, they can't get at it...There is no PIN for home savings".

Martin made clear that he still used his home savings because it was more accessible than M-PESA. He would use the money stored at home to make "small purchases" around Kibera. The rest of his money was stored in M-PESA, as he did not have a bank account.

John and Joyce also saved with M-PESA. However, they deposited a much smaller percentage of their income into their M-PESA accounts. Joyce explained that she preferred to invest her cash in her small business. She would often maintain low balances in all of her savings mechanisms. She explained that money stored at home was at risk of being stolen by her husband who was often

thirsty for *changa* [local brew]. She did not keep too much in her bank account because interest rates were low. The balance in her M-PESA account was the highest. She explained that she used this money for daily consumption and the "upkeep" of her rural relatives. Because an M-PESA agent was located close to her home, Joyce was able to accumulate money through weekly deposits. She would remit the money when she met her savings target for the month. The cash that was left over at end-month would be used to purchase something for the home. Joyce explained that the previous month she had purchased some utensils. This month, she planned to buy a new stool. For John the balance was kept low because, as mentioned above, M-PESA was just one of several mechanisms he used for savings.

Four of the urban participants did not use M-PESA for savings. Wyclif and Lawrence did not know that M-PESA could be used for this purpose. As was mentioned above, M-PESA was not designed or regulated as a savings mechanism. This is why Safaricom never advertised this option. Those who used M-PESA for savings discovered this function on their own, or heard about it from friends. Brown and Patrik said that they knew M-PESA could be used for savings, but had no use for this mechanism. Their existing portfolio of savings mechanisms was enough to meet their needs.

Some of the urban informants kept a bank account. Usually, they used the bank to accumulate money for future expenses. Many also wanted to build a relationship with the financial institution to access credit in the future. There were informants who explained that they did not keep an account by choice; rather, they had their salaries deposited directly. They explained that banks were too expensive and that fees were "eating up" their savings. Numerous informants wanted their salaries deposited directly into M-PESA. They explained that they took a risk each time they carried money from the bank, which was located outside of Kibera, to their homes.

In Rural Areas, Many Preferred to Keep Their Money in Circulation Rather Than Saving Their Cash; Saving in Kind Was Also More Common

In the villages, the home bank was the most popular mechanism for savings. On average 32 percent of rural household income was deposited into the home bank. Many preferred this method because it was accessible. The majority of banks and MFIs were located in the closest town, which was over 20 km away. Many of the rural dwellers noted that this was too far to travel. They also explained that the banks only catered to the "rich". The monthly fees and transaction costs were too high and would quickly wipe out their "small money". Those who kept accounts in the villages were usually cash crop farmers, who grew sugar cane. They would sell this cane to a nearby manufacturer who deposited their pay directly into a bank. These informants noted that they were displeased with this method of payment. It was expensive and time consuming for them to get their cash.

ROSCAs, also known as merry-go-rounds, were also popular in the villages. Four out of the six rural women were involved in a merry-go-

round. However, only 2 percent of rural inflows were stored in this mechanism. When asked why so little was stored, some of the rural respondents said that they were a part of the merry go round for social, rather than, financial reasons. Violet explained that she enjoyed the weekly meetings with the group, composed of women from her village. It gave her a chance to catch up with the women and discuss some of the village happenings. Others further noted that these group mechanisms "forced" them to save. Gaudezina explained:

I make sure to keep some cash in the merry go round. That way, I am sure there is something left over...and that I will save every week... But the problem is these groups are only for small money. So, you have to join many groups if you want to save. But then you spend all of your time going to the meetings. Then you have to think if this is eating too much time.

Many of the other women confirmed that these group savings models were time consuming. Some also noted that they were risky. Both Betty and Elizabeth had lost money when previous groups disbanded without warning. Betty explained that because of such risk, it is best to keep smaller amounts in the merry go round. It is also better to have "back-up" savings in other mechanisms such as the home bank.

Many of the rural women further asserted that they also invested a portion of their wealth into material items such as livestock. For example, Violet and Gaudezina both purchased chickens during the period. The women explained that they would use the eggs for their own consumption, or sell them to neighbours when they needed money. Some would also purchase and re-sell items such as bananas and sugar cane. They explained that they preferred to "make something small" with her money rather than keeping their cash idle. Violet explained that she only saved a "lump sum" when she had to make a larger purchase. The last time she did this, she continued, was when she had to pay school fees for her daughter. She further explained that she would "invest" the rest of her cash into sugar cane.

The rural informants explained that these in-kind savings were somewhat risky. There was no guarantee that the material good would be converted into wealth. A buyer had to be located, and a series of negotiations undertaken, before a sale occurred. Material forms of savings also rendered wealth more visible. The result was often an increase in the demands for money. Martin explained that he did not purchase too many cows for Margaret [his wife]. He wanted to reduce the risk of her being "hassled" for money by the neighbours.

None of the rural participants used M-PESA for savings. Again, most did not know that M-PESA could be used for this purpose. Those who did know claimed that the application was not suitable for savings. They noted frequent cash shortages in rural areas, and were concerned that money saved with M-PESA would be difficult to access. Because the majority of the M-PESA transactions in rural areas were withdrawals, agents often ran out of cash float. Some would maintain this float by making regular trips to the bank to "top up". Others, however, found such maintenance too

costly and time consuming. They instead chose to top up their float sporadically. This resulted in cash shortages. Betty explained:

"My husband told me that M-PESA is also for savings. He said I should store some small money there....Sometimes I go [to M-PESA agent] and have to wait for cash. Sometimes I wait for several days. That is the danger of storing with M-PESA... There is an emergency, you need cash, you don't want to wait for several days...It is better to keep the money close to you."

Other rural respondents confirmed that accessibility to cash was very important. For this reason, the home bank was one of the most popular savings mechanisms in rural areas. As is shown in Figure 3, all of the rural participants stored their money at home. These rural respondents further expressed a need for an affordable and accessible savings mechanism. As in the urban areas, they wanted to remove their cash from the household economy where it was prone to demands of relatives and neighbours.

Figure 3. Savings portfolio of rural diarists

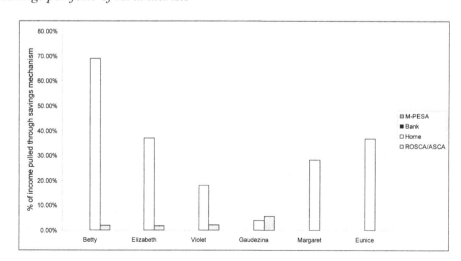

M-PESA Acted as a Complement, Rather than Substitute, for Many of the Other Mechanisms in the Savings Portfolio

For the participants who used M-PESA for savings, an interesting trend was noted. The application acted as a complement, rather than a substitute, to these other mechanisms. It was used in conjunction with the bank, home bank and ROSCA. M-PESA had a vital place in the savings portfolio of the poor informants—somewhere between the bank and the home bank. Unlike the bank, M-PESA was appropriate for the accumulation of small savings. There were no fees to deposit money or to maintain the account. The application was also more accessible than the bank. Customers could transact at over 10,000 agent outlets. Those living in Kibera, did not need to leave the informal settlement to make deposits or access their cash. They could also check their balance, at any time, using their mobile phone. Because M-PESA was accessible, it was used more often than the bank and ROSCA as is shown below. In some cases, deposits and withdrawals were made nearly every day. (see Table 3)

Many also noted that M-PESA was safer than the other mechanisms. Safaricom was less likely than the bank to crash. Money stored with M-PESA could also not be stolen by a husband who was thirsty for *changa* [local brew]. The applica-

Table 3. Number of monthly transactions per savings mechanism for M-PESA users

	M-PESA	**Bank**	**Home**	**ROSCA**
John	18	13	15	6
Sylvesta	25	17	0	31
Martin	6	0	24	9
Joyce	4	3	32	4
Total	53	33	71	50
Mean	**13**	**8**	**18**	**13**
Median	**16**	**8**	**20**	**8**

tion was further used to organize cash. For example, John used M-PESA to separate his business from his personal savings. Joyce used the application to accumulate money that would be sent to her rural relatives. Once M-PESA became integrated into the savings portfolio of the poor, there was a re-balancing of amounts in each of the savings mechanisms. For example, Martin began to store more in M-PESA and less in his home bank. Sylvester took a balance from his bank account and kept it with M-PESA. As mentioned above, many wanted to spread out their cash to decrease the risk of it being lost if one of the mechanisms failed.

It must be noted that M-PESA had some disadvantages as a savings mechanism. As was explained by John, it was not appropriate for "big savings". Interest was not paid on the money stored. Loans could also not be acquired from Safaricom. M-PESA was also dependent on the Safaricom network. Thus, when there were network issues money could not be accessed. This happened several times throughout the course of the fieldwork. Many informants explained that this dissuaded them from keeping larger amounts in M-PESA. Also, as mentioned above, many did not use M-PESA for savings in the rural areas because of frequent cash shortages. They instead chose to keep cash at home where it was accessible. John explained that unlike M-PESA his home bank "never closed". Furthermore, money stored in M-PESA is not adequately protected. As mentioned above, the service is not regulated by the Central Bank of Kenya. This is mainly because M-PESA was never designed to be a savings mechanism.

Safaricom can take various measures to improve the current M-PESA savings value proposition. In particular, there is the opportunity for M-PESA to be more than just a mechanism in the savings portfolio. The application can become the platform from which the entire portfolio of mechanisms can be accessed. This would provide poor savers with a centralized savings base on which they could accumulate, track, and manage, their small savings. It would also allow them to work with two forms of currency when organizing their finances—cash and electronic value. The latter would be advantageous because it would facilitate the movement of value across the numerous accounts. As was shown in the empirical findings, such movement has significant costs (time and money). The electronic value would also render wealth invisible, which would make it less prone to demands from friends and family. However, before M-PESA becomes a platform for savings, the system design needs to be altered and new partnerships must be cultivated.

Issuance of M-PESA Accounts by Banks or Third Parties

For M-PESA to become a centralized base for savings services, the opening and maintenance of accounts would have to be outsourced. This would allow banks and MFIs to tap into the M-PESA platform and offer services at scale. It would also provide customers with new opportunities to generate interest on their savings. Currently, M-PESA accounts are issued by Safaricom and thus not subject to full prudential scrutiny by bank supervisory authorities. It puts M-PESA in an unstable regulatory position, which prevents Safaricom from benefiting financially from the interest on float held. It further precludes Safaricom from paying interest on balances held, or promoting M-PESA as a savings service for fear of incurring more regulation. If accounts were formally issued in the name of a bank, or other financial institution, the arrangement would be regulatorily more sustainable as funds held in M-PESA would have the necessary prudential protections.

No change to the design, operation and branding of the service would be required except that the accounts would be issued in the name of a bank. Customer contracts would be issued by the bank but processed by Safaricom, in the same way as it processes the contracts today. Safaricom would

continue transferring all stored funds through M-PESA with the chosen bank, but now they would be stored on behalf of the M-PESA clients, not on behalf of M-PESA itself. Safaricom would still operate all individual accounts, and their collective value would be registered as a single line (pooled deposit account or account payable) in its ledger. This would be following the Smart Money model in the Philippines, where the service is operated and branded by mobile operator Smart Communications but the mobile wallet accounts are issued in the name of bank partner Banco de Oro. To make this possible, the Central Bank of Kenya would need to permit a high degree of outsourcing of bank operations to a non-bank.

Extending the outsourcing logic further, the mobile wallet or savings account could be co-branded ("licensed") by multiple third party institutions eager to acquire a "white label" savings service. Safaricom would manage the service end-to-end, and there would be a single issuer of the accounts (either Safaricom as at present or a lead bank as per above). The licensee could be grass-roots financial institutions thinking of transforming or larger banks thinking of downscaling. Their motive in licensing M-PESA's platform might be to acquire an entry-level savings service as they test markets and acquire early customers. It could also be non-financial players under co-branding arrangements, thereby opening up the sales and marketing of M-PESA to players who might be more actively targeting or have more affinity with poorer customers. To make this possible, Safaricom may need to differentiate the branding of the payment service (which would remain the core M-PESA service) from that of the wallet management (or savings) service. Nothing would need to change operationally from today.

The customer would benefit from this arrangement. They would be able to access a multitude of savings accounts, from different institutions, via their mobile phone. The value of M-PESA as a savings platform would also grow exponentially as more institutions use it to offer their savings products.

Creating Savings Sub-Accounts

Once M-PESA becomes a centralized savings base it could provide a link between people's goals and their savings by compartmentalizing these savings into a system of sub-accounts. Each of these would have a pre-defined purpose. When making a deposit, the agent would ask customers if they had a special purpose for the funds. If so, the agent would select the appropriate item from a limited set of pre-defined options on the M-PESA menu (home savings, school fees, house repairs, funeral, remittances, etc.) when requesting authorization for the deposit. These options could be based on the most common savings objectives according to local research. It would also possible for customers to pre-define their own objectives. When customers check balances through their mobile, their balance would be itemized by saving purpose (i.e. by sub-account). When making withdrawals or payments, customers would be able to select which sub-account to withdraw from. A ROSCA account could also be integrated. This could eliminate the need for cash exchanges at the meetings. The pay-out could also be provided in electronic value, rather than cash.

M-PESA could also facilitate the movement of funds between these various accounts. For example, the pay-out from the ROSCA could be immediately deposited into the school fees account. A remittance transfer made into the M-PESA wallet could also be moved into the account that is allocated to daily consumption. This could eliminate the need to physically move the money between the different mechanisms. It would also allow the poor to more easily diversify their savings base by the appropriation of various mechanisms and, in effect, spread out their risk. Disciplinary techniques could also be used to integrated into the system. For example, a text message could be sent to remind a saver who is accumulating cash that a deposit is due. Mechanisms that deter withdrawals on some accounts can also be incorporated. These could be in the form of higher withdrawal fees. They could also be in the form of time restrictions on withdrawals.

Enabling Micro-Transactions

The lowest amount that can currently be deposited into M-PESA is 100 KSh. This makes it more difficult for M-PESA to be used for the accumulation of "small savings". This is where the home bank, without any minimum deposit stipulations, has a significant advantage. By lowering this minimum deposit amount to around 10 Ksh, M-PESA could encourage poor savers to make more frequent deposits into the system. This would remove money from the household economy, where it is liable to theft and demands from relatives. Through appropriate partnerships new strategies can be found to provide interest on the money stored.

The pricing structure for withdrawals would also need to be altered. M-PESA's current fee structure penalizes smaller transactions. The smallest withdrawal fee is KSh 25=USD0.33, which makes it quite costly to withdraw amounts smaller than around USD10 (implying a fee of more than 3 percent). The single flat rate on P2P payments of KSh 30=USD0.40 has the same effect. Safaricom could create a more uniform fee structure as a percent of total transaction value by introducing more tranches or 'steps' in the pricing structure. For instance, creating a new withdrawal fee tranche of say KSh12=USD0.15 for transactions of up to KSh800=USD10, and a P2P transaction fee of KSh 15=USD0.20 for transactions under KSh800=USD10. These measures would increase the value of M-PESA as a savings mechanism.

Managing Liquidity

If M-PESA was to be used as a tool for the mobilization of savings, one of the greatest challenges for Safaricom would be to ensure the liquidity of M-PESA accounts. As was mentioned in the empirical findings, many rural dwellers did not use M-PESA for savings because of the frequent cash shortages. These shortages were especially prevalent in rural areas because agents were farther away from the banks. One strategy that could be taken to increase cash float is to increase the number of rural deposits. This could only be done by finding ways in which M-PESA could beat out the home bank as a savings mechanism. Facilitating access to accounts offering interest, and future loans, would be a good start. Banks could also work with Safaricom to help with liquidity management in rural areas. It is in their interest to ensure cash is readily available not only to keep customers happy but also to increase the number of transactions going through the system. The chapter showed in the empirical findings that banks had the lowest number of transactions amongst the numerous savings mechanisms.

FUTURE RESEARCH DIRECTIONS

This research revealed that M-PESA, when first integrated into the savings portfolio, acted as a complement to the other mechanisms. It would be interesting to examine whether this changes through time. For example, it can be argued that M-PESA may eventually act as a substitute for a formal account. Those who consider and use M-PESA as their "bank" may delay from entering the formal financial sector, especially if they see the application as a viable alternative to a formal account. This may limit their ability to build credit histories and to access credit from formal institutions in the future. It may also result in less diverse portfolio of savings mechanisms. As was mentioned previously, such diversity is important because it reduces the risk of savings being inaccessible if the one of the other mechanisms fails.

In some cases, the opposite may occur. The unbanked may realize the benefits of removing

cash from the household economy once adopting M-PESA. They may also become more familiar with the concepts and processes related to banking because of the application. For example, many of the unbanked were introduced to concepts such as PIN, account and balance after adopting M-PESA. However, more research is required to determine just how relationships between the unbanked and formal financial institutions are changing because of the introduction of M-PESA.

CONCLUSION

The findings presented here are broadly in line with the recent literature on the savings patterns of the poor. The poor 'push' and 'pull' income on a routine basis, often daily (Collins et al., 2009). The variety of instruments used to do so is partly due to the lack of reliable access to some instruments. Poor people learn to associate individual savings instruments with particular savings needs for which they have a relative advantage. I set out to test whether the addition of an electronic form of savings –accessible through the mobile phone—in any way altered these insights. The empirical findings confirmed that the poor use a variety of mechanisms to meet their unique savings needs. These are combined into a savings portfolio, in which each of the mechanisms acts as complements to the others. M-PESA has a vital role in this portfolio—somewhere between the bank and home bank. It is more accessible and cheaper than the bank. It also provides additional security to savers by removing the money from the home and rendering wealth invisible.

The chapter further suggested that M-PESA can have a much greater role in the mobilization of savings. Rather than just being a mechanism in the financial portfolio, it can provide a platform on which various savings mechanisms can be accessed. This is especially the case because it utilizes a new form of value—mobile money (or electronic money more broadly). As was shown in the empirical findings, this form functions as a complement to cash; savers only convert cash to mobile money when it provides them with some type of benefit. Usually, this benefit is added security. This work also made clear that mobile money can have additional benefits if M-PESA becomes a platform for savings. Most importantly, this new form of value would make it easier for savers to organize, and keep track of, their various accounts. Rather than going from one mechanism to the next to check balances, and make deposits and withdrawals, all the accounts would be centralized and made accessible via the mobile. It would also make it easier to move money between accounts. Accumulated amounts could be moved to a bank account to accrue interest; money in the bank could be moved to M-PESA for daily consumption. Mechanisms could also be built in to instil discipline. For example, a user accumulating cash could be sent a text message each time a payment was due. The user could immediately move value from one account to the next in reaction to this electronic reminder. There are thus endless possibilities for the formalization, and mobilization of savings with the mobile as a platform.

In this world of fairly specialized savings instruments, mobile money can exploit some key disadvantages of more established forms of savings. Once it has secured a toe-hold in poor people's lives, it is likely that we will see a slow but inexorable rise in its use for savings more broadly. Thus, savings through mobile money offerings will replicate the experience we are already seeing with mobile payments: from 'send money home' to a full range of payment applications; from larger to smaller payments. But this will require building ever more trust in the M-PESA savings proposition by strengthening the reliability of the technical platform and the liquidity options of users, and increasing the flexibility in how people can use the system to save.

REFERENCES

Ambes, S., & Treich, N. (2007). Roscas as financial agreements to cope with self-control problems. *Journal of Development Economics*, *82*, 120–137. doi:10.1016/j.jdeveco.2005.09.005

Ashraf, N., Gons, N., & Yin, W. (2003). A review of commitment savings products in developing countries. Financial Access Initiative.

Ashraf, N., Karlan, D., & Yin, W. (2008). Female empowerment: Impact of a commitment savings product in the Philippines. Working Paper 106. Boston, Harvard Business School.

Collins, D. (2005). Financial instruments for the poor: Initial findings from the financial diaries study. CSSR Working Paper. Cape Town, University of Cape Town.

Collins, D., Murdoch, J., Rutherford, S., & Ruthven, O. (2009). *Portfolios of the poor: How the world's poor live on $2/day*. Princeton: Princeton University Press.

Dupas, P & Robinson, J. (2009). Savings constraints and micro-enterprise development: Evidence from a field experiment in Kenya. Financial Access Initiative.

GSMA. (2009). Mobile Money for the Unbanked Annual Report 2009. London, UK.

Gugerty, M. K. (2007). You can't save alone: Commitment in rotating savings and credit associations in Kenya. *Economic Development and Cultural Change*, *55*, 251–282. doi:10.1086/508716

Hughes, N., & Lonie, S. (2007). M-PESA: Mobile money for the "unbanked". Turning cell phones into 24-hour tellers in Kenya. *Innovations: Technology, Governance, Globalization*, *2*, 63–81. doi:10.1162/itgg.2007.2.1-2.63

Ivatury, G., & Lyman, T. (2007). *Regulatory issues in branchless banking: The new frontier. Washington, D.C: CGAP.Ivatury, G. & Mas, I. (2008). The Early Experience with Branchless Banking.* Washington, D.C: CGAP.

Kenya, F. S. D. (2007). Financial access in Kenya: Results of a 2006 National Survey. Nairobi, Kenya.

Leishman, P. (2009). Understanding the unbanked customer and sizing the mobile money opportunity. In *Mobile Money for the Unbanked Annual Report 2009*. London, UK: GSMA.

Lyman, T. R., Ivatury, G., & Staschen, S. (2006). *Use of agents in branchless banking for the poor: Rewards, risks and regulation*. Washington, D.C: CGAP.

McNamara, P., & Shipton, P. (1995). Rural credit and savings. In McPherson, M., & Radelet, S. (Eds.), *Economic recovery in the Gambia: Insights for adjustments in sub-saharan Africa*. Cambridge: Harvard University Press.

Owuor, S. (2005). *Urban households ruralising their livelihoods: The changing nature of urban-rural linkages in an East African town*. Leiden: African Studies Centre Seminar Series.

Owuor, S. (2006). *Bridging the urban-rural divide: Multispatial livelihoods in Nakuru town*. Leiden: African Studies Center.

Rutherford, S. (1999). *The poor and their money: An essay about financial services for poor people*. Manchester: Institute for Development Policy and Management, University of Manchester.

Rutherford, S. (2002). Money talks: Conversations with poor households in Bangladesh about managing money. *Working Paper Series*. Manchester, Institute for Development Policy and Management.

Ruthven, O. (2002). Money mosaics: financial choice and strategy in a West Delhi squatter settlement. *Journal of International Development, 14*, 249–271. doi:10.1002/jid.875

Shipton, P. (1989). *Bitter money: Cultural economy and some African meanings of forbidden currencies*. New Hampshire: American Anthropological Association.

Shipton, P. (1995). How Gambians save: Culture and economic strategy at an ethnic crossroads. In Guyer, J. (Ed.), *Money matters: Instability, values and social payments in modern history of West African communities*. Portsmouth: Reed Elsevier.

Shipton, P. (2007). *The nature of entrustment: Intimacy, exchange and the sacred in Africa*. New Haven: Yale University Press.

ENDNOTES

[1] I would like to thank Ignacio Mas for his substantial contribution to this paper. Also, many thanks to the reviewers who provided excellent feedback on an earlier draft. This work was funded by Microsoft Research and the University of Edinburgh.

[2] A home bank is a small tin box that is used to store money. Usually, it has the label"home bank" inscribed on the front. These boxes were sold around Kibera and Bukura for around £.30-£.50.

Chapter 10

Can Information and Communication Technologies Improve the Performance of Microfinance Programs?
Further Evidence from Developing and Emerging Financial Markets

Fredj Jawadi
Amiens School of Management and EconomiX-University of Paris West, France

Nabila Jawadi
Amiens School of Management & CREPA, France

Ydriss Ziane
University of Paris 1 Pantheon Sorbonne & GREGOR Research Center, France

ABSTRACT

Given the important role played by microfinance institutions (MFIs), a growing number of studies have been recorded in this field. More specifically, researchers and practitioners are interested in factors that influence their performance in order to enhance the way they function and to ensure their sustainability. One of these factors concerns the use of information and communication technologies (ICT) in MFI programs. Despite the relevance of the topic, few studies have looked at the links between ICT use and the enhancement of MFI performance. In addition, ICT use in developing and emerging financial markets is also under studied. The purpose of this chapter is to fill this gap in the literature and to analyse how ICT can influence MFI performance. In this regard, three aspects of MFI performance are studied: efficiency, risk management and customer relationship management. The results of the survey conducted with MFI professionals in developing and emerging countries show that the implementation of ICTs enables MFIs to significantly improve their microfinance services, while enhancing work efficiency and customer relationship management in the same way as in other branches of financial services in general. However, our results give no empirical support to the contribution of ICTs in risk management or risk reduction.

DOI: 10.4018/978-1-61520-993-4.ch010

INTRODUCTION

Microfinance is a growing branch of financial intermediation with the specific and non-profitable goal of providing poor and excluded economic agents with small loans in order to satisfy their primary needs and/or finance their personal activities (Sriram, 2005). This type of intermediation first emerged in developing countries in order to reduce inequality and poverty (Hulme and Mosley, 1996). The first loans were allocated more than thirty years ago, but the movement reached its height during the 1980s when a lot of traditional bank systems were defaulting and microfinance appeared as a new regulation model where profit was no longer king (Morduch, 1999; Morduch, 2000; Labie, 2001). To achieve its social aims, microfinance products are generally provided in a local context by Microfinance Institutions (henceforth indicated as MFIs) such as banks, associations, mutual institutions, moneylenders, credit and savings cooperatives or local branches of mutual agricultural credit institutions.

Thanks to the success and the extensive contribution of some MFIs to national development, microfinance programs have increased rapidly. Their networks and subsidiaries have been introduced in several countries to satisfy the ever-increasing demands of clients worldwide. The first microcredit institution – the Grameen Bank – was developed by Muhammad Yunus in Bangladesh in 1974. It offered a small loan of $27 to a group of 42 Bangladeshi families in order to help them overcome serious famine.[1] Ten years later, it had become the "Bangladeshi Independent Bank." Nowadays, the bank counts over 7.3 million clients,[2] with a loan portfolio equal to €4.3 billon, and it continues to develop strong social projects nationwide. In 2006, the bank counted 2100 agencies in total. The bank now has an international dimension and has set up agencies in 60 countries across Africa, Asia and Latin America. Moreover, the Grameen Bank has provided the model for several MFIs that have sprung up around the globe to offer loans and microcredit to poor families with no financial security. The number of institutions providing microfinance products has increased considerably since the end of 1990 and MFIs are now present worldwide, including in several developing countries, but notably in countries where poverty and inequality are particularly rife.[3]

Overall, there are around 10,000 MFIs worldwide, serving more than 150 million poor people in 105 countries. The great success of the Grameen Bank experience motivated financial institutions not only in developing and emerging countries but also in the developed countries.[4]

MFIs initially began with small structures, dimensions and capital. They were not well developed and were often financially limited. Moreover, the aims of their initiatives with respect to poverty and inequality gave rise to a number of issues. Daley-Harris *et al.* (2007), among others, pointed out that few people believed in MFI programs and their purpose at first. This was a real challenge for MFIs as they had to introduce various rules and management practices to reduce running costs in order to enhance their effectiveness. Some MFIs were implicitly against the introduction of Information and Communication Technologies (ICTs) as initially they just dealt with small applications and projects and only provided small loans that did not need complicated operations or tools. The choice of not introducing ICTs was thus justifiable on two counts. On the one hand, they considered that ICTs were not really useful or that the MFI employees could easily manage all the applications and meet all the clients' demands without sophisticated tools. On the other hand, ICTs were costly and so many MFIs were unable to adopt such technologies in their daily activities. Indeed, ICT use would involve additional expenses and funding, and would also require the training of staff who often had few qualifications and so would not be very profitable.

However, the microfinance framework, as it was launched over thirty years ago, is no longer the same because of the huge development of, and increase in, MFI programs, activities, products, clients and networks. MFIs now have many characteristics (large client base, labor intensive activity, etc.) and needs (standardized procedures, better access to background information, etc.) that makes the use of ICTs more interesting. Such development also involves a large increase in client files and demand for microfinance products that can no longer be dealt with manually or with traditional tools. This development has generated an increase in intangible information, diversity and heterogeneity of client demand, and a large increase in the risks associated with microfinance products. It has become difficult to study all the clients' demands efficiently and in a timely manner using the traditional framework. It is also hard for MFI services to collect and examine all the information needed to ensure their efficiency.

Consequently, we believe that the introduction of ICTs provides an effective solution to the issue of data collection and analyses in MFIs. Such electronic tools are expected to improve the running of MFI operations by enhancing work efficiency, risk management,[5] and the development of customer relationship management. Indeed, the use of electronic tools in MFI current operations enables them to reduce transactions costs. Different applications make it easier to reach new clients where ever they are. Hence, MFI are not obliged to establish new physical branches in rural zones. In addition, information systems enable MFI to reduce operations time (such as examination of loan demands) as automation facilitates information collection and storage. This also helps microfinance professionals to better manage risk associated with unpaid loans and insolvent clients. Through data collected on past clients' behaviors and transactions, MFI could be well informed about their future situation and whether they are solvent or not. Previsions of future behaviors could be easily done. More interestingly, customer relationship management applications could help

MFI to better answer to clients requests and then to enhance their notoriety.

In all these situations, ICTs enable MFIs to reduce information asymmetry through improved data collection and storage, and enhanced handling of the different stakeholders (clients, banks, suppliers, public and legal authorities, etc.).

In this chapter, we explore these aspects by focusing on how ICT use impacts on MFI activities. We investigate whether the introduction of ICTs in the microfinance industry improves MFI services and reduces the risks associated with financial products and the information asymmetry inherent in inter-temporal financial exchanges. To our knowledge, academic research regarding the introduction of ICTs in the microfinance industry and their effects on MFI performance is still little developed. The contribution of this paper is thus twofold. Firstly, we discuss the economic and social aspects of microfinance, focusing on the interaction between microfinance services and those of formal financial institutions. Secondly, we explain the contribution of ICTs to reducing both information asymmetry and the risk of MFI products, and to improving MFI programs by limiting the impact of market imperfections (i.e. information costs).

The chapter is organized as follows. The background section briefly describes the economic and social advantages of microfinance. In the third section we present the contribution of ICTs to the microfinance industry on three levels: work efficiency, risk management and customer relationship management, leading to the formulation of testable research hypotheses. Then, we present an empirical investigation to test hypotheses based on both qualitative and quantitative studies. We also discuss our results regarding the implications of ICT use in the microfinance sector. Future avenues for research are presented in section 4 and the concluding remarks are summarized in section 5.

BACKGROUND

MFI are playing an important role both on economic and social sides. However, given the specificities of their clients characterised by poverty and social exclusion, it is crucial for MFI to ensure their performance. In this regard, ICT have an important contribution on several aspects. In this section, we first present MFI contribution to social and economic development before moving to explain to which extent ICT can enhance MFI efficiency, risk management and CRM.

MFI products are specific financial products and services such as microcredit, savings and microinsurance that are designed to provide financial support for the poorest populations (Rhyne, 1998; Robinson, 2001). These products address two specific types of clients. The first beneficiaries are generally families suffering from poverty and inequality that are often subject to credit rationing and redlining by traditional banks and financial institutions (Stiglitz and Weiss, 1981). The second type of public is investors and tradesmen who aim to create and develop productive and commercial activities. MFI clients are therefore populations which are most vulnerable to financial exclusion, generally without access to bank services, and living in developing and emerging countries: low-income households, the self-employed, small farmers, shopkeepers, service providers, craftsmen, street vendors, and home-based entrepreneurs (CGAP, 2006).[6]

Several previous studies have focused on microfinance products and examined the links between the microfinance industry and social challenges, mainly poverty and inequality. As demonstrated by Levine and Easterly (1997), poorer individuals on low incomes in developed countries are characterized by interest group polarization that leads to rent-seeking behaviors and reduces economic growth. For firms, as for individuals, better developed financial systems speed up growth and alleviate poverty; it has been established that financial development dispropor-

tionately helps the poor by improving their income faster than average per capita GDP growth (Beck *et al.* 2007). In this sense, microfinance improves – even basically – financial systems and increases both efficiency and equity by reducing income inequality (Townsend and Ueda, 2006). To this end, microfinance tries first to combat financial exclusion by giving the poorest populations and minorities access to conventional financial intermediation. According to Robinson (2001), 25% of the population are overbanked while 75% of the population are unbanked, suggesting a lack of access to financial services and the need for microcredit for micro and small businesses. In a global context, populations from developing countries are subject to a lack of consideration by banks, while those from developed countries are overbanked.

Therefore, microfinance products and informal financial services have both economic and social aims and aspects. From an economic point of view, MFIs offer financial services that can help to finance micro-projects and help micro-entrepreneurs to develop profitable activities. This in turns increases liquidity in the market and tends to stimulate investment and economic activity. In addition, by stimulating household consumption via MFI programs, we can also expect to see a positive link between the microfinance industry and the economic environment, even though such links are sometimes marginal because of the disequilibrium between the MFI client's needs and MFI program opportunities.

More interestingly, MFIs also offer a significant social service as they enable some social classes and families to increase their incomes, making many households better off. But can microfinance really reduce poverty? This question is the subject of lively debate in the literature and authors are far from unanimous about the effects of microcredit and the causality relationship between microfinance and economic and social development. Hashemi (1997) and Zaman (1999), for instance, show evidence of a significant and positive impact of microcredit. For these authors, MFI experiences have shown that microcredit has improved its customers' standard of living and reduced poverty and inequality. However, Hulme and Mosley (1996) consider that microcredit is too limited and short-lived to reduce poverty. More recently, Daley-Harris *et al.* (2007) suggested that microfinance will not resolve global poverty and that MFI programs alone cannot produce the empowerment needed. They suggest that microfinance may reduce poverty but that it is not able to resolve it. Thus, they argue that MFI programs can help some people to smooth out cash flow but not much more. They believe that small and medium-sized businesses need effective lending that will lead to job creation opportunities rather than micro-businesses in the informal sector.

Overall, it seems that although MFIs have recently considerably extended their reach, their missions have become harder, requiring improvements to their services. Indeed, MFIs still suffer from certain limitations and are exposed to numerous risks mainly associated with the increase in poverty and disparity and a rise in the frequency of microcredit repayment defaulting. In Morocco, for example, the unpaid rate of microcredit actually increased from 2% to 5%. This rate is still less than that of banks (12%), but is nonetheless considered as high and may be explained by the excess of indebtedness, insolvency, decrease in repayments, etc.

Despite the crucial role of MFIs in reducing poverty rates and social exclusion, they face serious challenges in their attempt to access larger population (Gupta, 2002; Hishigsuren, 2006). Indeed geographical dispersion of the population together with low density populations in rural areas, make it hard for MFIs to reach new clients and to present their programs. High transaction costs inhibit MFIs from establishing physical bank branches in rural regions. "*Recently, ICTs have emerged as a powerful tool to reduce operating costs, making it viable for financial institutions*

to expand into rural and low income areas" (Hishigsuren, 2006: p. 1).

MFI PROGRAMS USING ICTS

ICT features provide both MFIs and their clients with potential access to MFI programs in less time and with reduced operating costs. They enable financial institutions not only to enhance their performance but also to reach larger number of clients and to improve services. ICTs cover a large number of applications, enabling MFIs to perform different operations ranging from simple account opening to credit risk assessment.

Hishigsuren (2006) summed up ICT applications and their functions in microfinance operations in Table 1.

A. ICT Contributions to the Microfinance Industry

There has been some evidence of significant linkage between microfinance and ICTs over the last decade. MFI performance is quantitatively and qualitatively improved through ICTs. MFI services are more interactive, personalized, transparent, searchable and controllable, incorporating regulatory reporting, reliable analysis and consequently better corporate governance. ICT innovations are expected to improve the efficiency of microfinance operations and expand outreach by reducing transaction costs and bringing services closer to their clients (Hishigsuren, 2006).

Firstly, we believe that ICTs can improve MFI efficiency in terms of cost, security and operations, while promoting financial inclusion and transferring technology to financial services. Indeed, one of the factors inhibiting the establishment of MFIs is their transaction costs. The volume of business in some regions cannot support the cost of a bank branch. Low density populations and poor infrastructure discourage financial institutions from creating physical agencies. Operation costs are

Table 1. ICT applications in microfinance operations (Hishigsuren, 2006)

Functions	PDA/ Pal mPilot	Cards (magnetic and smart cards)	Phone Banking/ Internet Banking	ATM/ POS	MIS	Credit Scoring
Entering loan aplicaiotn data	■					
Recording payment transaction (e.g. passbook function	■	■	■			
Disbursing cash				■		
Money transfer between accounts			■	■		
Taking deposits				■		
Checking account balance/other inquiries			■	■		
Managing loan portfolio/other financial analysis					■	
Credit risk assessment						■

not covered by business profit and this may be harmful to the institution's overall performance. Using ICTs enables MFIs to cut down on these costs and to work with poor borrowers over a large area. Consequently, MFIs do not need to send their staff out for every new transaction. They only have to create a new client file through the Internet or by smart card, PDA, etc.

Gupta (2002) describes a pilot project conducted in an Indian bank that consists of a smart card delivered to new borrowers (with some conditions). According to the author, this technology enables the bank to register 70 new borrowers per month, which is three time higher than the existing lending channel, and at a third of the cost of the old channel. In the Philippines, the introduction of basic banking software products has enabled the administrative costs of rural bank operations to be cut by 60% (Kizito, 2007).

At the same time, technological applications enable MFIs to increase their efficiency by reducing operation times. They allow the staff to collect and process information more rapidly, thus increasing their productivity. Information management through ICTs is expected to help MFIs to collect more accurate information for more effective decision-making about strategic objectives and priorities, and then to monitor the performance.

This led us to formulate the first hypothesis regarding the impact of ICTs on MFI efficiency:

H1: *ICT use in MFI operations positively influences their efficiency.*

In addition to financial indicators, MFI performance is measured through its outreach evaluated by coverage of targeted households and the extent of services they receive (Arsyad, 2005). The institutional outreach is influenced by the quality of the relations with the clients and the effort made to satisfy them. In this regard, ICTs play an important role in facilitating and enhancing customer relationship management (CRM) and they give the clients better access to MFI services. Thanks to the Internet, correspondent banking and mobile banking, customers can reach MFI products more easily wherever they are. The quote below clearly illustrates this. *"Gangamma desperately needed a $10 loan to buy grocery items. She could not hope to get it from the commercial bank located in the village as no banks gave loans for less than $100. [...] She was very happy when she came to know about the Sudama project by BASIX in her* *village. Not only was the interest rate low but it was also easy to get the loan with dignity. It was made possible using BASIXPOT; a computer-based transaction-recording system introduced by BASIX in February 2002"* (Gupta, 2002: p. 2).

In addition, with ICTs it is possible to record transactions in distant areas and to transfer them easily to a central server (Mehta and Kalra, 2006). ICTs help MFIs to collect useful information for customer segmentation and decision making, and to develop data mining approaches for predictive modelling purposes. MFI managers can then develop specific commercial strategies to identify a client segment (Raihan, 2001).

Concerning communication services, ICTs can be used to reach new clients through advertising. Email can be used to facilitate communication with customers about movements and transactions in their accounts, information about new products, etc. (Kizito, 2007).

We can thus formulate the following hypothesis:

H2: *ICT use in MFI programs improves customer relationship management.*

The last performance factor analysed in this chapter concerns the contribution of ICTs to risk management. Cicchirillo (2008) posits that ICTs are very useful for MFIs as they enable them to assess the risk associated with microcredit more accurately. For example, customer information systems provide all the data regarding their profiles, their account movements, if they have past unpaid loans, etc. ICTs also enable MFI staff to

memorise all clients' past transactions and to draw up forecasts about the risks associated with their future behaviours. In this regard, we can say that ICTs help MFI managers to quantify credit risk and then to formulate appropriate action to avoid unpaid loans and to better manage "risky clients" (Brown, 2006; Peelen, 2006). Moreover, ICT use can also result in a significant reduction in risk related to microfinance products through further diversification of portfolio services (Mehta and Kalra, 2006).

The following hypothesis arises from these observations:

H3: *ICT use in MFI programs enhances risk management.*

The previous observations enabled us to draw up our research model as shown in Figure 1.

To summarise our development so far, ICT use impacts positively and significantly on MFIs because it allows them to deal with more and larger customers and to manage an increasing amount of data. Thanks to ICTs, MFI staff can conceptualize, develop, diversify and exploit their projects better, which in turn helps to reduce running costs. ICTs provide better credit information services, product innovation and scales of cost reduction. They lead to increased productivity and better access, choice and quality of services. Secondly, they ensure process standardization, lower costs and reduced service delivery time thanks to the online transaction processing and electronic platform.

Figure 1. Research model

While ICTs undoubtedly contribute to MFI performance, the effects may not be fully understood since they depend on many factors such as the level of access to ICTs, their cost, and the skills of MFI human capital. The inefficiency of e-microfinance often appears to be due to low levels of awareness (Cicchirillo, 2008; Sogala, 2008). In addition, not all MFIs or their customers are equipped with appropriate or even basic technologies for several reasons such as cost, computer illiteracy, available technology, etc.

Research Methodology

As discussed in the second section, checking the effectiveness of MFIs with ICTs could help MFI managers to think about ICT use in their work in order to enhance their performance. Thus, testing the contribution of ICTs with regard to the risks associated with MFI programs and customer relationships may help them to investigate possible ways of improving customer management and evaluate default probability and the rate of unpaid loans using ICTs.

Therefore, to test our research hypothesis, we conducted an empirical investigation based on both qualitative and quantitative studies. The former incorporated interviews with professionals from microfinance institutions in France. The latter used a large survey administered to professionals in the field in emerging countries. In this section, we present the details of these two studies and their contribution to achieving our aims.

Given the exploratory nature of our work, on the one hand, and the limited amount of research on the topic on the other, we chose to start the field investigation with a qualitative study, conducting 10 interviews with microfinance professionals from French institutions. To this end, we prepared a three-part interview guide. In the first part, the interviewees were asked general questions about the way their institutions function, the number of microcredits granted per year, the interest rates charged, customer profiles, etc. In the second

part, we investigated the advantages and risks related to microcredit and their possible future evolutions. In the third part, the interviewees were asked about the contribution of ICTs to enhancing the performance of microfinance institutions. All the questions were open-ended to give the interviewees greater freedom to provide more complete answers. The interviews lasted about one hour and all were recorded and transcribed in accordance with the recommendations made by Miles and Huberman (1994) to facilitate analyses. The results of this step will be discussed later.

The second step in the empirical study consisted of a survey based on a research questionnaire in three parts. The first part included questions about economic and social aspects of microfinance products such as their role in reducing poverty and social inequality. The second part focused on ICT use and its impact on microfinance institutions. Respondent were asked about the frequency of ICT use, factors influencing investment in ICTs, and the contribution of ICTs to efficiency at work, risk management and customer relationship management. In the third part, the questions were designed to provide socio-demographic information about respondents such as their gender, age, qualifications or degrees, etc. The survey included 47 items, measured on a 5-point Likert scale ranging from: ①-"I completely disagree" to ⑤-"I completely agree."[7] The questionnaire was administered in both French and English as our sample included both French and English-speaking individuals.

Data for the second step came from the Microfinance Information Exchange (MIX), a global microfinance information platform which provides news about thousands of MFIs in both developed and developing countries around the world. Created in 2002 under the supervision of the United Nations, the MIX offers standardized information on all types of MFIs to improve and stimulate microfinance performance and transparency. We focused on MFIs located in Africa and the Middle-East, two regions where poverty is high, microcredit is expanding and where ICTs are promoted to enhance trade and facilitate economic growth in financial services, in particular. As mentioned in the first appendix, we selected 347 MFIs from 43 different countries and we extracted demographic and financial data from the MIX as well as contact person details (contact name, position, direct phone and e-mail) to send our questionnaire. With regard to our sample, described in the first appendix, over 35% of our panel was composed of non-profit MFIs while 25% were non-bank financial institutions and 27% cooperative unions. Banks only represented 6% of our observations.

In the second appendix, we summarize the demographic and financial variables concerning our panel. We noted that, as social organizations, MFIs report negative returns for assets and equity as well as for profit margin. Gutiérrez-Nieto, Serrano-Cinca and Mar Molinero (2007) examined the nature of efficiency in microfinance institutions. This is particularly interesting in the case of social financial institutions driven by factors other than profit alone. Beyond simple financial ratios and using data envelopment analyses, the authors found that MFI efficiency is mainly guided by country-specific aspects and status.

Following this procedure, a total of 450 questionnaires were administered by e-mail. The questionnaire was web-based, using SPHINX software, and respondents had to fill it in and submit their answers through a URL link. After several trials, the number of surveys collected reached 81 leading to a response rate of 18%. One questionnaire was dropped as it was incomplete. The data collected from the survey was analyzed using SPSS 11.5 software. To test our research hypotheses, we conducted factor analyses, reliability and correlation analyses. The following section presents the details of both the qualitative and quantitative data analyses together with the results.

Analyses and Results

For the qualitative study, content analyses were conducted via interviews that achieved two purposes. On the one hand, data collected through the interviews helped us to apprehend the characteristics of microfinance institutions and to understand how they function and the type of customer they deal with. The interviewees pointed to the relevance of the products their institutions provide to individuals with limited revenues and how this can help them to deal with problems of poverty and social exclusion. In addition, they highlighted how ICTs enhance their performance by reducing their costs and the time dedicated to examining customers' requests, and developing better customer relationships and risk management.

The interviews also enabled us to prepare the second part of the empirical study as the answers helped us to determine our sample for the survey and to design the study questionnaire. The interviews indicated that microfinance products are most relevant in the context of developing and emerging countries. We therefore addressed our questionnaire to professionals in emerging countries in Africa and Asia such as Morocco, Tunisia, Egypt, Zimbabwe, Yemen, India, etc. The structure and the questions formulated in the survey were also inspired by the interviews. Thus, the qualitative steps helped us to prepare the tools we used in the quantitative study.

The quantitative analyses were conducted in three steps. First, descriptive statistics were used to examine the answers to the first part of the survey (social and economic contribution of microfinance products). Second, factor analyses were developed to assess the dimensionality and reliability of the variables introduced in the second part of the survey which included work efficiency, risk and customer relationship management. Finally, means comparison through ANOVA were applied to test our research hypothesis.

A. Descriptive Statistics

Based on means and frequency of answers, several findings should be noted. They concern the most appropriate population for microfinance products, the economic and social role of these products, and ICT use in microfinance institutions.

Firstly, our results show that microcredit is most suitable for women (m=3.56, σ=0.12), adults (m=3.46, σ=0.12) with a professional activity (m=3.46, σ=0.13), and developing a personal project (m=3.24, σ=0.12). The respondents disagreed about the appropriateness of microfinance products for men (m=2.45, σ=0.11), young or old people (respectively m=2.56, σ=0.11; m=2.26, σ=0.09) without any professional activity (m=2.69, σ=0.13), and for professional projects (m=2.9, σ=0.14).

Concerning the social and the economic role of microfinance products, the respondents in our sample agreed that these products contribute significantly to reducing poverty and inequality between social categories. The mean of answers and standard deviation are respectively (m=3.95, σ=0.10; m=3.69, σ=0.11). These results are not surprising given the initial purpose behind microfinance products. Indeed microcredit and microinsurance products are designed for people who have no access to other financial institutions (such as banks) to obtain loans and no favorable response to their applications. These people belong to low and middle income groups who use microcredit to develop projects that enhance their earnings and their social position.

Finally, a surprising result from the survey concerns ICT use in microfinance institutions. Indeed, the respondents said they believed that ICTs are generally well used in the microfinance sector (m=2.44, σ=0.08), but that they are poorly equipped and do not use ICTs frequently in their institutions since statistics for ICT availability and frequency of use are respectively (m=1.32, σ=0.06) and (m=1.14, σ=0.04). This result confirms our assumption regarding the contribution of ICTs to performance in microfinance institutions. Professionals in this domain do not appear to be convinced of the advantages of ICTs with respect to their institutions' operations, even though they are well equipped and generally use them in their everyday tasks. This result may be explained by a predominant idea that costs related to ICT investments are high and require specific skills. The answers also confirm this observation as statistics concerning links between ICT use and costs, skills, and availability respectively are (m=3.63, σ=0.11), (m=3.80, σ=0.10), and (m=3.66, σ=0.11).

B. Factor Analyses

The dimensionality of the scales related to the contribution of ICTs to work efficiency, risk management, and customer relationship management was assessed through an analysis of the principal components (APC) using Varimax rotation. In this stage, two items were dropped out as they have low factorial contributions. The first item is related to the contribution of ICTs to work efficacy and is formulated as follows: "*ICT use in work activities enables time reduction.*" Its factorial contribution is 0.4. The second item is related to the customer relationship management dimension and is formulated as follows: "*ICT use in work activities promotes accelerated commercialization of microfinance products.*" Its factorial contribution is 0.51. The three variables of work efficiency, risk management, and customer relationship management are unidimensional and account respectively for 75%, 56%, and 48% of the total variance explained.

The reliability and internal coherence of items constituting a single dimension were assessed through Cronbach's alpha coefficient. For work efficiency α = 0.82, for risk management α = 0.80, and for customer relationship management α = 0.73. These values are satisfactory according to Hair *et al.* (1998). The factor analyses' results are summarized in Table 2.

Table 2. Factor analysis results

Items	Total extracted variance	Factorial contribution	Cronbach Alpha
Work efficiency: - ICT use in work activities has no effect on deadlines. - ICT use in work activities promotes greater effectiveness. - ICT use in work activities has no effect on work effectiveness.	75%	0.89 0.78 0.88	0.82
Risk management: - ICT use in work activities enhances information about clients' situations and profiles. - ICT use in work activities has no effect on the degree of clients' knowledge and associated risks. - ICT use in work activities significantly reduces risk of unpaid loans. - ICT use in work activities enables risk to be centralized to protect clients and microfinance institutions. - ICT use in work activities enables risk to be limited for microfinance products and protection of clients and microfinance institutions.	56%	0.81 0.75 0.61 0.85 0.64	0.80
Customer relationship management: - ICT use in work activities enables costs related to client applications to be reduced. - ICT use in work activities reduces the number of clients' files. - ICT use in work activities reduces the time needed to seek information about clients. - ICT use in work activities enables clients to be contacted quickly.	48%	0.73 0.83 0.78 0.63	0.73

C. ANOVA Analyses

The relations between ICT use and its effects on microfinance institutions' performance were tested via an ANOVA analysis. ANOVA was run using ICT use as an independent variable and work efficiency, risk management, and customer relationship management respectively as dependent variables. ICT use appeared to be a strong predictor of work efficiency and customer relationship management ($F=25.9$, $\rho=0.000$; and $F=5.78$, $\rho=0.01$ respectively). However, no significant links were found between risk management and ICTs ($F=1.32$, $\rho=0.26$). These results enable us to validate H1 and H2. However, H3 is rejected.

These findings may be explained in several ways. Microfinance professionals have a positive perception of the role played by ICTs to enhance work efficacy by reducing time on work activities. They also believe that ICTs enable them to reduce the time dedicated to examining customers' files and help them to answer their requests quickly. This is achieved through quick and easy access to information about work and customers, which is collected and stored using technological tools. ICTs also provide features that facilitate data analyses and reduce the processing of requests and answers. They also considerably reduce distance to reach rural zones without the need for a physical agency.

Concerning the absence of a significant relationship between ICT use and risk management, this result may be explained by the characteristics of microfinance products. Indeed, microcredit and microinsurance have an inherently risky nature as they address individuals with low or no income and who are often insolvent. In this regard, ICTs cannot help MFIs to reduce risk as they are not able to change customers' profiles or provide them with guarantees to reduce the possibility of insolvent clients. For this reason, individuals in our sample perceive no relationship between ICT use and a reduction in the risk associated with microfinance products. However this result needs to be confirmed by other studies in other contexts.

These results enable us to formulate some managerial implications regarding ICT use in MFI programs. Information systems and technologies appear to play an important role in facilitating the running of MFIs and enhancing their performance. Managers need to ensure the availability of such tools in their institutions. They also need to provide staff with training to enable them to fully and effectively use ICTs. On the other hand, MFIs have to understand that most borrowers are ICT illiterate and lack access to ICTs. They therefore need to provide them with user-friendly technologies.

FUTURE RESEARCH DIRECTIONS

Despite the importance of the topic of microfinance and its social and economic impact, research in the field is limited both theoretically and empirically. Our paper attempted to contribute to the microfinance literature by studying possible links between ICT use and MFI performance. Although our results provide some interesting insights, some limitations need to be noted and addressed in future work.

In terms of theory, we were interested in the effects of ICTs on three performance variables, namely, work efficiency, risk management and customer relationship management. Although these variables include the most important issues in MFI operations, other variables may also play an important role in MFI performance and may be positively influenced by ICT implementation. Such variables may concern the global performance of MFIs, enhancement of their products, how they can be integrated as part of other financial products in traditional financial institutions, etc.

In addition, we analyzed the effects of all ICTs in general without specifying a single type. In future extensions, it would be interesting to focus on just one type of ICT, such as Internet or ERP, and to study its effects on MFI performance.

Another direction that could be explored concerns the barriers that hinder ICT implementation and use in MFIs. In this regard, we could investigate the effects of the characteristics of emerging financial markets with respect to ICTs such as poor infrastructures, inadequate regulations, low level of education and very local development based on personal relationships. These factors may considerably slow down ICT development and use in MFIs and hence reduce their performance.

In methodological terms, our empirical study may be enhanced on two levels. On the one hand, our sample comprised 81 individuals. Although this is a satisfying number for statistical purposes, future work should extend the sample in order to enhance the results and reach a larger population. In addition, our respondents were all MFI professionals. To reduce the possible bias arising from this limitation, the population needs to be more diversified, including other partners in MFI relationships such as customers and other financial institutions.

At the same time, the testing of hypotheses could be enhanced by using structural equation modeling. This method may provide more parsimonious results concerning ICT effects on MFI work efficiency, customer relationship management and risk management and the relative importance of each factor in determining MFI performance.

All the proposed extensions aim to enhance our understanding of the way microfinance works and the factors that influence MFIs and enhance their performance. They also constitute promising directions for developing the literature on microfinance and its social and economic effects.

CONCLUSION

This paper focuses on the study of microfinance programs with ICTs. After investigating the social and economic purposes of MFI services, we tested how ICTs impact on the effectiveness of microfinance and improve MFI services. In addition to the economic and social roles of MFIs suggested by our interviewees, our findings show further evidence of a significant reduction in time and information asymmetry for MFIs using ICTs. IMF staff argue that they can get faster access to customer files, obtain information more easily, and rapidly provide answers to clients' requests and demands using ICTs.

In addition, we identified a significant, positive and increasing impact of ICTs on the management of MFI customers since using sophisticated tools allows MFI staff not only to improve their work and the management of microfinance clients, but also to provide support in studying and developing their projects, defining the terms and conditions of microcredit repayment, and achieving their objectives. However, our study also suggested that the risks associated with microfinance products appear to remain the same even with ICTs. This, together with the topics developed in the previous section, could be explored in more depth and verified in future research, with more precise definition of what risk management implies for MFIs.

REFERENCES

Arsyad, L. (2005). An assessment of microfinance institution performance: The importance of the institutional environment. *Gadjah Mada International Journal of Business*, 7(3), 391–427.

Beck, T., & Demirguc-Kunt, A. & Peria. M. (2007). Banking Services for everyone? Barriers to bank acess and use around the world. *World Bank Policy Research*, Working Paper n° 4079.

Brown, S. (2006). *Customer Relationship Management*. Toronto, Canada: John Wiley & Sons.

CGAP. (2006). *Good Practice Guidelines for Funders of Microfinance*. CGAP.

Daley-Harris, S., Pollin, P., & Montgomery, F. (2007). *Debate on Microcredit*. Washington, DC: Foreign Policy in Focus.

Gupta, S. K. (2002). Information and Communication Technology (ICT) plus Finance Model for Rural Poor. *Working paper*.

Gutiérrez-Nieto, B., Serrano-Cinca, C., & MarMolinero, C. (2007). Microfinance Institutions and Efficiency. *Omega*, 35(2), 131–142. doi:10.1016/j.omega.2005.04.001

Hashemi, S. (1997). Those Left Behind: A Note on Targeting the Hardcore Poor. In Wood, G. D., & Sharif, I. A. (Eds.), *Who Needs Credit: Poverty and Finance in Bangladesh* (pp. 249–257). London: Zed Books.

Hishigsuren, G. (2006). *Information and Communication Technology and Microfinance: Options for Mongolia. Discussion paper n°42.* ADB Institute.

Hulme, H., & Mosley, P. (1996). *Finance Against Poverty (Vol. 1)*. London: Routledge.

Kizito, B. J. (2007). Practices of managing and using ICT services by village banks in Uganda. *Working paper, Kampala International University*.

Labie, M. (2001). Corporate Governance in Microfinance Organizations: a Long and Winding Road. *Management Decision*, 39(4), 296–301. doi:10.1108/00251740110391466

Levine, R., & Easterly, W. (1997). Africa's Growth Tragedy: Policies and Ethnic Divisions. *The Quarterly Journal of Economics*, 113(4), 1203–1250.

Mehta, S., & Kalra, M. (2006). Information and Communication Technologies: A bridge for social equity and sustainable development in India. *The International Information & Library Review*, 38, 147–160. doi:10.1016/j.iilr.2006.06.008

Miles, M. B., & Huberman, A. M. (1994). *Qualitative data analysis* (2nd ed.). Thousand Oaks, CA: Sage.

Morduch, J. (1999). The Microfinance Promise. *Journal of Economic Literature*, 37(4), 1569–1614.

Morduch, J. (2000). The Microfinance Schism. *World Development*, *28*(4), 617–629. doi:10.1016/ S0305-750X(99)00151-5

Peelen, E. (2006). *Customer Relationship Management*. Bruxelles, Benelux: Pearson Education.

Raihan, A. (2001). The State of E-Finance in developing Countries: Bangladesh perspective". Expert Group Meeting on "Improving Competitiveness of SMEs in Developing Countries: Role of Finance, including E-finance to Enhance Enterprise Development," Geneva, 22-24 October, 2001.

Rhyne, E. (1998). The Yin and Yang of Microfinance: Reaching the Poor and Sustainability. *MicroBanking Bulletin*, *2*(July), 6–9.

Robinson, M. S. (2001). *The Microfinance Revolution: Sustainable Finance for the Poor*. Washington: The World Bank.

Sriram, M. S. (2005). Information asymmetry and trust: A framework for studying microfinance in India. *Vikapla*, *30*(4), 77–85.

Stiglitz, J., & Weiss, A. (1981). Credit rationing in markets with imperfect information. *The American Economic Review*, *71*, 93–410.

Townsend, R. M., & Ueda, K. (2006). Financial Deepening, Inequality, and Growth: a Model-based Quantitative Evaluation. *The Review of Economic Studies*, *73*(1), 251–293. doi:10.1111/ j.1467-937X.2006.00376.x

Zaman, H. (1999). Assessing the poverty and vulnerability impact of microcredit in Bangladesh a case study of BRAC. *Background paper for the WDR 2000/2001*. Banque mondiale, Washington.

ADDITIONAL READING

CGAP. (2003). *Guiding principles on regulation and supervision of microfinance*. CGAP.

CGAP. (2004). *Key Principles of Microfinance*. CGAP.

Christen, R. P., & Rosenberg, R. (2000). The Rush to Regulate: Legal Frameworks for Microfinance. *Occasional Paper, vol. 14*. Washington, D.C.: CGAP.

Cull, R., Demirguc-Kunt, A., & Morduch, J. (2007). Financial Performance and Outreach: a Global Analysis of Leading Microbanks. *The Economic Journal*, *117*(517), 107–133. doi:10.1111/j.1468-0297.2007.02017.x

Demirguc-Kunt, A., & Maksimovic, V. (1996). Financial Constraints, Uses of Funds, and Firm Growth: An International Comparison. *The World Bank Policy Research Working Paper Series 1671*.

Hansmann, H. (1996). *The Ownership of Enterprise*. Cambridge, MA: The Belknap Press of Harvard University Press.

Hartarska, V. (2005). Governance and Performance of Microfinance Institutions in Central and Eastern Europe and the Newly Independent States. *World Development*, *33*(10), 1627–1643. doi:10.1016/j.worlddev.2005.06.001

Isern, J., Ritchie, A., Crenn, T., & Brown, M. (2003). *Review of Commercial Banks and Other Formal Financial Institutions Participation in Microfinance*. Washington, D.C.: CGAP.

Jansson, T., Rosales, R., & Westley, G. (2004). *Principles and Practices for Regulating and Supervising Microfinance*. Washington: Inter-American Development Bank.

Ledgerwood, J., & White, V. (2006). *Transforming Microfinance Institutions*. Washington, DC: The World Bank and The MicroFinance Network.

Mersland, R. (2007). Cost of Ownership in Microfinance Organizations. *University of Agder Working Paper Series*.

Mersland, R., & Strøm, R.Ø. (2009 forthcoming). Performance and Corporate Governance in Microfinance Institutions. *Journal of Banking and Finance*.

White, V., & Campion, A. (2002). Transformation: Journey from NGO to Regulated MFI. In D. Drake & E. Rhyne (Ed.), *The Commercialization of Microfinance* (pp. 22-45). Bloomfield: Kumarian Press.

ENDNOTES

[1] Muhammad Yunus and Grameen Bank were awarded the Nobel Prize in 2006 for their work in developing economic and social development.

[2] 97% of clients are women.

[3] In Morocco, for example, several microfinance institutions have been developed and four microfinance associations rank in the top 100 of global microfinance associations.

[4] According to the Grameen Bank, about 50% of microcredit borrowers in Bangladesh (50 million people) no longer suffer from poverty (all their children ago to school; the family members eat 3 meals a day, have sanitary facilities and access to drinking water) thanks to these loans. More importantly, the repayment rate exceeded 98.35% in 2007.

[5] We may define risk management as the reduction of information asymmetry between actors in order to limit the default probability

[6] According to Mohapatra (2008), about 43% of indebted farmers in India are excluded from formal financial services.

[7] Full possible answers are: ①I completely disagree, ②I disagree, ③Indifferent, ④I agree, ⑤I completely agree.

APPENDIX A

Composition of Data by MFIs Country and Type

MFIs Country	Number of MFIs	Percent	MFIs Type	Number of MFIs	Percent
Angola	2	0.58	Bank	21	6.05
Benin	19	5.48	Cooperative/credit union	94	27.09
Burkina Faso	4	1.15	Non-bank financial institution	89	25.65
Burundi	3	0.86	Non-profit organization	124	35.73
Cameroon	16	4.61	Other	16	4.61
Central African Republic	1	0.29	Rural bank	3	0.86
Chad	2	0.58	**Total**	**347**	**100**
Congo	15	4.32			
Egypt	13	3.75			
Ethiopia	16	4.61			
Gabon	1	0.29			
Gambia	1	0.29			
Ghana	14	4.03			
Guinea	8	2.31			
Iraq	2	0.58			
Ivory Coast	11	3.17			
Jordan	7	2.02			
Kenya	18	5.19			
Lebanon	3	0.86			
Liberia	1	0.29			
Madagascar	12	3.46			
Malawi	9	2.59			
Mali	14	4.03			
Morocco	10	2.88			
Mozambique	8	2.31			
Namibia	1	0.29			
Niger	5	1.44			
Nigeria	13	3.75			
Palestine	7	2.02			
Rwanda	7	2.02			
Senegal	17	4.90			
Sierra Leone	7	2.02			
South Africa	14	4.03			
Sudan	2	0.58			
Swaziland	2	0.58			
Syria	1	0.29			

continues on following page

Appendix A. continued

MFIs Country	Number of MFIs	Percent		MFIs Type	Number of MFIs	Percent
Tanzania	11	3.17				
Togo	14	4.03				
Tunisia	1	0.29				
Uganda	22	6.34				
Yemen	5	1.44				
Zambia	5	1.44				
Zimbabwe	3	0.86				
Total	**347**	**100**				

APPENDIX B

MFIs Demographic and Financial Variables

Variables	Mean	Median	Min.	Max.
Firm age	10	9	1	63
Number of personnel	245	99	1	2 800
Number of active borrowers	35 847	11 102	2	228 000
Average loan per borrower ($)	873	318	11	22 252
% of female borrowers	62	58	9	100
Number of savers	965	579	0	7 830
Average savings per saver ($)	256	184	0	5 991
Gross loan portfolio ($) Total assets ($)	12 561 511 17 162 710	8 157 125 11 321 025	239 239	53 900 895 64 189 455
Savings ($)	105 835	48 325	0	4 998 295
Total equity ($)	799 233	512 975	179	40 314 619
Debt/equity ratio (%)	11.8	5.4	7	144
Return on assets (%)	- 1.3	- 0.5	- 22.3	47
Return on equity (%) Profit margin (%) Loan loss reserve ratio (%)	- 3.7 - 20.4 2.4	- 1.4 - 7.5 1.8	- 35 - 184 0.1	19.8 70 6.4

Section 3
Online Financing for Microfinance

Introduction

Arvind Ashta

Burgundy School of Business (Groupe ESC Dijon-Bourgogne), France

Although innovative group and community lending schemes, among others, have helped overcome information symmetry and reduced the risk of lending to poor people, the cost of extending this credit is very high, with rates as high as 100% per annum creating controversies. The average annual interest rates are around 28%. The main reason for these high interest rates is the small size of the transaction. Therefore the fixed transaction costs are a high proportion of the interest rates. One possible solution to the reduction of interest rates would be the use of technology in reaching out to the poor. The book has already discussed two such technologies, namely dedicated and, perhaps, shared information systems and mobile telephone based solutions.

At the same time, it is estimated that the existing funding to this sector is about $ 5 billion while the needs are $ 250 billion. There is also a movement to wean the movement away from donors to commercial or social private investors. The question is how to bridge this gap and get more funds by getting retail investors to lend to this sector. This role is being attempted by web-based online lenders. This section of the book is addressing this section of the supply chain of online lending: how to raise funding for microfinance directly through individuals and how to create online networks which can reduce the cost of searching and finding an appropriate institutional partner.

The field of online lending is relatively new and started in 2005, after the failure of Egg, an experiment in online banking which was a bit ahead of its time. The typical supply chain for commercial online lending (examples: Zopa, Prosper, Lending Club) is that of a retail lender sending money to a website operator who then lends it to a borrower. This model doesn't work for the microfinance sector because the poor borrower in a poor country does not have a computer. Therefore the supply chain of online microcredit has another intermediary, the Microfinance Institution in the poor country who takes the money from the online operator (examples Kiva, Babyloan) and gives it to the borrower. Essentially, the website aggregator then funds a Microfinance Institution. New operators are entering to fill in gaps. For example, government regulations do not permit Kiva or Babyloan to enter India and we have seen Rang De and DhanaX starting operations there. Similalry, Wokai has entered to transfer donor funds from US citizens to Chinese microfinance agents and even more recently United Prosperity has entered to allow rich people to offer guarantees to banks on the behalf of poor borrowers, enabling banks to finance the related MFI to a greater extent.

The marketing trends of this sector of peer-to-peer microlending websites have been left largely unexplored during its rise to recognition. In Chapter 11, Djamchid Assadi and Meredith Hudson Claspill look at the field of online lending websites and indicate the different marketing strategies being adopted by the different online lending operators. Based on a sample of nine popular social lending sites, this exploratory chapter uses observational research methods to analyze the uncontrollable and controllable marketing elements of online social lending websites in order to better understand its present and future tendencies. It is hoped that a more comprehensive understanding based on similarities and differences of the marketing movement within this industry will be of benefit to students as well as practitioners who want to work in this field or to enter with new unmet needs.

In Chapter 12, Arvind Ashta and Djamchid Assadi then investigate whether social technologies of web 2.0 are being harnessed appropriately by these online lending websites to increase outreach and reduce financing costs for MFIs. Peer to Peer transactions and Web 2.0 have two things in common. The first common denominator is that both of them are rather newcomers in their respective fields and growing fast. The second is that they are both based on mutual and social exchanges between people instead of intermediary based relationships. The main objective of this chapter was to investigate whether peer to peer online lending transactions are integrated to support a higher level of social interactions and associations with a promise of reducing (transaction) costs through disintermediation and risk reduction. They find that "peer to peer" lending consists of diverse websites of microcredit (Kiva, Wokai, Babyloan), social investing (MicroPlace) as well as small loans at market rates (Prosper, Zopa, Lending Club), and even lending between friends and family members (Virgin Money). The chapter studies the use of web 2.0 technologies (blogs, interactivity between lenders and buyers, peers' reviews and comments, peers communities and chats) in seven such online lending sites. It finds that most of the so called "peer-to-peer" lenders are in fact intermediaries between the peers (lender and borrowers) and there is little direct contact between the peers. One website used none of the web 2.0 tools. None of the websites used all the web 2.0 tools. The impact on transaction costs should therefore be very little as there is neither disintermediation nor risk reduction. A discussion of difficulties in establishing platforms in this field and directions for future research are provided.

Going beyond the immediate subject of microfinance is an innovative online-offline solution provided by EDA CapitalConnect and Daniel Brett and Nikias Stefanakis include this as a case study in chapter 13. Since its inception in July 2008, EDA CapitalConnect (EDACC) has sought to address inefficiencies in the market for funding to social enterprises worldwide. To tackle these challenges, the company has developed an online platform that allows social enterprises and institutional funders to communicate with one another, initiate financial transactions, and analyze market trends. The platform seeks to increase deal flow and transparency in the social enterprise space by facilitating information dissemination and the exchange of funding offers between capital providers and seekers of all sizes. As the platform develops, the challenges of achieving financial sustainability and scale will require EDACC to continue to fine-tune its services to meet the evolving needs of the social enterprise community. EDACC's experience in its nascency suggests that technology providers to microfinance institutions and social enterprises – particularly start up organizations – must pay close attention to the behavior of their target users, and modify their services based upon trends in usage and market perceptions.

Although internet based solutions many not yet be optimally adapted to reaching poor people in developing countries, the potential efficacy of these initiatives will likely increase as the mobile telephone is gradually becoming a hand held computer device. It is likely, therefore, that only the direct interface will change, and people in more developed nations can work on their computers to link directly with the mobile telephones held by people living in the developing world. Given this forecast, the research presented in this section becomes even more relevant to the growth and maturation of the microfinance industry, and the resulting reduction of poverty worldwide.

Chapter 11
Marketing Analysis of Emerging Peer–to–Peer Microlending Websites

Djamchid Assadi
Burgundy School of Business (Groupe ESC Dijon-Bourgogne), France

Meredith Hudson
First United Bank in Durant, Oklahoma, USA

ABSTRACT

The marketing trends of the emerging sector of peer-to-peer microlending websites have been left largely unexplored during its rise to recognition. Based on a sample of nine popular social lending sites, this exploratory chapter uses observational research methods to analyze the uncontrollable and controllable marketing elements of online social lending websites in order to better understand its present and future tendencies. A more comprehensive understanding based on similarities and differences of the marketing movement within this industry will be the end result of this chapter, and therefore, a more reliable prediction of the future it holds.

INTRODUCTION

The sector of microfinance has been widely analyzed since its inception as an entrepreneurial approach to combat poorness. However, studies have been mainly related to the financial, economic, political and even humanitarian aspects of the microfinance, and much less to marketing. This is a considerable shortcoming because with the growth of competition in microfinance marketing becomes inevitable. The above failing has been even more alarming in the expanding field of peer-to-peer lending.

This chapter aims to proceed with a marketing analysis of the peer-to-peer lending on the Internet. The research method will be based on an exploratory method to discover the peculiarities of the juvenile and fast-changing sector of peer-to-peer (P2P) lending, along with a second step of observation to scrutinize the general orientation of the different peer-to-peer websites with regard to marketing mix elements. If citations are not specified, the information originates in the organization's website. The results should illustrate if the online P2P microlending represents

DOI: 10.4018/978-1-61520-993-4.ch011

specific marketing peculiarities in its deployment and development.

The marketing analysis of the websites in our sample will distinguish between two sets of factors: uncontrollable and controllable. We will first present microlending within its historical context, and then explore the uncontrollable and controllable variables which influence the evolution of P2P lending online.

BACKGROUND: FROM MICROFINANCE TO SOCIAL LENDING

To better understand the focus of our research, P2P lending, also known as social lending, it is important to differentiate between *microfinance* and *microcredit*. Microfinance is "the act of providing borrowers with financial services such as savings institutions and insurance policies," while microcredit is "the act of providing a loan" (Aubuchon & Sengupta, 2008). So, microfinance encompasses microcredit, synonymously referred to as *microlending*. P2P lending is an evolutionary tangent from the original idea that signifies lending and borrowing between peers and individuals.

History of Microfinance: From Jobra to the Internet

Microfinance began in underdeveloped countries; then it evolved into a business model in developed nations, and finally emigrated to the Internet to take the specific form of social (P2P) lending. To truly understand the character of social lending, one must first understand its roots.

Starting in the 1970s, programs in Bangladesh, Brazil, and a few other countries extended tiny loans to poor entrepreneurs, mainly, women, for income generating activities. These micro-lending" programs were based on solidarity group lending in which every member of a group guaranteed the repayment of all members. If Nobel winning

Grameen bank is one of the most famous, it was not the only institution with financial programs for the poor.

ACCION International, founded with by a law student, Joseph Blatchford, $90,000 raised from private companies, to address poverty in Latin America's cities, is now one of the premier microfinance organizations in the world, with a network of lending partners that spans Latin America, the United States and Africa. SEWA Bank, (SEWA for Self Employed Women's Association), was registered in 1972 as a trade union in Gujarat (India), with the main objective of improving income, employment and access to social security. In 1973, to address their lack of access to financial services, the members of SEWA decided to found a bank. Since then it has become a viable financial venture for providing banking services to poor, illiterate, self-employed women.

With Grameen Bank. Professor Muhammad Yunus designed an experimental credit programme to serve the poor in Bangladesh in 1976. It spread rapidly to hundreds of villages. In this chapter, the Grameen has been chosen as a background for further analysis because of its fame and the familiarity of the average reader with it.

Mohammed Yunus, Nobel Peace Laureate 2006, initially questioned the vagueness of the term "poverty" when designing the idea of microfinance. Working in Jobra, a city in Bangladesh, Yunus noticed that without providing a distinction between the different levels of poorness, the less poor reap advantages meant for poorest percentage of the population – and those with the least will remain at a disadvantage (Yunus, 2003).

Yunus, for this reason, differentiated levels of poverty in Bangladesh ranging from the absolute poor to the bottom 50 percent of the population. In this method the absolute poor are given the first advantage because of their economic distinction. The microfinance model came as so into existence.

Twenty-seven United States Dollars was all it took for forty-two people in the village of Jobra to get out from the suffocating grips of moneylenders in their area (Yunus, 2003). The Bangladeshi women used this money to buy the raw materials that they needed to perform their various tasks, such as making stools or baskets, and then selling them. In the past these women had needed to take out hefty loans from money-lenders, in which an entire day's work of making and selling their product would not pay off their loan plus interest, nor generate money for food or housing. A few dollars was all it amounted to, and all of a sudden, they were able to survive on their own.

Yunus thought group membership not only creates support and protection but also smoothes out the erratic behavior patterns of individual members, making each borrower more reliable in the process (Yunus, 2003). This prospect of group membership creates trust within each of the borrowers. This is a source of interdependence and motivation for the group. If one person defaults on a loan, the whole group defaults.

Another tactic to help toward the end of poverty was (and is) education. In order to secure a loan at Grameen, the bank that Yunus created for microlending in 1983, the individuals must complete a seven-day training course, and then pass an oral exam. This helps the borrowers understand the loan and repayment process, and therefore fosters confidence. As most of the borrowers in Grameen are women, usually widowed with children to care for and no assets, these loans can mean medicine and education for their children, not to mention a suitable home. The confidence in understanding how money works and how they can make it on their own not only inspires them, but also the next generation – their children.

The microfinance model as proposed by Yunus is demonstrated in Figure 1. Individuals form a group, educate themselves and pass their oral exam, and then the microfinance bank provides the first two members with their loans. When these two loans are repaid, the next two members are granted their loans, and so on. Default on a loan by one member of the group requires the fellow members of the group to pay off the debt, or all

subsequent loans are denied to every member of the group (Armendariz de Aghion, 2005).

Grameen Bank's repayment formula follows this outline (Yunus, 2003):

- Repayment period for loans is one year
- Installations are repaid weekly, to a local frontline bank worker, who travels to the village once a week to meet with groups and collect repayment.
- Repayment begins one week after the loan is given.
- The interest rate is 20 percent.
- Five percent of the loan is put into a "group fund" where members can withdraw money in the event of emergencies and repay the group without interest.
- Repayment amounts to two percent of the loan amount per week for 50 weeks.
- Interest rate payments were two taka a week for every 1000 taka.

After two decades of providing microloans to the poor, Nobel winning Gramen Bank, started offering saving products to its clients in 1998. Just seven years later, Grameen's clients started saving more than they borrowed – around $460 million (Banerjee, 2009).

Figure 1. The original microfinance model

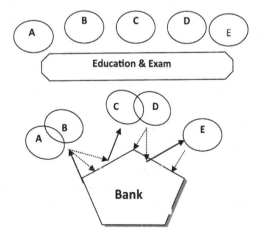

The group lending-based business model developed by the Grammen bank and its homologous has inspired many in more developed countries. Group lending historically originates in different cultures and countries: the "susus" (Ghana) and "tontines, djanggis" (Cameroun), "xitique" (Mozambique) in Africa; "tandas" (Mexico) and "pasanaku" (Bolivia) in Latin America; "tontines" (Cambodia), "arisan" (Indonesia), "chit funds" (India), "Gharse-ol-hasaneh" (Iran), "wichin gye" in Korea, "cheetu" (Sri Lanka), in Asia; as well as numerous savings clubs and burial societies found all over Europe. Now, this ubiquitous practice, under the name "Rotating Savings and Credit Association", ROSCA, is a modern economic concept. ROSCA means an assembly of individuals who agree to get together in order to save and borrow within the group. In such a group money is not idle and changes hands to satisfy both consumption and production needs.

The group-based micro-lending has not met the success in the developed countries as it did in the developing countries. The Good Faith Fund in the United States for example, was a pioneering project for group lending. Yet, it has not had the success that other microfinance organizations have come to see mainly because of the inability of clients in the United States to form groups. The Good Faith Fund was initially implemented in a rural community in Arkansas. Unlike Bangladesh, where population density is high and it is easy to find citizens in the same economic situation, the population of rural America is widely spread out, and finding five people in the same social class in a close distance of one another is more of a challenge. The economic situations of countries also account for microfinance. Where in the developing world jobs are scarce and many people rely on their individual skills to secure an income, jobs in developed countries (such as the United States) are usually available, and therefore the motivation for entrepreneurship is lower (Aubuchon & Sengupta, 2008). Credit card debt

is the main reason individuals are turning to P2P lending (Bruce, 2008).

Even if the reference or solidarity groups seem to be less dynamic in the developed countries than in the developing countries, it should be noticed that an online kind of reference group is on the rise in the P2P lending markets of the developed countries. LendingClub, launched in May 2007, mainly works with people in affiliated groups, matching up travel agents or MIT alums with peers.

As social lending in the developed countries mainly targets individual in liquidity difficulties, and not the poor of the bottom of pyramid, "trust groups" seem to be less important for concluding deals between lenders and borrowers. Here, the creditworthiness of the prospect is more important for the lender, as investor, than the reference group of his/her client. Moreover, electronic mechanisms enable assessing potential customers. LendingClub which uses traditional credit scoring also brings into play a propriety assessment of customers' reputations within their social networks.

In developed countries, generally, many people looking for a loan go directly to their conventional banks. Since the emergence of informational and particularly Web 2.0 technologies, the options for getting loans have expanded enormously to the online P2P social lending, especially for people with less appealing credit scoring. Over the last few years, online P2P online platforms have been popping up everywhere. Social banking platforms are expected to obtain a market share of ten percent of the worldwide market for retail lending and financial planning (Gartner Inc. 2008). The growth of the US P2P lending market is estimated to attain a volume of up to ten billion USD before 2017 (Bruene 2007).

These online networks use websites dedicated to social lending and generally include photos of the lenders and borrowers along with reasons for borrowing or lending, and other interactive features that may be unique to each specific site.

Zopa.com; and websites like it; are the newest step in the evolution of social lending. On Zopa.com, a site for the United Kingdom, Japan and Italy (closed in the United States), lenders and borrowers interact directly with regards to amounts, repayment periods and interest rates. Borrowers are required to have a certain credit score, and in the event they default, credit agencies will be notified and their credit score will drop.

MARKETING ANALYSIS OF ONLINE SOCIAL LENDING

Uncontrollable Marketing Factors

Uncontrollable marketing factors are composed of the market, along with competition and environment which will be analyzed in the following.

Market Analysis: Online P2P Lending

In 1998, it was estimated by Asheesh Advani, founder of CircleLending (now Virgin Money US), that for loans of $1000 or more, there was an estimated market of $300 billion and a market of $6 million person to person loans made in America alone each year (Bray, 2007). Still these growth projections are said to take into account only a small amount of the overall numbers in the market of small loans. The different sites appeal to different needs of the consumers they target, this allows for the market to be widespread and diverse. The volume of online social lending loans for 2008 is expected to reach $1.6 billion, and that number is furthermore expected to double in 2009 and reach nearly $6 billion in 2010.

Some more market-related data are provided in Table 1.

The process of becoming a lender or borrower on these sites is quick and easy and can be done conveniently at home. Those who have extra cash and want a return greater than what a bank can provide on a regular CD (Certificate of

Deposit) or a stock portfolio are interested as lenders. Others are attracted for the philanthropic nature of certain social lending sites. Borrowers are mainly attracted for the freedom and flexibility that comes with online lending, such as choosing the interest rate, payback periods, and so on.

The market segments for P2P lending are diverse. Kiva lends from wealthy to poor, while Zopa fosters many consumer and car loans in the United Kingdom. Many members at Lending Club and Prosper state credit card consolidation or small business loans as their purpose for loans. Virgin money focuses its attention on loans between family and friends.

Progressively, two major target markets are distinguishable within the sector of social small loans. In developing countries the main target is mainly composed of poor entrepreneurs; while in the developed countries, there is also a significant market which is made up of individuals who are not poor, but are in liquidity difficulties. With the emergence of the financial crisis in 2007 and ever since (by November 2009 at least), the banking system, mainly in the US, made it hard for even clients with the most excellent credit rating to get a good interest rate. So a rising number of them looking to consolidate debt, pay off a mortgage, or simply buy a consumer item, tries Internet to

Table 1. Data on Market and MFIs (December 31, 2007) (Source: State of Microcredit Summit Campaign 2009)

Number of MFIs Reporting (1997–2007):	3,552
Number of MFIs Reporting in 2008 Only:	861
Percent Poorest Clients Represented by MFIs Reporting in 2008:	83.4%
Total Number of Clients (as of 12/31/07):	154,825,825
Total Number of Women (as of 12/31/07):	109,898,894
Total Number of Poorest Clients (as of 12/31/07):	106,584,679
Total Number of Poorest Women (as of 12/31/07):	88,726,893

ask money from other people (Lee/St. John, 2008, Bogoslaw, 2009).

However, this does not mean that there is no poor entrepreneur or no loan offer for the poor in the developed countries. The business models of micro-lending for the poor entrepreneurs seem even to function efficiently in the US market. For example, ACCION USA targets business owners who are not able to obtain loans from traditional lenders, and provides them credit or alternative financing they need. The point is that in the developed countries, there is also a small loans market for "not-poor individuals" which is significant and developing.

The Table 2 illustrates different possible segments of P2P lending, based on levels of income and familiarity between lenders and borrowers.

Envisioned benefits are potentially another factor of segmentation. Each site pulls in members seeking specific benefits: Kiva is a not-for-profit website, while Zopa and Prosper are private companies.

Competition Analysis: Online P2P Lending Websites

The number of institutions of inclusive finance is now abundant. The Microcredit Summit Campaign reports the figure of 3552 reporting MFs (Daley-Harris, 2009). The lion share comes to the largest individual institutions. 76 largest MFI have served 94 million (88.2 percent) of the 106.6 million poorest clients in 2007. (see Table 3)

Despite the high number of them, the lending alternative financial institutions all fall into two basic business models: microfinance institutions and consumer lenders (Rhyne, 2009). While microfinance began with offering credit to the owners of tiny informal businesses, consumer lenders began by helping salaried workers, upper end of the "Bottom of Pyramid" market, buy things. Today, especially in Latin America, the two approaches are starting to meet and compete (Rhyne, 2009).

A third type of inclusive finance might be added to the above typology by including the business model of those which facilitate to provide credit

Table 2. Analysis of product's market placement

	Known to Known	*Unknown to Unknown*	*Affiliation*
Rich	Virgin Money, Lending Club	Zopa, Globefunder	Prosper, Fynanz
Poor		MyC4, Kiva, Microplace	

Table 3. MFIs by Size and clients (Source: State of Microcredit Summit Campaign 2009)

Size of Institution (in terms of poorest)	Number of Institutions	Combined Number of Poorest Clients	Percentage of Total Poorest
1 million or more	10	28,098,014	26.36
100,000–999,999	60	17,184,064	16.12
10,000–99,999	310	8,525,154	8.00
2,500–9,999	533	2,608,463	2.45
Fewer than 2,500	2,633	1,454,464	1.36
Networks (Including SERP, FWWB, NABARD, BRDB, ACCU, and TNCDW)	6	48,714,520	45.70

and loans, not for the bottom of the pyramid, but for individuals who are better off but in temporary liquidity difficulties. Zopa is most likely the most famous example in this category.

The actors are not less interested in online P2P social lending. As per March 2008, Ashta and Assadi (2008) had identified six specialized websites in peer-to-peer lending via the public domain Website Wikipedia, and a peer-reviewed and non peer-reviewed research on the academic EBSCO database: Circle Lending (now Virgin Money), Kiva, Lending Club, Microplace, Prosper, and Zopa.

GlobeFunder, Fynanz and MyC4 have come on the scene since then. Modest Needs (Modest-Needs.org) was studied and considered, however, was excluded due to the nature of the grants given by the sites, which needed no repayment. It was, therefore, dropped from our sample population.

As stated on their website, Kiva.org is a non-profit organization that was incorporated in November of 2005, founded by Matt and Jessica Flannery. The word "Kiva" is actually Swahili for "unity" or "agreement". As of April 2009, their site statistics include 472,765 lenders, 95,705 loans, 44 participating countries and the cumulative amount of loans funded since 2008 as just under 66 million USD.

Lending Club's CEO, Renaud LaPlanche, stated that his company has "been growing at a rate of 100 percent month-to-month" in 2008 (Bruce, 2008). The statistics on their online webpage disclosed that as of the first of April 2009 the amount of issued loans on LendingClub.com totaled 33,150,400 USD.

MicroPlace, a wholly-owned subsidiary of EBay, defines its mission as helping to alleviate global poverty by enabling everyday people to make investments in the world's working poor. Microplace began as an idea by Tracey Pettengill Turner after first having heard of microfinance and visiting Dhaka, Bangladesh to work for Grameen Bank. Upon her return, she envisioned Microplace.

In the summer of 2006 MicroPlace became part of the eBay Internet revolution.

Prosper began operation in February of 2006 and is currently America's largest online lending firm, according to its website, with as of July 2009 over 830,000 members within the United States and over US $178 million in loans funded since its inception (Press Release Point, 2008). In November 2008 Prosper received a Cease and Desist order from the Security Exchange Commission (SEC) in the United States because of mainly two supposed faults. Prosper, for one, does very minimal vetting of borrower's personal information that lenders rely on to make an investment decision. Secondly, Prosper sells its platform as an investment while it is marketed as a social lending website. A legal matter, "the Cease and Desist" order, prevented Prosper.com from accepting new lender registrations or new commitments from existing lenders for a while. On July 2009, Prosper.com was on its way back. The analysis put forth in this chapter is based upon the business model and activities of Prosper.com prior and after the "Cease and Desist" order.

Virgin Money USA differs from other online microfinance organizations, because it focuses on loans between people who are familiar with one another, such as family and friends.

Zopa has launched sites all over the world, beginning in Great Britain and expanding to the USA (closed in October 2008), Italy and Japan ("Zopa Membership"). Zopa's mission, as described in its website, is social finance to let a community of members help each other financially, via the tools of finance and social networking. The term of Zopa stands for "Zone of Possible Agreement" and is the overlap between one person's bottom line (the lowest price to sell something for) and another person's top line (the highest price to pay for). Zopa is most likely the world's first person to person online lending site.

The Zopa original model continued to doing well in Europe and Japan. Launched by a management team that comprised many of those that founded Egg in the UK in 2005, Zopa was the first P2P lending company: Lenders offer money at rates they set and borrowers might take up their offer or not. Zopa itself functions as an online social networking site and contibutes to spread loans between multiple lenders to ensure that no one is completely at risk if the borrower defaults. When a borrower's application comes in, Zopa checks their requirements and matches it to the best offers in the appropriate band. (see Table 4)

However, the Zopa original model continued to doing well in Europe and Japan. Launched by a management team that comprised many of those that founded Egg in the UK in 2005, Zopa was the first P2P lending company: Lenders offer money at rates they set and borrowers might take up their offer or not. Zopa itself functions as an online social networking site and contibutes to spread loans between multiple lenders to ensure that no one is completely at risk if the borrower defaults. When a borrower's application comes in, Zopa checks their requirements and matches it to the best offers in the appropriate band.

The Fynanz website considers itself an online auction site where students can get competitive rates on education loans. The borrowing students complete a loan request specifying the desired amount of their loan and interest rate, which lenders then bid on.

Globefunder shies away from being considered a "peer-to-peer" marketplace, and instead relies on the phrase "Direct-to-Consumer Lending (D2C)". The technology platform of Globefunder was launched in 2007 and the Retail Partnership Program launched in May of 2008. There are more than 1,000 clients served as of September 2008.

MyC4. an online microlending firm based in Copenhagen, Denmark, was founded by Mads Kjaer, and Tim Vang in May 2006. It allows anyone in any part of the world to provide microloans, however, these loans are specifically targeted to the poor in Africa. According to the website, the name of the organization "MyC4" refers to something or someone that you care for. Also the reference of "C4" in the title hints at the plastic explosive by the same name. This metaphorically symbolizes the potential of the small to medium size African business market that is ready to take-off. MyC4 hosts 6,734 investors from 68 countries who have currently provided EUR 3.8 million in more than 2,300 businesses in Uganda, Ivory Coast, and Kenya.

The market for P2P online lending is huge and growing, meaning the threat of new entrants into the market is high. Social lending sites will need to ensure repeat customers and pull new membership to survive the market. They will need to customize and offer unique and creative services from which the consumers will profit.

Table 4. Presentation of the peer-to-peer lending websites

	Created in	Founder(s)	Location
Fynanz	2007	Veterans of student loans	New York, US
Globefunder	2006	Benjamin Decio	Kalamazoo, US
Kiva	2005	Matt and Jessica Flannery	San Francisco, US
LendingClub	2006	Renaud Laplanche	Sunnyvale, US
Microplace	2006	Tracey Pettengill Turner & eBay	N/A
MyC4	2006	Mads Kjaer, Tim Vang	Copenhagen, Denmark
Prosper	2006	Chris Larsen	San Francisco, US
VirginMoney.	2000	Asheesh Advani	Waltham, US
Zopa	2005	Richard Duvall	London, England

Competition into the social lending world is introduced all the time with more sites appealing to different groups. The competition within the market is contributing to specific positioning strategies as an "act occupying a distinct competitive position in the target customers' minds" as shown in Table 3 (Kotler, 1997).

Analysis of the Macro-Environment of Online P2P Lending

This section seeks to construct a better understanding of the economic, legal, political and technological environments that surround online social lending.

Social lending sites are seeing quick success due to the economic situations throughout the world which is currently experiencing economic distress. It seems that Americans that are facing high amount of credit card debt are turning more to online social lending. This also comes along with a budding generation of technologically savvy and Internet-comfortable adults that are willing to interact limitlessly online.

Regulatory issues are complex when social lending firms operate simply within one country, and the complexity multiplies when they attempt cross-border operation. Banking licenses are required in the United States to make loans, even if these online sites are not necessarily banks. Some sites, such as Lending Club and Prosper, team up with online banks (Web Bank being the affiliate for the latter two firms).

Another big problem (at least, in the United States) is the simple question of to whom the loan actually belongs and how it is transferred. Lending Club was forced to shut down operations for a short time in April of 2006 when the U.S. Security Exchange Commission stepped in and raised some questions about the legitimacy of Lending Club's operations. The loan can either be owned by Lending Club, or by the lenders ("peers"), and it eventually may be transferred around, which would denote it being a "security".

Since Lending Club does not directly connect lenders to the borrowers, its borrowing practices can be interpreted as "sales of securities". This means that Lending Club needed a broker-dealer license from the SEC, which it now has. Securities are thoroughly regulated in the United States, and therefore, this "gray-area" of social lending caused some sticky and complex situations for sites like Lending Club, Prosper, and Zopa.

Zopa's United States debut was delayed because of the regulatory issues the site had to tackle. For regulatory reasons, Zopa deployed in 2007 an entirely different business model on the US market than that of its sister sites in the UK, Italy and Japan, based on online P2P lending. In the US, Zopa was in fact a lead-generation site for six credit unions as the sole lenders. Borrowers could obtain a loan via Zopa from one of the Credit Unions. The latter bought a Zopa "Certificate of Deposit" to help borrowers by reducing the amount of interest they had to pay. A Credit Union is owned and operated by its associates for promoting thrift and providing credit at reasonable rates to its members.. This means that in order to borrow a Zopa loan an individual needed to be or become a member of one of the affiliated credit unions. It was simply a click of a button on the website's "Partners" page to register. Yet, it added a bit of inconvenience to the process, and uncertainty to those who aren't aware of what credit unions are. When those credit unions became unable to adequately fund the leads due to *the* difficult consumer credit circumstances, Zopa US stopped its activity on October 8, 2008.

The National Credit Union Administration and many state authorities regulate all Zopa loans and Zopa CDs. Regulations that are complied with at Zopa include: the Equal Credit Opportunity Act, the Truth in Savings Act the Truth in Lending Act, the Fair Debt Collection Practices Act, as well as all consumer lending laws. Technically, however, Zopa is neither a bank nor a credit union.

Regulations by national, international and local governments can be party to pricing strategy, as well as macro economy. Authorities that regulate interest rates of banking and service firms exist all over the world, and have a major effect on pricing of international banking cooperatives. Furthermore, an international firm must take into account inflationary periods and the stability of monetary units of foreign currencies as well as their own currency when determining a pricing strategy.

Technologically speaking, the social lending revolution is constantly updating security services, online transactions, etc. For the market to further grow, Internet based technologies are to be utilized more by P2P lending websites: Web 2.0 and social networking websites. The term "Web 2.0" refers to the sharing and interacting between peers online and can concurrently have a considerable impact on P2P lending ("The Internet Giants," 2008).

The online social networking trend pertains to sites such as Facebook, MySpace, Flickr and Second Life, an online 3D virtual networking world with around 10 million members, and can promote interaction and transactions among peers on the Internet.

Controllable Marketing Factors

The controllable factors of the marketing mix, knowingly product, price, place and promotion, tend to obtain the marketing goals of P2P lending websites.

Product Policy Analysis of Online P2P Lending Websites

A *product* is "anything that is offered to a market to satisfy a want or need" (Kotler, 1997). Correlatively, in a market of financial services, the motivating reason for buying a product resides in its benefit solving a user's need or want, and provides value (Ledgerwood & White, 2006). Micro-lending as a product is a small loan offered to a person outside of the conventional banking and financial sector. The benefits of these loans

are higher returns for lenders and the ability to obtain loans for borrowers.

The Internet increases benefits in many ways to its users: convenience, personalization, and most importantly, knowledge enabling consumers to shop by comparison and competition (Frost and Strauss, 2001).

There is a sustainable relationship between the customer value hierarchy and the economic status of countries (Figure 2). Currently, most customer-value in developed countries such as in Europe resides in the product-plus services level, while in developing countries it is mostly based on the basic expected benefit of the product (Kotler, 1997). These differences in the focus of product marketing levels have been influential in the development of micro-lending in both developed and less developed countries. Simply obtaining the loan is almost all that is expected of the micro-lending companies in underdeveloped countries, not much online convenience services.

Micro-lending firms have product strategies in developed and underdeveloped countries due to the needs and wants that vary by economic conditions. Services offered by micro-lending organizations that are not specifically catered to the economic situation of the nation are not successful, as aforementioned in the instance of the Good Faith Fund in the United States. Zopa, as a microfinance institution would not foster in a poor country with its current business model which caters a better security of transactions, especially for lenders, for higher charges.

Some of the benefits added to online P2P lending websites are the support services. Customer support can actually be one of the main reasons a consumer chooses one online firm over another, especially when the is sophisticated and confusing a good quality firm will have customer support services that are easily accessible, available continuously, and facilitate customer usage. Support services are further examined in this chapter as a public relations medium. (see Table 5)

Figure 2. Customer value hierarchy & economic status

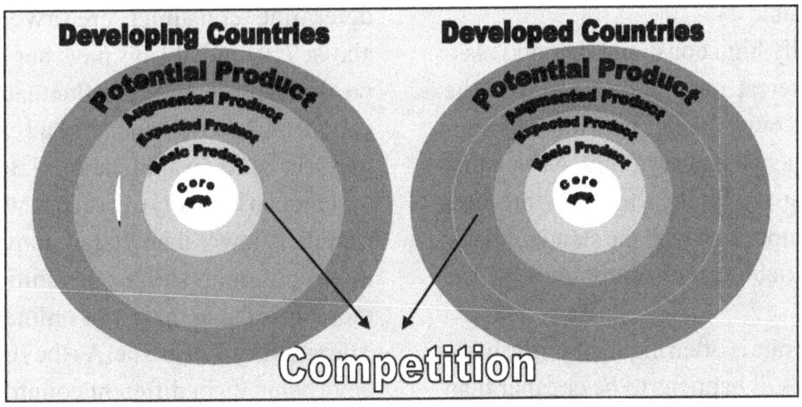

New products such as home equity loans and car loans are being specifically addressed on some sites while other sites have no specifications of where or for what the loan money will be used.

Pricing Analysis of Online P2P Lending

For customers, interest rates represent the cost or price of loans. This price, like other types of price, is influenced by factors such as: competitor's pricing, profitability targets, consumer's price sensitivity, cost of supplying the product to the market, and especially risks, regulations, and economic and social considerations within the banking industry. (see Table 6)

As of January 2009, the Prime Interest rate for the United States is currently 3.25 percent, with a 30 year fixed mortgage rate of 4.96 percent and a 15-year fixed mortgage of 4.62 percent. Foreign Prime Rates are shown in the table below.

Bankrate.com conducts weekly national surveys of large banks and thrifts in the USA. The below table indicates interest rates of five common consumer banking products in the United States during the weeks of September 4 – 10, 2008 and the interest rates on the same five products during the week of January 29 – February 4, 2009. This analysis indicates the volatility of American inter-

Table 5. Product analysis on online P2P lending websites

Brand or Name	Core Benefit & Positioning
Fynanz.com	Providing better rates for student loans
Globe-funder.com	Facilitating loans B2C between financial institutions and small businesses and their customers
Kiva.org	Humanitarian, lending to poor entrepreneurs
Lending-Club.com	Convenience, lower rates for borrowers, monetary gain for lenders
Microplace.com	Humanitarian, monetary gain for lenders
MyC4.com	Humanitarian for Sub-Saharan African entrepreneurs
Prosper.com	Lower rates for borrowers, monetary gain for lenders
VirginMon-eyUS.com	Convenience provided for family and friends loaning to each other
Zopa.com	Convenience, lower rates for borrowers, monetary gain for lenders

Table 6. Prime rates in selected countries

Country	September 2008	January 2009	November 2009
United States	5.00%	3.25%	3.25%
Japan	1.88%	1.88%	1.475%
Germany	4.00%	3.75%	3.75%
Britain	5.00%	5.00%	0.50%
Hong Kong	5.50%	5.50%	5.00%

est rates, especially during the current economic downturn. (see Table 7)

There is usually high consumer demand elasticity for low interest rates. Table 6 shows the average interest rates being provided by our sample websites as of January 2009. Notice that the interest rates given by the social lending sites are extremely competitive with the standard fixed and standard variable credit card rates in the United States.

If P2P interest rate is often higher than the basic conventional rates, it happens to be cheaper than conventional consumer credits. LendingClub's rate for the best credit risks was 7.88 percent in autumn 2009, while the bank rate in the US for personal loan, on average, was 13 percent. Consequently on the online P2P social lending, a credit-worthy borrower could get the money faster and for 5 percent less. In autumn 2008, a couple of clients who could not get an interest rate below 15 percent – even with credit scores in the 700s of 850 maximum – took finally most of their debt - $5000 – to LendingClub. They agreed to pay back $136 a month at a fixed 11.41 percent (Lee/St. John, 2008). Another example is not less instructive to understand the nature of this type of P2P social lending market: Anna Sinclair got a Lending Club loan for $20,000 in December (2008) to complete the financing for a house she bought. Even though she was putting up cash for 80% of the house's value, has a FICO (a credit

scoring model is used by many creditors to help determine consumer creditworthiness) score above 750, and always pays her credit-card bills on time and in full, the fluctuating income she earns from her own business had caused five banks to reject her loan applications (Bogoslaw, 2009).

One can logically expect that when online interest rate is lower than that of conventional banks, more consumers shift from traditional channels to more affordable option of online social lending. The contrary is also true. As the state and financial environments in different countries reduce basic interest rates to face the current financial crisis, one might wonder if the online P2P lending websites will remain attractive as lending and borrowing prospects. (see Table 8)

There are also some non-pecuniary psychic costs such as confusing websites, slow Internet, service speed, or other technical frustrating problems (Frost & Strauss, 2001). While administrative and financial costs usually provide the foundation for interest rates at a banking firm by using a percentage markup associated with the costs, risk is a large influencing factor in lending (Ledgerwood & White 2006). In order to offset the psychic cost of risk, banks charge interest rates at different levels corresponding to the market.

Table 7. American interest rates

United States	September 2008	January 2009	November 2009
One Year CD	2.4%	1.63%	1.73%
Five Year CD	3.58%	2.38%	2.91%
New car Loan (60 month)	7.10%	6.90%	6.29%
Credit Card (standard fixed)	13.42%	13.29%	13.46%
Credit Card (standard variable)	11.57%	10.87%	11.16%

Table 8. Interest rates available on P2P lending sites (January 2009)

Website	Interest Rate
Fynanz.com	2.50% to 7.50% borrowing rate range
Globefunder.com	Set by borrower
Kiva.org	0%
LendingClub.com	6.69%- 19.37% borrowing rates
Microplace.com	n/a
MyC4.com	Set by borrower
Prosper.com	7.68% borrowing rate
Virgin MoneyUScom	Lender sets rate
Zopa.com	8.75% to 16.99% borrowing rate range

The cost of producing online peer-to-peer lending services can originate in the following areas (Prosper Lending Review, 2007): Programming fees for updating products, services, and security; Maintenance of the site; Marketing of the site and Salaries.

The pricing objective and approach varies from company to company. Some site charge membership fees while others implement a percentage by transaction approach. Charitable organizations such as Kiva, do not charge a rate at all, while Zopa sets their own interest rates. Virgin Money's interest rates are set by the friend or family member giving the loan, and Prosper is an auction house for loans.

On the P2P lending websites in developed countries, loan amounts range from 200 USD to 10,000 USD, all for different reasons: getting out of credit card debt, buying a new oven for a small restaurant, or simply a college student buying books and looking to avoid credit card debt. The 200 USD someone needs to repair the truck he uses to get to work is not usually provided by conventional banks. Table four shows the comparison of the pricing strategies in our sample. (see Table 9)

Distribution Analysis of Online P2P Lending

Place, another element of the four P's, encompasses the various activities the company undertakes to make the product available to target customers, through channels of interdependent intermediaries, such as suppliers, wholesalers, brokers, resellers, agents, retailers, merchants, agents, facilitators, and so on (Kotler, 1997).

In the banking sector, intermediation functions achieve both high-tech, such as online banking, cell phones and ATMs, etc.; and high-touch strategies like face-to-face interactions between the customers and employees. Internet has pushed the high-tech strategy further resulting in market deconstruction, and types of new intermediaries (Frost & Strauss, 2001).

The basic intermediation role of social lending sites is exchange facilitation: a peer has an amount of money to lend at a certain return rate, and another peer looks for lenders with sufficient funds. However, the model of this undertaking assumes different forms. Here we study our different social lending websites in order to analytically compare

Table 9. Pricing strategy of online micro-lending firms

	Cost for Lender Servicing fee % of loan	Cost for borrower % of loan
Fynanz	1%,	Based on grades: 2.9% Platinum, 4.9% Gold, 6.9% Silver.
Globefunder	1.75% or $50 (whichever is greatest).	3.75% of loan or $200 (whichever is greatest).
Kiva	Lender fixes price, upon repayment lender chooses whether to donate funds, re-lend, or withdraw.	N/A
LendingClub	1% of all amounts repayments	Based on grades:.75% to 3%.
Microplace	N/A	N/A
MyC4	No fee for lenders	2% upon disbursement, then additional 2% of total when loan is completed.
Prosper	Depending on grades: 0.5 to 1%	Based on grades: 1%, 2%. Or fee: minimum of $25
VirginMoneyUS	Servicing fee of $9 per payment.	Depending on type of loan: $99 personal loan; $199 Small business; $699-$2000.
Zopa	No– users buy a Zopa CD.	Depending on CD

how the intermediation functions are assumed by each channel.

For a social lending site to be available to the public, it needs to have suppliers, which are also known in this type of industry as capital providers or investors. Charitable social lending organizations (such as Kiva) are funded by grants and group or individual philanthropic donations while others, such as Virgin Money, have been funded through a parent company. Many other companies funded by private lenders or investors.

On the borrowers' side, Kiva works with "Field Partners" which are local existing microfinance institutions; usually short on funds, but with the access and ability to choose qualified borrowers/entrepreneurs from world-wide impoverished communities. To become a "Field Partner", the postulating microfinance institution must currently serve at least 1,000 active microfinance borrowers, have a history of at least 2-3 years of lending to poor and/or vulnerable people for the purpose of alleviating poverty or reducing vulnerability, be registered as a legal entity in its country of operation and be able to show at least one year of financial audits and preferably be registered on the MIX Market (www.mixmarket.org).

On the lender side, Kiva encourages potential loan givers to choose directly among entrepreneur profiles uploaded onto the site and subsequently sponsor their business. On listings borrowers are presented in terms of name, age, country, business, conditions of repayment, etc. Lenders are also given the option to present themselves on the site. The course of a loan is usually between six to twelve months and its amount can be as little as $25 at a time. Once a loan is repaid, the lender can withdraw the funds or re-loan them to a new entrepreneur.

Kiva never promotes connections or the interaction and communication between lending and borrowing individuals. Of course, loan givers periodically hear back from their sponsored entrepreneur and remain informed on the progress of the entrepreneurship, yet not directly from the sponsored entrepreneurs, but via email and online journal updates. These updates are often written by partner representatives and loan officers.

Lending Club is presented on its website as a social lending network where lenders, both individuals and organizations, can earn money at better returns, and borrow money at better interest rates. Lenders will list the total amount they would like to loan and the risk level they can stand. The risk is measured on a scale of numbers one to five, where five represents the highest tolerance for risk. Then lenders can directly select individual borrowers or generate a portfolio of borrowers to reduce risk. There are seven main types of loans: A, B, C, D, E, F and G. The letter "A" refers to the highest credit scores with the lowest risk, and the letter "G" the lowest credit score with the highest risk.

Borrowers first register at Lending and provide information about his/her identity and creditworthiness. They need credit scores of at least 640 (of 850 maximum) and a debt-to-income ratio of 30 percent or less. Borrowers with a credit score above 640 might be turned down if their overall debt level is too high, or if they have less than twelve months of credit history. They then complete a loan request and instantly view the interest rate at which they pre-qualify. Borrowers who share their loan listings with their Facebook networks increase their chances of being funded and funded faster. Borrowers subsequently select a loan option, and Lending Club will post the loan request on the site for two weeks, during which time interested lenders will contribute portions of the amount you requested. The borrowers might re-list a loan, if the first one does not receive full funding.

Lending Club uses a "connections system" to secure transactions between lenders and borrowers, moreover, through membership in an association, network or group in Facebook, called affiliation. Lending Club manages the money movement between members, including loan repayment, and provides detailed reporting. Once a loan request is granted by one lender or by many, Lending Club deposits the loan into the borrower's bank account. Later, repayment will be taken directly out of that same bank account each month, and then transferred to the lender's account. Lenders can withdraw these funds or can select additional loans to fund. Borrowers will pay a processing fee that ranges from 0.75 percent to 2 percent of the loan amount. This fee will be deducted from the loan proceeds prior to depositing the loan in the borrower's bank account. In the instance a borrower fails to pay, Lending Club reports the borrower to credit agencies and utilizes a collections agency to recover the funds. If one borrower is late on a payment, Lending Club charges late fees on lender's behalf. After 30 days past due date, the borrower's account will be sent to Lending Club's collection agency partner and the late payment history will also be reported to the credit bureau partners.

On the site of Microplace, people purchase investments from security issuers and attribute their investment to a specific developing country's microfinance institution. Funds so generated are disbursed as small loans to the working poor who use the loans to start or expand small businesses and lift out of poverty.

Once the security issuers receive their loan plus interest, they pay back people who purchased original securities. Unlike Kiva, where lenders provide capital to microfinance institutions, MicroPlace is mainly a market for microfinance securities.

On the site Prosper, the term "lender" is used for the sake of simplicity. To place bids, "loan purchasers" have to transfer money to Prosper, as people transfer funds to their brokerage accounts before buying stocks. Loan purchasers can either choose a portfolio plan composed of several borrowers or choose directly from the listed borrowers. They can lend up to two million dollars at Prosper, but only $25,000 at a time, the most one borrower can have access to at a time. Prosper provides data on credit, employment, and income of the prospects.

Any individual can register as a borrower and build a profile. A borrower's loan might come from a single lender or several. For lending or borrowing, one should primarily be in a group – volunteer fire-fighters, for example. If a borrower is more than one month late on a payment, Prosper engages a collection agency on the lender's behalf and dings the borrower's credit score. Prosper charges fees when a borrower obtains a loan and when a lender receives repayment.

Prosper, like Kiva, does not play the role of facilitator between lenders and borrowers in its social network. Both sites have specific links to "Question and Answer" pages where lenders can ask questions and borrowers are supposed to answer. Still, the borrowers are not obliged to answer, and when they do, they are asked to do so under conditions of anonymity. Exposing borrower's identity to a lender may put the latter in a legally precarious situation, and consequently borrowers are firmly asked by Prosper to avoid it at all costs. The borrower is also given the option to post the answer for all lenders to read. This is again far from a mutual communication.

Virgin Money sets up the payment schedules and legal documents between individuals with a prior connection and then charges fees correspondingly. The borrowers and lenders on the site already know one another, and therefore they need less to use social networking tools.

An example of this procedure would be a grandmother loaning her grandson money to buy a car. While the grandmother and grandson set their own interest rates, repayment period and so on, Virgin Money registers both, sets up the framework for the loan and manages the loan between the two parties. There are certain legal guidelines they must follow.

On the Site Zopa in UK lenders offer their money to potential borrowers as a function of the risk and loan term. Each loan is spread across many borrowers in order to reduce the effect of any defaults. If a Borrower defaults, the debt is normally sold to a debt collection agency and Lenders will be paid a portion of any money recovered. Borrowers, after undergoing underwriting checks, state their loan projects, preferred interest rates and repayment schedules. Funds are then assigned to the potential borrower in a reverse-auction where the lowest interest rates win. The winner borrower can accept or reject the loan. Both Borrowers and Lenders are charged fees by Zopa.

The loans are originated by Fynanz and then sold to loan purchasers, rather than lenders. A lender with Fynanz must be a US resident over the age of eighteen with a US bank account and social security number. Again with Fynanz the term "lenders" is used loosely.

Fynanz designates FACS (the acronym of "Fynanz Academic Credit Score") to each borrower to help lenders determine the risk of default. These ratings composed of the academic characteristics of the student, such as GPA, school, class standing and year of study. The interest rate of a loan at Fynanz is constituted of the Base Rate, Margin and Lender Guarantee Fee. The site also charges a servicing fee to the lenders of one percent of the initial loan balance, and an upfront fee to borrowers based on their FACS Grade.

The lenders that bid on the student loans can be networked within alumni, friends and family. Fynanz caters to networked borrowers by instituting a Friends and Family Bid Match program, which rewards borrowers by matching the first $1,000 and bid half the amount for the next $3,000 if the lender of a loan identifies themselves a friend or family member of the borrower.

Globefunder caters toward banking institutions in order to provide them with a lower cost way to acquire customers. To lend at Globefunder, however, there is a rigid set of requirements. It is very clear through their registration process that they are not a P2P lending site but very much a direct-to-consumer (D2C) marketplace. Still, the process is social lending nonetheless. Globefunder also partakes in retail partnerships with businesses in order to provide them with more affordable financing solutions for their custom-

ers. One example is the collaboration with Cal Spas, a manufacturer of Home Resort products. In June of 2008, Cal Spas released C&S Financial through Globefunder as a way for the customers to finance their home renovations while saving on borrowing costs. Cal Spa used Globefunder to manage high loan volumes.

Focusing on Sub-Saharan Africa, MyC4 allows African entrepreneurs of small and medium size businesses to obtain loans through a network of local providers. All applicants must undergo a screening process before they are accepted into the MyC4 network.

MyC4 allows investors to see all potential borrowers, a description of the business, the amount of loan needed, and the maximum interest rate that can be afforded. Then a Dutch-style auction takes place among lenders who would like to provide the loan. This process ensures that the African entrepreneur is receiving the best deal possible.

Investing in the platform is free of charge, and it is free for the African business to secure a loan. MyC4, however, charges the African business two fees for providing the infrastructure. One flat fee of two percent payable when the loan is disbursed, and another fee of two percent of the amount repaid on the basis of a declining balance. Loans are repaid by the African entrepreneur on a monthly basis, with the incentive to repay as quickly as possible because the interest rate is applied on a declining balance basis. The currency used at MyC4 is typically the Euro, however, the local currency may be used depending on the amount of the loan issued.

Like MyC4 (Denmark), launched in 2007, other platforms which connect lenders to microentrepreneurs and allow the former to choose and support the latter have emerged on the Internet: Rang De and dhana X from India and Wokai which mainly targets China. Since the contribution on Wokai is a kind of donation, contributors in the United States may also get a tax-deduction.

On LendingClub, borrowers need credit scores of at least 640 of 850 maximum and a debt-to-income ratio of 30 percent or less. An average loan is about $9000. It is funded by approximately 22 to 25 people. On LendingClub, lenders list the total amount they like to loan and the risk level they stand. They, they select borrowers, or the site's "Lending Match" program will generate a portfolio. Lending Club was shuttered for six months in 2008 while it awaited the SEC's approval of its registration. It emerged with tougher qualifications for investors: minimum household income of $70,000 a year and net worth of at least $70,000, excluding a person's primary residence (Bogoslaw, 2009).

Communication and Promotion Analysis of Online P2P Lending

The fourth of the four P's is *promotion*, also known as communication, encompasses all activities such as advertising, promotion, direct marketing and public relations that the company undertakes to communicate and promote its products to the target market (Kotler, 1997). We will now consider the types of promotion being used by social lending sites.

Advertising for the P2P micro-lending websites is primarily based on Internet media, with a significant emphasis on news stories on financial websites such as the Financial Times, Bankrate. com, as well as TV news outlet segments (Fox News Financial Analysts, for example). A plethora of other advertising options are also available via the Internet. Registering with search engines, sending electronic press releases, links to other sites, etc.

For a social lending website, a lot of the attention comes from the satisfaction and excitement of individuals who have used the site and subsequently share the idea with others. Word of mouth and popularity are exceedingly important for their advertising. Luckily, it's also cheap! At many of the social lending sites we have examined in our sample, customers can promote their own profile to friends and family.

After typing in a number of key words regarding social lending into top search engines, it appeared that many of the P2P sites do not advertise with them, and the sites which do, did so only with very specific words. Table 8 indicates the keywords used in a search conducted on January 29, 2009. If advertisements for our sample sites were present after a keyword search, the site name is noted. If ads were present, however, the advertised organizations were not members of our sample, it is indicated by the term "ads present". Furthermore, if no ads were present at any part of the keyword search "no ads" appears in the corresponding column.

Corresponding to the keywords of "P2P lending", "social lending", and "peer lending", each search engine result revealed Wikipedia's link to its definition of "person to person lending" as its first result. Wikipedia's webpage explained the movement of social lending, as well as provided links to the main social lending sites – all members of our sample population.

The keywords "microcredit," "micro-lending" and "microfinance" returned the Wikipedia webpage for microcredit, which explained the movement and also included links to the main micro-lending sites. The sites outlined on the webpage contained brief summaries and links to Microplace and Kiva.

While there were multiples instances of no sites advertising, each keyword presented numerous articles in which the sample sites were mentioned directly. It appears this sort of indirect advertising is working as social lending gains popularity. The articles that correspond to the keywords peak interest, cause word of mouth and hence do the advertising. Furthermore, the "social" aspect of peer lending stimulates a grassroots movement of support in itself. (see Table 10)

Public relations on a social networking website is, naturally, very important. The sites are expected to be social with their customers. The support services, or "contact us" links are representative of these sites interacting with the con-

Table 10. Keyword search for P2P lending ad

Key Words	Google	Yahoo	Windows Live	Ask.com
P2P Lending	*No ads*	*No ads*	*No ads*	*No ads*
Social Lending	*No ads*	*No ads*	*No ads*	*No ads*
Peer Lending	*No ads*	*Ads present*	*No ads*	*No ads*
Microlending	*Kiva*	*No ads*	*No ads*	*Ads present*
Microcredit	*Kiva*	*No ads*	*Ads present*	*Ads present*
Microfinance	*Ads present*	*No ads*	*Ads present*	*No ads*
Personal Loans	*Ads present*	*No ads*	*No ads*	*Ads present*

sumers and displaying their public interactivity. Almost all members of our sample provide "blogs" that the executives of the business post on, while others have multiple email addresses, telephone numbers and links that connect them to representatives of the company. The closest these social lending sites can come is presenting a telephone number, or asking clients to send in a request form for an agent to contact them personally.

While Kiva proceeds to marketing and public relations toward both potential lenders and microfinance institutions, it does not practice the same kind of promotions. For prospect field partners, the Kiva's marketing strategy mainly consists of participating in international conferences and local public relations to increase awareness and notoriety. To attract potential lenders, Kiva executes a heavy marketing strategy online and offline. As of November 2009, over 130 field partners have collaborated with Kiva, dramatically extending its scope and reach. (see Table 11)

FUTURE RESEARCH

This is one of the first chapters on the marketing analysis of online social lending. Consequently, many questions can constitute directions of subsequent study: additional research surrounding the advertising strategies of social lending firms would be beneficial to the new market, as well as the advancements in Web 2.0 technologies that will change the face of the Internet and directly affect online P2P lending market platforms. Would these new applications garner more trust and spur the growth of online lending firms? Furthermore, with regard to economic performance, it would be interesting to see how online social lending firms perform alongside traditional banking firms and the stock market. As consumers withdraw their investments from the stock market or traditional CDs, will they invest in other people? Will borrowers reach out to their online peers more often? If so, that may suggest that online social lending is a phenomenon of its own – more applicable to the social networking trend than to the banking industry, revolutionizing both while personalizing what once was a faceless financial sector. Or finally, what specific marketing techniques should be employed to build a new P2P site for micro-lending and how can MFIs use the Web 2.0 tools to attract more funds?

Each section of this chapter, uncontrollable and controllable variables, can generate an axis of research. For uncontrollable factor of competition, a bigger sample can be considered containing among other: Qifang.cn (China), Pertuity.com, MatchSavings.com, Smava (Germany), Kokos and Monetto (Poland), etc.

Regarding controllable factors, marketing-mix elements in particular, the policies of selective, intensive or extensive distribution can be examined more broadly in online P2P lending. Selective policies allocate the product in focused geographic locations that are most beneficial to the sale of the product, while intensive policies saturate the

Table 11. Support services on online P2P lending sites

	Number of Email Links	Toll-free Telephone Number (Monday-Friday)	Mail Address	Other
Fynanz	Several corresponding to area of interest	Several corresponding to area of interest	-	
Globefunder	One for all inquiries	Provided	Provided	
Kiva	None	-	-	FAQ
LendingClub	Three for specific inquiries	8 am. to 5 p.m.	Provided	
Microplace	Two: customer service and a media inquiry	8 a.m. to 4 p.m.	-	Provide a "live chat" option M-F, 8 a.m. to 4 p.m. PST
MyC4	One for "info"	-	Provided	
Prosper	Only for members	-	-	
VirginMoneyUS	Two email links provided: support and sales.	9 a.m. to 7 p.m.	Provided	Provides a link to request a call from them
Zopa	Four for specific inquiries.	8 a.m. to 6 p.m.	Provided	

market using every available outlet, and exclusive policies highlight where the product can exclusively be found. When considering online loan services, these policies rely more heavily on the market niches and vision of the respective companies. In developed countries, where the trend of social lending is taking off, any service available online could be considered intensive distribution, since the service is available everywhere, to most everyone. For this reason, the distribution intensity must be determined by considering the type of consumer targeted by the P2P lending company. For instance, Fynanz targets students, Kiva and MyC4 target humanitarians and Globefunder is more of an entrepreneurial lending site. Zopa and Prosper, however, target everyone and therefore they have true intensive policies correlating to the online market of which they are a part.

Another example of supplementary research could be the communication strategy of P2P lending websites. The site might use pull strategy to gather their customer base of lenders and borrowers, or employ a push strategy to target different intermediaries in order to draw the awareness of lending and borrowing peers to the site.

CONCLUSION

Considerable differences and similarities between online social lending firms are prevalent in the market, as this marketing analysis has shown. For instance, at Prosper the financial transactions are made through loans that are sold and purchased through their marketplace. At Zopa, lenders purchase CDs, while Virgin Money acts as a legal facilitator for the parties involved. Each company has a different business model, which entails various uses of intermediaries.

The social lending sites studied in this chapter all centralize around the idea that the credit partners have control over their investments and loans – that the control can ultimately be in the hands of the consumer instead of the banking industry. This similarity in focus connects the websites; however, the differences between the specific websites and how they aim to provide benefits to their consumers are vast.

The types of Web 2.0 technologies utilized by the organization vary with the sites. They seem to be dominantly driven by Web 1.0 technology which looks for eyeballs rather than interactions.

Targeted audiences, validation of authorized lending and borrowing profiles, source and method of the interest rates fixations, etc. all constitute major differences among the social lending websites. These distinctions insure competition, and make the marketplace full of consumer benefits.

REFERENCES

Armendariz de Aghion, B. (2005). *The Economics of Microfnance*. Cambridge, MA: MIT Press.

Ashta, A. (2008). ASSADI D. (2008). Do Social Cause and Social Technology Meet? Impact of Web 2.0 Technologies on peer-to-peer lending transactions, Asia Microfinance Forum 2008 Hanoi, Vietnam, Microfinance in the 21st Century: Future Trends & Opportunities, Theme 4. *Technology (Elmsford, N.Y.)*, (August): 26–29.

Aubuchon, C. P., & Sengupta, R. (2008). The Microfinance Revolution: An Overview. *Federal Reserve Bank of St. Louis Review*, *90*(1), 9–30.

Banerjee, S. S. (2009). How Microfinance Changes the Lives of Millions. *Foreign Policy*, (October): 26. Retrieved from http://www.foreignpolicy.com/articles/2009/10/26/how_microfinance_changes_the_lives_of_millions.

Bogoslaw, D. (2009, April 6). Peer-to-Peer Lending: Problems and Promise. *Business Week*. Retrieved from http://www.businessweek.com/investor/content/apr2009/pi2009043_811816_page_3.htm

Bray, H. (2007, July 2). Need cash? Just ask. *The Boston Globe Online*. Retrieved September 1, 2008 from www.boston.com/business/personal-finance/articles/2007/07/02/need_cash_just_ask

Bruce, L. (2008, June 6). Peer-to-peer online lending grows in tight economy. Retrieved September 1, 2008 from www.bankrate.com/brm/news/investing/20080606_P2P-lending-growth-a2.asp

Bruene, J. (2007). Person-to-Person Lending 2.0: Disruptive Service or Market Niche? Online Financial Innovations, Online Banking Report: Seattle.

Daley-Harris, S. (2009). State of Microcredit Summit Campaign, Microcredit Summit Campaign, Washington, DC, United States of America. Retrieved November 6, 2009 from http://www.microcreditsummit.org/state_of_the_campaign_report/

Frost, R., & Strauss, J. (2001). *E-Marketing* (2nd ed.). Upper Saddle River, NJ: Prentice Hall.

Gartner Inc. (2008): Gartner Says Social Banking Platforms Threaten Traditional Banks for Control of Financial Relationships. *Gartner*. Retrieved from www.gartner.com/it/page.jsp?id=597907.

Idate Organization. (2008). The Internet Giants and Web 2.0. *DigiWorld 2008*. Retrieved from www.idate.org

Kotler, P. (1997). *Marketing Management* (9th ed.). Upper Saddle River, NJ: Prentice Hall.

Ledgerwood, J., & White, V. (2006). *Transforming Microfinance Institutions: Providing Full financial Services to the Poor*. Washington, D.C.: The International Bank for Reconstruction and Development/The World Bank.

Lee/St. John. J. (2008, February 29). Hey, Buddy, Can You Spare $10,000? *Time Magazine*. Retrieved at http://www.time.com/time/magazine/article/0,9171,1718569,00.html

Prosper Lending Review. (2007, July 23). How does Prosper make money? Retrieved September 1, 2008 from http://prosperlending.blogspot.com/2007/07/how-does-prosper-make-money.html

Rhyne, E. (2009). Microfinance for Banker & Investors: Understanding the Opportunity at the Bottom of the Pyramid, Underwritten by Visa Inc., Commissioned by the UN Advisors Group on Inclusive Financial Sectors. Retrieved November 6, 2009 from www.accion.org/Document. Doc?id=405

Yunus, M. (2003). *Banker to the Poor*. New York: PublicAffairs.

ADDITIONAL READING

Harper, M. (Ed.). (2003). *Microfinance: Evolution, Achievements and Challenges*. London: ITDG Publishing.

Prahalad, C. K. (2005). *The Fortune at the Bottom of the Pyramid*. Saddle River, NJ: Wharton School Publishing.

Yunus, M. (2007). *Creating a World Without Poverty*. New York: PublicAffairs.

Chapter 12
The Use of Web 2.0 Technologies in Online Lending and Impact on Different Components of Interest Rates

Arvind Ashta
Burgundy School of Business (Groupe ESC Dijon-Bourgogne), France

Djamchid Assadi
Burgundy School of Business (Groupe ESC Dijon-Bourgogne), France[1]

ABSTRACT

Microcredit interest costs remain higher than those of commercial banks in spite of significant donor funds, largely owing to transaction costs relative to small loan sizes. With the rise of Web 2.0 and online social interactivity, can these transaction costs be reduced through peer to peer lending? Peer to Peer transactions and Web 2.0 have two things in common. The first common denominator is that both of them are rather newcomers in their respective fields and growing fast. The second is that they are both based on mutual and social exchanges between people instead of intermediary based relationships. The main objective of this chapter was to investigate whether peer to peer online lending transactions are integrated to support a higher level of social interactions and associations with a promise of reducing (transaction) costs through disintermediation and risk reduction. We find that "peer to peer" lending consists of diverse websites of microcredit (Kiva, Wokai, Babyloan), social investing (MicroPlace) as well as small loans at market rates (Prosper, Zopa, Lending Club), and even lending between friends and family members (Virgin Money). The chapter studies the use of web 2.0 technologies (blogs, interactivity between lenders and buyers, peers' reviews and comments, peers communities and chats) in seven such online lending sites. It finds that most of the so called "peer-to-peer" lenders are in fact intermediaries between the peers (lender and borrowers) and there is little direct contact between the peers. One website used none of the web 2.0 tools. None of the websites used all the web 2.0 tools. The impact on transaction costs should therefore be very little as there is neither disintermediation nor risk reduction. A discussion of difficulties in establishing platforms in this field and directions for future research are provided.

DOI: 10.4018/978-1-61520-993-4.ch012

INTRODUCTION

The last few years have witnessed major changes in information and communication technologies which have created disruptive and radical innovations. New companies such as Facebook, YouTube and Flickr have emerged and caught the attention of the public and financial investors and are valued in millions or billions of dollars. Existing companies such as IBM, Amazon and Google have also taken to these new technologies profitably. These companies have been able to use information technologies to encourage users to create value, providing networks to multiply effects, allowing people to build connections and companies to capitalize on competencies and using new forms of collaborative innovations.

As illustrated in Figure 1 below, Shuen (2008) explains that the new internet technologies have led to democratized innovation, crowdsourcing, eco-system platform innovation and recombinant innovation. The major change in technologies facilitating this is termed "Web 2.0", often called "social technology". The point of the new Web 2.0 technologies is that they harness network effects and allow people to participate and share their own questions and ideas with a company through its website. As visitors participate, thanks to these technologies, innovation is not anymore the prerogative of the companies. Moreover, with a massive democratized participation of people, the bottom line is not the sum of them, but a new mechanism of innovation.

This technology includes blogs, interactivity, peers' reviews and comments, peers communities and chats. These technologies have led to direct transactions between peers and concomitantly reduced transaction costs in a number of ways: automating the procurement process and reducing paperwork; interoperability and multi-user communications; auctions to get best prices; collaborative planning leading to reduction of inventories; and collaborative design[2]. The spread of these technologies has been influenced by Social Contagion[3].

Our research question was whether these Web 2.0 techniques have led to a potential for reduction in interest costs or to an increase of credit availability by the lowering of transaction costs and overcoming information asymmetries in novel ways.

Figure 1. Transformation of innovation models

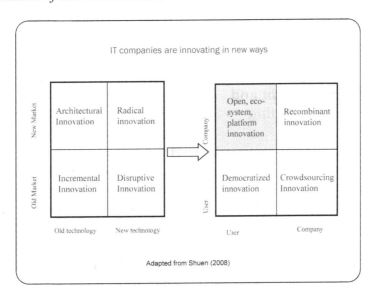

The main objective of this chapter is to document such sites and investigate whether the online websites have integrated the social networking tools of Web 2.0 to support the social interactions and associations of the peer-peer lending. In other words, the chapter aims to scrutinize whether the online websites make use of the social Web 2.0 tools to encourage mutual exchanges and cooperation between peers to lend and borrow money or whether, instead, they centralize the loan transactions. Is the overall performance leading to lower transaction costs and lower interest rate loans to poor people?

Directed by the above research objective, in the next section we will provide some background information on microfinance transaction costs and information asymmetry as well as an introduction to the use of web 2.0 techniques. Thereafter, we will see whether new online lending sites are using these techniques to further microfinance. In the subsequent section, we offer additional directions for further research. The final section would provide our conclusions.

BACKGROUND

In this section, we will provide a brief introduction to the transaction costs that create impediments to the growth of online lending and to the web 2.0 tools that are being used by online lending sites to overcome such transaction costs.

The High Costs of Microcredit and the Potential for Online Lending

One of the problems in lending situations is imperfect information: the lender does not know the borrower's situation as well as the borrower does. Within this imperfect information stream, there is a special case of asymmetry of information producing special problems such as adverse selection (Akerlof, 1970) and moral hazard (Stiglitz & Weiss, 1981)[4]. Some of these problems

can be reduced by screening, regular monitoring and enforcement. However, such monitoring is expensive and not practical for the small scale of loans given by a lender. Conventional solutions have included the development of guarantees, cautions and the development of intermediaries with private information[5]. An often cited example is the creation of stock exchanges who guarantee information flow from a company issuing securities to the investor who has little information on the companies.

Banks give loans to people based on different factors, including some assessment of risk. The lower the risk, the lower is the interest rate. With extremely high risk, there may even be no loans (we can say that interest rate is infinite). The mechanisms of risk mitigation used by banks include collateral, certified accounts, regular reporting, and even presence on the board of directors.

One way large companies lower interest rates is by bypassing the banks and directly issuing bonds. The public gets higher interest rates than that given by banks on deposits. At the same time, the companies pay lower rates than those charged by banks. One of the reasons large companies can do this is that they reduce the information asymmetries and the inherent mistrust because of their well known brand. Often, this is because they are already present in share markets and the stock exchange watchdogs (SEC in the USA, AMF in France) guarantee information flow and external auditors certify that the information is trustworthy. Although recent scandals have shaken confidence in the auditing system, the governments of various countries have quickly responded by new changes in legislation to reestablish trust (e.g., SOX in the US, NRE in France).

However, till recently, small firms and individuals faced large transaction and information asymmetry costs mainly because people didn't know them and so would not lend directly to them. The latter preferred to lend to banks that they knew. The banks, having private information on these firms and individuals, then assessed the risk of each borrower before lending. However, the banks were not used to taking high risks for small amounts, even at high rates of interest because of usury law limitations or cultural constraints (Attuel-Mendes & Ashta, 2008; Goudzwaard, 1968).

The advent of microfinance changed this situation. Through an extensive use of benevolent workers and donor funds, microfinance was able to considerably reduce transaction costs (Armendariz & Morduch, 2005; Ashta, 2007; 2009; Bernasek & Stanfield, 1997; Bhatt & Shui-Yan, 2001). By innovative schemes of staggered lending and progressive lending, as well as group monitoring, microfinance institutions were able to lower information asymmetry costs. The phenomenal growth of Microfinance from the first organization in the 1970s to 10,000 organizations today (World Bank estimation), testifies to the success of the different variants of the model. Even if only 175 of these microfinance operations are sufficiently scaled for financial sustainability, all are involved in achieving the function of transferring funds from people who have excess funds to people needing these funds.

However, interest rates of Microfinance continue to remain high and this creates controversies. It has been found that microfinance interest costs to final borrowers (including application processing fees, interest rates, opportunity cost of compulsory deposits) remain higher than those of commercial banks in spite of significant donor funds, largely owing to transaction costs associated with small loan sizes. These interest costs vary from country to country from 15% to 100%[6]. Administrative costs, including traveling from village to village, processing time, etc. represent two-thirds of the costs (Dieckmann, 2007). Since these high interest costs have poor ethical connotations (Ashta & Bush, 2009), they may keep socially responsible investors from financing microcredit institutions.

The interest costs of MFIs to final borrowers are a direct function of financing costs of the MFI, the loan loss reserve, the operating expense, taxes and the profit margin and an inverse function of

other income. A recent study by CGAP (Rosenberg, Gonsaez & Narain, 2009) estimated that the average interest rates of MFIs to final borrowers in 2006 were 28.3%. That study provides some details about the break-up but between the use of averages and medians, the totals do not always add up. The average funding cost of MFIs is about 8.3%, the loan loss reserve is about 2.3%, operating expenses are a median of 11.4% and profits are about 12.5% (Rosenberg et al., 2009).

The high transaction cost for small loans is best understood by an example. Imagine a rich person wants to borrow a thousand dollars for a year and it takes 30 minutes for a loan officer to interview him and fill up the documentation. Let's assume that the loan officer is paid 10 dollars an hour and that this, therefore, costs $5. The cost is therefore 5% of the loan amount. If, instead a poor borrower wanted a hundred dollar loan for a year, and the loan officer took the same 30 minutes to interview him and fill up the documentation, the extra cost would be 5%. Therefore, a loan from a Microfinance institution to a poor customer would cost 10 times higher than a loan from a bank to a rich borrower, because the loan is 10 times higher for the same time involved.

Therefore it is interesting to see whether through online lending, if the costs of lending could be reduced, notably by lowering their transaction costs component or further lowering the information asymmetry. One way to lower such transaction costs would be to reduce the number of intermediaries between the small saver and the final borrower. To understand the existing system of brick and mortar MFIs, a simplistic version of the supply chain of money in microcredit is shown on the left hand side of Figure 2 as a linear model. Individual donors/lenders give money to donor organizations / social intermediaries. These donors/investor intermediaries provide this money to Microfinance institutions and then these MFIs lend to individuals. Thus, there are at least two intermediaries between the lender and the ultimate borrower: the donor/investor organizations and the

Microfinance institution. The promise of peer to peer is to reduce these intermediaries. With the arrival of internet, it should now be technologically possible for small firms and individual borrowers to get access to a large number of individuals and institutions, thus bypassing the intermediating brokers/investors and banks/Microfinance institutions, thus reducing the financing cost element. The relative low cost of internet technology should make small transactions feasible, thus reducing the operating cost element. However, borrowers also need to overcome the asymmetric information problem. The question is whether new internet tools, termed Web 2.0 social tools, can contribute to overcome information asymmetries and reduce the inherent risk for building up a climate of trust for the parties of a microfinance exchange, without increasing the loan loss reserve.

Development of Online Lending

On the Internet, we find a new category of lending companies is indeed emerging, which has been termed "peer to peer lending". The field regroups a few institutions with different missions and different legislative constraints, but all based on the promotion of peer-to-peer contacts. We find that peer to peer lending consists of diverse websites of microfinance (Kiva, Wokai, Babyloan), social investing (MicroPlace) as well as small loans at commercial market rates (Prosper, Zopa, Lend-

ing Club), and even lending between friends and family members (Virgin Money).

This fledging Internet-based peer-to-peer lending industry is evolving rapidly: about $650 million in outstanding debt in 2007 (Lee-St. John, 2008) to which can be added another $100 million to $150 million for 15 online microfinance platforms, according to a spokesman from Babyloan. A rising number of individuals are now looking towards networks of friends or even strangers on the Internet to finance purchases, pay for one-time events (such as weddings or vacations), consolidate debt, finance their small business or pay off a mortgage. The nascent peer-to-peer lending business on the Internet is based on online facilitators and/or intermediaries who enable and encourage social exchange between borrowers who post a request, and lenders who indicate how much and at what interest rate they want to lend. The demand for funds still appears to outstrip supply, mainly because lending and borrowing peers very often come from different cultures and territories and consequently do not know each other and hesitate to conclude deals, fearing opportunism, risk and difficulty of litigation in a foreign country.

Our study was initiated in February 2008 based on a literature review of what existed then (Farrell, 2008; Freeman, 2006a; Holahan, 2007; Pratt, 2007; Sisk, 2008; Stetenfeld, 2008). Additional web-sites have emerged since then (Powers, Magnoni & Knapp, 2008), but we have added only Babyloan owing to close association during the last few

Figure 2. Models of peer-to-peer micro-lending distribution channels on the Internet

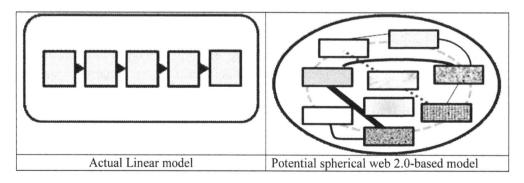

| Actual Linear model | Potential spherical web 2.0-based model |

months. Therefore, seven specialized websites in online lending constitute our sample: Kiva, Babyloan, Prosper, Zopa, Lending Club, Circle Lending (now Virgin Money) and MicroPlace.

As seen from Table 1, the first institution to be established was Circle Lending in 2002. At that time, it dealt with loans between families and friends who are already known to each other and the website was only a facilitator. Recently, this institution was taken over by Richard Branson and is now Virgin Money. The second institution to be started in 2005 was Kiva with founders Matt and Jessica Flannery, which has clearly taken the micro-credit niche. Babyloan, started in 2008, is a Kiva me-too, but with some differences. Two other institutions, Zopa and Prosper, which started in 2005 and 2006, respectively, are online mar-

ket places where borrowers and lenders who are unknown to each other come together. Although some of the loans on these websites may be small enough to be called micro, this is not the purpose. Another institution, similar to Zopa and Prosper, is more into community based lending: Lending Club (started in 2007). MicroPlace started in 2006 and is also concerned with financing microfinance institutions. One common denominator of all these websites is the repetition of the underlying philosophy of encouraging and promoting direct interaction and transactions between people. Although some of these have subsidiaries in other countries, we have covered only the parent country. We can also mention that for SEC regulation, some of these operations have had to close down (Zopa US, Prosper) and restart (Lending Club).

Table 1. Brief description of sample unit online finance operators

	Started	Status	General description	Interest rates to lenders	Online site Financed by	Role	Finance to	Model
Kiva,	2005	NGO	Microfinance	None	Donors or Grants and interest free loans	Broker/agent	Micro-finance institutions	Intermediary
Babyloan	2008	For-profit company	Microfinance	None, but service charges depending on volume of business	donors, Investors and interest free loans	Broker/agent	Micro-finance institutions	Intermediary
Microplace	2006	For-profit company	Social investing	1 to 3%	Individual investors	Broker/dealer	Security issuers	Intermediary
Prosper	2006	For-profit company	market place, auction	Market rates, depend on risk	security issuers	Broker/agent	Individuals	Intermediary
Zopa	2005	For-profit company	Market place, auction	Market rates, depend on risk	Lenders	Broker/agent	Individuals	Intermediary
Lending Club	2007	For-profit company	Market place	Market rates, depend on risk	Individual, business investors	Broker/agent	Individuals	Intermediary
Virgin Money (ex-Circle Lending)	2001/02	For-profit company	Social lending	Fixed Service fee for servicing between family or friends	Relatives, friends	Facilitator	Relatives friends	Direct

Some preliminary research states these sources of trust: (1) trustor or the one who trusts through his/her extravert, assertive and sociable personality; (2) trustee or the trust-inspiring partner of transaction who elates reliability and credibility because of his/her expertise and honesty and finally (3) third party certifiers who, by virtue of their cultural, legal and vocational statue, comply the transaction parties to loyalty and respect of commitments. It is hard to verify the personality of potential lenders and/or borrowers on the websites. Therefore, our focus is mainly on trustee and certifier.

This research finds that the sources of trust using online lending are often intermediary or institutional based. Trustor based sources of trust are not present on these websites (Assadi & Ashta, 2009). Trustee based sources of trust exist if these websites are facilitators: most are not. In facilitator websites, the information available in communities or groups could be harnessed through the use of web 2.0 tools such as automatic rating of peers by peers (borrowers by their friends) to devise risk rating. Such risk rating could also be impacted if some of the borrowers or lenders present on the website agree to be sponsor (act as guarantor) of the potential borrower. Thus, the use of webtools could use the information available in the community to reduce the asymmetric information part of risk. In this chapter, we examine whether these online websites are really using all the webtools at their disposal. We are not implying that the use of web2.0 tools is essential for trust: there could be other ways of building it, but this is the area in which we focus in this chapter.

The Web 2.0 Social Media

The term Web 2.0 is believed to have been coined by Dale Dougherty and then popularized by Tim O'Reilly[7](Lenrevie, Lévy & Lindon, 2006). It stands for a generation of social media that allows users to jointly create and manipulate content. Such media can take many forms, from the virtual worlds of Second Life, Microsoft Office-compatible Google Documents and Spreadsheets, blogs, wikis and group messaging software programs.

For solving problems, innovating, taking decisions, and even predicting the future, collaboration and aggregation of information in groups are considered to be better than the enlightenment of any elite few, no matter how brilliant (Surowiecki, 2004). Now, web 2.0 tools can enhance collaborative environments by making the practices of knowledge work more visible and accessible (McAfee, 2006). These tools enhance meaningful in-house dialogue and facilitate mass virtual collaboration to solve a problem or to improve an operation (Tapscott & Williams, 2006). Blogs, for example, can potentially bring organization and their constituencies together in a way that improves both image and bottom line (Scoble & Shel, 2006). Dell currently has several sites that support user-generated content and give its customers and community a voice (Armano, 2007). Many companies, such as Ernst & Young, recruit new employees primarily on Facebook (Hollis, 2007).

Empowered by the collaborative potential of the Web 2.0, many individuals now take the initiative to form communities and exchange directly on different issues. Moreover, a growing number of Web 2.0-equipped sites now enable Internet users to reward or punish corporations for their behavior and provide an opportunity to create brand affinity by driving communities to form around companies such as Harley-Davidson (Armano, 2007). Consumers on the internet share not only their purchase experiences with the rest of the world, but make their buying intentions transparent as well. Intentional buying groups show clearly their intentions. This phenomenon, dubbed "Intention Economy"[8] means letting consumers make their buying intentions known, and then inviting suppliers to bid for their business.

These applications create the possibility of strong collaboration. They enable distant peers to create, share, edit, categorize, and exchange information directly and independently. Every change or comment is preserved on the hosting web server. (Yu & Hui, 2007).

The revolutionary potential of these technologies reside in the ability to let atomistic individuals to form, by themselves, new groups, organizations, social networks and peer-to-peer collaborations. More than one billion consumers are now on the Internet. Many of them comment on commercial offers and post reviews and experiences, and are adding to the knowledge available on each brand and business. In fact, collaborating through Web 2.0 technologies is also referred to as "crowd sourcing" (Tapscott & Williams, 2006).

Through Web 2.0 technologies, distribution of data becomes spherical rather than linear, including horizontal and bottom-up, not just top-down communication. Furthermore, Web 2.0 open standards applications such as tagging, bookmarking, and user-generated content enable new forms of collaboration and new forms of information. The barriers between people have never been so thin. Web 2.0 technologies embrace the idea that the more people use a service or application, the stronger and more valuable it becomes, following "power laws". An illustration of such a network is provided in the right hand of Figure 2 as a potential spherical web2.0 based model, where people network with each other using the website as a platform to create content.

A McKinsey survey by Bughin & Manyika (2007) includes the following nine web 2.0 tools, ranked in order of respondents' interest and importance attached: web services, peer-to-peer networks, collective intelligence, social networks, podcasts, Blogs, RSS (Really Simple Syndication), Wikis and Mash-ups. Definitions of each tool are available in that survey. The survey points out that different industries use different tools. For example, Communications and media industries use RSS, Blogs and Podcasts more than the average user. Similarly, Knowledge-focused industries such as high-tech use Mash-ups, peer-to-peer networking, social networking, collective

intelligence and wikis more that average users. This is not to say that they lay less importance on Web services. Web services continue to be the most important, but both these industries use web-services as much as any other user. Thus, we can conclude that even if web 2.0 tools are used differently in different sectors, they all tend to favor horizontal collaborations and interactions between individuals and peers.

Our question is whether Web 2.0 tools are being used in the peer-to-peer (P2P) online lending websites to reduce information asymmetry and transaction costs in microfinance. Schematically, the question is whether the online lender's system resembles an intermediation linear chain as in the left hand side of Figure 2 or a platform spherical model as in the right hand side of Figure 2. The question is not only theoretical but also practically important because the ostensible mission of these websites is to encourage transactions between peers. In this chapter, we examine the web tools these website-based lenders use to build trust and reduce transaction costs.

IS ONLINE LENDING USING PLATFORM TECHNOLOGY TO REDUCE TRANSACTION COSTS?

Do Online Lending Sites resemble Web 2.0 Platforms or are they Intermediaries?

The first exploratory step of our research discovers specific business missions of the members of our sample and leads to discovering particular patterns in online lending. Our first question was whether these websites were actually peer-to-peer. From the description of the transactions on the various websites, we noted the movement of funds. From this it appears that the only facilitator dealing with peer to peer lending, without intermediary, is Virgin Money. In all the others, the so-called "peer-to peer" lending site is in fact an intermediary. In fact, four distinct online role models appear, which we will treat successively: microcredit, social investing, commercial market places and social lending. In the discussion below, we explore only the question of the business role by determining how money is transferred between entities. Further details of the operators may be obtained from their websites.

The Online Microcredit Model (Kiva, Babyloan)

For both Kiva and Babyloan, their objective is developmental in terms of mobilizing lower cost funds for MFIs in contrast to other sources of finance available to them. On their websites, individuals can choose to invest in one of the entrepreneurs who are profiled there.

Kiva is as an intermediary between lenders and borrowers. Its model is the linear one depicted in Figure 2. On the borrowers' side, Kiva works with, "Field Partners" which are microfinance institutions located in the country of the final borrower. Usually such microfinance institutions have limited funds, but have access to and ability to choose qualified borrowers / entrepreneurs from impoverished communities. Kiva does not distribute the funds itself to the final borrower. On the other side of Kiva, lenders can directly sponsor a business/borrower via an MFI, but sends the funds to Kiva. Therefore, the entire online process contains two intermediaries. The first is Kiva. org. When a lender loans, the funds are sent to Kiva.org via PayPal or a credit card. From Kiva. org the funds are sent to another intermediary, a field partner (a microfinance organization), which distributes the funds to the assigned entrepreneur. So, donors and interest-free lenders basically trust the intermediaries who facilitate the transfer and repayment of the microcredit. Trust may be less important on Kiva as essentially lenders are making donations. Their interest in getting the loans repaid is really so they can lend them out again and feel they are getting better "value" for

their donation. However, these donor-lenders may still want to verify that their philanthropic mission is fully satisfied through a transfer of loans to genuine entrepreneurs. This may explain the listing of entrepreneurs on the site of Kiva.org. Some field partners work with groups of entrepreneurs. Here, the group guarantees repayment of each individual member. No interest is currently charged or paid on loans from Kiva. Once a loan is repaid, lenders can re-loan or withdraw their funds. Kiva's running costs are paid by donors (including lenders who donate a small percentage of their loan), sponsors, as well as the interest on the float (money received but not yet lent or not yet reimbursed to lender).

Babyloan follows the same model as Kiva except that it has made modifications to conform with French legislation. It facilitates a contract between the lender and the MFI and charges a service fee to the donors as well as the MFIs. This is a 2.5% service charge to lenders and 2.5% to the borrowers, and it allows Babyloan to seek financial sustainability. Babyloan cannot charge interest because that is only allowed to banks as per French legislation. Moreover, since Babyloan is a for-profit company, it cannot solicit donations. Nor can it use volunteer workers as is the case with Kiva. Repayment from the borrower is made via the Babyloan system. This money does not go back to the original lenders till the end of the loan period and, then, the lenders have the option of lending again.

To become a Kiva or Babyloan "Field Partner", the prospective microfinance institution must currently serve at least 1,000 active microfinance borrowers; have a history (at least 2-3 years) of lending to poor, excluded, and/or vulnerable people for the purpose of alleviating poverty or reducing vulnerability; be registered as a legal entity in its country of operation; be able to show at least one year of financial audits; and preferably be registered on the MIX Market (www.mixmarket. org). Moreover, field visits by volunteer workers (in the case of Kiva) validate the existence of the

MFI. For Babyloan, the MFI's are supported by European technical assistance organizations and "Babyloan's Professional Network (BPN)"[9]. These requirements help to build trust with the ultimate lender, but are an expense borne by the donors of KIVA (volunteer time, donations).

On the lenders side, Kiva encourages potential loan givers to choose directly among uploaded entrepreneur profiles on the site and sponsor a business. The course of a loan is usually between 6-12 months and its amount can be as little as $25 at a time (20 Euros for Babyloan). Once a loan is repaid, the lender can withdraw the funds or re-loan them to a new entrepreneur. Lenders periodically hear back from their sponsored entrepreneur and remain informed on the progress of the enterprise, via email and online journal updates, often written by partner representatives and loan officers. Kiva never facilitates the interaction and communication between lending and borrowing individuals. The website of Kiva is not interactive and does not promote peer-to-peer connections.

Online Social Investing (MicroPlace)

MicroPlace distinguishes itself from Kiva and the other entities and refers to its lenders as "investors". These lenders invest in market notes of security issuers. These security issuers then provide the funds to microfinance institutions who lend the funds to poor people. The original investors get returns of 1 to 3%. MicroPlace is a registered broker-dealer which allows the social investors to buy the bonds of security issuers. Microplace earns a commission from the security issuer. It can take only funds from American retail investors. Microplace is therefore also following the linear model.

Once loan repayments are received by the MFI from its clients, the institutional investors receive their principal (plus interest) and can then pay back their own investors, i.e., people who purchased those original securities. Unlike Kiva and Babyloan, where lenders provide capital

to microfinance institutions directed to specific entrepreneurs, MicroPlace is mainly a market for microfinance securities, not just requests for loans, and the investors target specific Microfinance Institutions and not the ultimate entrepreneur (2008b).

In MicroPlace's case, their website suggests that they would like to view themselves as a platform where at the very least investors, security issuers and MFIs are present. It would be difficult for individual entrepreneurs/borrowers to be present because the poor may not have the literacy level to use internet to update their profiles. Kiva is using donors funds, volunteer time, its own employees and that of partner MFIs to upload borrower profiles[10.] MicroPlace has therefore obviated this expense by positioning itself in relation to lender/investors and MFIs.

However, even MFIs are not present on the platform directly. Since interest is being charged (as opposed to free "donor" loans in the case of Kiva and reduced cost loans in the case of Babyloan), the Securities and Exchange Commission does not allow MicroPlace to give loans to MFIs directly. As a result, MFIs have no interest in registering on their website. MicroPlace therefore has to attract Security Issuers who already have their contacts with MFIs. Moreover, MicroPlace does not have the capacity to rate the MFIs. For all these reasons, the MFI is not on the MicroPlace platform. A Microplace spokesman adds "MFI's are simply not sophisticated enough themselves to be able to create a security to offer to US investors. As you can appreciate, it's an expensive and complex process even for the largest organizations like Calvert or Oikocredit."

Even Security Issuers are not yet present on the MicroPlace platform. Since there are only two security issuers who are dealing with MicroPlace, it is too early to determine whether they are on a platform. One reason could be that there may not be many security issuers dealing with MFIs and therefore the market is too small a niche for the moment. A second reason could be that these two may be sufficiently large to attract all existing investors that MicroPlace has been able to mobilize thus far. The Microplace spokesman confirms that although the technology we are dealing with allows instantaneous communication and transfer of funds, it is embedded in an orthodox regulatory environment and for a new player such as MicroPlace, the attraction of security issuers and their involvement on the site is a long process: "We have many security issuers in the pipeline, but bringing a retail investment to market in the US involves many regulatory, cost and other hurdles. We try to lead security issues down the path and make it easy, but the fact is it just takes time and perseverance to get through all the necessary details and MicroPlace may be one of many competing distribution channels for them. As we have more issuers on the site, raise more capital, and develop more of a standard "toolkit" for completing the process, it will be easier- we're just enduring a few expected growing pains now".

This then brings us to the question of what measures are required to get lenders/investors to bring more funds to MicroPlace. As with security issuers, there are undoubtedly patterns of social interaction that are deeply embedded in systems of procurement, based on history, country, laws, institutions, geography and resources (2001). The role of these factors in influencing technology adoption may influence the development of web 2.0 in areas as conservative as investing, lending and borrowing money.

Online Commercial Lending Market Places (Zopa, Prosper and Lending Club)

Zopa, Prosper and Lending Club[11], three other members of our sample, provide a matchmaking service of introducing borrowers to lenders who previously did not know each other. According to the websites, this process helps borrowers to get lower rates than commercial credit and offer lenders higher rates than bank deposits (see the

Chapter by Assadi & Hudson in this book). The websites indicate that many borrowers would otherwise be unable to get any loans from banks: for example, new companies who have no financial history seem to have difficulty in getting loans from banks during the first two years because they do not have financial information to provide (Farrell, 2008)[12]. These firms find that they can get small loans from people on these websites, even without getting to know their lenders. Freeman (2006b) finds other similarities between Zopa and Prosper: "both vet potential borrowers, assess the credit risk, and distribute that risk among a number of different lenders, all individuals who determine how much money they wish to loan out at what level of return". Any individual can register as a borrower and can build a profile for himself/herself. Loans from a lender can be distributed to a single person or divided amongst several borrowers. Conversely, a borrower's loan might come from a single lender or several, to reduce risk. An auction mechanism is used to allow borrowers to get the lowest rates for their credit rating. They are all using the linear model. Most of the lending may be consumer lending. An important distinction between the commercial lending and the previous microlending models is that in these commercial models there is one level of intermediary (the web operator), while in the microlending models there were two levels of intermediaries, at least, because the local MFI was also required in addition to the web operator.

Online Social Lending (Virgin Money)

Virgin Money (USA) differs from the three previous online lenders because it focuses on loans between people who are familiar with one another (family and friends). The Virgin Money people deal with the paper work such as loan documents, payment processing, reminder emails, and year-end statements. Virgin Money is the only real peer to peer movement of funds as shown in the model of Figure 2. This distinction exists because the borrower and lender know each other before contacting Virgin Money. It is ironic that there is an absence of the Web 2.0 tools on its website to encourage direct contact and trust building between peers. In fact, people use Virgin Money because they wish to formalize transactions in a way that would otherwise be costly, i.e., it is not the information asymmetry they are dealing with, it is perhaps that formalizing the transactions reduces the risk of default (i.e., often friends might say they would pay back but the lender would find it virtually impossible to enforce repayment) and lowers the transactions costs of doing this. Also, another advantage is that it allows an informal borrower (within family) to create a good credit history by repaying in public.

The review of the four different online lending models indicates that the only real direct peer to peer lending is through Virgin Money, which is merely a facilitator offering services to the peers who already know each other. All the other five are intermediaries and money flows through them. However, the motivation of these five differs. Prosper, Zopa and Lending Club seek to maximize profits for their clients and for themselves. At the other extreme, Kiva is a not-for-profit and its lenders also do not receive interest. The essential difference in Babyloan and Kiva is that Babyloan is searching for a sustainable for-profit model in Microfinance while Kiva is donor driven (The founders of Babyloan prefer the social business image rather than a profit-mixmisation one). In between, MicroPlace is looking for a small return and falls into the category of social investors.

The last four columns of Table 1 summarize our findings of the different internet models used and the position in the chain of each operator.

Are These Social Lending Sites Using the Full Range of Web 2.0 Tools?

Our research objective was to determine whether peers build direct trust with each other on the microfinance websites through the Web 2.0 tech-

nologies which potentially enable direct, immediate and horizontal interactions and transactions. What are the performances of the members of our sample with regard to this issue?

Table 2 resumes our findings of the web tools being used to facilitate contact. We have not observed all the web 2.0 tools surveyed by Bughin and Manyika (2007) because some tools are typically used in-house and/or are not observable, while other tools are used to relate to external customers and are more visible. For example, peer-to-peer technology of sharing files across a number of users' computers rather than maintaining the files in a large central server, is not visible to the outside observer (such as us) unless the firm outlines such procedures explicitly on its website. Similarly, wikis are often used more for in-house collaboration and knowledge building than for sharing information with workers. We have classified the visible tools which we surveyed into blogs, interactivity, peers' reviews and comments, peers' communities and chats, as shown in table 3. We find that five sites use blogs, two sites have other means of interactivity, one site is using Wikis and three sites are offering Peer Community and Chat Services.

However, not all these blogs are interactive. Some are only one-way communication channels. For example, we note that blogs may be institutional; they may permit comments; and they may allow people to initiate new topics. Similarly Communities may be open only to lenders; only to borrowers; or to lenders and borrowers. The fact that the members of our sample do not use web 2.0 is surprising because these tools have the potential of promoting connections between peers, and one would expect that social lending websites to increase social transactions.

Although at first glance, it is surprising to see that Virgin Money does not use any web 2.0 tools, it must be remembered that the people using Virgin Money already know each other and may not need such tools.

Table 2. Web 2.0 social tools on the online lending websites

	Blog	Interactivity between lenders and buyers	Peers' reviews and comments	Peers Communities and chats
Kiva	Journals of entrepreneurs with photo, message. Possible link to the lenders' blogs. Kiva Blog, "Inside Kiva", an info. letter with links. No interactivity with readers.	None, but members may request for visiting their beneficiaries.	Comments on the journals of the entrepreneurs. No interactivity	Communities only for lenders (since August 2009)
Babyloan	The blog is maintained by an administrator. Readers can comment, but these comments are vetted by an administrator.	None, but members sometimes request visits to their beneficiaries, as indicated in blog.	None	Friends community system allowing lenders to invite and create friends network inside the web site
Lending Club	General blog for all members, allows comments and discussion by authorized people (we see the same person writing all the time).	No direct contact or exchange on the site Possible exchange via common out-of-site affiliations like FaceBook, MySpace.	Possible comments on borrowers or lenders in the out-of-site affiliations websites. None on their website.	None
MicroPlace	Institutional blog, personalized with pictures. Can comment but not initiate.	Listing of borrowers. No interactivity	General information on borrowers. No peer comment	None
Prosper	There are two types of blog on prosper.com: institutional blogs and affiliated and linked to blogs. The institutional blogs are not personalized. Still, they allow comments even if users cannot initiative new topics.	"Questions & Answers" on borrower's listing.	None	Prosper Groups, created by lenders and borrowers, Rated on repayment performance
Virgin Money	None	None	None	None
Zopa	Institutional blog for all members. Can comment.	The discussion board is interactive	Not on the site. Possible via the personal borrowers' blogs (if linked to the site's listing)	Discussion board for members
Total using tool	5	3	1	3
Updated September 25th, 2008, incorporated Babyloan reviewer updates March 2010 for Babyloan.				

When we compare to the McKinsey survey (Bughin & Manyika, 2007), we find that online lending sites use significantly more blogs than most websites. Other web 2.0 tools that we examined indicated that these lending sites are not significantly different to those found in the McKinsey survey. It may be interesting to discuss why online lending websites may not use the web2.0 technologies to promote direct P2P interaction. A notable reason could be that these web-site operators in our sample are intermediaries who make their money through intermediation. If there was direct connectivity and interactivity between borrowers and lenders, there would be no need for the intermediary. Another reason is that interaction, direct or indirect, using web 1.0 or web 2.0, is not sufficient to overcome the information asymmetry problem that requires knowing a person over time. As a result, a certifying intermediary will always have a role to play. Moreover, as the experience of Kiva shows, if the intermediary website is operating in more than one country, there is a need for a second intermediary in the country of the borrower who is aware of local rules and regulations for enforcement.

The McKinsey survey describes "webservices" as "information systems to make it easier for different systems to communicate with one another automatically in order to pass information or conduct transactions". They provide an example of a supplier and retailer updating each other's inventory. However, the retailer does not let the supplier update his or her customer's inventory. So, it is evident that this kind of webservices would not be found between borrowers and lenders that we studied because the intermediary is more in the position of retailer with the lender being the supplier and the borrower being the customer. However, such webservices may be being used between the website of the intermediary and the borrowers or between the intermediary and the lenders, without visibility to the public. Moreover, these technologies constitute the "plumbing" for information flow between two or more systems. Hence the question of using webservices for interaction between lenders and borrowers does no arise, as borrowers in the microfinance world are typically poor individuals or groups of individuals without access to advanced use of computers.

In a similar vein, it is useful to note that peer to peer lending websites do use more blogs, but these blogs are one-way instruments. As a result, there is no real possibility for comments and dialogue. So, the blogs provide only one-sided information and opinions. The blogs are serving a corporate advertising purpose and not a market feedback mechanism.

The online lenders recognize that they run the risk of increasing adverse selection and moral hazard – as of course the likelihood is that potential borrowers can post deliberately misleading information and make the problem harder. Thus the attempts by Kiva and Lending Club to use web 2.0 tools such as blogs and communities to create the kind of group information sharing which was the characteristic innovation of brick and mortar microfinance lending.

Has Online Lending Impacted Credit Availability, Interest Rates and Transaction Costs?

The commercial lending sites such as Lending Club, Prosper and Zopa, may result in lower rates of interests for borrowers and higher rates of interests for depositors than brick-and-mortar banks, but these banks would soon match them by banking online. Many of these sites are not explicitly aimed at the poor, except for MicroPlace, Babyloan and Kiva.

Even for the three sites aiming at the poor, in fact the MFI as well as the lending site continue to exist as intermediaries and there are no economies of shortening the supply chain of credit. Both these entities still need to have operating and financial sustainability. So, even if spreads are limited by this new online transaction method, they do not really reduce overhead costs of the Microfinance Institution, which is the biggest component of the transaction cost. It is admitted that with poor illiterate borrowers on one end of the spectrum, it is necessary, in this model, to have MFIs as an intermediary. But the question raised is whether Kiva, Babyloan and MicroPlace have a role to play.

Since the poor are not directly connected on the internet as they do not have the education level to use internet nor the complementary capital to access it, all the uploaded stories are written by the associated Microfinance institutions or by Kiva volunteer workers. This process adds to the costs of the system, even if the costs are borne by donors.

FUTURE RESEARCH DIRECTIONS

This is a first paper on this subject, in an evidently new field. Obviously, the number of questions for future research is numerous. We can at least advise the following fields of investigation.

One axis for development would be examining why P2P online lending websites do not promote direct interactions and transactions, which would lower interest costs and increase the volume of business. The research seems to be pertinent and urgent when one considers that a lot of other business is being done online.

A connected issue for research as well as experimentation could be whether multimedia solutions are possible for illiterate borrowers. In this case, they could record their stories directly on the website, bypassing the MFI. However, the cost of access to internet may still pose a problem, even though internet centers have opened up in urban and suburban areas. Moreover, they would still need a bank account to access the money of the online lender. Perhaps, with the development of mobile telephone based e-money, there could be an eventual direct link between the online website and the borrower.

Future research needs to explore issues such as whether lenders and donors are inhibited by culture from proclaiming that they are donors. Also, do borrowers and recipients feel any shame or other refraining emotions in openly disclosing that they need financial help? Although Kiva is helping build borrower profile in a bid to help the microcredit movement, do the illiterate borrowers understand and approve of their virtual images placed in public places? This last question is treated in a subsequent chapter in this book (Gajjala et al).

Surprisingly, almost all commercial sites we reviewed are national/domestic. Although we have focused on the American sites, many of the commercial sites also have presence in other countries with separate companies and separate websites. Therefore, except for donations, funds seem to be unable to move across borders. It may be interesting to compare national legislations (sometime State legislations within federal countries) to understand the blocks to a truly global economy allowing a truly social movement of funds from the rich to the poor. The successive suspending of Lending Club, Prosper and Zopa for SEC regulations means that there are important regulatory issues to be studied. An important

question is whether international/global legislation will follow or precede and facilitate the new reality being ushered in by these online lending operations, whether commercial, social or donor.

There are other research issues related to online lending which this chapter has not examined but are equally compelling. It will be very useful to actually compare the final lending rates to borrowers, between what is possible through an online lending site, and outside of it through older and more traditional channels of microfinance. It will also be useful to have information on whether the actual quantum of credit extended by online lenders to borrowers is higher (or lower) than the traditional channels.

CONCLUSION

The chapter pointed out that there are three major cost elements in interest rates to ultimate borrowers: financing costs, processing costs and costs of defaults related to information asymmetry. The commercial online lending sites indicate that there is a role for disintermediation from the banks and that financial inclusion (outreach) can be increased to people who the banks were not lending to or loans can be provided at lower rates than those of banks. Thus financing costs could be reduced. This is even more true for donor dependent or subsidized financing models used by the microfinance online websites, which permit MFIs to get lower interest cost financing, but with perhaps other servicing costs.

The processing costs of the brick and mortar MFIs are unaffected by the new technology since these websites are just another financing mechanism. The processing costs of commercial online lending sites could be lower than those of brick and mortar banks for small transaction amounts because of digitalization, automation and virtualization.

The risk associated with MFI level microfinance is also not affected since it's the same brick and mortar MFI providing funds to the final borrowers. However, the risks related to commercial online lending websites is a more serious question since they do not have the final face-to-face contact with a banker and they have been experimenting with the creation of communities and self-assessments to reduce risks.

The chapter studied the use of web 2.0 technologies (blogs, interactivity between lenders and buyers, peers' reviews and comments, peer communities and chats) in six online lending sites. It finds that most of the P2P lending websites are in fact intermediaries between the peers (lender and borrowers) and facilitate little direct contact between the peers. The only site which permitted direct contact was Virgin Money. However, this is because the borrower and lender are already known to each other in their model. As a result, perhaps, Virgin Money is the only website that did not use any of the web 2.0 tools. Since the peers are known to each other in their model, the facilitator did not need to use Web 2.0 tools to bring them together. The information asymmetry problem did not exist. All the other intermediaries use at least one Web 2.0 tool. None of the websites used all the web 2.0 tools. Indeed, they recognize that they run the risk of increasing adverse selection and moral hazard – as of course the likelihood is that potential borrowers can post deliberately misleading information and make the problem harder. Thus the attempts to use web 2.0 tools such as blogs and communities to create the kind of group information sharing which was the characteristic innovation of brick and mortar microfinance lending.

The chapter raises questions of why these websites, particularly those relating to microfinance (Microplace, Babyloan and Kiva), would keep their intermediation functions. Some institutional reasons are involved. These include illiteracy of the final borrower. As a result, the strength of online lending microfinance has been more in the promotion of the microfinance movement towards the small investors and permitting them

to be involved in the struggle against poverty, and perhaps mobile banking or other solutions examined elsewhere in the chapter may be more useful in reaching the other side: the final borrowers.

Immediate profit-making is the most likely reason for maintaining intermediation roles although web2.0 tools and lower costs give less need for such immediacy. With time, people may make websites which will permit people to borrow and lend directly. Government regulations may then become more relevant. As with Napster, other stakeholders may want to make money through such developments. Then stakeholders such as insurance companies and certifiers would become involved and regulation would need to balance these alternative stakeholder interests.

Additionally, there may be a failure to create the excitement necessary for social contagion[13]. This could be because people are hesitant to talk about money and giving to charity. Alternatively, it may be because these operators (Kiva, Babyloan and MicroPlace) have not been able to find the appropriate mavens or connectors[14] to spread the "buzz" effectively beyond the initial novelty impact[15]. According to our Microplace spokesman, in addition to buzz, viral marketing, culture and institutions, an essential issue is of understanding typical ecommerce behavior: "what's important to our customers, understanding what inspires them to invest etc. etc. However, it is possible that we are judging harshly a movement which will take time to be accepted for cultural reasons as well as overcoming legislative barriers and legal risk specific to international finance and perhaps the benefits of web 2.0 tools are to increase the users' enjoyment of the platforms and services - ultimately to the benefit of trust through transparency and open communication– and to help spread the word about the new platforms virally. Then again, it is possible that web 2.0 tools are only part of the story and many other marketing and product-mix factors go to explain the success or failure of online lending.

REFERENCES

Akerlof, G. A. (1970). The Market for "Lemons": Quality Uncertainty and the Market Mechanism. *The Quarterly Journal of Economics, 84*(3), 488–500. doi:10.2307/1879431

Armano, D. (2007). It's the Conversation Economy, Stupid. *Business Week Online* (p. 11).

Armendariz, B., & Morduch, J. (2005). *The Economics of Microfinance*. Cambridge, MA: MIT Press.

Ashta, A. (2007). An Introduction to Microcredit: Why Money is Flowing from the Rich to the Poor. *Cahiers du CEREN Working Paper 21*.

Ashta, A. (2009). Microcredit Capital Flows and Interest Rates: An Alternative Explanation. *Journal of Economic Issues (M.E. Sharpe Inc.), 43*(3), 661-683.

Ashta, A., & Bush, M. (2009, November). Ethical Issues of NGO Principals in Sustainability, Outreach and Impact of Microfinance: Lessons in Governance from the Banco Compartamos' IPO. *Management Online REview, vol. November*, 1-18.

Assadi, D., & Ashta, A. (2009). How do People Trust on Peer-to-Peer Lending Websites? Analysis of the Impacts of the Web 2.0 Technologies and Intermediation Roles. In Gera, R. (Ed.), *Advances in Technology and Innovation in Marketing* (pp. 49–69). Delhi: MacMillan Publishers India Ltd.

Attuel-Mendes, L., & Ashta, A. (2008). French Usury Legislation and the Development of Credit Availability for Microenterprise. *Global Journal of Business Research, 2*(2), 123–138.

Bernasek, A., & Stanfield, J. R. (1997). The Grameen Bank as Progressive Institutional Adjustment. *Journal of Economic Issues, 31*(2), 359–366.

Bhatt, N., & Shui-Yan, T. (2001). Designing Group-Based Microfinance Programs: Some Theoretical And Policy Considerations. *International Journal of Public Administration, 24*(10), 1103–1125. doi:10.1081/PAD-100105104

Bughin, J., & Manyika, J. (2007). *How businesses are using Web 2.0: A McKinsey Global Survey*. The McKinsey Quarterly.

Dieckmann, R. (2007). *Microfinance: An emerging investment opportunity: Uniting social investment and financial returns* (p. 20). Frankfurt: Deutsche Bank Research.

Farrell, M. (2008). *Banking 2.0: New Capital Connections for Entrepreneurs*. Forbes.

Freeman, L. (2006a). ZOPA: A Gigantic Opportunity. *Credit Union Journal, 10*(46), 1–17.

Freeman, L. (2006b). ZOPA: A Gigantic Opportunity - Are You Watching P2P Lending? You should Be. *The Credit Union Journal*.

Goudzwaard, M. B. (1968). Price Ceilings And Credit Rationing. *The Journal of Finance, 23*(1), 177–185. doi:10.2307/2325317

Holahan, C. (2007). EBay: The Place for Microfinance. *Business Week Online* (p. 24).

Hollis, T. (2007). *Social Media Advertising: No Direct Response Proposition*. ClickZ Experts.

2004How "Social Contagion" Affects Consumers' Willingness to Try Online Retailers. *Knowlege@Wharton*.

2008aKiva: Improving People's lives, One Small Loan at a Time. *Knowlege@Wharton*.

Lee-St. John, J. (2008). Hey, Buddy, Can You Spare $10,000? *Time, 171*(10), 58–58.

Lenrevie, J., Lévy, J., & Lindon, D. (2006). *Mercator*. Dunod.

Mahoney, P. G. (2002). Information Technology and the Organization of Securities Markets. *Working Papers -- Financial Institutions Center at The Wharton School* (p. 1).

McAfee, A. P. (2006). Enterprise 2.0: The Dawn of Emergent Collaboration. *MIT Sloan Management Review, 47*(3), 21–28.

Mishkin, F. S. (2004). *The economics of money, banking and Financial Markets*. Paris: Pearson Addison-Wesley.

2008bOpen Up Your Virtual Wallet: The buzz about online microlending. Microfinance Gateway.

Powers, J., Magnoni, B., & Knapp, S. (2008). *Person-To-Person Lending: Is Financial Democracy A Click Away?* (p. 43). US AID.

Pratt, M. K. (2007). Game Changer (cover story). *Computerworld, 41*(5), 31–32.

Rosenberg, R., Gonzalez, A., & Narain, S. (2009). The New Moneylenders: Are the Poor Being Exploited by High Microcredit Interest Rates? *Occasional Paper, 15*. Washington, D.C.: CGAP.

Scoble, R., & Shel, I. (2006). *Naked Conversation: How Blogs Are Changing the Way Businesses Talk with Consumers*. Wiley.

Shuen, A. (2008). *Web 2.0: A Strategy Guide*. Sebastopol, CA: O'Reilly Media Inc.

Sisk, M. (2008). The Rise of Lending Communities. *U.S. Banker, 118*(2), 18–20.

Stetenfeld, B. (2008). P2P Lending: Threat or Opportunity? (cover story). *Credit Union Magazine, 74*(1), 32–36.

Stiglitz, J. E., & Weiss, A. (1981). Credit Rationing in Markets with Imperfect Information. *The American Economic Review, 71*(3), 393–410.

Surowiecki, J. (2004). *The Wisdom of Crowds: Why the Many Are Smarter than the Few and How Collective Wisdom Shapes Business, Economies, Societies, and Nations*. New York: Doubleday.

Tapscott, D., & Williams, A. D. (2006). *Wikinomics: How Mass collaboration Changes Everything*. New York: Portfolio.

2001The Evolution of B2B: Lessons from the Auto Industry. *Knowlege@Wharton*.

2006The Intention Economy. *Searls Doc: Linux Journal*.

2005What's the Buzz About Buzz Marketing? *Knowledge@Wharton*.

Yu, C., & Hui, D. (2007). Welcome to the World of Web 2.0. *The CPA Journal*, 6–10.

ENDNOTES

[1]   Our thanks to Alain Bultez of the Facultés Universitaires Catholiques de Mons for his statistical analysis and to the participants at Asia Microfinance Forum in Hanoi, Vietnam: August 26-29, 2008, the participants at the Atout workshop organized by Jacques Thépot, as well as to Jonathan Greenacre, an anonymous MicroPlace correspondent for their reviews and comments, to Zopa for helping us understand further and Babyloan reviewers: Aurelie Duthoit, Arnaud Poissonnier and Margaux Goute. An earlier version of this paper was published by the internal working paper series of our school's research center Cahier du Ceren n°23 (June 2008).

[2]   (2001)

[3]   (2004) According to the Penguin dictionary of Pyschology, Social contagion is "the rapid spread of attitudes, ideas or moods through a group or a society, as, for example, through rumour".

4 The distinction between the two is that adverse selection is the problem faced by an agent before the event while moral hazard is the problem faced after an event (Mishkin, 2004).

5 For example, securities intermediaries such as stock exchanges create rules for doing business that add to information flow and to ethical norms for participating and their own credibility and reputation are a function of fixed and human capital invested in the exchanges (Mahoney, 2002) Value would be added to the society (in the Pareto optimality sense) if the adverse selection problem could be resolved by the provision of information. However, a free rider problem emerges if people with information provide this publicly. So some intermediaries (like banks) prefer to keep the information privately.

6 The interest rates also vary from author to author: For Example Dieckmann ((2007)) suggests a range of 15% to 70%. However, with Compartamos, Mexico having charged 100% the range is increased to 100% in line with Ashta (2009). There is some evidence that Compartamos may be an outlier and that normal interest rates have reduced from 35% to 28% from 2003 to 2006 ((Rosenberg, Gonzalez & Narain, 2009))

7 The Weblog of Tim O'Reilly can be viewed at < http://www.oreillynet.com/ >

8 (2006)

9 Information provided by Babyloan reviewers: Aurelie Duthoit, Arnaud Poissonnier and Margaux Goute.

10 (2008a)

11 In the US, SEC permission is required. This has entailed Lending Club and Prosper to close one by one. Lending Club has reopened after clearance.

12 However, this may vary from one weblender to another: it may be harder in credit risk (not liquidity) terms to get a loan from Zopa, for example, than a bank, as is borne out by their tiny levels of default below 0.2% of all funds ever lent (source Zopa).

13 (2004)

14 (2005)

15 In March 2009, after four years of operations, Kiva has served a little over 90,000 borrowers. With the power of internet's outreach at low costs, it seems that despite the best promotions, including testimonials by people like Bill Clinton and heavy subsidies, clearly Kiva has not tapped the power of Web 2.0.

Chapter 13

EDA CapitalConnect:
An Online Platform for Social Enterprise Financing

Daniel Brett
EDA CapitalConnect, USA

Nikias Stefanakis
EDA CapitalConnect, USA

ABSTRACT

Since its inception in July 2008, EDA CapitalConnect (EDACC) has sought to address inefficiencies in the market for funding to social enterprises worldwide. To tackle these challenges, the company has developed an online platform that allows social enterprises and institutional funders to communicate with one another, initiate financial transactions, and analyze market trends. The platform seeks to increase deal flow and transparency in the social enterprise space by facilitating information dissemination and the exchange of funding offers between capital providers and seekers of all sizes. As the platform develops, the challenges of achieving financial sustainability and scale will require EDACC to continue to fine-tune its services to meet the evolving needs of the social enterprise community. EDACC's experience in its nascency suggests that technology providers to microfinance institutions and social enterprises – particularly start up organizations – must pay close attention to the behavior of their target users, and modify their services based upon trends in usage and market perceptions.

INTRODUCTION

Over the last few decades, social enterprises[1] around the world have risen in prominence, as their impact on people's lives has become increasingly evident. These organizations are growing in scale, structure and reach, and their capital needs – both debt and equity – are increasing as well. In the

United States alone, there are roughly 1.5 million non-profit or social ventures which have combined revenues of $700 billion, and control assets valued at $2 trillion (Wei-Skillern, 2007). At the same time, the investing and lending community worldwide is becoming more socially responsible, and has increasingly sought to provide capital support to these social enterprises; by 2052, an estimated $6 trillion will flow directly to social enterprises in the United States alone (Thompson,

DOI: 10.4018/978-1-61520-993-4.ch013

2008). This growing interest has not been limited to socially responsible investors and lenders, as mainstream funders have also begun to provide greater amounts of capital to social enterprises.

Despite increasing interest and widespread growth in this sector, the flow of information between providers and seekers of capital remains imperfect and asymmetric[2] (Arzeni, 2004). Many social enterprises are unable to effectively engage institutional lenders and investors in the development sector because they are physically isolated, small, lack sufficient financial and human resources to effectively outreach to funders, or are unfamiliar with the funding process and do not know how to structure a funding offer. Similarly, many institutional funders are interested in investing in social enterprises but are unable to easily connect with the ones that meet their funding requirements.[3] This lack of information flow prevents many deserving organizations from obtaining the funds that they need, and hinders funders' ability to achieve the highest financial and social return on their investments.

To address these concerns and capitalize on the increasing prevalence of the internet throughout the developing world, EDA Rural Systems launched EDACC in 2008. The purpose of this interactive online marketplace is to facilitate the initiation of primary and secondary debt and equity transactions and partnerships, and increase information flow in the social enterprise sector. Combining elements of online auction and social networking sites, the platform allows social investors and enterprises to communicate, initiate financial transactions, and access market trends and benchmarks to further facilitate deal flow.

This chapter describes EDACC's journey to provide an innovative service to the social enterprise sector. Basic background information on EDACC will be provided, followed by current trends in the market, and lessons learned from reviewing the performance of similar online platforms, all of which contributed to the conceptualization of EDACC. The discussion will then cover EDACC's current offering and operations, the business model, the performance to date, and conclude with a discussion of the organization's key challenges, lessons learned and future goals.

BACKGROUND

EDACC was conceived by Director and Founder of EDA Rural Systems, Mr. Sanjay Sinha. In 1983, Sinha established EDA Rural Systems as a development sector consultancy, research and capacity-building organization. Through its trainings and academic publications, EDA Rural Systems became well-known in the development sector and in Asia's microfinance sector in particular. As the sector grew, Sinha observed that there was a pressing need to improve the availability and flow of information between microfinance institutions (MFIs) and other industry stakeholders, which he believed could reduce the information asymmetry in the market for capital.[4] From this observation and the success of EDA Rural, Sinha and his team launched Micro-Credit Ratings International Limited, (M-CRIL), which developed and implemented the concept of producing credit ratings of MFIs. In addition to a review of financial performance, these ratings include a risk assessment, projections of future performance, and recommendations for investment. Over its first decade of operations, M-CRIL expanded its services in terms of the number of MFIs rated and the quantity of funds channeled to MFIs. In 2005, EDA pioneered the assessment of the effectiveness of MFIs' systems and services for the achievement of its social objectives by developing the first social rating tool for MFIs (Sinha F., 2006).

As EDA and M-CRIL adapted to the substantial growth of the microfinance sector, Sinha and his team became increasingly aware of broader funding trends for social enterprise organizations – of which microfinance is a subset – and identified several inefficiencies that characterize this emerging and yet fragmented market.

Analyzing the Social Enterprise Sector

Most grassroots entities working in the social enterprise sector are traditionally formed as non-profit organizations, and rely upon grants as their primary sources of funding. As these organizations (and the sectors in which they operate) mature, they depend more on commercial funds than grants, for several reasons. Firstly, organizations do not typically grow without increasing their financial requirements. This requires them to access larger funds, most of which are commercial. Secondly, donors are increasingly seeking to reduce their involvement after early stage funding. Lastly, the financial success of organizations working in a young sector encourages more for-profit entities to enter that sector, and for-profit entities have a greater demand for commercial funds than do non-profit organizations.[5]

Empirical evidence from the microfinance sector in India is illustrative of social enterprise funding trends in the developing world is shown in Figure 1.

As Figure 1 indicates, the sector displays a trending away from the reliance on grants in favor of institutional or commercial debt. This shift is not only attributable to an increasing demand for commercial funding, but is also explained by capital providers' growing interest in providing commercial funds to the social enterprise sector. Where there were initially mostly foundations and government lending institutions (for instance, USAID and DFID), banks, individual and institutional investors and trusts are now key facilitators of capital flow into social enterprises (Bedson, 2009). Motivations for engaging in this sector range from philanthropic to commercial, but nonetheless they are now very active in providing both debt and equity. Box 1 provides a summary of the key players who fund social enterprises.

Despite increases in both the demand and supply of funding in the social enterprise capital market, serious inefficiencies in capital pricing and allocation continue to exist in this space. EDA Rural Systems' team completed a comprehensive review of the sector, and noted that these inefficiencies are primarily manifested in three forms: Inefficient Primary Markets, Inefficient Secondary Markets and an Absence of Industry-wide Benchmarks.[6]

Inefficient Primary Markets: Many social enterprises are unable to engage institutional lenders and investors in the development sector because these organizations are small, physically isolated, or unfamiliar with global financial markets. Similarly, many institutional funders seeking to expand their reach to a greater number of potential investees or recipients of their funds, struggle because their existing networks are not sufficiently large enough for them to find an adequate number of organizations that match their funding criteria. These constraints prevent many deserving organizations from obtaining the funds that they need.

Inefficient Secondary Markets: Lenders and investors find it challenging to sell their debt or equity, because they are unable to efficiently identify and communicate with a large number of the financial institutions who might be interested in purchasing their holdings. This restricted flow of information impedes funders' ability to liquidate their assets or diversify their portfolios, which curbs their incentives to lend or invest in social enterprises. These disincentives, in turn, reduce both the volume of capital flow and the efficiency of capital allocation in the social enterprise sector.

Absence of Benchmarks: Industry players cannot track the price and volume trends of financial transactions in the social sector, because no organization or entity collects this information. A lack of industry-wide benchmarks prevents industry players from knowing whether they will receive a competitive price for the capital they seek to raise, lend, or invest. This market inefficiency reduces the long-term viability of capital flow into the social enterprise sector.

Figure 1. Distribution of funding sources (as a percentage of total revenue) (Source: M-CRIL Microfinance India Review 2006, 2007, Used with Permission)

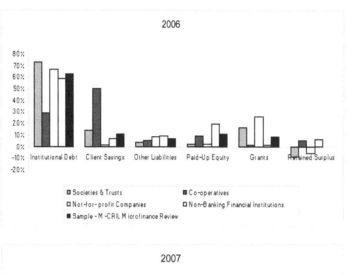

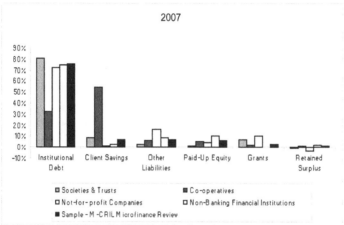

Along with the limited flow of information between *the providers and seekers* of capital in this sector, information flow is also lacking between *social enterprises*. While not directly related to the flow of capital, this communication gap reduces the sharing of innovation and best practices across the sector, which, in turn, reduces the sector's growth.

The Market for Institutional Funding

Every economic activity has a range of funding sources, which includes grants, equity, mezzanine capital[7], debt instruments, and loans. Each of these financial instruments can be raised from either retail or institutional capital providers[8]. Retail capital flows are highly regulated by Central Banks and Securities Exchange Commissions in most countries, while institutional capital flows, in many cases, have lower compliance requirements. While business' funding mix tends to shift over time, with young businesses predominantly relying on institutional funding and then accessing retail markets as they mature, most businesses receive some institutional funding.[9] Organizations raise capital from institutional funders primarily through one-to-one agreements (grants, loans), or through tradable instruments (equity, debt or

Box 1. Funders in the social enterprise sector

• *Government-run banks and lending institutions* (such as USAID, IFC, GTZ, DFID) seeking to meet their social targets. While often not the most dynamic in their approach, these entities are the largest providers of credit to social enterprises in most countries.
• *Banks and institutions* that are beginning to view this market segment as a different asset class.
• *Trusts and foundations* that – while having a largely philanthropic approach – usually provide a mix of grants and commercial funds.
• *Social investors* (both funds and private investors) who seek to fund activities which have both social and financial returns.
• *Mainstream investors* who view investment in social enterprises as an opportunity to generate financial returns.

mezzanine capital). Excluding grants, these transactions can broadly be categorized as either 'bank / term loans' or 'private placement transactions'.

Regulated exchanges, which facilitate both retail and institutional investments, lead to more symmetric information flow and effective price discovery of the listed debt and equity. In most economies, however, institutional transactions are characterized by pricing asymmetries, because they occur in the absence of established marketplaces. The absence of marketplaces also leads to high transaction costs – in the form of transaction and arranging fees – in both the primary and secondary institutional funding segments.

There have been a number of attempts to develop markets which would facilitate efficient price discovery, in both the private placement and bank loan segments. Some of the more prominent of these initiatives include 144A securities markets[10] in the US, mostly launched in 2007, such as the Nasdaq Portal Market, the Open Platform for Unregistered Securities (OPUS-5) launched by Citigroup, Lehman Brothers, Merrill Lynch, Morgan Stanley and the Bank of New York, GSTRuE (Goldman Sachs Tradable Unregistered Equity System), and JP Morgan's 144A Plus. Riskxpress.com and Debtonnet.com, launched in 1999/2000, were fixed income private placements platforms, targeting both the primary and secondary segments in India. Meanwhile, Immediance. com provides primary and secondary deal options for enterprises and Private Equity investors and Biz2credit.com aims to match small businesses with suitable bank loan schemes.

The initiatives described above have been met with varied degrees of success, or in some cases, failure, with their performance primarily determined by three key factors. First, target users' comfort with navigating the internet directly impacts their participation on the platform. The two initiatives in India, Riskxpress.com and Debtonnet.com, found that their target users had limited access to and lacked familiarity with the internet, which limited the success of their platforms. As these initiatives were launched 8 to 10 years ago, when internet usage was significantly less pervasive in India than it is today, they may have been ahead of their time.

Second, the influence of investment consultants, brokers, and other industry players facilitating private equity and debt transactions increase barriers to entry for platforms seeking to enter the market for facilitating financial transactions. These middle–men typically view private placement platforms as direct competition to their services, and actively discourage their clients from participating in these initiatives.

Third, these initiatives remove direct 'person-to-person' interactions from the transaction process; all of the organizations described above were developed for individuals or organizations to exchange offers with finalized deal terms, and did / do not allow their users to send early stage, exploratory offers with negotiable offer terms. Human psychology coupled with tradition has shaped the thinking of institutional funders; they often believe that unlisted transactions cannot be concluded until all parties have spoken with or met one another, especially in the case of primary transactions.[11] Concluding large transactions online runs contrary to this prevailing mindset.

Taking into account the inefficiencies in the social enterprise sector and the experience of the platforms serving mainstream capital markets to address similar challenges, Sinha decided that an initiative like EDACC could help facilitate solutions to the problems he observed in the social enterprise sector's capital market. He critically reviewed the institutional funding process (as is outlined above) and concluded that this process essentially entails the following steps:

1. Either providers or seekers of capital *scan the market to identify potential partners*
2. They *filter* this list of potential partners according to their specific criteria
3. They *identify* the current funding requirements / criteria of the potential counterparties
4. They gauge whether potential counterparties' requirements *match* their current funding position
5. They *analyze*, *discuss*, *finalize the terms*, and *conclude* the deal[12]

After evaluating this process with respect to the challenges faced by previously launched initiatives, Sinha reached the following conclusion: direct interaction between parties is most important during Step 5 of the process outlined above and is not necessary for Steps 1 to 4, and that these first four steps can be made more effective by communicating online. Sinha and his team concluded that developing a platform focused on identifying potential partners and filtering offers, rather than concluding transactions, would be the most effective approach to improving the efficiency of the institutional funding process.

Following the above analyses, EDA launched a platform, EDACC, that combines the features of an online auction site (such as eBay) with a social networking site (similar to Facebook); providers and seekers of capital communicate with one another to efficiently explore potential debt and equity transactions.

THE EDA CAPITALCONNECT OFFERING

With the objective of tackling the issues outlined in previous sections, EDACC seeks to provide three key services through its online application: enable users to initiate primary and secondary debt and equity transactions, facilitate discussions between enterprises to explore mutually beneficial partnerships, and provide regularly-updated trends and benchmarks for the social enterprise capital market.

The details of the service are discussed as follows.

Membership Criteria

Registration with EDACC is open to all institutional providers and seekers of social enterprise capital across the world. Members are categorized into three distinct groups. Social Enterprises are either for-profit or not-for-profit organizations working with a social objective, and seeking commercial funds. This broad category includes grassroots entities such as microfinance institutions, organizations active in the areas of education, healthcare, alternative energy, rural infrastructure, or any other activity with a direct social impact, as well as service providers to these organizations. Institutional Lenders & Investors are any registered institution that has already funded or is seeking to fund social enterprises. Banks, financial institutions, donors, multi-lateral agencies, trusts, and funds may register under this category. Promoter Investors are either joint stock companies[13] who have already invested in or seek to invest in social enterprises, or individuals who hold equity in existing social enterprises.

EDACC does not currently allow retail investors to register with its service, for two reasons. Firstly, EDACC is currently focused on the market for institutional funding to limit its scope in the initial stages of the platform's development. Secondly, retail investment regulations are stringent and vary substantially across countries, which imposes a risk of liability to EDACC, e.g. an individual invests in a social enterprise based on falsely-reported information that they obtained from the EDACC platform, loses money on their investment due to the fraudulent claims made by the social enterprise, and regulations in that investor's country of incorporation (or potentially the social enterprise's country of corporation) deem that EDACC is partially liable for their loss.

However, since promoters in their individual capacities hold a large share of equity in social enterprises, their participation on the EDACC platform plays an important role in the development of an active secondary market. For this reason, the team has allowed individual promoter investors to participate on the platform, with two limitations: they must have at least a 10% equity holding in a social enterprise when they register with the platform (but may subsequently hold less than a 10% equity holding), and may only send offers to offload existing holdings. The first restriction serves as an ad hoc threshold so that only more serious investors who understand the funding process – and its inherent risks – can use EDACC's service, while the second limitation aims to further reduce the risk of liability, since individual investors tend to have less experience and fewer resources than institutional investors that they can utilize to assess the potential financial return and risks of an investment opportunity.

Types of Subscriptions

The service fee on the platform could either be structured as a subscription fee – wherein all members bear some cost, independent of how valuable the service is for them – or as a transaction-based fee – wherein only those members who derive some tangible benefits (in this case, funds raised or placed) bear a cost. The challenges faced in structuring a fee model that is both equitable and profit-maximizing are further explored at the end of this case study.

Currently, EDACC offers three types of memberships:

1. No-Fee Trial Membership – full service access to the EDACC dashboard for 1 month, provided to all participants.
2. For-fee Full Service Membership – full service access following the trial period, once the participant pays the applicable subscription fee for a 12 month period.
3. No-fee Limited Access Membership – limited features service following the trial period, if the participant chooses to not pay the applicable fee for the Full Service Membership.

Full Service members can send and receive communications (either for funding or partnerships), whereas Limited Access members may only receive communications, and cannot respond to offers and messages sent to them through the EDACC dashboard.

EDACC's objective of creating these three subscription structures is to help build a strong membership base. Specifically, it aims to:

1. Attract organizations and individuals to register with EDACC by allowing them to use the service without any payment obligation.
2. Reduce the dropout rate by providing participants with a no-fee limited access option, and hopefully convert them to the for-fee service as the membership grows.

Features of the Service

The EDACC dashboard has four principal features: creating organization profiles, connecting with members, reporting transactions, and tracking market trends. First, members set up a profile, selecting which other members can view their detailed profile or send them written messages. Second, members connect with other participants on the platform by sending messages requesting

Box 2. Fee Structure

The following factors played a key role in EDACC's determination of the fee structure: 1. Differing levels of perceived need by enterprises and investors 2. Ability to pay 3. Fee structures of transaction advisory providers The current applicable fee structure is:	
Type of User	*Annual Membership Fee*
Social Enterprise	USD 500 or INR 20,000
Promoter Investors	USD 750 or INR 30,000
Institutional Lenders & Investors	USD 1,000 or INR 40,000

Note: as of August 2009

them to share their detailed profiles, or asking them to view their own detailed profiles. They can then initiate conversations to discuss potential business partnerships, or send offers to meet a variety of financial needs. These include raising fresh debt and equity, selling existing debt and equity, investing in fresh or secondary debt and equity, and exploring options for structured obligations[14].

Third, members provide EDACC information on how they have ultimately concluded the interactions that they initiated on the platform. This information can help the EDACC team evaluate the effectiveness of its service, both in terms of conversion rates (of conversations to deals) and also how the indicative rates compare with the final deal terms. An analysis of this data is shared with members in quarterly market reports. The EDACC team recognized that funders and social enterprises might be unwilling to voluntarily share the details of closed deals which they initiated on the platform, so a clause was included in a service agreement that members sign before completing the registration process, requiring them to provide final terms on EDACC platform-sourced deals.

Lastly, members have access to aggregated market data and analyses of all the transactions that occur between the members of EDACC, which they obtain through EDACC's quarterly market reports. These reports include aggregated analyses of members' detailed information, financial and non-financial interactions that occur on the platform, terms of debt and equity offers and counteroffers that are exchanged among members, and trends observed on the platform. To protect members' confidentiality requirements, EDACC does not disclose specific participant or deal information without receiving consent from relevant parties. Regular email updates to members, however, summarize recent activity on the platform that may be of specific interest to each member, including messages and offers that they have received.

By providing market reports and regular email updates to members, the EDACC team's objective's are threefold: to increase the awareness of the activity that is occurring on EDACC, to establish benchmarks that assist members in deciding between funding or investment options, and provide value to participants who are not currently seeking to raise or provide capital, but wish to have access to the latest information and trends in the market. EDACC believes that achieving each of these objectives will likely trigger more activity on the platform. User activity is an important determinant of the success of EDACC – as is true for most online social networking initiatives – because participation on the platform and value of the service are inextricably linked. Generating either more platform activity or service value increases both participation and members' utility, initiating a virtuous cycle which has the potential to benefit both EDACC and its members financially and in terms of social impact. This effect represents a substantial opportunity and challenge for EDACC and other online service providers, which will be explored in depth in subsequent sections of this chapter.

Competitive Landscape

Numerous consultants, merchant bankers, and other intermediaries facilitate institutional funding in the social enterprise sector, many of whom have created databases of interested providers and seekers of capital or consultancy services. Examples of these players include Grameen Capital, Unitus Capital, Altruistiq, BCorporation, and specialized Chartered Account firms such as Nagarajan & Associates in India. Since EDACC'sservice is continuous and real-time and not specific transaction focused, and fees for the service are not based upon the size of the financial transactions that it facilitates, the CapitalConnect platform has the potential to match funders and social enterprises with greater time and cost efficiency than do intermediaries who refer to a database of capital seekers and providers. For this reason, organizations that provide transaction advisory services can use EDACC on behalf of their clients, which broadens the scope and could improve the effectiveness of EDACC's service.

Still other organizations have created stock exchanges for the purposes of price discovery and establishing industry benchmarks. Examples include Green Stock Exchange (Canada), Mission Markets (USA), Social Stock Exchange (UK), SASIX (South Africa) and MFDAQ (Aruba). Most of the above stock exchanges maintain a more dedicated focus on facilitating funding of microfinance organizations or green businesses[15], or utilize a high fee structure per issue. Apart from the significant difference in price and scope, a key distinction between these organizations and EDACC is the structure of the service; EDACC offers an exploratory platform that is used to initiate the financial transaction process, whereas all platforms described above (with the exception of MissionMarkets) are for institutional players for subscription of listed issues.

Several online funding portals like Babyloan, Kiva, Global Giving. MyC4, Microplace, and Wokai, allow individuals to lend to clients of microfinance institutions or individuals. Since these platforms do not target institutional lenders and investors, there is no overlap between EDACC's target segments on the side of funding. Moreover, these organizations are focused only on primary issues of debt, and not secondary market activity or equity investments.

Business plan sites, such as the India Development Gateway, assist social entrepreneurs in developing their business models, and seek to connect them with investors. The participants on these platforms represent a sub-segment of EDACC's target users.

In most of the above cases, the focus is on the more evolved microfinance sector or the burgeoning green investment sector, while EDACC reaches out to a wider universe of social enterprises.

EDACC has established partnerships with a growing number of the aforementioned social enterprise service providers, so that it can collaborate (rather than compete) with similar organizations. These partners help connect their clients or affiliated organizations with the EDACC team if their clients communicate an unmet funding requirement or interest in the CapitalConnect platform, and EDACC in turn matches its members with partners whose service is likely to be of value to them. EDACC's partners currently include two financial advisory firms, Ayani and Unitus Capital, Babyloan, a peer-to-peer microlending site, SocialEarth, a weblog focusing on the work of for-profit social enterprises, and UnLtdWorld, an online information sharing platform for social entrepreneurs.

PERFORMANCE TO DATE

As of October 9th, 2009, EDACC had 116 members based in 26 countries across the world. The 105 registered social enterprises were based in twenty-six countries across Asia, Africa, Europe, and North America, and work in the fields of microfinance, healthcare, green technology, livelihood promotion, education, and human rights. Even as EDACC increases its network worldwide, it continues to deepen its presence in India – it has member organizations operating in 14 Indian states.

While a substantial number of enterprises are pure play[16] organizations focused on providing a single service to their clients, most offer multiple services, and while a majority[17] of the enterprises are registered as not-for-profit entities, the percentage of for-profit entities out of the total registered social enterprises has increased since EDACC published its first market update at the end of November, 2008.

The experience and organizational maturity of social enterprise members is spread across a wide spectrum, ranging from start-ups with less than a year of operation to enterprises with over 25 years of operations. Figure 2 displays the range of experience of registered members on the platform. The social enterprise members of EDACC also have diverse financial profiles, with scales spread across the spectrum from start-ups at one end to organizations with asset bases of over USD 100 million at the other. Correspondingly, revenues range from less than USD 10,000 to over USD10 million. Additionally an increasing number of mid-sized enterprises are also registering with the service. Finally, profitability of EDACC's membership organizations is quire varied as well, in terms of both net profit margins and return on assets; however, the distribution is skewed favorably towards positive and healthy returns.

As of the beginning of August 2009, there are 10 institutional funders and 1 promoter investor registered on the platform. The existing funding exposures of these entities together span across 26 countries. Together, the funders manage a total corpus[18] of over US$ 247 million, of which over US$ 175 million is yet to be invested. These investors are primarily interested in funding social enterprises in Asia and Africa, in a wide variety of sectors (see Table 1).

Activity on the Platform

From July 2008 through the end of August 2009, 8 equity offers (5 generic, 3 specific) and 19 debt offers (9 generic, 10 specific) were made on the EDACC platform. The relatively large number of debt offers reflects – to an extent – the fact that 65% of the social enterprises registered with EDACC were not-for-profit organizations, and could only receive debt investments.

- The types of offers exchanged on the platform, along with the terms of those offers are summarized in Figure 3.

Offers to borrow are significantly higher in number than offers to lend, reflecting the ratio of social enterprises to institutional funders registered on the platform (Figure 4).

From December 2008 through the end of August 2009, the interactions on the platform

Figure 2. Enterprises: Years of formation (Source: EDA CapitalConnect Newsletter, August 2009 (http:// edacapitalconnect.com/pdf/09_08%20CapitalConnect_Newsletter.pdf))

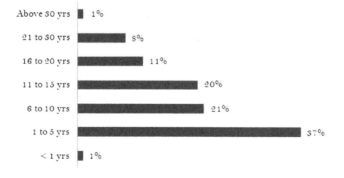

Table 1. Sectors in which funders are interested in investing

Agriculture	Housing
Alternative Energy	Light Manufacturing
Education & Skills	Market Linkages
Forestry	Technology / Telecommunications
Financial Services / Microfinance	Water / Sanitation
Healthcare	

have become more focused than they were from July 2008 through the end of November 2008; participants are choosing to make more offers to individual and select groups of organizations (i.e. they are sending specific offers), rather than to all the members of EDACC. While the 7 equity offers received only 2 responses so far, the 16 debt offers that were made on the platform have received a total of 26 responses.[19] Conversion rates between each stage of the debt offer process

Figure 3. Offer terms (as of the end of Jul'09) (Source: EDA CapitalConnect Newsletter, August 2009 (http://edacapitalconnect.com/pdf/09_08%20CapitalConnect_Newsletter.pdf))

Particulars	Debt	Equity
Offer Period (days)		
Minimum	8	12
Maximum	365	181
Average	78	77
Offer Amount (USD)		
Minimum	10,000	8,000
Maximum	30,00,000	30,00,000
Average	5,91,563	9,43,569
Median	1,50,000	5,47,500
Interest Rate %		
Minimum	0.00%	
Maximum	15.00%	
Average	11.10%	
Average Range	3.40%	
Loan Tenure (months)		
Minimum	3	
Maximum	60	
Average	26	

continue to be high (e.g. the percentage of initial offers that received counter offers), reflecting the fact that members are actively using the EDACC platform taking interest in the offers they receive.

CHALLENGES, AND LESSONS LEARNED

EDACC is faced with core challenges which represent the difficulty in achieving its two primary objectives: realization of a social impact by providing valuable services to clients, and generation of sufficient revenue allowing the organization to sustain itself financially and obtain its growth targets. The following sections explore the importance of, and relationships between, these obstacles and will identify practical lessons to guide technology providers and social enterprise start-up organizations in designing and implementing initiatives.

Creating Value

EDACC's principle challenge is to create services which will provide tangible benefits to its members. Unlike many other technology providers, EDACC and other online social networking initiatives cannot substantially affect the value of their products and services directly by modifying or improving their services, but instead must seek to indirectly increase their services' value by channeling a relatively large portion of its resources towards greater organization participation and active usage of the EDA CapitalConnect platform. Figure 5 defines each of the previously discussed services and features of the EDACC, and identifies the primary determinants of the value of each of these services and features: (1) the quantity and quality of member organizations, partners, and endorsements, and most importantly, (2) the number of interactions (i.e messages and offers) exchanged on the EDACC platform.

Figure 4. Types of offers (As of the end of Jul '09) (Source: EDA CapitalConnect Newsletter, August 2009 (http://edacapitalconnect.com/ pdf/09_08%20CapitalConnect_Newsletter.pdf))

Particulars	Debt	Equity
Transaction Type		
Buy/Lend	5	1
Sell/Borrow	14	7
Nature of Offer		
Fresh	18	7
Secondary	1	1
Recipient Type		
Specific	10	3
Generic	9	5

Figure 5 demonstrates that establishing partnerships with other transaction advisory service providers and increasing the size and quality of membership increases the value of EDACC's services by providing a greater number of offline services to members, and increasing the amount of available information on potential competitors or partners, respectively. The most important driver of service value, however, is the volume and quality of active member participation on the EDACC platform. Deals will not be discussed and closed, nor can trends in the funding market be established unless member organizations send one another a substantial number of realistic funding offers. Likewise, strategic partnerships and unofficial networks cannot be established unless members are directly communicating with each other. The primary challenge for the EDACC team, therefore, is increasing member usage of the platform. The importance of this obstacle is best illustrated by the fact that while a substantial number of offers have been exchanged on the EDACC platform, no funding deals have yet been finalized between members as of October 9th, 2009.

To assist readers in understanding the obstacles that EDACC has faced to achieve its primary goal – bringing capital to social enterprises – Figure 6 identifies all of the factors which affect the primary determinants of the value of EDACC's services, and highlights the causal relationships between each of these variables. These determinants have been conceptually divided between internal and external factors, i.e. those factors over which the EDACC team does and does not have direct control.

EDACC Inputs

Figure 6 demonstrates that there are three key areas in which EDACC can shape the value of its services: (1) provide offline services, such as

Figure 5. EDACC's Value

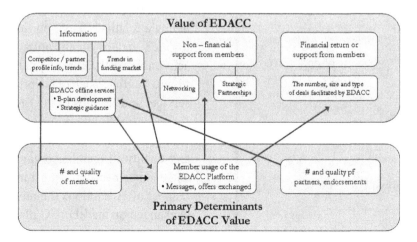

assistance with designing and exchanging funding offers, along with other offline services such as business plan development and strategic planning, which have the potential to directly benefit social enterprises in achieving their financial and social objectives, (2) structure the EDACC platform such that its features are complex and flexible enough to accomodate the widely differing strategic needs of funders and social enterprises, but also simple and intuitive enough such that most members – particularly social enterprises based in rural areas in developing countries – are able to effectively use the platform and, (3) engage in both direct and indirect outreach efforts with potential members and partners, such as attending conferences, scheduling in person and phone conversations, disseminating market reports and newsletters to stakeholders in the social enterprise sector, and utilizing other social networking sites and contacting media organizations to increase the international visibility of EDACC. The question then becomes: How can the EDACC team demonstrate the value of its services in the organizations' pilot phase when value is primarily determined by the participation of organizations who seek to join

and utilize the EDACC platform? This circular causal flow represents a key obstacle to EDACC, and will be explored in this section of the chapter.

Secondary and Tertiary Determinants of Value

While EDACC's direct inputs are obvious and crucial drivers of the depth of the organization's social impact, Figure 6 demonstrates that a variety of factors out of EDACC's direct realm of control affect the value of EDACC's services. The three secondary determinants of value (factors which directly affect the primary determinants of value) are the computer and internet literacy of potential and current members, the perceived value of EDACC's services, and the financial and human resources available to EDACC, its members, and its target market.

Potential clients' and members' lack of internet and computer literacy has been a substantial challenge in facilitating effective social enterprise usage of the platform, and has lead numerous organizations to request for assistance from the EDACC team with online registration, logging into

Figure 6. Determinant of EDACC's value

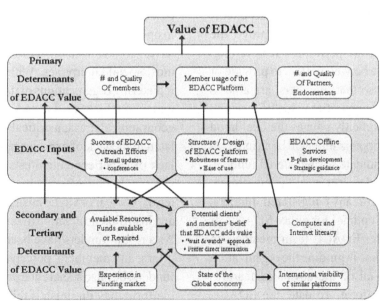

the website, viewing their profiles, and using the platform's features. Lack of internet proficiency has lead several organizations to mistakenly send offers to obtain funding to other social enterprises seeking funding, which has engendered false expectations among certain members, potentially reducing their perceived value of the platform. Other members have failed to send offers to other participating organizations whom might be interested in discussing partnership or funding opportunities, because they did not understand how to review these other members' profiles and / or send them offers. Most importantly, members' and potential client's difficulties with understanding and appropriately using the platforms' features have required the EDACC team to dedicate a substantial portion of their limited human resources to resolving these issues – resources which could be better utilized in developing or improving platform features, providing more productive offline services, or engaging in outreach. It is this continued challenge of maximizing the use and availability of limited resources – both from the EDACC and member perspective – that is critical to the success of the platform and will be discussed in greater detail below.

To address this critical issue pertaining to the usability of the EDACC platform, the EDACC team reviews technical problems that its clients encounter to determine how to improve the precise structure of the platform's feature (e.g. clearly differentiate between offers to provide or to obtain funding, so that members' are able to easily determine the potential value of received offers), and also explicitly gauges the likelihood that the struggling organization will be an interesting investment candidate for registered funders. If the organization does not meet the investment criteria of many (or any) registered funders, then it may not be optimal for either EDACC or the organization, for EDACC team members to spend substantial time in guiding the organization to effectively use all of the advanced features of the EDACC platform. To date, the EDACC

team has observed that most of the members with internet and computer literacy issues are non-profit organizations which do not match the funding criteria of registered funders, since these social enterprises nearly all seek small amounts of debt funding while registered funders want to make larger investments, primarily in equity. Responding to this trend, the EDACC team currently invests relatively fewer human resources in assisting members with technical issues than they did over the course of the organization's first six months of operations.

To more rigorously analyze the drivers of EDACC, tertiary factors which represent the effects of the broader operating landscape have been included in Figure 6. While the EDACC team – like many similar organizations – lacks the capacity to find solutions to these larger issues, the discussion of these additional factors offers critical insight into the social enterprise sector. These three factors directly affect (and are often the primary cause) of the previously discussed secondary determinants of EDACC value: the lack of member experience in the funding market, the downturn in the global economy, and the visibility and subsequent credibility of similar international platforms.

As displayed in Figure 2, the majority of EDACC's social enterprise members have been in operation between one and five years and often have a greater need for additional funding than do most social enterprises. With a large number of registering organizations of this level of maturity, many of which are located in under-developed geographical areas, a critical issue has arisen related to the lack of experience with funding. This lack of experience manifests itself in numerous ways including: offers being sent with unrealistic terms, unclear or vague business plans/proposals, and insufficient attention to funders requirements. As a result, funders have been less responsive to offers, and members' perceived value (primarily funders, but also social enterprises) of the EDACC platform may diminish if this trend continues.

The EDACC team has begun to address this issue by offering the aforementioned offline advisory services to members. EDACC team members review and collaborate with members to improve the structure of offers, profiles and assist with business plan development. The lack of experience among social enterprises paradoxically represents an issue and an opportunity of great magnitude, as maximizing all social enterprise members' ability to engage with funders currently exceeds the capacity of the EDACC team, yet transaction advisory support is precisely the service which EDACC can provide to directly achieve social impact. Solutions to address lack of member experience will need to be considered with an eye to a long-term, resource-efficient approach.

The global financial downturn which began in 2007 similarly affects the value of the EDACC platform. Diminished funding resources available in the social enterprise sector has created a landscape in which a majority of institutional funders are more selective in engaging in financial transactions. The corollary result of this 'credit crunch' is that many social enterprises have fewer resources to invest in outreach and employee capacity building, exacerbating the previously discussed issues that arise from social enterprises' lack of experience. EDACC is no exception to this trend; the scarcity of capital as a result of the global state of the economy has impeded EDACC's ability to obtain additional funding, which would assist the organization to improve the quality and provide a greater number of services to most efficiently facilitate deal flow.

Finally, while platforms of this nature have received substantial media attention and have drawn widespread public interest in developed countries in recent years, they have not yet established a strong presence in many developing countries. The relative novelty and lack of visibility of online financial platforms represents another key factor in determining EDACC's value, because individuals' preconceptions about similar platforms – if they have any – directly shape their perceptions of the potential value of the EDACC platform. Since similar platforms are just beginning to increase in usage and visibility, users do not entirely understand the EDACC model or believe that can benefit them, leading them to adopt the "Wait and See" approach. This trend will be further discussed in the next section of this chapter.

The Trouble with Perceptions

Out of all the challenges facing EDACC, demonstrating to both potential clients and members that the platform is effective in facilitating communication and deal flow between strategic and funding partners is the most fundamental and complex obstacle facing the organization. It is a fundamental challenge because it both affects and is affected by nearly all of the other determinants of EDACC's value (see Figure 6). It is complex because tackling this challenge requires that the team identify and clearly understand the strategic and psychological factors which limit incentives to join and actively participate on the platform, and shape the offering to reduce these disincentives. Two key challenges related to the perception of the EDACC platform's value are discussed below. The first obstacle highlights the important role that perceptions play in determining the 'real' value of the platform, and the second demonstrates the difficulty that the EDACC team faces in changing stakeholder's perceptions.

The first major obstacle is the "Wait and See" approach taken by both funders and social enterprises with regards to the development of the CapitalConnect platform. The intrinsic value of a platform like EDACC is its ability to connect a network of institutions that vary in location, offering, and financial maturity and provide them with a virtual space to initiate business transactions. Since this value is primarily determined by the quantity and quality of participants interacting on the platform (see Figure 5), EDACC faces a 'Catch-22' dilemma; the platform will have little value if only a small number of enterprises and investors register with the service, but the vast majority of enterprises and (especially) investors will only join the platform if they perceive immediate value in the service. Many potential partners, even if they are in support of the EDACC model, will wait to see if the concept matures into a robust platform, and if and when it does, will then consider registering. To address this pivotal challenge, EDACC has taken an outreach approach similar to those adopted by other online networking sites: targeting niche users who have substantial demand for the platform's services and will therefore be more likely to join the service even if immediate benefits are not apparent (i.e., social enterprises with a critical need for funding, and private equity firms who seek more exposure), while also leveraging existing professional relationships from EDACC's parent organization, EDA Rural Systems and EDACC's partner organizations to improve the success of outreach initiatives.

The second challenge is industry players' preference for personal interaction with potential counterparties. In the social enterprise space, investments have traditionally been initiated and concluded through face-to-face interactions between funding parties. Institutional funders, particularly those seeking to make equity investments, understand the inherent risks of investing in social enterprises that often have limited track records and experience, and would prefer to directly communicate with potential investees to gauge important unquantifiable factors which affect the return on investment, namely the competency and vision of the fund seekers' management team. Most enterprises do not need to thoroughly evaluate the subjective strengths and weaknesses of potential investors, but want to understand their requirements and expectations. Hence, some investors and social enterprises struggle to understand the benefit of EDACC's online platform, because they believe that the personal assurances that they require cannot be achieved through online communication.

Additionally, if one considers the diverse number of economic and social activities that traditionally required personal interactions between partners to establish trust, but now have become substantially more cost and time-efficient through the use of online platforms (e.g., purchasing automobiles on eBay, finding a romantic partner on Match.com, or obtaining a university degree online), one can see that exploring funding opportunities online is not as removed from current human behavior as skeptics of this model might claim. As the prevalence of trust-fostering online platforms that increase information flow continues to increase – no matter their target sector, and whether or not they target institutional or individual clients – uncertainty towards the concept of an online marketplace for the social enterprise sector should diminish.

EDACC has begun to address the concerns outlined above by structuring the offering so that transactions are finalized offline (the fifth step in the aforementioned institutional funding process – refer to the Background section), thereby facilitating the direct interaction of parties to a transaction. Moreover, EDACC has maintained the practice of vetting the financial records of all members, to promote members' successful completion of steps 1 through 4 of the institutional funding process online.

To date, none of the 9 registered funders have sent any indicative offers to any of the 105 social enterprise members. Several factors could be contributing to this paucity of investor participation, including many of the secondary and tertiary determinants discussed. Although these factors do appear to be impacting funders' use of the EDACC platform (as confirmed through informal discussions with registered funders), an additional factor which appears to be a major source of funders' passivity is more troubling, because it runs contrary to the institutional funding process that Sinha and Vishwanatham observed and explicitly defined prior to EDACC's launch. Institutional funders simply may not want to send indicative offers to social enterprises before they communicate with them via written messages, telephonic discussions, and / or personal meetings. This discrepancy between the original market research and the observed trends in potential clients' reactions and members' usage of the platform has been the most important lesson for the EDACC team over the course of its operation. Understanding the potential for discrepancy between assumptions and past observations and current market behavior, and maintaining the practice of continually calibrating EDACC's services to match the needs of clients is essential for the team to generate and maintain value and revenue flows over the long term. EDACC believes that all organizations, particularly those with relatively untested models operating in emerging markets, must place a strong emphasis upon this process of continuous evaluation of their clients' behavior, and should not solely rely upon the findings of initial market studies or occasional program evaluations.

While EDACC has no control over funder's outstanding funding requirements or specific funding criteria and therefore cannot affect many of the factors described above, the team can (and has) reshape the EDACC offering to match the needs of funders. To date, the EDACC team has begun to communicate with registered funders regarding their funding criteria, and is directly providing them with detailed financial information from the social enterprise members who match these criteria. Although this offline matching process undermines the utility of the online platform because it provides disincentives for funders to use the platform at all, the EDACC team believes that what is most critical for the success of this organization is facilitating the closure of deals, which may have an immensely positive impact on the perceived value of the organization's services, and will likely lead to greater membership growth and activity on the online platform.

A secondary approach to facilitating investor participation and therefore increasing capital flows

is EDACC's decision to restructure the features of the platform for registered members. Currently, investors and social enterprises cannot exchange written messages until after one party has sent an initial offer and the other party has responded to that offer. The logic behind this communication format is that it would increase the utility of the EDACC platform because member organizations would be required to send more formal, structured offers to one another which would make conversations more efficient, taking into account that inexperienced social enterprises would now need to consider all of the factors which make up investors' funding criteria (e.g. size of loan, interest rate, length of term, purpose of loan, collateral, etc.). Secondly, requiring members to exchange indicative offers before they can verbally communicate provides the EDACC team with more data, allowing them to more effectively establish funding benchmarks for the social enterprise sector. If members are allowed to communicate directly before exchanging this information, it will be much more challenging for the EDACC team to achieve its objective of identifying trends in the funding market.

Despite the benefits of requiring all members to exchange indicative offers before messages, the EDACC team has decided to allow funders to send messages to social enterprises at any time; social enterprises will still be required to send indicative offers before they can write messages to members, encouraging them to carefully consider their requests before sending them, and while less data will be readily available to the EDACC team to establish benchmarks, EDACC expects that funder participation on the platform will increase as a result of the restructured communication features.

Financial Sustainability

Even if EDACC overcomes the aforementioned challenges and major industry players perceive enough value in the platform to register and buy and sell capital to its members– EDACC will still need to evaluate how to most effectively derive financial sustainability from its membership base in a medium in which consumers typically expect to obtain value from products and services for free. EDACC needs revenue to support necessary website maintenance, customer service, operations staff, product development, and marketing. In this evolving sector, there are no industry benchmarks by which to gauge consumers' willingness to pay for EDACC's services. Assessing the challenge of achieving financial sustainability, online platforms of this nature have primarily incorporated one of three potential funding avenues (Anderson, 2009):

1. Cross-Subsidy/Advertising Revenue: The majority of free services on the internet generate revenue from advertising or other cross-subsidies. Brand companies identify high visibility partners on the internet and for a combination of upfront and pay-per click payments, the website generates enough revenue to sustain its business. Google is the archetype of this business model, having created a multi-billion dollar enterprise almost entirely through cross-subsidies (Anderson, 2009). For EDACC, adding sponsored content or advertisements to generate revenue is expected in years to come and will be difficult to predict, since revenue size will largely depend on the rate of membership growth, and members' projected spending on advertised products. Even if EDACC is able to achieve rapid membership growth and the projected spending of its members on advertised products is substantial, it is unlikely that advertising revenue will significantly contribute to EDACC's revenue, for two reasons. Firstly, as noted in a recent New York Times article, advertising revenue in the developing world (the platform's core target demographic) might not be a viable model due to diminishing returns for advertisers (Stone and Helft, 2009). Secondly, with the

sensitivity of materials on the platform, including financial reports and contact details, many members who are inexperienced with online products and services might be wary of privacy and security with the presence of advertising banners, even if these advertisers cannot access the information. Such a model will therefore need to be reserved for long-term consideration.

2. Transaction Fees: Fees on transactions would provide an alternative revenue model: participants would be provided membership free of charge and would only be charged a percentage of total transaction value if they complete a financial transaction with another member. While theoretically sound, this model presents significant logistical and regulatory challenges. Since financial transactions are not completed on the platform, the final terms of an offer made on EDACC do not necessarily reflect the finalized terms of the resulting financial transaction. EDACC includes a clause in its service agreement that requires members to report information on all financial transactions that occur on the platform for the purpose of producing aggregated market information, but such an arrangement is difficult to enforce. Additionally, if EDACC implements a transaction-based system through which deals are finalized on the platform, it would be subject to regulations on worldwide financial transactions, thus increasing the organization's liability.

3. Membership Fees: Ultimately, as previously discussed, EDACC determined that charging participants a flat annual fee for membership would be the most feasible model to maximize consumer satisfaction and achieve financial sustainability. The current fee structure is tiered to accommodate different types of users. In first few months after EDACC's launch, the EDACC team expected a large number of participants to resist paying for membership until they perceived immediate

value (e.g. productive conversations with funding partners) which led to the creation of a no-fee limited access membership which members can select after their trial period has expired. EDACC believes that adding a free membership option will aid the organization to increase its membership growth and reach financial sustainability because the free service will substantially reduce the member dropout rate, and because the EDACC team believes that they will require fewer resources to convert Limited Access members into paying members than recently-registered organizations. However, the challenge remains to further facilitate paid membership, which continues to be one of EDACC's core business considerations and remains a critical factor to ensure the financial sustainability of the organization.

To this end, the financial viability of the organization will be primarily determined by members' perceived value of the service, as opposed to the services' real value. For example, an increased number of paying members will improve the perceived value of the service because paying members will presumably use the EDACC platform more frequently, increasing the probability of establishing quality partnerships or closing deals. This improved perceived value among members and potential clients will likely lead to a greater number of full member registrations, increasing revenue for the platform which will allow the team to develop improved services. These improved services may then facilitate greater value (both real and perceived), leading to more revenue and so on in a 'virtuous cycle'.

There are other obstacles that EDACC will need to identify and mitigate in the years to come. Ensuring transaction integrity and facing the need for strategic investment planning[20], while salient to this discussion, are less critical in the short term or will diminish with time.

THE FUTURE OF EDA CAPITALCONNECT

In addition to improving the platform's ease-of-use and addressing the issues of value creation and financial sustainability, the EDACC team expects to make several key value additions to the platform in the short-term. Seeking to facilitate an efficient, effective, and secure network, the hope is to introduce metrics to quantify participants' usage of the platform. These metrics, similar to eBay's feedback and detailed seller ratings, will allow participants to evaluate other members' usage of the platform, helping them gauge the success of their interactions by measuring conversion rates and response times to messages and offers.

EDACC also plans to offer a service to coordinate online meetings between members once they have exchanged offers, counteroffers, and messages through the dashboard, thereby facilitating the continuation of conversations outside of the online platform. Finally, EDACC expects to develop a module for grant funding offers in addition to debt and equity. The organization recognizes that grants are still a critical early stage source of funding for social enterprises, and by excluding them from the platform, it is currently not serving a crucial present need of this sector.

Technological innovations and the social enterprise sector will both evolve in unexpected ways, creating new challenges and opportunities for this organization and for the social enterprise space. Sinha acknowledges that his team at EDACC must remain agile and continue to fine-tune its offering to tackle these new challenges and accommodate the evolving needs of this growing sector.

REFERENCES

Anderson, C. (2009). *Free: The Future of a Radical Price*. New York: Hyperion.

Arzeni, S. (2004). *Entrepreneurship: A Catalyst for Urban Regeneration.* Paris: Organization for Economic Co-operation and Development.

Bedson, J. (Ed.). (2009). Microfinance in Asia: Trends, Challenges, and Opportunities. The Foundation for Development Cooperation. Retrieved August 12, 2009, from http://www.bwtp.org/files/MF_Trends_Challenges_Opportunities_ELECTRONIC.pdf.

Sinha, F. (2006). *Social Rating and Social Performance Reporting in Microfinance: Towards a Common Framework.* Washington DC, USA: EDA/M-Cril, Argidius, and the SEEP Network. Retrieved August 11, 2009 from http://www.m-cril.com/pdf/Framework- for-Social-Performance-Rating-and-Reporting.pdf

Stone, B., & Helft, M. (2009). In Developing Countries, Web Grows without Profit. *The New York Times.* Retrieved April 27, 2009 from http://www.nytimes.com/2009/04/27/technology/startups/27global.html?_r=2&ref=global-home.

Thompson, R. (2008). The Coming Transformation of Social Enterprise. *Harvard Business School: Working Knowledge.* Retrieved April 29, 2009 from http://hbswk.hbs.edu/item/5986.html.

Wei-Skillern, J., Austin, J. E., Leonard, H., & Stevenson, H. (2007). *Entrepreneurship in the Social Sector.* Thousand Oaks, CA: SAGE publications. Retrieved April 27, 2009 from http://hbswk.hbs.edu/item/5782.html.

ADDITIONAL READING

Titley, B. (Ed.). (2008). Comparative Advantage in Green Business. *United Kingdom Department for Business Enterprise and Regulatory Reform.* London: Ernst and Young. Retrieved August 13, 2009 from http://www.berr.gov.uk/files/file46793.pdf

ENDNOTES

[1] Social enterprises are organizations that advance a social mission through entrepreneurial, earned income strategies. (http://www.nonprofitsassistancefund.org/pages/glossary)

[2] Information asymmetries arise when at least one party to a transaction has relevant information which the other(s) do not possess.

[3] Information obtained from an interview with Aparna Vishwanatham and Sanjay Sinha. (2008, October, D. Brett, Interviewer.)

[4] Information obtained from an interview with Aparna Vishwanatham and Sanjay Sinha. (2008, October, D. Brett, Interviewer)

[5] Information obtained from an interview with Aparna Vishwanatham and Sanjay Sinha. (2008, October, D. Brett, Interviewer)

[6] Information obtained from an interview with Aparna Vishwanatham and Sanjay Sinha. (2008, October, D. Brett, Interviewer)

[7] Mezzanine Capital can be structured as either subordinated debt, which has a lower priority than other bonds of the issuer in case of liquidation during bankruptcy, or preferred equity, which typically pay cash and / or payable in kind (PIK) interest. PIK interest increases the principle amount by the amount of the interest, rather than paying in cash.

[8] A retail capital provider refers to individuals or institutions that provide services directly to the end user or consumer usually in smaller quantities.

[9] Information obtained from an interview with Aparna Vishwanatham and Sanjay Sinha. (2008, October, D. Brett, Interviewer)

[10] Rule 144A is an exemption provision of the Securities Act in the United States whereby securities can be sold through private placement to qualified institutional buyers within the United States without SEC registration.

[11] Information obtained from an interview with Aparna Vishwanatham and Sanjay Sinha. (2008, October, D. Brett, Interviewer)

[12] Funding needs are dynamic for both providers and seekers of capital, so the above cycle is a continuous one.

[13] A joint stock company is broadly defined as a company which has the capital of its members pooled in a common fund; transferable shares represent ownership interest and shareholders are legally liable for all debts of the company (http://wordnetweb.princeton.edu/perl/webwn?s=joint-stock company)

[14] A Structured obligation is an investment created by bundling a pool of similar loans into a single investment that can be bought or sold. Often in the form of a Collateralized Debt Obligation (CDO), investors that purchase this obligation own a right to a part of this pool's interest income and principal. (http://www.wikinvest.com/wiki/CDO).

[15] Broadly defined as those businesses that, across the whole economy, have made efforts to introduce low carbon, resource efficient, and/or re-manufactured products, processes, and services, and business models, which allow them to operate in a significantly more sustainable way than their closest competitors. (Titley, 2008)

[16] Pure play organizations are defined as organizations which have a singular business focus or single core competency.

[17] As of the beginning of March, 2009.

[18] Total corpus is the sum of funds earmarked for investment and lending, and those that have already been invested or lent.

[19] As of the beginning of March, 2009.

[20] We define this term as the internal considerations an organization must make in assessing where, when, and how much they invest.

Section 4
Technical, Regional and Sectoral Issues

Introduction

Glòria Estapé-Dubreuil
Universitat Autònoma de Barcelona, Spain

Previous sections of this book deal with Information and Communication Technologies for MFIs, looking at some of the more recent advances on Technology and how they can be applied to the benefit of microfinance and their clients. But like the multiple facets of a high quality diamond, the MFIs and their missions can profit, and actually are profiting, from advanced technologies in a lot of different ways. This last section of the book will be devoted to the study of some of them.

When considering Information Technologies, in general, and Management Information Systems (MIS) in particular, efficiency should be the main concern. As it has already been pointed out in this book, costs are a large component of efficiency, but the main goal of a MIS should be to provide an efficient tool to help a given organization to fulfill its own mission and organizational objectives (CGAP, 2008). Efficiency in MFIs means a delicate balance between cost of implementation and usefulness and ease of use within the organization. It also means that IT and MIS should indeed be designed to manage internal organizational needs related to accountancy and operability, but also to reap the expected benefits of their introduction, an aspect that has lately been questioned in the literature (Booth & Philip, 2005) and is often related to an incomplete specification of requirements to be meet by the designed MIS (Sobczak & Berry, 2007).

Through this last section of the book, two main concerns relating IT and MIS design are addressed. The first one is linked to the design of governance tools to deal specifically with risk. Both risk of the borrower and risk of the individual are critical to measure in order to separate the good from the poor risk. Such aspects lie in the foundation of the two first chapters of this section. A second and equally important aspect of IT and MIS design refers to their client-orientation. MIS should be specifically designed to serve clients efficiently, taking into account their main characteristics and interests, be it individual clients or collectivities. And this point is indeed a common denominator of the last three chapters of this section, since each one of them deal with the identification of such needs and interests of both potential and real MFI clients, focusing on a specific economic region or sector. Let me introduce each one of the chapters in turn, to provide an overview of what is going in Section 4.

The two first chapters of this section present readers with two proposals concerning mathematical and statistical tools to look after or to improve MFIs' performance. A detailed discussion of the opportunity, potential benefits of and controversies around the use of credit scoring technologies in microfinance can be found in Chapter 14, authored by Lilian Simbaqueba, Gehiner Salamanca & Vitalie Bumacov. Starting with a simple but expressive example, the authors introduce the basis of credit scoring as a tool to assess the credit risk of potential borrowers. The chapter goes on differentiating between classical scoring and credit scoring for microlending, offering a detailed discussion on the requirements to the suggested use of first judgmental and then statistical scorecards in MFIs, explaining their main technical aspects and pointing out tradeoffs between expected benefits and implementation and maintenance efforts. Recommendations concerning scoring strategies to be adopted by a given Institution, as well as proceedings to handle scoring practices in electronic format are also found in the chapter. It concludes with references to several already implemented examples where some benefits had been found in the use of the scorecards, suggesting that the technique can help MFIs reach self-sustainability.

Carmen Lozano & Federico Fuentes, in Chapter 15, also deal with MFIs' performance, but from an external evaluator's point of view. The authors propose a methodology to measure the impact of a given microcredit program based on fuzzy logic, in an attempt to overcome the problems encountered in the assessment of some of the social achievements of the MFIs' borrowers, which are of a qualitative nature. A brief outline of fuzzy sets and fuzzy logic, together with some arguments in favor of its use in the context of microfinance, form the first section of the chapter. Its main topic deals with the proposed model of impact measurement, in which the evaluation of the MFI's impact on the borrower, his/her household and the economic impact of the microcredit investment are combined through the additional use of system dynamic techniques.

The next two chapters lead us to yet another facet of the alleged diamond. In Chapter 16, Samanthala Hettihewa & Chris S. Wright deal with the appropriate tools, approaches and strategies to be followed in the design and deployment of microfinance in developed countries. To be able to develop their proposals, the authors start with a discussion of the socio-economic differences between less developed countries and developed countries. They argue that microfinance programs in developed countries must, along with lending money, provide social, financial and administrative intermediation to their borrowers, in a process that is revealingly compared to the support provided by most venture capitalists to their entrepreneur clients. Among other aspects, they discuss the higher risks incurred by micro-entrepreneurs in developed countries as a source for needed intermediation. Such issues are highlighted by indirectly confronting a case example of a micro-enterprise in a less developed country with three cases of micro-enterprises in developed countries, intuitively showing the effects of different regimes of regulation and taxes. Those are limiting aspects that appear to be generally under-appreciated, but are in fact important issues determining the success of developed countries' MFIs according to the thesis sustained by the authors of the chapter.

Discussion on microfinance in developed countries is also pursued by our next chapter, focused in the Spanish microcredit industry. Indeed, in Chapter 17, Consol Torreguitart-Mirada and I deal with the use of internet and other IT practices by microfinance firms in Spain, an area that has scarcely been researched before, nor in neighboring countries. After a brief description of the composition and practices within the microcredit sector, we describe the sector status for the basic IT resource factors: organizational IT infrastructure, IT software competences, electronic communication media and website uses and capabilities. Data obtained through a direct questionnaire to the researched MFIs is also compared to similar statistical data available for other relevant Spanish sectors. A discussion of the impact of IT use in the management of the MFIs, and of their strategic use of IT complete the portrait of IT use in Spanish microfinance sector organizations. Conclusions concerning the role of Spanish MFIs in IT intermediation within micro-entrepreneurs link the final remarks of this chapter to the more general claims about intermediation on the part of developed countries' microcredit programs made in the precedent chapter.

Last but not least, Chapter 18, authored by Jack Sim and Karl Dayson, makes readers turn their attention again to the "real challenge of microfinance", as the authors put it: whether microfinance can be used to transform major social issues. And the authors do so while focusing on the sanitation crisis striking less developed countries, and on the health problems related to it. The chapter presents three case studies from different parts of the world in which innovation in toilet supply mechanisms is found, showing the opportunities but also the challenges in developing sanitation market places. The authors argue that microfinance "credit-plus" institutions could make a difference in this area too, provided that the major organizational and cultural problems arising from that market could be at least partially overcame. To so do, the authors go on suggesting an IT solution to it, through an Internet Portal designed to fill the existing gap in information dissemination, thus facilitating the linkages across all market actors in the sanitation segment, including the possible use of microfinance to fuel the market and the MFIs acting as key intermediaries between clients and suppliers or those involved in infrastructure development.

Is there anything more exciting than concluding this book not with a closed account of accomplished targets but with an open call to use IT and microfinance to yet achieve another social challenge? If the readers agree with me in that point, I can ensure them a pleasant and interesting tour alongside microfinance and IT issues in this section of the book.

REFERENCES

Booth, M. E. & Philip, G. (2005), Information systems management: role of planning, alignment and leadership. *Behaviour & Information Technology, 24*(5), 391-404.

CGAP (2008). *Information Systems: Implementation Guidelines. A practical guide to the development life of microfinance information systems.*CGAP. Retrieved from www.cgap.org.

Sobczak, A. & Berry, D.M. (2007), Distributed priority ranking of strategic preliminary requirements for management information systems in economic organizations. *Information and Software Technology, 49*, 960-984.

Chapter 14
The Role of Credit Scoring in Micro Lending

Lilian Simbaqueba
LiSim, Colombia

Gehiner Salamanca
LiSim, Colombia

Vitalie Bumacov
LiSim, Moldova

ABSTRACT

This chapter aims to present credit scoring as a technology meant to improve micro lending significantly. We consider that credit scoring is an advanced technology because statistical procedures, some sophisticated, are required to design powerful scorecards. In the same time, we want to show that scoring is not an elitist tool. It is not for every institution, as some prerequisites are required, but we are convinced that there is an enormous potential market for credit scoring in micro lending. Credit scoring can be efficient only in massive homogeneous markets. Microfinance usually addresses this kind of markets. This is the opportunity we want to exploit. On the other hand, quantitative measurements, required for statistical developments, suffer from the fact that micro-entrepreneurs operate mostly in the informal or semi-formal sectors. Some variables like the profit of the business or the turnover cannot be measured accurately because there is no reliable source. This is a challenge. Implementation of credit scoring and follow-up in an environment that has limited access to data infrastructure solutions could also be considered as a challenge. Here we describe in detail possible applications of credit scoring in micro lending. We explain main technical aspects and point expected benefits versus implementation and maintenance efforts. This chapter is written from the point of view of several scoring experts that develop credit scoring models for micro and SME lending on a commercial basis.

DOI: 10.4018/978-1-61520-993-4.ch014

INTRODUCTION

In microfinance there are two things that are supposed to be big: the impact on poor people and transaction costs. Micro credit accounts for the biggest share of the success of microfinance. In micro lending, a long-term impact on borrowers and their environment can be achieved only through self-sustainability. Not sustainable micro credit providers depend on external financial support – a fact that makes them vulnerable and their success fragile.

The fundamental sustainability equation states that own revenues should at least equal costs. The equation is simple, but it is not easy to apply this principle in practice as costs are high in microfinance while margins are small. The search for intensive growth of revenues is not always compatible with the common purposes of microfinance. Extensive growth and constant effort to lower transaction costs are seen by the authors as the perfect solution. Mainly these goals are pursued when microfinance institutions decide to introduce credit scoring.

We distinguish three stages of the cycle of the micro borrower where credit scoring can be used. The first, called evaluation stage, refers to the moment when the financial institution meets the potential micro borrower for the first time. Credit scoring is used to assess his credit risk.

The second stage, called renewal stage, refers to the moment when the client is renewing his micro loan. The microfinance institution has to take the decision whether to disburse a new loan or not. Credit scoring is used to assess the same risk of the client. The difference is that at this point, past credit behavior of the borrower with the institution is known, and by consequence, the forecast of the risk is more accurate.

A third stage, called collection, refers to the moment when the institution is dealing with delinquent clients. Credit scoring is used to forecast the behavior of the clients that are late with scheduled payments. The institution will give priority to cases with higher chances of default.

In this chapter we will focus on the first two stages, as we are more frequently confronted with demands from microfinance institutions to develop evaluation and renewal scoring. This does not mean that collection scoring has lower added value for clients, but since institutions choose to implement evaluation and renewal credit scoring first, a successful implementation will have strong positive impact on delinquency and by consequence the collection problem loses its important for the institution.

BACKGROUND

Scoring is a methodology that offers an objective way to assess risk. It estimates the probability that an event will occur, by giving grades to known characteristics that have impact on the event. In the case of credit scoring, the forecasted event is the bad credit behavior of the client that can lead him to default. This is one of the main risks in lending: Will the client be able to repay integrally the loan and due interest on time?

Bad credit behavior, called also negative credit behavior, is when the borrower registers delinquency. He fails to meet his obligations with respect to the due principal and interest. This fact has the following consequences: the institution cannot use the money it was expecting; penalties start to be calculated on the overdue amount; and the institution starts to take actions to recover the money. Short delinquencies are not dangerous for the client and for the institution, but long or frequent delinquencies are risky because they can lead the client to default. The institution risks losing the money, while the micro entrepreneur risks to lose the business that, in many cases, is the only source of income for his household.

At the moment of credit approval nobody can certify that the client will repay on time and integrally the loan and due interest. In fact, nobody can certify that recovery actions undertaken by the institution, once the client in delinquency, will give any result. In these conditions the losses of the lender can be even bigger, as the institution besides lent money could invest in collection activities and have no return. This is why financial institutions require collateral, cosigners and other guaranties meant to give a possibility to recover credit amounts if clients fail to pay. But even these guaranties cannot save the institutions from losses generated by bad loans.

In these conditions, credit scoring appears to be a very useful tool. That is why it is so popular, if not a must, in mainstream finance, where this technique is used not only to help approve loans but also it is widely applied in marketing, debt recovery, provisions, fraud detection and churn prevention.

Credit scoring is not new. We don't know when for the first time it became an official tool to evaluate credit risk, but we know for sure that it existed for decades in the heads of loan officers and influenced their way of judging the credit-worthiness of loan applicants based on similar past experiences. In fact this is the assumption on which credit scoring is built: future credit behavior of clients is supposed to be similar to the credit behavior of past clients with similar characteristics.

Since the late 90s, credit scoring gradually finds its place in microfinance. It proved its use in approval of micro loans to new micro entrepreneurs. It also proved its use in loan renewal. We must admit that there are challenges for scoring in micro lending. Some are different from those in classical credit scoring, but there are much more arguments in favor of credit scoring.

HOW DOES CREDIT SCORING FOR MICROFINANCE WORK?

Basic Principles of Credit Scoring for Microfinance

Like in classical credit scoring, the scoring tools for microfinance rely on scorecards and scoring

strategies. A scorecard is a selection of characteristics that could be found in the borrower's profile. The profile of the borrower is basically all we know about a certain potential or current client. This information refers to his socio-demographic data, business-demographic data, the information about his previous loans, also the information about the product he is applying for and other similar information that allows the institution to know this client.

This information can be structured in variables and their corresponding characteristics. Let's take the case of a married, 28 years old male that is earning 10,000 rupees per year from selling vegetables in the market as example. He just reimbursed without any delay the first loan and wants to renew it. We have a variable "age" and the corresponding characteristic is "28 years". We have another variable "gender" with the characteristic "male". The variable "annual income" has the characteristic "10,000 INR". Other variables and corresponding characteristics are: marital status – married, business activity – vegetable vendor, business place – market. We have also several behavioral variables: previous loans with the institution – 1, maximal delinquency registered during the previous loan – 0 days, number of times delinquent during the previous loan – 0 times.

In the scorecard are included only characteristics that have risk predictive power. Each characteristic, if incorporated, has a grade assigned. As example we can take this imaginable renewal scorecard which includes 6 variables with 9 characteristics. (see Table 1)

If the applicant has in his profile some characteristics included in the scorecard, he will receive the points corresponding to each characteristic that matched his profile. The sum of all grades received plus the initial score represents his final credit score. It indicates on a scale specific for credit scoring the probability of bad behavior of this applicant. As we mentioned previously bad behavior does not mean the fact to register short arrears, it is the situation when, because of the arrears, the client risks to default. A bad credit

Table 1.

Initial score		800
Variable	**Characteristic**	**Grade**
Age (years)	18 - 30	- 10
Marital status	Single	- 5
	Divorced	+ 5
Business activity	Manufacturing	- 10
Business place	Market	+ 10
Annual income (INR)	10,000 +	+ 15
Previous loans with the institution	3 +	+ 20
Maximal delinquency during the last loan	15 - 30	- 20
	31 +	- 30

behavior could also mean frequent arrears that make the loan unprofitable for the institution due to frequent reminding and investigation actions.

The credit score of the applicant from the example above will be: $800 - 10 + 10 + 15 = 815$. Please note that in this case the variable "gender" was not considered relevant for credit risk estimation. In some countries the law prohibits the use of variables that are considered discriminative, but for microfinance these cases are rare.

Characteristics in the scorecard can have assigned positive or negative grades, meaning that a characteristic can make the client more or less risky. If a high credit score indicates high probability of good credit behavior, a negative grade means that the characteristic is predicting bad behavior, so the probability of good behavior will be lower.

Let us imagine that the applicant from the example above would have been in arrears for 40 days once during the previous loan. In these conditions, his credit score would be: $800 - 10 + 10 + 15 - 30 = 785$. This figure is lower than the first result, which is 815. By consequence, his credit risk is higher.

Even if the borrower doesn't have, in his profile, any of the characteristics included in the scorecard, he'll get the initial score that will be his final score. The initial score gives the probability

that the forecasted event will occur to subjects whose profiles don't have any of the characteristics included in the scorecard. In fact we always say that credit scoring estimates the probability of an applicant to be bad, but in reality it gives the probability of the subject to be good. It is because these two probabilities are interrelated and it is easier to understand that a higher score means a better client.

Statistically speaking, the probability that an event will occur during a given time can be represented by a number ranging from 0 to 1, where 0 indicates no chances for the event to occur and 1 indicates absolute certainty that the event will occur during the given time. A number between 0 and 1 indicates more or less chances for a certain outcome. As example: a probability of 0.25 indicates 25% chances for the event to occur.

If the probability of an applicant to be good is 0, than the probability to be bad is 1. If the probability of the applicant to be good is x, the probability to be bad is $1 - x$. In credit scoring, to simplify the understanding of the figures, experts usually work with numbers ranging from 0 to 1,000, where 0 will be the equivalent that the bad behavior will certainly occur and 1'000 indicates no chances for bad behavior during the given frame of time. Scores between these limits indicate proportionally a certain probability of bad behavior. Please note that we speak about forecasted bad behavior and not delinquency. In these conditions, subjects with high scores will be less risky than subjects with low scores.

Difference with Classical Credit Scoring

If we take the example of consumer lending in developed countries, the information on income of the borrowers is available from trusted sources. The same is for credit history. If the borrower has a stable source of income and positive credit history, basically money surplus of his household will decide the amount and the term of the loan.

Socio-demographic variables play a secondary role.

Micro entrepreneurs usually operate in the informal or semi-formal sectors. Many don't have official or trustful income statements. The assets owed by micro entrepreneurs are not reflected in the bookkeeping documents. All quantitative measurements of the business have to be estimated or calculated indirectly. That is why a visit of a loan officer to the business place of the micro entrepreneur is a mandatory stage for every loan demand. Home and neighborhood visit is also a common practice.

The loan officer, based on the information collected from the potential new or renewal borrower, from his clients and suppliers, from his business neighbors, from the home visit, will generate the income statement, the balance sheet and different ratios that are required by internal policies and legislation. The loan officer will try to determine if the borrower has a credit history with other financial institutions or informal lenders.

In the end, some estimated quantitative measurements will give an important insight on the ability of the borrower to repay the loan. Due to the fact that these measurements are approximated, the socio-demographic variables have an important weight in the evaluation of the demand for micro credits.

To compensate this lack of trustful data, loan officers use qualitative indicators like the impression from the visit, the perception of the borrower by the neighbors, presence of conflicts in the family, presence of vices in the family and so on. Although are subjective, these variables, if quantified using ranks, help predict credit risk and have their place in the scorecards for micro lending.

Statistical scorecards can be developed based on the profiles of past borrowers which should imperatively include their detailed credit behavior. Behavior and variables are linked using statistical software to identify characteristics that predict bad credit behavior. If the credit behavior or the characteristics of past clients are not available in electronic format, information should be transposed to a database. If the behavior of past clients is lost or key figures from the borrowers' profiles are missing and manual collection of a sample of data is not an option, a statistical development is not possible at this stage. The alternative to this situation is judgmental credit scoring.

To summarize, it's all about information. The biggest difference between classical scoring and credit scoring for micro lending represents the availability of data – data asymmetry. This is one of the causes of disparity between costs and earnings. Another big difference is in data gathering and treatment. Microfinance lenders do not capture many variables from the borrower's profile. Also it is common to see that the information is not transferred to a functional database from paper support. The same happens with the behavior of the clients. Not so rare are the cases when arrears are managed manually and records are made only in clients' paper files. The "2008 Microfinance Technology Survey" conducted by CGAP on a sample of 152 microfinance institutions worldwide revealed that 4% of the respondents manage the loan portfolio manually. A similar survey was conducted in 2004 and showed that from 270 voluntary responses from MFIs 11% declared to use manual procedures in portfolio management while 35% were using spreadsheets.

Judgmental Scorecards

Judgmental scorecards, called also expert scorecards, have shown good results in microfinance. As the name indicates, an expert scorecard is the result of the work of several different experts that have, as their main objective, identified and grouped risk predictive variables. Based on observations, personal experience, information from similar markets or pure judgment, these experts decide to assign grades to characteristics with estimated risk discrimination power. Several rules apply, but these will be detailed later in this chapter.

The main source of inspiration is the knowledge of the loan officers who work daily with micro loans. The most experienced ones have in mind clear patterns of good and bad clients. Scoring experts are crucial. They know from experience in similar markets which variables and characteristics statistically proved to have predictive power. Other actors, like managers of risk department, credit department or debt recovery department, can participate and help identify relevant characteristics and estimate their weights.

If a characteristic is supposed to predict future good credit behavior of the applicant, the grade corresponding to this characteristic will be positive. Grades will depend on the power to predict behavior. One common possibility is to have five levels of power: high, above-average, average, below-average and low predictive power. To low predictive power corresponds 5 points. High predictive power implies a grade of 25 points, with a pace of 5 points between levels. If a characteristic is predicting a future bad behavior, the grade corresponding to this characteristic will have negative sign, but same power levels. An example would be: -20 points for a characteristic with above-average power to predict bad behavior.

Each scorecard, besides the grades corresponding to the selected characteristics, has an initial score. This score should represent the probability of good behavior of loan applicants that don't have in their profiles any characteristic included in the scorecard. As this probability is difficult to estimate, it is common to use the probability of good behavior of the entire population of clients, which is usually known. Knowing the number of bad loans, it is easy to calculate the bad rate of the population and the rate of good behavior.

The set of characteristics is, by consequence, adjusted to avoid giving grades to characteristics that are observed for the majority of clients. Instead, the other characteristics observed in less then 50% of the population must be considered. Let's take the following example. Experts know that the variable "gender" is important in predicting

the credit risk. In their MFI women have better credit behavior and this characteristic is judged to have average level of predictive power: 15 points. If women represent the majority of the micro borrowers, the experts will prefer to give -15 points to the characteristic "man".

Once the judgmental scorecard is ready it could be tested on a sample of borrowers from a similar market. It is important to know which loans from this sample are bad and which are good. In this way it will be possible to observe how the scorecard predicts bad loans. These results can inspire the experts in fixing the cut-off.

The cut-off is initially fixed by the experts, but later could be adjusted by the institution based on real credit behavior of the clients that received loans after being scored by the expert scorecard. In consumer lending the cut-off is meant to determine who qualifies for the loan and who doesn't. In microfinance the applicants that receive scores below the cut-off should be denied the loan but should not be refused. Alternatives should be provided like group loans and trainings in order to meet their needs and also help applicants improve their borrowing profile.

Expert credit scoring should be seen as a temporary solution before the implementation of statistical scorecards. The implementation of credit scoring, even if based on a judgmental scorecard, brings a "data culture" to the institution. Scoring imposes a systematized collection of data related to the profiles of the borrowers and their credit behavior. All this information can be used to develop a statistical scoring model to replace the existing judgmental as soon as a sufficient sample of good and bad loans is collected.

Statistical Scorecards

A statistical scorecard better forecasts the credit risk because it gives statistical odds that a loan applicant will be good if he receives a certain credit score. Statistics are used to link the credit behavior of past clients with the characteristics of their profiles. As mentioned earlier, the assumption that future behavior of the clients will be similar to the behavior of past clients with similar characteristics stands.

It is a common rule in scoring to have the smallest sample of data to develop a scorecard of 1,000 to 1,500 bad client profiles and at least a similar quantity of good profiles. From experience we know that powerful scorecards can be developed with smaller samples, but we must highlight the importance and advantages of big samples.

The data from the profile of the borrower should be collected at the moment of application for the loan as in the future the statistical credit scoring will be used at the same moment of application for the loan. Statisticians link the characteristics from the profiles with the behavior registered by their loans. They will assume that future clients with same characteristics will behave as past clients did. It is important to exclude old profiles from the sample to avoid making conclusions using data that could be irrelevant in the present. Generally, loans disbursed more than 2-3 years ago could be considered as old.

There is a definition for bad loans and a definition for good loans. Bad loans and correspondingly bad clients are those that are not desired by the institution. If the institution only knew that these clients will behave as they did, they would be refused at the moment of loan application or loan renewal. Usually these clients generate losses to the institution. In fact, the definition of a bad client depends on the financial institution that could define it differently, but if credit behavior is to be forecasted, than the definition should be based on a quantitative representation of credit behavior.

There are statistical methodologies to determine accurate definitions of bad clients. The "deterioration matrix" is one of these. Analyzing it, the scoring expert can identify after how many consecutive days in arrear a client has more chances to aggravate his delinquency than to recover. This number of days can be used in the definition of bad loans. In microfinance, a common definition

of a bad client is at least one time in arrear for more than 30 consecutive calendar days.

Bi-dimensional definitions of bad loans, like 15 consecutive days in arrears at least 2 times, are also common. The introduction of the second dimension like number of times in arrear, average delinquency or percentage of time in delinquency, is meant to improve the definition of bad loans by excluding good loans that accidentally registered delinquencies.

In the sample can be included also some current loans. If a borrower registered enough delinquent credit behavior to consider his loan as a bad, his profile could be included in the sample. If a loan becomes bad, it remains bad till the end. On the contrary, if a loan didn't register any bad behavior at the beginning, we could not consider such loan to be good as bad behavior could follow.

We observed that in microfinance loans require up to 6 - 8 months to show bad behavior. If during this time the borrower didn't register bad behavior, chances are low that he will have bad behavior later. This period depends on different factors like country, product or institution specifics. We call it "maturity period" and it is not difficult to estimate it. We group all current loans, including recently disbursed, by month of disbursal. We analyze the percentage of bad loans in each group and we observe that the percentage of bad loans is very low in recent months but increases gradually till it stabilizes at a certain level. This level is the bad rate of our population of borrowers and the time needed to reach this level is our maturity period. Loans that passed this period without bad behavior could be considered as good loans even if borrowers still have several installments to reimburse.

The percentage of bad loans in the sample should be equal to the bad rate of the entire population of borrowers. The sample of bad and good loans is analyzed to identify all the characteristics that have predictive power. This is a laborious task. Firstly, variables are analyzed individually. Discrete variables are easier to analyze. Gender and marital status are perfect examples of discrete variables. For each characteristic we calculate the weight of evidence, called also percentage of reference (%ref). The formula is simple: *%ref = 1 – (bad rate of loans that have the characteristic / bad rate)*. This indicator shows characteristics that are gathering bigger proportions of good loans or bigger proportions of bad loans. This operation is done to simplify the statistical treatment that will follow. If the %ref of a characteristic in absolute value exceeds 20%, it is clear that this characteristic has power to predict credit behavior. As in the case of judgmental scorecards, characteristics observed for the majority of subjects in the sample are ignored.

Continuous variables require bigger effort. Age and income are perfect examples. Variables are segmented in ranges and %ref is calculated for every segment. It is important to find logical explanations and see expected trends in the results of this selection. As an example, it is normal to see the bad rate diminishing while business experience of the borrower increases. If some ranges show ambiguous results and there is no logical explanation, the variable should not be used for further statistics. Variables with more than 10% of missing data also should not be used. Variables could be crossed and each combination checked for better results in matter of risk discrimination.

The selection of characteristics is used for regression. Regression analysis refers to several techniques for modeling functions that can determine the value of a dependent variable using values of independent variables. Logit, also called logistic regression is a common regression technique in credit scoring. It is used to estimate the probability that an event will occur by entering the values of the independent variables in the logistic function. The dependent variable is the probability of good behavior and independent variables are the selected characteristics. As the result of the function is a probability (number ranging from 0 to 1), to convert it to the common scoring base, we multiply this number by 1,000.

Regression analysis requires the assumptions that the sample is representative of the population of clients and variables are not correlated. This fact requires additional statistical analysis and data treatment. Because there are inevitably strongly correlated variables, some characteristics are excluded from the scorecard. Are also excluded the characteristics that have insignificant statistical impact on the outcome.

Data

As mentioned previously, the profile of the borrower makes credit scoring different in micro lending. Socio-demographic variables are very important. Obviously, business-related variables, if quantified accurately are also important. Many qualitative variables that describe in a subjective way the applicant and his business have power to predict future behavior. That is why such variables find their place in statistical scorecards for microfinance.

The variables used to develop scorecards for micro lending can be organized in the following categories: socio-demographic variables, business-demographic variables, financial indicators, loan variables and past credit behavior. Past credit behavior could come from credit bureaus, which is rare in microfinance, or from the institution itself in case of loan renewal.

Socio-demographic variables describe the applicant and his household. Business variables describe the business of the micro entrepreneur. Financial indicators are meant to describe the financial situation of the borrower. The characteristics of the loan that the micro entrepreneur is applying for have an impact on the credit risk. Loan term, repayment frequency, currency, grace period and other loan variables are frequently included in statistical and judgmental scorecards.

Credit bureaus for micro entrepreneurs are rare, but if available, variables quantifying past credit behavior of the applicant with other financial institutions have important weights in scorecards.

It is known that past credit behavior of the applicant has strong predictive power. If a client was several times delinquent previously, there are high chances that he will be late with his payments in the future. The same if the client didn't register any delinquency during his previous loans, chances are low that this client will register bad behavior in the future, unless the clients wants to fraud and created artificially a good credit behavior to get access to bigger amounts of money.

For loan applicants that want to renew their micro loans, past credit behavior with the institution is available. This type of information is very important because it is more detailed and accurate than credit bureau data. Information of each delinquency is available and the behavior can be quantified accurately.

Scoring models that are built using behavior variables are called behavioral models. These models have better discrimination power. Discrimination in this context means ability to separate good clients from bad. The difference between evaluation scoring which is used to approve micro loans to new clients and behavioral scoring used to approve demands for loan renewal are described below.

Evaluation Scoring

Evaluation scoring, as we call each credit scoring model used to assess the creditworthiness of new applicants, has an important added value for the MFI. Using a set of variables from the profile of the applicant, the scoring model forecasts the probability of good behavior of the potential client. This information is extremely useful for the loan officer who evaluates the loan demand, as it gives an objective view on the credit risk of application.

If the loan application receives a high score, the institution can approve it in a simplified way. Knowing that the applicant is from a low risk category, the MFI will do less effort to decide what amount to disburse. As result transaction costs reduce while amounts disbursed increase.

We can imagine a sort of auto-approval technique where low-risk applications are treated by the loan officer solely. The resources of credit committees are saved for more difficult cases.

A low score, below a certain cut-off, indicates a high probability of bad behavior. For the institution, it is obvious that the micro loan should not be approved. The MFI in this case will save money, avoiding costly evaluation procedures, delinquency management and probable collection actions. In microfinance, it is difficult to simply refuse a client even if self-sustainability is a priority. MFIs continue to be socially-committed and redirect refused applicants to different programs where micro entrepreneurs can build a saving and credit history participating in group loans.

Average score indicates average credit risk. Such loan demands will be probably analyzed in the same way as before the implementation of credit scoring, where all applications required the decision of the credit committee. The difference is that the credit committee should have more time to analyze each application as no time will be wasted on high-risk and low-risk applications. Also the score will help take the decision being the "third voice in the credit committee" (Schreiner, M. 2002, p.7).

In conclusion, evaluation scoring will estimate the credit risk of the applicant helping recommend the most appropriate credit product, protecting the institution and the applicant from default. The institution will prevent the client from taking extra risk and by consequence, will lower its own risk. In the same time the institution can avoid refusing the micro entrepreneur by proposing a different, more appropriate product. The client feels a more personal relation with the institution, which in reality is reducing micromanagement to cut operational costs.

Renewal Scoring

The same added value is generated by behavioral scoring models used for loan renewal. An important advantage can be seen in the fact that the institution can increase revenues by offering auto-renewal. This proactive process can be automated. Besides increasing revenues and lowering transaction costs, it has an impact on clients' loyalty.

Before the current loan is fully reimbursed, the credit score of the borrower is calculated, taking into account his recent credit behavior. If the score is high enough, the micro-entrepreneur receives the approval of a new micro loan. Many borrowers will find difficult to refuse such offers, feeling a personal relation with the institution. Such measures can prevent the churn of the best clients.

Group Lending

Credit scoring can be used in group lending also. In fact, the credit score of a group will be the lowest score obtained by each member of the group. Because amounts are small and delinquency rates are much below those registered in individual micro lending, credit scoring is not popular for group loans. Often MFIs don't register individual credit behavior of group members but only the behavior of the group as an entity. Information about individual credit behavior is crucial for the development of statistical scorecards and for later follow-up.

In conditions with almost perfect credit behavior, credit scoring finds its utility in microfinance seen from a different perspective. MFIs understand that extremely low delinquency levels could mean than micro borrowers do not take full advantage of the leverage offered by micro loans. On the other hand, loan officers are afraid to disburse bigger amounts, to maintain delinquency low. In these conditions, credit scoring is used to justify the ability of certain borrowers to receive bigger individual loans. It is a sort of graduation from group loans to individual loans – the opposite of the situation of high risk individual loan applica-

tions that are denied the individual loan but can enroll in group lending.

Score Distribution and Tests

It is a procedure to be performed with each scorecard after it is developed. Statisticians recommend using a separate sample of good and bad loans for tests. If the test sample is not available, the initial sample which was used to develop the scorecard can be used. Each loan from the sample is scored using the scorecard. Loans are organized in an ascendant order of resulting scores. Loans are grouped by ranges of score in sets of 5 to15% depending on the bad rate of the range. (see Figure 1)

We can observe that as the score increases, the percentage of bad clients diminishes. Inevitably there are small quantities of good clients that received low scores and also few bad clients with high scores. The score distribution helps us evaluate the quality of the scorecard. There are also specific tests to evaluate the scorecard, but the fact that the distribution has this shape is a good sign.

In fact this is the advantage of using a scorecard. For every score (or score range) we can estimate the odds of good behavior of the applicant. The score distribution is used to establish the cut-offs. Depending on the strategy of the institution, the rejection cut-off could be increased for a more strict approval policy or can be decreased for a more permissive approach.

Besides the analysis of the distribution, it is common to test the scorecard using the Kolmogorov–Smirnov test (K–S test), GINI coefficient or similar indicators that can measure the discrimination power of the scorecard. For judgmental scorecards, if profiles of the borrowers match, samples of loans from similar markets can be used to see the distribution and test the scorecard. Also smaller samples that were not big enough for a statistical development can be used for tests.

Figure 1. Example of a score distribution of a statistical scorecard developed for micro lending

Score range	Good loans	% Good (Row)	Bad loans	% Bad (Row)	Total Row	% Total
<= 293	105	21.88%	375	78.13%	480	5.5%
294 - 458	195	36.11%	345	63.89%	540	6.2%
459 - 570	390	52.00%	360	48.00%	750	8.6%
571 - 703	585	62.90%	345	37.10%	930	10.7%
704 - 765	570	77.55%	165	22.45%	735	8.4%
766 - 826	720	82.76%	150	17.24%	870	10.0%
827 - 876	840	84.85%	150	15.15%	990	11.4%
877 - 919	1110	90.24%	120	9.76%	1230	14.1%
920 - 946	1185	90.80%	120	9.20%	1305	15.0%
947+	810	93.10%	60	6.90%	870	10.0%
Total	**6510**	**75%**	**2190**	**25%**	**8700**	**100%**

Scoring Strategies

Scoring strategies are seen as the ultimate goal of credit scoring. Through these strategies institutions can reduce transaction costs and increase the number of clients while maintaining the credit risk at acceptable level. Risk based pricing can also be achieved by using scoring strategies. We distinguish two types of strategies: decision strategies and product definition strategies.

Decision strategies are meant to organize the decision process. The most important is "decision level" strategy. It indicates the authority to decide the approval or rejection of the application. Usually, the loan officer prepares the documents and a credit committee decides to approve, amend or reject the loan demand. The decision level strategy is based on the credit score and the required loan amount. It recommends different decision levels for different combinations of risk and amount. (see Table 2)

For applications that received high scores and require low amounts, the loan officer will have the right to decide whether to disburse the loan. Simplified credit committees will be able to decide on applications that received average scores and demand average loan amounts. The most difficult cases are those with a low score and high required loan amount. These loan demands will be assigned

to credit committees. In this way, the most experienced resources, which are the most expensive, are focused on applications that require them.

The benefits are obvious. The MFI makes economies on low risk applications, speeding-up the disbursal process. On the other hand, high risk applications are analyzed by experienced teams that should make accurate credit decisions keeping the credit risk within the limits.

One decision strategy could recommend intensive verification of applications with high risk and simplified verifications or no verification for low risk application. Another strategy, mostly for renewal applicants, could abandon the home visit for low risk profiles, or even the visit to the business place. Visits are one expensive component in the approval process, so an accurate strategy that focuses the resources of the loan officers on risky applications can help make big savings with no incidence on the risk indicators.

Product definition strategies can help MFIs implement risk based pricing and risk based selection of loan conditions. In risk based pricing, the interest will be higher for riskier applicants and lower for clients with a high score. Same principle could be applied for loan maturity, required guaranties, grace period and minimal cash contribution to the project.

Table 2. Example of "decision level" strategy

Decision Taking Authority	Loan Amount		
	Low	Average	High
High Risk	Reject	Reject	Reject
Average-High Risk	Level 3	Level 3	Reject
Average Risk	Level 3	Level 3	Level 3
Average-Low Risk	Level 2	Level 2	Level 2
Low Risk	Level 1	Level 1	Level 2

Level 1 – the loan officer;
Level 2 – simplified credit committee composed by the loan officer + 1 senior loan officer;
Level 3 – credit committee – a full scale credit committee.

In fact, the mere role of product definition strategies is to adjust loan conditions to meet the needs of the applicant and limit the credit risk at the same time. Table 3 gives an example of a strategy that based on the credit score and required loan amount defines the minimal guaranty level that the applicant should provide in order to get the loan.

This strategy introduces collateral-free lending without increasing much the risks of the financial institution.

Once the strategies approved, the scoring tool has to be implemented. The lending process flow is adjusted to fit the operations required to calculate the credit score and take the actions indicated by the scoring strategies. Changes do not affect much of the work of the staff involved in lending. People tend to be opposed to changes and this can be an obstacle to correct implementation and use of scoring. That is why the implementation of scoring should be accompanied by intensive communication and training. Scoring could be considered by loan officers as a substitute for their work. In microfinance that is hardly imaginable. Scoring can never replace a loan officer. It is a tool that helps take correct credit decisions. This message should be transmitted to the end users of the credit scoring tool.

Reports

Each scorecard has to be monitored constantly to ensure that it maintains the expected credit risk estimation power over time. There are several reports that help monitor the performance of the scorecard. Some reports are similar to the operations completed during the development of the scorecard. Current and initial results are compared. Big differences indicate modifications in

Table 3. Example of one scoring strategy that defines the minimal guaranty level based on the credit score and required loan amount

Minimal Guaranty Level	Loan Amount		
	Low	Average	High
High Risk	No Renewal	No Renewal	No Renewal
Average-High Risk	1 Cosigner	1 Cosigner	No Renewal
Average Risk	1 Cosigner	1 Cosigner	Collateral
Average-Low Risk	No Guaranty	No Guaranty	1 Cosigner
Low Risk	No Guaranty	No Guaranty	No Guaranty-

the behavior of the clients and/or in the structure of the clients.

Data reports monitor the quality of the information used by the scorecard. Through these reports, it is possible to observe changes in the structure of the population of clients. Also, it is possible to observe if the loan officers collect the data accurately.

Scorecard evaluation reports follow-up the scoring model itself. The score distribution is analyzed periodically using mature loans that were disbursed using credit scoring. Current distribution is compared with the initial distribution.

Additional managerial reports like the rejection report or the report on overwrites help monitor other aspects of the use of credit scoring in the institution.

Issues, Controversies, Problems

There are two categories of issues related to credit scoring in micro lending. A first type regroups objective problems related to technical issues, the second type of subjective issues is related to the application of scoring in practice.

As we stated initially, credit scoring is not for every MFI. Firstly, scoring should fill a need – the need for correct estimation of credit risk. The credit risk is compared with the risk of loosing the opportunity to serve the micro entrepreneur. If the credit risk is lower than the opportunity risk, the loan should be disbursed. If credit risk is not an issue, credit scoring is useless. The same happens if the institution is not experiencing any opportunity risk.

To forecast accurately the risk, advanced statistics are required to link past credit behavior with the characteristics of the corresponding past clients. All these clients should form a homogeneous population and the environment should not change too fast, as we assume that similar credit behavior will be registered by future clients. Statistical requirements affect the population of clients, the sample of good and bad loans and the

quality of the data, which consists of profiles of the borrowers, including their credit behavior.

The implementation of credit scoring could suffer from the limitations of the institutions in matter of information technologies. It is highly desirable that credit scoring runs on a MIS platform that allows the calculation of the score once all required information is available. The MIS should also be able to register and store data about the behavior of the clients, in addition to the profiles of the borrowers.

Subjective issues can have their origin in the resistance of the loan officers to use credit scoring. The tool can be seen as a threat, meant to replace the loan officers. On the other hand, loan officers can be tempted to manipulate the tool. They can intentionally overestimate or underestimate several important variables to increase the final score and finally approve a loan that normally they would not be authorized to do.

If the institution is striving to reach self-sustainability, it will try to avoid bad loans. In credit scoring this procedure is done through fixing accurate cut-offs. Clients that receive a score below a certain limit are denied the micro loan. Applications on the limit or slightly above are analyzed intensively as their credit risk is high. Using the score distribution we can estimate the percentage of bad loans that will be refused at every score level where the cut-off can be fixed. The question here is, "what is the right level?"

Solutions and Recommendations

There are solutions for the majority of the identified issues. For institutions that don't meet the statistical requirements, the solution is a temporary judgmental scoring tool. We say that the micro lending market should be massive, because in massive markets the cost of credit scoring per loan disbursed can be low enough to make possible and economically viable the implementation of credit scoring. If the MFI can identify for a specific loan product a sample of bad loans big enough for a statistical development of a scorecard, we can consider that the concerned population of clients is massive enough for credit scoring.

Population should be homogeneous. This can be determined by analyzing the profiles of the borrowers, especially; the size and field of business, the amount and purpose of the loan, and the patterns of credit behavior. We can assume that in every MFI the clients of distinct micro credit products form distinct homogeneous populations. We used to divide micro borrowers in two distinct populations: agro and non-agro clients. Due to business-specific variables, the profile of agro borrowers is different from the profile of non agro micro borrowers.

Training, transparent communication and verification procedures are meant to cut the resistance of the users of scoring. Credit scoring cannot replace a loan officer, especially in microfinance. Even more so, if the institution decides to implement scoring strategies that allow loan officers to approve certain credit applications, the role of the loan officer becomes more important. In these conditions credit scoring can be seen as a tool that augments the importance of the loan officer, and not the reverse.

To discourage any manipulation of the scoring tool, the scorecard should not be known by the users. This fact doesn't meet the "transparency requirement" but, as rule, scorecards are secret. A scorecard in its essence is a short description of the know-how of the institution and competitors could be interested to copy it for own use. To avoid and prevent manipulations by loan officers, random verifications could be organized by the institution. To engage the responsibility of a second loan officer, the institution can implement the principle of "four eyes verification" before disbursal. These actions can be included in a decision scoring strategy, knowing that this will raise the cost and time required for disbursal.

Loan officers should also know that cases of manipulation can be identified later, as the loans disbursed fraudulently are riskier than should

be and there are reports that identify them. It is important to know that due to an important number of variables included in the scorecard, the manipulation of one or two characteristics doesn't have a decisive impact on the result. Applications that barely pass the rejection cut-off are supposed to be analyzed profoundly by credit committees.

Theoretically, credit scoring can be used on paper. While the loan officer is completing the evaluation form of the applicant, he can calculate his credit score. The big advantage is that the risk of the micro entrepreneur can be assessed directly on the ground and if the decision of the credit committee is not required, the disbursal can be done immediately. The disadvantage is that in this case the scorecard becomes known to the loan officers. To have the same advantages but keep the scorecard hidden, MFIs give portable devices to loan officers. These tools calculate the score once the loan officer entered the profile of the applicant. The data is saved in an electronic format and can be transferred automatically to a database, for later reports and statistics.

Microsoft Excel is a common platform for credit scoring in microfinance. The disadvantage is that credit application should be stored in separate files and credit behavior added manually to each. For reports, the information from the files should be collected and organized in a database.

FUTURE RESEARCH DIRECTIONS

Even if we found solutions for major issues related to the use of credit scoring in micro lending, there is room for research and analysis to find better alternatives. Statistics remain the preferential area of interest for researchers. There is still need for additional regression techniques more suitable for the microfinance environment, which is characterized by small samples, poor quality of the data, few reliable quantitative measurements of key business indicators and abundance of subjective qualitative measurements.

The costs of the visits to the business and the home of the potential borrower are high. In microfinance these stages seem to be mandatory for every loan demand coming from new applicants. To quantify the business performance of a micro entrepreneur, a loan officer can spend a full day measuring the real turnover or visit randomly the applicant several times to count his cash. This effort could be in vain if the loan officer is not convinced or the credit committee refuses the disbursal. Methodologies oriented to evaluate the business accurately in less time and with less effort are needed.

If microfinance institutions could identify trustful indicators of the business performance that could be estimated in the office, it is possible to modify the process flow and introduce pre-scoring: the scorecard is divided in two sections as the application form is. First part of the application form is completed by new applicants in the branch. If the pre-score passes the cut-off, the loan officer continues the evaluation process with the home and business visit and completes the second section of the application form. This procedure is meant to screen bad clients before expensive activities are undertaken. At the end the entire application form is scored and the final credit score used to take the decision.

If credit bureaus for micro entrepreneurs are possible, then credit scoring for these bureaus is also imaginable. In a study conducted in 2004 on the Nicaraguan microfinance market, we showed empirical evidence of benefits from sharing credit information among providers of credit to low-income segments. We also showed the importance of use of credit scoring to forecast the credit risk of micro borrowers.

Simulating credit expansion and risk reduction in financial institutions providing retail micro loans, we obtained a 58% increase of good borrowers and a reduction of the default rate to 26.39% from 46.17%. For the simulation we supposed that concerned loan providers shared positive and negative credit information and used credit scoring to decide the disbursal of loans.

One important topic related to credit scoring is discrimination, in its primary sense, different from the one used frequently in this chapter, which is statistical discrimination. Discrimination means giving a treatment to one person differentiated from the treatment received by another person in same circumstances just because the first possesses an attribute, which is unrelated to the situation. Racial discrimination is the most known form. Besides the race, in advanced financial markets anti-discrimination rules restrict the use of other variables for credit scoring, like the gender or the age of the applicant. Microfinance seems to be far from such rules.

On the other hand, microfinance appears to be more vulnerable to discrimination and one eminent example is gender discrimination. In many regions of the world women have limited access to micro loans because they are subjectively judged less capable of running micro businesses. In these conditions, if statistics clearly show a better credit behavior for women, this fact will be included in the scoring model and this argument will be used to promote a different approach toward the subject. In fact, we reflected only one aspect of this problem. More research is needed to analyze from a multi dimension perspective the relation between credit scoring and discrimination.

CONCLUSION

"Credit scoring is one of the most important uses of technology that may affect microfinance", as per Rhyne, E. and Christen, R.P. (1999). We fully agree and we think that credit scoring has an important role to play in micro lending because it can help MFIs reach self-sustainability. Self-sustainability is important because it facilitates the increase of the outreach of the MFIs without additional resources. The consequence is augmentation of revenues. The transaction cost per unit follows a descendent trend based on the effects of economies of scale and also based on economies realized using appropriate scoring strategies. Due to an accurate estimation of credit risk, costs generated by bad credit behavior of the clients are expected to have negative or moderate growth.

All these benefits have a cost composed of three components: development, implementation and maintenance of credit scoring. Certainly, for small institutions credit scoring could be a bad investment as it could be bad investment for institutions with low credit and opportunity risks. However, institutions with low delinquency levels can find own advantages in scoring. The accurate and objective assessment of risk can determine lenders increase loan amounts so that capable micro entrepreneurs can take full advantage of this leverage and escape poverty.

As a result of the technical assistance from IFC, in November 2006 the Egyptian MFI Alexandria Business Association / Small & Micro Enterprise Project (ABA/SME) started the use of credit scoring for a part of its micro lending operations. At the 2007 Next Generation Access to Finance conference hosted by the World Bank the Executive Director of ABA/SME declared that in the first eight months following the implementation of scoring ABA/SME registered 15% increase in numbers and 30% increase in amounts of loans disbursed over same period of the previous year. ABA/SME experienced a minor drop in administrative costs per loan disbursed and repayment rate on concerned credits was almost 99.5%. These results convinced ABA/SME to use credit scoring for all demands of micro and small credits.

The example of the Peruvian bank Mibanco shows a different side of use of credit scoring in microfinance. Although the institution reported to have reduced by almost 10% the costs of approval, Salazar, D. (2004), in the first year following implementation of credit scoring, at the same conference, Mr. Ferreyra - the business manager of Mibanco highlighted a number of problems the bank experienced during implementation and

afterwards. The main difficulties were related to quality of the data and principles of use of scoring. Mibanco found difficult to create a "culture" of use of credit scoring, as well as to keep secret the scorecards. The follow-up of the new process of loan approval was much more difficult than expected. The same for dealing with overwrites. In spite of problems, credit scoring helped Mibanco reduce time of approval and delinquency levels and an increase of the productivity of loan officers was registered. Ferreyra concludes that credit scoring is a good tool but loan officers must learn to apply it correctly.

REFERENCES

El Tabba, M. (2007). *Introducing Credit Scoring in Microlending in ABA/SME.* Presentation made at the 2007 IFC Conference: Next Generation Access to Finance.

EU/ACP Microfinance Programme. (2009). *2008 Microfinance Technology Survey.* Washington D.C.: CGAP, from: www.cgap.org/gm/document-1.9.34552/2008%20Microfinance%20Technology%20Survey.pdf

Ferreyra, J. (2007). *Credit Scoring. Implementación en Mibanco - Perú.* Presentation made at the 2007 IFC Conference: Next Generation Access to Finance.

IFC Conference proceedings. (2007). *Next Generation Access to Finance.* Retrieved from www.ifc.org/ifcext/gfm.nsf/AttachmentsByTitle/FI-CB-NextGenProceedings-Dec08/$FILE/FI-CB-NextGenProceedings-Dec08.pdf

Rhyne, E., & Christen, R. P. (1999). *Microfinance enters the Marketplace.* USA: USAID Microenterprise Publications. Retrieved from www.uncdf.org/mfdl/readings/Marketplace.pdf

Salazar, D. (2004). Credit Scoring. CGAP IT Innovation Series, Washington D.C.: CGAP. Retrieved from www.microfinancegateway.org/content/article/detail/18047

Schreiner, M. (2002). *Scoring: The Next Breakthrough in Microcredit?* Washington D.C.: CGAP, Retrieved from www.microfinance.com/English/Papers/Scoring_Breakthrough.pdf

ADDITIONAL READING

Berger, A., Barrers, M., Parsons, L., & Klein, J. (2007). *Credit Scoring for Microenterprise Lenders*. USA: Microenterprise Fund for Innovation, Effectiveness, Learning and Dissemination.

Goldberg, N. (2005). *Measuring the Impact of Microfinance: Taking Stock of What We Know.*

Schreiner, M. (2000). *Credit Scoring for Microfinance: Can It Work?* Paper presented at the III Foro Interamericana de la Microempresa, Barcelona, Spain, from: http://www.microfinance.com/English/Papers/Scoring_Can_It_Work.pdf

Siddiqi, N. (2005). *Credit Risk Scorecards: Developing and Implementing Intelligent Credit Scoring*. USA: Wiley.

USA. Grameen Foundation Karlan, D. & Zinman, J. (2007). *Expanding Credit Access: Improving Microfinance Operations and Measuring Impact with Credit Scoring*. USA: Financial Access Initiative.

Chapter 15

A Systemic–Fuzzy Model to Evaluate the Social Impact of Microcredits

Carmen Lozano
Polytechnic University of Cartagena, Spain

Federico Fuentes
Polytechnic University of Cartagena, Spain

ABSTRACT

This chapter presents an application of systemic-fuzzy models to evaluate the social impact of a microcredit program. The goal of our research is to supply a complement to effectiveness indicators (traditionally based on profitability and portfolio quality) by measuring personal and family achievements, and through consideration of the economic consequences derived from microcredits. We will thus attempt to offer a more complete and transparent image of the activity of such institutions.

INTRODUCTION

The microfinance industry has undergone a significant development and growth in the last years, which has meant a larger concern on the part of investors, donors and regulators, that maximum transparency is achieved in the judgement of rating agencies in charge of gathering and spreading such companies' work and performance, while at the same time openly showing perspectives and risks that may be faced.

Microfinance Industry Rating began at the end of the last decade and it has experienced its own evolution. Many have been the debates, studies

and opinions trying to find the best assessment indicators of financial situation, risk and yield of rated companies. The task is not simple, if one keeps in mind the wide variety of tasks carried out by such companies, of task contexts, size differences and differences in accounting practices, which make it difficult to establish comparisons between companies and may distort the net worth view. All this has motivated the absence of universal indicators particularly in microfinancial companies.

In 2003 MicroRate (rating agency specialized in microfinance), the Interamerican Development Bank (IDB), the Consultative Group to Assist the Poor (CGAP), the United States Agency for International Development (USAID) and rating

DOI: 10.4018/978-1-61520-993-4.ch015

agencies MCRIL and PlaNet Rating, concluded after a round table in the publication of a list of twenty performance indicators, their definitions, applications and weaknesses. The purpose of this technical guide is relatively narrow. It highlights 14 of the most commonly used definitions published by the Roundtable Group and illustrates how they are used. It provides some explanation and analysis of the indicators for those who are interested in understanding their application as well as weaknesses. For each indicator, the Guide presents the proposed definition, interprets its meaning, identifies potential pitfalls in its use, and provides benchmark values for 29 Latin American microfinance institutions compiled by MicroRate (the "MicroRate 29"). It should be noted, however, that these added sections are the work of MicroRate and the IDB, and do not necessarily or automatically reflect the opinion or position of the other entities participating in the Roundtable discussions.

These indicators basically referred to four main categories: quality of the portfolio, efficiency and productivity, financial management and profitability. Their aim is to offer an image of the risk and financial situation of the microfinance companies analysed.

One of the analysis areas that has suffered from the lack of indicators (due to its difficult quantification) involves the qualitative aspects that consider and influence the strength of microfinance companies. Management quality, market opportunities, research and development of new products, knowledge about the market, measurements of organizational performance, clients' satisfaction… would be some of them. All analysts agree that these aspects should be treated as a complement to reports involving more quantifiable aspects. Interviews through on-site visits to companies by rating agents could be a way of summarizing information, although no method is able to handle such information and incorporate it in reports with the importance that it should be given. Let us keep in mind that a microfinance

company may be carrying out important work in a depressed area with a high index of poverty and low capital ratios, infrastructure or turnover, and however receive a bad rating that makes it difficult to find financing for its objectives.

The only result indicators commonly used to evaluate microcredit programs' effectiveness assess the profitability of a credit institution and the quality of its portfolio, but they neither tell us anything about social impact (improvements relating to the individual and to his family unit), nor about the economic influence that these programs generate. Such information may indeed be included in reports of performance evaluation of some of these institutions, through surveys which are mostly treated with scarce statistical rigor (small samples, slanted by absence of comparisons to control groups, dubious choice of variables…etc).

A very frequent error made when performance impact is being evaluated, is that only isolated parts of the problem are generally kept in mind, and just the symptom of the problem rather than its cause is treated. Under this reasoning, decisions offer symptomatic solutions that temporarily improve the system, without eliminating the root of the problem, since only the parts but not the whole have been considered. Systemic thinking approaches entireties and structures underlying complex situations, and therefore supports decision taking that aims at significant and durable improvements.

In the particular case of microcredit institutions, complexity is specially critical in order to evaluate the consequences of performance, knowing that social, spiritual, political and economic dimensions are involved. The social repercussion of a microcredit program can be inferred from information coming from the client and/or the user of such services, and must be analyzed under the premise that after borrowers receive their credits, there is a specific expected response, such as improvement in borrower's revenues because of having received the loan. However, we may get confronted with the paradox that the individual often behaves counter-intuitively, in a manner revealing that credit involves debt, which might just as easily be deemed as destructive rather than the opposite.

Therefore, lack of steady rules limits the evaluator's ability to use his expertise, invalidating the effectiveness of intuition. Mental models must be corrected and/or improved by means of a learning process. System Dynamics[1] translates those mental models into computerized processes, enabling researchers to deduce the consequences of system components' interaction - consequences which usually escape our understanding. These models in turn are corrected and perfected by means of a learning process.

This chapter introduces a technique based on System Dynamics that "maps" the following three mental models: (1) impact that microcredit and subsequent investment has on the borrower; (2) consequences experienced by the family unit after the new economic situation originated by the microcredit, and (3) general economic impact exerted by the microcredit program developed by an institution. The systemic definition of these impacts and their processing by a simulation program will allow for the analysis and study of their behavior in the face of various distortions, thus yielding a useful tool for controlling this type of institutions.

Since mental models deal with qualitative knowledge, fuzzy logic is a natural candidate for their computer representation. The methodology we propose is based on the application of the theory of fuzzy subsets. Our approach makes use of logical outlines, with are flexible enough to attempt more realistic assessments - which is indispensable in a context clearly defined by complexity and uncertainty.

The possibilities which the fuzzy sub-sets offer to tackle either the problems of decision making in which the appearance of vagueness is fundamental or those problems which are characterized by the non-existence of repetitive guidelines which force to take possible outcomes and then probability into consideration, have been a reason why we have decided to use these techniques. In addition they can be enriched and complemented with systemic approaches which reflect the existing interdependence (we assume that it exists) among the considered variables. In this way we consider the company as a system in motion.

In the last part of the article a determination of the order of importance of such variables is carried out, allowing for a better knowledge of the possibilities and limitations presented by each company, from the point of view of attractiveness to the company's projects' founders. The presence of each variable and its relative importance will be evaluated within the company. Different MFIs from the same sector will then be compared, basing on the relative distance between the presence of each variable and the sector's ideal profile conformed by founders' analysis of risks.

The possibilities which the fuzzy sub-sets offer to tackle either the problems of decision making in which the appearance of vagueness is fundamental or those problems which are characterized by the non-existence of repetitive guidelines which force to take possible outcomes and then probability into consideration, have been or reason why we have decided to use these techniques. In addition they can be enriched and complemented with systemic approaches which reflect the existing interdependence (we assume that it exists) among the considered variables. In this way we consider the company as a system in motion.

BACKGROUND: PRINCIPLES AND ELEMENTS OF SYSTEM DYNAMICS AND FUZZY LOGIC IN THE ASSESSMENT OF MICROFINANCE PROGRAMS' IMPACT

Most of the reviewed studies that aimed at testing the impact of microcredit on the socio-economic wellbeing of the beneficiaries used quantitative methods in the form of correlation and regression analyses where the indicators of wellbeing represented the dependant variables. Therefore, in our research, correlation was performed in order to test the existence of associations between the microcredit and our chosen dependent qualitative variables and indicate the possible effect sizes. Then, regressions were performed in order to test the causality and significance of such associations. It is worth noting that because our sample is relatively small, generalization should be avoided. However, given that very few if not at all studies were previously done to measure the impact of microcredit programs on beneficiaries; our hope was to shed some light on the following questions:

- What can be expected from the offer of microcredit on the welfare of recipients?
- Under what conditions would such an offer be more beneficial[2]?

A number of different types of rating scales or scale formats are available to measure the intensity of concepts or attitudes (e.g. semantic differential, Stapel scale, Likert scale, Thurstone scale, and the direct rating scale). They generate numbers that represent a rough ordinal level of the attribute at the most, while data processes involve indices and parameters implying that the resulting scores are real numbers. In fact, there are many approaches to measure the direction and strength of an attitude.

The Likert scale poses, in fact, many problems. The presence/absence of the neutral point denoted by syntagms such as «same as now», «right amount», «I don't mind» is a debated issue. It is often eliminated to press respondents to choose a sharp alternative instead of allowing refuge in a middle position, assuming that (1) it attracts people who have no opinion or prefer a noncommittal position rather than saying «I don't know», (2) respondents tend toward one or the other polar alternative, (3) people who really are neutral, randomly choose one of the two nearest alternatives (Schuman, Presser, 1996). A scale without a middle position has no position equal to "zero" and the alternative options are no longer equidistant, but its inclusion does not solve the difficulties of using option values as real numbers.

Fuzzy Logic was first developed in 1965 by Lotfi A. Zadeh, a professor of computer science at the University of California, Berkeley. Basically, Fuzzy Logic (FL) is a multivalue logic that allows intermediate values to be defined between conventional evaluations like true/false, yes/no, high/low, etc. Notions like rather tall or very fast can be formulated mathematically and processed by computers, in order to apply a more human−like way of thinking in the programming of computers. Fuzzy logic perfectly adapts to the non lineal requirements resulting from the presence of qualitative variables.

The Fuzzy Sets Logic (FS) is a flexible method to obtain a numerical value from ordinal variables, such as course evaluation data, and presents no problems regarding some difficulties typical of many scales such as the issue of a middle position, which vanishes in the FS operating procedure. FS design could easily incorporate the knowledge of an expert in the fuzzification of input and in the building-up of control block-rules, as they allow for the best adaptability. These are strengths, but also weaknesses as they involve extremely subjective, ambiguous, and «private» decisions, when scientific procedures should be objective, unambiguous, and public. Actually, the architecture of the FS could be public, but, for example, the number of rules grows exponentially and their control is arduous. Furthermore, the aggregation of variables proceeds through a tree, varying nonlinearly their impact on the output, as their influence depends on the levels of the knot where they enter. The responses are a sort of weighted average with «unknowable» weights. However, in spite of these difficulties, the FS could be a valid and reliable tool to represent situations described by qualitative ordinal variables comparable with others.

System Dynamics constitutes an approach that reproduces the interdependences that exist within a system, revealing the existence of a great variety of alternative decisions potentially applicable to certain events. The great potential of System Dynamics comes from using dynamic models -i.e. focusing on time- allowing for the observation of adopted decisions' consequences taking place in the short, medium and long run.

There are three fundamental principles on which System Dynamics is based. The first principle concerns the existence of feedback loops, since the environment or situation of the system determines a decision whose result is an action that influences this environment in turn, and therefore future decisions.

The second principle concerns the existence of non-linearity in relationships among variables. It is not useful to analyze isolated variables but variables as a whole, because the alteration of one of them may cause the variation of the combined behavior.

The final principle is the existence of delays in relationships among variables. The symptom of a problem frequently appears far away in time and space from the action that originated it. The existence of delays in relationships among variables implies that the effects of the decisions taken are not reflected in an immediate manner, which makes it difficult to discern cause-effect relationships.

The method begins with the identification of the problematic situation and the purpose of the model, and ends with the design of a solution or the implementation of changes in some company policies, i.e. decision making. There are seven steps in the use of a model of System Dynamics for decision taking.

The first step is identification of the problem and purpose of the model, which involves identifying input and output variables and the determination of fuzzy sets. This first phase is fundamental and decisive, because if we identify all aspects involved correctly, we will be able to elaborate a dynamic model that is representative of the impact of a microfinance program, thus allowing to simulate different alternative policies, and subsequently know which one of them is more suitable for future application.

The second step is conceptualization of the system, by which a method will be selected for fuzzification[3] and defuzzification[4]. In this step, the limits of the system must be specified; that is to say, discern which factors will be included in the model (and which will be excluded), choosing those that intuitively seem to be most significant.

The third step required the formulation of the model and estimation of parameters, creating a knowledge base through the use of IF_THEN_ rules.

The fourth step is concerned with the analysis of the behavior of the model through the design of an inference mechanism.

The fifth step involves the evaluation of the model.

The sixth step uses or implement the model and feedback of information. It is necessary to point out that this definition doesn't make reference to conscious or explicit decisions but also to unconscious or implicit decisions. The advantage in studying feedback is the possibility to understand how fluctuating or unstable behaviors are originated by corrective actions and delays between action and effect within the interconnected components of a system. The model is perfected by means of a learning process that takes place both during the construction of the model and in later simulations. By means of the simulation, the model is set "in motion"; that is to say, we reproduce the prospective behavior of the organization or problem in a virtual context, in order to observe the impact of decisions, policies, changes of scenario, etc, on the relevant indicators, and take a glance at the effects of decisions in time and space. There are computer tools currently available that let us develop and simulate such models.

The last step involves applying the optimized policies from the previous phase.

We will now evaluate the impact of a microcredit program of a hypothetical institution on its clientele, using the methodology based on System Dynamics and Fuzzy Logic that we have just introduced.

MEASURING THE IMPACT OF A MICROCREDIT PROGRAM UNDER A SYSTEMIC APPROACH USING FUZZY LOGIC

The problematic situation under analysis was how little poverty was alleviated through microfinancing. So as to find a solution to this problem with the suggested methods, a computer simulation model was developed in order to represent the system under evaluation. The goal of the model was to explain system behavior, basing on indicators of social impact under the influence of economic, social and empowerment variables.

The solution found was to create a model comprising three subsystems as shown in Figure 1. The goal of the first subsystem was to represent the impact the microcredit program had on the borrower; the goal of the second subsystem was to represent the transformation experienced by the borrower's family unit as a consequence of starting the investment project undertaken with the received microcredit (measured in terms of

health, education, food security or housing); the third subsystem reflects the consequences on employment, investment, level of revenues in the region that take place after starting a microcredit program.

The first subsystem was modeled using System Dynamics techniques. The impact on the borrower was measured in terms of self-esteem, development of managerial skills and economic empowering as indicated in Figure 2. The appreciations in his behavior were elements and relationships taken into account in the second subsystem, which analyzed the impact on the borrower's family unit regarding improvements in family income, home assets, food security, health, education, or housing conditions. This second subsystem was modeled using Fuzzy Logic techniques. In the third subsystem, the economic repercussions of starting up the microcredit program were considered, measured in terms of employment creation or investment.

At the moment, the relationship between the number of credits that the institution has granted and the number of credits that have brought about economic and social improvement, is not known with accuracy, although it is accepted to be quasi-linear. Borrower's satisfaction (positive impact) will be used as vague knowledge for the creation of the fuzzy intervals that determine the

Figure 1. Model to evaluate the impact of microcredits

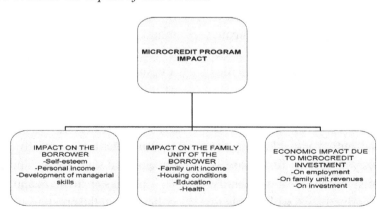

Figure 2. Fuzzy model of microcredit program impact

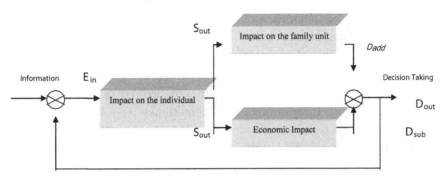

static component (input and output variables) of the model.

The subsystem dealing with "Impact on the individual", accepts variable *Ein* as input, (which represents the relevant parameters, such as: self-esteem, development of managerial abilities, economic empowering, and yields variable *Sout* as output, which corresponds to the level of achievement of a satisfactory state which the borrower will transfer to the family unit. Both the input and the output variables have been divided into intervals, making up the inference rules of the subsystem.

The second subsystem - "Impact on the borrower's family unit"- is defined by input variable *Sout* and output variable *Dadd* corresponding to the level of improvement of education, health and housing conditions and property experienced

by the family unit as a direct consequence of the microcredit received by one of its members.

Finally, the *Economic Impact* subsystem receives variable *Sout* as input and yields output variable *Dsub*, that corresponds to employment generation caused by starting the microcredit, creation of companies, estimated monetary value of the assets of the economic unit.

Figure 3 shows the system as a whole. Input variable *Ein* corresponds to information obtained through a test applied to microcredit clients, whereas variable *Dout* represents the level of economic, social, and cultural improvement that the microcredit program has generated, i.e. its social impact.

The impact of the microfinance program is reflected by variable *Sout*, which is defined as the borrower's net available financial resources (gen-

Figure 3. Dadd and Dsub graph

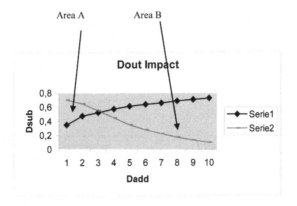

erated and consumed) at the start-up of the economic project that is going to be financed with the microcredit. For the following impact evaluation, variable *Dout* is fed back into the system as input *Ein* of the first subsystem.

Output variables Dadd and Dsub are presented in the central value of the triangular fuzzy number that represents them.

A cut off point (0,35) can be observed in Figure 3, dividing it in two sections: area A and area B. In area A, the impact that the microcredit program has generated at a social or economic level on borrowers of a microcredit program, doesn't noticeably differ from the situation of other people unrelated to this program. A low impact (located in area A) might indicate the urgent necessity to undertake amendments within the microfinance institution towards increasing quality level, and the study could orient about aspects not initially considered in which the program is failing. In area B, the situation is inverted and program impact is high. Therefore granting microcredits is generating a clear satisfaction to clients and their environment, as well as an improvement in the economy of the area.

The model based on Fuzzy Logic has been implemented using Simulink, a tool from the Matlab platform (a copyright of The Math Works, Inc). Processing the fuzzy system involves three steps: (1) using mapping rules so as to assign membership degrees to input variables with regard to fuzzy sets; (2) inferring actions to carry out; and (3) initiating the estimated corrective action, interpreting the membership degrees of output variables. According to that, the first group of experiments managed to prove the system's ability to achieve a level of desirable impact. The second

series of experiments was aimed at studying the system's ability to return to an appropriate impact level after an instantaneous impact distortion is introduced (e.g. the launching of a new product in the market; the appearance a new company in the competition; or the tightening of microcredits conditions).

Results show that the model reacts properly in the face of different levels of satisfaction and concession of microcredits until achieving the steady state, so that such a state is reached gradually, never abruptly. Besides, once that state is reached, the model is capable of holding impact levels.

It is worth remembering that in order to implement the model, only a minimal set of knowledge items regarding the relationship among variables was considered, while determining inference rules that handle the behavior of the three subsystems in an appropriate manner, without needing a high amount of empiric data.

Evaluation of the Company and Comparison with the Sector

1ST variable: Impact that the Microcredit Program has generated at a Social or Economic level on Borrowers of a Microcredit Program

The average profile in the sector relating to individual borrower is represented in Table 1:

Whereas in the four considered simulated companies the average value obtained in the different subvariables are (see Table 2):

We can now proceed to determine the *"differences"* which exist between the fulfilment of the subvariables for each one of the four considered companies and the average of the sector. This will demand a comparison between the two subsets

Table 1.

Sector	Subvariable 1: *Impact on the individual*	Subvariable 2: *Impact on the family unit*	Subvariable 3: *Economic impact*
Variable: Economic impact	0. 8	0.4	0.3

Table 2.

Company A		Subvariable 1	Subvariable 2	Subvariable 3
	Variable: 1	1	0.3	0.6
Company B		Subvariable 1	Subvariable 2	Subvariable 3
	Variable: 1	0.5	0.3	0.4
Company C		Subvariable 1	Subvariable 2	Subvariable 3
	Variable: 1	0.2	0.6	1
Company D		Subvariable 1	Subvariable 2	Subvariable 3
	Variable: 1	0.5	0.4	0.1

of the same referential for which the mathematical concept of distance is used. In this present study, the so-called HAMMING's distance which gives an indication as to how the two subsets differ (normal or fuzzy) will be used.

If we take *"Hamming's relative distance"*, i.e. the total distance divided by 4 (cardinal of P) between each one of the 4 considered companies, we will obtain:

$$\sigma(\tilde{A}_i, \tilde{C}) = \frac{1}{4} \sum |\mu_{\tilde{A}} - \mu_{\tilde{C}}| \qquad (1)$$

$$\sigma(\tilde{A}_A, \tilde{C}) = 1/4 \left(|1 - 0.8| + |0.3 - 0.4| + |0.6 - 0.3| + |1 - 1| \right) = 0.15$$

$$\sigma(\tilde{A}_B, \tilde{C}) = 0.275$$

$$\sigma(\tilde{A}_C, \tilde{C}) = 0.425$$

$$\sigma(\tilde{A}_D, \tilde{C}) = 0.325$$

Thus we will achieve the following order: $\tilde{A}_A > \tilde{A}_B > \tilde{A}_C > \tilde{A}_D$ which means that Company *A* is the one which adjusts better to the levels of the average economic impact profile, whereas Company *C* is the one which adjusts less to this average profile. (see Figure 4)

Identification of Intangibles in the Value of Microfinance Institution

A classification of the risk and its valuation cannot grant itself being based exclusively on financial analysis, since these would not reflect the true potential of the microfinancial entities; that is why

Figure 4. Comparison with the sector

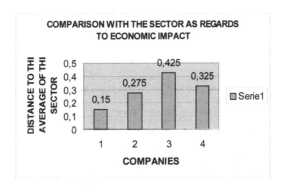

275

the quantitative analysis should be supplemented with qualitative aspects, with the purpose of arriving at an appropriate classification.

Among the qualitative aspects that influence the financial strength of the MFIs, we could point out, in a first approach to the topic, the four following: the quality of the administration, the clients' satisfaction, plans and strategies of the company and market opportunities, the staff's experience.

The empirical study which will next be carried out, starts from simulated data since, in this first phase, it has tried to articulate the model of valuation of intangibles and its inclusion in the Invisible Balance Sheet of the company, in order to, in a second phase, put it into practice by using real data obtained from opinion polls. (see Figure 5)

After the realization of surveys for the generation of qualitative information in the four selected variables, a comparison of the results obtained in microfinancing companies that present similar performance indicators in their four basic categories (as any company): portfolio quality, efficiency and productivity, financial management and profitability, could be carried out. In the

Figure 5. Identification of variables, companies to be compared, sample data

Name of the variable	Identificator
A.- CLIENT SATISFACTION	1
1.- Reduction of poverty level	
2.- Materialization of expectations	
3.- Employment generation	
4.- Participation in the taking of decisions and recognition in their activity field	
B.- QUALITY OF THE ADMINISTRATION	2
5.- Ease and agility in credits concession	
6.- Specialized staff, evaluation methodology, appropriate internal controls and computer systems that allow to offer a package of financial products.	
7.- Wide offer of financial services, beyond credit or saving, for the managers of low resources and their homes, adapting for this new sector, products already existent in the banks.	
C.- MARKET KNOWLEDGE	3
8.- To know the client and the market sector deeply, what will allow the development of specialized products that respond to the necessities of the clients and an appropriate sector risk handling	
9.- To possess some appropriate distribution channels that combine the existent branches of the banks, points of attention of minimum investment and alliances with other institutions	
10.- To be up to date in the events that can influence in the microfinancial sector, changes in fiscal and accounting normative, international agreements... .etc.	
11.- Excellent relations with Governments of the country, companies and institutions	
D.- HUMAN FACTORS	4
12.- Profesionalism and proximity to the client's problem and their context	
13.- Impartiality: if banks microfinancing is motivated by political or obligatory reasons, the risk exists that the banks carry out this task improperly or simply that they don't carry it out.	
14.- Employees that are able to take advantage of the existent infrastructure of the bank and at the same time to develop new capacities necessary for the development of their work in a more efficient way	

methodology that will be used to carry out this comparison, we will use four companies symbolically denominated A,B,C,D.

The sample of the observations carried out reveals the number of times each subvariable has been selected as a priority in one company rather than another. The results are shown in the following chart. For the variables client satisfaction, defined by 4 subvariables: poverty reduction level, expectative materialization, employment creation, participation in decisions making and recognition in their activity field, the following matrix given in Table 3 is considered:

The interpretation of the results, which appear in the above matrix, would be: in the subvariable 2- personalized attention- Company A has been highly valued -three times greater than the rest of the companies. Company D however, has been valued even more highly- five times greater than the rest- and so on.

A similar matrix representation of the fuzzy preference relation would be carried out between a company and another of the comparison for every one of the variables: Client Satisfaction, Quality of the Administration, Know Market, Human Recours. These measurements contribute to measure internal attributes and at the same time identify the comparative advantages both between companies and the average of the sector. See Appendix 1 for mathematical processing comparison.

In these previous phases a contribution to the measurement of the microfinance institutions has been carried out, although we have only considered non-monetary indexes and values. However, it would be a big step forward if the contribution of each one of the above mentioned intangibles could be measured in monetary terms.

FUTURE RESEARCH DIRECTIONS

Qualitative methods for data collection play an important role in impact evaluation by providing information useful to understand the processes behind observed results and assess changes in people's perceptions of their well-being. Furthermore qualitative methods can be used to improve the quality of survey-based quantitative evaluations by helping generate evaluation hypothesis; strengthening the design of survey questionnaires and expanding or clarifying quantitative evaluation findings.

Our results outline the possibility to design an intelligent system able to start the necessary actions to achieve a level of general impact desired by microfinancing institutions, when confronted with different levels of borrowers' satisfaction.

The qualitative qualification of the performance of a microfinance institution, constitutes a valuable complement to the representative tradional indicators of the financial situation and risk.

CONCLUSION

It has been shown how System Dynamics supplemented with a fuzzy treatment enables modeling and implementation of evaluation mechanisms of microcredit programs' impact: a complex system affected by a high number of variables, some of

Table 3.

Companies	Subvariable 1	Subvariable 2	Subvariable 3	Subvariable 4
A	1	3	0.8	1
B	0.3	0.5	2	2
C	1	0.8	1	1
D	1	5	0.6	0.5

them lacking clearly defined behavior patterns. At the moment we are improving the empiric study by including time and space restrictions in the model in order to make it more realistic.

The perceptions of participants in a microcredit program have been made explicit, mapped and compared with perceptions of other people unrelated to these programs, after which we finally assessed the true impact of such programs.

This model maintains the balance between model complexity and fidelity of behavior. Mathematically, the model is a non-linear system of fourth differential order, highly coupled in its closed loops.

Learning generated during modeling -in which the processes of eliciting[5], reflection and dialogue of assumptions and policies were present- was a result of great value. Developing the model led to structured dialogues that generated participation and consent, identification of key improvement points and new conclusions.

Although the mental model of the participants was presented, research must continue for the validation of the model under the perceived reality. This process will require data collection and new adjustments of the model.

Modeling of complex systems using System Dynamics and Fuzzy Logic offers a feasible alternative to represent tacit knowledge, letting microfinancing organizations share experiences among their different business units. The results obtained showed feasibility, as well as learning potentiality during a modeling process using computer simulators.

The selection of performance indicators presents a more complete image of the microfinance company, has been a task not exempt of debates and proposals. Many attempts have been taking place in order to arrive at the determination of some universal indicators, but there is still quite a lot to be done before their inclusion in a list, but qualitative indicators representing the quality of the service of the company, the quality of their team manager and their organizational structure,

the knowledge of the market or the convenience of their projects in the socio-economic context of the country in which they are developed…, these indicators can end up being important, even more than those referred to a more quantifiable reality (revenues, expenses, slowness in paying….). The selection should be made under the premise that any qualitative indicator that is used should contribute confidence, viability and good cost-effectiveness relationship with the performance of these institutions.

Several tools and available methodologies of qualitative investigation exist although unfortunately they are very scarce and not very well-known. The present work is inserted in the field of the qualitative or structural methodology, and it therefore supposes a search for a solution to the evaluation of these institutions and their comparison.

The convenience of this and other future works that could arise in the same investigation line is reasonable if we start from the conviction that there is a long way to go in the attainment of the objective of showing the most transparent image of the MFI.

REFERENCES

Gil Aluja, J. (1999). *Elementos para una Teoría de la Decisión en la Incertidumbre*. Pontevedra, Spain: Milladoiro.

Schuman, H., & Presser, S. (1996). *Questions and Answers in Attitude Surveys: Experiments on Question Form, Wording, and Context*. Thousand Oaks, CA: Sage.

Stauffenberg, D V.,Jansson, T.,Kenyon, N., & Barluenga-Badiola, María-Cruz (2003) *Indicadores de desempeño para instituciones microfinancieras*. Microrate y Banco Interamericano de Desarrollo (Departamento de Desarrollo Sostenible).

ADDITIONAL READING

Barnes, C. (1996). *Assets and the Impact of Microenterprise Finance Programs*. Washington, DC: Management Systems International.

Beuningen, C. V. (1997). *Outline for Impact Assessment in the Credit Line. Consultative Group to Assist the Poorest*. Washington, DC: CGAP.

Bharadwaj, B. (2007). Development of a fuzzy Likert scale for the WHO ICF to include categorical definitions on the basis of a continuum. *ETD Collection for Wayne State University*. Paper AAI1442894. Retrieved from http://digitalcommons.wayne.edu/dissertations/AAI1442894

Burkun, M. (2000). Los activos intangibles desde la perspectiva estratégica. *Management & Empresa, 37* (2).

Cheston, S. (1999, June). *Medición de la transformación: Evaluación y mejora del impactodel microcrédito*. Paper presented at the meeting of the Microcredit Summit (Abidjan)

Davies, P. (1996). *Qualitative Tools and Microenterprise Impact Evaluation*. New York: Work Paper of SEEP.

Emami, M. R., Goldenberg, A. A., & Turksen, I. B. (2000)... *Engineering Applications of Artificial Intelligence, 13*(1). doi:10.1016/S0952-1976(99)00031-7

Garcia Parra, M., Simo Guzman, P., Mundent Hiern, J., & Guzman Conesa, J. (2004). A Technical Guide to Developing and Delivering Money Transfers. Retrieved November 12, 2004 from the CGAP Web site (http://www.cgap.org/) publications page.

Harvey, M. G., & Lusch, R. F. (1999). Balancing the intellectual capital books: Intangible liabilities. *European Management Journal, 17*(1). doi:10.1016/S0263-2373(98)00065-6

Isern, J., Donges, W., & Smith, J. (2008). Making Money Transfers Work for Microfinance Institutions: A Technical Guide to Developing and Delivering Money Transfers. Retrieved January, 2009 from the CGAP Web site (http://www.cgap.org/) publications page.

Jansson, T. (1998). La regulación financiera y su importancia para la microfinanza en América Latina y el Caribe. Retrieved May 2000 from www.gdrc.org/icm/govern/Jansson- spanish.rtf.

Lainez Gadea, J. A. & Cuéllar Fernandez, B. (2002). Factores determinantes del ratio Book-To-Market. *Revista española de financiación y contabilidad, XXI(*112)

Lev, B. (2002). Remarks on the Measurement, Valuation, and Reporting of Intangible Assets. Federal Reserve Bank of New York, *Economic Policy Review*. Retrieved from http://www.newyorkfed.org/rmaghome/econ_pol/2002/1202lev.pdf

Lo Vuolo, R. (2001). *Alternativas, la Economía como cuestión social*. Buenos Aires, Argentina: Altamira.

Matin, I., Hulme, D., & Rutherford, S. (2002). Finance for the Poor: From Microcredit to Microfinancial Services. *Journal of International Development*, 14.

Otero, M., & Stearns, K. (1990). *La conexión clave. El gobierno, las entidades privadas y el sector informal en América Latina*. ACCION Internacional. Serie Monografías, 5. Washington.

Quintana, M. A. (2003). *Modelo híbrido para los procesos de Data Mining en el apoyo a la toma de decisiones basados en tecnologías inteligentes conexionistas y difusas*. Paper presented at the meeting of the XVII Simposio Brasileiro de Redes Neurais.

Serrani, E. (2004). *El microcrédito como instrumento de autogestión y desarrollo humano*. Buenos Aires, Argentina: IUGD-FONCAP.

Sinha, F. (2006). *Social Rating and Social Performance Reporting in Microfinance*. Ed: EDA(UK) Ltd., in association with Micro-Credit Ratings International Ltd., and the Social Performance Task Force Sub-committee on Social Rating and Reporting

Smithson, M. J. (1988). Fuzzy set theory and the social sciences: the scope for applications. *Fuzzy Sets and Systems, 26*(1). doi:10.1016/0165-0114(88)90002-4

Sveiby, H. E. (1997). The Intangible Assets Monitor. *Journal of Human Resource Costing and Accounting, 2*(1).

Westover, J. (2008). The Effectiveness/Ineffectiveness of Microfinance Programs as a Means of Alleviating Poverty. *Electronic Journal of Sociology, 3*.

Yunus, M. (1999). *Hacia un mundo sin pobreza*. Santiago de Chile: Andrés Bello.

ENDNOTES

[1] Emami et al, 2000
[2] Bharadwaj, 2007
[3] Fuzzyfication: conversion from a numerical value of mesure to a linguistical variable
[4] Desfuzzification: conversion from a linguistical variable to a numerical value
[5] Eliciting: getting information

APPENDIX 1

Mathematical Processing Comparison among Companies

For every subvariable C_j, j= 1,2,...,n (table n° 2), a comparison of pairs of companies is carried out, by means of a quotient which determines the number of times which a company is preferred to another for each subvariable. In this way $\mu_{ik} = \dfrac{f_i}{f_k}$ for i, k = 1,2,3,...n. will represent the number of times which C_i is preferred to C_k., evidently $\mu_{ki} = \dfrac{f_k}{f_i} = \dfrac{1}{\mu_{ik}}$ is the combination of all μi_k and it will be a matrix for every subvariable C_j, which will be reciprocal by construction. Remembering that a matrix is reciprocal if:

$$\mu_{ii}=1 \ y \ \mu_{ik} = \frac{1}{\mu_{ki}} \ para \ \mu_{ik} \in R_0^+ , \ i, \ k= 1,2,...,n \tag{1}$$

When it is fulfilled that $\forall i,k \in \{1,2,...,n\}$ and $\dfrac{f_i}{f_k} \cdot \dfrac{f_k}{f_1} = \dfrac{f_i}{f_1}$, i.e. $\mu_{ik} \cdot \mu_{k1} = \mu_{i1}$, it is said that the matrix is "coherent" or "consistent".

When a matrix in R_0^+ is reciprocal and coherent, it possesses some very elemental properties, useful for our objectives:

1. $\displaystyle\sum_{k=1}^{n} \mu_{ik} \cdot f_k = \sum_{k=1}^{n} \frac{f_i}{f_k} \cdot f_k = n \cdot f_i.$

2. All its rows (and also its columns) are proportional to the first row (and also to the first column), therefore each row (and each column) is equal to another row (and another column) multiplied by a coefficient (Gil Aluja, 1999).

For each subvariable C_j, j= 1,2,3,...,n a reciprocal matrix can be obtained but is not necessarily coherent. Any positive square matrix has its own positive real value, whose module is superior to all of the rest which can be real or complex. This particular real or positive dominant value, which will be called λ, is unique according to Perron-Frobenius's theorem[1]. If n is the order, the matrix will be $\lambda_1 \geq n$ The particular vector which corresponds to the particular dominant value λ_1 – by which the relative preference of the products in relation to their respective characteristics is shown- will be formed by positive terms and when it is normalized will be unique. In this sense, if we have a positive and reciprocal square matrix with an n order its dominant value will be λ_1. When λ_1 is very close to n, it can be said the matrix is almost coherent and then becomes suitable for our object. The coherence index is usually established as follows:

$$I_c = \frac{\lambda_1 - n}{n} \tag{2}$$

In this way, from the referential sites to be arranged - X- and the subvariables C a reciprocal matrix will be obtained for each subvariable, with an particular value $\lambda_1^{(j)}$ and a coherence index for each one. If this coherence index is sufficiently reduced, the corresponding particular vector will be accepted.

To sum up, the matrix will have a dominant own value $\lambda_1^{©}$ and a corresponding vector [V©] as representative of the importance of each characteristic which affects the decision. This vector can be the ponderation term of our scheme for which -according to the methodology of ordination followed by Gil Aluja (1999) its normalization will be necessary with a sum equal to the unit.

Having obtained the matrix [V] and the normalized vector [N©] it will be enough to multiply [V]* [N©] to obtain the new vector [D] whose value will allow an ordination according to the competitive priorities of the companies- bearing in mind the relative importance assigned to each subvariable.

Chapter 16
Microfinance from LDCs to DCs:
Are Socio–Economic Differences Important?

Samanthala Hettihewa
University of Ballarat, Australia

Christopher S. Wright
University of Ballarat, Australia

ABSTRACT

Microfinance (MF) has demonstrated great success in poverty-relief in less-developed countries (LDCs) and is experiencing rapid growth and interest in developed countries (DCs). However, the current literature on DC MF leaves a general impression that DC MF is failing and its original core intent of poverty relief is being diluted by survival concerns. Descriptive analysis is used in this chapter to infer that DC MF must be redesigned to meet DC socio-economic conditions, if it is to avoid a reputation of being too poorly focused, ineffective, and inefficient for use in DCs. After demonstrating that poverty in LDCs is harsher than in DCs, this chapter reviews current-performance concerns of DC MF, discusses how it can still effectively relieve poverty in DCs, examines how regulatory and other socio-economic factors affect micro-enterprise, and concludes that MF should be refocused before DCs commit to further developing/adapting MF infrastructure.

INTRODUCTION

Microfinance (MF) has a long history of successful deployment in lesser developed countries (LDCs). However, MF has different meanings for different people and interest groups, that vary from micro-credit (for micro-enterprise development and consumer durables) to insurance and income protection, to social enlightenment

DOI: 10.4018/978-1-61520-993-4.ch016

(Burkett, 2003). This chapter corrals this diversity of meaning into a broad definition where MF is conceptualized as a set of tools, approaches and strategies developed in LDCs to give a *hand-up* to people who are trapped in poverty because, for various reasons, they are excluded from accessing mainstream financial services. Buckland & Dong (2008) note that financially excluded people (by definition) rely almost entirely on non-mainstream and informal financial services. The well-documented profound success of MF, in helping many poor in LDCs escape the poverty trap, has sparked debate on how such powerful tools can be, or have been, imported to developed countries (DCs) for similar service—for details see Servon, 1997 and 2006; Bhatt & Tang, 2001; Hung, 2003; and Dubreuil & Mirada, 2008.

The literature on DC MF projects, as noted later in this chapter, gives the general impression that MF in DCs is failing to achieve both its financial and poverty-relief objectives. Many researchers attribute these difficulties to high administration costs, nonperforming and/or defaulted loans, adverse-selection of clients, cost-recovery issues, difficulty developing appropriate administrative tools (e.g. use of peer-groups), and confusion over its client base and role in society. However, the thesis in this chapter is that these issues are symptoms and that, unless the fundamental cause of these symptoms is resolved, the progression of DC MF setbacks will continue and likely turn to a general rejection of DC MF by fund providers and mainstream DC finance.

This chapter flows from the premise that a tool designed for a specific purpose and for use under specific conditions can fail catastrophically if it is applied toward a different purpose with different prevailing conditions. The objective of this chapter is to show that the root causes of poverty differ between LDCs and DCs and that those differences are important to the design and deployment of MF tools in DCs. This chapter is organized as follows:

a background discussion on how MF works, an evaluation of socio-economic differences between LDCs and DCs (in particular how poverty differs between them), a review of current performance concerns of DC MF, consideration of whether MF can be and/or is being adapted to effectively relieve poverty in DCs, and a conclusion that MF should be refocused before DCs commit to developing/ adapting infrastructure for MF.

BACKGROUND

How Does Microfinance Work?

It is vital, from the outset, to understand that MF works best when it helps the poor surmount restrictions on their ability to access main-stream financial services and that lack of access was either holding them in poverty or putting them at risk of falling into poverty. A non-exhaustive selection of these *at-risk groups* in DCs, include those who are isolated by real or perceived attributes associated, among other things, with[1] (see Table 1):

Thus, for MF to work in DCs: (1) difficulties in accessing mainstream-financial services must be a significant cause of DC poverty; (2) access problems of one or more *at-risk* groups must be targeted; and 3) the MF process must be sustainable. The absence of any or all of these attributes risks making DC MF an innovative variant of

Table 1.

Issue	Examples/description
Culture, ethnicity, or religion	European Gypsies, Australian Aborigines, Aboriginals in the Americas (e.g. the First Nations of Canada and Native American of the USA), multi-generational welfare families, and new migrants with language issues. Ageism (50+ or young adults) or sexism (often, but not always, female) are also common issues.
Educational challenges	Illiterate, innumerate, inarticulate, unskilled in a trade or a profession.
Poor employment prospects	Unaccredited and/or inexperienced in the work-force (often directly closely related to the educational challenges above).
Ill-health, disability, or disfigurement	Mental or physical difficulties arising from disease, accident, age, or congenital issues.
Family obligations	Single parent households, the role of wife in a traditional extended family, adult children with disabled parent(s).

welfare and/or a *boondoggle* where net gain goes mostly to the MF-service providers (in the form of employment, power, and status), at great cost to the public and little or no gain to MF recipients. However, MF is often expected to provide much more than mere financial stability. Specifically, socio-political issues are often more important to those who fund the non-governmental organizations (NGOs) providing MF services. Helms (2006) found that three-of-four common MF-program-funding providers in Asia, Africa and Latin America are very strongly interested in social development and the fourth is likely to promote itself as having such an interest or as having been pressured to have that interest by government requirements (Goodwin-Groen, 1998; Pitt, et al., 2003; Dunford, 2006; Pitt, et al., 2006; Deaton, 2009).

The Effect of Socio-Economic Differences on MF in LDCs and DCs

Understanding the socio-economic differences between LDCs and DCs is vital to understanding why MF (a tool developed for LDCs) is having difficulty adapting to the socio-economic realities of DCs. As noted later in this chapter, individuals in LDCs often have much higher social capital and place more value on that capital than individuals in DCs (Banerjee & Duflo, 2007)—much of this social capital arises from village setting and the reduced mobility. Specifically, families may live in the same village for generations and, as a result, reputation is very important and can be used as collateral. In contrast, people in DCs tend to live in large, impersonal urban settings and move frequently (in many cases the moves are over great distances, to other cities or even countries). As a result, reputation often has little or no long-term value as collateral. Also, differences in the nature and causes of poverty (the main target of MF) in LDCs and DCs will profoundly affect how well MF works in a DC setting. Thus, the sociology component is as important as the economic com-

ponent in the socio-economic factors that will determine the success or failure of DC MF.

Individuals, who move from one culture to another, often have a better understanding of the socio-economic differences between those cultures than a person who was born, raised, and lives in one culture. Thus, while this study is not about migrants, seeing through the eyes of a LDC migrant to a DC is a good means to compare and contrast the socio-economic differences between LDCs and DCs.

Initially, many migrants from LDCs tend to see their new DC home as a land of hope and opportunity, where access to credit and opportunities to prosper via work or trade appear to be ubiquitous. As a result, often newly-arrived migrants to DCs are, after they find work, confused as to how poverty can persist or even exist in such a land, other than through wilful laziness on the part of those who are poor. Further, when a migrant from a LDC sees how the DC poor live and what they own, they are confused because, in their former country, such a lifestyle was only aspired to by those in the lower-middle class, middle class, or above. Also, the poor in their former land are very much poorer than the poor in their new land. The important issues raised through this perspective are: firstly, that poverty is more contextual and relative than absolute[2]; secondly, that poverty is more physically severe in LDCs than DCs; and thirdly, that poverty is caused in DCs by different and often more subtle factors than poverty in LDCs. As Cabraal, et al. (2006, p.3) note: "Poverty is not only about the income levels of individuals, but about their ability to make informed choices".

Figures 1, 2, and 3, confirm the forgoing assertion that the physical reality of poverty in DCs differs greatly from poverty in LDCs; i.e. it involves significantly less absolute deprivation than poverty in LDCs. As depicted in Figure 1, the poor in LDCs are at much greater risk of starvation (the risk of death by malnutrition falls sharply in the emerging countries and in DCs). In DCs, charities and government support programs seek to ensure that death by malnutrition is uncommon in DCs and is mostly due to such disease processes as anorexia, celiac, Crohn's disease, etc., rather than being a direct outcome of poverty.

As per Figures 2 and 3, the LCD poor work longer (if they find work) to earn an equivalent purchasing power, than do DC working poor.[3] In Figure 2, the minimum wage rises exponentially with GDP per capita until 28,000 (USD) GDP per capita, after which, it continues rising at a declining rate. In terms of the litres of vegetable oil that can be bought with an hour's wages, Figure 3 shows that the working poor in LDCs have less earning power than the working poor in DCs.

Figures 1, 2 and 3, demonstrate that the DC poor are physically better-off in terms of access to the means to satisfy basic needs, than the LDC poor and their potential earning power (i.e. their wage per hour times their purchasing power) is significantly greater. However, these realities do not lessen the case for assisting the poor in DCs; such a case rests on any or all of the following broad foundations: *Charity* – the relief of suf-fering is always meritorious, unless reducing the pain of poverty reduces the will to struggle out of poverty; *Economic Equity* – the relative deprivation in DCs is still deprivation and, as it is stressful and emotionally hurtful to live in relative poverty, it affects health (Finkelstein, et al., 2002), increases the burden of health budgets, and reduce the ability to struggle out of poverty; and *Enlightened Self-interest* – the net wealth of the nation rises when people escape poverty by creating tradable wealth/services; as a result, there is more to share, the net tax burden falls, net employment rises, and (just as a rising tide raises all boats) almost everyone benefits.

Sen (1999, p.20) asserts that poverty is the "...deprivation of basic capabilities, rather than merely...a consequence of low income. Deprivation of [these] elementary capabilities can be reflected in pre-mature mortality, significant under-nourishment, ...persistent morbidity, widespread illiteracy and other failures". These consequences of poverty are not limited to LDCs, in that, even with the significant charity and income transfer

Figure 1. Malnutrition death-rate vs. GDP per capita (Sources: WHO, 2004 and CIA World Factbook, 2008)

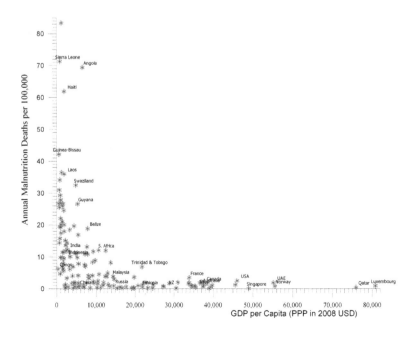

Figure 2. Minimum wage for workers in basic metal working (Sources: IMF, 2008 and CIA World Factbook, 2008[4])

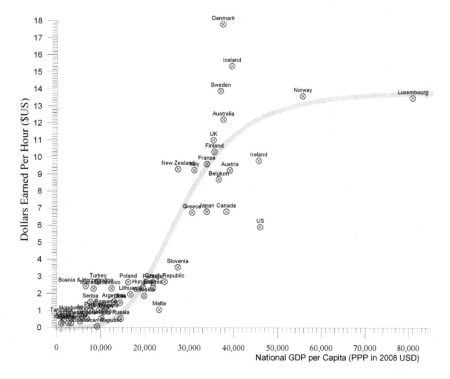

Figure 3. Earning power of workers in basic metal working (Sources: IMF, 2008 and CIA World Factbook, 2008)

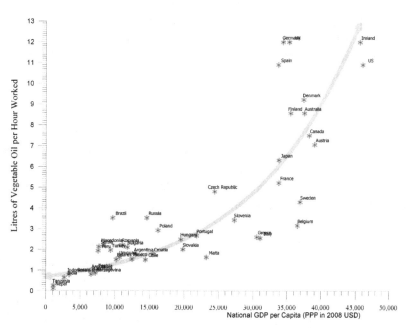

programs of DCs, the poor in DCs still suffer higher mortality and morbidity rates in addition to restricted opportunities.[5]

Can MF Strike at a Root Cause of Poverty?

"There are a thousand hacking at the branches of evil to one who is striking at the root..." (Thoreau, 1854, p.80).

Unlike charity, which only temporarily relieves the consequences of poverty, the intent of MF is to strike at a root cause of poverty. However, as previously noted, the nature of poverty is less absolute and more contextual and relative to the society in which it is found and/or defined. Thus, it is not surprising that the root cause of poverty may differ according to the socio-economic environment in which it occurs.

Specifically, the LDC poverty trap can be due to a vicious cycle, in which the poor are the victims of ignorance, prejudice, disease and corruption, which act to further deepen poverty, which again increases the harm of ignorance, prejudice, disease and corruption, which then further deepens poverty, and so forth. In such a vicious cycle, MF can provide an initial access to credit that is a hand-up from an ever deepening pit of despair into a *virtuous-cycle* of co-operative learning, earning and reinvestment that enables individuals to escape their part of the pit of poverty and, often, to pull others up with them. In contrast, the DC poverty trap has more relative than absolute depravation and escape from it often requires an extended investment of effort, time, and modified consumption/savings patterns (Matin, et al., 2002) that, for a variety of reason (peculiar to DCs) often provides little immediate return and much more frustration and heartbreak than what is experienced by the more indolent poor.

If MF programs are to have any reasonable success in resolving poverty in DCs, they must identify, target, and resolve the peculiarities that cause and sustain DC poverty. Most studies of MF in DCs (Servon, 1997 and 2006; Bhatt & Tang, 2001; Hung, 2003; Dubreuil & Mirada, 2008) note that like similar MF programs in LDCs, DC MF programs need to do more than lend money to alleviate poverty; they must provide three types of "[risk-] intermediation" (Bhatt & Tang, 2001, pp.231-236): *Social Intermediation* to build up the social and human capital of their clients so as to make them more loan-ready; *Financial Intermediation* to assess and manage the credit worthiness and default risk of their clients; and *Administrative Intermediation* to control, govern and optimize their internal procedures and processes.

As part of the risk intermediation, DC MF programs need to triage their clients, so as to put their program's limited resources to their best use (Servon, 2006) and recognize that they cannot eliminate poverty, even when acting as *lenders of last resort* to the entrepreneurial poor who cannot obtain credit through traditional means. Specifically, MF programs have a delicate balancing act where, on one hand, they must exclude those *with ready access to other reasonable sources of credit* and, on the other, they must ensure the ongoing financial viability of the MF program by excluding the *truly disadvantaged*, because they lack the means to pay interest and repay what was loaned. Increasingly MF programs are channelled into serving the working poor, who have both the experience and other resources to leverage the limited resources made available by a MF program into success (Servon, 1997; Khandker, 1999; Bhatt & Tang, 2001; Burkett, 2003; Hung, 2003). Part of the MF triage process is recognizing that lending to those with no means or prospect of repaying what is lent, may be profoundly harmful; e.g. via deepening the debt load of their clients, stressing or fraying their social capital (ties to family, friends, and peers) and deepening feelings of failure, despair, and disadvantage (Frankiewicz, 2001). In this process of triage, many DC MF programs have largely abandoned "...their original mission of assisting the most disadvantaged [poor, after

they protect their loan capital by screening]…
out those who are not willing or able to repay the
loans" (Bhatt & Tang, 2001, pp.230-231). Hung
(2003) and Servon (1997) note that, as part of being more sustainable, many DC MF programs are
now requiring their clients to have some regular
income, some experience in a trade and some
credit history—this practice is shifting their focus
from helping people escape welfare to assisting
the entrepreneurial working poor.

The provision of the above three types of intermediation mean that DC MF programs must,
along with lending money, provide similar support to their entrepreneur clients as is commonly
provided by most venture capitalists (see Sayd &
Hettihewa, 2007, for details on venture capital).

THE EFFECT OF SOCIO-ECONOMIC CONDITIONS ON MF

Different Root Causes of Poverty Require Different MF Tools

As noted previously, poverty in DCs has different and often more subtle causes than poverty in
LDCs. As a result, MF programs in DCs require
significant revisions and refocusing away from
their LDC origin. The literature shows that MF
in DCs faces different challenges from their
counterparts in LDCs. Servon (1999 and 2006)
assert that MF standards were developed in the
early stages of MF, while it was in LDCs, and that
those standards are less appropriate for the DC
MF movement. Servon's assertion is affirmed by

Table 2.

Information Asymmetry	• **Work with clients who have significantly less social capital** (Putnam, 1993; Bhatt & Tang, 2001; Hung, 2003, Burkett, 2003). In DCs, for example, extended families are largely absent, people move more frequently than people in LDCs, and clients in DCs are more likely to live in densely populated impersonal urban settings that often lack the inter-personal ties and commitments that are common within a village setting (Frankiewicz, 2001).
Moral Hazard	• They **loan significantly larger amounts**—e.g. 500-10,000 USD (Servon, 1997; Bhatt & Tang, 2001; Frankiewicz, 2001; and Burkett 2003), to tens of thousands of USD (Servon, 2006); and in the European Union, 10,000-30,00 € (Dubreuil & Mirada, 2008). In contrast, LDC MF loans tend to average 50 USD, per client (MIE, 2007).
	• **Have much higher loan delinquency and default rates.** Servon (1997), Hung (2003) gave an example of a program that experienced delinquency rates of 30 percent, Bhatt and Tang (2001) noted that another program's loan losses averaged 18 percent, during 1992-1994, Frankiewicz (2001) observed that 25 percent of Metrofund clients defaulted, and Bhatt and Tang (2001) discussed a program that had loan losses of 60 percent over an eight year period. In contrast, to the experience of DC MF programs, the delinquencies and losses of LDC MF loans can be as low as (respectively) 0.9 and 0.3 percent (MIE, 2007; Hung, 2003). While the Australian experience by National Australia Bank (of 1.9 percent default rate on 876 loans averaging 2,700 AUD) is much better than the average experienced in Canada and the US, that program only started in 2004 and Metrofund Canadian had similarly encouraging low default rates of 3.5 percent, at that early stage of its program (Frankiewicz, 2001).
Transaction Size	• **Incur much higher administrative costs** (NAB, 2008) and Bhatt & Tang (2001) noted that one MF program had administrative costs averaging 325.4 percent of the value loaned during 1992-1994. These high costs are reflective of clients who are "quite needy and [demand] … a lot of time and energy from loan officers and other staff members [with staff often acting like]…. social workers and councillors to help customers work through emotional and financial crises" (Frankiewicz, 2001, p. 31).
	• **Have cost-recovery issues** due to an inability to "charge interest rates and fees that can cover their risks and administrative cost structures" (Frankiewicz, 2001, p.48). This inability to recover costs is largely due to the poor credit quality of the DC MF customers, which necessitate high fees and interest, to cover costs, but such charges conflict with the stated philosophy of DC MF of supporting and facilitating the poor to escape the poverty trap. An estimate of what interest rates are needed for cost recovery can be seen in GE Finance (a for-profit lender that targets the same socio-economic group as the DC MF programs) and has interest rates that (in effective terms) approach or even exceed 50 percent per annum.

a plethora of studies that note, in contrast to MF in LDCs, DC MF programs experience a number of issues that (per Gueyié & Fischer, 2009) can be separated into (see Table 2):

A common theme in many studies on MF in DCs, are the consequences that arise from combining the conflicting goals of lending, economic development and poverty alleviation (Servon, 1997 and 2006; Bhatt & Tang, 2001; Chowdhury, 2007). Several studies have suggested that these consequences can be mitigated if each MF program were to make either lending or social development their core competency and stopped trying to do both, and doing them badly. While such specialization is good business sense, it is likely to frustrate MF's intended role. Specifically, a MF program is more than either a lending agency or a charity—it blurs the line between economic development and poverty alleviation. As Servon (1997, p.178) notes, the MF *raison de etra* (reason to exist) is to combat poverty, by changing:

"...the mind-set of people by creating a forward motion, giving them the hope they need to take charge of their own lives.... By helping people begin to think strategically about creating better futures for themselves and providing them with the tools necessary to make that happen, these programs shift the focus from maintenance to investment."

Credit from commercial lenders is rarely completely inaccessible in DCs (Frankiewicz, 2001; Burkett, 2003; Buckland & Dong, 2008). Servon (2006) asserts that low and moderate income groups are increasingly being served by such fringe income financial services as check cashing operations, payday lenders, and rent-to-own operations and those services are enormously profitable. Further, advances in technology have decreased transaction costs and allowed mainstream financial institutions to move into shallower waters to serve lower income groups. Also, partnerships between MF programs and mainstream banking and other main-stream-banking-MF initiatives are beginning to occur—e.g. in Australia[6]: the Brotherhood of St. Laurence has developed a matched savings program with the ANZ Bank (Burkett, 2003); the Westpack Bank worked with the Indigenous Enterprise Partnerships (IEP) and the Good Shepherd Society to establish a MF program for the Aboriginal community at Cape York in 2001 (Andrikonis, 2005; IEP, 2005); the National Australian Bank (NAB) started *Step Up Loans* in 2004 in conjunction with the Good Shepherd Youth & Family service Australia that provided low interest loans of between $800-3,000 (AUD); the NAB launched a 30 million (AUD), three-year commitment to not-for-profit micro-credit program in 2006, providing loans (via community groups) of up to 1,000 (AUD) for low-income Australians (NAB, 2008).

Frankiewicz (2001) cites Calmeadow's five-year experience in Canada to illustrate the point that DC MF programs that seek to specialise as *for-profit* lenders are unlikely to create much social value in that role or find that there is much need/demand for it. As evidenced by the recent *subprime lending crisis*, lending to the destitute or to those otherwise unable or unwilling to repay the loan can, on balance, do more harm than good (Frankiewicz, 2001); by perpetuating or accelerating a vicious cycle of failure, poverty, and dependency. Similarly, while welfare, charity, and other purely social-development programs can alleviate many of the worst physical hardships of poverty, they can also perpetuate a vicious and often inter-generational cycle of indolence, irresponsibility and dependency. Thus, it is the conflicting and often unstable mix of services offered by MF (credit, training, and development) that make possible the opportunities MF offers to its clients and society.

What MF Cannot and Can Offer to the DC Poor

The previous section shows that DC MF programs have run into several unexpected challenges. These challenges prevent DC MF from being a low cost self-sustaining cure-all for poverty; many programs have failed because they attempted to solve *the urban poverty problem*. As previously noted, DC MF programs can make themselves more financially sustainable if they restrict their focus to the working poor and limit their involvement with their original target group of those who are the most disadvantaged and, hence, less likely to succeed (Servon, 1997; Bhatt & Tang, 2001; Hung, 2003). Current DC MF programs face several sustainability issues.

Loan delinquency and loss rates are many times what was expected and are often several orders of magnitude higher than the experience of MF programs in LDCs (Tang, 2001; Bhatt & Tang, 2001; Hung, 2003; MIE, 2007). This problem is compounded because loan delinquencies and losses are difficult to predict and the outcomes of regression models have been inconsistent (Frankiewicz, 2001). There have been difficulties in adopting the LDC use of peer-groups to reduce loan delinquency and loss rates in DC MF (Servon, 1997; Hung, 2003 and 2006; Burkett, 2003). These problems likely occurred because (as noted elsewhere in this chapter) MF clients in DCs tend to have significantly less social capital than their counterparts in LCDs. Administrative costs are much higher than expected; often 100 percent of the value loaned (NAB, 2008) and can run as high as three to four times that amount (Bhatt and Tang, 2001). This leads to breakeven points which are so high as to be difficult or even impossible to achieve and/or sustain. These issues are complicated by the legal and regulatory environment in which many MF programs operate (Burkett, 2003). There has been a fragmented focus on what specific services, or combination thereof, to offer; a fragmented approach as to whom and how services are offered; and fragmented criteria as to what constitutes success. This fragmentation reflects the absence of program accreditation, regulation, standards of care and/or rules for transparent reporting. The funding flows have been inconsistent or unreliable, including (given the high rates of nonperforming and defaulted loans) cash flows from the repayment of loans and interest payments (Servon, 1997 and 2006; Bhatt & Tang, 2001; Helms, 2006). There has been a generally inadequate response to the need for ongoing innovation; Specifically, given that customer bases shift and needs change, it is important that non-profits (like MF programs) think hard about innovation (Servon, 2006; Burkett, 2003), if they are to avoid becoming obsolete or socially irrelevant. A lack of appropriate technology development and application to assist MF administrators – e.g. a lack of *automated-credit-scoring programs* to assess and match the needs and attributes of clients with specific MF programs (Servon, 2006).

MF loans leave many borrowers worse off – Frankiewicz (2001) noted that even where a borrower's net worth improved, it was often achieved through a significant increase in their liabilities, which rendered them more vulnerable to a *hard landing* in the next economic downturn.

A self-inflicted adverse selection problem leading to increased loan losses as the better credit-quality clients gradually left (as they either gained sufficient credit-worthiness to access the mainstream financial institutions or grew their business beyond the need for MF credit). This process leaves MF programs with an ever degrading loan portfolio and DC MF may prove to be a *Bubble Industry* that continually sheds its best clients and accumulates a rising burden of ever-less-credit-worthy loans (Frankiewicz, 2001).

MF clients have many problems that are complex, inter-related and difficult to resolve rather than only an access-to-credit problem. Thus, resolving one problem for a client often uncovers a tangle of more pernicious problems that must be resolved for the client to succeed.

For example, when a client's welfare benefits are subject to *means testing*, their income needs to either remain below the cut-off point at which their welfare payments are affected or it needs to rise high enough to compensate for any lost welfare benefits (Burkett, 2003). These multiple problems are likely a significant part of why the failure rates of DC micro-enterprise is much higher than the experience in LDCs (Burkett, 2003).

Micro-entrepreneurs in DCs often face more complicated regulatory barriers, very sophisticated, competitive and fast evolving markets, and exacting consumer quality standards (Frankiewicz, 2001) than those faced by LDC microentrepreneurs.

Despite these challenges, a well-designed MF program offers something special for the relief of DC poverty—a reasonable hope for some of the poor, that they can develop sufficient self-reliance to enable them to not only escape the poverty trap, but to offer fair and gainful employment to other poor. Some highly focused MF programs have offered social development via a re-balancing of relative power, by gender, ethnicity, or other key attribute; e.g. Dubreuil and Mirada (2008) suggest that Spanish MF programs significantly improved the well-being of many families by re-balancing financial power in favour of poorer women, particularly immigrants. Empirical studies by Banerjee, et al. (2009) and Karlan & Zinman (2009) found that, after self-selection and other confounding factors were corrected, MF provided only a negligible reduction in poverty in, respectively, Bangladesh and the Philippines. Other recent studies suggesting that much of the purported success of LDC MF may be more expectations, good public relations, poor internal controls and poor experimental design, than from actual performance include Roodman & Morduch (2009), Chemin (2008), Banerjee & Duflo (2008) and Coleman (2006). However, these studies and a review of some of them in the Economist (2009), suggest that even if its short-run effects are small, MF can reduce poverty in the long run, by tak-ing risks on entrepreneurial individuals who lack other means to start a business. Thus, while MF in both LDCs and DCs cannot eliminate poverty, it can provide a hand-up, by which a very select few of the more entrepreneurial poor may escape the poverty trap.

Micro-Enterprise Development Cases: A Tale of Two Cities

The previous section showed that DC MF programs have been forced to choose between either being true to their original intent of providing a *hand-up* to the poor or maintaining their financial viability by lending only to those with the means to succeed at micro-enterprise. In either case, DC MF programs must recognise that they owe an important *duty of care* to their clients. Specifically they must carefully evaluate how the proposed investment projects fit their DC socio-economic setting and to restrict the loans and resources offered to clients whose projects do not have a reasonable likelihood of success (Servon, 1997; Bhatt & Tang, 2001). Failure in this duty of care: 1) can harm MF clients by deepening their debt loads, stressing or fraying their social contacts/capital/collateral and aggravating feelings of failure, despair and disadvantage (Frankiewicz, 2001); and 2) can harm the MF program via increased defaults which, by reducing the capacity of the MF program to issue future loans, also disadvantages future poor entrepreneurs—e.g. the non-viability of "borrowers' businesses...was a key reason why the agency's [Women's Development Association Program] portfolio suffered from high risks...and default rates" (Bhatt & Tang, 2001, p.233).

Thus, evaluation and management of risk is an important duty for DC MF programs. While project risk "...refers to the borrower's ability to run a successful business [it also] includes exogenous factors such as the local, regional, or national economy" (Hung, 2003, p. 384). This chapter contends that the micro-enterprise risk in DC socio-economic setting is much greater than what is experienced by their counterparts in LDCs and that a large part of that higher risk is due to barriers created by regulations, laws, taxes, and user-pay fees for government services (that are made mandatory by regulation). This assertion is demonstrated in the following case-studies. As part of evaluating why DC MF have experienced more difficulty than LDC MF, these cases use an example of a micro-enterprise in a LDC and three cases in a DC. A LDC migrant to a DC was used in the later three cases, not to highlight migration itself, but to contrast the socio-economic conditions (especially differences in regulation and bureaucracy) between LDCs and DCs. While it might be argued that a migrant will be hampered by a lack of knowledge about rules and regulations in his/her adopted country, the level of ignorance of other MF *at-risk-groups* is likely to be just as great, if not greater. The cases are crafted as a collage/ assemblage of many experiences (rather than being the experience of a single person). Cases are used for their intuitive appeal and ease of understanding. While an empirical study on the effect of differing regimes of regulation and taxes on micro-enterprise would be useful as a future area of research, it is beyond the scope of the chapter.

Case 1. Micro-Enterprise in a LDC: From Nut Peddler to Upper Middleclass

Ms. M lives in an LDC, where she established a micro-enterprise with help from a LDC MF

program. Ms. M realized that there might be a market for hulled, roasted Kottamba nuts (Terminalia *catappa*). Traditionally, Kottamba nuts (also known as the *Indian almond*) were considered the *food of the poor*, as only the destitute would gather them from the ground for food. However, growth and rising prosperity over recent decades had propelled many of the formerly poor and/or their children into positions of power and affluence. These *nouveau riche* remembered Kottamba nuts favourably from their days in poverty and wanted to snack on them—but only if their nature was not readily apparent to others. The business case was simple: (see Table 3)

Ms. M was surprised that her monthly revenue of Sri Lankan Rupees 21,667 (Rs 1,000 x 5 days x 52 weeks/12 months) was roughly the monthly wage of a mid-level government office worker and even more surprised as her microenterprise, selling a product commonly associated with poverty, expanded after 5 years to 8 carts (with many employees and casual workers) and her one-third share (Rs 7,222 per cart per week x 8 carts) propelled her into real wealth.

Case 2: Micro-Enterprise in a DC: Death by Set-Up Requirements and Costs

Mr. K a former acquaintance of Ms. M, now lives in a coastal city in a DC. After paying $30.00 for a *green-metallic-king-cobra guppy* fish for his daughter's *tropical-fish* aquarium, Mr K. had an

Table 3. Estimated Daily Cash Flows for Ms. M

Expected Daily Revenues – based on 500 bags of 200 grams (gm) of hulled, roasted Kottamba nuts selling at Sri Lankan Rupees 25 per bag (Rs 25x500).	Rs 12,500
Expected Daily-Raw-Material Production Costs – based on Kottamba nuts being freely available for gathering from the ground by neighbours, who can be paid Sri Lankan Rupees 20 per kilogram (kg) of raw nuts. After hulling, salting, and roasting, the finished-product pack-out is 20 percent of the weight of raw nuts. Therefore, a 200gm bag requires 1.0 kg of raw nuts (Rs20 x 500bags x1kg).	Rs 10,000
Other Costs – oil, salt, paper bags, kerosene, rental of a hand-cart with a kerosene cooker, and sundry costs.	Rs 1,500
Expected Daily Net Revenues to the Entrepreneur	Rs 1,000

inspiration for what should be a real winner of a business. Specifically, he knew where this species of fish could be bought in his former country could be bought for the equivalent of 30 cents each. A 100-fold mark-up on cost (10,000 percent) meant little or no risk, and he would create jobs back in the *old country*. After studying the associated import fees, quarantine costs, costs of delays in-transit, paperwork costs, stock losses, fish-health-certification costs, air-freight costs and finding that the wholesale price was $10.00 (tropical- fish retailers need a big mark-up) and only for *certified virus-free stock*, he determined that it would cost him $8.00 to import the fish. Mr. K thought that, with volume, he might just be able to make enough profit for the project to be worthwhile. However, as he was exploring that possibility, a local green-activist group ran ads against the harvest of endangered tropical fish. Mr. K's daughter, after seeing the ads, threatened to never speak to him again if he started a business of kidnapping and selling wild fish. A final blow fell when the national fisheries management department of his adopted country sent him a letter informing him that the Department's current interpretation of a newly enacted "precautionary management approach" would prevent him from importing live fish into the country unless he or someone else proved that the fish were not endangered. Recognizing that the study would cost tens of thousands of dollars that he did not have, Mr. K abandoned the live-fish importing business and suffered net losses of $5,000 plus a year of planning and effort.

Case 3: Micro-Enterprise in a DC: *The Verst is Yet to Come*

Having learned the pitfalls of importing (especially, live fish), Mr. K yearned for a safer business. He remembered the push-carts back home from which a host of tasty treats were sold and noted that they were virtually absent from his new home. Rather than limit his market or risk import issues, Mr. K choose to sell locally made Kransky sausages on local buns with local chopped onions and national brand relishes from a push cart in a downtown park near the major office complexes. Being handy with tools he made his own pushcart, wood cutting boards, on a kerosene stove and he set his price at $6.50 per Kransky—yielding a healthy 200 percent mark-up on food costs.

The first day sales were brisk until an official from the city-hall told him that to sell in the city parks he would need to buy a $2,000 license every two months and that fire-safety rule dictate that he must use a bottled-gas cooker instead of a kerosene one.

Two weeks later, having paid his park-seller's license fee and put a bottled-gas cooker in his push cart, he was back in the park and sales were again brisk, until the restaurant food safety inspector shut him down, fined him $1,000 and told him that he needed to pass a food safety inspection every four months and, with the new user-pay policy of the state and city governments, he would have to pay $500 for that inspection.

Six weeks later, having had the food-safety inspection and three re-inspections (at $500 each) his push cart was *brought-up-to-code* by adding a small refrigerator, changing the wood cutting boards to the code-specified plastic and tempered-glass ones and painting the inside of the push cart with special and costly food-safe paints, he was back in the park and sales were again brisk, until the employment safety inspector informed him that his two children were not property certified to serve food to the public and that the electrical points on the carts would have to be inspected at a user-pay cost of $800.

Two weeks later, having changed the power points to meet code, he was back in the park and sales were again rapid, until an official from the city hall fined him $1,500 for not having an up-to-date park-seller's license.

A week later, having paid for two more months of park-seller's license fee, he was back in the park and sales were again vigorous, until a vegan/animal rights group (who were protesting the eating of meat) dumped rotten offal over his cart. A food-safety inspector (who had observed the attack) commiserated with Mr. K, but then informed him he would be unable to adequately clean the cart to meet current health regulations and he would need to replace everything and have the new cart inspected for food-safety and employment safety. When Mr. K took the fouled push cart to the dump, he was charged $30 user-pay tipping fee plus a $300 toxic waste user-pay disposal fee.

Mr. K, unwilling to continue the frustrations of the business, gave it up and suffered net losses of $10,000 and another year of planning and effort.

Case 4: Micro-Enterprise in a DC: More than the Yabbies are Pinching

Having learned the pitfalls of importing and of trying to sell hot food in a city park, Mr. K desired a much safer business. He knew that in his new home, a delicacy called yabbies (i.e. crayfish) were abundant and, in his former country and throughout South-east Asia, increasing tourism and rising incomes were increasing the number of French restaurants—who were, at great cost, importing large amounts of crayfish, from France and Louisiana (US). Mr. K reasoned that he could make money by acting as an intermediary between the farmers who had yabby ponds and the foreign restaurants who needed them and, because the exports would benefit his new country, he should be reasonably free from bureaucratic interference.

After six months he had 50 farmers interested in harvesting yabbies from their dams and ponds—they would harvest and process yabbies (i.e. purged and transport ready) for a gross of $10,000 per farmer and Mr. K's 50 percent mark-up on that cost would cover the transport and border inspections that he had already contracted, and leave him with $30,000 a year.

After a year, when contracts were in place and everything was ready, Mr. K heard from the farmers that, due to new taxes and user-pay fees,

they could not afford to harvest yabbies (Grow-fish, 2004; Mether, 2004). Specifically, harvesting yabbies from a dam or pond would now convert it to a commercial-use impoundment and attract a new $125 annual fee (per dam) plus a new $200 annual yabby-pond license fee (holding and cleaning ponds were not exempt). Also, a $200 annual fee was added for inspecting each processing site. Given that each farmer had ten dams/ponds, their annual government licensing and inspection fees for harvesting yabbies would be $3,450 (10 x (125+200) + 200) per farmer. These fees reduced the farmer's gross revenues by 34.5 percent, from a viable $10,000 per farmer to a nonviable $6,550.

After, paying cancelation and penalty fees, and quitting the business, Mr. K incurred a loss of $30,000 and yet another year of planning and effort.

Micro-Enterprise in a DC Case Epilogue

Mr. K decided that he has had enough of business ventures and will focus on getting a job. In his former country, Mr. K was a wealthy engineer, but the debts from his failed ventures force him into getting a job as a night watchman in his adopted homeland. In the following year, after an audit by the Federal Revenue authorities, Mr. K was informed that none of his business losses in the prior three years were deductible for tax purposes, because the lack of a profit over three years demonstrated that, for tax purposes, his businesses were more of a hobby than serious business investments. As a result, Mr. K had to repay the tax on the investment income he had offset against his business losses, along with interest and penalties.

Mr. K observed: no wonder this is such a land of *untapped* opportunity—he had turned from paid employment, to pick-up an opportunity to make something of it, for himself and others, but was left with little more than a fist-full of *tax nettles*, *regulatory thistles* and *user-pay-fee burrs*—and after being taxed, regulated, and *user-fee'd* out of business was given yet another tax-kick for failing to show profit.

SUGGESTIONS FOR FUTURE RESEARCH

Empirical investigation is needed on the how differences in the socio-economics of LDCs and DCs affect MF programs and work should, also, be done on finding solutions for the adverse effects. In addition, research is needed on the socio-economic, and political effects of lightening the regulatory, administrative, and tax burdens of DC micro-entrepreneurs. Studies on the relation between migration and MF would, also, be interesting.

CONCLUSION AND RECOMENDATIONS

This chapter uses descriptive analysis to consider the performance and sustainability of MF in DCs. It is suggested that the imperfect fit of a LDC solution to a related but importantly different DC problem is creating difficulties for DC MF that can squander resources and severely damage the public view of the capacity of MF to serve the needs of DCs.

Even though the physical reality of poverty is often less harsh in DCs and DC poor are significantly more affluent than the poor in LDCs, this study suggests there are still many sound reasons to develop and support programs to alleviate poverty in DCs. However, as evidenced throughout the operations and academic literature on DC MF, reality appears to be deflecting DC MF programs from their original social objectives (e.g. service to the poor, gender equality, and social education) to economic survival.

In recognition that DCs are in more need of the MF social objectives being effectively serviced than they need more free-market providers of loans and given the large differences in the socio-economics of LDCs and DCs, DC MF programs must develop and be held to different standards than those that have become common to LDC MF programs. Further, recent research is suggesting that much of the purported success of LDC MF may be more expectations, good public relations, poor internal controls and poor experimental design, than actual performance.

While the above issues are well considered in the literature on MF, there is another fundamental difference between the LDC and DC micro-enterprise environments that appears to be under-appreciated. Specifically, the regulation, fees, taxes, red-tape, record-keeping rules, other bureaucratic intrusion (e.g. health and safety, endangered species and environmental protection acts), and the threats and reality of legal action (e.g. lawsuits, torte actions, and injunctions) are many orders of magnitude higher in DCs than they are in LDCs. As a result of this issue, DC micro-entrepreneurs face many more and much higher risks, start-up costs, start-up delays, and surprises than their LDC counterparts. Many MF adherents suggest that such problems are limitations of micro-entrepreneurs, and (as such) are beyond the scope of MF. However, these problems contribute greatly to the failure rates experienced by DC micro-entrepreneurs and, thus, are important issues determining the success or otherwise of DC MF programs.

The effort to identify and resolve what troubles DC MF is worthwhile. Specifically, while charity can often only trim and ease the worst consequences of poverty, MF provides a means to strike at a root cause of poverty and can provide some (but not all) impoverished individuals with the tools to escape poverty. Ultimately, DC MF needs to be more than a *for-profit* lender of last resort, they must provide a host of costly support services and provide (on an as-needed basis) counselling and social work to help clients work through the roller-coaster of emotional, financial, and confidence crises that are all too often a part of the DC micro-enterprise experience.

REFERENCES

Andrikonis, C. (2005). Westpac Bank Cape York Experience. In Landvogt (Ed.), Microcredit: *More than just small change*. Conference Proceedings, Melbourne, Good Shepherd Youth and Family Services, Melbourne.

Banerjee, A. V., & Duflo, E. (2007). The Economic Lives of the Poor. *The Journal of Economic Perspectives, 21*(1), 141–167. doi:10.1257/jep.21.1.141

Banerjee, A. V., & Duflo, E. (2008). *The Experimental Approach to Development Economics*. Working Paper. Cambridge, MA: MIT Department of Economics.

Banerjee, A. V., & Duflo, E. Glennerster, R., & Kinnan, C. (2009). *The Miracle of Microfinance? Evidence from a Randomized Evaluation*. Working Paper. Cambridge, MA: MIT Department of Economics.

Bhatt, N., & Tang, S.-Y. (2001, August). Making microcredit work in the United States: Social, financial, and administrative dimensions. *Economic Development Quarterly*, 351–367.

Buckland, J., & Dong, X.-Y. (2008). Banking on the margin in Canada. *Economic Development Quarterly, 22*(3), 252–263. doi:10.1177/0891242408318738

Burkett, I. 2003. *Microfinance in Australia*. Working Paper, School of Social Work and Social Policy, University of Queensland, Australia. May 12, 2003.

Cabraal, A., Russell, R., & Singh, S. (2006). Microfinance: Development as freedom. *Financial Literacy, Banking and Identity Conference*. RMIT University, Melbourne, Australia, Oct. 25-26, 2006.

Chemin, M. (2008). The benefits and costs of microfinance: Evidence from Bangladesh. *The Journal of Development Studies, 44*(4), 463–484. doi:10.1080/00220380701846735

Chowdhury, F. (2007). The Metamorphosis of the micro-credit debtor. *New Age Journal*. 24 Jun/07. Retrieved March 25, 2009, from http://www.newagebd.com/2007/jun/24/oped.html

CIA. (2008). *CIA World Factbook* - Unless otherwise noted, information in this page is accurate as of January 1, 2008. Retrieved January 08, 2009, from http://indexmundi.com/g/r.aspx?c=be&v=6 or https://www.cia.gov/library/publications/the-world-factbook/

Coleman, B. E. (2006). Microfinance in Northeast Thailand: Who benefits and how much? *World Development, 34*(9), 1612–1638. doi:10.1016/j.worlddev.2006.01.006

Deaton, A. (2009). Instruments of development: randomization in the tropics, and the search for the elusive keys to economic development. Working Paper 14690. Cambridge, MA: National Bureau of Economic Research.

Dubreuil, G. E., & Mirada, C. T. (2008). Microfinance and gender considerations in developed countries: The case of Catalonia. *ISTR 2008 International Conference*. Barcelona, Spain. July, 2008.

Dunford, C. (2006). *Evidence of microfinance's contribution to achieving the millennium development goals*. Davis, CA: Freedom from Hunger.

Economist. (2009, July 18). Microcredit may not work wonders but it does help the entrepreneurial poor. Finance and Economics, *Economist*, 68.

Finkelstein, M., Jerrett, M., DeLuca, P., Finkelstein, N., Verma, D., Chapman, K., & Sears, M. (2002, September 2). Relation between income, air pollution and mortality: A cohort study. *CMAJ (Canadian Medical Association Journal), 169*(5). Retrieved August 19, 2004, from http://cmaj.ca/cgi/content/ full/169/5/397

Frankiewicz, C., (2001, February). Calmeadow Metrofund: A Canadian experiment in sustainable microfinance. Calmeadow, Nova Scotia, Canada.

Goodwin-Groen, R. (1998). *The role of Commercial Banks in Microfinance: Asia-Pacific Region.* The Foundation for Development Cooperation Ltd.

Growfish. (2004, June 23). Victorian yabby growers pushed to the wall. *Gippsland Aquaculture Industry Network – GAIN.* Retrieved July 10, 2009, from http://www.growfish.com.au/content. asp?contentid=1864

Gueyié, J.-P., & Fischer, K. P. (2009). Microfinance and market-oriented microfinance institutions. *Canadian Journal of Development Studies, 29*(1-2), 23–40.

Helms, B. (2006). *Access for All: Building Inclusive Financial Systems.* Washington, DC: CGAP/ World Bank.

Hung, C. H. (2003, November). Loan performance of group-based microcredit programs in the United States. *Economic Development Quarterly, 17*(4), 383–395. doi:10.1177/0891242403255364

Hung, C. H. (2006). Rules and actions: Determinants of peer group and staff actions in group-based microcredit programs in the United States. *Economic Development Quarterly,* (Feb): 75–96. doi:10.1177/0891242405279361

IEP. (2005). *Breakthrough.* Indigenous Enterprise Partnerships. Retrieved June 20, 2009, from www.positiveoutcomes.com.au/uploads/ files/1126158084404_0.5922729914425602.pdf

IMF. (2008). *The Purchasing Power of Working Time 2008 – An international Comparison.* International Metalworkers' Federation. Retrieved February 28, 2009, from http://www.imfmetal.org

Karlan, D., & Zinman, J. (2009). *Expanding Microenterprise Credit Access: Using Randomized Supply Decisions to Estimate the Impacts in Manila.* Yale Economics Dept. Working Paper No. 68, Yale University, New Haven, USA.

Khandker, S. R. (1999). *Fighting Poverty with Microcredit (Bangladesh edition).* Dhaka: The University Press Ltd.

Lynch, J., Smith, G., & Kaplan, G., & House. J. (2000). Income inequality and mortality: importance to health of individual income, psychosocial environment, or material conditions. *British Medical Journal, 320,* 1200–1204. doi:10.1136/ bmj.320.7243.1200

Matin, I., Hulme, D., & Rutherford, S. (2002). Finance for the poor: from microcredit to microfinancial services. *Journal of International Development, 14*(2), 273–294. doi:10.1002/jid.874

Mether, L. (2004). Yabby farms to close. *Growfish.* Gippsland Aquaculture Industry Network – GAIN. Retrieved July 10, 2009, from http://www.growfish.com.au/content.asp?contentid=1991

MIE. (2007). The microfinance information exchange. *MicroBanking Bulletin, 15.*

NAB. (2008). Micro Finance. *National Australia Bank Annual Report.* Retrieved February 03, 2009, from http://nab2008annualreports.textpacific.com.au/corporate_responsibility_review/ microfinance. asp

Pitt, M., Shahidur, M., Khandker, R., & Cartwright, J. (2006). Empowering women with micro finance: Evidence from Bangladesh. *Economic Development and Cultural Change, 54*(4), 791–831. doi:10.1086/503580

Pitt, M., Shahidur, M., Khandker, R., Chowdhury, O. H., & Millimet, D. L. (2003). Credit Programs for the Poor and the Health Status of Children in Rural Bangladesh. *International Economic Review, 44*(1), 87–118. doi:10.1111/1468-2354. t01-1-00063

Putnam, R. (1993). The prosperous community: Social capital and public life. *The American Prospect, 13*, 35–42.

Roodman, R., & Morduch, J. (2009). *The Impact of Microcredit on the Poor in Bangladesh: Revisiting the Evidence.* CGD Working Paper 174. Washington, DC: Center for Global Development. from http://www.cgdev.org/content/publications/detail/1422302.

Sayd, N., & Hettihewa, S. (2007). Venture capital or private equity? The Asian experience. *Business Horizons, 50*(4), 335–345. doi:10.1016/j.bushor.2007.03.001

Sen, A. (1999). *Development as Freedom.* Oxford University Press.

Servon, L. J. (1997, May). Microenterprise programs in U.S. inner cities: economic development or social welfare? *Economic Development Quarterly, ly*, 166–180. doi:10.1177/089124249701100205

Servon, L. J. (1999). *Bootstrap Capital: Microenterprises and the American Poor.* Washington, DC: Brookings Institution Press, Washington, DC.

Servon, L. J. (2006, November). Microenterprise development in the United States: Current challenges and new directions. *Economic Development Quarterly*, 351–367. doi:10.1177/0891242406289355

Thoreau, H. D. (1854). Economy. *Walden.* Retrieved August 10, 2008, from http://xroads.virginia.edu/~hyper/walden/walden.html

WHO. (2004). Table 3: Estimated deaths per 100,000 population by cause, and member state, 2002. In *Estimates of death rates for 2002 by cause for WHO Member States*, World Health Organization. (WHO), Dept of Measurement and Health Information Dec/04. Retrieved February 26, 2009, from http://www.who.int/whosis/indicators/compendium/2008/1mst/en.

ADDITIONAL READING

Armendáriz de Aghion, B., & Morduch, J. (2000). Microfinance beyond group lending. *Economics of Transition, 8*, 401–420. doi:10.1111/1468-0351.00049

Armendáriz de Aghion, B., & Morduch, J. (2005). *The Economics of Microfinance.* Cambridge, MA: MIT Press.

Bateman, M. (2008, December 20). Microfinance's 'iron law' – local economies reduced to poverty. *Financial Times.*

Carr, J., & Kolluri, L. (2001). *Predatory Lending: An Overview.* Washington, DC: Fannie Mae Foundation.

Carr, J., & Schuetz, J. (2001). *Financial Services in Distressed Communities: Issues and Answers.* Washington, DC: Fannie Mae Foundation.

Churchill, C. (1999). *Client-Focused Lending: The Art of Individual Lending.* Toronto: Calmeadow.

Clark, P., Kays, A., & Zandniapour, L. Soto, E. & Doyle, K. (1999). *Microenterprise and the Poor: Findings from the Self-employment Learning Project.* Washington, DC: Aspen Institute.

Consultative Group to Assist the Poor. (2009). *What Do We Know about the Impact of Microfinance?* Retrieved November 4, 2009, from http://www.egap.org/p/site/c/templete.rc/1.26.1306/

Daley-Harris, S. (2009). *State of Microcredit Summit Campaign Report 2009.* Microcredit Summit Campaign, Washington, DC.

Edgcomb, E. L., & Klein, J. A. (2005). *Opening Opportunities, Building Ownership: Fulfilling the Promise of Microenterprise in the United States.* Washington, DC: Aspen Institute.

Frank, R. (1999). *Luxury Fever.* New York: Free Press.

Giné, X. And Karlan, D. (2006) *Group versus Individual Liability: Long Term Evidence from Philippine Microcredit Lending Groups*. Yale University working paper.

Laffont, J. J., & N'Gessan, T. T. (2000). Group lending with adverse selection. *European Economic Review, 44*(4-6), 773–784. doi:10.1016/S0014-2921(99)00041-0

Lichtenstein, G. A., & Lyons, T. S. (2001). The entrepreneurial development system: Transforming business talent and community economies. *Economic Development Quarterly, 15*, 3–20. doi:10.1177/089124240101500101

Marmot, M., & Wilkinson, R. (2000). *Social Determinants of Health*. Oxford, UK: Oxford University Press.

Marmot, M., & Wilkinson, R. (2001). Psychosocial and material pathways in the relation between income and health: A response to Lynch et al. *BMJ (British Medical Journal), 322*, 1236-1240. Retrieved August 20, 2009, from http://bmj.bmjjournals.com/cgi/content/full/322/7296/1233.

Morduch, J. (1999). The microfinance promise. *Journal of Economic Literature, 37*, 1569–1614.

Mt. Auburn Associates. (1994). *An Evaluation of the Working Capital Micro-enterprise Lending Program*. Report prepared for the Institute for Cooperative Development, New Hampshire College.

OECD. (2006). *OECD Economic Surveys: Australia*, 2006(12), OECD, Paris.

Rowe, B. R., Haynes, G. W., & Stafford, K. (1999). The contribution of home-based business income to rural and urban economies. *Economic Development Quarterly, 13*, 66–77. doi:10.1177/089124249901300109

Rutherford, S. (20000. *The Poor and Their Money*. New Delhi: Oxford University Press.

Schreiner, M. (1998). Self-employment, microenterprise, and the poorest. *The Social Service Review, 73*(4), 496–523.

Servon, L. J., & Bates, T. (1998). Microenterprise as an exit route from poverty: Recommendations for programs and policy makers. *Journal of Urban Affairs, 20*(4), 419–441. doi:10.1111/j.1467-9906.1998.tb00430.x

Servon, L. J., & Dosha, J. P. (2000). Microenterprise and the economic development tool kit: A small part of the big picture. *Journal of Developmental Entrepreneurship, 5*(3), 183–208.

Sherraden, M. S., Sanders, C. K., & Sherraden, M. (2004). *Kitchen Capitalism: Microenterprise in Low- income Households*. Albany, NY: State University of New York Press.

Wright, G. A. N. (1998). Beyond Basic Credit and Savings: Developing New Financial Service Products for the Poor. Retrieved November 04, 2009, from http://www.gdrc.org/icm/ppp/buro-0.html

ENDNOTES

[1] See Burkett (2003, p.25) and Buckland and Dong (2008, pp. 255-261) for a listing of additional *at-risk* groups in Australia and Canada.

[2] The notion of poverty being a relative concept is captured in the Merriam-Webster Online (2009) definition of poverty being "...the state of one who lacks a usual or socially acceptable amount of money or material possessions".

[3] Figure 2 and 3 are developed from an IMF study comparing minimum wages and

purchasing power for workers across 50 countries. Minimum wage and purchasing power for workers in basic metal working was selected for the graph, because it is common to 50 countries and the technology/ capital per worker is less likely than many other industries to be a confounding factor across countries.

[4]   Ibid, end note 2.

[5]   See Frank (1999), Lynch, et al. (2000), and Marmot and Wilkinson (2000 and 2001) for studies on the social, psychological, and physical effects of income gradients in DCs.

[6]   See Cabraal, et al. (2006) for a more complete listing and discussion of Australian MF initiatives.

Chapter 17

Information Technology and Microfinance in Developed Countries:
The Spanish Case, with a Focus on Catalonia

Glòria Estapé-Dubreuil
Universitat Autònoma de Barcelona, Spain

Consol Torreguitart-Mirada
Universitat Autònoma de Barcelona, Spain

ABSTRACT

As Information Technology becomes increasingly more present in the so called Information Society, its potential to constitute a strategic resource also increases. Whether, and to what extent, strategic changes linked to the adoption of IT have effectively reached specific economic sectors or industries is therefore of interest. This chapter is meant as a contribution in that area, analyzing the relationships between IT and microfinance, focusing on the microfinance sector in Spain. Our study shows that the microfinance sector's basic IT infrastructures are above the Spanish average. Two main uses of IT tools are revealed: (1) to provide information, both to prospective clients and to those sustaining microfinance, and (2) as a management and support tool, including on-line direct support to would-be entrepreneurs. Strategic use of IT is less widespread, related primarily to financial transparency issues, more clearly shown by MFIs linked to the social economy. Finally, depth of outreach related to the actual IT use in the sector is also discussed.

INTRODUCTION

As technical changes, such as information systems or information technologies, become increasingly available, their potential power to transform organizations has also increased. The term "information system", or management information system, is used to encompass all kinds of organization-wide systems designed to manage all major functions of an enterprise. Meanwhile, "information technologies" stand for a large array

DOI: 10.4018/978-1-61520-993-4.ch017

of communication media and devices (e-mail, video-conferences, the internet, groupware and corporate intranets, mobile phones, and so on). As has become conventional in the literature, the term information technology (IT) shall be used here in its broader sense, to include both information systems and information technologies, since they are often inextricably linked (Dewett & Jones, 2001; Hackler & Saxton, 2007).

Literature has widely examined different roles played by IT in organizations, especially in large firms, but also in small firms and in nonprofit organizations. IT knowledge entails its use as a vehicle for the storage or communication of information, but also the enhancement of administrative and operational efficiency and effectiveness of the organization (Lee, Kim, Choi & Lee, 2009). As IT becomes more and more affordable, powerful and accessible, technical knowledge and expertise are likely to be amongst the critical resource dependencies of many organizations (McLoughlin, 1999). At the same time, advanced IT has the potential to support innovative and strategic responses to the challenges faced by the organizations (Castells, 2000).

Currently, IT has been explicitly regarded as a strategic resource for public, private and nonprofit organizations alike, in a number of recent theoretical and empirical works. Measures of performance nevertheless differ between for-profit and nonprofit organizations. While financial performance is a basic guide to strategy development in the for-profit sector, it has to be replaced with other measures, such as efficiency and effectiveness in achieving its mission, in the nonprofit and public sectors (Moore, 2000). Based on several profit and cost-based performance measures, results of a well known study conducted by Bharadwaj (2000) on a group of large firms indicate better performance of firms with high IT capability. Similar findings are reported by Ragowsky & Gefen (2008) concerning the competitive advantage provided by the use of information systems in (large) manufacturing companies, stressing

their strategic impact in increasingly complex environments. Those results also matter to small businesses, as shown by Smith (1999) or Lee *et al.* (2009) amongst others, correlating the knowledge and use of IT to the firm's performance.

The use and effects of technology on non-profit organizations have also been studied to some extent in the literature. Results indicate that significant numbers of voluntary organizations show a "relatively low use and application of the core networking technologies, [... thus] under-exploiting the transformational and learning capabilities inherent within these technologies" (Burt & Taylor, 2000, p. 132, referring also to Gordon, 1998). Saidel & Cour (2003) report on nonprofit organizations' awareness of the effect of IT on their missions, although "it is not clear [...] just how carefully decision makers examine the relationship between mission and technology" (p. 22). Basic use of IT is widespread among nonprofit organizations; even though their employment of IT to help fulfill the organizational mission is significantly lower (Hackler & Saxton, 2007). Strategic change in several nonprofit organizations has nevertheless been encountered and studied in the literature (Elliot, Katsioloudes & Weldon, 1998; Burt & Taylor, 2000, 2003; Finn, Maher & Forster, 2006).

Specifically regarding microfinance, reported uses of IT include the adoption of several technical devices for operational purposes. Among them, the use of Smart Cards to reach clients more efficiently (Cecchinni & Scott, 2003) or the development of remote hand-held transaction systems to process on the spot loan applications and approvals (Claessens, 2006) could be mentioned. Improvements in specific information infrastructures allow technology to bring down transaction costs (Beck, Demirgüç-Kunt & Honohan, 2009; Attali, 2000). Nevertheless, the overall presence of Microfinance Institutions (MFIs) on the internet is scarce. According to Gutiérrez-Nieto, Fuertes-Callén & Serrano-Cinca (2008), only large MFIs have high degrees of public exposure on the internet and, on the whole, levels of financial or social disclosure of MFIs' programs are to be considered low. Quite expectedly, they also found a positive correlation between the levels of development of a country and MFIs' use of the internet (for reporting).

This chapter is meant as a contribution to the analysis of the relationships between IT and microfinance. It is of particular interest because it deals with the use of internet by microfinance firms in Spain, an area which has not been researched before, nor in neighboring countries. Its main objective is the study of the actual use of IT in the sector, focusing both on IT-related management of its organizations and the analysis of the strategic uses of IT within the sector. Prior to that, composition of and practices within the microfinance sector in Spain are described. The background section also includes some general references to the adoption of IT by Spanish organizations, where the intention is merely to contextualize IT microfinance use.

BACKGROUND

In the analysis of the impact and prospective benefits of the use of IT tools in the Spanish microfinance sector, two different and complementary contextualization angles are needed. A certain degree of IT use is to be expected in the sector, obviously due to its location in an economically developed country. Its measurement should therefore be compared to the degree of organizational IT use in Spain. Its concise description will accordingly constitute the first part of our contextualization. The second part is devoted to a brief account of the microfinance sector itself. The roles played by institutions with diverse social and economic backgrounds will be highlighted, since differences in aims and missions have to be taken into account in their regard for and actual use of IT.

Organizational Use of IT in Spain

Data related to the actual exploitation of IT in Spain are available at different levels. The Spanish *Instituto Nacional de Estadística* maintains annual statistics aimed at the analysis of use and implementation of IT in Spain, including the business sector[1]. Other relevant sources consist of various reports from the Spanish *Ministerio de Industria, Turismo y Comercio* (ONTSI, 2008 and Red.es, 2007), as well as the analysis of IT use in the Spanish Public Administration (IRIA, 2008). Regarding IT use in Spanish nonprofit organizations, unfortunately, to our knowledge there is no data available.

Our starting point will be a brief description of the Spanish business sector. Most Spanish firms (94.1%) are to be considered micro-businesses, having less than 10 workers[2]. Large firms account for only 0.19% of the total. Going into more detailed information, 51.3% of Spanish micro-businesses do not have salaried workers; whereas only 14.8% have more than 3 workers (DIRCE, 2008). Small and medium enterprises employ 62.7% of the total work force, while the remaining 37.3% are employed in large firms (PYME, 2007).

By the end of 2007, most medium-sized and large Spanish firms had incorporated the basic technical infrastructure and IT resources. Studies show that the 98.1% have some kind of computers, and 94.3% access to the Internet (ONTSI, 2008). Primary uses of the internet within those firms include searching for information (96.1%) and access to banking and other financial services (85.8%). E-commerce is used for buying purposes in almost 20% of Spanish firms, and for selling purposes in only 9% of them. A sizable number have internet presence through corporate websites, attaining almost 87% in large firms, and 68% in medium-size enterprises (52% for all firms employing more than 10 people). However, there are differences between industries, both the computer industry and the financial industry being leaders in internet presence among Spanish enterprises.

Data from Spanish micro-enterprises have a high degree of variability, largely depending on the number of employees at the firm (Red. es, 2007). Overall, only 60.6% of firms use computers on a regular basis, only 44.8% have access to the internet and 42% e-mail addresses. Those figures increase notably when only firms employing between 3 and 9 people are considered. Among these, 88.5% do have at least one computer, 72.3% access to the internet, and 68.5% have e-mail. Differences are also remarkable between industries. For instance, firms in the retail trade, which accounts for more than 18% of the total Spanish micro-enterprises, or in the construction industry (14%), have a small degree of IT presence. In both industries, less than 50% of the firms have computers, and internet access is limited to the range between 30% and 35%. Consulting services are one of the industries with the largest IT-presence, ranges of computer usage being between 83% (legal services, etc.) and 97% (IT-consultants and similar).

Among firms with internet access, 86% have high-speed broadband connections. Primary internet uses do not differ from those attested in larger firms, although financial services are less used (65.7% in micro-firms). Corporate websites are nevertheless scarce in micro-firms, only a meager 20.8% of those firms having internet access. The figure reaches 31.8% when considering micro-firms with more than 3 employees. Differences between industries are also observed. Basic software, including word processing and spreadsheet applications, are used in 60% of micro-business, a figure that almost matches the total number of micro-business with desktop computers. More sophisticated software is limited; the subsequent outstanding figures dropping to around 30% of micro-businesses having some kind of business software, such as accounting software (27.7%).

Major aspects limiting IT adoption amongst micro-enterprises include misperception of its actual utility within micro-firms, which is especially acute in such industries as retail trade. Financial aspects, related to IT acquisition and yield, are also mentioned by more than 30% of firms (Red.es, 2007).

Within nation-wide public administration agencies, IT infrastructure and use are widespread. Of the total fleet of Spanish computers, State administration agencies own 11.2% of the mainframe computers, 23.8% of midrange computers and 7.6% of the total number of personal computers. Local administration exhibits some differences, depending on the size of the municipality. For instance, almost all municipalities with more than 30,000 habitants have their own website, whereas this is the case only in 39% of the municipalities with less than 10,000 habitants (IRIA, 2008).

The Spanish Microfinance Sector

The presence of Microcredit programs and Microfinance Institutions (MFI) has been attested in Spain since the early 1980s. As in most European countries, in Spain there is no specific legislation on microcredit (European Commission, 2007). Therefore a definition of the Microfinance Institution in Spain through its legal status can not be provided. Different institutions have been identified as suppliers of microcredit, including savings banks, foundations and diverse types of nonprofit associations. All of these will be considered MFIs for the purpose of this chapter.

The pioneer MFI was established in Catalonia in 1981. As its name suggests, *Acció Solidària contra l'Atur* (ASCA) funded a "solidarity bank" aimed to alleviate poverty, providing microcredits to unemployed people without collateral, either to purchase work tools or to start-up a micro-business. This pioneer initiative was followed years later by other institutions of the social economy. Based primarily in Catalonia, and more recently extending their offers to other parts of Spain directly or in association with others, their promotion of social credit has its roots in their own missions. Targets are nevertheless dissimilar, usually focusing either on minority groups (women, immigrants, unemployed, etc.) or nonprofit institutions promoting social reintegration.

From 2001 on, microcredit programs in Spain entered a new stage. In 2001, through one of its foundations (*Fundació Un Sol Món*, FUSM, *Caixa Catalunya*), a savings bank promoted a microcredit program in the Catalan area, extended to other regions of Spain three years after. Somewhat later, in 2002, the Spanish Official Credit Institute (*Instituto de Credito Oficial*, ICO) also launched a program to promote entrepreneurship among individuals without collateral. As is usual with the ICO programs, it was designed as a mediation line, signing specific agreements with other financial institutions to effectively run the program. As a partial consequence, the Spanish Confederation of Savings Banks, *Confederación Española de Cajas de Ahorro*, set up a working group in 2004 to promote microfinance in Spanish savings banks. By 2007, one third of Spanish savings banks offered some kind of microcredit line within their social programs (*Obra Social*).

By the end of 2008, the Spanish microfinance sector was therefore structured in three clusters: programs linked to organizations of the social economy, those promoted by savings banks, and the microcredit public program. Several characteristics are common for all MFIs, while others are primarily determined by their social and economic background.

Among the common characteristics exhibited by the whole Spanish microfinance sector, the four most significant will be considered. The first matches some of the standard world-wide practices: microcredits are awarded (only) to financially excluded people, and granted without collateral. Moreover, microcredits are endowed in Spain without the disbursement fees or early repayment fees that are usually associated with loans in the traditional banking system[3]. Secondly, owing to its origins, the Spanish microfinance sector is less focused on operational objectives (cost structure minimization, economic sustainability, the maintenance of a high quality portfolio, etc.) than on social and financial support for poverty and joblessness. Consequently, self employment is one of the main goals of Spanish microcredit programs, a feature shared by other MFIs in Western European countries (Guichandut, 2006; European Commission Report, 2003). As a third point, therefore, it shall be noted that loans must be aimed at the start-up, consolidation or expansion of recently created micro-businesses[4]. As a result, in the Spanish case most microcredits are granted as individual loans, and both personal and business-related guarantees are required as substitutes for material collateral. In particular, the presentation of a detailed business plan, independently checked for economic viability, is always required. Thus, our fourth point is that social mechanisms widely used in MFIs in other parts of the world to ensure repayment, such as group-based loans, or joint-liability contracts (Bhatt & Tang, 2001; Conlin, 1999; Ghatak & Guinnane, 1999; Morduch, 1999), or the granting of progressive loans (Jain & Mansuri, 2003), have not been considered in the Spanish microfinance sector.

On the differentiation side, sources of the funds used to endow microcredit programs have to be put forward. Each of the social economy MFIs has sought its own financing scheme. Donations, as well as fund-raising and grant-seeking activities, are the starting point for some microcredit programs. Other organizations act as ethical banks, therefore using savings programs as funding sources for their lending programs. Alternatively, some institutions' microcredit programs are established through an agreement with traditional banks, in which the organization itself is considered the social collateral.

For MFIs linked to the traditional banking system, either savings banks or the public bank, financial sources are very clearly stated. As is customary in governmental programs, ICO's microcredit program has been opened for specific periods of time (2002-2004; 2005-2006; 2007-2008), with a closed budget for each edition. Likewise, savings banks offering a microcredit program have annually endowed them, following more general strategies of their own social programs. It is worth saying that Spanish savings banks, although part of the traditional banking system and usually privately owned, have a special legal status as nonprofit institutions. By law, then, Spanish sav-ings banks must assign part of their annual profits to cultural or social initiatives, managed through their *Obras Sociales*. Such microcredit programs therefore have the infrastructural back-up of their "mother" institutions.

Figure 1 provides some details concerning the most relevant microcredit programs operating in Spain, including totals disbursed during program

Figure 1. Some relevant characteristics of the microcredit programs analyzed

	MFI	Program initiated in	Totals during program life (–,2007)		Disbursed in 2007		Loan conditions of the Microcredit Programs (2008)			
			# operations	total awarded	# operations	total awarded	max. loan amount	annual interest rate	disburse-ment fee	repayment term
Social economy organizations	ASCA	1984	600 mc 1,700 w.tools	n.a.	22 mc 62 w.tools	€ 221,374 € 34,157	–	0%	0%	according to feasibility
	COOP57	1996	235	€ 7,206,560	56	€ 2,249,721	€ 180,000	6.8%	0%	7 years
MFIs linked to savings banks	FIDEM	1999	161	€ 1,853,889	16	€ 211,050	€ 25,000	5.0%	0.50% + 0.25%	5 years
	FUSM	2001	1,259	€ 11,523,724	250	€ 2,223,724	€ 30,000	5.0%	0%	5 years
	Caja Granada (*)	2002	471	€ 4,178,117	93	€ 793,648	€ 12,000	fix 4.0%	0%	5 years
	BBK	2003	216	€ 13,704,471	60	€ 6,715,383	€ 30,000	Euribor + 0.5%	0%	according to feasibility
	Caixa Galicia	2003	394	€ 3,600,000	95	€ 900,000	€ 25,000	fix 5.0%	0%	5 years
	Caja España	2004	n.a.	n.a.	n.a.		€ 24,000	fix 4.0%	0%	5 years
	Caixa Tarragona	2005	41	€ 725,000	35	€ 661,000	€ 25,000	5.5%	0%	5 years
	Caixa Sabadell (*)	2005	8	€ 93,750	3	€ 24,000	€ 15,000	according to actual values	0%	4 years
	CajaSol	2005	n.a.	n.a.	52	n.a.	€ 15,000	4.0%	0%	6 years
	CAM (*)	2007	73	€ 1,499,010	22	€ 438,573	€ 25,000	Euribor + 2%	0%	5 years
	La Caixa / MicroBank	2000 / 2007	2,624	€ 36,400,000	539	€ 7,100,000	€ 25,000	5.75%	1%	7 years
Public program	ICO	2002	1,285	€ 24,562,321	32	€ 600,000	€ 25,000	ICO ref.+3%	0%	7 years
Totals for the 14 MFIs (data available)			**9,067**	**€ 105,346,842**	**1,337**	**€ 22,172,630**			(*) totals include data from 2008	

307

life and current loan conditions of each one[5]. It primarily includes self-employment microcredit loans. Funds granted to nonprofit organizations promoting social reintegration are also considered, though only three MFIs currently grant such projects (Asca, Coop57 and BBK). In Asca's case, data concerning its program aimed at the acquisition of work tools has also been added, owing to its direct relationship with self-employment. Data has been provided directly by the MFIs or, in a few cases, obtained through their annual reports.

As a second differentiating trait, the geographical scope of the microcredit programs has to be considered. Some of them act Spain-wide (ICO, MicroBank/La Caixa[6]), some on a multi-regional level (*FUSM* in Catalonia and Madrid; *Caixa Galicia* in Galicia and Madrid; *Caja de Ahorros del Mediterráno*, CAM, in Valencia and Murcia) or regional level (*Caja Granada* in Andalusia, *Bilbao Bizkaia Kutxa*, BBK, in the Basque Country; *Caja España* in Castile-León). Several even have a sub-regional scope, as it is the case for *Caixa Tarragona* or *Caixa Sabadell*, both in Catalonia, and *CajaSol* in Andalusia[7]. Catalonia is the geographical origin of all MFIs linked to the social economy mentioned in Figure 1. Nevertheless, FIDEM's scope is Spain-wide, having signed agreements with governmental agencies and other similar associations. Coop57 has likewise enlarged its geographical scope from Catalonia to other regions of Spain, including nowadays Aragon, Madrid and recently Andalusia.

Finally, a third factor of differentiation between Spanish microcredit programs is the current management of microcredit applications. For the social economy MFIs, the appraisal of loan applications is made by voluntary or regular staff, usually meeting with the would-be entrepreneurs to assess their business-like "capacities" and actual experience, as well as the economic viability of the business project. Loan approval is made in accordance with its own mission and requirements.

As for the MFIs linked to the traditional banking system, most of them have created networks of non governmental organizations (NGOs) and local public development agencies[8]. Organizations within the network of a given microcredit program usually assist at least in the appraisal process of the applications, advising would-be entrepreneurs on the configuration of their business plans. The final approval process is nevertheless typically made by the microcredit program's own staff, sometimes rejecting projects that had previously received the "green light" from their nonprofit associates. Some programs require additional letters of introduction either from NGOs or from previous employers, establishing the *bona fides* of the would-be entrepreneur. Routine queries to the Central Credit Register maintained by the official *Banco de España* are generally also made.

IS THERE A STRATEGIC USE OF INFORMATION TECHNOLOGY IN THE SPANISH MICROFINANCE SECTOR?

The main goal of the chapter is to study the intensity of IT use in the Spanish microfinance sector. At the same time, we shall consider whether such use adds effective value to the performance of some or all Spanish MFIs; that is, whether the analyzed IT use can be regarded as strategic.

To proceed, four different and complementary factors will be examined. Considered together, these factors show an increasing tendency of technological strength within an organization. To begin with, organizational IT infrastructure must be considered, including desktop computers, networking and Internet access capabilities. Secondly, the software available to the organization is of interest, as well as its level of use. Thirdly, intensity of use of electronic communication media such as e-mail, mobile phones or intranet is discussed. The fourth and last item is related to the uses and capabilities of the organizational websites of the MFIs. Highly developed Internet and Web-based usage and capabilities are among the core competencies of IT-savvy organizations that are able to translate IT resources into substantive strategic outcomes (Hackler & Saxton, 2007).

Intensity of use of those combined IT resources undoubtedly has an influence both on the internal management of the organization and on microcredit clients' support. Ultimately, it can have a considerable impact on MFI performance. This chain of relationships is shown in Figure 2.

Our starting point shall be the description of the research methodology. The actual microfinance sector status for each one of the IT resource factors will subsequently be examined, making distinctions between the MFIs in terms of their social and economic background whenever necessary. Next, the impact of IT use for the management of microcredit programs will be focused on, both on an internal level and when considering the clients of micro-loans, two aspects that are critical to MFI performance. The final part of the section examines our findings focusing on the strategic use of IT in Spanish microfinance sector organizations.

Data and Research Methodology

Our data is based on both direct and indirect sources. Primary information is used to portray technological exploitation in the Spanish micro-

finance sector, while analysis of website content is made through secondary information.

The most relevant Spanish microcredit programs have been considered, including all of those based in Catalonia. Being the pioneer region in offering such programs, the Catalan microcredit sector exhibits a wider spectrum of MFIs in terms of dimension, therefore enriching the study. Data from 14 microcredit programs has been compiled, the complete list of which is described in Figure 1. The ICO's microcredit program had to be disregarded, since it was no longer active[9] in February 2009. All of the remaining 13 organizations in the sample were contacted by e-mail or telephone. Afterwards, a detailed semi-structured questionnaire was e-mailed, combining questions with a pre-fixed selection of answers with other open-ended questions. A total of 10 responses were obtained, 3 from social economy organizations, and 7 from microcredit programs linked to savings banks. All respondents were subsequently contacted through personal or phone interviews to further comment on their answers.

The questionnaire was based on the standard model designed by the *Instituto Nacional de Estadística* to annually measure IT use and impact in Spanish enterprises[10], following methodological recommendations from *Eurostat*. The aim was to provide comparability of our results with more

Figure 2. Relationship between IT resources and MFI performance

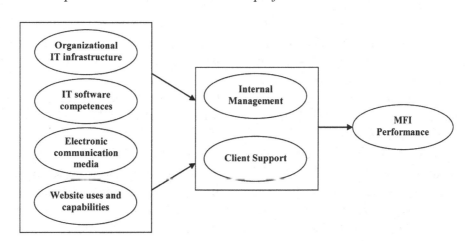

general outcomes obtained on a Spanish level. Nevertheless, several aspects of the original questionnaire had to be modified in order to fit the special characteristics of the microfinance sector. At the same time other sections of the questionnaire, such as the one reserved for the firm's electronic commerce, were of very limited interest to our particular study. Therefore, we ended up with a questionnaire in 6 sections, three of which were very similar to the standard, and three other more specific sections. Parameters providing general information about the microcredit program constitute the first section. Information about IT systems and software available to the MFIs formed the second section. Respondents were asked about the average number of employees and voluntary workers using computers at least once a week; about various dimensions of IT usage (computers, LAN, Intranet, Extranet, mobile phones), plus others related to the basic characteristics of software applications available. The third section was devoted to MFI's use of Internet: type of external internet connection; whether different varieties of Internet uses were applicable; as well as several questions about services and facilities provided through its own website.

Additional questions were addressed to the IT relationships established between the microcredit program and would be entrepreneurs, including average e-mail use to obtain information about the program, existence of IT application processes, and level of IT interaction with micro-lenders. Questions also probed the degree of internal IT management concerning applications. A final group of questions asked whether the MFI was considering further IT development, or had medium-term IT planning. It was followed by an open-ended question to provide additional comments or special information about the MFI that was not included in the previous sections of the questionnaire.

We regarded MFI website content to be a significant component of our study. Therefore we decided to complement data obtained through the questionnaire with other data gathered by our own analysis of all concerned websites. The corporate website of the ICO's program was also considered, using a version stored in January 2009 for the analysis. The authors' own choice of codes has been used, in an interactive process during the website assessment. This has led to a final classification of contents, together with some relevant interactivity properties. For some items we not only acknowledged their presence, but also appraised their intensity. Easiness of web surfing or quality of reported information are examples of such items. Since assessment can be subjective, each author coded each one independently, and the results were compared and revised as we moved along the process. Final revision of the corporate websites was made during the last week of March 2009, and whenever possible compared with data obtained in the questionnaires.

Because of the size and composition of the Spanish microfinance sector, only qualitative methods can be applied to our analysis. Statistical approaches cannot be of use, since inferential analysis could not be performed with such a small sample. For this reason, percentages provided thereafter must be considered only to be descriptive of the relative significance of a given characteristic. We could have used a case study approach, thus providing more insight into specific measures of performance, but our conclusions would have only been orientated on a micro-level. Instead, our priority has been to obtain a general portrait of IT usage within the Spanish microfinance sector. For that purpose, general qualitative methods are better suited (Creswell, 2003; Flick, 2006).

Findings and Discussion: Attested use of IT

To give a general portrait of IT usage in the Spanish microfinance sector, the above mentioned four complementary factors (see Figure 2) are successively presented. First, the organizational IT infrastructure is considered, since it constitutes the basis both for software and electronic communication media use, the second and third factors respectively. The fourth factor examined is related to the organizational websites of the MFIs.

The Spanish microfinance sector exhibits a fair degree of IT infrastructure. All organizations report the use of desktop computers with internet connections, which are used on a regular basis by 100% of the employees supporting the microcredit program in each MFI. In virtually all cases there is also a local area network (LAN) interconnecting all personal computers used. Furthermore, all MFIs have high-speed broadband connections to the Internet. Use of mobile phones is less extensive in the sector. In fact, only microcredit programs linked to savings banks report the use of mobile phones for "business purposes", and only half of them had mobile connections to the internet.

Almost all organizations use standard operative systems, open source software based on Linux being mentioned only in one case. Quite obviously given the context, at least the basic business software is installed in all MFI computers, including word processing and spreadsheet applications and accounting software. Specific database applications are also common. Nonetheless, more sophisticated service-oriented architectures to support company-wide computer software systems of the Enterprise Resource Planning (ERP) type are not reported.

Specific software for internal management is reported in all but two MFIs, both of which were organizations linked to the social economy. As for the remaining MFIs, three different models of software use arise. In the first, outsourced software, selected and purchased by the MFIs, is used. Either software products oriented at small-size Spanish cooperative and credit Unions (less than 5,000 clients) or Spanish banking standards intended for payment orders to client bank accounts are reported. The second model uses customer-adapted software to link with the Institutional banking software of the savings bank funding the MFI. In this model, the management of the microcredit is

made through the standard institutional software and the customized one is intended to provide reporting and monitoring facilities to the MFI. In the third model, found only in the smallest MFIs linked to the traditional banking system, there is no specific software. Reporting is made through spreadsheet applications and software management of microcredits is like that of any ordinary loan.

Considering all data presented together, we must conclude that the technical infrastructure and basic computerization of the Spanish microfinance sector is satisfactory. All staff are able to make use of computers with high-speed Internet access and software to perform their daily chores.

The MFIs' technological status can also be favorably compared with that of average Spanish enterprises' IT levels. Only taking into account employees to specifically support the microcredit programs, all Spanish MFIs will be considered micro-enterprises (see footnote 2), most of them having between 2 and 5 members of staff[11]. Of course, microcredit programs linked to savings banks cannot be considered independent organizations on their own, and all Spanish savings banks are large enterprises. Their "Obra Social", often independently administered through Social Foundations, should nonetheless fall into the small business category. In any case, the fact that computers with internet access and ample software are extensively used puts the microfinance sector in an advantageous position with respect to the average Spanish firm, both considering micro- and small enterprises. Furthermore, the IT level of the sector in terms of internal management software is similar to that of the traditional Spanish banking industry, since standard banking software applications are available in 80% of the MFIs considered.

Intensity of e-communication has also been reported by Spanish MFIs. Two different variables have been considered to measure such intensity. First, the adoption of the Internet by the sector as a user or consumer of several services has been appraised. Second, data regarding specific uses of e-mail, mobile phones and intranet or internal websites is also analyzed.

As a consumer of Internet services, the search for information, and the use of banking and financial services (wherever applicable), are widely reported by all MFIs. There is no distinction between MFIs and the average Spanish firm concerning other internet uses, such as training and education or purchasing e-services and products.

E-mail uses concerning the microcredit program include both incoming mail from would-be entrepreneurs asking for information about the program, and outgoing e-mails to monitor current clients (to answer occasional questions, to make appointments, etc.). According to the information provided, all MFIs have an e-mail address available for enquires. However, the actual number of incoming e-mails is not very large in any case. In fact their frequency is qualified as "low" in two thirds of the MFIs, while for the remaining, it is considered "infrequent" to receive such e-mail inquiries. It has to be pointed out than some MFIs report increments of e-enquiries of approximately 20% in recent years.

Use of e-mail to contact the program's clients is also present in all MFIs. Frequencies have unfortunately not been reported, although they are considered part of the corporate policy of all organizations. A similar statement can be applied to the use of mobile phones, reported in all but one MFI, probably due to the high costs associated with their use as standard communication devices. Finally, the use of intranets to communicate with clients is only mentioned by two organizations.

All in all, we must again stress that the use of e-communication media in the microfinance sector is clearly higher than average in the Spanish entourage. If fact, its level (if not its intensity of use) is comparable to the IT use made by large Spanish firms, both considering microcredit programs linked to savings banks and most relevantly those belonging to the social economy.

Let us now turn our attention to the websites that are maintained by the microfinance sector. Websites appear to be the main IT instrument used by MFIs to diffuse information about their programs, with only one notable exception: one of the programs offered by a savings banks (*Caixa Taragona*) does not have any kind of presence in its institutional website. In the following paragraphs, therefore, all sentences and conclusions must be interpreted in the context of *all but one* MFI.

Pre-eminence of this IT-vehicle is also confirmed by the fact that almost all microcredit programs that started their activities from 2001 on have simultaneously included at least one page in their website publicizing the program. Quite understandably, the corporate websites of the pioneer social economy MFIs were established some years after the introduction of their respective microcredit programs: ASCA's in 1998, COOP57's in 2001 and FIDEM's in 2003.

Figure 3 summarizes the main characteristics of the websites analyzed. Five different topics constitute the basis of our study. Since the microcredit program is not the only service offered by the organizations analyzed, a first group of items refer to the web surfing facilities to search for information about the program. A second is related to the contact information provided on the "home page" of the microcredit program, if available. The third analyzes the descriptive information that can be found in the microcredit program's web pages, including a general description the microcredit concept, the financial conditions for loans and the program's requirements for being granted a micro-loan. Application facilities found in the website constitute the fourth item considered, and the types of reporting information encountered in electronic format are the fifth and last.

A first conclusion that can be drawn from our study is that in general microcredit programs are not easy to find in corporate websites. In fact, only the social economy MFIs and MicroBank have their microcredit programs in a relevant position within their corporate websites. Trying to find the

Figure 3. Main characteristics of Macro-credit programs' websites

		ASCA	COOP57	FIDEM	FUSM	Caja Granada	BBK	Caixa Galicia	Caja España	C.Tarragona	Caixa Sabadell	CajaSOL	CAM	Micro Bank	ICO (+)
INTERACTIVITY — Surfing Facilities	Access to the microcredit program's home page	direct	direct	direct	indirect	direct	direct	indirect	indirect	no access	direct	indirect	indirect	direct	indirect
	Easiness of surf	M	H	H	H	L/M	M	H	M	-	M	L	M	H	M
	Level of content structure	M	M/H	M	M	M	L	H	H	-	M	M	M	H	M
	Site map	no	no	no	yes	yes	yes	yes	yes	yes	yes	yes	yes	no	yes
	Searching facilities	no	H	L	H	L	L	L	H	yes	H	L	no	H	H
Contact Information	Telephone number	yes	yes	yes	yes	yes	yes	yes	*	-	yes	no	no	no	yes
	E-mail address	yes	yes	yes	yes	yes	*	yes	*	-	yes	yes	yes	no	no
	Postal address	no	yes	yes	*	yes	yes	yes	*	-	yes	yes	no	yes	yes
	Support associations information	-	-	yes	yes	yes	no	yes	yes	-	no	no	yes	yes	yes
WEB CONTENT — Descriptive Information	General information	yes	yes	yes	yes	yes	yes	yes	yes	-	yes	yes	yes	yes	yes
	Financial conditions	yes	yes	yes	yes	yes	no	yes	yes	-	yes	yes	yes	no detail	no
	Entry requirements	yes	yes	yes	yes	yes	no	yes	yes	-	yes	yes	yes	no	yes
	Background information	no	no	no	yes	no	no	yes	no	-	no	no	no	no	no
	FAQs	no	yes	no	no	no	no	yes	no	-	no	no	no	no	yes
Application Facilities	Applications forms	no	e-form	word	no	excel	no	pdf	pdf	-	no	no	no	no	no
	Business Plan guiding information	no	no	word	no	excel	no	e-form	pdf	-	no	no	no	no	no
	Links & Contacts to elaborate Business Plan	no	no	no	no	yes	no	yes	no	-	no	no	yes	no	no
Reporting	Statistical Information	H	H	L	M (ar)	H (ar)	M (ar)	M (ar)	no	M (ar)	no	M (ar)	M (ar)	M (ar)	L (ar)
	Financial Information	yes	yes	no	(ar)	(ar)	(ar)	(ar)	no	(ar)	no	no	(ar)	no	(ar)
	Social Information	yes	yes	yes	yes	yes	yes	yes	no	yes	no	yes	yes	yes	(ar)

Legends: H (high); M (medium); L (low); (ar): found in the organization's Annual report; * found only in the home page of the corporate Web site (+) as in the end of 2008

microcredit program's home page either using the internal website engine or through direct surfing within the website can also be hard (see Figure 3 for the coded levels of difficulty). Finally, it must be said that most of the websites fit basic requirements with respect to content structure once the appropriate home page has been found.

The electronic contact facilities supplied are found to be neither specific nor widely publicized on the microcredit program's pages. On the contrary, almost all websites do provide information and contact details about nonprofit associations or other support organizations able to help would-be entrepreneurs, particularly in the design of their business plans.

Information on microcredit programs provided on the corporate websites has also been analyzed. Most webs contain relatively detailed general information about the program, entry requirements and also financial conditions for loans. Strikingly, the ICO's public program is one of the few where accurate information about financial conditions is not provided, even though this was done in previous editions (Estapé-Dubreuil & Torreguitart-Mirada, 2008). All in all, less specific information about the program is usually also correlated to poor performance in other characteristics, such as web content structure or contact details.

Comparatively, MFIs from the social economy are far more active in providing on-line facilities to their would-be clients. Electronic application forms or files with detailed information on business plans elaboration are maintained on their websites. The public sector microcredit program had none of these facilities, even though some sectors of the Spanish public administration are leaders in the field of on-line interaction. The same has to be said about the vast majority of microcredit programs in the savings banks group. Exceptions must nevertheless be signaled, two very active organizations having made recent changes to introduce useful e-forms on their websites[12]. Given the variety of free on-line software available to design and present a business plan, not to mention the relative ease to design an e-form, the scarcity of their presence on the MFIs websites is notable.

A final item of special interest about the MFIs' corporate websites is their use to disclose reports about their microcredit programs. Detailed financial statements or reports on portfolio quality, based on world-wide recommended standards (for example CGAP, 2003), are not found in the Spanish microcredit sector. Nevertheless, several levels of external reporting must be taken into account. Statistical data concerning several

characteristics of micro-loan clients, such as age, geographical origin, economic sector of their business, etc, constitute a first level of disclosure. A deeper one is related to the financial information provided, considering not only general annual financial statements, but specific information on their microcredit programs (disbursed amounts, etc.). Reporting of social aspects of their microfinance activities, such as illustrative examples and descriptions of successful clients' histories, is considered a complementary level of disclosure.

Reporting levels on the MFIs linked to savings banks are relatively similar and not very extensive. Furthermore, when provided, the disclosure of financial information on the internet is made only indirectly through the organization's annual social report, which is not linked to the microcredit program's home page. It is usually a wide report in which only fragmented information on a given program is available, more likely in statistical format. Disclosure of social information is encountered more often, including access to videos. However, the social economy MFIs do provide comparatively more statistical and financial information about their microcredit programs and do so in a more detailed and comprehensive way than those linked to the traditional banking system do (see Figure 3).

A final point regarding corporate websites must be made. As was the case with basic technical infrastructure, the presence of websites within the microfinance sector is far superior to the average within micro-businesses in Spain (30% considering firms with more than three people employed, see background section). Nevertheless, facilities provided by the websites are similar, a corporate presentation of the firm being encountered in virtually all cases. Only 20% of the firms' websites provide other more sophisticated services (Red. es, 2007), a percentage similar to the equivalent e-forms and other software encountered in the microfinance sector.

Impact of IT Use in the Management of MFIs

The section will focus on IT use both for internal management and for relationships with the MFIs' clients. Regarding internal management, aspects related to the management of applications are outlined. Other activities in which IT use for internal management is reported are also discussed.

E-applications are not of standardized use in the Spanish microfinance sector, as is to be expected given the few on-line facilities encountered in the MFIs corporate websites. Half of the MFIs require instead standard paper forms that have to be physically submitted; while for the other half on-line forms are also admitted. For social economy organizations, the proportions are slightly favorable to electronic forms. On average, nonetheless, the number of e-forms is considerably lower compared to those applications submitted in paper. Approximately the same rule applies to the additional documentation required (business plans, letters of introduction, etc.). Digital documentation is nonetheless admitted in almost all organizations, in some cases transmitted only via e-mail.

Concerning the application evaluation process, social economy MFIs have no pre-fixed electronic system to be followed; both paper and digital forms are currently used for evaluation purposes in all cases. In the case of savings banks' microcredit programs, it should be noted that a great deal of the application and evaluation process is handled by their network of support entities. When those associations are in charge of the entire evaluation process, the MFI usually only accepts digital information concerning the applications, transmitted either by e-mail or through their intranet. Otherwise, both digital evaluation forms and paper ones are admitted.

The use of IT as an enabler in the internal management of MFIs is our next analyzed parameter. Certainly, all MFIs are able to accurately control their clients' loan repayments, mostly through the specific banking software reported. Efficiency of data management for other purposes, nevertheless, is contingent on the software model adopted by the MFI. In particular, the elaboration of internal and external reports is reported to require the use of additional software (e.g. spreadsheets) in most MFIs. This is the result of the general banking orientation of the software used, instead of more specific microfinance software products (CGAP, 2009). It has to be said that the trade-off between the cost of purchasing or customizing software with enough report facilities and the cost of semi-manual reporting is contingent on the size of the MFI's client portfolio. Cost issues in this case seem to favor the adoption of the latter strategy in all MFIs studied. Furthermore, the well acknowledged role played by IT in the minimization of transaction costs is regarded here to be a secondary issue, mostly due to the role of voluntary labor within Spanish MFIs.

Some remarks regarding the degree of technological relationship established between MFIs and their clients during the repayment period will conclude the section. As in previous items, differences relating to the type of MFI considered must be put forward. Since the application and evaluation process is usually not made directly by employees in charge of the microcredit programs linked to savings banks, a low level of relationship is found. Typically it is limited to practical aspects related to the management of the loan (notification of loan-repayment dates, loan fees, admission of deferred payments if applicable, etc.). In all cases, IT communication media are used (mobile phones, e-mail), especially Short Message Service (SMS) technologies and e-mails to send messages. IT use for client support in social economy MFIs is also usually very limited, but for different reasons. The explanation here is linked to the higher degree of personal contact (interviews, etc.) occurring during the assessment process, which is maintained during the repayment period, in some cases through a specific accompanying off-line program.

Strategic Issues

From the above discussion it is clear that all organizations in the Spanish microfinance sector have enough capacity, in terms of IT hardware and software, to be able to use them for strategic purposes. Such levels are especially remarkable in social economy organizations, being themselves micro-enterprises. In the last five or six years we have seen a major change in their administrative dealings, nowadays being almost fully computer-based procedures. LAN is also present in all organizations, enabling them to share electronic information with all computers in the office. Spanish authorities consider both LAN and high-speed broadband internet access to be an indication of potential competitive advantage within micro-businesses (Red.es, 2007). Whether these changes are at least induced by the presence of other MFIs in the sector is unknown, but the fact is that they have adapted well to the new situation, a sign in itself of successful strategic use of IT.

Maintaining a corporate website *per se* does not have any strategic meaning, but its content may be the result of a strategic outcome. In that sense, the comparative high level attained by the websites of some MFIs must be signaled. One of them has held from the outset a prominent position within the savings banks association in promoting microcredit programs. A website with useful and successful instruments to support micro-entrepreneurship should therefore constitute a strategically competitive advantage.

The specific aspects of external reporting that each MFI chooses to disclose in its website also have a strategic significance, linked to their corporate communication strategies. Disclosure of social aspects, including the high visual impact of videos telling stories about successful clients, plays a major role in the websites of MFIs linked to savings banks. The central aim, nevertheless, is to publicize their investments in social issues as a form of differentiation between savings banks and other commercial banks. Financial details

concerning such investments seem accordingly less relevant. As a consequence, financial reporting is usually not emphasized.

Strategic reasons linked to management transparency objectives should be considered in social economy MFIs, since IT enables the attainment of a very high level of diffusion at a relatively low cost. Coop57's website is used to publish a biannual electronic gazette with detailed financial information, including particulars of every project that has been granted a loan. Website use to publicly give account of MFI funds management should therefore be considered strategic; particularly considering that solidarity banks' fund-raising depends on the prospective collaboration of new members. IT potential to communicate with stakeholders and other donors through electronic networks has also started to be acknowledged by other social economy MFIs. Recent changes made to their websites are a clear indication in that sense. The detailed quarterly report made by ASCA in its website since mid 2008, complementing its annual printed report, is one instance of such changes.

Answers related to MFIs' plans for future IT development, our final enquiry in the field questionnaire, may also give hints related to their strategic view of IT. According to them, MFIs linked to savings banks do not seem to have planned further significant changes either to their IT infrastructure or IT services offered in their microcredit programs. Undoubtedly, being part of the traditional financial system, an industry leader in Spain in technological innovation, is a reason for that. In fact, the few IT changes reported (for example introduction of a Service-Oriented Architecture) have a more general scope than the microcredit program itself.

Within social economy MFIs, positions are again somewhat different, most likely because of their more modest dimension. Here, answers denote a much higher degree of concern for technological innovation. Strategic changes such as substantial improvements to the facilities provided by the corporate website, or structural changes in the electronic internal management of the organization are mentioned.

Nonetheless, neither IT-experts in permanent positions nor regular IT-consultancy have been reported. IT decisions are usually made by the executive board, especially in social economy MFIs, or transferred to the savings bank IT-experts. Although the small size of most MFIs must surely be considered, it is also a sign of low strategic concern regarding IT-investments.

FUTURE RESEARCH DIRECTIONS

Several different research directions arise directly from the present study. Among them, we shall mention one related to depth, a second linked to geographical scope and a third to time. Greater levels of depth in the understanding of the role played by IT in the Spanish microfinance sector can be attained through a more detailed study of nonprofit organizations linked to the MFIs. Both strategic IT use and their e-links with would-be entrepreneurs should be considered. Of special interest is seeing whether IT knowledge on the part of nonprofit organizations is actually "passed on" to the micro-entrepreneurs, thus enhancing IT strategic uses in their micro-business. In-depth insight of the question of whether the efficiency of MFIs in Spain is enhanced by the use of IT can also be obtained using a more quantitative approach, considering both financial and social performance.

As an alternative view, taking a broader approach, a comparative study of IT use by microfinance industries on a European level should also be of interest. Finally, given the short tradition of the microfinance sector in Spain as a whole, a temporal analysis could also be relevant. Identification of links between further technological developments, their intensity of IT use and strategic outputs could be of benefit for the sector.

CONCLUSION

The present chapter enables us to draw conclusions on three different and complementary levels. The first is related to the observed use of Information Technologies in the Spanish microfinance sector, whereas the second refers to their reported strategic use. We will finish with some considerations of the current depth of outreach of the microfinance sector related to IT use by micro-entrepreneurs.

The Spanish microfinance sector's basic technical infrastructure is above the Spanish average, both taking into account economic sector and firm size. Likewise, their use of Internet, website content and facilities is at least significant. We have identified two different goals related to actual IT use. Information Technologies have indeed been used as a tool to provide information, both to prospective clients and with a more general scope. Furthermore, improvements on management due to IT use have also been encountered. We have identified several instances at this level, among them on-line direct support to would-be entrepreneurs through specific software.

Strategic use of IT is more clearly shown by social economy MFIs. Its use as a financial transparency tool, as well as publicly account offing for the MFI fund management must be emphasized. Furthermore, its potential use to increment fund-raising has been increasingly recognized. Likewise, their effort in the improvement both of IT infrastructure and internal use of software has a clear strategic component, centered on better reaching and serving their potential clients.

For MFIs in the traditional banking system, strategic issues are instead most probably linked to their social strategy in general. The diverse extension and accuracy of information of their microcredit program web pages, or the encountered differences in the software used for internal management, are a clear expression of the relative relevance of each program.

Concerning the Spanish microfinance sector's depth of outreach, it must be considered that there is currently a technological gap between MFIs and their intended clients. Among other reasons, limited capacity to access the Internet, shown both on household and micro-enterprises levels, must be put forward. As a consequence, the diffusion of microcredit programs based exclusively on IT would have the side effect of low outreach to their target population, who most likely do not have internet access or skills.

Once an individual or group has become an MFI client, however, Information Technologies should be considered a facilitating factor of strategic changes in the micro-enterprises thus created. The promotion of IT among MFI clients through IT monitoring will therefore help them to overcome likely short-term competitive disadvantages. It would also be advisable to promote (free) software intended for the internal management of firms. Encouragement of IT use must not, however, deter personal relationship, which is especially advisable with marginalized clients who constitute a sizable majority of Spanish MFI clients.

All in all, our results indicate that more effort has been made to diffuse microcredit programs than in the IT-support division. Of course diffusion has lower costs, since IT management would need the development of specific software. To their credit, all the same, most microcredit programs are "young" in their experience, most likely still at a developmental stage in which IT enhancement will play a predominant role.

REFERENCES

Attali, J. (2000). A Market Solution to Poverty: Microfinance and the Internet. *New Perspectives Quarterly*, *17*(1), 31–33. doi:10.1111/0893-7850.00235

Beck, T., Demirgüç-Kunt, A. & Honohan, P. (2009). Access to Financial Services: Measurement, Impact, and Policies. *The World Bank Research Observer*, forthcoming (advance published February 27, 2009).

Bharadwaj, A. S. (2000). A Resource-Based Perspective on Information Technology Capability and Firm Performance: An Empirical Investigation. *Management Information Systems Quarterly*, *24*(1), 169–196. doi:10.2307/3250983

Bhatt, N., & Tang, S.-Y. (2001). Designing group-based microfinance programs: some theoretical and policy considerations. *International Journal of Public Administration*, *24*(10), 1103. doi:10.1081/PAD-100105104

Burt, E., & Taylor, J. A. (2000). Information and Communication Technologies. Reshaping Voluntary Organizations? *Nonprofit Management & Leadership*, *11*(2), 131–143. doi:10.1002/nml.11201

Burt, E., & Taylor, J. A. (2003). New Technologies, Embedded Values, and Strategic Change: Evidence from the U.K. Voluntary Sector. *Nonprofit and Voluntary Sector Quarterly*, *32*(1), 115–127. doi:10.1177/0899764002250009

Castells, M. (2000). *The rise of the network society*. Oxford, UK: Basil Blackwell publishing.

Cecchinni, S., & Scott, C. (2003). Can information and communication technology applications contribute to reduce poverty? Lessons from rural India. *Information Technology for Development*, *10*(1), 73–84. doi:10.1002/itdj.1590100203

CGAP. (2003). *Disclosure Guidelines for Financial Reporting by Microfinance Institutions. Microfinance Consensus Guidelines*, published by CGAP/The World Bank Group, available at www.cgap.org.

CGAP. (2009). Information systems: Software Listings and Reviews. Retrieved July 10, 2009, from http://www.cgap.org/p/site/c/template.rc/1.11.103251/1.26.3104/.

Claessens, S. (2006). Access to Financial Services: A Review of the Issues and Public Policy Objectives. [from http://ec.europa.eu/enterprise/enterprise_policy/sme_definition/index_en.htm]. *The World Bank Research Observer, 21*(2), 207–240. Retrieved March 15, 2009. doi:10.1093/wbro/lkl004

Conlin, M. (1999). Peer group micro-lending programs in Canada and the United States. *Journal of Development Economics, 60*(1), 249–269. doi:10.1016/S0304-3878(99)00043-7

Creswell, J. N. (2003). *Research Design: Qualitative, Quantitative, and Mixed Methods Approaches* (2nd ed.). Thousand Oaks, CA: Sage Publications Ltd.

Dewett, T., & Jones, G. R. (2001). The role of information technology in the organization: a review, model, and assessment. *Journal of Management, 27*, 313–346. doi:10.1016/S0149-2063(01)00094-0

DIRCE. (2008). Corporate Structure and Demography. Central Companies Directory at 1 January 2008. *Instituto Nacional de Estadística.* Retrieved March 18, 2009, from http://www.ine.es/en/inebmenu/mnu_empresas_en.htm.

Eliot, B., Katsioloudes, M., & Weldon, R. (1998). Nonprofit Organizations and the Internet. *Nonprofit Management & Leadership, 8*(3), 297–303. doi:10.1002/nml.8308

Estapé-Dubreuil, G., & Torreguitart-Mirada, C. (2008, September). *An analysis of the public initiatives to support self-employment business activities of the less favoured: Is there a public policy to support the micro-credit sector in developed countries? The case of Catalonia and Spain.* Paper presented at the European Network on Industrial Policy International Conference, San Sebastián, Spain

Estapé-Dubreuil, G. & Torreguitart-Mirada, C. (2009). L'esperit emprenedor i el microcrèdit: deuanys de microcrèdit a Catalunya (1998-2007). *Revista econòmica de Catalunya, 52* (forthcoming)

European Commission (2003). Commission Recommendation of 6 May 2003 concerning the definition of micro, small and medium-sized enterprises, 2003/316/EC. *Official Journal of the European Union 20.5.2003.*

European Commission (2007). *The Regulation of Microcredit in Europe.* Expert Group Report.

European Commission Report. (2003). *Microcredit for small business and business creation: Bridging a market gap.* Enterprise Directorate General of the European Commission.

Finn, S., Maher, J. K., & Forster, J. (2006). Indicators of Information and Communication Technology Adoption in the Nonprofit Sector. Changes Between 2000 and 2004. *Nonprofit Management & Leadership, 16*(3), 277–295. doi:10.1002/nml.107

Flick, U. (2006). *An introduction to qualitative research* (3rd ed.). Thousand Oaks, CA: Sage Publications Ltd.

Ghatak, M., & Guinnane, T. W. (1999). The economics of lending with joint liability: theory and practice. *Journal of Development Economics, 60*(1), 195–228. doi:10.1016/S0304-3878(99)00041-3

Gordon, L. (1998). Tech Wise: Nonprofits Join the Revolution. *Nonprofit World, 16*(5), 37–41.

Guichandut, P. (2006). Europe occidentale et reste du monde: parle-t-on des mêmes pratiques?, *Finance & The Common Good / Bien Commun, 25*(3), 54-113.

Gutiérrez-Nieto, B., Fuertes-Callén, Y., & Serrano-Cinca, C. (2008). Internet reporting in microfinance institutions. *Online Information Review, 32*(3), 417–436. doi:10.1108/14684520810889709

Hackler, D., & Saxton, G. D. (2007). The Strategic Use of Information Technology by Nonprofit Organizations: Increasing Capacity and Untapped Potential. *Public Administration Review*, *67*(3), 474–487. doi:10.1111/j.1540-6210.2007.00730.x

IRIA. (2008). Informe IRIA 2008. *Consejo Superior de Administración Electrónica. Ministerio de Administraciones Públicas*. Retrieved March 15, 2009, from http://www.csi.map.es/csi/iria_2008/

Jain, S., & Mansuri, G. (2003). A little at a time: the use of regularly scheduled repayments in microfinance programs. *Journal of Development Economics*, *72*(1), 253–279. doi:10.1016/S0304-3878(03)00076-2

Lee, S. M., Kim, J., Choi, Y., & Lee, S.-G. (2009). Effects of IT knowledge and media selection on operational performance of small firms. *Small Business Economics*, *32*(3), 214–257. doi:10.1007/s11187-007-9095-5

McLoughlin, I. (1999). *The shaping of Technology and Organizations*. New York: Routledge. doi:10.4324/9780203019870

Moore, M. (2000). Managing for Value: Organizational Strategy in For-Profit, Nonprofit, and Governmental Organizations. *Nonprofit and Voluntary Sector Quarterly*, *29*(1), 183–208. doi:10.1177/089976400773746391

Morduch, J. (1999). The Microfinance Promise. *Journal of Economic Literature*, *37*, 993–1006.

ONTSI. (2008). The Network Society in Spain-Annual Report 2007. *Spanish Observatory for Telecommunications and Information Society. Ministerio de Industria, Turismo y Comercio*. Retrieved February 25, 2009, from http://observatorio.red.es/annual-reports/articles/1449.

PYME. (2007). Informe sobre la PYME. Colección Panorama PYME, 12. *Dirección General de Política de la Pequeña y Mediana Empresa. Ministerio de Industria, Turismo y Comercio*. Retrieved March 21, 2009, from http://www.ipyme.org/IPYME/es- ES/QuienesSomos/Publicaciones2.

Ragowsky, A., & Gefen, D. (2008). What Makes the Competitive Contribution of ERP Strategic. *The Data Base for Advances in Information Systems*, *39*(2), 33–49.

Red.es. (2007). Tecnologías de la Información y las Comunicaciones en la microempresa española. Análisis por sector de actividad y Comunidad Autónoma. *Observatorio de las Telecomunicaciones y de la Sociedad de la Información. Ministerio de Industria, Turismo y Comercio*. Retrieved March 2, 2009, from http://observatorio.red.es/empresas/articles/id/422/

Saidel, J. R., & Cour, S. (2003). Information Technology and the Voluntary Sector Workplace. *Nonprofit and Voluntary Sector Quarterly*, *32*(1), 5–24. doi:10.1177/0899764002250004

Smith, J. (1999). Information Technology in the small business: Establishing the basis for a management information system. *Journal of Small Business and Enterprise Development*, *6*(4), 326–340, 400. doi:10.1108/EUM0000000006684

ENDNOTES

[1] Statistical series title is "Encuesta de uso de TIC y comercio electrónico en las empresas". It has been available at the official INE website, http://www.ine.es/inebmenu/mnu_tic.htm#1, since 2002.

[2] In using the term "micro-business" we are following the actual standard use in the European Union (European Commission, 2003). While staff numbers are central to the definition of the size of an enterprise, finan-

cial criteria concerning annual turnover and balance sheet totals are also used "in order to grasp the real scale and performance of an enterprise" (p.36). Nevertheless, only the first criterion is mentioned in the reported information on IT use in enterprises.

3   There is one notable exception to this rule, the microcredit program sponsored by one savings bank, La Caixa. As a consequence, it is also the case for FIDEM, since its funds are in fact linked to the former microcredit program. Fees are nevertheless somewhat dissimilar, see Figure 1, following special agreements signed between Fidem and La Caixa as a provider of its funds.

4   A few MFIs have a wide offer, including microcredits to cover "special needs", unforeseen financial problems or others related to vital needs (repayment of debts in loaner's country of origin, tenancy deposits, health care payments, etc.). Both ASCA and the savings banks of the Basque country (Bilbao Bizkaia Kutxa, Gipuzkoa Donostia Kutxa, Vital Kutxa) offer these on a regular basis. MicroBank has also recently added it to its offer.

5   Unfortunately, data related to portfolio growth or portfolio quality could not be included in Figure 1, due to the reporting policy of most MFIs, which do not include such data in their annual reports. See nevertheless some data elaborated on an aggregate Catalan level in Estapé-Dubreuil & Torreguitart-Mirada (2009).

6   *La Caixa*, with its headquarters in Barcelona, is currently the leading savings bank in Spain and the third largest financial entity in the country (http://portal.lacaixa.es/infocorporativa/bienvenido_en.html, accessed March 10, 2009). It initiated a microcredit program with FIDEM at the end of 2000, which was rapidly extended to collaboration with other nonprofit organizations in Catalonia, and in Spain years after. In 2007 one of its satellite

banks was re-defined to make it an MFI, and named it MicroBank. MicroBank does not have specific branches, operating through the regular branches of *La Caixa* instead, and remains linked to its Obra Social.

7   Other Spanish savings banks have also recently established a microcredit program. *Vital Kutxa* in the Basque County, *Caja Segovia* in Castile-León and *La Caja de Canarias* in the Canary Islands have some information on their respective websites about their microcredit programs.

8   In fact, the ICO's microcredit program had a double network. The second consisted of commercial and savings banks charged with further study of the economic viability of a project and in due course provision of financial services to its promoters. From 2005 on, the network of nonprofit organizations has been disregarded, leaving the whole assessment process to the agreed traditional banks.

9   To our knowledge, there has been no official communication that the ICO dropped its microcredit line, but there is no further mention of it on its website, where there was before. Some comments have been made on the Internet, one of which is available at the Internet address http://noticiasemprendedores.blogspot.com/2009/02/donde-esta-la-linea-ico-microcreditos.html (accessed February 24, 2009). Titled "Where is the ICO microcredit line?" it cites official sources of ICO in saying that the microcredit program will not be available during 2009, and that no date has been announced for its relaunch.

10   Official questionnaires can be found in Spanish at INE's website www.ine.es/metodologia/t09/eticce1_06.pdf. We have also used the bilingual version used in Catalonia, provided by the *Institut d'Estadística de Catalunya*, ww.fobsic.net/opencms/export/sites/fobsic_site/ca/Documentos/TIC_Empreses/2006_2007_TIC_Empreses/

ETICCE1-EC-06.pdf (accessed February 27, 2009).

[11] It should nevertheless be pointed out that voluntary staff also have a role in most Spanish MFIs. For example, ASCA reports a total number of 23 regular voluntary collaborators, but had difficulty translating their total work load into a full-time equivalent. This is also the case for all microcredit programs linked to savings banks, due to the number of (voluntary) people collaborating in their affiliated support organizations.

[12] As shown in Figure 3, a third MFI does provide a detailed application form including the business plan to be presented. However, the closed PDF format prevents users from directly filling it in on a desktop, thus undermining its real utility.

Chapter 18
Portal to Portaloo:
Can Microfinance and IT Help Solve the World's Sanitation Crisis?

Jack Sim
World Toilet Organization, Singapore

Karl Dayson
University of Salford, UK

ABSTRACT

2.5 billion people do not have access to a toilet; instead they have no choice but to practice open defecation, having a potentially detrimental effect on their health. The chapter asks whether microfinance and IT can play a role in tackling the problem. Drawing on the experience of Grameen Telephone it is argued that this is analogous with attempts to promote the purchase of toilets, in particular the technological leap where expensive infrastructure is bypassed. Drawing on three case studies we show that such a process is underway and while there are a limited number of microfinance institutions (MFIs) engaged in this market it is insufficient to address the myriad of both organizational and cultural problems. However, the use of a prospective web portal may help create the environment for a viable market to emerge.

INTRODUCTION

While most of the preceding chapters discuss how IT is being used to improve the efficiency and efficacy of microfinance services the real challenge is whether IT and microfinance can be used to transform major social issues. This chapter deals with one such issue: sanitation and the use of toilets. There's probably nothing bigger than the sanitation crisis. According to the 2006 United Nations Human Development Report 2.5 billion

people do not have a toilet, representing 40 percent of the world's population with no access to proper sanitation. For most of us in the developed world the toilet is a convenience, a necessity, and a basic right; and when nature calls, our biggest worry is whether or not we will encounter an unpleasant stench or a lack of toilet paper. But for 2.5 billion people the call of nature becomes a threat to dignity, safety, income, and health. But what role can microfinance and IT play? We will argue that it is analogous with mobile phone technology which has found a market in the developing world, in particular in Bangladesh where Grameen

DOI: 10.4018/978-1-61520-993-4.ch018

Bank have used microfinance to sell these new products. Furthermore, through the use of three case studies and examples of microfinance providers engaged in this area we will highlight the elements preventing the establishment of a viable market, ultimately suggesting that an interactive web portal along with MFIs committed to social objectives could play a crucial role.

As many microfinance initiatives evolved from development NGOs there has always been a commitment to improvements in health. From the work of Freedom from Hunger to the social impact work of CGAP there is extensive evidence of microfinance interventions improving the health of service users (Littlefield et al 2003, Dunford et al 2007). There are numerous studies that indicate households of microfinance users have better health and nutrition, particularly in relation to breastfeeding (Khandker 2005, MKNelly & Dunford 1999, MkNelly & Dunford 1998, Barnes et al 2001, Chowdhury & Bhuiya 2001). Collectively there is significant evidence that microfinance contributes to the United Nations' Millennium Development Goals (Simonwitz 2002). However Littlefield et al's (2003) bibliographic summary of microfinance social impact confirmed that they had not found any studies showing a connection between microfinance and sanitation, though some programs did offer loans for toilets. They noted that partnership between private sanitation infrastructure providers and MFIs was a 'promising option' for exploration. It is a topic that will be explored later in the chapter, but first it is necessary to understand why there is still a problem.

BACKGROUND: OPEN DEFECATION—SCOURGE OF THE POOR

In 'Clean: a history of personal hygiene and purity' (2008) Virginia Smith details the evolution of cleanliness from the Neolithic period. However, though the book is a social and cultural history

Smith reminds readers that human waste is a chemical reaction:

"..the kidneys filter the blood and keep the cellular water pool clean, excreting the waste products as urine. By the time the food reaches the colon whatever remains is surplus to requirements, and ready to be rejected via the bowels through the anus. Human excreta or dung consists mostly of water dead bacteria, and cells, indigestible matter, and various gases and chemicals, such as bilirubin, which is made when the body takes old cells apart – bilirubin is a brown color" (p11)

It is one thing accepting that the body excretes 'toxins' and 'poisons' (Smith 2008), quite another to change behaviour, or indeed increase supply of loos. Yet in most societies there is cultural avoidance of human waste, thus those involved in working with this material invariably have a low social status (McLaughlin 1971, George 2008, Smith 2008). It would seem that our responses to human waste are both a product of nature and nurture. Elias describes the latter as a civilizing process in which habits of cleanliness are first imposed from without before being internalized through self-compulsion. That's not to say it cannot retrench, as during the seventeenth century when hygiene declined due the legitimate fear of water borne diseases, reducing the use of public bathhouses. (2000[1939]: 520, n.128).

Today in the developed world it is assumed that households have access to their own toilet, but the assumption that going to the toilet is a private affair is disputed by evidence from classical Rome where public and communal latrines were the norm. Gradually over the following centuries there was a separation of space that led to toilet usage being conducted away from other human activities. First, in an external building but, ultimately in a specific room within the home linked to a highly sophisticated technology – a sewage system (Smith 2008). This is not the experience in the developing world where there is a preponderance of open defecation—that is, answering the call of nature behind a bush or in any other open area, where they can minimize the likelihood of prying eyes.

Open defecation attracts flies, spreads pathogens, and contaminates water used for drinking, washing and bathing. The health statistics are stark: poor sanitation, hygiene, and water supply lead to diarrheal diseases that cause 1.8 million deaths a year, of which ninety percent are children under the age of five (UNDP Report 2006). What's more, up to 400 million school children suffer intestinal worms that rob them of their nutrition, worms that often propagate through fecal contamination. In total diarrhea kills more children under five than HIV, malaria and tuberculosis (George 2008).

Beyond the staggering health costs, a lack of sanitation takes a high toll on the comfort and dignity of the people who have so little to begin with. Open defecation is a humiliating and dangerous experience, especially for women, who as they undress and relieve themselves have to suffer the gaze of men. In fact, access to the privacy of toilets has been shown to be a big determinant of school attendance, particularly for young girls during puberty (Rukunga et al, undated).

All this ill health has an economic cost. Those with access to toilets have fewer days off work and use health services less. According to Hutton et al (2007) every dollar spent on sanitation brings $5-12 of economic benefit in the developing world (an average of $9). Globally universal sanitation would cost $95 billion but save $660 billion. (George 2008). The UN has set its Millennium Development Goal (MDG) for water to halve the global proportion of people without access to improved sanitation by 2015. The cost of not meeting this goal is estimated to be US$38 billion a year, with sanitation accounting for 92% of this (Frost 2007, Hutton et al 2007). This comes from money spent on health care, reduced productivity, and premature death, as well as environmental degradation and social impact.

Clearly poor housing and availability of land are serious barriers to the construction of more toilets. In addition, there are cultural barriers around sanitation that have long been recognized by anthropologists in which available provision 'affords a set of markers within a temporal and spatial frame' (Douglas & Isherwood 1996). Thus social as well as accessibility factors matter and while land reform is a long term objective, addressing the cultural issues can be perceived as the more pragmatic response. This is probably most pronounced in India where religious ritual and caste system influences the treatment of waste (Khare 1962, George 2008). Paul (1958) describes the social gatherings of women in India linked to going to the toilet in open fields and the difficulty of changing culturally embedded habits, not least because there was only limited understanding of '*connection between faeces and enteric diseases*' (p1504). More contemporary sources found that Baigas women were reluctant to wash their hands after defecation believing it was harmful (Dwivedi & Sharma 2007). These examples from just one nation demonstrate the cultural challenges faced by those wanting to encourage toilet usage.

A MARKETPLACE-BASED SOLUTION

Given the health imperatives attached to the provision of toilets it should be possible to create a market. At the current rate of progress the world will miss its Millennium Development Goal commitment for improved sanitation by over half-a-billion people (UN 2008). That is due in part to the fact that donors have traditionally thought that top-down, supply-driven toilet construction programs and a focus on technical solutions would produce healthy people who used, maintained, and enjoyed proper sanitation. But that has not been the case (WEDC, undated). In fact, without training and sensitization, many poor people saw the value of their gift of an enclosed and waterproof toilet structure as the perfect general storeroom (Hindu- Indian National Newspaper 19 Oct 2009). This exemplifies the cultural changes required. Therefore it is insufficient to just provide the hardware for a transformation to occur. Instead, the foundation for change also needs to be laid, in the form of creating demand for toilets among those who would most benefit from them. If one of the challenges faced by sanitation is overcoming these cultural barriers then it will be essential to engender trust of suppliers and products. MFIs could play an important contribution as they have a track record of building these types of relationships (Fisher & Sriram 2002).

There is evidence, mainly from West Bengal, that suggests that poor people who finance household latrines and are involved in the construction process are more likely to use and maintain them (UNICEF 2002, Government of Orissa, undated). In other words, people will utilize an improved sanitary situation if they have both a desire and a sense of ownership. And herein lays an opportunity to change lives and create a market at the same time. By driving demand (and working to build and support a supply chain), we can trigger a change in behavior that will ensure homegrown solutions evolve through innovation and competition, driving adoption up and prices down. Probably, the most effective way to approach the problem is not to see 2.5 billion people who are in a dire situation, but instead to see 2.5 billion customers who currently are not being served by the marketplace. The market grows when adding toilets at workplaces, schools, transport centers, markets, religious buildings, recreation centers; and it expands again when factoring in sanitation treatment, installation, maintenance, and the supply chain channeling of raw materials into finished products. Then there's promotion, distribution, and investment and cashflow financing. Furthermore, there is the upgrade market, the disaster market, the military market, the refugee market, and the market for recycling waste into fertilizer. All told,

this becomes a market worth nearly US$1 trillion (World Toilet Summit 2008, Macao).

Why hasn't this market developed on its own? George (2008) suggests it is because of the taboo nature of sanitation: in so many countries, the act itself is unspeakable or associated with the lowest of the low. This has stifled the development of the market, creating a dysfunctional economy in which suppliers do not exist to stimulate demand and demand does not exist to stimulate supply, even though this is one of the most basic needs.

Creating demand will probably require employing both health and cultural stimuli. The World Toilet Organization (WTO)[1] members found it much more effective to personalize human waste when explaining the benefit of toilets to potential clients, i.e. they are effectively eating their neighbor's excreta; this it is claimed tends to trigger demand. The villagers cannot bear the thought of eating the excretion of their mother-in-law, or anyone else. This is before they are told about the risk of disease. The other angle involves marketing toilets as status symbols and objects of desire, creating a trend that drives emotional appeal in functions, colors and designs. Few people want to appear out of step with their neighbors, so the market mechanism is driven by aspirational marketing coupled with good affordable products and services. Jealousy is indeed a powerful universal marketing tool.

Unlike many other prospective markets, the supply of toilets already has economies of scale on proven, patent-free technologies. In addition, distribution channels have already been developed. Once demand is created it should be possible to franchise, promote, supply, install, and maintain toilets at a local level. Engineering and enterprise know-how exists as well, but it's still too abstract and work needs to be undertaken to facilitate transferring this knowledge into a simple, picture-based form that even the unschooled entrepreneur can learn and utilize.

Much like the way mobile phone technology has spread, so sanitation technology can find its way into every corner of every village on the globe. And while microfinance will not play much of a role in creating the demand for sanitation it could play a tremendous role in helping the demand find a supply. But as will be noted in the following section the process of selling a third-party's product inevitably involves negotiations with suppliers to ensure it can be marketed and sold. In this way the expertise of the microfinance provider in understanding the client group and their needs can be utilized to provide a feedback loop for the product design, manufacture and distribution. The main barrier to the microfinancing of household toilets has been the perspective that sanitation is expenditure, not an investment, but in reality sanitation is probably the cheapest preventative medicine: an investment with immediate payback. However, achieving this and making this technological step may require drawing on the lessons from another technological leap.

Leapfrogging Technology: Grameen Phone as a Parallel Example

With his Grameen Phone's Village Program, Muhammad Yunus has proven that micro-loans for this type of expenditure can work: that the poor will pay back the money they borrow for purchases of technological assets. Located in Bangladesh, the Grameen Phone's Village Program provides the credit necessary (around $500 per borrower, usually a poor village woman,) to purchase a phone, with the expectation that other villagers will pay her for using it. Grameen Phone also resells airtime at cost to the merchant, helping her realize a quick return on investment. 150 villages participated in a pilot program that proved the viability of this concept. Each of these operators made around $2 a day, or $700, after covering their costs. This is more than twice Bangladesh's annual per-capita income (Yunus 2008).

Initial skepticism focused on demand for mobile phone communications in villages that have no conventional landlines. After all, whom would the customers be calling? But demand quickly proved itself in the form of calls between villages, as well as calls to cities for information about prices in the commercial centers. Today, with more than 200 phones per village in operation, this program has impacted on the entire village market structure. Traders are now paying higher prices both for raw materials and for hand-crafted goods because villagers now have better information about pricing. What's more, currency exchange rates are improving in villages with telephone access.

The Grameen Phone's Village Program can be viewed as a comparable method to a sanitation delivery model as there are a number of similarities in both approaches. First, the assumption that demand was limited. Yunus (2008) describes how a consultant predicted a market of 250,000 when it turned out to be 7 million. Equally, an affordable toilet has the potential to sell millions of units. Second, contrary to external predictions poor people invested in complex technology. Something that is essential if the more innovative waste disposal toilets are to be used. Third, the selling of individual calls is equivalent to charging for every use of a public toilet. In theory a model could be established in which one villager purchases a toilet that others pay to use. Fourth, access to information via the internet can change behaviour and increase economic performance. For clients of sanitation this would involve material that overcame embedded cultures' resistance to toilet use and fewer days off through ill health. Fifth, both services provide dignity to users through either proving a link to the outside world in the case of Grameen Phone, or by private toilet space for sanitation providers. Sixth, Grameen were selling a third-party's product and not just providing credit that the client can use freely. This meant Grameen was involved in negotiations with both the manufactures and the suppliers to ensure the product, service and partnership agreement were appropriate for Grameen and their clients. This process was not without its difficulties and it took Grameen beyond the provision of ordinary credit products. An important lesson for microfinance providers wanting to sell toilets is that they have expertise (detailed knowledge of potential clients) that can be used as leverage to improve products, services and distribution, to aid the credit provision to their clients.

As will be noted in the Sulbah Toilet case study it can be run as a for-profit social-business, which cuts the bureaucratic bottleneck of government services and lets the poor take ownership of their environmental standards. This is similar to Yunus' desire to create a social business owned by the poor for Grameen Telephone. Another possible transferable lesson from Grameen is the evidence that the poor, when given the opportunity, act like consumers, being discerning in their choices based on a range of motivations. Finally, in the past, getting a phone line to rural areas was rarely possible due to the absence of infrastructure. But cellular phones eliminate the need for such infrastructure—which has allowed these villages to leap past the capital-intensive barrier to entry. Equally, the need for a sewage pipeline can be eliminated by using appropriate sanitation technology for rural toilets, along with small on-site sewage treatment systems.

For the lessons from Grameen Telephone to be transferred to another field it is essential that there are suppliers capable of delivering a technologically advanced product, finance and service methodology. This needs to be supplemented by a medium for the collation of all the available information and subsequently translated into an understandable form for potential clients and intermediaries. What follows are three short case studies detailing the current innovation in toilet supply mechanisms, a discussion about the role of microfinance including examples of where it is being used to purchase the product and details of the proposed web portal for clients and sellers that WTO is developing.

Sulabh Toilet: Proving the Demand for Toilets

Sulabh International, a 40-year-old movement promoting low-cost sanitation throughout India, employs over 50,000 associates and presently operates in 26 states. The organization had revenues approaching $32 million in 2005, with approximately $5 million in surplus. An estimated ten million people use its facilities across the country every day. Sulabh has also trained 19,000 masons who build low-cost, twin-pit toilets using locally available materials. One of the greatest social contributions of Sulabh's program is the liberation of the low-caste "untouchables" from the humiliating practice of removing human fecal waste by hand. Sulabh has helped 60,000 people transcend their caste, "liberating them" in their terminology, from the indignity of scavenging.

When Sulabh started, the big question was demand: why would poor people pay to do something in a building they can do for free in a field? But Sulabh has shown that even poor people have a price for dignity. By collecting a marginal fee from users, the 6,500 public toilets run by local Sulabh entrepreneurs break even within eight to nine months, as facilities in prominent places are highly profitable. And now, state governments that used to invite Sulabh into single-party tenders have started inviting competitive bids to build and run public toilets. In addition to supporting local entrepreneurs, Sulabh also sells and installs household toilets. Here they have also had success, installing 1.4 million household toilets by 2006. Clearly there is ample scope for replication and even scaling up of the Sulabh model, because it has proven three important things: that poor people will pay to install household toilets, as well as using community toilets and related facilities; that low-cost hygiene solutions exist; and that the poor can find access to finance for sanitation.

The initial pilot project developed by Sulabh demonstrated the popularity of pay-per-use toilet facilities in the urban areas in Bihar, one of India's poorest and least developed states, pioneering the low-cost toilet for installation in poor residential areas. Next, it constructed a museum in Delhi to get international attention and planned for a sanitation university, while training other NGOs and starting a policy dialogue with governments. Sulabh's lobbying influenced the central government decision to construct over 100,000 public toilets, in addition to providing toilet-related loans and subsidies.

Zero-Subsidy, 100% Demand: Community Led Total Sanitation

Dr Kamal Kar is the father of Community Led Total Sanitation (CLTS) in Bangladesh, an organization that motivates entire villages to build their own toilets and become one hundred percent open-defecation free. This program advocates a zero-subsidy approach; instead it relies on the power of demand to create solutions. It developed from the recognition that just providing a toilet does not guarantee usage, which, as noted earlier, confirms that toilets alone are not enough to improve sanitation and hygiene. Without stimulating demand, earlier approaches to sanitation led to uneven adoption, problems with long-term sustainability, and only partial use. It also created a culture of dependence on subsidies, while open defecation and the cycle of fecal–oral contamination continued to spread disease.

CLTS concentrates on behavioral change. It invests in community mobilization instead of hardware, and shifts from a focus on individual households to whole "open defecation-free" villages. It seeks to raise awareness that even when a minority practice open defecation, the whole village is at risk. This instigates change from the villagers, encouraging them to innovate and provide mutual support to find appropriate solutions to the problem.

The problem with CLTS is that while habits may change, the first toilets are often very ru-

dimentary and do not always survive the rainy season. Moreover, due to their limited lifespan there is minimal, if any, maintenance training. Therefore CLTS require demand from clients to justify investment in better toilet superstructure: in other words, a functioning sanitation marketplace. The greater lesson is clear: you cannot just give toilets away and holistic solutions will by definition involve many organizations. Only if there is demand will users feel a sense of ownership, and only if there is ownership will people continue to engage in sanitary habits and seek to upgrade the product.

Not just Asia: The Case for African Demand

Another case study comes from David Kuria, a young social entrepreneur from Kenya who started IKO-Public Toilets, which are funded by cross-subsidizing the toilets with earnings gained from on-site shoe-shine, newspaper, and snack kiosks. His key concept was what he calls the ABCD of sanitation: Architecture, Behavior change, Cleanliness and Disposal technologies as the new package for sustainability.

Most sanitation development has failed in Kenya and elsewhere in Africa due to the strong cultural taboo associated with it. The ABCD offers a wide range of innovative solutions: appropriate architecture creates a public image that attracts users into the built space, helping them identify with it and feel part of the whole. This atmosphere is complemented by add-on services like shoe shines, newspaper vendors, and soft drink sellers to create a "Toilet Mall" concept. Improved management through franchise mechanisms ensure locals are involved in operations and accrued benefits. It also helps enhance hygiene levels. In these Toilet Malls, human waste utilization is a valued addition, as it can be harvested in the form of biogas from digesters, urea can be converted to a fertilizer, and compost can be made from the sludge.

Kuria's organization has engaged the municipality and local schools in a new partnership arrangement: Build Operate Transfer (BOT). This involves these firms in sanitation infrastructure construction, management, and operations for a period of five years, during which time the program will develop through incubation of franchises to ensure new knowledge on sanitation management is in place for now and the future. Kuria has signed contracts with ten local authorities for the initial 100 units and has engaged different corporations to sponsor each of them. A local university will assist in the development of a week-long module for capacity development of franchisees. They are also planning to extend this model to the slums and public schools in Kenya.

Their ultimate strategy is to scale up in the entire country, with a particular focus on the urban slums, schools, and refugee camps. The demand is large with 10,000 targeted public schools and slums in almost all urban centers in Kenya. Corporations will adopt several facilities for the prominent advertising space or corporate social responsibility (CSR) branding, bringing further income to the franchisees. The Acumen Fund has already disbursed loans for the IKO-Toilet expansion program at very moderate interest rates.

All three examples demonstrate the opportunities but also the challenges in developing a sanitation marketplace. It is a many-faceted task requiring a continuous search for willing stakeholders to align their multiple missions towards product design and related issues, manufacture and logistics, and marketing and changing consumer behavior. This is made difficult because the somewhat fragmented approach of much of the global humanitarian community, with projects being done in isolation, supported by different organizations, nations and funding streams. In addition, many of the skills required are more likely to be found in the private sector rather than among development agencies.

It is also necessary to develop solutions that reflect local cultures as no one solution fits all

situations. That is why the current silo based services did not work well in serving the poverty sanitation sector. A customer-centered approach with an understanding of the culture, habits and affordability will allow design and supply of products that are both emotionally appealing and operationally compatible to the location, its hydrology and its people.

Sanitation as an Income-Generator: The Case for Microfinance

All three initiatives demonstrate that there is a market but there are also problems to be overcome, so what engagement have MFIs had? Although only a limited number of initiatives have been implemented, recently more microfinance institutions are realizing that sustainable businesses can be established in water supply and sanitation projects.

Perhaps most hopefully for MFIs there is some evidence that clients do repay their loans. Centre Régional pour l'Eau Potable et l'Assainissement à faible coût (CREPA) reported in 2005 that their Côte d'Ivoire branch saw its US$ 10,800 worth of loans for drinking water connections for 300 households in Abidjan paid back within 17 months. In Togo, microfinance has paid for household water points and seen seventy percent of loans repaid within six months, with householders selling drinking water to create revenue for their payback. In a low-income neighborhood in Burkina Faso, a savings-credit initiative was set up for the household management of domestic waste. Once people were made aware of the need for sustained sanitation services, repayment rates rose to eighty percent, and are anticipated to increase to a profit-making level (Trémolet et al, 2007).

TSPI (*Tulay Sa Pagunlad,* or Bridge Towards Progress) is a microfinance NGO in the Philippines. In 2007, TSPI started offering loans for housing and sanitation, and has already seen demand increase to the point where TSPI had to build its internal capacity and hire 20 Project Officers.

After a modest couple of years the service began to attract a more substantial take-up in the first nine months of 2009, with US$ 201,216 released among 292 clients in the form of construction materials and cash for labor and overhead costs. In addition to the sanitary benefits, this project generates employment for local carpenters and foremen (TSPI 2009).

In Cambodia WTO is currently testing a rotating credit and savings association (ROSCA) in which 16 households form a savings group. Each pays $5 a month into a common pool fund. As each completed toilet with treatment services cost $80, one household gets a toilet each month. After 16 months, everybody has a toilet at home. To avoid disputes, who gets the first toilet is decided by lottery.

MFIs have also had opportunities when the sanitation services were upgraded. In Lesotho, sanitation coverage has increased from 20 percent to 53 percent in the last twenty years (Pearson 2002). This is due in part from the shifting of subsidies away from latrines and towards promotion and training. The government supplies basic latrine components at cost to rural households and operates a loss-making pit-emptying service. Similarly, Mozambique's subsidies were shifted to focus on the delivery of the latrine slab, the biggest barrier for many household latrines. In both cases there was an opportunity for microfinance institutions to lend to those who wanted an upgraded product. Another example was UN-HABITAT and Manus Coffey Associates who designed a machine to empty pits in densely-populated low income areas. The UN-HABITAT Vacutug is build specifically for narrow, unpaved streets where larger vehicles cannot pass. Initial studies pointed towards substantial demand for small-scale entrepreneurs in many parts of the world (Alabaster & Issaias, 2003). Again, there is an opening for a MFI to fund the expansion of this innovation through financing microentrepreneurs to own and operate the vehicles.

Should MFIs be Involved in Sanitation Services?

There has been a longstanding debate about the efficacy of microcredit with regards to development (Morduch 2000, Martin et al 2002). At one extreme stand the 'minimalists' that argue MFIs should concentrate on delivering an efficient credit service, which will ultimately deliver an improved economic situation for their clients. The alternative perspective believes that MFIs should have much broader objectives, including social development (Copestone 1995, Fisher and Sriram 2002). These are known as maximalists. Such dichotomies can become entrenched and prevent microfinance from achieving either aim (Fisher and Sriram 2002). For example, a risk of relying on a narrow range of credit products is that it excludes those who may need different services than the ones available (Matin et al 2002).

Fortunately, MFIs have sought to break out of this ideological cage and between these extremes are organizations which can be described as 'credit plus' institutions delivering a wider range of financial products, such as savings and insurance (Rutherford 2000). In recent years there has been much criticism of the minimalist approach (Dichter and Harper 2007) as its claims of sustainability (Von Pischke 2007) and impact (Meyer 2007) came under scrutiny. By contrast 'credit plus' can be perceived as the 'third way' for the sector. However, the most famous microfinance providers, Grameen Bank and BRAC, continue to be involved in social programs, though the former was described as a finance minimalist organization and the later as 'finance plus' (Hulme & Moore 2006). The latter nomenclature moves beyond a specific product (credit) to connect with development goals. It is these initiatives that may offer a model for the delivery of sanitation services in the developing world.

An example of a 'finance plus' approach is BRAC's livestock artificial insemination program which was delivered by volunteers from village organisations. BRAC recruited, trained and provided the equipment and infrastructure support for the livestock artificial insemination workers. As their businesses have grown BRAC is now lending them money to purchase mobile phones to keep in contact with smallholding farmers in need of the service (Matin et al 2007). Such an approach is not dissimilar to the microfranchising model developed by Stephen W. Gibson, which '*is the systematization and replication of microenterprises with the intent to alleviate poverty*' (Fairbourne 2006). Though the initial microfranchises are in cellular phones and spectacles there is no reason why this cannot be extended to sanitation, providing there are uniform standards, detailed operating systems and support and mentoring by the franchiser. This will help overcome the skills shortage faced by sanitation companies seeking to develop new marketplaces in the developing world. Clearly, as microfranchising is a relatively new concept it is too soon to have a full appreciation of both its potential and disadvantages. However, given that microfranchises require funding and that business supported by a larger organization will have a 'greatly' reduced risk of loan default the proponents believe that it can have a '*symbiotic*' (p23) relationship with microfinance (Fairbourne 2006).

One of the criticisms of 'finance plus' microfinance, particularly in its original incarnation as development NGOs, is that it distorted the financial services part of the firm leading to inefficiency (Johnson & Rogaly 1997). However, by having a completely distinct management structure for the grant services, while keeping it closely coordinated with microfinance delivery BRAC has shown that it is possible to maintain a viable socially focused MFI (Matin et al 2007). Of course this does lead to strategic choices that could dampen the microfinance market. For example, instead of selling insurance a MFI could focus on health preventative measures, such as sanitation. Alternatively a MFI that wanted to remain a financial institution (what Von Pischke calls a Type II) could work in partnership with NGO who can promote the MFI and provide expertise in a social field (Johnson & Rogaly 1997, Fisher & Sriram 2002).

The other alleged fear of MFI minimalists is that a broader set of corporate objectives will result in lower interest rates and increased subsidy, as self-sustainability is sacrificed for more ephemeral social goals. Moreover, subsidized interest rates 'trigger' credit rationing which favors borrowers able to repay at the expense of poorer more marginal clients (Von Pischke 1991, Christen and Pearce 2005). This argument was deconstructed by Jonathan Morduch (2000) citing evidence that very few MFIs were financially sustainable and that the logic of pursuing sustainability did not withstand scrutiny. Rather MFIs may need to vary their services, including lowering interest rates, to ensure they serve those their donors most want them to support. Other programs have found 'substantial benefits' by incorporating education within financial products (Morduch 2000). Again this offers support for MFIs wishing to explore the possibility of connecting financial services to sanitation provision.

However, one of the advantages of the minimalist approach is that employees can be trained to do a single task well, say issuing financial services products, rather than take on additional roles, such as training (Morduch & Rutherford 2003). By contrast, finance plus MFIs can engender stronger user loyalty, which can lead to these firms having better repayment rates during periods of economic turbulence (Velasce & Marconi 2004, Marconi & Mosley 2006). Therefore, though there are strong arguments endorsing a minimalist approach, there is inadequate support for the thesis that minimalist strategy is the most effective way to manage a MFI. Equally there are risks attached to the 'finance plus' strategy that MFIs must be fully cognizant of when designing their management and governance systems. In both cases, according to Murdoch (2000), the essential elements of a successful program are '*efficiency, transparency, and appropriate management incentives*' (p619), and *'having a hard budget constraint, something possible even with subsidies'* (p626).

As noted in the introduction, there have been only modest attempts to provide microfinance for improved sanitation. One explanation is that the cost of the sanitation products and the delivery of the associated training are prohibitive once the pilot funded subsidy is removed (Fonesca et al 2007). Consequently, most initiatives tend to be small scale and, as was evident in the case studies, lack sufficient financial performance data. Without this information from early-implementers it makes it difficult for MFIs considering entering the market to properly assess the risks. Despite this some lessons are discernable.

An urban sanitation project in Wogodogo in Burkina Faso struggled to secure repayments (only 5 of 35 households repaid the loans) because it had not fully explained to the borrowers that these were required to finance the waste infrastructure that supported their latrines (Kouassi-Komlan & Fonesca 2004). In addition, the pilot suggests that strong MFI financial management is required, which becomes more difficult if clients have not been culturally sensitized to the benefits of sanitation services. Therefore, there is a need for MFIs both to understand the sanitation products they are financing and utilize NGO expertise in training and technical support. Another issue is that infrastructure programs will require some interaction with local government and other local stakeholders and landowners (Kouassi-Komlan & Fonesca 2004). Again this may be done through a NGO partner but the MFI needs to be aware of the progress and likely problems if it is to properly price risk. Given the high costs of many sanitation products relative to the income of potential clients MFIs will need to consider the nature of credit services provided. Most borrowers are unlikely to have any collateral and therefore some other guarantees may be needed, perhaps from a third party. In Europe credit for businesses is often attached to state-backed guarantees for a proportion of the loan and there is no reason why a similar model cannot be utilized for sanitation services in the developing world.

Another challenge faced by MFIs wanting to enter this market is their limited outreach in the poorest areas, especially Sub-Saharan Africa, where many of those most in need in sanitation services reside (Fonesca et al 2007). However, given the scale of the problem and the complexities of any solutions it may be more practicable for MFIs to start with their existing clients before extending the service to harder to reach groups. Ironically, there is a much clearer market for MFIs once the sanitation infrastructure is in place as a range of support services will then be required. These include waste collection and disposal, toilet cleaning and maintenance, and toiletries, which all could be delivered by micro-entrepreneurs in receipt of MFI credit. Thus, asset creation and infrastructure offer new opportunities for MFIs in helping clients invest in the home, improve their health and facilitate a new micro-enterprise industry. But to be successful MFIs have to be involved in a whole systems approach even if they only deliver the financial part of the service. One example where this is beginning to emerge is a partnership in India involving BASIX and a self-help group, Gramalya, both of whom helped create a partnership (Water Partnership International) that facilitates strategic support, donor funding and technical expertise. Subsequently Gramalya train villagers in cement fabrication and brick making for the construction of toilets, while BASIX created a dedicated MFI, Guardian, to provide the loan finance (George 2009). These types of arrangements draw on the conventional strengths of MFIs, while helping them work collaboratively with strategic partners to address pressing social needs. Perhaps this offers a productive way out of the dichotomy of minimalist versus maximalist MFIs.

Another challenge is that selling a small micro-loan can incur high overheads for the lender. Traveling between poorly-connected villages for sales and fulfillment purposes is a costly affair in relation to the loan size. Since a larger loan size will certainly mean lower overheads per dollar, one option is to draw on the experience of Grameen Telephone and bundle the micro-loan with the toilet product itself, turning the financer into a hire-purchase vendor through a microfranchise approach. In this way, the selling costs of both products are combined, which will reduce overheads and allow the vendor/financer to reduce its costs. Therefore, the savings through bundling products and micro-loans may result in lower interest charges for the borrower as well as additional product margin profit for the lender selling the sanitation systems.

The Big Goal: Towards an Efficient Sanitation Marketplace

The preceding section shows that there is innovation in design and supply of toilets, while the possible use of microfinance to fuel this market is increasingly apparent, if only on a limited scale. But, as discussed, there are considerable barriers to the opening of a viable market. It is here that we believe that IT could play a significant role.

As discussed in the section on market-based solution, the sanitation marketplace is dysfunctional, predominantly due to the taboos surrounding it. Strong demand will help overcome this taboo, but this will expose, unless they are addressed, the problems of supply. Some products already exist and a wide range of good sustainable sanitation designs and technologies are available without a patent. These designs need to be either mass-produced in centralized locations, or manufactured in a more decentralized approach. In each case, it will require a concerted effort to suppress costs due to the limited income of the end clients. It is possible that efficiency can be achieved through "intelligent components" that connect suppliers in centralized locations with locally available, grown, or produced materials. However, the sanitation marketplace is so big and underdeveloped that there is enough business for both large and small enterprises. Ideally, big companies like IKEA and TATA could exercise their huge manufacturing prowess while local smaller operators could concentrate on distribution. Alternatively, it is possible to have micro-factories near regional markets to generate jobs in local economies. With the potential of 2.5 billion customers, if bulk buying or co-buying is coordinated it should be possible to drive costs lower than the current small volume purchases, in particular for raw materials such as cement and steel. This could be achieved by a centralized web-ordering center with decentralized distribution.

As discussed earlier there are two kinds of appeals that will generate demand: rational drivers and emotional drivers. And when it comes to toilets, both kinds of drivers have their place. Rational drivers are all about the benefits toilets bring you: the improvements in health and the reduced expenditure associated with it, convenience and ease of use for sick or elderly people, increased income and productivity from improved health, improved environment and reduced pollution of your well and other water bodies, and privacy and safety, especially for females. The risk of snakebites is another common rational reason to own a toilet. However, as discussed earlier emotional drivers are critical to changing habits. Aspirational marketing for sanitation includes creating a trend such that having a toilet becomes a marker of distinction and social status. Emotional drivers can outweigh rational drivers in the bottom-of-pyramid markets just like they do in the upper classes, where people buy things like designer clothes for status and prestige. Both rational and emotional drivers will vary across country, region, and also an individual's family context. Sanitation marketing should be designed to reflect the wealth strata, social norms and habits, family demographics, competition of priorities and availability of supplies and promoters.

Not every toilet is the same. What will work in the rainforests will not work in the deserts. What is more, defecation habits vary between cultures, and are also influenced by attitudes on gender, religion, washing and/or wiping habits, and more. Therefore it's very important that the right technology be identified before the investment is made. As markets develop, there is a risk that price-cutting is realized by lowering the quality of goods. Some quality benchmarking and recommendations by trusted intermediaries, such as a MFI, would reduce this risk. Sanitation cannot be given—it must be owned and maintained by the local population. Therefore, a possible approach is through microfranchising as a way of connecting localities to a wider distribution network. Members of the community are recruited to open franchises, selling hardware as well as construction, training, and maintenance. Given the preceding discussion about the struggles faced by incipient MFI sanitation products it is important in building this network that the infrastructure is subsidized, though not the hardware itself. This is because people highly value and maintain what they pay for and, in the case of big purchases like this, what they sacrifice, while infrastructure that connects multiple households is at best owned collectively and less likely to inspire strong levels of commitment. In order to help sellers achieve volumes, it may be necessary to subsidize early losses to create market momentum. However, this is not the same as simply paying for the toilets and dropping them at someone's doorstep—this is more of a mutual partnership, which means that the subsidizer is investing as much as the buyer or the seller. Within this nexus of investment, costs and products, MFIs could act as key intermediaries between clients and suppliers or those involved in infrastructure development. The objective should be the creation of a sustainable market and not one in which donors 'dump' products on communities without any evidence of demand, training and sensitization.

Alternative Zero-Interest Financing Model

World Toilet Organization has now a new way of selling toilets in Kampung Speu in Cambodia. Instead of borrowing money to buy latrines immediately, these 2-pits latrines were sold not by micro-finance but by a "Tontine System" where many households pool equal amount of money together every month and take turns to own the toilets. Each week there are now about 100 units sold comprising of 2-pits latrines including the squat pan, costing US$35 each set..The superstructure option is also available at another US$ 45 but the homeowner can also build his own super-structure in any manner he prefers. This method of funding has long been practiced in this part of Asia and applying it to selling toilets means "micro-financing" without incurring any interest rate charges.

Supporting the Creation of Demand and Supply: The Role of IT Portal

Though the aforementioned are enormous challenges all of them could at least be partially offset through extensive use of existing IT technologies. We start from the premise that the people who would most benefit from access to improved sanitation do not have ready access to the Internet. However, many of the people who are dedicated to helping these people, like local and community leaders, NGOs, and governments, would benefit from an online portal designed to spread localized information that will generate the kind of demand for toilets that could bring about positive change.

This World Toilet Portal would be a first pure sanitation portal in the field[2] a one-stop portal for the development of the market for trading, training, financing, knowledge and best-practice sharing, volunteer, talent matching, donor funding, etc. Designed to fill the gap that exists in global sanitation information dissemination, the portal could be a comprehensive unified open source web platform that facilitates linkages across all market actors in the sanitation segment (including NGOs, governments, and community leaders, as well as for-profit entities) with the primary objective of creating and developing the bottom of pyramid sanitation market. This database could include all existing private sector products both from large and small enterprises targeting the marketplace. Key components of the portal could include: database of latrine components and systems available in Asia, gradually expanding to include a wider geographic area in later stages. Database services could incorporate information on costs per unit and bulk purchase options; a latrine design database with design specifications, and bills of quantities and user reviews. To facilitate connections and networking a directory of manufacturers, material suppliers and latrine components, including contact details, and an interactive map of distribution channels of large market players and medium size enterprises. There should be space for an open source "Latrine Designer's Corner" for designers and inventors to share latrine design innovations, and a password-protected discussion group where technical field workers can post questions and discuss technical aspects of latrine construction. To assist those involved in support functions there could be sections to address needs and concerns of suppliers, distributors, logistics, business planning, maintenance, training, and quality control. All this could be connected to donor matching, MFIs and the support platform for a World Sanitation Funding Facility currently under development by organizations including WSSCC, Ashoka, World Toilet Organization, UNICEF, and World Bank WSP. The portal would also need to engage those involved in outreach. To help with education and skills development it could include picture-based pedagogic tools for the local community leaders and NGO staff to use when training the unschooled poor to learn to become

sanitation craftsmen, installers, entrepreneurs, etc. and other on-line community events and sharing. One place where the portal could provide an essential resource is supporting the development of microfranchise operations. Such an approach has already been suggested in connection with distance learning and a small exploratory project is underway in Nepal (Ivins 2008).

The scale of the project would help create a critical mass of information and become an essential resource for all those involved in the sector. The most innovative part of this portal could be the use of visual mnemonics and other tools to ensure the information transcends the language in which it is written. To change habits of less literate people, for instance, the portal could have picture-based instructions on the dangers of poor sanitation and the benefits of improved sanitation. The website could provide instructions to facilitate local organizations in creating localized versions of the information with the aim of developing a demand for sanitation. In this model, information technology's role is clear: to provide a template for the activist to customize the generic signs with language and names, while retaining the universal pictograms.

Another role for IT would be in matching toilet products to local regions. There are hundreds of different models of low-cost toilets, encompassing variations on superstructure, toilet pan, and treatment, each appropriate for different regions, environments, incomes, and cultural values. To facilitate the growth of the sanitary marketplace, IT would be used to build a matrix that would easily allow vendors to identify the proper technology for their area. Overall, an IT portal could have a substantial impact on local markets and prices, and supply chains for low-cost toilets. This is in addition to being a hub for driving both product and supply chain innovation, including new microfinance products tailored to this market.

FURTHER RESEARCH DIRECTIONS

The development of the portal is an obvious example of a potential action research project and there could be opportunities to explore the relationship among and between the various sub-communities that could access it. Clearly there is an evaluative question on whether the web portal infrastructure delivers enhanced and more numerical links between prospective manufacturers and indigenous entrepreneurs (i.e. does it replicate the Grameen Telephone lady model). Furthermore, can on-line purchasing of toilets and repayment of loans via mobile phones be developed and, if so, what opportunities are there for mainstream financial providers. There are also questions about cultural issues related to sanitation and a need to thoroughly test the hypothesis that visual prompts along with personalized messages can overcome the cultural resistance to toilet use. Finally, for MFIs there could be numerous studies exploring the impact on the organization of financial plus approaches and what mechanisms are employed to overcome fiscal tension and distortions of the wider business. In addition, work could look at the products designed and ask whether this informs the development of products offered in a MFIs traditional business?

CONCLUSION: "9-TO-1": THE RETURNS ON SANITATION INVESTMENT

The chapter has sought to argue that the sanitation crisis can draw on the lessons from Grameen Telephone and use microfinance and IT to overcome current weaknesses in the market. All the technical innovations suggested for the portal are used in different areas across the internet. The task is to draw them together and tackle this most socially taboo of subjects. But surely the measure of a technology's success, both social and IT, is when it transforms from the exotic to the mundane. Together IT and microfinance could be used more extensively to encourage toilet usage among the forgotten 2.5 billion people.

As mentioned earlier, in terms of health and other economic costs, there is an estimated $9 return on every $1 invested in sanitation. Through sanitation 'market-making', the economic benefits for local suppliers of latrine components and other members of the supply chain are also significant. What's more, access to sanitation is well known to substantially reduce incidence of diarrheal diseases and the 1.8 million deaths per year they account for globally.

Adequate sanitation is essential for human dignity, safety, security and comfort and is closely linked to proper nutrition, education and poverty reduction. And with the help of microfinance and IT, the Millennium Development Goal to reduce by half the number of people without sanitation might after all be in reach. As people have proper sanitation, they become healthier and earn more money; their children get better education, work in better jobs, and move to middle incomes. Equally, there are potential benefits to MFIs that break free from the dichotomy of minimalist and maximalist approaches, and instead adopt a 'finance plus' strategy. The work may open new markets and opportunities for those that build effective partnerships. But MFIs should not enter the field lightly and should anticipate the need to overcome many challenges, not least the requirement to rely on others to construct a viable market. However, the main benefit is that it will reengage a MFI with its original purpose of helping those most in need.

REFERENCES

Alabaster, G., & Issaias, I. (2003). Case Studies: Removing human waste – the Vacutug solution. *Habitat Debate, 9*(3), 17.

Barnes, C., & Gaile, G. (2001). *The Impact of Three Microfinance Programs in Uganda: USAID/ Uganda*. Washington, D.C.: AIMS.

Chowdhury, A. M. R., & Bhuiya, A. (2001). Do Poverty Alleviation Programmes Reduce Inequality in Health: Lessons from Bangladesh. In Leon, D., & Walt, G. (Eds.), *Poverty Inequality and Health*. Oxford: OUP.

Christen Peck, R., & Perce, D. (2005). *Managing Risk and Designing Products for Agricultural Microfinance: Features of an Emerging Market*. CGAP Occasional Paper No. 11 Washington D.C. USA: CGAP.

Copestone, J. (1995). Poverty Oriented Financial Services Programmes: Room for Improvement? *Savings and Development*, *19*(4), 417–435.

Dichter, T., & Harper, M. (Eds.). (2007). *What's Wrong with Micro-finance? Practical Action: Rugby*.

Douglas, M., & Isherwood, B. (1996). *The World of Goods: Towards an Anthropology of Consumption* (2nd ed.). London: Routledge.

Dunford, C. Leatherman, S. Sinclair, M.R., Metcalfe, M., Gray, B. & Vor der Bruegge, E. (2007). How Microfinance can Work for the Poor. In *Freedom for Hunger*.

Dwivedi, P., & Sharma, A. N. (2007). A Study on Environmental Sanitation, Sanitary Habits and Personal Hygiene among the Baigas of Samnapur Block of Dindori District, Madhya Pradesh. *Journal of Human Ecology (Delhi, India)*, *22*(1), 7–10.

Elias, N. (2000). *The Civilising Process: Sociogenetic and Psychogenetic Investigations*. London: Wiley/Blackwell. (Original work published 1939)

Fairbourne, J. S. (2006). Microfranchising: A New Tool for Creating Economic Self-Reliance. ESR. *RE:view*, *8*(1).

Fisher, T., & Sriram, M. S. (2002). *Beyond Micro-Credit: Putting Development Back into Micro-Finance*. Oxford: Oxfam.

Fonseca, C., Adank, M., Casella, D., Jeths, M., van der Linde, P. & Dijkshoorn, B. (2007). *Microfinance for Water, Sanitation and Hygiene: An Introduction*.

Frost, B. (2007) Water and Sanitation: The Silent Emergency, *United Nations Chronicle* Vol XLIV (4) accessed at: http://www.un.org/wcm/content/site/chronicle/cache/bypass/home/archive/issues2007/themdgsareweontrack/waterandsanitationthesilentemergency?ctnscroll_articleContainerList=1_0&ctnlistpagination_articleContainerList=true

George, M. M. (2009). *A Blue Revolution: Microfinance, Water and Sanitation in India. Microfinance Insights* (*Vol. 10*). Jan/Feb.

George, R. (2008). *The Big Necessity: Adventures in the World of Human Waste*. London: Portobello Books. Government of Orissa (undated) Total Sanitation Campaign http://www.orissa.gov.in/RD/sanitation/tsc.html

Hulme, D. & Moore, K. (2006). *Why has Microfinance Been a Policy Success? Bangladesh and Beyond*. paper presented at ESRC Seminar, Statecraft in the South: Public Policy Success in Developing Countries, University of Manchester, May 20, 2005.

Hutton, G., Haller, L., & Bartram, J. (2007). Global cost-benefit analysis of water supply and sanitation interventions. *Journal of Water and Health*, *5*(4), 481–502. doi:10.2166/wh.2007.009

Ivins, T. Z. (2008). Microfranchising Microlending Centers: A Sustainable Model for Expanding the Right to Education in Developing Countries? *Journal of Asynchronous Learning Networks*, *12*(1).

Khandker, S.R. (2005) Microfinance and Poverty: Evidence Using Panel Data from Bangladesh, *The World Bank Economic Review* 19(2) 263:283

Khare, R. S. (1962). The Ritual Purity and Pollution in relation to Domestic Sanitation. *The Eastern Anthropologist, 15*(2), 125–139.

Kouassi-Komlan, E., & Fonseca, C. (2004). *Micro Finance for Water and Sanitation in West Africa.* 30th WEDC International Conference, Vientiane, Laos. Johnson, S. & Rogaly, B. (1997). *Microfinance and Poverty Reduction.* Oxford: Oxfam.

Littfield, E. Morduch, J. & Hashemi, S. (2003). *Is Microfinance an Effective Strategy to Reach the Millennium Development Goals.* CGAP: Focus Note 24.

Marconi, R., & Mosley, P. (2006). Bolivia During the Global Crisis 1998-2004: Towards Macroeconomics of Microfinance. *Journal of International Development, 18*, 237–261. doi:10.1002/jid.1218

Matin, I., Hulme, D., & Rutherford, S. (2002). Finance for the Poor: From Microcredit to Micro financial Services. *Journal of International Development, 14*, 273–294. doi:10.1002/jid.874

McLaughlin, T. (1971). *Coprophilia or a Peck of Dirt.* London: Cassell.

Meyer, R. L. (2007). Measuring the Impact of Microfinance. In Dichter, T., & Harper, M. (Eds.), *What's Wrong with Micro-finance, Rugby: Practical Action.*

MKNelly. B. & Dunford, C. (1998). *Impact of Credit with Education on Mothers and Their Young Children's Nutrition: Lower Pra Bank Credit with Education in Ghana.* Freedom from Hunger Research paper, No. 4 Davis, CA, USA.

MKNelly. B. & Dunford, C. (1999). *Impact of Credit with Education on Mothers and Their Young Children's Nutrition: CRECER Credit with Education Program in Bolivia.* Freedom from Hunger Research paper, No. 5 Davis, CA, USA.

Morduch, J. (2000). The Microfinance Schism. *World Development, 28*(4), 617–629. doi:10.1016/S0305-750X(99)00151-5

Morduch, J., & Rutherford, S. (2003). *Microfinance: Analytical Issues for India background paper prepared for the World Bank.* Washington, DC: World Bank.

Paul, B. D. (1958). The Role of Beliefs and Customs in Sanitation Programs. *American Journal of Public Health, 48*(11), 1502–1506. doi:10.2105/AJPH.48.11_Pt_1.1502

Pearson, I. (2002). *The National Sanitation Programme in Lesotho: How political Leadership Achieved Long-term Results.* Washington: World Bank.

Rukunga, G., Mutethia, D., & Kioko, T. (n.d.). *Why the water and sanitation sector in East Africa should consider disabled people*, WELL Country Note 12.1 (F. Odhiambo, Ed.) Loughborough: WEDC Loughborough University. Retrieved from http://www.lboro.ac.uk/well/resources/Publications/Country%20Notes/CN12.1.htm

Rutherford, S. (2000). *The Poor and Their Money.* New Delhi, India: OUP.

Simonwitz, A. (2002). *Appraising the Poverty Outreach of microfinance: A Review of the CGAP Poverty Assessment Tool (PAT).* Brighton: ImpAct, Institute of Development Studies.

Smith, V. (2008). *Clean: A History of Personal Hygiene and Purity.* Oxford: OUP.

Trémolet, S., Cardone, R., da Silva, C., & Fonseca, C. (2007). Innovations in Financing Urban Water & Sanitation. Paper presented at the Global Urban Summit "Financing Shelter, Water and sanitation, July 1-6, 2007, Bellagio, Italy. Rockefeller Foundation Center for Sustainable Urban Development of Columbia University. http://www.earth.columbia.edu/csud/documents/Final%20Papers/Week%201/Week1_Finance_IRC.pdf

TSPI. (2009) Microfinance Innovation: Housing & sanitation Program for the Poor presentation at *Philippine Symposium on Sustainable Sanitation and Global Handwashing Day,* Metro Manila, Philippines, 15-16 October.

UNICEF. (2002) *Learning from Experience: Water and Sanitation in India.* UNICEF: New York, accessed at: http://www.unicef.org/publications/files/pub_wes_en.pdf

United Nations. (2008). *Millenium Develoment Goals report.* New York: UN Statistics Division.

United Nations Human Development Report. (2006). *Beyond Scarcity: Power, Poverty and the Global Water Crisis.* New York: United Nations.

Velasco, C., & Marconi, R. (2004). Group Dynamics and Gender Development in Bolivia. *Journal of International Development, 16,* 519–528. doi:10.1002/jid.1089

Von Pischke, J. D. (1991). *Finance at the Frontier: Debt Capital and the Role of Credit in the Private Economy.* Washington, DC: World Bank Economic Development Institute.

Von Pisschke, J. D. (2007). Methodenstreit and Sustainability in Microfinance: Generalizations Describing Institutional Frameworks. In Dichter, T., & Harper, M. (Eds.), *What's Wrong with Microfinance, Rugby: Practical Action.*

Yunus, M. (2008). *Creating a World Without Poverty: How Social Business Can transforms our Lives.* New York: PublicAffairs.

ADDITIONAL READING

Adams, D., Graham, D., & von Pischke, J. D. (1984). *Undermining Rural Development with Cheap Credit. Boulder, Co.* USA: Westview Press.

Morduch, J. (1999). The Microfinance Promise. *Journal of Economic Literature, 37*(4), 569–1614.

Mosley, P. (2001). Microfinance and Poverty in Bolivia. *The Journal of Development Studies, 37,* 101–132. doi:10.1080/00220380412331322061

Otero, M., & Rhyne, E. (Eds.). (1994). *New World of Microenterprise Finance: Building Healthy Financial Institutions for the Poor.* West Hartford, CT, USA: Kumarian Press.

ENDNOTES

[1] The WTO is a global non-profit committed to improving toilet and sanitation conditions worldwide.

[2] The only service we could indentify operating in this field was a water and sanitation website run by a Dutch charitable partnership (Akro)

Compilation of References

Adamson, I., & Shine, J. (2003). *Extending the New Technology Acceptance Model to measure the End User Information Systems Satisfaction in a Mandatory Environment: A Bank's Treasury*. Taylor & Francis Ltd.

Agarwal, R., & Prasad, J. (1999). Are individual differences germane to the acceptance of new information technologies? *Decision Sciences*, *30*(2), 361–391. doi:10.1111/j.1540-5915.1999.tb01614.x

Agarwal, R., Sambamurthy, V., & Stair, R. M. (2000). Research report: The evolving relationship between general and specific computer self-efficacy – An empirical assessment. *Information Systems Research*, *11*(4), 418–430. doi:10.1287/isre.11.4.418.11876

Aghion, P., Howitt, P., & Mayer-Foulkes, D. (2005). The Effect of Financial Development on Convergence: Theory and Evidence. *The Quarterly Journal of Economics*, *120*, 173–222.

Ajzen, I. (1991). The theory of planned behavior. *Organizational Behavior and Human Decision Processes*, *50*, 179–211. doi:10.1016/0749-5978(91)90020-T

Ajzen, I., & Fishbein, M. (1980). *Understanding the attitudes and predicting social behaviour*. Englewood Cliffs, NJ: Prentice-Hall Inc.

Akerlof, G. A. (1970). The Market for "Lemons": Quality Uncertainty and the Market Mechanism. *The Quarterly Journal of Economics*, *84*(3), 488–500. doi:10.2307/1879431

Alabaster, G., & Issaias, I. (2003). Case Studies: Removing human waste – the Vacutug solution. *Habitat Debate*, *9*(3), 17.

Ali, A. (2008). *Managed Information System (MIS) for Microfinance*. The First MicrofinanceBank Ltd. BWTP Network. Retrieved December 25, 2008 from http://www.bwtp.org/pdfs/arcm/5Ahmad.pdf

Ambes, S., & Treich, N. (2007). Roscas as financial agreements to cope with self-control problems. *Journal of Development Economics*, *82*, 120–137. doi:10.1016/j.jdeveco.2005.09.005

Anderson, C. (2009). *Free: The Future of a Radical Price*. New York: Hyperion.

Andrikonis, C. (2005). Westpac Bank Cape York Experience. In Landvogt (Ed.), Microcredit: *More than just small change*. Conference Proceedings, Melbourne, Good Shepherd Youth and Family Services, Melbourne.

Annan, K. (2005). *In larger freedom: towards development, security and human rights for all. Report of the Secretary-General, 21 March 2005*. United Nations.

Armano, D. (2007). It's the Conversation Economy, Stupid. *Business Week Online* (p. 11).

Armendariz, B., & Morduch, J. (2005). *The Economics of Microfinance*. Cambridge, MA: MIT Press.

Arsyad, L. (2005). An assessment of microfinance institution performance: The importance of the institutional environment. *Gadjah Mada International Journal of Business*, *7*(3), 391–427.

Arunachalam, R. S. (2007). *Microfinance and Technology – Critical Issues, Lessons and Future Implications*. MCG Research Note Series in Low Income Financial Services, Research Note # 1. Tamil Nadu, India, Microfinance Consulting Group (MCG).

Arzeni, S. (2004). *Entrepreneurship: A Catalyst for Urban Regeneration*. Paris: Organization for Economic Co-operation and Development.

ASA. (1997). *Causes of Default in Microcredit*. Dhaka, Bangladesh: ASA.

Ashraf, N., Gons, N., & Yin, W. (2003). A review of commitment savings products in developing countries. Financial Access Initiative.

Ashraf, N., Karlan, D., & Yin, W. (2008). Female empowerment: Impact of a commitment savings product in the Philippines. Working Paper 106. Boston, Harvard Business School.

Ashta, A. (2008). ASSADI D. (2008). Do Social Cause and Social Technology Meet? Impact of Web 2.0 Technologies on peer-to-peer lending transactions, Asia Microfinance Forum 2008 Hanoi, Vietnam, Microfinance in the 21st Century: Future Trends & Opportunities, Theme 4. *Technology (Elmsford, N.Y.)*, (August): 26–29.

Ashta, A. (2007). An Introduction to Microcredit: Why Money is Flowing from the Rich to the Poor. *Cahiers du CEREN Working Paper 21*.

Ashta, A. (2009). Microcredit Capital Flows and Interest Rates: An Alternative Explanation. *Journal of Economic Issues (M.E. Sharpe Inc.), 43*(3), 661-683.

Ashta, A., & Bush, M. (2009, November). Ethical Issues of NGO Principals in Sustainability, Outreach and Impact of Microfinance: Lessons in Governance from the Banco Compartamos' I P O. *Management Online REview, vol. November*, 1-18.

Asian Development Bank. (2007). *Proposed Loans and Guarantees REG: Micro- and Small Enterprise Financing Facility: Report and Recommendation of the President to the Board of Directors*. Asian Development Bank.

Assadi, D., & Ashta, A. (2009). How do People Trust on Peer-to-Peer Lending Websites? Analysis of the Impacts of the Web 2.0 Technologies and Intermediation Roles. In Gera, R. (Ed.), *Advances in Technology and Innovation in Marketing* (pp. 49–69). Delhi: MacMillan Publishers India Ltd.

Attali, J. (2000). A Market Solution to Poverty: Microfinance and the Internet. *New Perspectives Quarterly, 17*(1), 31–33. doi:10.1111/0893-7850.00235

Attuel-Mendes, L., & Ashta, A. (2008). French Usury Legislation and the Development of Credit Availability for Microenterprise. *Global Journal of Business Research, 2*(2), 123–138.

Aubuchon, C. P., & Sengupta, R. (2008). The Microfinance Revolution: An Overview. *Federal Reserve Bank of St. Louis Review, 90*(1), 9–30.

Augsburg, B., & Schmidt, J. P. (2006). *Free & Open Source Software for Microfinance: Increasing Efficiency and Extending Benefits to the Poor*. Policy Innovations Retrieved September 15, 2008, from http://www.policy-innovations.org

BAI. (2004). *Transaction Cost per Distribution Channel*. Chigaco: BAI.

Banerjee, S. S. (2009). How Microfinance Changes the Lives of Millions. *Foreign Policy*, (October): 26. Retrieved from http://www.foreignpolicy.com/articles/2009/10/26/how_microfinance_changes_the_lives_of_millions.

Banerjee, A. V., & Duflo, E. (2007). The Economic Lives of the Poor. *The Journal of Economic Perspectives, 21*(1), 141–167. doi:10.1257/jep.21.1.141

Banerjee, A. V., & Duflo, E. (2008). *The Experimental Approach to Development Economics*. Working Paper. Cambridge, MA: MIT Department of Economics.

Banerjee, A. V., & Duflo, E. Glennerster, R., & Kinnan, C. (2009). *The Miracle of Microfinance? Evidence from a Randomized Evaluation*. Working Paper. Cambridge, MA: MIT Department of Economics.

Barnes, C., & Gaile, G. (2001). *The Impact of Three Microfinance Programs in Uganda: USAID/Uganda*. Washington, D.C.: AIMS.

Beck, T., & Demirguc-Kunt, A. & Peria. M. (2007). Banking Services for everyone? Barriers to bank acess and use around the world. *World Bank Policy Research*, Working Paper n° 4079.

Beck, T., Demirgüç-Kunt, A. & Honohan, P. (2009). Access to Financial Services: Measurement, Impact, and Policies. *The World Bank Research Observer*, forthcoming (advance published February 27, 2009).

Bedson, J. (Ed.). (2009). Microfinance in Asia: Trends, Challenges, and Opportunities. The Foundation for Development Cooperation. Retrieved August 12, 2009, from http://www.bwtp.org/files/MF_Trends_Challenges_Opportunities_ELECTRONIC.pdf.

Benkler, Y. (2002). Coase's Penguin, or, Linux and The Nature of the Firm. *The Yale Law, 112*.

Bernasek, A., & Stanfield, J. R. (1997). The Grameen Bank as Progressive Institutional Adjustment. *Journal of Economic Issues, 31*(2), 359–366.

Berry, D., Hungate, C., & Temple, T. (2003). *Delivering Expected Value to Users and Stakeholders with User Engineering*. IBM Systems Journal.

Bharadwaj, A. S. (2000). A Resource-Based Perspective on Information Technology Capability and Firm Performance: An Empirical Investigation. *Management Information Systems Quarterly, 24*(1), 169–196. doi:10.2307/3250983

Bhatt, N., & Shui-Yan, T. (2001). Designing Group-Based Microfinance Programs: Some Theoretical And Policy Considerations. *International Journal of Public Administration, 24*(10), 1103–1125. doi:10.1081/PAD-100105104

Bhatt, N., & Tang, S.-Y. (2001, August). Making microcredit work in the United States: Social, financial, and administrative dimensions. *Economic Development Quarterly*, 351–367.

Bhatt, N., & Tang, S.-Y. (2001). Designing group-based microfinance programs: some theoretical and policy considerations. *International Journal of Public Administration, 24*(10), 1103. doi:10.1081/PAD-100105104

Biskup, J. (2009). *Security in Computer Systems: Challenges, Approaches and Solutions*. Berlin, Heidelberg: Springer-Verlag.

Bogoslaw, D. (2009, April 6). Peer-to-Peer Lending: Problems and Promise. *Business Week*. Retrieved from http://www.businessweek.com/investor/content/apr2009/pi2009043_811816_page_3.htm

Booz Allen. (2003). *Processing Cost per Transaction*. New York: Booz Allen.

Bray, H. (2007, July 2). Need cash? Just ask. *The Boston Globe Online*. Retrieved September 1, 2008 from www.boston.com/business/personalfinance/articles/2007/07/02/need_cash_just_ask

Brown, I., Cajee, Z., Davies, D., & Stroebel, S. (2003). Cell phone banking: predictors of adoption in South Africa-an exploratory study. *International Journal of Information Management, 23*, 381–394. doi:10.1016/S0268-4012(03)00065-3

Brown, S. (2006). *Customer Relationship Management*. Toronto, Canada: John Wiley & Sons.

Bruce, L. (2008, June 6). Peer-to-peer online lending grows in tight economy. Retrieved September 1, 2008 from www.bankrate.com/brm/news/investing/20080606_P2P-lending-growth-a2.asp

Bruene, J. (2007). Person-to-Person Lending 2.0: Disruptive Service or Market Niche? Online Financial Innovations, Online Banking Report: Seattle.

Buckland, J., & Dong, X.-Y. (2008). Banking on the margin in Canada. *Economic Development Quarterly, 22*(3), 252–263. doi:10.1177/0891242408318738

Bughin, J., & Manyika, J. (2007). *How businesses are using Web 2.0: A McKinsey Global Survey*. The McKinsey Quarterly.

Burkett, I. 2003. *Microfinance in Australia*. Working Paper, School of Social Work and Social Policy, University of Queensland, Australia. May 12, 2003.

Burt, E., & Taylor, J. A. (2000). Information and Communication Technologies. Reshaping Voluntary Organizations? *Nonprofit Management & Leadership, 11*(2), 131–143. doi:10.1002/nml.11201

Burt, E., & Taylor, J. A. (2003). New Technologies, Embedded Values, and Strategic Change: Evidence from the U.K. Voluntary Sector. *Nonprofit and Voluntary Sector Quarterly, 32*(1), 115–127. doi:10.1177/0899764002250009

Cabraal, A., Russell, R., & Singh, S. (2006). Microfinance: Development as freedom. *Financial Literacy, Banking and Identity Conference*. RMIT University, Melbourne, Australia, Oct. 25- 26, 2006.

Castells, M. (2000). *The rise of the network society*. Oxford, UK: Basil Blackwell publishing.

Cecchinni, S., & Scott, C. (2003). Can information and communication technology applications contribute to reduce poverty? Lessons from rural India. *Information Technology for Development, 10*(1), 73–84. doi:10.1002/itdj.1590100203

Center for the Study of Financial Innovations. (2009). *Microfinance Banana Skins 2009: Confronting Crisis and Change*. New York: Center for the Study of Financial Innovations.

CGAP. (2006). *Good Practice Guidelines for Funders of Microfinance*. CGAP.

CGAP. (2008). *2008 Microfinance Funders Survey, Global Results*. Washington, D.C.: CGAP.

CGAP. (2003). *Disclosure Guidelines for Financial Reporting by Microfinance Institutions. Microfinance Consensus Guidelines*, published by CGAP/The World Bank Group, available at www.cgap.org.

CGAP. (2008). *Press Release: Study on Evolving Opportunities for Microfinance Investment Funds*. Retrieved September 6, 2009 from http://www.cgap.org/p/site/c/template.rc/1.26.3406/. Washington, D.C.: CGAP.

CGAP. (2009). Information systems: Software Listings and Reviews. Retrieved July 10, 2009, from http://www.cgap.org/p/site/c/template.rc/1.11.103251/1.26.3104/.

CGAP. (2009). *Software Product Dashboard*. Retrieved from CGAP: http://collab2.cgap.org/gm/ISFund_Software_Product_Dashboard

Charitonenko, S. & Campion (2003). *Expanding Commercial Microfinance in Rural Areas: Constraints and Opportunities. A. Rural Finance Expansion: Experience in Commercialization*. Chemonics Int. Retrieved September 25, 2009, from http://dec.usaid.gov

Chemin, M. (2008). The benefits and costs of microfinance: Evidence from Bangladesh. *The Journal of Development Studies, 44*(4), 463–484. doi:10.1080/00220380701846735

Chowdhury, A. M. R., & Bhuiya, A. (2001). Do Poverty Alleviation Programmes Reduce Inequality in Health: Lessons from Bangladesh. In Leon, D., & Walt, G. (Eds.), *Poverty Inequality and Health*. Oxford: OUP.

Chowdhury, F. (2007). The Metamorphosis of the microcredit debtor. *New Age Journal*. 24 Jun/07. Retrieved March 25, 2009, from http://www.newagebd.com/2007/jun/24/oped.html

Christen, R. P., & Drake, D. (2002). Commercialization: The New Reality of Microfinance? In Drake, D., & Rhyne, E. (Eds.), *The Commercialization of Microfinance: Balancing Business and Development*. ACCION International.

Christen Peck, R., & Perce, D. (2005). *Managing Risk and Designing Products for Agricultural Microfinance: Features of an Emerging Market*. CGAP Occasional Paper No. 11 Washington D.C. USA: CGAP.

CIA. (2008). *CIA World Factbook* - Unless otherwise noted, information in this page is accurate as of January 1, 2008. Retrieved January 08, 2009, from http://index-mundi.com/g/r.aspx?c=be&v=6 or https://www.cia.gov/library/publications/the-world-factbook/

CIA. (2008). *South Africa*. Retrieved Nov 10, 2008, from CIA - World Fact Book: https://www.cia.gov/library/publications/the-world-factbook/geos/sf.html

Claessens, S. (2006). Access to Financial Services: A Review of the Issues and Public Policy Objectives. [from http://ec.europa.eu/enterprise/enterprise_policy/sme_definition/index_en.htm]. *The World Bank Research Observer, 21*(2), 207–240. Retrieved March 15, 2009. doi:10.1093/wbro/lkl004

Coleman, B. E. (2006). Microfinance in Northeast Thailand: Who benefits and how much? *World Development, 34*(9), 1612–1638. doi:10.1016/j.worlddev.2006.01.006

Collins, D., Murdoch, J., Rutherford, S., & Ruthven, O. (2009). *Portfolios of the poor: How the world's poor live on $2/day*. Princeton: Princeton University Press.

Collins, D. (2005). Financial instruments for the poor: Initial findings from the financial diaries study. CSSR Working Paper. Cape Town, University of Cape Town.

Conlin, M. (1999). Peer group micro-lending programs in Canada and the United States. *Journal of Development Economics, 60*(1), 249–269. doi:10.1016/S0304-3878(99)00043-7

Copestone, J. (1995). Poverty Oriented Financial Services Programmes: Room for Improvement? *Savings and Development, 19*(4), 417–435.

Creswell, J. N. (2003). *Research Design: Qualitative, Quantitative, and Mixed Methods Approaches* (2nd ed.). Thousand Oaks, CA: Sage Publications Ltd.

Daley-Harris, S., Pollin, P., & Montgomery, F. (2007). *Debate on Microcredit*. Washington, DC: Foreign Policy in Focus.

Daley-Harris, S. (2002). State of the Microcredit Summit Campaign Report 2002. Retrieved October 5, 2009, from http://www.microcreditsummit.org

Davies, E., & Roy, A. (2008). *Does Meeting Repay? Early Repayment and Default in Microfinance: Evidence from India.* Presentation made by the Institute for Financial Management and Research (IFMR), India.

Davis, F. (1989). Perceived usefulness, perceived ease of use, and user acceptance of information technology. *Management Information Systems Quarterly, 13*, 318–339. doi:10.2307/249008

Deaton, A. (2009). Instruments of development: randomization in the tropics, and the search for the elusive keys to economic development. Working Paper 14690. Cambridge, MA: National Bureau of Economic Research.

Demirguc-Kunt, A., Beck, T., & Honohan, P. (2007). *Policy research report on Access to Finance*. Washington, DC: World Bank.

Dewett, T., & Jones, G. R. (2001). The role of information technology in the organization: a review, model, and assessment. *Journal of Management, 27*, 313–346. doi:10.1016/S0149-2063(01)00094-0

Dichter, T., & Harper, M. (Eds.). (2007). *What's Wrong with Micro-finance? Practical Action: Rugby.*

Dieckmann, R. (2007). *Microfinance: An emerging investment opportunity: Uniting social investment and financial returns* (p. 20). Frankfurt: Deutsche Bank Research.

DIRCE. (2008). Corporate Structure and Demography. Central Companies Directory at 1 January 2008. *Instituto Nacional de Estadística*. Retrieved March 18, 2009, from http://www.ine.es/en/inebmenu/mnu_empresas_en.htm.

Douglas, M., & Isherwood, B. (1996). *The World of Goods: Towards an Anthropology of Consumption* (2nd ed.). London: Routledge.

Dubreuil, G. E., & Mirada, C. T. (2008). Microfinance and gender considerations in developed countries: The case of Catalonia. *ISTR 2008 International Conference.* Barcelona, Spain. July, 2008.

Dunford, C. (2006). *Evidence of microfinance's contribution to achieving the millennium development goals.* Davis, CA: Freedom from Hunger.

Dunford, C. Leatherman, S. Sinclair, M.R., Metcalfe, M., Gray, B. & Vor der Bruegge, E. (2007). How Microfinance can Work for the Poor. In *Freedom for Hunger.*

Dupas, P & Robinson, J. (2009). Savings constraints and micro-enterprise development: Evidence from a field experiment in Kenya. Financial Access Initiative.

Dwivedi, P., & Sharma, A. N. (2007). A Study on Environmental Sanitation, Sanitary Habits and Personal Hygiene among the Baigas of Samnapur Block of Dindori District, Madhya Pradesh. *Journal of Human Ecology (Delhi, India), 22*(1), 7–10.

Economist. (2009, July 18). Microcredit may not work wonders but it does help the entrepreneurial poor. Finance and Economics, *Economist*, 68.

El Tabba, M. (2007). *Introducing Credit Scoring in Microlending in ABA/SME*. Presentation made at the 2007 IFC Conference: Next Generation Access to Finance.

Elias, N. (2000). *The Civilising Process: Sociogenetic and Psychogenetic Investigations*. London: Wiley/Blackwell. (Original work published 1939)

Eliot, B., Katsioloudes, M., & Weldon, R. (1998). Nonprofit Organizations and the Internet. *Nonprofit Management & Leadership, 8*(3), 297–303. doi:10.1002/nml.8308

Estapé-Dubreuil, G. & Torreguitart-Mirada, C. (2009). L'esperit emprenedor i el microcrèdit: deuanys de microcrèdit a Catalunya (1998-2007). *Revista econòmica de Catalunya, 52* (forthcoming)

Estapé-Dubreuil, G., & Torreguitart-Mirada, C. (2008, September). *An analysis of the public initiatives to support self-employment business activities of the less favoured: Is there a public policy to support the micro-credit sector in developed countries? The case of Catalonia and Spain*. Paper presented at the European Network on Industrial Policy International Conference, San Sebastián, Spain

EU/ACP Microfinance Programme. (2009). *2008 Microfinance Technology Survey*. Washington D.C.: CGAP, from: www.cgap.org/gm/document-1.9.34552/2008%20Microfinance%20Technology%20Survey.pdf

European Commission (2003). Commission Recommendation of 6 May 2003 concerning the definition of micro, small and medium-sized enterprises, 2003/316/EC. *Official Journal of the European Union 20.5.2003.*

European Commission (2007). *The Regulation of Microcredit in Europe*. Expert Group Report.

European Commission Report. (2003). *Microcredit for small business and business creation: Bridging a market gap*. Enterprise Directorate General of the European Commission.

Fairbourne, J. S. (2006). Microfranchising: A New Tool for Creating Economic Self-Reliance. ESR. *RE:view, 8*(1).

Farrell, M. (2008). *Banking 2.0: New Capital Connections for Entrepreneurs*. Forbes.

Ferreyra, J. (2007). *Credit Scoring. Implementación en Mibanco - Perú*. Presentation made at the 2007 IFC Conference: Next Generation Access to Finance.

Finkelstein, M., Jerrett, M., DeLuca, P., Finkelstein, N., Verma, D., Chapman, K., & Sears, M. (2002, September 2). Relation between income, air pollution and mortality: A cohort study. *CMAJ (Canadian Medical Association Journal), 169*(5). Retrieved August 19, 2004, from http://cmaj.ca/cgi/content/ full/169/5/397

Finn, S., Maher, J. K., & Forster, J. (2006). Indicators of Information and Communication Technology Adoption in the Nonprofit Sector. Changes Between 2000 and 2004. *Nonprofit Management & Leadership, 16*(3), 277–295. doi:10.1002/nml.107

Finscope. (2008). *FinScope SA 2008 Survey Findings Launch*. Johannesburg: FinMark Trust.

Fishbein, M., & Ajzen, I. (1975). *Belief, attitude, intention and behavior: An introduction to theory and research*. Reading, MA: Addison-Wesley.

Fisher, T., & Sriram, M. S. (2002). *Beyond Micro-Credit: Putting Development Back into Micro-Finance*. Oxford: Oxfam.

Fleisig, H. W., & de la Peña, N. (2003). *Legal and Regulatory Requirements for Effective Rural Financial Markets*. Paper presented at the USAID/WOCCU International Conference on Best Practices: Paving the Way Forward in Rural Finance, Washington, D.C. Retrieved October 10, 2009, from www.fao.org

Flick, U. (2006). *An introduction to qualitative research* (3rd ed.). Thousand Oaks, CA: Sage Publications Ltd.

Fonseca, C., Adank, M., Casella, D., Jeths, M., van der Linde, P. & Dijkshoorn, B. (2007). *Micro-finance for Water, Sanitation and Hygiene: An Introduction*.

Fountain, J. E. (2003). *Information, Institutions and Governance: Advancing a Basic Social Science Research Program for Digital Government*. Working paper series No. RWP 03-004, John F. Kennedy School of Government, Cambridge, MA, USA.

Frankiewicz, C., (2001, February). Calmeadow Metrofund: A Canadian experiment in sustainable microfinance. Calmeadow, Nova Scotia, Canada.

Freeman, L. (2006a). ZOPA: A Gigantic Opportunity. *Credit Union Journal*, *10*(46), 1–17.

Frost, R., & Strauss, J. (2001). *E-Marketing* (2nd ed.). Upper Saddle River, NJ: Prentice Hall.

Frost, B. (2007) Water and Sanitation: The Silent Emergency, *United Nations Chronicle* Vol XLIV (4) accessed at: http://www.un.org/wcm/content/site/chronicle/cache/bypass/home/archive/issues2007/themdgsareweontrack/waterandsanitationthesilentemergency?ctnscroll_articleContainerList=1_0&ctnlistpagination_articleContainerList=true

Gartner Inc. (2008): Gartner Says Social Banking Platforms Threaten Traditional Banks for Control of Financial Relationships. *Gartner*. Retrieved from www.gartner.com/it/page.jsp?id=597907.

George, M. M. (2009). *A Blue Revolution: Microfinance, Water and Sanitation in India. Microfinance Insights* (*Vol. 10*). Jan/Feb.

George, R. (2008). *The Big Necessity: Adventures in the World of Human Waste*. London: Portobello Books. Government of Orissa (undated) Total Sanitation Campaign http://www.orissa.gov.in/RD/sanitation/tsc.html

Ghatak, M., & Guinnane, T. W. (1999). The economics of lending with joint liability: theory and practice. *Journal of Development Economics*, *60*(1), 195–228. doi:10.1016/S0304-3878(99)00041-3

Ghosh, R. A. (2005). *Free/Libre/Open Source Software for developing countries: skills, employment and costs*. Paper presented at International Conference on Open Source ICOS 2005, Taipei. November 10, 2005. Retrieved October 20, 2009 from http://www.infonomics.nl/FLOSS/papers/20051110/rishabGHOSH-icos05.pdf

Gil Aluja, J. (1999). *Elementos para una Teoría de la Decisión en la Incertidumbre*. Pontevedra, Spain: Milladoiro.

Gilb, T. (2005). *Competitive Engineering*. Oxford, MA: Butterworth Heinemann.

Global Envision. (2006). The Basics on microfinance. Retrieved October 20, 2009 from http://www.mcenterprises.org/userimages/file/basics_on_microfinance_global_envision_2006.pdf

Goodwin-Groen, R. (1998). *The role of Commercial Banks in Microfinance: Asia-Pacific Region*. The Foundation for Development Cooperation Ltd.

Gordon, L. (1998). Tech Wise: Nonprofits Join the Revolution. *Nonprofit World*, *16*(5), 37–41.

Goudzwaard, M. B. (1968). Price Ceilings And Credit Rationing. *The Journal of Finance*, *23*(1), 177–185. doi:10.2307/2325317

Gray, V. (2007). *Africa, ICT Indicators, 2007*. Retrieved on 1 November 2009 from http://www.itu.int/ITU- D/ict/statistics/at_glance/af_ictindicators_2007.html ITU

Growfish. (2004, June 23). Victorian yabby growers pushed to the wall. *Gippsland Aquaculture Industry Network – GAIN*. Retrieved July 10, 2009, from http://www.growfish.com.au/content.asp?contentid=1864

GSMA. (2009). Mobile Money for the Unbanked Annual Report 2009. London, UK.

Gueyié, J.-P., & Fischer, K. P. (2009). Microfinance and market-oriented microfinance institutions. *Canadian Journal of Development Studies*, *29*(1-2), 23–40.

Gugerty, M. K. (2007). You can't save alone: Commitment in rotating savings and credit associations in Kenya. *Economic Development and Cultural Change*, *55*, 251–282. doi:10.1086/508716

Guichandut, P. (2006). Europe occidentale et reste du monde: parle-t-on des mêmes pratiques?, *Finance & The Common Good / Bien Commun*, *25*(3), 54-113.

Gupta, S. K. (2002). Information and Communication Technology (ICT) plus Finance Model for Rural Poor. *Working paper*.

Gutiérrez-Nieto, B., Serrano-Cinca, C., & MarMolinero, C. (2007). Microfinance Institutions and Efficiency. *Omega, 35*(2), 131–142. doi:10.1016/j.omega.2005.04.001

Gutiérrez-Nieto, B., Fuertes-Callén, Y., & Serrano-Cinca, C. (2008). Internet reporting in microfinance institutions. *Online Information Review, 32*(3), 417–436. doi:10.1108/14684520810889709

Haaland, R. (2003). Licence fees and GDP per capita: the case for open source in developing countries. *First Monday, 8*(12). Retrieved October 20, 2009 from http://firstmonday.org/htbin/cgiwrap/bin/ojs/index.php/fm/issue/view/165

Hackler, D., & Saxton, G. D. (2007). The Strategic Use of Information Technology by Nonprofit Organizations: Increasing Capacity and Untapped Potential. *Public Administration Review, 67*(3), 474–487. doi:10.1111/j.1540-6210.2007.00730.x

Hasan, M. E., Nuremowla, S. A., & Musa, A. S. M. (2004). *Come To Save (CTS) Cooperatives Limited – A Vision: A Case Study on Poverty Focused Microfinance Program.* Dhaka: Plan Bangladesh.

Hashemi, S. (1997). Those Left Behind: A Note on Targeting the Hardcore Poor. In Wood, G. D., & Sharif, I. A. (Eds.), *Who Needs Credit: Poverty and Finance in Bangladesh* (pp. 249–257). London: Zed Books.

Helms, B. (2006). *Access for All: Building Inclusive Financial Systems.* Washington, DC: CGAP/World Bank.

Hishigsuren, G. (2006). *Information and Communication Technology and Microfinance: Options for Mongolia.* ADB Institute Discussion Paper No. 42. Tokyo, Japan, Asian Development Bank.

Holahan, C. (2007). EBay: The Place for Microfinance. *Business Week Online* (p. 24).

Hollis, T. (2007). *Social Media Advertising: No Direct Response Proposition.* ClickZ Experts.

Hong, W., Thong, J. Y., Wong, W. M., & Tam, K. (2001). Determinants of user acceptance of digital libraries: An empirical examination of individual differences and system characteristics. *Journal of Management Information Systems, 18*(3), 97–124.

Hughes, N., & Lonie, S. (2007). M-PESA: Mobile money for the "unbanked". Turning cell phones into 24-hour tellers in Kenya. *Innovations: Technology, Governance, Globalization, 2*, 63–81. doi:10.1162/itgg.2007.2.1-2.63

Hulme, H., & Mosley, P. (1996). *Finance Against Poverty (Vol. 1).* London: Routledge.

Hulme, D. & Moore, K. (2006). *Why has Microfinance Been a Policy Success? Bangladesh and Beyond.* paper presented at ESRC Seminar, Statecraft in the South: Public Policy Success in Developing Countries, University of Manchester, May 20, 2005.

Hung, C. H. (2003, November). Loan performance of group-based microcredit programs in the United States. *Economic Development Quarterly, 17*(4), 383–395. doi:10.1177/0891242403255364

Hung, C. H. (2006). Rules and actions: Determinants of peer group and staff actions in group-based microcredit programs in the United States. *Economic Development Quarterly,* (Feb): 75–96. doi:10.1177/0891242405279361

Hutton, G., Haller, L., & Bartram, J. (2007). Global cost-benefit analysis of water supply and sanitation interventions. *Journal of Water and Health, 5*(4), 481–502. doi:10.2166/wh.2007.009

Idate Organization. (2008). The Internet Giants and Web 2.0. *DigiWorld 2008.* Retrieved from www.idate.org

IEP. (2005). *Breakthrough.* Indigenous Enterprise Partnerships. Retrieved June 20, 2009, from www.positiveoutcomes.com.au/uploads/files/1126158084404_0.5922729914425602.pdf

IFC Conference proceedings. (2007). *Next Generation Access to Finance.* Retrieved from www.ifc.org/ifcext/gfm.nsf/AttachmentsByTitle/FI-CB-NextGenProceedings-Dec08/$FILE/FI-CB-NextGenProceedings-Dec08.pdf

IMF. (2008). *The Purchasing Power of Working Time 2008 – An international Comparison.* International Metalworkers' Federation. Retrieved February 28, 2009, from http://www.imfmetal.org

IRIA. (2008). Informe IRIA 2008. *Consejo Superior de Administración Electrónica. Ministerio de Administraciones Públicas*. Retrieved March 15, 2009, from http://www.csi.map.es/csi/iria_2008/

Islam, R., et al. (2008). *Internal Assessment of CTS: Microfinance Software and Handheld Device*. Unpublished, Plan Bangladesh and Come To Save (CTS) Cooperatives Limited, Bangladesh.

Ivatury, G., & Mas, I. (2008). *The Early Experience with Branchless Banking*. Washington, D.C.: CGAP.

Ivatury, G., & Pickens, M. (2006). *Mobile Phone Banking and Low-Income Customers: Evidence from South Africa*. Washington, DC: CGAP.

Ivatury, G., & Lyman, T. (2007). *Regulatory issues in branchless banking: The new frontier. Washington, D.C: CGAP.Ivatury, G. & Mas, I. (2008). The Early Experience with Branchless Banking*. Washington, D.C: CGAP.

Ivatury, G. (2005). Using Electronic Payments to Build Inclusive Financial Systems. *CGAP Technology Center*. Retrieved March 17, 2009, from www.cgap.org/technology.html

Ivatury, G. (2006). Using Technology to Build Inclusive Financial Systems. *Microfinance Gateway Library*. Retrieved March 17, 2009, from http://www.microfinancegateway.org/p/site/m/library.html

Ivins, T. Z. (2008). Microfranchising Microlending Centers: A Sustainable Model for Expanding the Right to Education in Developing Countries? *Journal of Asynchronous Learning Networks, 12*(1).

Jackson, C. M., Chow, S., & Leitch, R. A. (1997). Toward an understanding of the behavioral intention to use an information system. *Decision Sciences, 28*(2), 357–389. doi:10.1111/j.1540-5915.1997.tb01315.x

Jain, S., & Mansuri, G. (2003). A little at a time: the use of regularly scheduled repayments in microfinance programs. *Journal of Development Economics, 72*(1), 253–279. doi:10.1016/S0304-3878(03)00076-2

Jensen, M. C. (2000). *Value Maximization and Stakeholder Theory* (Working Paper-HBS Working Knowledge). Cambridge, MA:Harvard Business School.

Karlan, D., & Zinman, J. (2009). *Expanding Microenterprise Credit Access: Using Randomized Supply Decisions to Estimate the Impacts in Manila*. Yale Economics Dept. Working Paper No. 68, Yale University, New Haven, USA.

Kaufman, R. J., & Kriebel, C. H. (1988). *Identifying Business Value Linkages for Information Technology: An Exploratory Application to Treasury Workstations*. Information Systems working paper series, NYU working paper no. IS-88-47. NY, USA.

Kenya, F. S. D. (2007). Financial access in Kenya: Results of a 2006 National Survey. Nairobi, Kenya.

Ketley, R., & Duminy, B. (2003). Meeting the Challenge the Impact of Changing Technology on MicroFinance Institutions (MFIs). *MicroSave Briefing*. Retrieved October 10, 2009 from http://www.microsave.org/

Khandker, S. R. (1999). *Fighting Poverty with Microcredit (Bangladesh edition)*. Dhaka: The University Press Ltd.

Khandker, S.R. (2005) Microfinance and Poverty: Evidence Using Panel Data from Bangladesh, *The World Bank Economic Review* 19(2) 263:283

Khare, R. S. (1962). The Ritual Purity and Pollution in relation to Domestic Sanitation. *The Eastern Anthropologist, 15*(2), 125–139.

Kiva: Improving People's lives, One Small Loan at a Time. *Knowlege@Wharton*.

Kizito, B. J. (2007). Practices of managing and using ICT services by village banks in Uganda. *Working paper, Kampala International University*.

Kotler, P. (1997). *Marketing Management* (9th ed.). Upper Saddle River, NJ: Prentice Hall.

Kouassi-Komlan, E., & Fonseca, C. (2004). *Micro Finance for Water and Sanitation in West Africa*. 30th WEDC International Conference, Vientiane, Laos. Johnson, S. & Rogaly, B. (1997). *Micro-finance and Poverty Reduction*. Oxford: Oxfam.

Labie, M. (2001). Corporate Governance in Microfinance Organizations: a Long and Winding Road. *Management Decision, 39*(4), 296–301. doi:10.1108/00251740110391466

Langer, A. M. (2008). *Analysis and Design of Information Systems*. London: Springer-Verlag.

Ledgerwood, J. (1998). *Microfinance Handbook*. Washington, DC: The World Bank. doi:10.1596/978-0-8213-4306-7

Ledgerwood, J., & White, V. (2006). *Transforming Microfinance Institutions: Providing Full financial Services to the Poor*. Washington, D.C.: The International Bank for Reconstruction and Development/The World Bank.

Lee, G. K., & Cole, R. E. (2003). From a firm-based to a community based model of knowledge creation: The case of the Linux kernel development. *Organization Science, 14*, 633–649. doi:10.1287/orsc.14.6.633.24866

Lee, S. M., Kim, J., Choi, Y., & Lee, S.-G. (2009). Effects of IT knowledge and media selection on operational performance of small firms. *Small Business Economics, 32*(3), 214–257. doi:10.1007/s11187-007-9095-5

Lee-St. John, J. (2008). Hey, Buddy, Can You Spare $10,000? *Time, 171*(10), 58–58.

Leishman, P. (2009). Understanding the unbanked customer and sizing the mobile money opportunity. In *Mobile Money for the Unbanked Annual Report 2009*. London, UK: GSMA.

Lenrevie, J., Lévy, J., & Lindon, D. (2006). *Mercator*. Dunod.

Levine, R., & Easterly, W. (1997). Africa's Growth Tragedy: Policies and Ethnic Divisions. *The Quarterly Journal of Economics, 113*(4), 1203–1250.

Littfield, E. Morduch, J. & Hashemi, S. (2003). *Is Microfinance an Effective Strategy to Reach the Millennium Development Goals*. CGAP: Focus Note 24.

Luarn, P., & Lin, H. (2005). Toward an understanding of the behavioural intention to use mobile banking. *Computers in Human Behavior, 21*, 873–891. doi:10.1016/j.chb.2004.03.003

Lui, A., Pertet, R., & White, V. (2006). *Technology for the Poor: Challenges and Benefits of PDAs, ATMs and More for Microfinance Institutes.* Paper presented at a USAID Learning Conference: Microenterprise Development in a Global World. USAID.

Lyman, T. R., Ivatury, G., & Staschen, S. (2006). *Use of agents in branchless banking for the poor: Rewards, risks and regulation*. Washington, D.C: CGAP.

Lynch, J., Smith, G., & Kaplan, G., & House. J. (2000). Income inequality and mortality: importance to health of individual income, psychosocial environment, or material conditions. *British Medical Journal, 320*, 1200–1204. doi:10.1136/bmj.320.7243.1200

Mahoney, P. G. (2002). Information Technology and the Organization of Securities Markets. *Working Papers -- Financial Institutions Center at The Wharton School* (p. 1).

Mainhart, A. (1999). *Management Information Systems for Microfinance*. Development Alternatives, Inc.

Mainhart, A. (1999). *Management Information System for Microfinance: An Evaluation Framework*. A work supported by the U.S. Agency for International Development, Bureau for Global Programs, Center for Economic Growth and Agricultural Development, Office of Microenterprise Development, through funding to the Microenterprise Best Practices (MBP) Project, contract number PCE-C-00-96-90004-00. Retrieved August 6, 2006 from http://www.cgap.org

Majewsky, G., & Usoro, A. (2008). *Microfinance Monitoring, Reporting and Group Lending as Challenges for the Data Warehousing Technology*. Paper presented at eRA – 3 Proceedings: The Contribution of Information Technology to Science, Economy, Society & Education. T. E. I. of Piraeus, Spetses Island, Greece.

Marconi, R., & Mosley, P. (2006). Bolivia During the Global Crisis 1998-2004: Towards Macroeconomics of Microfinance. *Journal of International Development, 18*, 237–261. doi:10.1002/jid.1218

Mathieson, K. (1991). Predicting user intentions: comparing the technology acceptance model with the theory of planned behaviour. *Information Systems Research, 2*, 173–191. doi:10.1287/isre.2.3.173

Mathieson, K., Peacock, E., & Chin, W. W. (2001). Extending the technology acceptance model: The influence of perceived user resources. *ACM SIGMIS Database, 32*(3), 86–112. doi:10.1145/506724.506730

Mathison, S. (2005). *Increasing the Outreach and Sustainability of Microfinance through ICT Innovation*. Brisbane, Australia, Foundation for Development Cooperation (FDC).

Mathison, S. (2007). *Increasing the Outreach and Sustainability of Microfinance through ICT Innovation*. Papers from Electronic Banking with the Poor: Increasing the Outreach and Sustainability of microfinance through ICT Innovation, The Foundation for Development Cooperation. Retrieved on August 15th 2009, from http://www.fdc.org.au/

Matin, I., Hulme, D., & Rutherford, S. (2002). Finance for the Poor: From Microcredit to Micro financial Services. *Journal of International Development, 14*, 273–294. doi:10.1002/jid.874

Matthews, P. (2007). Platform for Improving Service Delivery or an Expensive Distraction. *Rural e-services*. Retrieved March 19, 2009, from http://linux.odi.org.uk/eservblog/?

McAfee, A. P. (2006). Enterprise 2.0: The Dawn of Emergent Collaboration. *MIT Sloan Management Review, 47*(3), 21–28.

McKnight, D., Choudhury, V., & Kacmar, C. (2002). Developing and validating trust measures for e- commerce: An integrative typology. *Information Systems Research, 13*(3), 334–359. doi:10.1287/isre.13.3.334.81

McLaughlin, T. (1971). *Coprophilia or a Peck of Dirt*. London: Cassell.

McLoughlin, I. (1999). *The shaping of Technology and Organizations*. New York: Routledge. doi:10.4324/9780203019870

McNamara, P., & Shipton, P. (1995). Rural credit and savings. In McPherson, M., & Radelet, S. (Eds.), *Economic recovery in the Gambia: Insights for adjustments in sub-saharan Africa*. Cambridge: Harvard University Press.

Mehta, S., & Kalra, M. (2006). Information and Communication Technologies: A bridge for social equity and sustainable development in India. *The International Information & Library Review, 38*, 147–160. doi:10.1016/j.iilr.2006.06.008

Mether, L. (2004). Yabby farms to close. *Growfish*. Gippsland Aquaculture Industry Network – GAIN. Retrieved July 10, 2009, from http://www.growfish.com.au/content.asp?contentid=1991

Meyer, R. L. (2007). Measuring the Impact of Microfinance. In Dichter, T., & Harper, M. (Eds.), *What's Wrong with Micro-finance, Rugby: Practical Action*.

MIE. (2007). The microfinance information exchange. *MicroBanking Bulletin, 15*.

Miles, M. B., & Huberman, A. M. (1994). *Qualitative data analysis* (2nd ed.). Thousand Oaks, CA: Sage.

Ministry of Statistics and Program Implementation. (2002). *Report on Village Facilities*. New Delhi, NCR: National Sample Survey Organisation of India

Mishkin, F. S. (2004). *The economics of money, banking and Financial Markets*. Paris: Pearson Addison-Wesley.

Mithas, S., Krishnan, M. S., & Fornell, C. (2005). *Effect of Information Technology Investments on Customer Satisfaction: Theory and Evidence*. Stephen M. Ross School of Business working paper no. 971, University of Michigan, MI, USA.

Mithas, S., Ramasubbu, N., & Sambamurthy, V. (2008). *Information Management Capability and Firm Performance: An Empirical Analysis*. Robert H. Smith School of Business Research Paper No. RHS 06-071, University of Maryland, MD, USA.

Mize, J., & Hallam, C. (2002). *Stakeholder Value Metrics (Module to support Team Assignment in Course 16.852J/ESD.61.J-Fall 2002 "Integrating the Lean Enterprise")*. Cambridge, MA: Massachusetts Institute of Technology.

MKNelly. B. & Dunford, C. (1998). *Impact of Credit with Education on Mothers and Their Young Children's Nutrition: Lower Pra Bank Credit with Education in Ghana.* Freedom from Hunger Research paper, No. 4 Davis, CA, USA.

MKNelly. B. & Dunford, C. (1999). *Impact of Credit with Education on Mothers and Their Young Children's Nutrition: CRECER Credit with Education Program in Bolivia.* Freedom from Hunger Research paper, No. 5 Davis, CA, USA.

Moore, G. C., & Benbasat, I. (1991). Development of an Instrument to Measure the Perceptions of Adopting an Information Technology Innovation. *Information Systems Research, 2*(3), 192–222. doi:10.1287/isre.2.3.192

Moore, M. (2000). Managing for Value: Organizational Strategy in For-Profit, Nonprofit, and Governmental Organizations. *Nonprofit and Voluntary Sector Quarterly, 29*(1), 183–208. doi:10.1177/089976400773746391

Morduch, J. (2000). The Microfinance Schism. *World Development, 28*(4), 617–629. doi:10.1016/S0305-750X(99)00151-5

Morduch, J. (1999). The Microfinance Promise. *Journal of Economic Literature, 37*(4), 1569–1614.

Morduch, J., & Rutherford, S. (2003). *Micro-finance: Analytical Issues for India background paper prepared for the World Bank.* Washington, DC: World Bank.

Morduch, J. (1998). *Does Microfinance Really Help the Poor? New Evidence on Flagship Programs in Bangladesh.* MacArthur Foundation project on inequality working paper, Princeton University, draft. Retrieved April 17, 2006 from http://www.nyu.edu/projects/morduch/documents/microfinance/Does_Microfinance_Really_Help.pdf

Naagesh, N. (2009). *FINO launches MITRA.* India Microfinance News Retrieved August 10, 2009, from http://www.microfinancefocus.com

NAB. (2008). Micro Finance. *National Australia Bank Annual Report.* Retrieved February 03, 2009, from http://nab2008annualreports.textpacific.com.au/corporate_responsibility_review/microfinance. asp

NABARD. (2008). *Report of the Committee on Financial Inclusion.* New Delhi, NCR: NABARD

News, E. F. Y. March (2007). *Janalakshmi Gets Smart Card Solution from IBM, FINO.* Retrieved March 7, 2007, from http://www.efytimes.com/e1/fullnews.asp?edid=17699

O'Brien, J. (Indian Reprint 1996). *Management Information Systems.* New Delhi: Galgotia Publications.

ONTSI. (2008). The Network Society in Spain-Annual Report 2007. *Spanish Observatory for Telecommunications and Information Society. Ministerio de Industria, Turismo y Comercio.* Retrieved February 25, 2009, from http://observatorio.red.es/annual-reports/articles/1449.

Owuor, S. (2005). *Urban households ruralising their livelihoods: The changing nature of urban-rural linkages in an East African town.* Leiden: African Studies Centre Seminar Series.

Owuor, S. (2006). *Bridging the urban-rural divide: Multispatial livelihoods in Nakuru town.* Leiden: African Studies Center.

Parikh, T. (2005). *Rural Microfinance Service Delivery: Gaps, Inefficiencies and Emerging Solutions,* University of Washington. Retrieved October 5, 2009, from http://www.fdc.org.au

Paul, B. D. (1958). The Role of Beliefs and Customs in Sanitation Programs. *American Journal of Public Health, 48*(11), 1502–1506. doi:10.2105/AJPH.48.11_Pt_1.1502

Pearson, I. (2002). *The National Sanitation Programme in Lesotho: How political Leadership Achieved Long-term Results.* Washington: World Bank.

Peelen, E. (2006). *Customer Relationship Management.* Bruxelles, Benelux: Pearson Education.

Pitt, M., Shahidur, M., Khandker, R., & Cartwright, J. (2006). Empowering women with micro finance: Evidence from Bangladesh. *Economic Development and Cultural Change, 54*(4), 791–831. doi:10.1086/503580

Pitt, M., Shahidur, M., Khandker, R., Chowdhury, O. H., & Millimet, D. L. (2003). Credit Programs for the Poor and the Health Status of Children in Rural Bangladesh. *International Economic Review, 44*(1), 87–118. doi:10.1111/1468-2354.t01-1-00063

Plan Bangladesh. (2007). *Annual Report 2007*. Dhaka: Plan Bangladesh.

Powers, J., Magnoni, B., & Knapp, S. (2008). *Person-To-Person Lending: Is Financial Democracy A Click Away?* (p. 43). US AID.

Prahalad, C. (2004). *The Fortune at the Bottom of the Pyramid: Eradicating Poverty Through Profits*. Wharton, USA: Wharton School Publishing.

Pratt, M. K. (2007). Game Changer (cover story). *Computerworld, 41*(5), 31–32.

Prosper Lending Review. (2007, July 23). How does Prosper make money? Retrieved September 1, 2008 from http://prosperlending.blogspot.com/2007/07/how-does-prosper-make-money.html

Putnam, R. (1993). The prosperous community: Social capital and public life. *The American Prospect, 13*, 35–42.

PYME. (2007). Informe sobre la PYME. Colección Panorama PYME, 12. *Dirección General de Política de la Pequeña y Mediana Empresa. Ministerio de Industria, Turismo y Comercio*. Retrieved March 21, 2009, from http://www.ipyme.org/IPYME/es- ES/QuienesSomos/Publicaciones2.

Ragowsky, A., & Gefen, D. (2008). What Makes the Competitive Contribution of ERP Strategic. *The Data Base for Advances in Information Systems, 39*(2), 33–49.

Raihan, A. (2001). The State of E-Finance in developing Countries: Bangladesh perspective". Expert Group Meeting on "Improving Competitiveness of SMEs in Developing Countries: Role of Finance, including E-finance to Enhance Enterprise Development," Geneva, 22-24 October, 2001.

Ramana-Murthy, G. V., & Bagchi, S. (2005). *Delimiting Microfinance through Effective MIS*. Paper presented at ICT for Communities: Learning Workshop Series - I, 2005 MIS for Community Based Financial Institutions - Innovations & Experiences. Retrieved April 25, 2009, from www.microfinancegateway.org

Rao, K. M. (2004). *Microfinance Institutions in India*. An article presented at the APRACA Seminar on Regulation of MFIs, Manila, Philippines.

Red.es. (2007). Tecnologías de la Información y las Comunicaciones en la microempresa española. Análisis por sector de actividad y Comunidad Autónoma. *Observatorio de las Telecomunicaciones y de la Sociedad de la Información. Ministerio de Industria, Turismo y Comercio.* Retrieved March 2, 2009, from http://observatorio.red.es/empresas/articles/id/422/

Reenskaug, T. (1979). MODELS - VIEWS - CONTROLLERS. http://folk.uio.no/trygver/1979/mvc-2/1979-12-MVC.pdf

Regy, P.V. & Mahajan, V. (2006). IT at BASIX: Successes and Failures, a Retrospective, *Information for Development, 4*(5).

Reille, X., & Forster, S. (2008). *Foreign Capital Investment in Microfinance: Balancing Social and Financial Returns. Focus Note 44.* Washington, D.C.: CGAP.

Reille, X. (2008). *Technology Revolutionizing the Industry*. Presentation made at SANABEL 5th Annual Conference; "State of the Industry and Presentation of the Conference Themes." Tunis, Tunisia.

Rekha Misra Sa-Dhan Association. (2008). *Bharat Micro Finance Report*. New Delhi, NCR: Sa-Dhan Microfinance Resource Centre

Rhyne, E. (1998). The Yin and Yang of Microfinance: Reaching the Poor and Sustainability. *MicroBanking Bulletin, 2*(July), 6–9.

Rhyne, E. (2009). Microfinance for Banker & Investors: Understanding the Opportunity at the Bottom of the Pyramid, Underwritten by Visa Inc., Commissioned by the UN Advisors Group on Inclusive Financial Sectors. Retrieved November 6, 2009 from www.accion.org/Document.Doc?id=405

Rhyne, E., & Christen, R. P. (1999). *Microfinance enters the Marketplace.* USA: USAID Microenterprise Publications. Retrieved from www.uncdf.org/mfdl/readings/Marketplace.pdf

Robinson, M. S. (2001). *The Microfinance Revolution: Sustainable Finance for the Poor.* Washington: The World Bank.

Rogers, E. M. (1995). *Diffusion of Innovations* (4th ed.). New York: The Free Press.

Roodman, R., & Morduch, J. (2009). *The Impact of Microcredit on the Poor in Bangladesh: Revisiting the Evidence.* CGD Working Paper 174. Washington, DC: Center for Global Development. from http://www.cgdev.org/content/publications/detail/1422302.

Rosenberg, R., Gonzalez, A., & Narain, S. (2009). The New Moneylenders: Are the Poor Being Exploited by High Microcredit Interest Rates? *Occasional Paper, 15.* Washington, D.C.: CGAP.

Rosenberg, R., Mwangi, P., Christen, R. P. & Nasr, M. (July 2003). *Disclosure Guidelines for Financial Reporting by Microfinance Institutions.* Washington D.C.: CGAP.

Rukunga, G., Mutethia, D., & Kioko, T. (n.d.). *Why the water and sanitation sector in East Africa should consider disabled people,* WELL Country Note 12.1 (F. Odhiambo, Ed.) Loughborough: WEDC Loughborough University. Retrieved from http://www.lboro.ac.uk/well/resources/Publications/Country%20Notes/CN12.1.htm

Rutherford, S. (1999). *The poor and their money: An essay about financial services for poor people.* Manchester: Institute for Development Policy and Management, University of Manchester.

Rutherford, S. (2002). Money talks: Conversations with poor households in Bangladesh about managing money. *Working Paper Series.* Manchester, Institute for Development Policy and Management.

Ruthven, O. (2002). Money mosaics: financial choice and strategy in a West Delhi squatter settlement. *Journal of International Development, 14,* 249–271. doi:10.1002/jid.875

Saidel, J. R., & Cour, S. (2003). Information Technology and the Voluntary Sector Workplace. *Nonprofit and Voluntary Sector Quarterly, 32*(1), 5–24. doi:10.1177/0899764002250004

Salazar, D. (2004). Credit Scoring. CGAP IT Innovation Series, Washington D.C.: CGAP. Retrieved from www.microfinancegateway.org/content/article/detail/18047

Sanchez, E. C. (2003). Microfinance and technology: The way to greater financial access Retrieved August 1, 2006 from http://www.itmatters.com.ph/features.php?id=091503

Sayd, N., & Hettihewa, S. (2007). Venture capital or private equity? The Asian experience. *Business Horizons, 50*(4), 335–345. doi:10.1016/j.bushor.2007.03.001

Schreiner, M. (2002). *Scoring: The Next Breakthrough in Microcredit?* Washington D.C.: CGAP, Retrieved from www.microfinance.com/English/Papers/Scoring_Breakthrough.pdf

Schuman, H., & Presser, S. (1996). *Questions and Answers in Attitude Surveys: Experiments on Question Form, Wording, and Context.* Thousand Oaks, CA: Sage.

Scoble, R., & Shel, I. (2006). *Naked Conversation: How Blogs Are Changing the Way Businesses Talk with Consumers.* Wiley.

Sen, A. (1999). *Development as Freedom.* Oxford University Press.

Servon, L. J. (1997, May). Microenterprise programs in U.S. inner cities: economic development or social welfare? *Economic Development Quarterly,* 166–180. doi:10.1177/089124249701100205

Servon, L. J. (2006, November). Microenterprise development in the United States: Current challenges and new directions. *Economic Development Quarterly*, 351–367. doi:10.1177/0891242406289355

Servon, L. J. (1999). *Bootstrap Capital: Microenterprises and the American Poor*. Washington, DC: Brookings Institution Press, Washington, DC.

Setboonsarng, S., & Zhang, J. (2006). *Using ICT in Capacity Building for Poverty Reduction in Asia: Lessons Learned from the Microfinance Training of Trainers Course*. ADB Institute Discussion Paper No. 50. Tokyo, Japan, Asian Development Bank.

Shipton, P. (1989). *Bitter money: Cultural economy and some African meanings of forbidden currencies*. New Hampshire: American Anthropological Association.

Shipton, P. (2007). *The nature of entrustment: Intimacy, exchange and the sacred in Africa*. New Haven: Yale University Press.

Shipton, P. (1995). How Gambians save: Culture and economic strategy at an ethnic crossroads. In Guyer, J. (Ed.), *Money matters: Instability, values and social payments in modern history of West African communities*. Portsmouth: Reed Elsevier.

Shuen, A. (2008). *Web 2.0: A Strategy Guide*. Sebastopol, CA: O'Reilly Media Inc.

Silva, S. (2002). *Quantum Leap: Microcredit Boosted by Technology*. Microenterprise Americas Magazine. Friday, May 27, 2005/Saturday, June 4, 2005.

Simonwitz, A. (2002). *Appraising the Poverty Outreach of microfinance: A Review of the CGAP Poverty Assessment Tool (PAT)*. Brighton: Imp-Act, Institute of Development Studies.

Sinha, F. (2006). *Social Rating and Social Performance Reporting in Microfinance: Towards a Common Framework*. Washington DC, USA: EDA/M-Cril, Argidius, and the SEEP Network. Retrieved August 11, 2009 from http://www.m-cril.com/pdf/Framework- for-Social-Performance-Rating-and-Reporting.pdf

Sisk, M. (2008). The Rise of Lending Communities. *U.S. Banker*, *118*(2), 18–20.

Smeaton, R. (2003). *Splitting of database: How and why*. The Access User Group of San Diego (AUGSD). Retrieved August 15, 2008, from http://www.augsd.org/sampleapps/Splitting%20a%20Database.ppt

Smith, J. (1999). Information Technology in the small business: Establishing the basis for a management information system. *Journal of Small Business and Enterprise Development*, *6*(4), 326–340, 400. doi:10.1108/EUM0000000006684

Smith, V. (2008). *Clean: A History of Personal Hygiene and Purity*. Oxford: OUP.

Srinivasan, N. (2008). *Microfinance India: State of the Sector Report 2008*. New Delhi, India: Sage Publications.

Sriram, M. S. (2005). Information asymmetry and trust: A framework for studying microfinance in India. *Vikapla*, *30*(4), 77–85.

SSA. (2008). *Mid-year population estimates*. South Africa: Statistics South Africa.

Stauffenberg, D V., Jansson, T., Kenyon, N., & Barluenga-Badiola, María-Cruz (2003) *Indicadores de desempeño para instituciones microfinancieras*. Microrate y Banco Interamericano de Desarrollo (Departamento de Desarrollo Sostenible).

Stetenfeld, B. (2008). P2P Lending: Threat or Opportunity? (cover story). *Credit Union Magazine*, *74*(1), 32–36.

Stiglitz, J. E., & Weiss, A. (1981). Credit Rationing in Markets with Imperfect Information. *The American Economic Review*, *71*(3), 393–410.

Stone, B., & Helft, M. (2009). In Developing Countries, Web Grows without Profit. *The New York Times*. Retrieved April 27, 2009 from http://www.nytimes.com/2009/04/27/technology/start-ups/27global.html?_r=2&ref=global-home.

Sundaresan, S. (Ed.). (2008). *Microfinance: Emerging Trends and Challenges* (1st ed.). Cheltenham, UK: Edward Elgar Publishing Limited.

Surowiecki, J. (2004). *The Wisdom of Crowds: Why the Many Are Smarter than the Few and How Collective Wisdom Shapes Business, Economies, Societies, and Nations*. New York: Doubleday.

Tan, M., & Teo, T. (2000). Factors influencing the adoption of Internet banking. *Journal of the Association for Information Systems, 1*(5), 1–42.

Tapscott, D., & Williams, A. D. (2006). *Wikinomics: How Mass collaboration Changes Everything*. New York: Portfolio.

The World Bank. (2008). *World Development Indicators 2008: Poverty Data, A supplement to World Development Indicators 2008*. Washington, D.C.: Development Data Group, The World Bank.

Thompson, R. (2008). The Coming Transformation of Social Enterprise. *Harvard Business School: Working Knowledge*. Retrieved April 29, 2009 from http://hbswk.hbs.edu/item/5986.html.

Thoreau, H. D. (1854). Economy. *Walden*. Retrieved August 10, 2008, from http://xroads.virginia.edu/~hyper/walden/walden.html

Tiwari, R., & Buse, S. (2007). *The Mobile Commerce Prospects: A Strategic Analysis of Opportunities in the Banking Sector*. Hamburg, Germany: Hamburg University Press.

Townsend, R. M., & Ueda, K. (2006). Financial Deepening, Inequality, and Growth: a Model-based Quantitative Evaluation. *The Review of Economic Studies, 73*(1), 251–293. doi:10.1111/j.1467-937X.2006.00376.x

Trémolet, S., Cardone, R., da Silva, C., & Fonseca, C. (2007). Innovations in Financing Urban Water & Sanitation. Paper presented at the Global Urban Summit "Financing Shelter, Water and sanitation, July 1-6, 2007, Bellagio, Italy. Rockefeller Foundation Center for Sustainable Urban Development of Columbia University. http://www.earth.columbia.edu/csud/documents/Final%20Papers/Week%201/Week1_Finance_IRC.pdf

TSPI. (2009) Microfinance Innovation: Housing & sanitation Program for the Poor presentation at *Philippine Symposium on Sustainable Sanitation and Global Handwashing Day,* Metro Manila, Philippines, 15-16 October.

UNICEF. (2002) *Learning from Experience: Water and Sanitation in India*. UNICEF: New York, accessed at: http://www.unicef.org/publications/files/pub_wes_en.pdf

United Nations. (2008). *Millenium Develoment Goals report*. New York: UN Statistics Division.

United Nations Human Development Report. (2006). *Beyond Scarcity: Power, Poverty and the Global Water Crisis*. New York: United Nations.

Velasco, C., & Marconi, R. (2004). Group Dynamics and Gender Development in Bolivia. *Journal of International Development, 16*, 519–528. doi:10.1002/jid.1089

Venkatesh, V., & Davis, F. D. (1996). A model of the antecedents of perceived ease of use: Development and test. *Decision Sciences, 27*(3), 451–481. doi:10.1111/j.1540-5915.1996.tb01822.x

Venkatesh, V., & Morris, M. G. (2000). Why don't men ever stop to ask for directions? Gender, social influence, and their role in technology acceptance and usage behavior. *Management Information Systems Quarterly, 24*(1), 115–139. doi:10.2307/3250981

Von Pischke, J. D. (1991). *Finance at the Frontier: Debt Capital and the Role of Credit in the Private Economy*. Washington, DC: World Bank Economic Development Institute.

Von Pisschke, J. D. (2007). Methodenstreit and Sustainability in Microfinance: Generalizations Describing Institutional Frameworks. In Dichter, T., & Harper, M. (Eds.), *What's Wrong with Micro-finance, Rugby: Practical Action.*

Wang, Y., Wang, Y.-M., Lin, H.-H., & Tang, T. I. (2003). Determinants of user acceptance of internet banking: An empirical study. *International Journal of Service Industry Management, 14*(5), 501–519. doi:10.1108/09564230310500192

Waterfield, C., & Ramsing, N. (1998). *Management Information Systems for Microfinance Institutes: A Handbook.* CGAP.

Waterfield, C., & Sheldon, T. (1997). *Assessing and Selecting Loan Tracking Software Systems.* New York: Women's World Banking.

Waterfield, C., & Ramsing, N. (1998). Handbook for Management Information Systems for Microfinance Institutions, CGAP Technical Tool Series No. 1, February 1998 Retrieved August 19, 2009, from www.microfinancegateway.org

Wei-Skillern, J., Austin, J. E., Leonard, H., & Stevenson, H. (2007). *Entrepreneurship in the Social Sector.* Thousand Oaks, CA: SAGE publications. Retrieved April 27, 2009 from http://hbswk.hbs.edu/item/5782.html.

Whelan, S. (2003). CGAP IT Innovation Series: Smart Cards. *CGAP Technology Center.* Retrieved March 15, 2009, from www.cgap.org/technology.html

WHO. (2004). Table 3: Estimated deaths per 100,000 population by cause, and member state, 2002. In *Estimates of death rates for 2002 by cause for WHO Member States,* World Health Organization. (WHO), Dept of Measurement and Health Information Dec/04. Retrieved February 26, 2009, from http://www.who.int/whosis/indicators/compendium/2008/1mst/en.

Yu, C., & Hui, D. (2007). Welcome to the World of Web 2.0. *The CPA Journal,* 6–10.

Yunus, M. (2003). *Banker to the Poor.* New York: PublicAffairs.

Yunus, M. (2008). *Creating a World Without Poverty: How Social Business Can transforms our Lives.* New York: PublicAffairs.

Zaman, H. (1999). Assessing the poverty and vulnerability impact of microcredit in Bangladesh a case study of BRAC. *Background paper for the WDR 2000/2001.* Banque mondiale, Washington.

About the Contributors

Arvind Ashta holds the Microfinance Chair of the Burgundy School of Business (Groupe ESC Dijon-Bourgogne), France. He is a professor of finance, control and law and is member of its research center CEREN. He offers courses in Microfinance and this is currently his main field of research (regulatory aspects of Microfinance and advanced technology in Microfinance). He has taught Microfinance as visiting faculty in Chicago (US), Pforzheim (Germany) and Brussels (Belgium). He holds a B.A. (Hons) in Economics from St. Stephen's College, Delhi University, a PGDM from IIM Calcutta and a Doctorat in Law from the University of Paris 2 (Panthéon-Assas). He worked 17 years in Corporate Enterprises in India and France in the fields on Management Control and Accounting before entering academics. He has a number of publications in International journals in behavioural finance, corporate social responsibility and in microfinance.

* * *

Djamchid Assadi is higher education professor and researcher at Groupe ESC Dijon-Bourgogne, France. He authored five books in French and published more than one hundred scholarly and professional articles in English and French. He is also member of several editorial boards publishing journal in English and French. Professor Djamchid ASSADI has delivered many lectures on business and marketing strategies.

Britta Augsburg is a research economist at the Centre for the Evaluation of Development (Institute for Fiscal Studies, London) and also working with the United Nations University/Merit, in the Netherlands. She recently completed her PhD in Social Protection Policy at the Maastricht Graduate School of Governance and previously did her degree in Econometrics at the University of Maastricht. In line with her PhD work, her present research looks at the effectiveness of development interventions, with a special focus on microfinance. She is currently involved in evaluating programs in Bosnia, Mongolia and India – in India also doing the implementation of the household surveys, to be used for the academic quantitative impact analysis. Topics addressed include joint versus individual lending, extending the client base, integrated microfinance programmes and sanitation interventions.

Daniel Brett is a Fulbright Research Fellow based in Santiago, Chile, and is investigating market based approaches to reducing the environmental, social, and health impacts of Chile's growing aquaculture industry. Prior to beginning this scholarship, Daniel managed operations at EDA CapitalConnect, a start up organization which has launched an online platform for social enterprise financing. Daniel has economic research experience in the fields of environmental policy and industrial organization; he worked with Redefining Progress, a U.S. - based public policy think tank, and with Compass Lexecon, a leading economic consulting firm. Daniel graduated from Tufts University with honors with a Bachelor of Arts in economics, and a Bachelor of Science in environmental science.

Puspadhar Das is heading the Information Technology division of Asomi Finance Private Limited, a non-banking finance company based in Assam, India and providing micro-credit to unserved markets in Assam. He is also a software consultant to various projects requiring management information system and GIS capability. He holds a B.Sc. (Hons) in Physics from St. Stephen's College, Delhi, India and a PGDM from Indian Institute of Management, Bangalore, India. He has 12 years of experience in diverse fields like agriculture, microfinance, software development, geographic information systems development.

Kevin Day is a microfinance investor, mobile internet specialist and social entrepreneur. Kevin founded Riskebiz Internet Services in 1999, a company which developed web applications for the insurance industry and which now manages the technical services facility for the Riskebiz Microfinance Fund, a MIV that leverages mobile technologies to implement microinsurance schemes at MFIs. Kevin has knowledge of running both private and public companies and has been actively involved in private financings as well as taking companies public. He has a degree in Political Science from the University of British Columbia. Kevin is also currently serving as a Committee Member of the Canadian Captive Insurance Association, a Director of Beauty Night Society, and as an advisor to FrontlineSMS:Credit and Pro-Microfinance International.

Glòria Estapé-Dubreuil is professor at the Faculty of Economics and Business, Universitat Autònoma de Barcelona, in Spain, and a member of the Business Efficiency and Competitiveness Research Group. She teaches several subjects on quantitative methods of management within the Business Economics Department, and also coordinates the recently created EHEA Business and Technology undergraduate studies. Her basic degree is in Mathematics, obtained from the University of Barcelona. She received her PhD in Economics and Business Administration from the Universitat Autònoma de Barcelona. She has also had several years of experience working with third sector organizations in Spain. Her present research interests lie in the areas of social credit, third sector organizations management, gender issues, and the development of models and applications of quantitative analysis to decision-making issues. She has a number of publications; some in international journals such as Management Research News, and actively participates in international conferences.

Federico Fuentes is an Industrial Technical Engineer and Economist, a Doctor in Economic Sciences for the University of Paris (Nanterre). He has carried out a professional work during 15 years in International Banking, developing this activity in Madrid, Paris and Moscow. For 15 years he has been a University Professor imparting, among others, the subject of World Economy. Since 1996, he is a professor at the Polytechnic University of Cartagena-Spain. His extensive investigating career is developed in the environment of the complex economy.

Samanthala Hettihewa - Senior Lecturer in Finance at the University of Ballarat (Australia). In earlier posts, Dr. Hettihewa served at the University of Western Sydney, (Australia) University of Canterbury (NZ), Lakehead University (Canada), the University of Colombo (Sri Lanka) and the University of Sri Jayawardenapura (Sri Lanka). Dr. Hettihewa is a F. FINSIA (the largest industry organisation in finance in the Australasian region), a Chartered Financial Analyst (CFA), and a Financial Planner Australia (FPA). Dr. Hettihewa has extensive publications in finance, small business, business ethics and corporate governance. She has also served on the boards of many NGOs and university bodies and has founded two NGOs and one academic conference.

Meredith Hudson is a Banking Officer and Management Trainee at First United Bank in Durant, Oklahoma. She received her International MBA through Schiller International University in Paris, France, and obtained her undergraduate degree in Government at the University of Texas at Austin. With a significant background in politics and passion for microfinancial endeavors, she plans to continue researching, supporting, and promoting awareness of microfinancial business models in rural areas of the United States.

Kishen Iyengar is a full time instructor at the Leeds school of Business, University of Colorado at Boulder. He completed his PhD in information systems from the University of Texas at Arlington. He has taught information systems and statistics for four years. His research interests include Agile software development, Information security, CIO executive leadership and IT value. He has a Master's from the University of Texas at Dallas and an MBA from Osmania University. His publications include several refereed conference proceedings.

Fredj Jawadi is currently an Assistant Professor at Amiens School of Management and a Researcher at EconomiX at the University of Paris Ouest Nanterre La Defense (France). He holds a Master in Econometrics and a PhD in financial econometrics from the University of Paris X Nanterre (France). His research topics cover modelling asset price dynamics, nonlinear econometrics, international finance and financial integration in developed and emerging countries. He has published in international refereed journals such as Journal of Risk and Insurance, Applied Financial Economics, Finance, Economics Bulletin, a book in finance and several book chapters.

Nabila Jawadi is a PhD in Management Information Systems and Assistant Professor at Amiens School of Management (France). Her current research and teaching interests include virtual team management, e-leadership, trust and performance management of virtual teams. Her overall interest field includes impacts of ICT on organization management. She also teaches in the area of virtual teams, leadership and IS for enterprises.

Karl Dayson is a Director of Sociology and the Executive Director of Community Finance Solutions, a research and development unit within the University of Salford. Community Finance Solutions specialises in researching and developing community based solutions to issues of asset ownership, control, and accessibility. They won the Times Higher Award for Outstanding Contribution to the Local Community in 2005 and they have been involved in the creation of 13 microfinance institutions across England. In 2008, with Pål Vik, he won the European Microfinance Networks; Research Paper of the Year for their work on sustainability of microfinance institutions. Karl was the author of 'Community Finance Initiatives: A Policy Success Story' (2004) and a co-author of 'Investing in People and Places' (1999), 'Investing in People and Land' (2001), 'Tackling Financial Exclusion – the case for the Community Banking Partnership approach' (2005) and co-editor of European Microfinance: A Handbook (Edger Allen, 2010).

Saleh Khan is the Country Director of Nigeria for ASA International where he is responsible for overseeing microfinance lending operations in Nigeria, as well as Ghana. Before taking up this post, he was a Junior Investment Director in Catalyst Microfinance Investor's (CMI) Bangladesh Office, where he was responsible for strategizing the fund's investments in Asian and African MFIs and monitoring their performances. Saleh has over 10 years of working experience and joined CMI after completing an assignment with the World Bank as a 'technology in microfinance' consultant, where he was an integral part of a team which evaluated the prospects of introducing a need-responsive and holistic MIS for MFIs in Bangladesh. Prior to this, he was the Country Manager of Bangladesh for MicroFinance ClearingHouse, a US based company that provides access to capital markets for MFIs around the world. Saleh has a degree in Business Administration with a focus on MIS."

Karuna Krishnaswamy is a microfinance research and technology consultant, currently with the CGAP Technology Program. He currently manages and conducts research on mobile and agent banking projects in the Philippines, Maldives and India. He has earlier consulted for MFIs and done research in microfinance specifically on issues of competition, multiple borrowing and outreach at various research centers in India. He has a B.Tech. in Electronics from IIT Madras and Masters degrees in Computing Sciences and in Economics.

Nandu Kulkarni is an independent consultant in banking and Microfinance technology, based in Pune, India. He has had extensive experience at strategic as well as project operational levels in building technology solutions for Payments, Retail Banking and Cash Management. The last position that he held before becoming an independent consultant, was Senior Vice President, Retail Banking Products at i-flex solutions ltd. (now Oracle Financial Services Software Limited. He currently advises several software product and services companies with focus on banking, payments and Microfinance. He holds a Bachelors degree in Electrical Engineering from the Indian Institute of Technology, Mumbai, and a PGDM from IIM, Calcutta.

Raghavan Kunigahalli has more than 20 years of experience that included senior technology management roles as Vice President, Chief Architect and Chief Technology Officer. As a VP - Information Officer at American International Group (AIG) Dr. Kunigahalli planned and executed AIG eBusiness technology strategy. As a Chief Technology Officer of SBA Technologies, Dr. Kunigahalli developed innovative technology patent applications to address the interoperability and security challenges of Mobile Banking. As a Lead Systems Architect at The Bank of New York, Dr. Kunigahalli architected one of the first Internet transactional applications of the Bank. Dr. Kunigahalli received his Doctoral degree from the University of Wisconsin - Madison. Dr. Kunigahalli has delivered several presentations that include keynote address to international conference on Banking & Payments Technology. Dr. Kunigahalli has authored numerous publications including newspaper & magazine articles, journals and handbooks.

Carmen Lozano is an economist. She has a doctorate in Economic and Managerial Sciences for the Polytechnic University of Cartagena (Spain). She has worked for 21 years as a regular teacher in the Polytechnic University of Cartagena. Author of diverse books, her scientific publications follow an investigation line on the problem of the valuation of intangible in the company of Internet, like previous step to the determination of the true value of these companies, the improvement of their competitive strategy or for the financing achievement.

Abu Saleh Mohammad Musa is currently working as the Country Coordinator of Bangladesh for the South Asian Microfinance Network (SAMN), which is a regional microfinance network hosted by Agency for Technical Cooperation and Development (ACTED). Mr. Musa combines strong analytical, financial and management skills with expertise in fund management; financial management, participatory appraisal & training; product development; technology innovation; product costing; microfinance; microenterprise and business development. He is good at providing training, program oversights including budget management, developing technical and financial proposals for projects targeting to improve the livelihoods of the poor. Mr. Musa also has gained hands-on experience on water & sanitation, disaster risk reduction and process monitoring during his professional attachment with several organizations. He is a Certified Service Provider (CSP) for MicroSave in Market Research for Microfinance Toolkit. Mr. Musa has completed his MBA in Finance from the University of Dhaka, Bangladesh.

Olga Morawczynski is a PhD candidate in the discipline of Science and Technology Studies at the University of Edinburgh. She has been conducting research in the field of ICTD for the past six years and has received recognition for her work. She was awarded a PhD scholarship by Microsoft Research. Her paper was also noted by the GSMA Development Fund Report as being in the "top 20" the field. Olga continues to publish in peer-reviewed journals, present at international conferences and undertake consultancy opportunities.

Krishna Nyapati is the Managing Director of Microsense Software Pvt Ltd, Bangalore, India(www.microsensesoftware.com).He has over 30 years of professional experience, following a degree in Engineering from Indian Institute of Technology, Madras and a post graduate diploma in Management from Indian Institute of Management, Kolkata. Much of his experience is related to software development and software marketing, addressing clients in India, USA and Europe. His expertise includes software quality management, project management and systems engineering and his current interests include evolutionary techniques, quantification of requirement specifications, and non functional requirements. In addition to professional interests in the area of software solutions, Krishna has been active in the areas of development economics and clean energy related issues. He serves as a Director of the Centre for Budget and Policy Studies (www.cbps.in) and as Chairman of the Technology Informatics Development Endeavour (www.tide-india.org).

S. M. Najmullah Quadri is a software consultant at Credit Suisse, Singapore. He is Test Manager and is responsible for Testing & Deployment for the Private Banking applications. He has over 3 years of experience as a software consultant in Banking and Financial Domain. He is certified in National Stock Exchange (NSE) in Financial Markets. He has done six technical paper presentations across different universities in India. He is also certified in ISTQB (International Software Testing Qualification Board). He holds a Bachelor of Engineering Degree (Hons.) in Computer Science stream from Oriental Institute of Science & Technology, Bhopal, India.

Mostafa Saidur Rahim Khan is currently working as an Assistant Professor in the Department of Business Administration of Stamford University, Bangladesh. Mr. Khan has completed his BBA in Finance & Banking and MBA in Banking from the University of Dhaka, Bangladesh. He is teaching finance and business courses for more than five years. His areas of interest are efficiency of financial markets, efficiency & profitability of banking institutions, corporate governance, corporate disclosure, stock market operations and microfinance. His current area of interest include assessment and determination of allocative and operational efficiency of microfinance institutions. He has published several research paper in the area of finance, banking and corporate governance. Before starting the career as an academician, he worked for the banking industry.

Jan Philipp Schmidt is a researcher of open education, commons-based peer production, and open source software communities. He has managed open education projects at the University of the Western Cape and the United Nations University MERIT and is based in Cape Town, South Africa. Philipp is a board member of the OpenCourseWare Consortium, a Shuttleworth Foundation fellow and recently founded the Peer 2 Peer University. Philipp holds a degree in Computer Science and is working towards a doctorate in Economics. He blogs at http://bokaap.net.

Prateek Shrivastava is an expert in mobile finance solutions. As Director, Emerging Markets at Monitise Group plc, he is responsible for developing and deploying mobile banking and payments technology in Africa, South Asia, Latin America and Asia Pacific. Since 1994, Prateek has worked in over 20 countries across all continents developing new products and delivery channels as well as creating technology solutions to improve the efficiency of organisations. Prior to joining Monitise, Prateek founded WiFinance Limited, a consultancy focussed on microfinance and wireless banking solutions. He worked for ABSA in South Africa to improve the adoption of mobile banking and helped implement Barclays Bank's Micro Banking Strategy in Ghana. Prior to this he was Manager, Global E-Business Strategy with Swiss-based Schindler Corporation. Prior to Schindler, Prateek successfully built and sold two Australian based ventures that developed groupware solutions for multinational companies. He holds an MBA in Microfinance and Mobile Banking from Henley Management College, a BSc in Computing and MSc in Information Technology, both from the University of Western Sydney.

Jack Sim is the Founder of World Toilet Organization, the global advocacy group that broke to taboo on the subject of toilet and sanitation since 2001 engaging the global media through his unique mix of humor, serious facts, headlines and interesting photo angles. He hosted 9 annualWorld Toilet Summits, and also declared 19 November each year as World Toilet Day. He is a Schwab Fellow of the World Economic Forum, an Ashoka Global Fellow, Ashoka-Lemelson Fellow, member of World Entrepreneurship Forum, Clinton Global Initiatives, and many other global platforms. He was named Hero of the Environment 2008 by Time Magazine. Jack holds a Post-Graduate Diploma in International Marketing from University of Strathclyde and is now a Masters Public Administration student at Lee Kuan Yew School of Public Policy. Jack is now rallying global stakeholders to see the issue of 2.5 billion people without access to proper sanitation as a market opportunity."

Vikas Kumar Singh is a Business Analyst at BNP Paribas, Singapore. He is responsible for Analysis and Development of the Wealth Management applications. He has worked for over 6 years as a Software Consultant for Investment Banking and Fund Management organization in India and in Singapore. He has also worked for two and half years in Head office of SKS Microfinance Pvt. Ltd., Hyderabad and developed Microfinance applications. He holds a B.Sc (Hons) in Mathematics from Magadh University, Bodhgaya, an MBA (IT) from Vinayaka University, Salem, Tamilandu and Diploma (DNIIT) in Web Technology from National Institute of Information Technology. He is a Microsoft Certified Solution Developer.

Nikias Stefanakis is an Associate with EDA CapitalConnect with several years of experience in Economic Development and Nonprofit management. His primary experience has been with international NGOs where he began as a researcher in Conflict Mitigation in Boston, MA and has worked in Washington, DC on foreign affairs policy development. Just prior to joining CapitalConnect, Nikias managed microenterprise programs in Urban Jakarta, Indonesia and Dili, Timor L'este. Nikias holds a Bachelor's Degree from Tufts University with honors in Economics and International Relations.

Consol Torreguitart-Mirada is currently professor at the Faculty of Economics and Business at Universitat Autònoma de Barcelona. She teaches in the area of management, her regular subjects being finance and business organization and administration. She has a MBA in Political Science as well as a PhD in Economics and Management, both from the Universitat Autònoma de Barcelona in Spain. She actively collaborates with local development agencies in the design and implementation of formative actions for entrepreneurs and micro entrepreneurs. Her research interests plough in all areas of entrepreneurship, especially micro-entrepreneurship. She studies financial support problems encountered by the companies of new creation, social credit and Microfinancial Institutions. At present, Microfinance is her main field of research. She actively publishes articles, present papers and participates in national and international congresses and conferences.

Christopher S. Wright has a multi-disciplinary PhD in Fisheries Management & Accounting Systems, has taught Accounting, Economics and Fisheries at the Undergrad and Post-grad university level for over 30 years. Dr Wright is currently a visiting researcher with the Centre for Regional Innovation and Competitiveness (CRIC; University of Ballarat, Victoria, Australia) and was the Professor of Accounting for Lincoln University (NZ). Dr. Wright was, also, an internal auditor with a large international forestry company for five years and worked in agriculture, fisheries, and services. Dr. Wright owned and operated three SMEs, has served on the boards of many NGOs, and has been extensively involved in applying for, receiving, reviewing, and granting research-focused government grants.

Ydriss Ziane is an Associate Professor of Finance at the Sorbonne Graduate Business School of the University of Paris 1 Pantheon-Sorbonne, in Paris, France. He received a Ph.D. in Finance from the University of Paris X-Nanterre in 2004. He is currently a member of the GREGOR Center Research. His interests concern financial governance of commercial firms, especially small and medium-sized ones. He is particularly interested in bank-firm long term lending relationships, trade credit relationships, microcredit and household indebtedness.

Index

A

B

C